T0368315

The Radical Revolutionary Strategic Management Matrix For Predators

Revolutionising Strategic Management.

By:

Defining Radical and Revolutionary Strategic Management Competencies and Matrix Principles for Predators, and

Applying the Sociological Approach.

Order this book online at www.trafford.com
or email orders@trafford.com

Most Trafford titles are also available at major online book retailers.

Printed in the United States of America.

ISBN: 978-1-4269-5992-9 (sc)
ISBN: 978-1-4269-5993-6 (e)

Library of Congress Control Number: 2011903780

Trafford rev. 03/11/2011

 www.trafford.com

North America & international
toll-free: 1 888 232 4444 (USA & Canada)
phone: 250 383 6864 ♦ fax: 812 355 4082

"Strategic excellence is not as much an art as what it is a journey of discovering new ways towards doing old things better" - *Reinier Geel*

To the readers

This book was written in such a fashion, so that seemingly unrelated bits and pieces of management philosophy, collectively tell a more compelling tale, of a strategic reality that use to exist as fog only. I have attempted to clear the fog of war, and paint the strategic landscape clearer, more detailed for all to see, and most importantly understand.

I have attempted to take the reader to the deep end of the knowledge pool without drowning them in too much detail.

Some chapters might appeal to all and some only to a few, never the less, keep reading it makes for a delightful journey.

The journey of life is made-up of many dissimilar and dark roads we have travelled, that has made up our being, so too the chapters connect likewise, to give you a total holistic concept, rather than just one few.

Reinier Geel

Author: Reinier Geel

Email: Strategicrevolution@gmail.com
Twitter mobi; StrategicManagement@Bookstrategic
Twitter Internet; http://twitter.com/bookstrategic
BLOG; Bookstrategic.wordpress.com

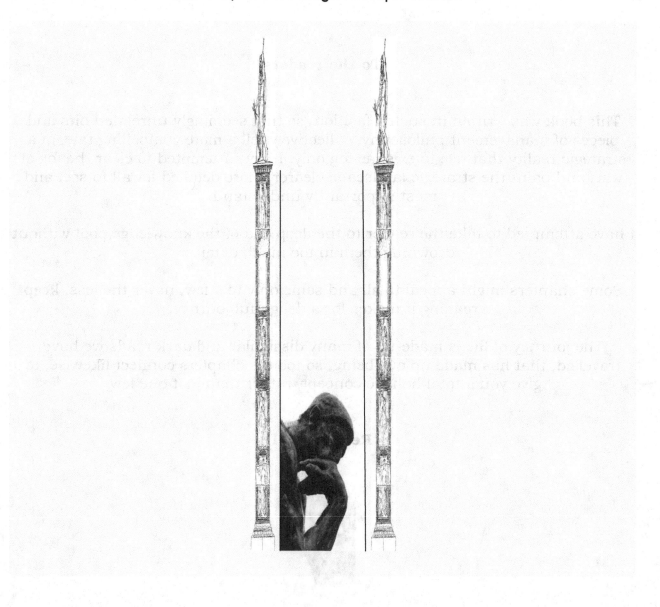

Introduction

Traditional strategic planning and methodology to some extent has given way to strategic thinking; the ability to identify the relevant strategic competencies required for a specific strategic project.

Termed **"The Strategic Management Matrix Faculty"**. Based on the assumption that three identified critical functions of strategy need to be present all the time; namely the alignment of operations, the continual improvement and innovation of systems design, and the allocation of effective recourses. Studies have shown that strategy formulation and execution requires very specific strategic competencies, in order for any strategic plan to work. It is no longer just about the strategic getaway and the big plan.

Six required competencies for strategic genius have been identified.

1. *Perception management and alignment*; is a companion to business philosophy, and planning good strategy. If we depart from the assumption that everything we deal with is based on someone's perception, then perception is of either things or "facts". Furthermore, a strategy points into a direction, that direction is based on some form of bias and alignment, of strongly held perceptions. Then alignment is of either belief, or orientation. These aspects have become focal in strategic circles, where strategies are now concentrating on both things that people believe in or perceive to be real and "fact", that they get from being orientated towards a belief or science, and aligning this with objectives. Perception management, a term that originated in the U. S. military. The definition relates to actions consistent to convey and/or deny selected information and indicators to foreign audiences. Specifically aimed at influencing, emotions, motives, independent reasoning, as well as intelligence, systems, and leaders at all levels. Furthermore, the aim is to influence people's beliefs, and opinions, that ultimately result in a desired altered behaviour. Consequently, altered behaviour brings about actions favourable to the originator's own objectives. In utilising various ways, perception can be manipulated – managed - to combine bits of "truths" about things and "facts", so that eventually it becomes a new reality and fact.

2. *The open systems perspective* refers to us being able to understand the implications of planning, and strategic actions. As well as its far reaching effects and importance. Strategic thinkers have to have the abilities of mental modelling, the ability to see creation in the mind, and relations in steps, and be able to design systems that will deliver on the completed end state, we need architects that can design complete systems from cradle to grave - with systematic planning. In order to be able to design systems with value creation, and quality in mind, they need to be open, to connect to attributes and essentials, as well as new resources at any given time.

3. The third competency is *creating focused intent;* which means looking at ways of getting more leverage, and initiative. By focusing our efforts faster and narrower; the ability to focus our attention as a collective, to resist diversion of efforts, through structured engagement and focused intent, and to concentrate all our efforts as a whole for as long as it takes to achieve our main objectives.

4. ***Thinking in time spirals*** means being able to bring past, present and future assumptions, and all relevant aspects into the strategic equation, to create better decision-making models and speedup implementation. "Strategy" is not just driven by future focused intent, action, and vision alone. It is also the opportunity that it creates, to close some gaps between today's problems and tomorrow's reality, and our intent for the future that is critical. It also serves as a learning experience that creates an awareness of old problems addressed in new ways. By being aware of time, and how to utilise it best as a valuable resource.

5. ***Critical thinking***, the fifth strategic competency is being skills development driven, by ensuring that both academical and practical skills are taught and transferred, by developing intellectual capital, with both imaginative and critical thinking.

6. The final strategic thinking competency is ***emotional intelligence***; By specifically identifying personal attributes that enable people to succeed in life, and developing them, and this also including self-awareness, empathy, self-confidence, life skills and self-control which means being entrepreneurial, and focused on network creation, we create human capital and emotional intelligence.

Get all your "Strategic Competency" issues addressed

- In this book, we will be getting to grips with strategy where it counts and becomes relevant and critical, by addressing very specific strategic competencies.
- Perceptions, emotions, and actions are a balanced trinity, essential for awareness and strong strategy. By creating a deeper understanding of why and how things become significant and addressing these and other competencies, chapter by chapter required from strategist today.
- Strategic thinking is just not enough; we require critical thinking, perception management, skills, reframing, tactics, structure, systems, action and planning, all attributes of success, and when combined they deliver...results.
- Do you have unanswered questions?
  - o Are you still trying to solve old problems the same way you created them?
  - o Has strategic roles and functions become mixed, and blurred, who is responsible for what?
  - o Are you surviving or thriving in your organisation, find out why?
  - o Battling with too many change initiatives, and diversification?
  - o Still attempting to secure your own organisational survival or just achieving some balance?
  - o Do top down strategies still determine how business gets done today?
- What's more important – growing expertise and strategic thinkers, or having a perfect strategy and chasing production figures?
- Frustrated with the strategic buzz words used, then break the mould!

What you will find in this book;

1. The art of strategic conceptualisation –the "Art of War" – CAPS and GAP the roots of all strategy.
2. Well explained to the very core, all the concepts of strategy; chapter by chapter, we cover...

   a) Visualisation and perception - how to see it, understand it, believe it, then plan it, and sell it.

b) Utilising conceptualisation to understand "why" rather than "how" better, by using – CAPS, (**C**oncepts, **A**ttributes, **P**erceptions, **S**ystems) – that gives you a formula for dissecting and working with the variables of design and change.

c) Learning to plan – with acronyms – then everyone speaks the same battle language.

d) Implementation, going over to action – Military styled ways to get people to implement precision styled plans.

e) Management and strategic control – understanding what it requires and all it entails.

f) Realignment of the strategic plan- with the OODA cycle.

3. Dealing with the gravity and complexity of strategy;

a) By reinventing thought processes – thinking strategic, with critical thinking for the professional.

b) Designing systems that work in collaboration, resilient, like an army on the move.

c) Aligning values and production output without becoming cliché.

d) Are we still confusing operational effectiveness, and tactics, with good strategy?

e) Defining the roles of management – and proper systems design.

f) Understand strategy from cradle to grave.

g) Become a corporate politician -start networks to deal with office politics.

h) Be radical in your thinking and more systematically inclined in your approach – and get your strategies working.

i) Make an impression with your insight – and gain recognition.

j) Maintain creative control of your work, and widen your control span.

k) Learn new problem solving techniques.

l) Dealing with change, without stressing it.

m) Errors in corporate strategy are often self-inflicted – are you the cause?

n) Strategy and Competitiveness are linked to personal and managerial traits.

o) The art of critical thinking...explained.

p) Grave strategic errors come from within – by relying on a flawed definition of what is strategy.

q) If you cannot get it right at the coalface then you will never turn it around.

r) A good strategist is a leader that is aware, and good at understanding influences – and even better at communication and networking – the A,B,C of progress and resolve.

The Radical Revolutionary Strategic Management Matrix For Predators

Contents Index:

Foreword	Revolutionising Strategic Management

Revolution is at the heart of human nature and Strategic Management

o   This miscellany is a study of cardinal influences that equates to the "make or break" factors in planning strategy, and the competencies required to execute perfect strategy.

o   Sets a new paradigm for the strategic management arena, backed up with essential knowledge that will empower individuals to behave like "Predators" on a strategic landscape, in a strategic society that has become increasingly complex, competitive and yet complacent. This book will capacitate you to deal with extremes. The new "Predator" paradigm, teaches us required Radical and Revolutionary insight for handling today's flux.

The significance of this required Revolution

We require more "revolutionary" ideas from entrepreneurs to think creatively, and thrive in this day and age. The very essence of **"Revolutionary"** ideas, have chartered the course of history and humanity, from Newton, to Picasso, from science to art. It only took a few unique men to challenge the boundaries of our existence, to ultimately influence the course of human history for good and evidently life, as we know it today. Ask yourself, if it was not for these men and their revolutionary ideas, where would we have been today. These "Predators" have set in motion a powerful surge of thinkers and apprentices to carry on with their ground-breaking work, they have inspired future generations of thinkers, which ultimately continues to spiral us forward and onward to the next level of existence. What is truly significant and remarkable about the evolution of humanity? It's our ability to evolved in leaps and bounds, at every completion of an evolution, we gained new knowledge and insight, both essential and required, to cope with the challenges of the new, to elevate us and prepare us for the challenges of the following new leap of evolution. This is the essence of strategy, its revival.

By looking back in time and history, we can see the relevance of this acquisitioned process of knowledge, both require and essential to capacitate us for the next evolution. Life has become a constant relay of cycles in a spiral of change, that increase in dimensions and speed as knowledge and wisdom grow in parallel with our evolution. With the inevitable completion of a cycle, we have already started the groundwork, unknowingly at times it seems, for the next cycle to start. In this manner, we have gone from intro to epilogue and we have started a never-ending seamless journey of growth and development, just like seasons change we change, and grow, in all spheres of our existence - since the beginning of time. Evolution is our survival, it has, and we can safely presume will always be at the centre of our existence.

The one thing that remains constant in this process is ever changing strategy. If we at first do not succeed, we try and try again, until we do. We have thus far relied on our ability to adapt to this continuum. To strategise and to adapt, in order to continue the epic of continued reinvention of knowledge, from the one to the next generation we have passed it on. To ultimately survive everything, from cold, disease, war, and hunger to taxes and demand for payment, life and living - it is all about strategy.

Throughout the ice age, on to the information age today, we have adapted and overcome our circumstances successfully, repeatedly, just by adapting our strategy. Our unique evolutional process and ability to influence our surroundings, has become our pinnacle mechanism for survival.

The threat now it seems is time, time itself, that aspect of keeping up with the time, we just do not seem to have enough time anymore. Time - has fast been catching up with us, we are running the risk of falling behind time within the following cycles or seasons of life, with every advancement we have made, time accelerates. We get more done in less time, but we still have much more to do, and not much time left doing it...

Survival and revival is at the very heart of man's evolutionary existence...and programming.

"Choice" - has been the only strategic mechanism standing between the two options in life - chaos and order.

Does strategy have to be Radical to be effective?

The word **"Radical"** within the strategic ambit refers to a required critical catalyst necessary for revolutionising our thinking, it opens us up to evolution and new ideas. Without the need for change and more innovation, we would still have been cave dwellers some believe. Human nature itself is not passive; we are greedy, we want things, and by satisfying our wants, we have become radical. Therefore, this makes the process of strategic thought so much more essential and far-reaching to manage change. Change, has forced our total adaptation; without it there would have been no need for our evolution, but, if anything, the forces of nature have taught us that change is inevitable and very necessary. This necessity to adapt to changes, no longer just requires skill and knowledge to be cultivated and passed on, we have to cultivate essential effective strategies to fuse it altogether in order for us to cope. We have come to the realisation that we require this catalyst, to open up the portal to more advanced forms of knowledge to cope, and in turn, it gave birth to us following **"Strategic"** principles.

Strategy

Strategy therefore became a law in its own right. A subject and knowledge field based on fundamental principles derived from our collective experience; by coping with change in many forms, we have grown in our evolutionary universal knowledge. It became part and parcel of man's being in the 21st century, solidified and imprinted in our DNA; it has become the vehicle of choice to exploit advantage by all man. We have realised that strategy diminishes risk. Strategy is calculated and both analytical, it gives us the ability to plan. The importance of strategy has also brought about the realisation, that strategy gives form to the abstracts of reasoning and shapes the world of thought and communication. All the while, the mental evolution of thinking strategically has been speeding ahead, regardless of time and of history itself. Our physical dimension has become trapped. The one thing that was left out, that changed our views on strategy and its usefulness, has become very apparent, and that is that all strategic thought requires is a sturdy rigid mental and ethical compass to steer it. We have come to a juncture, pertaining to the application of strategic thought and introduced the concept of **"Management"**.

Management, where does it fit into strategy?

Management, the concept of management is supposed to guide the strategic brilliance of man, to give it a required wisdom, understanding and direction by incorporating time. When the two merge we measure, and we start gauging performance against a certain criteria. This adaptiveness of man, his innate ability to improvise, adapt and overcome - has served us well, some hailed it man's greatest legacy. Strangely enough, strategy is also the guidance of thoughts, the thinking about thinking. In addition, although it does recognise the concept of time, it can function without it. Is this not the reason we have to leave this body to escape the consequence of time itself? Moreover, until then we will have to struggle with time and the one thing that keeps it all in balance, the capability of the human mind to think. To work with strategy one must be able to think critical, to negotiate any complexity and chaos. With the help of strategy, we have combined our whole being, to devise an amicable solution. This very aspect is what separates us from beast, this strategic distinction that has given birth to all of man's greatest accomplishments and failures by the same token, for we have been given our own free will, to choose our destiny. The ability to choose, to understand, to make sense of our surroundings and to find our purpose, this is all done by choice. Choosing has become the predicament of modern day man; we all get to face choices daily. Do we overcome our kin, our nature and ourselves? Well it is our choice. Do we have to grow knowledgeable, or not? Do we have to use knowledge effectively, or not? This is all by choice, we get to make the decisions, and this ability to choose has been given. Man stands at the eve of his greatest legacy, choosing his salvation; it is no longer a question of survival but a question of ethical and moral predicaments. Somehow, time has caught up with us and the only thing standing between our salvation and us is choice. This is not a simple thing either, choice is predominantly influenced by our perception and perception in turn is enforced by our choice, as it is enforced it eventually becomes our habit, and our reality. To understand perception then is to understand reality and the consequence of our thoughts and thinking itself.

Why a Matrix?

The **"Matrix"** in this book defines the boundaries of our thinking and living, by defining our perceptions and why they exist, by dissecting it to its core, starting with natural and universal laws that apply to everything we do, hear, say and experience. The Matrix defines all the physical and mental limitations of this cycle of thought and the forces that influence and guide our perceptions. Ultimately, we get to analyse every aspect of perception in detail and how we can apply choice with reasoning, by learning to think critical. Filtered against the influences of civilised norms and ethics and common manmade laws to help keep influences intact. The Matrix addresses the confines of what has become our perceptual boundaries in strategy formulation, man-made boundaries and the confines of our inner spiritual being, confronted by reality, and that which guides our beliefs and belief system. The matrix addresses further still, aspects of our perceptualization, that which so powerfully influences the moral fibre of society and its dignity. Those subtle restraints, that are of moral and ethical value. Then there are also the social barriers, which complicate the anomalies of what's deemed expectable. Perceptions challenges everything we are, do, and say, they get tested and formed by our interactions, the various stages of our growth, both mental and physical, from birth to adulthood - the anomalies we experience right through life. Those stages of interaction and solitude - our various states of existence are tested. The only thing that still exists to rid us from the burden of perception is our free will, our ability to think rationally, to think critically and to think outside perceptions. This realm of manmade perception – where we create our own reality. The Matrix teaches us that perceptions and imagination combined can conjure up irrational thought-inhibiting processes that will rob us of our opportunities in life. They are all free willed agents as well, in other words, they pop up at random, they mainly manifest our insecurities and inability to control our perceptions and insecurities effectively in nasty and ugly ways when challenged. What this implies is that only by choice do they become our reality; they have no natural or common boundaries opposing them, only mental. They reflect our desires and thinking, they control our subconscious and emotional reactions. They have roots that go back to the birth of the universe, yet they do not have a focal point of existence within the moral or ethical. They change and grow as we change and grow... Until we reach the "strategic mental maturity", to understand that perceptions have to be controlled.

Why the Predator within us?

The **"Predator"** within us, has to be awakened, as he has the true spirit of choice and action. Unlike sheep following the flock, sheep are soft, vulnerable, susceptible and gullible. They live and work in a world of denial and perception. Predators are individuals, seeking truth, they realise the importance of moral, spiritual and ethical living. The think and live outside the realm of "normality". By enhancing our Predatory instincts, they can serve us well still, in our modern day roles, as specialist tacticians, leaders, managers and master strategist; we inherited this skill from our ancestors. We were ultimately engineered to adapt and exploit our habitat to our advantage. We were born to hunt, to dominate, to ascertain knowledge, to lead and affect change and to survive any complexity that change presents, even at varying degrees, throughout our life cycle. In strategic terms, a chosen learned mental enhanced state of existence. The predatory instincts within us, drives us still today, to prey, the only changed aspect is a higher sense of prey, knowledge. To ultimately satisfy our modern day "predatorial" need for order and balance in the pack status of society. The only thing that has to change is our mental sight or insight. The pursuit is more moral and ethical standards – paradigms- of living, for everyone, especially our children. The Predator drive and frame of mind radiates vigilance. This field of predatory expertise is called Epistemology today and it is better explained as: the study of knowledge and its acquisition. All human's to a greater or lesser extent has perused this through the ages, the hunt and pursuit of knowledge, the growth of wisdom and understanding, the wanting to know. The earnest desire, to live a life of purpose and balance in all its facets is a spiritual one. We all want to survive and succeed, no matter how great the odds and still remain faithful to our virtues.

Chapter 1:

Looking at the Relevance of Human Cognitive Models

Not everything in life is always "Black or White" but a shade thereof, this chapter teaches us how to deal with this aspect of human cognitive modelling.

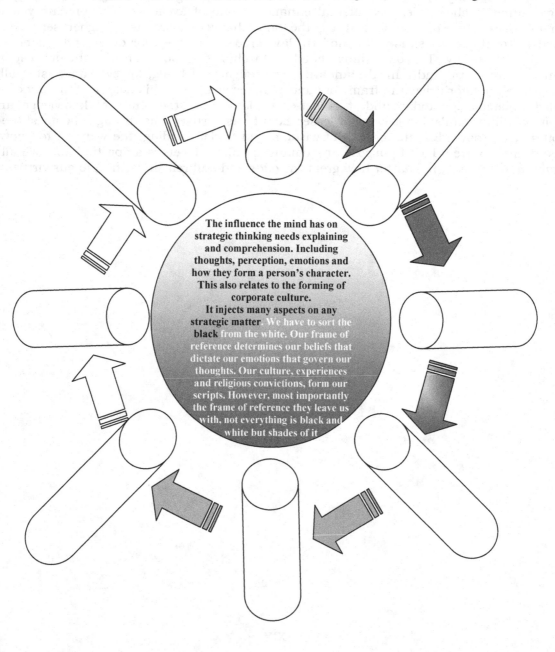

The influence the mind has on strategic thinking needs explaining and comprehension. Including thoughts, perception, emotions and how they form a person's character. This also relates to the forming of corporate culture.

It injects many aspects on any strategic matter. We have to sort the black from the white. Our frame of reference determines our beliefs that dictate our emotions that govern our thoughts. Our culture, experiences and religious convictions, form our scripts. However, most importantly the frame of reference they leave us with, not everything is black and white but shades of it

Looking at the Relevance of Human Cognitive Models

In order to **understand what really influences and informs strategy;** we need to be able to "see" strategy as it exist, and relate with it through conversation. This type of conversation must revolve around a model for it to become meaningful and entrenched in culture. Strategic conversation needs structure and reference points that join people with the whole aspect of communicating purposefully. Strategic conversation deals with concepts. Now, if we see a specific concept mentally, then we are engaged in "paradigm" reasoning. Therefore, if we understand what "paradigms" are, and how they influence our strategic communication, then we are on our way to "seeing" relationships where others only "see" complexity.

What is a Paradigm then, and how do they become so significant in strategic culture?

Paradigms have great power and influence on our thinking and reasoning. First, we need to understand what makes up paradigms. How we perceive something will determine how we will think about it in the future - because of the way we have regarded - perceived it - in the past.

The point to make here about perception is this; we have many informal perceptions – presumptions – that form daily, things floating in and out of our minds that we have no proof of, nonetheless its useful information, and we can use it as the premises on which we make decisions, or conversation over. Especially when we communicate with others, read, listen, watch shows, any sensory input creates both informal paradigms – uncertainties; in the form of suspicion, worries, doubts, and formal paradigms – certainties; belief, certainty, and trust to name but a few interchangeable examples. Perceptions are cognitive attempts at creating insights and eventually understanding. Perceptions also refer to our ability to observe with all our senses. Observing things refers to; noticing them, seeing things, and putting them into context, even our biases towards certain things are mostly influenced by our perceptions. Current and prevailing perceptions will also determine how we look at our world and ourselves, at any given moment, perception makes us stand in judgement of others, the situation and ourselves.

Perceptions become the building blocks of bigger frames of thinking, called paradigms, all the bits and pieces of information that gets collected through our senses work towards forming our perceptions, and eventually forming a concept of things, and our thinking on them, called a total paradigm. Like bits and pieces of a puzzle. Perceptions still influences our overall consciousness, the place where we are reasoning from, it is all governed by these perceptions we have developed or adopted. We tend to be very flexible on informal perceptions or information opposed to formal perceptions called facts. However, with formal perceptions – "facts" - we deal with conviction, because they are the building blocks of our personality and character, our culture. This is the power of perception; it persuades us on a subconscious level and moves us on our own, to think on a conscious level, if we are not guarded, we can get into trouble. Information is perception, not fact, in the absence of clarity, and certainty, people make up their own reality – then we call it their perception. Perception is someone's opinion, view, observation of something. When we get many perceptions that are related and on topic, then it becomes a paradigm.

A paradigm is a way of thinking about something specific that is critical.

The type of thinking that keeps informing us of something specific is called a paradigm, it is focused on specifics. Jip, no matter which way you are looking at solutions, or from which side or angle, it stays one thing, a critical evaluation of specifics, called a paradigm. In order to explain paradigm thinking, we need to understand what it comprises of. Let's say we are talking of war and tactics for instance. Then we will say that we are in a "warring" paradigm, or frame of mind. It is focused reasoning and thinking. Paradigms are made up of perceptions. New perceptions are created where thinking and discussions are current and on a specific topic, whenever we become engaged, then a perception is formed, and as the engagement continues, the perception evolves and devolves. A perception is of a current awareness of a specific situation; a mental representation of what is perceived – known, believed or understood about a specific topic, like the problems and situations at hand. When we are aware of the influence at play then we create perceptions, and magnify paradigms, then we see things better mentally. Paradigms engage all our senses to gather information for us. Now we are starting to observe with all our senses, the situation, the conversation, the information and our options, all become clear if our collective reasoning is sound. We become more aware when we set our paradigm, to the situation. It's like tuning into a radio station, tuning, then fine tuning, until it becomes perfect, with no noise. Only then do we become aware of its influences, and components of strategy and manipulation etc…These influences are the first building stone of reality, called the precept.

Percept is an exercise in validating our reality; it is a perception in action. It informs a perception as to whether it is still valid or not. It is important to discern percept from stimuli or their absence. Stimuli are not necessarily translated into a percept and rarely does a single stimulus translate into a percept. A mental impression of something perceived by the senses, viewed as the basic component in the formation of concepts – lips moving and sound emitting equals talking – a concept. Precept also changes or enforces our reality; this exercise never stops. Whilst life and living is playing itself out daily, we get into new situations that we only perceived in one manner, however it normally plays out to a totally new and different reality, from the perception we had of how it, things should look, from our viewpoint. Normally, things do not exactly play out as you expected them to or had contemplated beforehand, if it is not a run of the mill daily routine. This then becomes a percept, a pre-conceived-idea of how things should work, are, or could be. An experience of something that drives a specific reality, not all reality, and it either enforces an old perception or creates a new. Alternatively it destroys a total paradigm, and starts with a perception and eventually creates a totally new paradigm. Perceptions require precepts and an experience to enforce them to become a belief and ultimately a reality, of how we are experiencing something specific now, to reinforce them again and again. The basic components in the formation of a concept of strategy will emerge only when we have tested and strong precepts, that informs our perceptions and ultimately our opinions, which will become our new Reality.

When we are asked to engage strategically, then the wheels come off. Everyone having the ability to think perceives themselves having the ability to think strategically and having good strategic abilities and wisdom. Systemically and both strategically we are all thinking "strategy" when we join for a strategic session, however we are not on the same paradigm, even worse, tactically everyone is still doing a different thing, because they are experiencing things differently, their precepts are different, because their paradigms are different.

Strategic focus and alignment is paramount to strategic success. We need to be able to orientate people first. We need a solid foundation to depart from. Foundations are built from paradigm alignment, and it should be first on the strategic agenda, before we can reach our or any reality, and contemplate moulding strategy. This aspect is entrenched in all undeveloped strategic corporate culture. Where we have either; muscle or muscles, people muscling others around, instead of combining our strength and getting muscle. This is the point; no two people share the same reality if their paradigms, perceptions, and precepts are not the same, and aligned. We have to deal with a vast array of influences already, we cannot cope with a vast array of inputs and outputs that are dissimilar because we all want a say – that is organised chaos. Where certainty becomes the state of things we discuss, focused on things that informs us of reality as it actually exist, and not just in the mind, or may appear to us personally, then we have made great progress, how we think and give strategy thought then makes it an ultimate reality that we all can visit, and relate to.

A phrase that comes up a lot nowadays is "Perception is Reality." Our paradigms become so powerful, that we can influence a vast amount of people in a short space of time, just via perceptions, methods of communication, and it also touches the way we design, our world, lives our life, even interact with others. Paradigms interpret our experiments and observations with others and us, as scientists in our own right and as humans experiencing emotion, this creates several realities' daily, all in its own right. Although this concept might be wrong on a factual basis, it is still an informer of reality for all, a way of perceiving the world. Only by growing an awareness or consciousness, can we plan and follow a sustainable life path. A lack of awareness will be our downfall. The process of becoming aware of the world around you through your senses – is not a simple thing, it is very complex and complicated thing, and impacts on everything we are, have done and say. There are a whole lot of external reality's that exist out there that we need to become aware of, forever changing, that will and have impacted on us...

How do we make our decisions then, based on experience, or percept? The answer is both. Good decisions are a joint product of both the stimulation we experience and of the process of assimilation itself. Where assimilation deals with; experience, knowledge, wisdom and perception which generate beliefs, or perceptions, and stimulation is the emotional empathy we experience, how strong we feel about something, is it worth dying for, or not? It has a knock on effect, the one leads to the next and so forth and so on, from precept to precept, changing our perception, thus influencing our paradigms. The more experience we gain, the more knowledge we need, and the more perceptions we generate, the more beliefs we have to deal with, now we need systems or models to be and stay effective...at making good and then better decisions.

Why is it that attempting to get people to go over to action becomes such a difficult part of strategy? Mostly, it's because people lose sight of the plot, when we start changing things too much without giving it structure, we change the nature of it. Changing people's paradigms should be the first priority of any strategy. One of the deepest problems with leading intellectuals is that of gaining greater understanding of how people make sense of the vast amount of raw data constantly bombarding and influencing them from the internal and both external environment, and influencing our individual and social paradigms. We need to understand the internal as well as external environment, and the perceptions they create and hold that impact on our thinking. It's a process of consultation, mediation and then we move on. Even if we are of one mind, our individual characters also have been taught different ways of going over to action, and doing things, or getting them done. Everyone has a different approach – with tactics and bright ideas. Ideas lead to actions, or precepts – ways or approaches of doing things – that create more perception, if we become aware of more, we will own the process, if we design the perception and manage it, then we control the outcome. Starting and working with precepts, precepts evolve because of more or less involvement or influence from external inputs, drawing meaning out of situations that in turn influence personal perception to become habit. A great paradigm shift can be brought on by designing change that becomes habit or culture, change that willingly unites people to think with the same paradigm, informed by one vision. Where we have no common vision we only have chaos. Therefore elect a vision that will keep us focused... focus creates greater situational awareness. When we are aware we align ourselves to channel our energy in a specific direction, energy goes where attention flows. Once we get the creative and positive energies flowing, we can channel it with perception alignment and management. Interfacing people's contributions and energy with a plan, and then a system, is a trigger to growth. This growth needs to start with self-realisation.

If we are responsible for ourselves and accountable to others, then we are progressing fast as individuals. If we can duplicate this aspect we will have many growing fast. Otherwise we become change battered, the us and them situation, everyone for himself. Remember, all things being equal in this analogy, no two men in a room of plenty will share the exact same view on how to implement and construct strategy. Paradigms may be one way to explain a characteristic or elements of strategy that informs us how to align our thinking, and set it to thinking strategic, but still our perceptions are divergent and inclusive of elements of individual nature and own knowledge, as well as experience...and beliefs. This aspect of individual identity is a small aspect compared to changing a culture. Culture is the biggest inhibitor of strategy, cultural beliefs and dogma is entrenched and become a way of life. They share the same beliefs and therefore fears and reality. In the presence of fear creativity will die... fear is normally a result of perceptions that are not always true or even validated, due to a lack of proper communication and perception management. Perceptions need to be managed through structured strategic communication.

The four pillars of strategic communication

Why do strategists need to know and understand paradigms, when the simple truth is this, if you cannot persuade someone that something is possible, or even plausible – then you have no power over him. If you cannot change a person's perception, how will you change a total paradigm and influence a group or culture? We need to be able to sell concepts and attributes based on perceptions, all of which must be comprehended and be at least seemingly achievable, otherwise the plan of strategy will have failed altogether, because we have failed to communicate the plot. We need all three weapons of mind; *perceptions, emotions, and actions*. Perceptions, emotions, and actions are a balanced trinity, essential for total awareness and delivering strong strategy.

Perception management – *pillar one*

To explain a perception, is to **sell a concept**. In more practical terms, perceptions are like chapters in a book, whereas "Informal" perceptions are just notes... the one has substance the other is open to interpretation. Formal perceptions are internalised, part of who we are and it makes sense to us, it has meaning. As we write our own chapters throughout life, a formal perception is eventually created and we build on it, we shape and edit it from time to time but we do not change it much.

Component integration into perception – *pillar two*.

Many *"informal"* perceptions become *"formal"* where we integrate substance, or components into it. Where a component of emotion, sensory or knowledge or any combination hereof is integrated, we start formalising perceptions. They become our reference "books" once completed. Using the example of cooking. We experience the art of cooking from infancy at all three levels, **emotional, sensory and knowledge**, as we grow older and start learning to prepare food ourselves and master it; the knowledge level is then also incorporated, so it is safe to say that we have now formed a formal paradigm on cooking. - (we understand the concept of cooking). Therefore, when we want to cook, say fish for instance, we refer to the cookbook (a paradigm) on cooking and we then refer to the chapters (the perception) that tells us how to, where to, when to, what to and why, etc. Our insight or perception comes from prior learning and experience, the traditional trial and error method, or from knowledge we gained by observation and or studying things, these are the components necessary to formalise perceptions. Paradigms also influence the way we "see" things in their relation to the world. They also relate back to our experience of certain emotional interactions that create feelings, and how it left us after the experience.

Validate perceptions to create balance – *pillar three*.

If we want to test perceptions, and formalise them, so that they may be validated, then we have to check how they were modelled. Perception modelling is an internal against the external perceptions challenge. Where we are at two minds about what would be the best course of action. For instance, dealing with change and how we go about changing our or others paradigms as circumstances challenge them, faced with the current reality and us. We have to realise that we cannot control all circumstance in life, we also have the ability to create circumstance, or to avoid them, and then there are times where we have no choice, or do we?

Circumstance can be changed by changing our thinking, our perceptions and our paradigms. Mao said create an inner force to counter an outer force. Our mental actions determine our own actions and how outer forces will act upon us. By shifting our perceptions and paradigms, we will shift all other things in relation to it.

How we refer to a relative explanation of something (anything), be it abstract, emotional or concrete, will give it the power to create perception. For instance "love", when we look for the cognitive explanation; relating to the process of acquiring knowledge by the use of;

- **Reasoning** - is influenced by wisdom,
- our **intuition** – implying making use of the senses,
- then only do we resort to creating perception – that in turn influences our paradigms.

Our Paradigms relate to the way we are connecting at the sensory level with concepts – *pillar four.*

- All your thoughts and feelings have created who we are now, what you feel, think and attract.
- If we shift our awareness to visualisation and visualise the concept we are thinking of and then visualise them in a different ways then we project different energies and it affects every aspect of our overall energy.
- We have a choice, in all matters of mind, even what we focus on, and with which senses. This will eventually perpetuate as a new perception and paradigm – we can change how we feel or think by changing how we assimilate with our sense, then feel and ultimately think.
- Once we call on all our perceptions and paradigms as they manifest at any particular time and apply choice; then we channel what we want, via our visualisation of it into what we desire, and see, or envision.
- We have to focus more on the vision, of what we want rather than the decisions to get it, what you visualise you materialise, as it becomes a focal point of our energy.

This conscious application of vision over thinking about choice pushes aside all our former perceptions and influences, our new course and paradigms. If we want to move away or toward something, we need energy, we have to realise that we become what we think about, and energy goes where attention flows. We have a tendency to want things and we give them power by channelling them energy, we need to move energy with the end in mind, only then we have shifted focus and started to affect change internally, by creating order, and balance, the way we want it, just by shifting to focus we have shifted energy...

This is the creative process that models concepts; concepts (perceptions) become paradigms, which become things. When we look at human interaction as a premise for understanding perceptions and paradigms better; then we create impressions, small bits of energy we impart to others. Through our powers of observation, we create energy and we see and feel energy, we feel things better than what we see them, the ability to notice or discern things that escape the notice of most people, is the power of observation brought about by feeling it, or seeing it. Most people define themselves as objects to others, or as concepts – a doctor, a nurse, a manager. Instead, we are better defined as forms of energy, positive and negatively connected; we can create power and respect, when we create a presence with energy. Achievement is channelling this power of energy, in the way, or direction we want things to be, because we have the power and energy to change how we see ourselves, our beliefs and how we get others to see it and feel it. This will create the experience for us. We all deal from a paradigm of freedom and security. However, we seem to go about imposing barriers for ourselves and become objects, no object can change by choice and objects only change with physical intervention. In other words, a concept we have formed from our impression, was formed from the energy that flowed at that time, when we came into contact with things, energy flows where attention goes. Thoughts become things; things become concepts that in turn create the energy we project. We attract that which we think about. The way we think is determined by the concepts we have formed to understand these things. Our paradigms are determined not only by our thoughts, or governed by our emotions, they are also influenced by the physical attributes we attach, and attract to them. Our physical chemistry also creates feelings of pain and pleasure as we experience these things in the physical, these things and their experiences affects what we believe to be implicit meaning or by implication, only when we have the experience to go with it, then the result, the feedback of our thinking, is altered as if for the first time.

The question is, is this true, for all? Well no. It cannot be, we all have similarity as we also have differences in our understanding of things; concepts and paradigms. In all we perceive and understand to be true, everything relates back to how our perceptions were formed by our thinking and our own paradigms in the first place. This process was dictated by our growth and how much we were exposed to the concept and then this specific perception becomes a formal paradigm.

How this works is, we first mirror what we see, or test what we see, thereby forming many informal perceptions, the process of using the senses to acquire information about the surrounding environment or situation and forming a concept. Once we place all these perceptions together we form a paradigm. Take the paradigm on "love", according to our understanding; we start building informal perceptions in this way, of what constitutes "love", until we can define and mature it for ourselves, until then we mimic it and create the feeling we associate with the understanding. It is only during puberty that we start forming formal concepts; back to the concept of love on what it implies to be loved and to give love, and then we start formalising the formal paradigm. Why, well we now have the means, the body chemistry, intellect and structure to precipitate the emotional, physical and intellectual attributes associated with this concept. Only by understanding the formative process of perceptions surrounding love, do we grasp the forming of our paradigm on love. What we see, feel experience and understand love to be for ourselves for the first time, this is an on-going process of observation, orientation, decision and acting it out. The concept of love can only mature further from this point on to become a formal paradigm, as we have linked it with a feeling, emotion, and mental stimulus. Mental and personal maturity, will dictate the complexity of any paradigm formed by that individual. The stages of maturity. Yet with more perceptions forming as we grow, we evolve more formal perceptions, as we get to know the new, we replace the old, sharing, giving and commitment, takes on new meaning, as we now not only have an emotional connection to all, we now have a spiritual, moral, and ethical cognitive connection that influence our perceptions. The point is a paradigm is a complexity formed by many perceptions, or rather a culmination of many perceptions; that all have many attributes and origins. The way in which we will express ourselves through our views and our feelings in relation to words or by using gestures, will be strongly influenced by our beliefs – our formal perceptions that grew as we did, that builds our personality, our character traits.

People in general form very complex concepts of what is deemed acceptable and what is totally unacceptable – enter morality. **Morality** is therefore the *"constitution"* of formal paradigms, it has other stronger influences that will also try to shape and guide it, but morality stays pinnacle to how we think about all things in context, we will check all our perceptions and paradigms against a form of morality, it becomes a benchmark - before we move on to a new premise. This aspect is not cast in stone either, depending on where we find them in any particular equation that is to say on the winning or receiving end, or on the losing or giving end. Example: This aspect will again shift our mental gears. The way in which we view our situation in context, stems from the facts we incorporated towards finding our solution by sifting all our paradigms. Circumstances we endured throughout our life are also strong emotional catalysts, which have left us with informal paradigms that still influence our formal thinking, the way we express and relate, our preferred choice – the formal paradigm. The mind, subsequently derives directly from all our formal paradigms of reference as our scripts, before the resolution becomes concurrent with the solution to any problem, we give it thought. We decide on the best course of action generally. Repeatedly we test the validity of our thinking. This is mostly in accordance with our experiences of how to best handle situations of any particular nature successfully, therefore we can conclude, by saying that perceptions influence our informal paradigms and informal paradigms influence formal. They are not separated...

The second aspect of reasoning is an attempt to find or define "truth", what is truth, or is it just our reality - match with paradigm that best goes with it.

It was Friedrich Nietzsche (Zarathustra) that remarked: Everyone being allowed to learn to read, ruined in the long run not only writing but also thinking. Once spirit was God, then it became man and now it even becomes common people. If I wished to shake this tree with my hands, I should not be able to do so. But the wind, which we see not, troubled and bended it as it listened. We are sorest bent and troubled by invisible hands."

Morality vs. Truth; Then "What is truth" is it just our perception of a perceived reality -the fourth pillar.

One can safely say that the truth is neither here nor there, but still out there. Truth has become unimportant in modern day society, because there are so many flavours of the truth to be found these days that it is just not true or truth anymore. The real truth then, is what we perceive it to be; it does not necessarily hold the same meaning for everyone else. If it did then we would have lived in Utopia, so let us not fool ourselves on this, by believing that we are all truthful to the same standard. It has been estimated that as much as 70% of the content of a hardened criminal's dialogue is purely not true, they have adopted a natural defence against being caught out, by living in denial and by fabricating the truth that they like best. The worst of it all is that they believe and will defend to the end of that belief, the lie they live being far better than the real-truth or reality. By repetition, they enforce the new self-image and personality they created around a lie, or even several. They become the actors of the scripts they wrote to give meaning to their worthless selves. If this were true and accurate, then why can't normal people be at a lesser degree of truth but for the very same reason and be acting it out with some lies, from time to time. By adopting this way of living, we start living a life of portions of truth and untruth, a white and black life; it then becomes a life of absolute denial...all grey, next to living in emotional pain as the only alternative to facing up to reality. Because the truth is just too painful or ugly to be lived and worse told. Therefore, truths, or the variation thereof, will all depend on the situation and the person's character as well as motive. Whether he or she perceives a white lie to be acceptable or not given the circumstances we endure. For instance, will this situation exploit my vulnerability or not, should I be telling the whole truth and nothing but the truth so help me God? Alternatively, will a variety of truth get me by? This is why we find so many flavours of the truth, people force people to lie, we put people into situations, where we force them to act out scripts they had as children, because we see truthfulness from our own perspective and force it on others as the only truth to exist. With effect, that the other person eventually believes his or her truth to be a lie, a fabrication. Alternatively, they mask their truth, by telling little white lies, out of fear of whatever the reason...or insecurity. Every untruth starts out as a half-truth or more, just a little white lie and eventually it gets to snowball out of proportion. This last aspect has everything to do with our ethnic culture, our religious culture and our social and political culture and status, which forms our belief systems or value systems as well as our concepts of truth. Humans are in the business of measuring, we give every person a weighted worth score, that we pass on to the few we trust. He is worthy of our trust, because of ...She is not worthy of our trust because of...

"That, by which we measure ourselves another's truth and worth with, becomes a yardstick for every personal interaction."

The scales of truth and justice are blind and for good reason (we see her, the symbol for justice as a blindfolded maiden holding a scale and a sword) for she refers to law and not emotion as her measure to judge. Imagine how much time we would have spent in court if we were to have reasoned (- emotionally), by referring to the very paradigms we refer to and form daily in defence and attack. That which becomes our mental point of departure whenever we engage each other, in active or conceptual reasoning, refers to our paradigms. Therefore, the word paradigm will be used extensively throughout the book to refer to how we see things or perceive them, in relation to how we build concepts, form hypothesis and perceive reality. Therefore –thought/ thinking is directed by our paradigms, and the perceptions they create. As strategist, we have to learn the art of *"Perception Modelling"*.

What is Perception modelling?

We need to fully understand the concept of **"perception modelling"** without just reducing it to a mere definition, to understand its influences on any thinking and how powerful its role is in our daily lives, let us first see how we perceive "change". What is our perception on change? Strategy deals with change. Changes come in many forms; we will only address two primary forms at the two opposing ends of the spectrum. **Radical change** *is a change that is far-reaching and always very traumatic*, for instance a bomb going off and many are subsequently killed as a result, senselessly, or a natural catastrophes of epic proportions like a Tsunami. What is our first response? Yes always emotional. This type of change that comes about due to a chain of events that we cannot control scares the living breath out of all of us, or anything that cannot be foreseen or seen; events that happen in our lives that occur in the blink of an eye. This is called or referred to as "Radical change".

Radical change activates – **"Primitive perception"**; it activates the primitive mind immediately, we kick into survival mode, we fear the consequences because they fall far outside our sphere of our control and we become/ feel vulnerable, anything that resides or resembles such a change is reason for great concern. Why? Because, it seems to threatens our survivability as a person or race. However, if we were to be trained or conditioned mentally and physically we would react immediately, in the correct and appropriate manner, this is referred to as an automated response, or a trained response. In the military, responses are drill into soldiers until they become reflex responses, until they become second nature. If not, then the "Fight or Flight" response will be observed where there is no reflex, we will either first freeze up, or act in "Fight or Flight" response, all primitive, or just surrender to the threat in total, rendering us ineffective in dealing with sudden change.

Strategists have the cunning ability to overcome this aspect of human nature, the fear of change, by formulating and modelling a soft landing.

Either way, we have to understand our primitive nature, the "Fight or Flight" response normally kicks in as a primary response, before we can act rationally, or reflexive to sudden change. In instances where people have no "fight or flee" option, the person will just freeze up; we call this "the surrender state". The perception of the perceived threat is just overwhelming, the mind has reached its limit, the mental capacity is breached, and there is nothing beyond that, just emptiness. The person perceives in his mind a state of hopelessness, just as when a computer crashes, we have all experienced that feeling; this concept aligns with that feeling of hopelessness it is well beyond the person's personal capacity.

We have to make sure that when and where we step in to effect change that we don not enact this attribute in people. We have to deal with them truthfully, and not try to hide the obvious. Instead, we have to offer alternatives...and change perception.

IF YOU BELIEVE THAT YOU CAN DO A THING, OR IF YOU CANNOT, IN EITHER CASE YOU ARE RIGHT – HENRY FORD

How our natural experiences influence our primitive and rational perception:

Experiences influence perception. Therefore, how we experience things will determine how we see and react. The richness or poverty of every experience we have had leaves us with cardinal knowledge that filters into our thought making process. This phenomenon is attributed to the brains ability to utilise every bit of information it has ever gained, either – sensory, emotionally, physically, and mentally to influence and form reasoning with. The mind takes much longer to respond in the absence of experience - to get to the appropriate response. When not conditioned (not having had many experience in life) or trained (not having gained knowledge via tutoring or informative source), a person will not be able to function as intellectually proficient as one who has been exposed to an array of experiences, as people intelligent people.

Then there is also a thing that disregards our intelligence, called stimulus that activates/ influences our perceptions and responses. This stands in stark contrast to the norm of engaging in reasoning, as explained above. We also get reactive responses to a potential "threat" - that activates our primal nature, to fight, flee or surrender. Deeper than this we get frustrated, emotional, depress, and irrational. What makes these responses critical and significant is that people see people and their way in which they communicate, as either friendly, neutral or hostile,(to name a few) and then we decide how we will react, before we bring in reason. Perception is all-powerful, it dictates who, what, where, when and how, we will do, say or act, and in what manner. Regardless of our intelligence. In the time it takes the mind from the initial stimulus to the actual response, we have thought about how we will act, at times, it is beyond that point and we act automatically it seems. To understand this we have to picture a space being created in our minds by virtue of any stimulus, seeking an "appropriate" response. This "space" will become our next focal point of interest and discussion.

The space; or "Gap", where perception and choice originate.

The space or "Gap" that originates because of any stimulus needs to be filled. The "filling" is referred to as "our preferred choice", this is the one thing we have control over, the type of filling we are going to use between stimulus and response and this is also where we have a conscious pause to choose the relevant action that will follow.

In this "gap", we find the existence of multiple choices, as well as the realisation of their consequences. The mind has stored in it a host of "our preferred choices" to recurring stimulus. Because it learns from experience that these responses satisfy a particular stimulus, therefore it becomes a relevant choice and is stored for future use and reference.

This is once again a question of personal perception, on the part of the person; it is not to say that the responses stored (habits) are actually relevant and expected responses in general.

Perceptions formed by choices become "Habits" over time.

With this knowledge, we will form the new strategic managers, this is cliché, and the truth of the matter is old habits die-hard. We have to be realistic, where we give people too many choices; we end up with very little action. We all commonly accept and desire the ability to have a say in every matter, however, it is humanly impossible to listen to what everyone has to say to have something simple done. Re-engineered thinking; concentrates on changing perception, so that a group adapts the same views. Starting with changing opinions that change attitudes that change people, one at a time. People all have opinions, some very strong - based on their perceptions, and the way they say and feel about things, this aspect could become a source of contest and strife. The question is, what do we stand to benefit by changing perceptions – we create focus. Having a focal point channels all perceptions towards one goal, it creates a sense of purposeful and yet meaningful ways to change effectively as a collective and it becomes habitual.

By changing ourselves, we revolutionize the way we see others, the world, and change as being our opportunity at growth and gain, with this mind-set we accept any change and deal with it more effectively. Change has to be seen as opportunity by everyone, this should be a mind-set. Our mental point of departure will take time to form – people are very reluctant to change - and only through desire and practice will we succeed, in fine tuning paradigms on change. We all reside within our own fears, which keep us captive; they blur our vision of the near future, when faced with change. Now that we have found the key to the portal - that takes us from the one dimension - that of personal mental captivity and restraint to the next. Freeing us of our own unfounded paradigms on fear, on to the next advanced level of thinking, where we have to learn to reframe our thinking altogether, in order to fill the gaps we have created between reality and personal issues.

However, before we do, we have to understand that the subconscious mind also has more tricks to play. We have to become aware of this aspect, where fear keeps us captive. Where the subconscious mind tries to bring things into perspective that have no significance / bearing or relevance. The mind creates a hypothesis from former experiences, rendering anything new irrelevant in an instant. Then it becomes an emotionally charged train ride, where we struggle to make sense of what is and what is not applicable due to this input, emotional influence on our lives are strong, if not all the initial arguments, we create with thinking about change. Our own unique insecurities and personal beliefs dictate our next course of action. The point to make here is this; our entrenched perceptions will dictate what reality should look like from our own perspective. Therefore, we should become guarded, in our presumptions and try not to change reality to suit us all the time, but rather try to understand that we all live with altered states of what we perceive reality to be. We have to guard against automated responses and rather deal with every interaction on its own merit. First, seek to understand before seeking to be understood – this is the definition of "perception modelling", perceptions must be real or seemingly real to be effective, it deals with logic, emotion and fear and how things are universally understood.

Our universal knowledge becomes our logical perception.

Secondly, we have logical change, when something dies; it needs to make way for the new or better option- easy. Here the logical brain takes preference, where previously the historic and subconscious brain had preference in altering and influencing our thinking on perception. We will seek through data for a solution to the problem, but we will be rational our deduction and application. Therefore, everything in life is in the eyes of the beholder it is said, and no two people will do something in response to the same given situation in the same manner. The reason for this is perception. Perception is the way we ultimately see our reality, or want to perceive it to be. The other aspect is that of denial; denial is a defence of the truth. We all have "personal issues" so if the truth is too painful or the consequence thereof, then we will alter it with a denial. This is what makes strategy so interesting, we have to deal with three levels of the brain, how it "thinks", and how the person "sees" life, living and reality. We can relay this to movie clips of us growing up, or by referring to it as our "scripts". Every time the brain gets a response or stimulus, the stimulus is dispatched to all three regions of the brain.

  On to the final step in strategic management communication; we need to be aware that we are dealing with paradigms more than what we are dealing with people... once you have all the perceptions covered, only then do you have a green light to move onto talking strategy.

The power of Paradigms; they are the culmination of perceptions:

A final word on paradigms. Paradigms form when the mind looks through all the clips and scripts to find a fitting response. Perceptions therefore influence paradigms, either positively or negatively because perceptions are emotionally generated to colour in our paradigm, to give it life. Perceptions appeal to all our senses of taste and smell, but mostly scent, scent influences 75% of our emotional state. We can all effectively recall the smell of the ocean, or the stench of rotten fish and this could very well be why we do not like fish for instance. Consequently, it stands to reason that this person has a paradigm that is not consistent with how others view fish.

Now. some more practical example of a paradigm having formed, taking the Police as an example. The Police do not tackle crime to eradicate it, this type of thinking is not logical; in fact, they merely police the perception of crime in the media. The media has become a perception-altering agent. In other words, the media influences us to think in line with certain norms, right or wrong; it does not really matter to them.

We have to be aware that the media does not endorse the truth or the concept of the truth; they concern themselves only with the perception of the truth. The media wants to "show" the stench of rotting fish, regardless of its consequences. Whereas, the Police in this regard merely try to hide the bad smell of rotting fish from us. They are influencing the way we look at crime, by altering our perception of crime, so that our paradigm of crime may be changed. Consequently, if a Police spokesperson tells the media that they have had a 100% reduction in rape for this month and then it stands to reason that the Police have done an exceptional job in this regard. Wherein actual fact this is not the case, it is merely a perception generated that this area is rape free. In reality though, as many as six rapes in that area may have occurred over a specific period. The police work on statistical data that they compare to the previous year, and now they are down 100% on the previous year. Therefore, where perception meets reality everything is marginalized. The Police work on eventuality and perception, for instance a 12% average will be deemed as an acceptable level of crime for a specific category of crime in a certain area. The Police may allow for four to six rapes – as the norm and eventuality, due to the socio economic problems that exist in that particular community. Anything above that becomes statistics. This is perception management, perception is not "reality", it is what we want reality to ultimately be like, or what we are told or taught it should be like. Accordingly, we are not living in a "real world", we are living in a "perceived reality of the real world", where perception management becomes our reality... Let us see how it works and firstly take a scientific journey to discover more about this aspect of controlling thinking and altering it through perception management. These "things" will ultimately culminate and influence our Paradigm.

"According to your faith, shall it be done unto you – biblical -belief creates the actual fact" – *William James.*

What are we seeing; Perception, or Reality or have we become mentally blind by living a life of denial?

What actually forms perception, or "Percepts?"

Percepts – is the sum of influences - something that is perceived by the senses – to form a "Perception" – this is the process of using the senses to acquire information about the surrounding environment or situation. Precepts are influenced by:

- The *quality*; of the stimuli on the senses (seeing, hearing, smelling, tasting and touching)
- The *intensity*; of the stimuli dark vs. light, loud vs. soft and strong vs. weak
- *Duration*; time and distance as well as speed
- *Place*; have associations coupled to them, good vs. bad, hot vs. cold and loving vs. scary.
- *Self- awareness*; awareness of the self is man's greatest attribute, to the extent to which man's self is involved depends on the extent to which he is subjectively involved with the conceptual content of his perceptions. The "I" like, need, want, etc.
- *The symbolism*, the nature of perception;

Percepts are present and constituted whenever we perceive people, things, ideas, or situations physically present, they are symbolic representations of the perceived reality-out-there that forms our perception of it.

Strategy also creates stress due to the changes we require...

Therefore, we say, "You are what you see in the mirror"; by changing our beliefs, we are in fact changing our reality. In order to accomplish great things, we must not only act, but also dream; not only plan, but also believe. To achieve goals, we have to identify clearly, what we want first. To create the right perception, we have to dream it up and see it - "what we vividly imagine, ardently desire, we will evidently achieve". Consequently, it stands to reason, "If we don't see it, then it does not exist". This in itself is very important, we tell people our worth, and we tell them how to treat us and how to "see" us and most importantly how we see ourselves. We become the culmination of every second of our total living experience, what we read, understand, believe and experience. We create a perception of who we are and sell that.

The second dimension of perception is the symbolic component that influences percepts – what we see by adding symbols. The perception centre is where we keep all our perceptions generated, like a library of perceptions also called scripts. The role played by activating our memory with information is the perceptual process of imprinting stimuli, in other words forming habits are strongly influenced by our memory during early stages of life in the forming of perceptions, e.g. established attitudes, norms, values, needs and opinions, thus, percepts are not pure sense impressions. They are also aligned with our roles we perform like actors, from scripts that we wrote in similar situations - that reoccur along life's path, the shape shifting we do, from the one role to the next, whenever we enter into new debates etc. These roles were written by our interactions with others, by mimicking our parents and role models, they have become our frame of reference, our experiences and our thinking.

Change creates a stressed mind and lifestyle that influences our ability to think, strategists need to stay on top of their game as thinking critically is both mentally and physically exhausting and it therefore affects our bodies.

Now enter the hormones, Homoeostasis, the body is a big chemical factory that requires balance.

Homeostasis refers to the **interaction between the body and the mind**, the two halves that meet to form one whole, the one influencing the other. The body is a truly complex thinking machine governed by chemicals.

Therefore, we need to look at the mind and the body's interaction to understand the significance. A condition called Psychological homeostasis – (is a state of equilibrium, or a tendency to reach equilibrium between the two, the body and the mind that is).

Tension;

The first aspect is tension. This does not mean that a complete absence of tension becomes prevalent; on the contrary, for effective functioning of our minds and bodies a certain degree of tension is necessary to ascertain balance. Consequently, psychological homoeostasis and biological homoeostasis run in parallel. This simply means that the one promotes the other and visa-versa, it also means that if we suffer mental problems for instance such as fatigue it could manifest itself in the physical, as an ulcer, panic attack and tension etc. – all physical forms or manifestations of tension. The reverse is also true if we suffer physical pain and trauma it relates back to the emotional and manifests itself as emotional ailments. Consequently, the mind and body are interrelated and has a mutual effect on our mental ability and health or a lack thereof, as well as our physical health.

The defence system to tension and pain;

The body's defence system to pain either mental or physical and stresses is hormones. The body has its own chemical factory, which produces healing chemicals to help us cope. **Hormones** form a natural buffer system or psychological defence (psychological homeostasis). This could be extraordinarily effective in preserving emotional and endocrine homeostasis; relating to how our glands secrete a variety of hormones internally directly into the bloodstream to address issues related to our health, almost like feel good drugs, all in an effort to fight off pain and stressors.

Serotonin for instance makes us feel calm when we become stressed, or acts as pain reliever whilst **endorphins** - meaning morphine from within - kills pain and were found to have pain-reducing effects. Whereas **adrenalin** triggers survival, producing heightened strength and stamina – the "fight-flight" hormone. Endorphins are now known universally as stress or catecholamine, relieving hormones, which act much like the opiate drugs Opium, Morphine, and Heroin. When the brain detects stress it sends out signals, or opiates, which bind at the receptor sites and then pain is alleviated.

Why we get "High" on tension and stress.

Feelings of euphoria follow on and soon become apparent where athletes starts working on their "second wind", by working harder to get to the second body hit, where they do not experience any pain whilst running for instance, where the brain starts flooding the body with natural endorphins. Endorphins much like the drugs that they mimic have the phenomenon of eliciting the proverbial "body hit" or "high", which is why abuse is possible. It is known and obvious that structures in the body have evolved through the decades. Evidence of changes within the brains structures become apparent where humans learn to adapt to situations in order to survive situations of pain. The brain evokes an endorphin rush, which in turn allows a person to either stay or fight or run away, that furthermore evokes an adrenaline rush, either by trained choice or by natural phenomenon, all quite beneficial to survival of the individual. Afterwards, endorphins also allow the person to be able to work with the pain its body is feeling and to recover. These ground-breaking studies opened many doors for the scientific community to be able to study various angles of pain, depression, happiness, abuse/obsession and potential and homeostatic processes such as eating and exercise, many angles, which were previously barely understood.

The system of endorphins physically consists of chains of amino acids, which make-up the chemical messengers known as neuropeptides. The transmissions of pain and/or pleasurable feelings exist within the brain due to nerve impulses. These impulses are relayed via neurotransmitter chemicals thus causing the release of neuromodulator chemicals, such as endorphins. These messengers differ from neurotransmitters in the fact that they modulate feelings of pain and pleasure, rather than convey the actual feelings. In order to change the feelings of pleasure and block off pain, the endorphins must reduce activity in the thalamus and cerebral cortex. This occurs by the neuromodulators affecting the dopamine pathway by binding to a specific opiate receptor site. Endorphins "shut off" the nerves in the frontal lobe, inhibiting feelings of pain and allow this area to flood with dopamine, hence the feelings of euphoria.

Even in the face of what is perceived to be very severe stresses, we have as a defence endocrine homeostasis, a chemical laboratory of internal medicines to stop and overcome as well as cure the brain and body from stress.

Therefore, we can deduce that man was designed to cope with change and the pain it creates. We can furthermore appreciate that the body and mind exist and function independently of each other, but need one another. What's more, by saying this, we are referring to the interdependent nature of the two entities; the fact that imbalances occurring in either, will affect the overall balance. The ideal is to find balance, or homeostasis here.

General sources of strain, stress, or pain

Some individuals are better equipped to deal with stress than what others are. By saying this, we are implying that there are noticeable causes. By identify the underlying causes we can create distinctions between different forms of tension that are quite arbitrary, because they cannot be linked to one specific arousal response. In most cases a conglomeration of inputs evoke responses that sets off a chain of events, that evokes spontaneous responses. Most commonly observed stress related ailments manifests in the form of a nervous breakdown, angina and depression or total withdrawal. More severe; nevertheless not uncommon, are spontaneous outbursts of rage and anger by expressing ones frustration, all the result of overwhelming pressure, strains, and stress manifesting in different ways.

Tension has to be effectively controlled and managed. We have to have tension, we cannot function without it, and here are some identified forms of tension:

Forms of Tension

General Psychological tension;

Every stimulus; sight, sound, pain etc. evokes psychological tension of some sorts in the whole body – also referred to as general psychological stress.

Specific Physiological tension;

As the title suggests, this is a physical response and specific reaction in the presence of a specific stressor. Where the individual repeatedly reacts or shows the same psychological reaction pattern; fight or flight, the physical reaction or response. Nevertheless, what is significant about the response is that it is individualized in symptoms, manifestation, and character, in comparison to a study with a group of people in the same situation faced with the same common catalyst. Therefore, in general terms no two people will react exactly the same to any trigger that calls for a response of a physical nature or reaction. Therefore, every response to tension in this regard is specific to the individual.

Psychological tension;

By psychological tension we simply refer to conscious feelings of tenseness, an individual experiences it in the presence of emotional inducers; like anxiety, tenderness, fear, and grief. This happens daily, but what is significant about it is that here we have choice, as to how it will affect us, how we will react to it, cope with it, or give into it... Physical symptoms such as; headaches, stiff neck, watery eyes, tight chest and chest pains may develop. The antidote lies in the way we structure our lives. These are the manifestations of overworked, overstressed people just taking it too far for too long. The antidote is physical exercises, rearranging our lives, thinking, revisiting our daily priorities, to see if we are in balance, and taking stock of our emotional bank balances.

How much credit do we have with our children, our spouses, our brothers, sisters, parents and friends, or are we running into a debit. When you are overdrawn, you are on a subconscious level continuously sweating the deterioration of that bond that was so special, the one we had with our spouses, before the kids came, or our friends - before the big job opportunity came, before we became career orientated. Well the repossession of personal trust and love will be spiralling towards - the take back situation – where all ties are disrupted, turned off or withdrawn. This is just the nature of relationships; you have to be there to be engaged physically. The saying of "out of sight is out of mind" and "absence makes the heart grow fonder". These clichés come from noble-minded ideas and perceptions about truth and relationships. The truth is simple, no interaction, no feedback no relationship. Just as in real life if bills are not paid, the bank will reposes the house and the car etc. likewise with emotional banks, if you do not fulfil your commitments, they will become your burdens and haunt you.

Take note of the relationship between physiological and psychological tension when looking for people that can cope with stress.

Understanding the relationship between physiological; (relating to the way that living things function, rather than to their shape or structure) and psychological; (the emotional side - existing only in the mind, without having a physical basis) that creates or relieves tension. This begs the question of who has the right temperament for the job, and why we have to discriminate in this regard on the grounds of the different stress thresholds required for a specific job function. Temperament is the person's state of mind, where character, is an emotional condition, or predisposition of a particular kind. In order to find the best suitable candidate for the specialized unit's in the Police and Military for instance, they employ strict physical and mental criteria firstly and then only academic and other qualifications are reviewed. You should also note (with concern) the relationship between temperament and the concepts of emotional ability and stability to cope with high stress situations. Temperament also refers to a characteristic trait to deal with emotional and physical discomfort given a specific situations or stimulation. Like customary strength and speed of response, the quality of this ability to bounce back is commonly referred to as resilience. Resilience also relates to and does not exclude the ability to recover quickly from setbacks, the ability of a person to spring back quickly into the fully operational and capable shape after being bent, stretched, or deformed by an event. These qualities are hard to find, and have been observed to occur in tandem with our constitutional makeup, largely dependent on our inherent origin, you either have it or you do not.

The relevance and relationship between imprinting and exhaustion threshold.

When tension is created in a work environment by a stressor and is prolonged and repeated a "Plateau" is reached and the mind switches off, in order to restart, recalibrate, and make sense of the current situation. Mental fatigue is no joke. This is normally experienced with prolonged periods of work, where we reach our threshold and still have to function. Certain numbness overcomes us, but we fight it, adrenalin is re-injected, the alarm phase sets in, this causes agitated ness, sleepiness, or withdrawal. This is called the resistance phase, where the glucose levels are tapped. Very few police officers have not at some stage of their careers experienced the resistance phase; this is the phase where people make mistakes because they are exhausted, both mentally and physically. It is interesting to note that during this threshold limit, the stressors have a greater effect psychologically than what they do on the physical body; the body's ability to adapt and regulate its limits to changes in climate is exceptional. Nevertheless, the body has a limited programmed capacity as well, where reservoirs for mentally and physically troubling times are kept - from where it taps into under periods of extreme stress. This is where imprinting plays a role. "Mind over Matter" "if you don't mind it does not matter". This saying or maxim's hold many truths. Soldiers and cops are, or should be programmed to keep fighting and not stop once they feel pain or get hurt in the heat of battle. This comes with imprinting during advanced tactical training, where action and reactions are automated by doing "drills' over and over under varying conditions. Symbols are enforced and pain is induced to trigger the revival of the fighting spirit scripts, the survival scripts. This has everything to do with survival and staying in the fight or withdrawing. If not trained under extreme conditions of exertion and exhaustion the body will not be able to cope. The stressors will last too long during a real fight; a point is reached where the defences and resources of the body will collapse. An example of this type of behaviour can be observed where people assume the fetal position when attacked. So, when testing candidates test them to see how they would react in a "three on one" street fight type of situation, if they run, they will keep running, if they surrender they will keep surrendering but if they fight, train them to keep on fighting. Both genetically and mentally, this candidate is predisposed to fight for survival, as they are now programmed to react with more fight and encrypted to survive by knowing how to handle the threshold. It is in his/her DNA, he is a "Sheep Dog" a predator amongst men. How does one relate this back to a corporate environment? The organisation will have to take the initiative here, we had a programme where we taught people self-defence, knife fighting, and anti-hijacking techniques in work time, it started very slow, it's a sold out class now. If the corporate culture endorsed the principle of win-win fighting, then employees win in the way that they feel more secure in their ability to defend themselves, build camaraderie, and relieve stress. The more they interact with one another on a social and physical level, the stronger their camaraderie will become – and the more they want to keep doing it. Employees could spar; and get rid of their frustrations at the amusement of the rest of the staff. Because each one of our perceptions represents an experience that offers a precious nugget of wisdom; it is only human nature to be afraid when looking at our losses and setbacks in life. Because it generates an emotional response, but to do so constantly is to turn your back on the possibilities of gaining experience from it. Negativity and failure affects everyone; however, the most successful people take their setbacks in their stride. They don't ignore them instead they learn from them and rather choose to focus on them as reminders to shift their attention to creating energy to build on their greatest strengths in developing them to achieve new goals, and not repeat their mistakes, rather than dwelling on the past. We also have a need to understand our feelings; where they come from and how to make contact with their source. However, one thing that our minds do well and all the time, is to decide what is important enough for us to notice and what is not. This aspect creates inner turmoil, if we didn't discriminate against our own perception we would all be at sea, therefore, we need to take conscious decisions and go with the result. If not, we would get overwhelmed with too much information, so our minds are habituated to sort things and thoughts in order of importance, the wheat from the chaff, so that we notice what is important to us and not the rest. The trouble with this system of thinking is that the mind thinks what really matters is anything that is a threat, or a perceived threat, and wants us to act on it... now. This is in conflict with reality; things that don't matter are the things that don't change. Things that change and move and create drama get our attention first, whilst the simple unmoving true nature of the people and things around us are not deemed to be worthy of our attention. No wonder we are having a hard time staying calm and getting all stressed up about things! Only once thinking about thinking takes prevalence, where we start thinking critical, does this process of higher order thinking start opening our perception to new alternative thought. To intentionally put a portion of our attention, to where we want our energy to flow, on that which truly matters to us. This thinking about thinking becomes a steering mechanism to align us with what we truly need and want. We have become lazy to a very large extent to think clearly, we leave it to others, to a certain degree we resort to automated responses and allow our minds to go to hell. We allow emotions and perceptions as thought-based processors to rule our world for us. We have become spectators, the world in chaos has shrouded our ability to think critically, we numb our minds not to think, only to all think alike as the norm, and in the process we hide ourselves behind a "truth", our worth and our energy expires, and we become depressed.

Influences at work in an ever-changing Strategic Landscape. Thinking of strategy on a three dimensional scale reveals how influences work in on it.

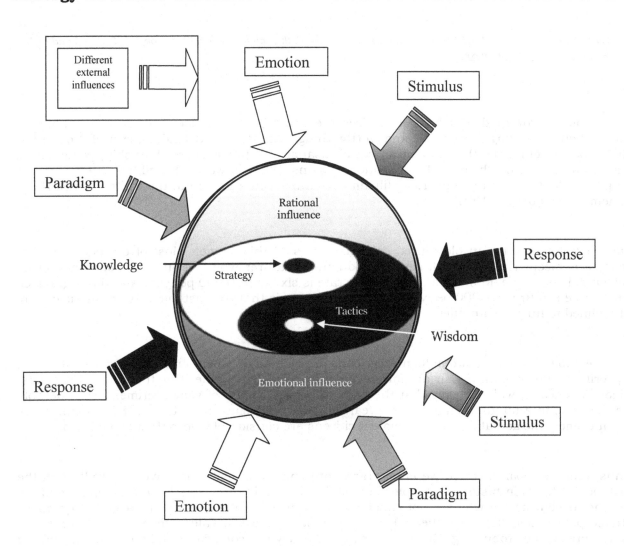

The influence of Denial and Vigilance – is powerfully illustrated in:

ON SHEEP, WOLVES and SHEEPDOGS

By LTC (RET) Dave Grossman, RANGER, Ph.D., author of "On Killing". (It is an extract from his book, "On Combat" and he has his own web site www.killology.com)

Honour never grows old and honour rejoices the heart of age. It does so because honour is, finally, about defending those noble and worthy things that deserve defending, even if it comes at a high cost. In our time, that may mean social disapproval, public scorn, hardship, persecution, or as always, even death itself. The question remains: What is worth defending? What is worth dying for? What is worth living for? - William J. Bennett – in a lecture to the United States Naval Academy November 24, 1997.

One Vietnam veteran, an old retired colonel, once said this to me: "Most of the people in our society are sheep. They are kind, gentle, productive creatures who can only hurt one another by accident." This is true. Remember, the murder rate is six per 100,000 per year and the aggravated assault rate is four per 1,000 per year. What this means is that the vast majority of Americans are not inclined to hurt one another.

Some estimates say that two million Americans are victims of violent crimes every year, a tragic, staggering number, perhaps an all-time record rate of violent crime. But there are almost 300 million Americans, which means that the odds of being a victim of violent crime is considerably less than one in a hundred on any given year. Furthermore, since repeat offenders commit many violent crimes, the actual numbers of violent citizens are considerably less than two million.

Thus, there is a paradox and we must grasp both ends of the situation: We may well be in the most violent times in history, but violence is still remarkably rare. This is because most citizens are kind, decent people who are not capable of hurting each other, except by accident or under extreme provocation. They are sheep. I mean nothing negative by calling them sheep. To me it is like the pretty, blue robin's egg. Inside it is soft and gooey but someday it will grow into something wonderful. However, the egg cannot survive without its hard blue shell. Police officers, soldiers and other warriors are like that shell and someday the civilization they protect will grow into something wonderful? For now, though, they need warriors to protect them from the predators.

Thus, by observing and identifying these influences, we could create counter measures, from outside, by creating the countering influences from inside and visa-versa. In order to change an

~ 23 ~

inner-influence we have to create an outer. This works the same in reverse. Forces determine balance and equilibrium, if one force becomes too much, or diminishes by too much, then the equilibrium becomes distorted. With strategy, we always strive to get our proportions in balance.

"Then there are the wolves," the old war veteran said" and the wolves feed on the sheep without mercy". Do you believe there are wolves out there that will feed on the flock without mercy? You had better believe it. There are evil men in this world and they are capable of evil deeds. The moment you forget that or pretend it is not so, you become a sheep. There is no safety in denial. "Then there are sheepdogs," he went on" and I'm a sheepdog. I live to protect the flock and confront the wolf."

If you have no capacity for violence then you are a healthy productive citizen, a sheep. If you have a capacity for violence and no empathy for your fellow citizens, then you have defined an aggressive sociopath, a wolf. However, what if you have a capacity for violence and a deep love for your fellow citizens? What do you have then? A sheepdog, a warrior, someone who is walking the hero's path. Someone who can walk into the heart of darkness, into the universal human phobia and walk out unscathed.

Let me expand on this old soldier's excellent model of the sheep, wolves and sheepdogs. We know that the sheep live in denial that is what makes them sheep. They do not want to believe that there is evil in the world. They can accept the fact that fires can happen, which is why they want fire extinguishers, fire sprinklers, fire alarms and fire exit's throughout their kids' schools.

But many of them are outraged at the idea of putting an armed police officer in their kid's school. Our children are thousands of times more likely to be killed or seriously injured by school violence than fire, but the sheep's only response to the possibility of violence is denial. The idea of someone coming to kill or harm their child is just too hard and so they chose the path of denial.

The sheep generally do not like the sheepdog. He looks a lot like the wolf. He has fangs and the capacity for violence. The difference, though, is that the sheepdog must not, cannot and will not ever harm the sheep. Any sheep dog who intentionally harms the lowliest little lamb will be punished and removed. The world cannot work any other way, at least not in a representative democracy or a republic such as ours.

Still, the sheepdog disturbs the sheep. He is a constant reminder that there are wolves in the land. They would prefer that he didn't tell them where to go, or give them traffic tickets, or stand at the ready in our airports in camouflage fatigues holding an M-16. The sheep would much rather have the sheepdog cash in his fangs, spray paint himself white and go, "Baa". Until the wolf shows up. Then the entire flock tries desperately to hide behind one lonely sheepdog.

The students, the victims, at Columbine High School were big, tough high school students and under ordinary circumstances, they would not have had the time of day for a police officer. They were not bad kids; they just had nothing to say to a cop. When the school was under attack, however and SWAT teams were clearing the rooms and hallways, the officers had to physically peel those clinging, sobbing kids off them. This is how the little lambs feel about their sheepdog when the wolf is at the door.

The Radical Revolutionary Strategic Management Matrix For Predators

Look at what happened after September 11, 2001 when the wolf pounded hard on the door. Remember how America, more than ever before, felt differently about their law enforcement officers and military personnel? Remember how many times you heard the word hero?

Understand that there is nothing morally superior about being a sheepdog; it is just what you choose to be. Also understand that a sheepdog is a funny critter: He is always sniffing around out on the perimeter, checking the breeze, barking at things that go bump in the night and yearning for a righteous battle. That is, the young sheepdogs yearn for a righteous battle. The old sheepdogs are a little older and wiser, but they move to the sound of the guns when needed right along with the young ones.

Here is how the sheep and the sheepdog think differently. The sheep pretend the wolf will never come, but the sheepdog lives for that day. After the attacks on September 11, 2001, most of the sheep, that is, most citizens in America said, "Thank God I wasn't on one of those planes." The sheepdogs, the warriors, said, "Dear God, I wish I could have been on one of those planes. Maybe I could have made a difference." When you are truly transformed into a warrior and have truly invested yourself into warrior hood, you want to be there. You want to be able to make a difference.

There is nothing morally superior about the sheepdog, the warrior, but he does have one real advantage. Only one and that is that he is able to survive and thrive in an environment that destroys 98 percent of the population. There was research conducted a few years ago with individuals convicted of violent crimes. These cons were in prison for serious, predatory crimes of violence: assaults, murders and killing law enforcement officers. The vast majority said that they specifically targeted victims by body language: slumped walk, passive behaviour and lack of awareness. They chose their victims like big cats do in Africa, when they select one out of the herd that is least able to protect itself. Some people may be destined to be sheep another's might be genetically primed to be wolves or sheepdogs. Nevertheless, I believe that most people can choose which one they want to be and I'm proud to say that more and more Americans are choosing to become sheepdogs.

Seven months after the attack on September 11, 2001, Todd Beamer was honoured in his hometown of Cranbury, New Jersey. Todd, as you recall, was the man on Flight 93 over Pennsylvania who called on his cellphone to alert an operator from United Airlines about the hijacking. When he learned of the other three passenger planes that had been used as weapons, Todd dropped his phone and uttered the words, "Let's roll", which authorities believe was a signal to the other passengers to confront the terrorist hijackers.

In one hour, a transformation occurred among the passengers - athletes, business people and parents. -- From sheep to sheepdogs and together they fought the wolves, ultimately saving an unknown number of lives on the ground. There is no safety for honest men except by believing all possible evil of evil men. - Edmund Burke. Here is the point I like to emphasize, especially to the thousands of police officers and soldiers I speak to each year. In nature the sheep, real sheep, are born as sheep. Sheepdogs are born that way and so are wolves. They didn't have a choice. However, you are not a critter. As a human being, you can be whatever you want to be. It is a conscious, moral decision.

If you want to be a sheep, then you can be a sheep and that is okay, but you must understand the price you pay. When the wolf comes, you and your loved ones are going to die if there is not a sheepdog there to protect you. If you want to be a wolf, you can be one, but the sheepdogs are going to hunt you down and you will never have rest, safety, trust, or love. But if you want to be a sheepdog and walk the warrior's path, then you must make a conscious and moral decision every day to dedicate, equip and prepare yourself to thrive in that toxic, corrosive moment when the wolf comes knocking at the door. For example, many officers carry their weapons in church.

They are well concealed in ankle holsters, shoulder holsters or inside-the-belt holsters tucked into the small of their backs. Anytime you go to some form of religious service, there is a very good chance that a police officer in your congregation is carrying. You will never know if there is such an individual in your place of worship, until the wolf appears to massacre you and your loved ones.

I was training a group of police officers in Texas and during the break, one officer asked his friend if he carried his weapon in church. The other cop replied, "I will never be caught without my gun in church." I asked why he felt so strongly about this and he told me about a cop he knew who was at a church massacre in Ft. Worth, Texas in 1999.

In that incident, a mentally deranged individual came into the church and opened fire, gunning down fourteen people. He said that officer believed he could have saved every life that day if he had been carrying his gun. His own son was shot and all he could do was throw himself on the boy's body and wait to die. That cop looked me in the eye and said, "Do you have any idea how hard it would be to live with yourself after that?"

Some individuals would be horrified if they knew this police officer was carrying a weapon in church. They might call him paranoid and would probably scorn him. Yet, these same individuals would be enraged and would call for "heads to roll" if they found out that the airbags in their cars were defective, or that the fire extinguisher and fire sprinklers in their kids' school did not work. They can accept the fact that fires and traffic accidents can happen and that there must be safeguards against them.

Their only response to the wolf, though, is denial and all too often, their response to the sheepdog is scorn and disdain. But the sheepdog quietly asks himself, "Do you have and idea how hard it would be to live with yourself if your loved ones attacked and killed and you had to stand there helplessly because you were unprepared for that day?" It is denial that turns people into sheep. Sheep are psychologically destroyed by combat because their only defence is denial, which is counterproductive and destructive, resulting in fear, helplessness and horror when the wolf shows up.

Denial kills you twice. It kills you once, at your moment of truth when you are not physically prepared: you didn't bring your gun, you didn't train. Your only defence was wishful thinking. Hope is not a strategy. Denial kills you a second time because even if you do physically survive, you are psychologically shattered by your own fear, the sense of helplessness and horror at your moment of truth when you realise that you were not ready to be tested.

Gavin de Becker puts it like this in Fear Less, his superb post-9/11 book, which should be required reading for anyone trying to come to terms with our current world situation: "...denial can be seductive, but it has an insidious side effect. For all the peace of mind deniers think they get by saying it isn't so, the fall they take when faced with new violence is all the more unsettling."

Denial is a save-now-pay-later scheme, a contract written entirely in small print, for in the long run, the denying person knows the truth on some level. Therefore, the warrior must strive to confront denial in all aspects of his life and prepare himself for the day when evil comes. If you are a warrior who is legally authorized to carry a weapon and you step outside without that weapon, then you become a sheep, pretending that the bad man will not come today. No one can be "on" 24/7, for a lifetime. Everyone needs down time. However, if you are authorized to carry a weapon and you walk outside without it, just take a deep breath and say this to yourself..."Baa".

This business of being a sheep or a sheep dog is not a yes-no dichotomy. It is not an all-or-nothing, either-or choice. It is a matter of degrees, a continuum. On one end is an abject, head-in-the-sand-sheep and on the other end is the ultimate warrior. Few people exist completely on one end or the other. Most of us live somewhere in between. Since 9-11 almost everyone in America took a step up that continuum, away from denial. The sheep took a few steps toward accepting and appreciating their warriors and the warriors started taking their job more seriously. The degree to which you move up that continuum, away from sheep hood and denial, is the degree to which you and your loved ones will survive, physically and psychologically at your moment of truth.

Forming individuals;

By making them aware of how they themselves influence strategy. Yes, we are still on the individual/s that create strategy; we will now look at other influences that govern our strategy makers, we have however covered extensively our abstract mental nature in chapter one, now we will move onto our formative mental nature.

Overcoming the influence of their stagnation

Subsequently, the four formative aspects we have to consider when we evaluate our ideal candidate would be:

a) **General activity level**; referring to the person's energy levels, how active or passive the person is at work; look into his medical history and physical wellbeing if necessary.
b) **Emotional stability**; how emotional or unemotional the individual is, does he take statements personal or not, here we are only concerned with the persons reaction to very intense stimuli when tested.
c) **Sociability**; referring to sociability as opposed to lack of involvement. Whereas one individual likes to be with people and the other prefers to work alone.
d) **Impulsiveness**; Reactivity, referring to how impulsive or retained and or deliberate the individual is in his reaction. This dimension is concerned with mainly the speed of an

individual's reaction time to stun stimuli and the appropriateness of the choice of reaction to the perceived threat.

1. **Overcoming lukewarm-ness by incorporating evolution**

Temperament: *Discipline does more in war than enthusiasm.* - **Machiavelli, the Art of War.**

Although it is true that "temperament traits" are largely determined by the inherited characteristics of the individuals' nervous and endocrine system, this does however not mean that traits remain unchanged throughout an individual's life – we do evolve. Through training and learning by way of new experiences and socialization, basic temperaments and tendencies may be modified and tempered. Just by starting with that very end product in mind and reverse engineering it, all strategy starts with people and this is why we will concentrate on this aspect first, from the forming process to the very first step of recruitment and building in temperament trait testing and evaluation.

2. **Darwin's Theory of Evolution by Natural Selection constitutes the following belief system:**

a) More individuals are produced in each generation that can survive.
b) Phenotypic variation exists among individuals and the variation is heritable.
c) Those individuals with heritable traits better suited to the environment will survive.
d) When reproductive isolation occurs, new species will form.

Darwin just missed one critical point, evolution does not exist in one continuous cycle, it happens in leaps and bounds.

"Variation is a feature of natural populations and every population produces more progeny than its environment can manage. The consequence of this overproduction is that those individuals with the best genetic fitness for the environment will produce offspring that can more successfully compete in that environment. Thus the subsequent generation will have a higher representation of these offspring and the population will have evolved."- Darwin.

3. The creation of our strategic Predator

Most people today just want to get on with life and living, change and strategy is not something they want or care much for. Their living stays mundane and their endless debating changes nothing about their terrible lives, world politics and crime... The fittest of the fit will survive; in business as in life, and it is said that business is just another battlefield.

4. The organisation seen as an individual entity and its role on strategy:

We will introduce basic forms of strategy and tactics first, derived directly from doctrines on war in the following chapters based on the model of guerrilla warfare. We will mature them with concepts, skills, and tactics as we progress and discuss means of balancing influences on strategy... and people involved.

 Therefore, it makes good sense to get the "Right stuff "from our candidate that has to lead us. In Military terms, this maxim holds many truths, good strategist win wars. However we as nations will appoint leaders based on a perception that has nothing to do with competence – yet another perception. The question is now, why do we not apply the same logic – when looking for "a few good men" to lead us - in business where everyone should be seen as a proficient leader? The reason is that in war, our sights, both mental and physical, are focused primarily on our survival; a highest order need, our imprinted scripts have served us well in this regard, for we are still surviving, although still making war. However, when we enter into a business mind-set, we tend to lower our sights onto a pure political perspective – perception - that is, we tend to lose our perspective and instinct of survival, and we lose sight on how important the knowledge of war is, and the credibility of our leadership and their competence.

Business is War! In addition, even basic business has many attributes of war, not just good leadership; although not all blood and guts, we trade those attributes of war for more subtle sacrifices like sweat, effort and time.

 War covers many subject fields and forms of attack, defence, entrenchment, fortification, camouflage, reconnaissance, communication, attrition and so forth. Why then are we only concerned with one or two of the most obvious aspects of war when it comes to business, have we lost sight of all the other skills - and unfortunately they are perishable skills. This aspect constitutes a great strategic disadvantage – self-inflicted - and therefore becomes the point of departure in this chapter. We require leaders that can grasp all of this, call it the essence of war, or the art of war, use it, master it, and apply it as a commander would at war, all within the confines of a corporate environment.

Now that we know what to look for in a strategist and leader, we need to develop these "predatory instincts", all war like attributes starting from an elementary premise, or point of view. We start by assuming nothing about our candidates, his or her schooling, or knowledge based on their academic qualifications. Most companies (get it all wrong) they hire degrees and doctorates based on an elementary job specification and hope that these candidates will solve the problems, by throwing expertise at it. This principle is fine, but re-train them from this elementary level in "your war like doctrine, culture and language". A leader is only as strong as what his people are wise and willing. This is why we are focusing on selection mind-set and people first.

We will begin with skills development, knowledge, strategic communication, and symbolism. What does this have to do with strategy you may ask, well everything? It becomes the vehicle of choice. Businesses all within the last decade have invested great amounts of their wealth in strategic advisors that practice 360-degree strategic orientation. They have realised that business is no longer a "Fair game", a gentlemen's world of trust and honour. It is only about who eats who to get to the top, nothing is enough. Corruption and fraud have become daily labels of most that is in power, but who elected them? Transactions and contracts are terminated in the wink of an eye, spelling out sure disaster. The introduction of defensive and offensive strategy has become the norm in strategic planning and our armour for survival, rather than the exception to the norm, for doing business. We have become an extremely litigations society, we take action and fear being prosecuted at the risk of being too adventurous, nothing is done at face value anymore and the handshake has become a pure formality.

5. The first major influence – is character traits;

On overcoming oneself: An elderly Cherokee was teaching his grandchildren about life;

He said to them, "A fight is going on inside all of us, it is a terrible fight and it is between two wolves." "One wolf is evil... he is fear, anger, envy, sorrow, regret, greed, arrogance, self-pity, guilt, resentment, inferiority, lies, false pride, competition, superiority and ego. The other is good... he is joy, peace, love, hope, sharing, serenity, humility, kindness, benevolence, friendship, empathy, generosity, truth, compassion and faith. The same fight is going on inside you and every other person, too. They thought about it for a minute and then one child asked his grandfather, "Which wolf will win?"

The old Cherokee simply replied, "The one you feed".

The fundamental principles of War

Now we move onto the bigger picture - the fundamental principles of war, to get the better perspective of what is at stake here, by looking at the elements of Guerrilla warfare: (McCuen - Based on a model of Mao). On the left, we have the military principles; on the right, we have enterprise principles.

Strategy: Strategic goals: Military	Enterprise
Self-preservation and annihilation of the enemy.	1. Devising a doctrine and strategic intent, that is both defensive and forceful, that can enforce discipline and dissolve uncertainty. In other words, everyone is following the company Constitution. Drafted in collaboration; with shared beliefs and values, which ties people in with the vision of the enterprise.
Establishing of strategic basis.	2. Diversify ways of achieving means do not rely on one source, supplier, or advisor. The media is you tool, or your grim reaper, depending on your relationship with them. Network, tell people your vision and generate support. Get allies that share the same vision.
Mobilization of the masses	3. Through dogma and doctrine, unify your corporate culture to become one political culture, with one set of values and rules for all. One vision, one mission.
Looking for external support	4. Network with inner and outer cells, collaborate and establish good ties with employees and clients as well suppliers.
Unity of action	5. The vision, mission and strategic intent must be entrenched, to unify all strategy to compliment the strategic intent of the organisation.
Tactics: Tactical goals: Military	Enterprise
Initiative	1. Support initiative, risk taking and creative thinking, take on stewardships roles that groom leaders and mangers.
Information	2. Eradicate information and communication system bottlenecks, by having an excellent technology based information system that links all role players. Standardised data management and warehousing. Information and communication, is only as good as it is accurate, timely and consistent.
Mobility	3. Mobility of thinking delegates responsibility with accountability along with resources and the required authority. By gaining the initiative we gain more mobility of thought. The key to mobility is initiative taking.
Surprise	4. Marketing, branding and competitiveness grows with the acquisition of knowledge and development of skills. Creating surprisingly good results, both internally and externally

Influences challenge your thinking; this whole book is written in such a manner as to open up your mind, to other possibilities; to influence you to utilise alternative thought to solve problems with. To "see" the possibilities that are abound and around you, within you, to look at strategy with new eyes. Potential exists abundantly and possibilities are endless when we start thinking with a strategic management matrix hat on. Should you get to choose, life will become that which you choose of your own accord, much easier than living a life of someone else's dictation. For I truly believe that all problems that we are faced with daily are events that are brought on our paths, created by people, we term them problems or challenges. Once organised, we call them opportunities, for their relationship has now been rationally resolved – that it was manmade - with a solution that makes sense. By having tapped into our potential, by starting with concept thinking, we conceptualise our thoughts to be able to envision it. It is a known fact that action beats reaction, that measuring twice and cutting once is a sound carpenter's law. However, we are ourselves all mixed up in "facts" (rather than concepts) that are not relevant when we are trying to draw a rational conclusion to a perceived problem. At times, we feel pressured by our internal forces – perceptions - that guide our rational and emotional as well as primitive thinking. We arrive at conclusions at stages in our lives that are not in coherence with our true nature and views because of distorted facts. A variety of mixed feelings whelms up and they challenge our core fundamental beliefs when faced with choice.

Choice challenges our internal influences; that challenges our worth, authority and trigger internal turmoil. For instance, when we are confronted with the choice of being "charged" or "rewarded" for being too conservative, or alternatively too liberal, too forceful or too diplomatic. How do we deal with these situations of having to choose right when we are not convinced within ourselves as to where we stand on a certain aspect. However things need to be done and we are forced to choose, therefore which is it going to be, we are pushed to choose. The situation requires an immediate response from us, conservative or liberal? We have all found ourselves in situations like this and I am sure will again. Now, the question is this; are they, or are they not two opposing entities, referring to being liberal and conservative? Well, it depends on how we look at them, our structure of civilization and social class and status will influence our behaviour in this regard when confronted to give an opinion on this accordingly. This in itself is a very strong influence – ego - our importance indicator – the halo effect. We acknowledge that politically viewed these two are at different ends of the spectrum, which makes them incompatible views. Secondly, we realise that both parties have made good and bad decisions on our behalf in the past and that they do find ways of working out problems together – that is politically thinking/speaking. However, we are not in a political arena now, we are in business and this could be a discussion/ decision with consequences for us. Should we choose the one over the other then we will in effect be siding. In my heart, I am thinking i am conservative in certain instances, pertaining to my choice of clothing, but I have been seen wearing a bright neon outfit on the beach, so what does this make me? I am sure everyone can tell a story of personal experiences. On the other hand, have we ever contemplated a neutral stance in this regard?

The influence of fear; When we are confronted with primal fear; we have three choices, run, fight, or surrender. Most of us will surrender, that is because it is the polite (diplomatic) thing to do, but this neutralises your credibility. All business is about credibility and so are relationships – never go back on your word/credibility. Aristotle was the one who said, "Man is a political animal" and our foundation stems from those political beliefs we hold dear, we should apply them in business as well. Every man is entitled to his opinion, right or wrong. The very same principle applies with political views. Masquerading is as old an art practiced by evil men itself, they take up the neutral corner and watch the left and right wing battle it out, just to leave with the proverbial "bone", " two dogs fighting over a bone just so that the third one gets to run off with it" type of scenario. We find this everywhere in corporate life, the point I am trying to make is this, you will have to choose, make sure you choose that which is in your heart and not in your mind.

The Radical Revolutionary Strategic Management Matrix For Predators

For someone once said; "birds of a feather flock together". So don't partner or side with vultures if you are a seagull, somewhere-somehow it will all fall back in your lap. The fullest potential of man is to be found in his political freedom, every man and woman is entitled to his own opinion. This also equates to business where politics are rife, if we open ourselves up and express our views freely, we will become part of a free business democracy, we will choose the hierarchical structures we desire and fill them with men and woman that will be liken us – open minded, who thrive on diversity and conflict, of their own choosing. This creates vibrancy that dissolves Luke warmness to boiling point. The argument is this, if the sum of the whole is bigger than the individual, if all the parts of a device obey the laws of physics regardless of their nature then the device as a whole must obey the laws of physics as well. Such should be the nature of a matrix enterprise, the one unto the other, regardless of race, culture, religion or belief. Could we ever hope to duplicate conditions like this in enterprise, like these laws of nature? The answer is yes. The law of conservation holds that if all obey the *laws of physics* then we will never face imminent collapse.

Therefore, it stands to reason; if we as people in an organisation can withstand the extremes of;

- work-*pressure*,
- the *magnetic fields* of company politics and diversity,
- the *temperature* of personalities,
- the *speed* of change and growth,
- and still keep course with all the influences in the *changes in direction* we experience daily
- and still be able to *revolve* securely around our own principled centre of living,

We will surly survive as a person, why not as an organisation. If only we stick to the fundamental rules of the law of physics and of conservation. For one thing, it is all natural law and secondly, we can relate to all of its aspects daily as it governs the influences and force of nature itself. Maybe this is why it is said that man is a truly conceptual entity (this is why we need concepts) and not a perceptual one (not facts). Animals on the other hand are deemed purely perceptual, therein rests the true distinction. Fact, animals are cognisant of other animals, they are not however cognisant of other animals views, politics and perceptions on existences and subsistence, or their philosophy. This is purely the abstract sum of the principles of human thought and human nature. Therefore, if we are cognisant of one another's conceptuality, we may just find a resolve to all social problems we are experiencing - when we align ourselves from this perspective. Man on the other hand, has the ability to reason and understands that thought and contemplation may lead to a plan of action by which he may or may not be successful in obtaining his desired goals - without neglecting his duty to his fellow man by doing so. This brings us back to the importance of setting goals, both strategic and tactical goals that predatorily instincts can follow, in this instance the strategic and tactical goals. Goals, viewed within the framework of traditional Guerrilla Warfare firstly. Later on, we will study the much desired form or strategic style of Guerrilla warfare namely "Protracted Guerrilla Warfare" as a concept.

The Nexus (connection or focus) of war and business:

The attributes;

The Strategic goals of unconventional war or guerrilla warfare:
Self-preservation and total annihilation of the enemy.
This aspect is clear and self-explanatory, total annihilation of the opponent its resources and means. We can quite clearly derive that this first aspect cannot and will not fit into the modern business world. However, be sure someone somewhere does, has and will, resort to this type of tactics. So prepare and incorporate alternatives, into all aspects of the strategic plan.
Establishing of strategic basis.
These are launching and training camps, which serve the role of recruitment posts, training camps and fulfils the role of logistical and essential aspects.
Mobilization of the masses.
Through a doctrine of what the cause is fighting/ striving for, propaganda is used as a primary means to entice and persuade potential recruits and to get more support, as well as financing. Cells form, that bloat and give rise to more and even more cells. From these cells, members are then carefully identified, selected and tested for their characteristics and convictions and trained accordingly to become leaders, or to further the cause and its aspirations.
Looking for external support
Drumming up support from sectors that are fighting similar fights, or that are championing same styled agendas, by forming alliances becomes the norm. From these unions they arrive at mutually beneficial agreements and the union becomes a network.
Unity of action
They carefully plan multilateral prongs towards achieving their aims, political, propaganda, pressure groups, violence, attacks, disruption and call for embargoes, etc.

Tactical goals:
Initiative – action beats reaction, you cannot fight that which you cannot see, measure, control and understand, so they try to remain faceless and characterless until they are fully mobilised and entrenched, for as long as possible. Whoever holds the element of surprise and the freedom of mobility has the initiative. The more unpredictable, the more fear you strike at the heart of your enemy.
Information – disinformation and over emphasis on weakness, rapid dissemination of relevant information to get widespread coverage.
Mobility – mobilisation of mass actions, cells and pressure groups, via media involvement, churches, community leaders and academical institutions. Any susceptible medium open to utilisation.
Surprise – attacks, mass action and disruption, the core aim is destabilisation and the creation of fear and anxiety. Thus causing a perception of lawlessness and ineffectiveness, they literally set out to create total chaos

Why it works -"Protracted Guerrilla Warfare"

Guerrilla tactics are the University of War; they teach us that the collective have greater power if we can create one common purpose, or symbol of reasoning. Strength is found only once you have "fought" several times, both valiantly and aggressively then it becomes worth. Therefore, if you exercise your worth, you may become a leader of people and there will be many well-known regular people, who will no longer be your peers. The more "battles" you win the more prestige and recognition you get, because rank or designation will no longer dictate your competence and importance, your work ethic and output as well as success at solving problems will become the formal measure. Without question, the fountainhead of guerrilla warfare is in the full utilisation of the masses of the people and their collective intelligence. By organising themselves and finding solutions directly from within their own ranks, people learn work ethic between themselves and it just keeps ballooning into a better self-organised and disciplined workforce. Adults want to experience freedom, however they also require structure, and they know what is expected and have to create working environments where the people closest to the task can use their initiative. Guided by frameworks within which freedom may be exercised in order for them to explore and grow. Opposed to someone looking over their shoulder, as parents do with children, we tend to take on the childlike mentality and only work when watched, or supervised. We have to surrender this type of over "well-meaning" control style and trust and by surrendering; we will experience growth over time and become leaders.

The importance of the leader's character;

Officers and leaders should have the following qualities:

- Great powers of endurance and resilience so that in spite of any hardships; he sets an example to his men and be a model for them
- He must be able to mix easily with his people; his spirit and that of the men must be one in strengthening the policy.
- If he wishes to gain victories, he must study tactics. A guerrilla grouped with officers of this calibre would be unbeatable.
- The officers must be naturally endowed with good qualities, which can be developed during the course of campaigning.
- The most important natural quality is that of complete loyalty to the idea of people's emancipation. If this is present, the others will develop; if it is not present, nothing can be done.
- When selecting candidates for performance positions, first establish the qualities that will be required of the post, what will be required of the people to work effectively.
- Before focussing on their qualifications, "the qualities of people" should receive particular attention. The argument is this; these people will become your future leaders and managers, if you choose average people, you can only expect average results.
- The better the people's qualities are, the higher the expectations and results will be. If there are insufficient good qualifications amongst the select to become officers, an effort must be made to train and educate people so these qualities may be developed and the pool potential officer material increase.

- There can be no disagreements between officers. As long as a person is willing to fight (work), his social situation or position is of no consideration.
- A soldier who habitually breaks regulations must be dismissed from the army.
- Vagabonds and vicious people must not be accepted for service and a soldier who cannot break himself of any addiction or bad habit should be dismissed.
- Victory in guerrilla war is conditioned upon keeping the membership pure and clean. It is a fact that during the war the enemy may take advantage of certain people who are lacking in the moral and ethical consciousness and end up becoming liabilities, such as betraying their own.
- Officers must therefore, continually educate the soldiers and inculcate patriotism in them. This will prevent the success of traitors. This procedure will serve as well as a warning to the other soldiers.
- If an officer is discovered to be a traitor, some prudence must be used in the punishment adjudged.
- Soldiers should be well treated and treated with respect, however care should be used during their reorientation to distinguish those whose idea is to fight (work), from those who may be present for other reasons.

Two pronged approach:

The aim is to address both military and political matters, an armed wing, a self-defence wing and a political wing. Of which the first two will sort under one banner.

How does this concept become relevant to business?

Firstly, the fundamental deduction from protracted Guerrilla warfare is this: Guerrilla Warfare teaches us fundamentals, that firstly "Unity is strength" and people create or distort unity – **and not systems, strategies and an abomination of controls.**

Secondly, that the leaders are the make or break factor, if they do not possess knowledge and wisdom, all is lost. If they are not groomed and skilled, the people under their control will suffer. – "You cannot take a person and put him on a horse, dress him up and then expect him to become a jockey and compete with other "jockeys" and win races." Leadership requires specifics, just like jockeys; as being of small build, armed with extensive knowledge of horses, their ability and nature as well as experience in riding – complying with the specifics of the requirements for "jockeys" - leaders.

Lastly, a leader without followers is like a shepherd without a flock, the one pretty useless without the other. We require the unity of culture, business culture, interpersonal culture and effective corporate politics. Good leaders are known for their ability to communicate effectively. We will also require a master tactician, a predator, to organise our defences and our attack doctrines through our strategic intentions. Leaders have new roles today; they have to be the team Captain.

Today's leaders face a new challenge altogether; they have to break out of the stereotype traditional roles of only managing with systems and statistics. We still need to, on occasion, direct and exercise control. Playing the dictator or police officer role only challenges your people to find ways – creatively - to bypass the system. Rather be approachable and offer positive open communication – from the model of **"Protracted Guerrilla warfare"**. Discipline is part and parcel of leadership. Nevertheless, be consistent and act within the spirit of problem solving and fair practice. The last aspect is our political leadership role; managers have to play roles outside their normal auspices and streamline company politics - in order to unify and solidify corporate culture. They can no longer distance themselves from the role as active politician of company politics.

Additionally, we are not oblivious to the fact that not all our staff will have and share the same levels of education, skills, income and experience. Thus these seemingly insignificant aspects of level of income and education will also impact directly on ethics and culture, for everyone measures within these confines of their own means their worth and potential. We reason according to our social class and level of education. What this implies is, we revert back to how we as "poor" people do things traditionally. How do we form one culture then? In the next chapter, we will start the process of revolutionising a company's culture.

Aristotle said ... If you want to win people over, state your case in "their thoughts, their beliefs and their attitudes".

Chapter 3:   The *"Revolutionary"* Strategic Management Principle explained

The principle of "Revolutionising" things; and how we can use it creatively in business.

The principle of revolution is nothing new; it is as old as man and history itself.

Many of us do not fully realize the true meaning and significance of any planned "Revolution". This is where interests are served, be it political, commercial, or otherwise. Our focus will be on harnessing this aspect of revolution to build an attack and defence doctrine for our enterprise. The point is there will always be a price to pay, at the cost of many things - good and bad - dependant on the architect's aims when contemplating revolution... Conversely, if we do not contemplate any revolution, or revolt, either from within or from outside, we will never see it coming until it is too late. Only the blind man has a valid excuse for not being able to see. The rest of us do not. With any sudden revolution, or rebellion from within, the norm is that "heads roll and walls of resistance are broken down". The term "stone walling" "favouritism" and "racism" and many other tricks are played to lobby for support, followed by a period of total uncertainty and then chaos ultimately sets in – this aspect is clearly depicted in the life cycle of. -**"Protracted Guerrilla warfare"**

   This is the process of constant internal and external influences clashing, two ideals at war, the one influences the other - and when not checked - has become many a big enterprises demise, for they never contemplate such a threat, especially from within, they just don't see it coming. Their circumstances blind them, like being surrounded and under siege. Conflict can be channelled to a positive, by changing the focus to view it as a process of evolution.

Evolution in the true sense is the natural process of living and life, the process of growth and mutation that emulates better characteristics through change. Change is very essential in today's life, where the speed of change dictates how we work, live and function. If our organisation is slow at change, then all our processes will follow suit. True *Revolution* is something very different altogether and very far removed from *Evolution;* in the true sense and meaning of the word and what it implicitly represents. We are confronted, daily with an onslaught of many forms of revolution. When we contemplate revolution as an effective means to an end; even change could prove to be disastrous if it does not fit in with the circumstance that are prevailing, we should be very wary of the consequences. For revolution in essence could be seen as a multitude of evolutions, taking place almost simultaneously and giving rise to a chain reaction of events. Which in turn produce new progeny, seldom before witnessed. No one should just start any revolutionary process for the sake of change or in the name of progress. Mostly with any revolutionary processes having taken place there will be observable consequences and irreversible implications we never could have contemplated - some even far-reaching. Professional Revolutionary ideas strive for advances emulating working concepts much sought after, the rather *tried and tested variety*. This is what we seek and desire with radical revolutionary change, we want to optimise the parts that are working and replace the parts that are not. What we do not want to see is a group of bright-eyed individuals seeing a symbol they desire and pursuing it feverously, in order to become great at any cost. They just vanquish everything old in their path to get there, leaving a trail of disaster in pursuit of their newfound cause, mostly ending in obliviousness. The truth of the matter is that things normally have to change radically in order for symbols to prevail or come into being. Literally, we are talking about ground-breaking processes having to occur, things never before even contemplated, it is a quantum leap in an altogether different direction and dimension, especially in dimension with new faster and improved thinking and systems. Here dimension refers to; the shape, the focus, the thinking, as well as the ideology that will make-up new paradigm. Everything needs to change in parallel – the systems and the people. This requires careful consideration and planning. Because, when revolution starts, it is not subtle, it is violent and we are not just implying minor adjustments to be made, but contemplate a total overall, a holistic adjustment. Even on a personal level, pertaining to new perceptions required. We have to change the very way we see, feel and reason as a collective. Let us review the diagram of traditional revolution and then work from it to create this understanding.

We will firstly get to know how radicalism functions in a political context and then the aspects used to conjure up a revolt with will be explained. Thereafter, we will construct our own revolutionary doctrine by following the elements without losing sight of the moral and ethical standards of modern day living and doing business. Revolution has become the inevitable ingredient in modern day business; a prerequisite in order to not just survive, but also to succeed by the same margin and thinking. Only he, who sees it, can grab it, his ticket to destiny.

The basic elements for a Revolution:

In order for a Revolution to begin one requires:
1. **At** least two opposing sides
2. **Access** to "weapons" – technology, means, finances, infrastructure, databases, human resources, suppliers and political backing or - in our case a strategic agenda that needs sustenance.
3. **Aims** expressed in a slogan and with symbols - in our case our vision, mission and goals to reach greater productivity, service, strength etc.
4. **Accomplished** leaders, battle hardened generals – same thing all around, just the titles that differ
5. **Ailments,** a perceived disease, either present socially, economically and or politically. (Corruption, aids, starvation etc.) – or in our case a strategic move / motive

The Life Cycle of Revolution

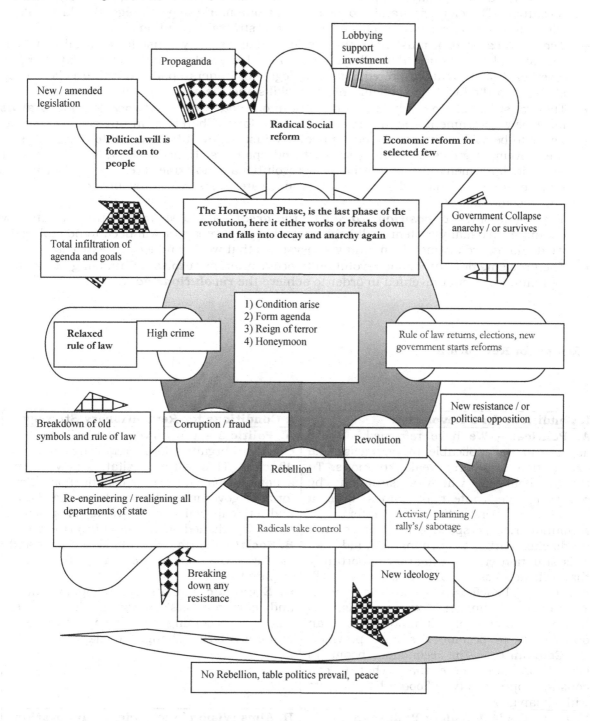

In Order For a Revolution to be successful, one requires certain attributes to be present.

- The *aims* of the Revolution need to be defined before we propagate it. (We demand - liberty, freedom, equality, etc.). The slogan; advertising is to business, as propaganda is to revolution. Therefore, it stands to reason that our marketing strategy should be aligned with our vision, mission and goals as well as our strategic intentions.
- *The leaders* we pick must have three prime qualities; they must have social status and educational background that allows them to hold the subsequent government (company) together. Consequently a prerequisite is a degree of leadership skills, with excellent people skills, topped off with good communication skills and the ability to network.
- They must be able to produce a framework and a *coalition* – **network of collaborators** - for a new government - management team - to form. Therefore, in our case the strategy needs to be sold to the people, our employees, just as revolution is sold to the masses and the movement grows by gaining support and sponsors. Hence, take this knowledge and apply it, implement it. It is the basis of revolutionary doctrine; the type of doctrine that toppled great nations and has formed even greater ones. We must break with mediocre and become radical.
- The degree of the *opposition cannot be too great, or too strong*, or the revolution will continue - too many systems will be destroyed beyond repair or will need to be replaced - if we do not guard against dismantling subsystems that work, and loosing expertise.
- The problems present for the revolution to occur must be resolved. Stumbling blocks must be removed, or circumvented in order to achieve the *revolutions goal*.

The Recipe for Revolution

I. Conditions for a Revolution	I. Conditions for Revolutionary Strategy
A. Political – We have reframed - these aspects to be applicable to business. The exploitation of others, weak situations. To bring about a win/win situation by reframing the context of things from a business perspective, versus a revolutionaries perspective i.e. – a country needs cheap drugs to curb malaria, aids etc. This situation creates a market opportunity that will address a political issue as well, mutually beneficial area to-explore. **B. Social** – hunger, overcrowding, no houses, water, or infrastructure, an opportunity to become a service provider. **C. Economic** – the economic boom in China, produces more than what it can consume, opportunity to flood other markets with cheap goods	**A. Political** – unresolved people issues –in effective organisation, requiring a new direction. This will necessitate a new vision, a new dogma and a new constitution. (New form of governance that reflects the moral and ethical beliefs and views of people). Mutually aligned with the enterprise aims. **B. Social** – reform cultural indifferences and clashes. One corporate cultural identity required. **C. Economic** – reforms, new opportunities and new markets emerging. The market place is becoming very competitive; and requires internal changes to adapt.
II. Aims (Goals, Vision or Philosophy)	**II. Aims (Vision before Ideas = Innovation)**

A. Must be clearly defined 1. Made into a **slogan**	A. The development of a powerful encompassing strategic plan, of what the future should look like. 1. Made into a **envision;** "Encompassing vision"
B. Leaders (**Accomplished** leaders)	B. Leaders (**Accomplished** leaders)
Must have social and educational background that allows them to hold the subsequent government together	Must be able to understand and reflect peoples, needs, wants and interests as well as satisfy them whilst performing at accomplishing objectives.
Must be able to produce a framework and a coalition for a new government	Must be able to lead effectively, enable and empower, whilst keeping people energised
The degree of the opposition cannot be too great nor too strong, or the revolution will continue.	The degree of the opposition cannot be too great nor too strong, people must follow willingly. Coercion should not be used.
III. Steps (stages) through the political spectrum	**III. Steps, Phased implementation**
A. Symbolic onset (big event that makes everyone mad) September 11 B. Initial event with a general base of support	A. Explaining the Vision
1. Must have **access to weapons** (don't have to use them but must threaten with them)	1. Workshop aspects that will threaten or enhance the probability of success. Form winning concepts.
C. Begun by the Liberals	C. Paradigm shift -Begun with the Leaders first
1. Must make some changes. 2. Must attempt to forge a constitution	1. Necessity for change collaborates with conservatives and incorporate safe guards. 2. Must attempt to forge a coalition, before attempting to formulate constitution.
D. Rule of the Moderates	D. Allow Rule of the Middle Management
1. Begin rule under new constitution 2. Usually split rule	1. Begin rule under new constitution. 2. Usually split rule – delegate and empower.
E. Challenge of the Conservatives	E. Challenge of the Conservatives – manage critique
1. Try to take over and stop changes	1. Explain that changes are necessary and inevitable to survive and prosper.
F. Radicals take control	F. Radicals take control – the changes are not phased and ironed out. Become problematic.
1. Reign of Terror	1. Ruptures occur and breakdown of systems sets in – no realignment and

	objectivity is noticeable, "if it does not work, it does not work" carry on regardless.
Radicals make too many changes too fast people attempt to revolt and the Radicals must begin eliminating political opposition	Too many radical changes too fast people lose sight and direction. They become uncertain, disillusioned and attempt to revolt, to go back to what was.
G. Reactionary	G. Reactionary
Small group of people usually from aristocracy make small changes that give the appearance that the conditions present are being resolved but actually, attempts are made to return to the prior situation	Small group of people usually conservatives make small changes that give the appearance that the conditions present are being resolved but actually, attempts are made to return to the prior situation
2. Corruption is present	2. Corruption becomes institutionalise and present
3. Economic instability occurs	3. Undisciplined leadership and instability occurs
H. Conservative One Man Rule	H. A new leader emerges
1. Must have support of the military. 2. Makes changes to keep the current government in control	1. Must have support of the enterprise. 2. Makes changes to keep the current enterprise in control
IV. Honeymoon Phase	**IV. Honeymoon Phase**
Monarchy or original government but in an altered form	New dispensation or original management but in an altered form
Monarch, dictator, or oligarchy amends some of the changes of the revolution	Minor adjustments and calibration takes place
2. Liberals then begin to question	More leaders emerge Effective systems develop Effective strategies role out New culture is born
Conditions corrected enough by reform then stability returns	Conditions corrected enough by reform then stability returns
Or Revolution begins again	Or Revolution begins again

The Business Revolution Model

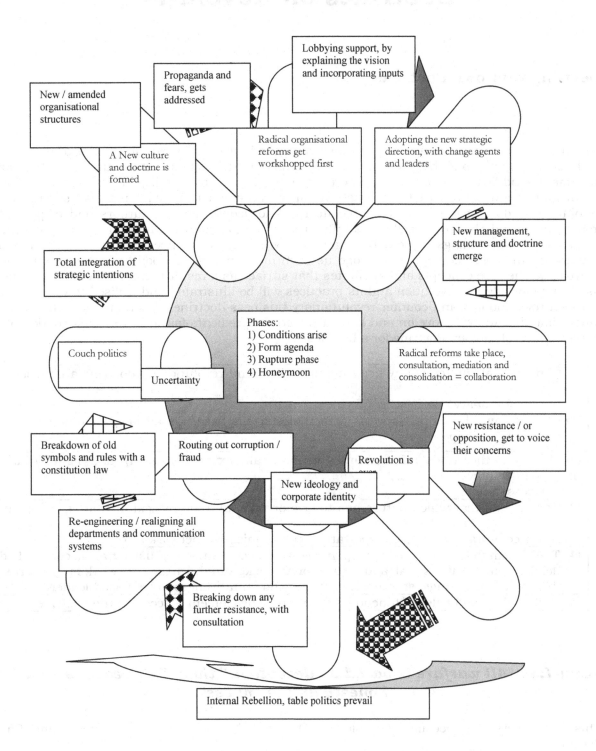

Lobbying support, by explaining the vision and incorporating inputs

Propaganda and fears, gets addressed

New / amended organisational structures

A New culture and doctrine is formed

Radical organisational reforms get workshopped first

Adopting the new strategic direction, with change agents and leaders

New management, structure and doctrine emerge

Total integration of strategic intentions

Phases:
1) Conditions arise
2) Form agenda
3) Rupture phase
4) Honeymoon

Couch politics

Uncertainty

Radical reforms take place, consultation, mediation and consolidation = collaboration

New resistance / or opposition, get to voice their concerns

Breakdown of old symbols and rules with a constitution law

Routing out corruption / fraud

Revolution is

New ideology and corporate identity

Re-engineering / realigning all departments and communication systems

Breaking down any further resistance, with consultation

Internal Rebellion, table politics prevail

Doctrines on Revolution

Devising your own Doctrine

Why a doctrine? Well, how many times have you asked, or been asked for a policy or a procedure or business plan - and have come up dry? Only to rush off and draw up some haphazard document - riddled with red type - where no one takes accountability or responsibility for the policy and or procedure - that only exist on paper in a cabinet. After having read several radical revolutionary doctrines, we must appreciate the knowledge that the authors had of perception management and change as well as its influence on human nature. The utilization of the human weakness to want things; by creating emotion, with words are used to create very emotional statements that become keys to dislodge us from our fundamental point of view - very thought provoking. The core concepts and attributes that surface as a result thereof are of consequence to us. This knowledge of revolution and its practices will be illustrated and utilised towards devising our own revolutionary and counter revolutionary business doctrines. Therefore, we will not waste much time, but we will move on and look at the core ingredients found in the construction of any successful revolutionary doctrine for a business:

The core attributes of any doctrine: all radical and revolutionary doctrine architects of many a revolutionary manifest had 5 rules:
The Moral Law; the moral aspect - with the next emphases on all law, including that of nature, instilling hope.
(2) Heaven; the rules of for and against, all extremes, good/bad, light /dark, profit/bankruptcy, success/failure
(3) Earth; - all that which nature has to give or take, all the physical attributes of a plan, time, resource, infrastructure, transportation, communication networks etc.
(4) The Commander; the person responsible and accountable – must be an accomplished leader, must have social and educational background, virtues of wisdom, sincerity, benevolence, courage, strictness, vigilance and imitativeness to be a good leader.
(5) Methodology and rules of functional discipline, engagement – becomes the doctrine

Sun-Tzu: "All warfare is based on deception." thus, "all peace is based on honesty and openness".

This might very well become your slogan. Dealing with honesty and openness and finding deception.

The Two Critical Components of a working Doctrine and Dogma: The Symbolic value and the conceptual value.

1) The Symbolic Meaning and the Power of Symbolism.

The power of symbolism has been with man since the beginning of time and in many cases, we even relate and interact with them on a subconscious level. A Symbol performs substitutive functions with regard to concrete objects and abstract ideas. It becomes powerful when used to promote propaganda, or promote an agenda, or hide an underground movement. It can unite or divide; it can be simple or complex with hidden meaning. Such is the nature of symbols. Tyranny the serpent (often, in ancient times, a **symbol** of divine wisdom) taught Adam and Eve to resist...

Background info:

The REVOLUTIONS catalysts; Occultists the world over believe that once a symbol is created, it acquires a power of its own and even more power is generated when such symbol(s) are created without anyone knowing about it. In addition, the greatest power of all is created in symbol(s), if they remain secret, uninitiated, undiscovered, then that symbol exists with innate power. The very secret society called the "Illuminati", whose motto is "Ordo Ab Chao" or "Out of Chaos Comes Order"- which literally means if you breakdown the existing structure and cause the people to look for order and structure again, you will emerge as the victor they seek. When you supply the solution to their problem – the solution becomes a symbol. Increasingly more numbers of people understand the essence of this concept. Looking at Lenin's political maxim: *"**Without revolutionary theory, there can be no real revolutionary movement". It is an inevitable cycle of good and evil – breaking down and re-building.***

Just how much power is in a Symbol then we may ask?

Let us take a practical example, Russia - Why did the "Big Bear" fall? Well in the middle of the 1980's, in Soviet society there were many problems that needed to be resolved and these problems were seriously deforming socialism in the USSR. Above all, the main deformation was to abandon the spreading of goods produced based on the principle of quantity and quality. Instead of resolving this problem, Gorbachev instituted the question of private ownership on the means of production. This meant abandoning socialist symbols and socialism and the resurrection of capitalism by promoting capitalist symbols. This did not need to happen; according to specialists and analysts, they had enough goods produced in all forms to last until the end of the century. Therefore, someone had a vested interest and saw an opportunity to enact a symbol – Liberty.

This became a very easy symbol to sell, because it had many icons. Therefore, by selling the "symbol" people liked best, they opened the floodgate for capitalism. Logos, symbols and maxims all have this quality; they are silent but hold unbelievable powers of persuasion. All humans have something in common we "want" something. It does not stop with wanting; we also have the power to devise the means to get it.

Big business has refined the art of symbolism from war and has woven it into their business strategy, we have seen them, BMW, VW and Mercedes Benz are universal symbols in the motor vehicle industry for instances.

Why do we need to know this? In order to understand the nature of "strategic and symbolic things" as catalysts in strategy. We need to know how they influence and relate to our schemes in the bigger context of things and how they form symbols and influences of their own. The vision of a strategy becomes a symbol in its own right. This skill makes the smaller things seem so much simpler when we can use this knowledge to embed deeper significance into strategy formulation by utilising emotional catalysts. Strategists therefore need to know and understand the relationship of parts; and if symbols form part of these parts, then they have unique elements that give them power. Moreover, they need to know how to fit them into a strategic plan, to give them a market edge over the competition. Nowhere on earth will the school of strategy be taught more graphically than in history itself, history combined with revolution and enclosed in military doctrine, becomes strategy. Therefore, many endeavour to hover over history briefly because they see no significance for it, and thus do not find the core fundamental principles they require. Military leaders study history to perceive future outcomes. Academics, study all academical schools of thought on strategy to derive some form of cause and effect theory, as if this is the golden mean to success and to highlight the importance of Strategy. Study, without understanding strategy's fluid nature – its symbols and catalysts – is futile. Very few have shaken off the pattern of the tailor made strategy, the step-by-step concept of the West, because it is easy and it works, but for how long? Nevertheless, most important in Radical strategy, we have to shake things up; otherwise, it is just an alteration to an existing plan, not pure strategy. The word strategy and strategic has been raped, due to uninformed managers just using it as "buzz word". It has to be radical to be powerful, to be successful, and to be called strategy.

By looking at the roots of strategy, the core ideas on the "following of symbolic strategy" utilised in revolutionary doctrine; and how they are used in business strategy today, we can get insight into the subtleness of using hard and soft techniques to get people to follow sublimely.

The Armed leg of Revolution:

"Colonialism was a gift to Africa and the world", it brought with it religion, crafts, and skills and industrialization, irrigation and farming. Africa in general is a pathetic continent, because it has adopted a culture of "hand-outs", we are the needy. In addition, has Africa forgotten which handled them and fed them into the twentieth century? This could be stated to be a revolutionary statement, because it could elicit an emotional response – yes. In addition, even spark a revolution.

Let us take some time here and look at Guerrilla Warfare: as well as how it relates to aspects found in Radical Strategy.

"Guerrilla Warfare" steps out of the bounds of tactics and knocks at the door of strategy, demanding that problems of guerrilla warfare be considered from a strategic viewpoint. What deserves our particular attention is that there is a distinctive difference between "Guerrilla Warfare" and "Protracted Guerrilla Warfare". The first is bent on total annihilation; with no concern of the impact on the community. Where the second, namely "Protracted Guerrilla Warfare" has a distinctive, marked difference, in that it is more calculated and guided by the moral and ethical. Protracted guerrilla warfare is quite a new thing, seen in the whole scope of history and war, if our enemy neglects to take this into account he will certainly come to grief! – Mao Tse-Tung.

Wow! This is my point; do you "see it yet"? The relevance and connection that is made here, between a symbol and the spoken, that creates an emotion that sparks action. Humans are born violent, we are taught to suppress our warmonger attributes. Nothing under this sun is new, this concept is simple yet very effective, just re-invented, re- incarnated and masked by our perception of how things are, and should be, and then change them towards how things should be according to societies rules and norms. Not so, strategic minds are lateral thinking, they are most effective in certain environments where we fall into the trap of repeating things that just do not work - generally situations where there is little or no established procedure for success or situations where the solution must be discovered, or fine-tuned as opposed to merely repeated along other routes. We will cover all these aspects later on in detail, but just take note of them for now. What we have now is the "Tree of revolution", with all its branches, we now require leaves to make it complete, herein lays the secret, the formulation of symbols that will form catalysts to action.

The influence of dogma and doctrine:

Understanding the Components of a Doctrine: The Political Leg;

Doctrine the concept and conceptual value. All trees have branches that make them trees but what makes them distinctive are their leaves. The leaf, a second characteristic or attribute of a doctrine, which coincides with the above, is that they are not necessarily accurate representations of concrete things and abstract ideas. Leaves all look the same at a distance, but when compared with another on the same tree they have distinctive differences. When we think, we use concepts - leaves, which serve as symbols for concrete things and abstract ideas that we desire to create or form. Concepts are systems used for the categorization of information, so that it makes sense. The abstract concept "Democracy" for instance, is not directly observable yet we can think of it in terms of symbols – leaf, describe it and argue it.

Opposed to a "horse", which is directly observable – that gives it meaning and context. In the absence of the "horse" we may think about it and recall images of it; its scent, rhythm, facial expressions, body posture and behavioural trait's, it may even elicit some emotional response, because we have already acquired the concept of "horse". We have experienced "horse", or been in contact with the very source. In stark contrast to formulating a concept, for a doctrine on Democracy that will differ as if leaves, but still the branches will tell us it is a democratic tree.

From an understanding of the nature of things, of concepts and concept thinking we must first take note of the concept of Abstraction. Abstraction; the essence of abstraction is contained in the phrase; "to leave out so many things". Therefore, it does not make rational sense, it is not arranged understandably, or in a concrete manner - a "thing" like a "horse" that you can touch. It has attributes - a quality and a property, even characteristic of somebody or something – that are unique. So when formulating a symbol or a concept you have to give it life, by giving it attributes.

The minimum value of three attributes will form a concept.

People who are good at grasping concept thinking and information and handling it are the visionary people, the corporate politicians, the one's that goes yes I see and not uhh?, when confronted with a concept - still abstract. Concepts are normally based on other concepts and or other models that people can relate to, which will be used as points of reference to elaborate, or illustrate the detail of the new concept.

Concepts are enacted and supported by "principles". A principle describes the statement so that it relates to the involved parties frames of reference; which expresses the relationship between two or more concepts and then brings in this new concept that connects seamlessly, or so it seems. Thus, categorising it, for instance in a spiritual manner, it could be made more expectable, or digestible for a lack of a better word, so that it will be accepted and not challenged outright. In summary, any new concept will try to mask itself with already endorsed and understood concepts, thus gaining approval by hiding itself between two extremes as the best alternative.

Let us recap; we have already been referred in the direction of two components, that of the symbolic mediation processes - creating images or symbols to live by - and concepts – good, ethical and professional - the political tools of the trade. The last component is the use of language to carry the symbols and concepts with. The units of language are words, phrases and sentences. The relationship between language and thinking has been heavily debated. Many regard language as an essential component of our thinking apparatus, which determines not only the content of our thoughts but also their structure. Language seen as a delivery system of symbols provides us with the skill of thinking, and expressing symbolically our thoughts; in other words, symbols with attributes relates to something, either images and or concepts. This becomes especially true and relevant in the formulation of new thought processes, when dealing with abstract thinking. In this section, we shall confine ourselves to only a few aspects of language and thinking.

In order to comprehend cognitively the language message of others, to become more or less emotionally involved and to produce the required understanding, we must learn at least three aspects of the art of politics;

1. To relate speech sounds to their intended meanings;
2. To relate words to the things and ideas (concepts) (images) (symbols) to which they refer; and
3. To master the rules (principles) according to which words in a language must be combined to form sentences

We have almost completed the introduction on utilising the concept of "revolution" and just before you drop the book, do not! Guaranteed, it will become more interesting from this point forward. To make sound arguments towards the reasons why strategies in a modelled form works – 'the type of just pour water and stir" - approach of the eighties and nineties just won't hold its own anymore, is this. It is just no longer a matter of using a proven business template and tracing the edges to form a company - it is no longer a prevalent form of designing and forming a business based on pure research. In one short phrase, "it has become just too conventional", everyone is doing it so we will be competing with ourselves. Templates were never designed to cope with the challenges and influences of the new era of enterprise and we require more flexible forms of wisdom and reasoning to speed up business progress. Moreover, the old strategies are too rigid to compete in a fast moving world, that is rapidly speeding up daily and shape shifting, old strategic models seem to get lost and trapped in "time" and "space". Somehow, somewhere, along the strategic path – it forces haphazard thinking on us that leads us into the lion's den of crisis management. Have a look around, is your organisation showing the signs, of haphazard thinking, and loosing focus? Have you become very proficient at crisis management of late? Thanks to the template that you use to run your business. I am sure most of us having degrees in crisis management by now; we have done so much, for so many, with so little, that it has become second nature. In this case, radical strategy was designed to circumvent and incorporate these aspects shortcomings. Radical strategy is so powerful because of its duality, it embraces the creative mental aspects of human nature first, enforces the uninhibited free flow of initiative, which gives it total flexibility to choose its form. Entrenched in a deep understanding of time-honoured military and militia's thought triggers on how to move on the strategic landscape. The second attribute is its empowering matrix; it focuses on the seamless fusion of concepts, to compliment man and systems. Opposed to the current situation that is the complete opposite, where systems have preference over man and his creative nature, man has to adapt to the systems and control, which makes it inflexible. This was derived from an in-depth study of great leaders of man, right throughout history we can find many great men, from common backgrounds that shaped the future with radical visions and doctrines. Therefore, we require the ability to recognise the human element or component in strategy first, as a departing idea, then to understand why. Something that transcends just human capital, resides in the ability to move man to do greater things, to get him to see and arrive at overall consciousness, this is the nexus of this new age of wisdom and information management. We have to start thinking "people" before anything else, this will only be accomplished with a well thought-out and clearly understood vision and doctrine. Vision without doctrine, is like a plane without fuel. When we start governing, we stop managing and this is where we create bottlenecks for the organisation and ourselves. This aspect historically speaking inspired men to lay down their lives for the cause to fight for freedom. Why not in the business arena, why don't we have the freedom to think, design, create and thrive... This is the essence; the lifeblood we need to re-capture into our business strategy as a catalyst the emancipation of enterprise and realise that the human perception about freedom, even in the workplace, dictates their will to work and go over to action – a big motivator. We need more leaders that are qualified in formulating such visions and that have such vision. We have relied far too heavily on the maxim of designs, systems, policies and procedures – all classic forms of control – that of Governing - and we are starting to fall and falter with it. We have done far too little for too long, on enhancing people's intellectual and spiritual capital. For if said, that "faith" "is the ability to believe in that which you cannot see, the effect hereof is that you will see that which you cannot believe". Therefore, we require leaders with "Faith". Consequently, all this was just to start you off, by introducing you to the core concepts that form the ingenious basic ingredients of "The Revolutionary Radical Strategic Management Matrix.

The formulation of such a revolutionary idea: becomes "The Business Doctrine".

More critical -What is doctrine?

"Put most simply, doctrine is what is taught, it is furthermore described as the fundamental principles by which the organisation guides their actions in support of their objectives."

The function of doctrine.

Its aim;

- Is to impart straightforward instruction sets, at one level, or standard operating procedures.
- Is to impart specific knowledge fields that will be required in specific circumstances.
- Is to combine both aforementioned, to have one system to be followed throughout.
- It is concerned with conveying unifying understanding of processes and how they relate to others and not just pure instructions.

Doctrine or dogma is the code of fundamental beliefs, a constitution of understanding; it helps everyone understand its implication and application within a context. Doctrine is broken up into levels, to make it specific and concise to its field of application.

- At the top level of doctrine – referred to the **"Higher-level Doctrine"**, we have – principles that govern the conduct, we lead by principles, rather than rules. "Rules" are rigid and uncompromising. "Principles" are empowering and flexible.
- The next level and main component, is "The **Operational Doctrine".** Here we have the essentials of the managerial function, planning and co-ordinating in the same fashion, whether it is for a specialised or common unit.

The Pyramid diagram depicts the components of effective business doctrine:

Strategic Intent Document = Aimed at understanding required direction and changes in direction. With weekly and monthly progress reports, the format, information required, statistics and intelligence. etc. "The Business Character".

Stratagem; Aimed at, unifying of diversified efforts, processes and through proper Command and Control protocol, communication and systems designed to manage information effectively. To assimilate and disseminate information and data

High-Level Doctrine; Aimed at creating common understanding, the corporate direction, aims, goals are explained, as well as the vision and mission, broken down into objectives, goals and action items. Which are timed phased and specific with the desired deliverables? – Coupled to the project management/ budgeting and approval criteria

The Standard Operational Procedure (SOP) Manual: Aimed at departing directives; orders and guidelines, in a systematic way. It also covers legislative parameters and incorporates these requirements. Furthermore, explaining and teaching principles and principled management.

The Methodology of the "Strategic Targeting" - document; Aimed at creating operational competence, managerial skills and leadership qualities. Enterprise objectives are entrenched in all training. Capacitating overall strategic and tactical excellence from within, by following a predetermined career path, individuals are developed unilaterally.

The Tactical and Field Training Manual. Aimed at unification of specialisation and specialised training, unit interactions and requirements. Systems management through environmental design is based on concepts, avoiding bottlenecks. The who, is responsible for doing what, where, when and how?

Research & Development. Projects, tenders and procurement. Policy and procedure manual

Logistics and Supplies procedural Manual, The who, when, how, what and why.

The finer aspects:

Finally forming the Revolutions doctrine with Words, Concepts, Symbols, Principles, Images and giving them the right intended powerful meaning by tapping into Nero Linguistic Programming NLP. – "By coining it".

Changing the paradigm of management from instruction sets to concept thinking.

It is certainly true, that there is a close relationship between words and concepts, but they are not the same. Concepts have emotional attributes - take the concept "*dog*" for instance; it may have extensional and intentional attributes. Suppose one now confronts a person who was bitten by a dog, the extensional attributes would come to mind first from the word "dog", meaning four legs, furry and of a certain design or build, looking like a dog. Nevertheless, the intentional attributes could be different pertaining from perception; it could be "bite", "terrible", "pain", or "repulsive". Thus, from this example make sure that when defining concepts that you consider this aspect. Therefore, subjective experiences may differ from person to person, so for every word and concept there maybe two, or more interpretations, or types of meaning: meaning relating to the *denotation* and *connotation* of a word or concept.

The difference between Denotations and Connotations:

Denotation: In linguistics, this is the most specific or literal meaning of a word, as opposed to its figurative senses or connotations, or explained as, when you are sitting at a table in a restaurant and you ask someone to please pass you the bread, they do, you don't get a potato or an onion. This is derived from a *universal* denotation to the meaning as understood to commonly - meaning one thing only.

Connotation: an additional sense or senses associated with or suggested by a word or phrase. Connotations are sometimes - but not always - fixed and are often subjective, implying, or suggestive of an additional meaning for a word or phrase apart from the explicit meaning. The "connotation" of a word is its emotive power – the feelings that it arouses because of our experiences and associations with the word and what it stands for. For instance, "dog" as described previously, could also imply danger, but also protection from danger.

Onto forming your "Revolutionary" concepts;

Symbol: Otherwise, known as productive thinking, the phases of productive thinking:	**Concept:** Otherwise known as encompassing vision thinking:
The Conceptual phase starts with:	The Conceptual phase starts with:
The defining of a concept or a new design and then formulating it into a plan or map.	Creating an Envision; Encompassing Vision, Showing what will be Showing how to become Showing how to arrive
Alternatively, the defining of a problem into a problem statement, with attributes.	Alternatively, concept – with attributes or both. Defining all the requirements, both operationally, logistically, organisationally etc.
The Research and development phase:	The Enabling phase: devising the;
The testing and selection of best practices, adopting ISO standards for instance. Finding new ways of doing old things faster, cheaper, smarter and more cost effective.	Operational, - Doctrine and Training Logistical – Requirement and Specification Organisational – Rights and Disciplinary Code Political – Company Constitution Financial – Procurement Policy
The formulation of alternatives, solutions or hypotheses	The formulation of alternatives, solutions, or hypotheses – on Command and Control, who does what, where, when and how. Role and function definitions and descriptions.
The Execution phase:	The Execution and empowering phase:
Decision making and implementation of the accepted hypotheses or, standards or best practice.	Testing and decision-making as well as implementation of the accepted hypotheses or, standards or best practice.

Brainstorming Tricks:

When brainstorming concepts and symbols with words, (referring to its denotation and connotation) to be used in the vision and mission statement formulation, then every sentence must be made up of concepts and must be cemented with symbolic words:

1. The amount of information is not prevalent to the solution. People are often bewildered by the redundant or irrelevant information given and consequently take longer to formulate the problem and take even longer still to find the solution to the problem.
2. Guard against habitual activity and be alert to new points of view. One cannot equip a person with the ability to form solutions, but one can train him or her to clear the ground so that the solution is not prevented. Keep your mind open to find new meaning, you cannot force solution patterns to crystallize in the brain, you have to evoke them by surrendering to them.
3. Previous learning experience has no apparent immediate impact on finding solutions, but previous experiences have on finding immediate solutions to problems. Therefore, we will all be equal at this point. Only later on when we develop the resolutions does training and academical qualifications come into play.
4. Frustration creates tension, which in turn hampers the cognitive processes. The frustrated person focuses all his attention so intently on the facts that he cannot solve the problem. In addition, strips himself of any alternative reasoning.

"Genius is the capacity for seeing relationships where lesser men see none."~ William James

The Evolution of a Revolutionary Doctrine: Reasoning inside and outside the box.

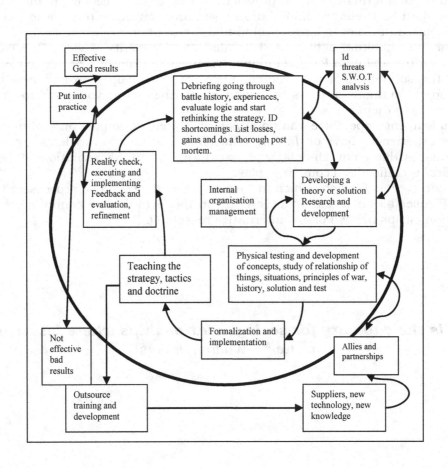

"The development of a doctrine is an essential part of revolutionary success"

Explaining; The difference in reasoning style, when reasoning with; Logic, Truth and Accuracy in mind.

A known fact, various factors influence correct judgment, one of the most important being the emotional meaning the situation elicits. The premise of a syllogism - a formal deductive argument made up of a major premise, a minor premise and a conclusion. An example is "all birds have feathers, penguins are birds and therefore penguins have feathers".

When reasoning from the general to the specific, if the person regards the premise of a syllogism as true and accurate, he often judges the conclusion as valid, whereas according to the rules of logic it is invalid. Therefore, if he regards the premise as untrue or inaccurate, he rejects the conclusion even though according to the rules of logic it is valid.

Therefore, to conclude:

1. Leaders have to incorporate symbolism with good communication skills, open-ended communication that stimulates more interaction and personal insight,
2. Leaders have to get personally involved, the true open door policy, by establishing open communication networks throughout the organisation and not by leaving the office door open, this is not an open door policy. An open door policy is rather better referred to as an open person policy,
3. Leaders have to endorse, apply and preach, principle centred decision making and living
4. Leaders have to be visible, by using unifying goals and vision statements that are radical
5. Leaders have to lead, give support and direction all in the same instance.
6. Leaders have to facilitate lateral thinking and guide ambition and drive to serve our ideas and us as a group to elevate the growth potential of all individuals.
7. Leaders have to be aware of the effect of cultural influences, diversity and formulate one corporate culture.
8. Leaders have to guide reasoning by influencing perceptions and managing them daily.

"Leaders have to focus their endeavours on Doctrines, Principles, Wisdom and Character and not Perceptions, to achieve true accuracy and goals – by developing - the human core first – the emotional reactivity and nature of thinking critically will spawn new ideas all the time."

Chapter 4:

Enhancing our Survivability;
On both Offence as well as Defence

The "CAPS" Diagram

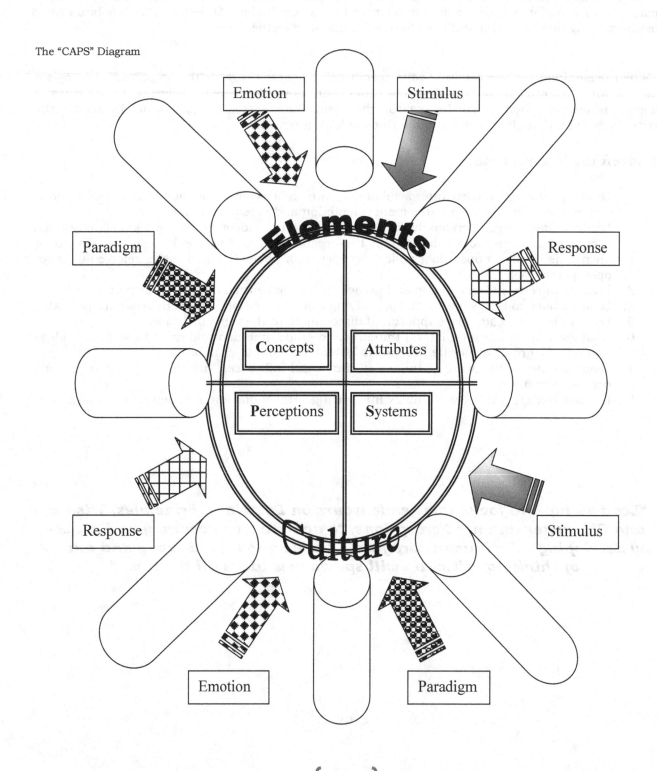

In our current day-to-day life and work situations, we face many intellectual challenges, both strategically and mentally challenging.

Many seem to feel lost at the sight of too much **complexity** and **conflict**. We purely surrender to its onslaught and feel overcome by its magnitude, so much so that we become anxious in our ability and ourselves. This disrupts our natural inner balance at the core.

In order to survive such challenges, one requires consistent and non-perishable "hovering strategies" – (we will deal with this concept later) call it core forming habits based on sound principles. It becomes a strategy in itself, with which to effectively counter such events that evolve and spiral us out of control. Liken seed becoming a tree and the tree becoming a forest... Any other strategy that requires a full-maintenance plan has become mentally exhausting, for it requires a driver, us, a force that will keep it alive.

By virtue of us having enlisted a magnitude of old corporate strategies and management principles as a norm, normally all diverse with no connectivity or over-arching objectives. Because of these aspects, we have formed many bad habits and strategies, the managerial positions have become to a certain extent exhausted in the face of the snowballing task of keeping up and rolling out plans, just to keep the burners of perishable strategy alive. To counter this exhausting aspect of managing too many strategies, we looked at some military acronyms and explored its value in this regard to streamline work performance. They were found to be non-perishable strategies that require little to no maintenance in order to prevail. The idea is not to dictate the process but the required results, how you achieve them is up to you. This type of radical thinking becomes meaningful and indispensable in the arsenal of weapons of mind and management. Firstly, to understand its strategic usefulness we have to understand its purpose first. We have to acknowledge that complexity and conflict go hand in hand and has everything to do with our paradigms on reasoning. If we want to understand complexity then and deal with the conflict it creates, we have to be able to break it down into its simplest understandable form -parts. Complexity is best described as a huge "rock" blocking our path in the gorge of progress. Seemingly, there is no way around it; it has the cliffs of circumstances that surround it.

It was "Hannibal", who encountered such a physical obstacle, on one of his quests, whilst marching his armies through mountain passes. He encountered a huge rock that blocked such a pass. He resorted to making fire under the rock. He then gave the command that vinegar be poured onto the hot rock. This caused it to crack and the rock was broken up.

From this type of insight we deduct workable solutions, we find its "white and black" parts, its strengths and its weakness, *for all complexity is just pure "rock" made up of parts*. It is only by breaking up the task at hand, into its understandable concepts, that we see the solutions required to the problems and challenges they reveal at a dissected level. Only here does complexity reveal itself, and it becomes unproblematic, because it becomes manageable in its smaller parts. The lesson is that all things consist of parts. Let us take this aspect a step forward.

Part one: The Conflict;

Conflict resolution; first, we have to deal with the conflict part, before we seek the strategic solutions.

Conflict is the emotional part of complexity, consequently; if we look at the latter, being conflict, then conflict can only be resolved if it is defused. In order to defuse conflict we need to acknowledge it first and foremost. We have to feed it that which it requires, namely empathy. The aim is to get the initiative on your side; the one that has the initiative takes the lead and subsequently the control. He then has to his advantage the freedom of movement and mobility of mind. In other words, he will then be able to "lead by the nose and kick by the rear". Therefore, in essence we have to totally relinquish our former command and control model, seemingly, to purposefully deal with the human element first. This sounds simple, but it takes practice, the first step in conflict resolution is to "listen with intent" and acknowledge everything all the way, by recapping and relating it back, to confirm that we are following, listening and acknowledging, until the fire of irrationality has burned itself out and awareness of the self enters. Verbal conflict is a means of control and staying in control. We have to surrender to the fight, so that the fighter has no reason or motivation to fight. He must perceive that he has won.

This does not necessarily imply that we have to agree; we just have to *acknowledge* that we understand the reasoning and paradigm of their reasoning. In other words, agree to agree, but not necessarily agree with what is said. We merely affirm that what is said whilst we are listening. Yes, this is the plain vanilla flavour of it in a nutshell, it works to varying degrees, but it is not a complete failsafe method either. The simple matter of the fact is, many books exist on dealing with conflict, the problem is the time involved, we simply do not have time, we are simply not mentally and emotionally always geared for this facade, or either workload and time does not afford us such luxury. Well then – we have to punch him in the face and let us see what happens – mentally speaking – this is something not taught in the class room for MBA's where diplomacy is taught. However, where diplomacy ends fighting starts, so why always go the route of public relations when one can clearly see that the opposition wants to be right and fight it out, this is a rule, you will always find someone that knows best, knows it all, or just wants to reinvent the wheel. How many of us know how to fight the good fight with these characters and win?

Part two: Dealing effectively with the Complexity of strategy;

Let us change the paradigm – to that of the acquisitioning of the ability to fight and defend. Our inability to resolve conflict that surrounds complexity, will ultimately affect our precision as well – "if I can't do this no one else can". This is undesirable; it then becomes an internal disabling element of our thinking and personality, which spreads into our corporate culture. Now, what if the conflict situation has spiralled out of control and we have drawn our lines in the sand. This is human nature at its best; there are certain times when we just have to draw the line, here we resort to settling disputes in business, as we did at school, on the school grounds as it were, we draw our line in the dirt and face the challenge, cross the line and see what happens. We have to realise that conflict is at times very necessary and useful, a natural phenomenon. When we are mentally geared for revolution, we contemplate irresolvable conflict. We plan our defences accordingly and our offences; we pick our battles well and defend our gains ferociously. This is the nature of radical revolutionary strategic management; it deals with the reality of things, without having to sugar-coat them to become palatable, our strategies do not require any maintenance, we become proactive and assume nothing, our encounters are brief and precise – like that of a predator.

Enhancing our "Predatorily traits"

Predators are focused on a - Revolutionary Radical Strategy – that is always well conceived, well planned, time-phased and engineered to be flexible, with true resilience and vigilance thus epitomising the symbol of the predator character. Where we act cool and calm, calculated in our aims, we are preserving our strength and not showing our weakness until the decisive moment. Designed and equipped for precision styled work. The predator waits his turn; he ambushes his prey and avoids conflict by doing so. Poised for that decisive moment, at which a calculated blow should be rendered, with precision; towards the "strategic target" of the body. Here he uses all his strength, power and tactics – to make the conclusion - final and the conflict brief. His strategy reduces any possibility of on-going confrontation, thus avoiding tension, as well as avoiding the possibility of injury to himself or allow the objective to escape and evade.

When on the attack: we require precision; this type of precision is echoed with the incorporation of "CAPS". Whenever we contemplate a strategic attack, we analyse our strategic targets and their strategic value first and foremost. We analyse it from two perspectives; the first, as if we were the aggressor and the second as if we were the prey. We do not waste our energies on crisis management as a means to an end, because of political influences. The objective is clear; the rest is only noise we have to start solving "rock in the path" problems, which becomes the end of the perceived threat in itself when we show others the means, and the way. Solving "rock" problems requires insight, the ability to confront problems and challenges for what they are, and not by the way, they are perceived as huge "rocks". We rely on precision military styled work ethic and planning to carry us through "Rock hard" times. This is where "CAPS" come in; it focuses all our energies and recourses in a structured manner towards resolving potential threats, or towards devising plans of attack, or both. "CAPS should become our doctrine; whenever we start dealing with strategy formulation, strategic targeting and conflict resolution.

CAPS:

Why CAPS, it defines the process, and principles that the military follow to identify their targets.

The first principle of war is to dislodge the head from the body, or to clamp the command and control elements, the neck, by suffocating it, as well as all its communication components, the major arteries and air way, a body becomes useless when the brain becomes dislodged, or starves from a lack of oxygen - information. Thus, we shift from the whole to the parts of the problem.

"CAPS" incorporates all the ingredients of effective strategy; it deals with "strategic targeting" in terms of its:

CAPS: stands for,
Concepts,
Attributes,
Perceptions and
Systems - (supporting a structure to bring it into effect or to make it effective in its purpose.)

CAPS works best when we apply "Strategic Targeting" first. With "**Strategic Targeting**" we try to find and identify our aim clearly; it is the mental process of - *Identify, Clarify, Quantify* and defining of our objectives and goals first. "Only fools rush in" – so that they are clearly understood when seeking a solution. Solutions become clear only when we have a concept to work with. The concept must be fully encompassing, and be a total solution. The collective envisions the contemplated solution against; what we know now, have assumed, and have to work with, vs. who, where, what, when, and how this will solve the problem - and "who" will be responsible. Only then planning becomes specific in direction - towards that which is becoming *significant* – and worthy of our effort and time spent – only then planning becomes a useful exercise. If the "envision" (the end–vision), if not significant (exciting, or a real total solution), then we are wasting our time planning for it. We might as well just do it and see what happens. We want to assure ourselves of uncompromising victories, at every stage of our offensive and not just a measure of success – that is left to chance. "It's all or nothing." Only when we have found our strategic target do we require planning.

"Strategic Targeting" first - then CAPS.

"Strategic Targeting" - is aimed at using the whole organisation. Strategic targeting systematically seeks out the capabilities and expertise that will be enhancing our chances as a collective to achieve the common objectives. The aim is to throw the whole fist and not just a finger, at our target, by drawing from our collective strength and experience, in the most comprehensive and conceivable manner. We do not do the obvious here either; we do not just "shoot" at the main target, we explore and plan several approaches.

We realise and factor in that there could be obstacles, obstacles yet unseen, liken to attributes and circumstances, in our path to the envisaged target if we merely plan a direct frontal attack, we understand that we could be seen and ambushed or stopped along the way. The point to make here is that strategic targeting helps us to look before we leap. Plan before we move, we therefore take the routes of least resistance; we come to the total realisation and awareness that even business could benefit just like any Army, from tactical wisdom and to get everyone to their predetermined strategic battle positions, takes time and contemplation. Then to get every component at the ready before the attack starts, takes even more time, time in training and developing abilities that will be required - needs to be factored in. In some instance – training and preparation is required beforehand. Covey calls it "The law of the harvest". Before we can even contemplate making any decisive radical moves, just like attacking with any Army, we have to prepare. You first train, and arm yourself and be able to re-supply before contemplating war, then only move to the best strategical point on the battle field, in other words position yourself first. This is the difference between two extremes, that of *becoming prepared* and really *being prepared* for whatever.

Battle is not the place where you want to find out that you were not ready to be tested.

"Failure is more costly, than preparation."

Becoming and being prepared.

"Becoming prepared" and **"Being prepared"** are two essential elements in War. That becomes one as we enter battle; our Preparedness – makes us **Vigilant**.

1. *The first aspect* of vigilance is the ***becoming prepared – developing sight***. Becoming prepared is a perishable skill and must be taught, trained and practiced recurrently until it develops into a trait. Becoming prepared is the physical part – it takes time - of preparation for the battle. Take athletes for instance, they train right through the year in the run up to the main event. The point is, if you are not physically well prepared to act mentally, then you are simply just not prepared. This implies that perishable skills; doctrines and tactics, must be recurrently practiced until it becomes second nature to the team. Training and tutoring has one beginning and no end. This aspect will give us the ability to see, seeing with the mind's eye that is. This required distinguished ability to "see" clearly with the mind's eye is only developed through rigorous and continued training. The relationships of things as they exist around us can only be seen with a trained mind's eye, if not trained we merely see complexity at every junction. This aspect is referred to as **becoming prepared**.

2. *The second aspect* is ***being prepared – developing fight***. This is the process of – or principle rather, of War. Training people on the job – in the environment they work in with the tools at their disposal and making sure that they know how to use resources effectively and correctly – as well as to its maximum potential. This aspect is very essential, as we are only as strong as our weakest link. Then we also have to make people comfortable with their tasks and familiarise them with the doctrine, until it becomes one seeming less recurring process. We have to teach, train and develop our human component to its full- "intended purpose" like wise. Although, here is a twist, just like with farming, if we take short cuts in doing so and cut corners, like not preparing the soil, then quality and the quantity of the "crop" will diminish – the combined intellectual coefficient will be questionable. You cannot want excellence without feeding it, to develop potential. If you want results, you have to get the right people and equipment, the right-minded managers and streamlined process, all have to be in place, only the diligent will delay gratification, to reap the continuous fruits of his labour. The fool will reap and eat all of the first crops. If you give mangers average people and average equipment, expect average results. However, if you give him exceptional people and equipment – expect excellence. This is the process of **being prepared** - or preparing holistically all the functioning…within the organisation.

From these two observations, we draw one conclusion; parts form systems. In true strategic terms, the equation of all strategic things should equate:

Strategic implying – being prepared – it gives us the required synergised vision, to see with the mind, by being able to see, we can find our targets, - targeting- then becomes easy. By being prepared – we can fight the fight alone, or as a collective and still achieve the goal - this gives us the required ability to think and fight three dimensional, - in military style with predatory precision, to evade and or overcome complexity, both of which are very beneficial to survival and excellence.

This way it does not leave us with either "collateral damage" – a lot of bruised and dented ego's-, or in financial ruin. We no longer have to seek out the smaller splintered parts of our goals that we missed, that get lost in the everyday noise of haphazard management, due to incompetence. Managers miss attempts at goal, because they could not see them, target them, prepare for them, as a result of poor strategic understanding of the importance of targeting. They just go after goals, they are "goal orientated" and driven.

Targeting vs. Targets

Rules for good targeting; you cannot target that which is not seen and clearly identifiable. Targets are multifaceted concepts that require three-dimensional evaluation of its nature. All targets have identity, size and is at a distance, they have components and parts that comprises the whole target. Targets are concepts that have attributes that give them their identity. Targeting on the other hand has to deal with all this complexity of directing strategy. Targeting is focused on both goals and objectives, in order to identify them. When hunting meat, hunters aim for the head, when hunting trophy, they shoot for the hart. Why? because these attributes of head and hart become significant when looking at specific outcomes. In this instance, any shot to the head or hart should kill the animal. This is the common *objective (the aim) of hunting*, however the *goals* (the motivation behind killing) in relation to what the purpose was for the hunt, could differ. The one hunter killed because he was after the meat the other the trophy. However, what happens daily? We are all hunting objectives – along different paradigms - on the strategic landscape – daily. Without knowing exactly what attributes to focus on implicitly when seeking our targets. Just take aim and shoot, it has become a hit and miss affair. Then we also tend to either aim to high or too low with our strategies, we strike at the target on pure assumption, without having confirmed its identity - that will deliver the attributes we seek. Taking this back to hunting, old animals make great trophies, younger animals supply tender meat. Then we also shoot because it feels right, the strategic "animal" gets hit in the neck and runs off, our effort was not good enough, the calibre of rifle we used was not adequate, the shot did not count. By the time we find our objective, it is ruined by circumstance. When our aim is to secure objectives, we need to secure it in full. We have to be more specific in our approaches to diminish waste and risk in ascertaining objectives. Targeting multifaceted objectives with one specific attribute is like hunting all types of game with one calibre rifle. Daily companies miss their targets, their opportunities, because of poor strategic targeting skills or understand of concepts. They lack strategic targeting as a doctrine.

They are either only focused on developing their sight, without developing their fight, or visa-versa.

By applying "Strategic targeting", we kill crisis management at its embryonic stage. We do not make one-sided decisions – referring to people who are either conservative or liberal, that reason from the same perspective, paradigm, which shares the same perception, based purely on one paradigm of thinking. Strategic targeting does not allow this; the obvious to take preference. In other words, the direct route from A to Z to prevail. No, we demand creativity and spontaneity. Strategic targeting does not overlook all the letters in between A and Z; it breaks it up into smaller manageable steps, or objectives, before we strike at the targeted objective, or our strategic objective. This ensures us of a steady footing, if we had to back step, we would still be in a favourable position. We have to close the distance, so that we have the best possible shot. Opposed to the norm of strategies, that jumps the Grand Canyon in one step, and hope they land on their feet. If anything goes wrong, if the situation changes, they have no place to back step to, this is the principle of strategic targeting and herein remains its flexibility. It can move with great speed over known terrain and tread carefully over unknown.

It moves from this premise, that one cannot measure that which one cannot **see;** one cannot fight that which we cannot **find – or target.** This evokes criticism in people, they cannot see what management wants, so they cannot target it, lock on to it, so they shoot blindly at their own targets, and get lost in the fight. Both these aspects have to form one whole. Then we can safely move on, we do not have to resort to crisis management repeatedly because people just cannot see or target by themselves and as a result do not plan effectively – **See.** Remember - action beats reaction. In the quest for better and faster, we have to develop people to do things either on their own accord, or as a collective, both gelling at some point. Even though we may follow many different avenues towards "targeting", we stay focused on precision activities by virtue of our strategy, our principles and with the full utilisation of our resources. We have to arrive at workable, practical solutions and not just theory. We secure for ourselves the best possible strategic outcome – by defining the mythology required, and entrenching it.

Therefore, Strategic Targeting is precision styled planning, collaboration, intelligence gathering and execution guide by simple principles.

"The only way to develop thought which is abstract in nature is to give it form, by writing it down, by giving it colour, by mapping it, putting it together like pieces of a puzzle – this is the secret of seeing relationships".

Hence the motivation for strategic targeting;

1. It generates full optimisation of organisational resources.
2. It becomes effective when addressing and managing perceptions.
3. It is focused on battles rather than wars – processes rather than results - driven by military precision like planning and execution.
4. It forces people towards re-organisation and collaboration to align with priority strategic intent.

5. It is diverse, multiple pronged, intelligence driven, collection, correlation & evaluation strategy making based on a formula shared within the organisation by all - CAPS.
6. It circumvents personal perception and agendas – because everyone is targeting strategic targets that are predefined in the corporate strategy.
7. It forces total collaboration from all the systems, subsystems and organisation towards achieving specifics.
8. It is synchronised, flexible directives, instruction sets, command and control.
9. It relies on predefined rules of engagement, parameters and mandates.

Strategic Targeting, questions our motives and conclusions.

1. Which methods exist, or can be developed, to target the market and new resources?
2. How have these methods been applied in the past and were they successful?
3. What is the criteria for targeting – Are we focusing on weakness or strengths; capacitating or incapacitating, attributes?
4. What are the success margins and benefits derived from this application? Was it designated by targeting methods, in comparison to conventional alternatives of regular stereo typed meetings giving directives, in terms of time, labour and cost involved?

The Strategic target - *is the one with the most emotional and capacitating attributes.*

When either destroyed, or compromised; or on the other hand been defended successfully and staying un-compromised - in military terms. Success influences morale, sustainability and survival. Therefore, in summary, the very-way strategic targeting works in the military is what makes it work for us. It is both, introspective - abstract and retrospective - formative / progressive - as it grows as a concept in the mind. It looks at all things in terms of its significance and its parts and their significance in relation to the concept; its pro's and con's - power and weakness... Strategic targeting is mainly used at resolving very complex issues that have no obvious immediate workable solution available. It could be argued that it is too time consuming to use in all instance to resolve all types of problems with – yes, true. It is the proverbial heavy artillery, like artillery it requires exact, precise co-ordinates and target designation to be effective. It is also more costly and slower – nevertheless remains the most effective. Yet, the effect is much more superior that any other existing alternative. It "literally" blows complexity to pieces. Leaving us with only answers, we never had, if not for the process, we followed.

It also has a spin-off effect, it becomes a corporate habit over time that is watered down to a personal doctrine on thinking innovatively, at a personal level, and we all become empowered to fight complexity along the same lines. With the same principles being applied throughout the organisation, unknowingly at times it seems, we start developing essential battle language, we communicate better, faster and more effective and we "see" better, fight better. It becomes a new habit and eventually we use it to solve all problems with, the "seed" becomes the "forest". Why, because we pollinate one another's thinking, now like never before, because of our similarity in thinking, planning, communication and reasoning, towards solving problems.

Let us get practical here and explain this by a simple example, to get us to understand better the principle that is involved here. When the US- Military were planning to invade Iraq, specifically Baghdad.

They were faced with the challenge of extreme complexity, the rock in the path problem. Firstly, they had to deal with the "targets" – and they had billions. In order to find the ones strategically significant, they looked at each targets concept. In terms of its military concept and strategic significance, they were looking for strengths and weakness.

However, they had to work within the frame work, of civilised war, - if something like that really exists – by factoring in the civilian population, their culture, the coastline and the mountainous terrain where they live; the military aspects, their radar defences and early warning systems, as well as the anti-aircraft batteries etc...

Then they planned their offences, by factoring in what they have and how can they use it to achieve the goal - and how effective certain units are at doing what? Let us not get to complicated; we get the idea of the short cut analysis. They then planned smaller objectives, leading up to their main objective, liberation. The final result was the "Systematically" advancement of the objective. Having several prongs with several objectives - leading up and towards an overall objective – equates to several ways of gaining sure success. This is the very essence of strategy we are trying to get across, certain primary objective require smaller objectives to be reached first. Stage one of the offensives, was to knockout Baghdad's defences and offensive systems that prohibited air supremacy and freedom – thus prohibiting initiative. By looking at the first target in this regard, let us say radar stations as a pre-primary objective, to achieve the secondary main goal of air supremacy...and ultimately taking the city and the country.

In business terms, strategic targeting is also referred to as the process of integrating your short-term plans with your long-term plans, your dream maker. A dream catcher of sorts, which brings about a ritual of scenarios (schemes), to guide you from the implicit, to the more explicit, your final destination, with greater certainty.

The system and levers of "Strategic Targeting"

Strategic targeting uses our IQ, - spelt IQ'Q. We rely on our IQ - **IQ'Q**. (*Identify, Quantify and Qualify*). To define the target firstly, then we mix the findings up with a **GAP analysis.**

We make our decisions based on intelligence and not on information. Intelligence is information that has been tested to make sure it is accurate. Then we analyse the target / objective within the following open ended principles:

- **Identify the concept**
- **Quantify its attributes**
- **Qualify your deductions**

Then we put it to the **GAP analysis:**

G – Geography (its natural features, infrastructure, suppliers, service providers etc.)

A – Attributes of geography (distance, reliability, maintenance, strategic position etc.)

P – Perceptions surrounding the concept and forgone conclusions.

The intelligence gathered from this simple exercise, is open ended, you decide where to stop, which direction to take, it keeps conversation strategic and focused and it becomes the focal point for departure.

We have designed a concept to deal with complexity simply called CAPS.

Let us first use it in the military context, to get a feel for it and then relate it back to the business context. Objectives are planned in phases, CAPS helps us to plan them at every stage.

Phase 1

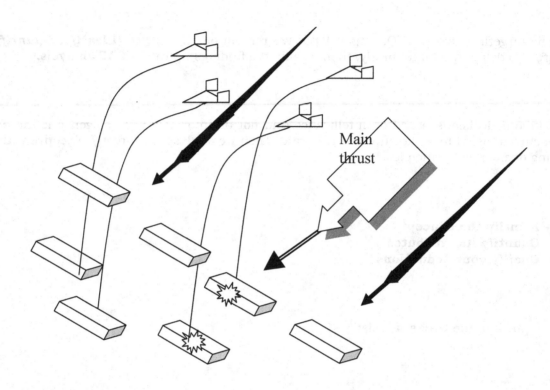

Phase 2

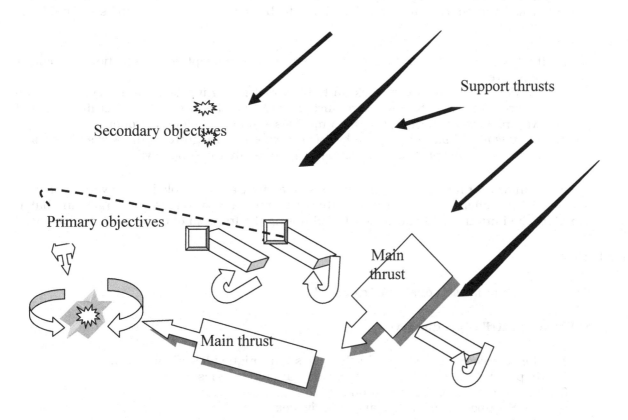

C.A.P.S –The Military Example

Concept

The Radar Station example again, to get to what is a strategic targets, – **"concept"**: every concept has three purposes strategically speaking, which we have to find and identify; otherwise, it is not a strategic target... If we do not arrive at this deduction, then we have over analysed the concept and we then have to back step until it becomes definable by these terms;

1. Its *"main purpose"* is to detect any aircraft – concept one, detection – ability - defensive
2. Its *"default purpose"* is to lock on to its target giving it a bearing, range, speed and quality – referring to how many aircraft or/ and the size of the aircraft – concept two, tracking and orientating Sam missiles – ability – defensive/ offensive.
3. Its *"integrated purpose"*, (in other words when it integrates with a system or sub systems) – concept three – target designation – ability – offensive.

Now we know that it can act in defence as well as play a major role in the overall defences and by default offence. Strategically it thus becomes a very important target, in that it prohibits the initiative of the attacker, by inhibiting the freedom of choice and movement.

Attributes

Dissecting the radar stations - **"Attributes"**

a) Physical attributes; dissected;

1. The complete radar station itself – gives it a unique identifiable form.
2. Its power source – what are they. Generators, batteries, solar, etc.
3. Its platform – mobile or stationary
4. The Sam batteries – range and effectiveness.
5. The low level advanced radar site – its range and inhibiting attributes – weather etc.
6. Its fire control and command centre – on or off site.
7. Its support system, gunnery batteries, helicopter gunships, crew etc.

b) Emotional/ symbolic attributes;

Abilities – offensive and defensive – early warning system.

c) Derivation or innate attributes;

The manufacture / architects specification will tell us more about its predisposed ability.

e) Objective and subjective attributes;

If utilised to its optimum capacity. What will its full potential be and how well is it be utilised currently?

Perception

Starting with;

What is perceived; about the target, as well as how is it perceived. We analyse the "perception" of any target firstly, to understand its primary perceived purpose within the context. We break it up into logical sectors we assume nothing.

1. **Value** - Mission critical or not – to the defence of the city.
2. **Purpose** – primary, secondary -to stop any air threat.
3. **Capacity** – It has great range and is a proven means of defence.

Attributes:

Enabling

- o Will show attacking aircraft.
- o Could direct missiles towards the attacking aircraft.
- o Could focus all efforts in the main direction of attack

Disabling

- o Without electrical power, it has no effect.
- o Without crew, it has no effect.
- o The use of "Stealth technology" against it.

Systems

Systems: supporting this structure to bring it into effect, or to make it effective in its purpose.

- o Communications – effectiveness
- o Supplies and logistics - effectiveness
- o Organisational diagram – if applicable
- o Infrastructure – available in support of target.
- o Hierarchy's influence on target' or its autonomy.
- o Elements, of culture that could have an effect on the targets effectiveness.
- o *Elements of our Intellectual Culture influence our perception on CAPS, communication and command and control.*

Applying the Principles of C.A.P.S – in Business.

Let us use an example here that everyone can relate to; I call it the "Equestrian Unit".

The scenario: We are a local law enforcement agency and we have been tasked to form an effective equestrian unit; well normally we would look for the obvious first, the horses... wrong apply CAPS and see how it will change your paradigm on reverse engineering.

Concept

- Its *"main purpose"* **is to;** Provide an alternative method of policing.
- Its *"default purpose"* **is to;** Provide patrols- rural, urban, - and crowd control.
- Its *"integrated purpose",* **is to;** serve as a Force multiplier at a ratio of 1-10.

Attributes

- *Physical attributes; dissected;* Riders, Horse, Stables, Vehicles, Horseboxes, Equipment, Stable hands, Manger, Vet, Arena, Lunging ring, feed, etc.,
- *Emotional/ symbolic attributes;* Power, Beauty and a force to be reckoned with.
- *Derivation or innate attributes;* Speed, power, agility, diversity and height increasing view, interactive with public.
- *Objective and subjective attributes;* Arguments for and against. Do the maths.

Perception

Starting with;

What is Perceived; about the targets;

- *Value - Mission critical or not* – Could be if utilised during a Olympic event, or World Cup event
- *Purpose – primary, secondary* – Patrol, high visibility, saturation
- *Capacity* – All terrain, All weather, Day and night time utilisation
- *Attributes:*

- *Enabling* – Rider/ food/ shelter/ training/ transportation.
- *Disabling* – Illness / injury / pregnancy / inoculation / real bad weather

Systems

- **Systems:** *supporting this structure to bring it into effect, or to make it effective in its purpose.*
- **Communications – effectiveness;** Essential
- **Supplies and logistics –** effectiveness – delivery and freshness of food/quality
- **Organisational diagram – if applicable –** will it require changes, if so what?
- **Infrastructure – available in support of target.** Land, vehicles, buildings, water, electricity, roads, etc.
- **Hierarchy's influence on target' or its autonomy.** Who will take it? Where will it slot into the organisation?
- **Elements, of culture that could have an effect on the targets effectiveness.** Cultural bias against horses, manure, police, riders, or the manner in which they will, or could be utilised.
-

We will explore this concept further – first we need to cover other important bases...

Handling the cognitive part of the plan

This section covers the required attributes to plan; this is the paralleled route to the CAPS diagram that runs in sync with the guideline we will cover in this section, the proverbial flipside of the coin:

Total preparation; culture forming and habit forming – influence strategy making.

Illustrated by focusing on Spartacus, the lord of slaves, born from noble blood, captured into slavery, then turned gladiator, who almost brought the Roman Empire to ruin. Spartacus being a farmer's son understood "the law of the harvest" and so did Genghis Khan, the greatest leader of men. He established an empire far greater than that of the Roman legacy. Through the *unification* of many tribes and in Spartacus situation, slaves, *unity was their strength*, but it was by their unified culture that they created, that they ultimately brought it altogether. Focus was on *discipline and principles* – freedom of movement and intuitive - that kept it altogether.

Without a unified principled-guided culture, the organisation will bear little fruits of mind. It will not yield any record harvest. They will not understand the law of the harvest. Principles and concepts take time to mature and so do forming one unified culture. Therefore, the concept of a new culture, a new unified corporate culture that is, will evidently also take time. Culture is made up of basic concepts, or essential elements.

"The law of the harvest" should be entrenched in corporate culture as a principle.

Liken the natural nutrients that need to be present in the soil; the soil being the organisation in this regard, the nutrients, being corporate culture. Put together they become the land. Farming is a high-risk business; you cannot store good weather, or even order it. Therefore, you have to plan, study and learn from its life cycle and the time it takes to complete cycles. This will eventually give one the required wisdom to farm. The problem is a practical one.

How to prepare; the soil and plan the crop:

Using Reframing as a principle imprinting tool, Reframing has all the ingredients needed to alter the reality of things from what they are to what they need to be in order for a specific 'AGENDA 'to prevail. Now this is a two-sided sword and can be used for good and evil.

Fact and point, large media companies are used in this manner to influence, beliefs, culture and ultimately perception in most countries. The process is referred to as behavioural shaping, or "reframing".

Reframing as a Perception changing tool; – "Let's unpack this to add value". Reframing is altering the meaning or value of something; by altering its context or description as it relates to reality, or rather the perception of reality. There are two basic kinds of reframes: contextual reframing and content reframing. Both can alter our internal representations of events or situations. Abraham Maslow's instinctoid theory of motivation may be described as a reaction to the prevailing influence of the behaviour and analytical approaches used - particularly where needs vs. one's instincts are prevalent. His hierarchy of needs pyramid is universally known, it starts with; Physiological needs, next the need for safety, then love, esteem and then lastly self-actualisation. However, we all know that satisfied needs do not nearly motivate us as much as unsatisfied needs do and they force us beyond our normal modes of operation, character and personality.

Reframing is such a powerful change agent, it helps us to realise the changes required to go from satisfied to a quenching mind-set, means that we have to deal with fear. Fear is pain and not something we like much. It changes our perceptions radically. Nevertheless, the ultimate question; does changing our symbolic representations of the real world actually change anything in the real world itself? The drive theory could better explain this question: The concept of **"drive"** is in many ways merely a substitute for the concept of **"instinct",** the primal basic survival needs of man. These include curiosity, exploration, manipulation and maternal drives. The significance of drives are that they are the attributes of success, they help us to overcome our fear, by virtue of its intensity, the level at which that specific drive instigates man to behave without fear, or to manifest a certain type of behaviour that overcomes fear.

"Even if the organism has not yet had the opportunity to learn that, such behavioural patterns are followed by primary drive satisfaction. Thus, for example a hungry rat will run about sniff and investigate – even though this behaviour has not yet produced a habit when wanting to satisfy a primal need". Bolles (1967).

How are Habits formed?

If we want to change behaviour, we have to change habits. Behaviourists approach this question from the source. Stimuli, and external response occur together and are followed by reinforcement; a relationship between stimuli and response is then enforced and formed. This relationship is then strengthened or established by the fact that the connection between stimuli and response is mediated internally, by the nervous system (Hull 1943 -1952). *Dr Leandro Herrero.*

"The only real change management is behavioural and procedures need to be **reinforced** *with rewards".*

Reframing – deals with changing people's attitudes by addressing their inhibitions and fears; feelings or beliefs that prevents somebody from behaving spontaneously or speaking freely. Perceived inabilities, and fear affect our mental orientation. Reframing dislodges minds from this belief to arrive with better alternatives, to perceive and deal with additional information accurately and more effectively. Before arriving at any point where reframing of paradigms can start, we have to have criteria that spawn critical focused thinking, by look at problems and their solutions from one perspective;

- o Retrospectively; to understand lessons learned from past conflicts, the interpretation of history and facts in relation to what we are busy with now
- o Perspectively; guiding choices by implementing mitigation steps towards solving conflicts that are likely or expected to happen

Advanced reasoning and pertinent solutions are sought in this fashion by utilising specific criteria for deduction and consensus building, the framework for reasoning freed from inhibitions and fear. Consensus is the critical building element within teams, in both the conflict assessment and resolution arena. Strategic intervention starts with reasoning with similar dynamic, we all have to see one picture with the same attributes, in simple terms it levels the playing field so that more people can get to have insight and understanding of what was previously misunderstood or vague. Everyone had their own picture as they perceived it "contained" as a problem.

Breaking out of our mental containment

Let us illustrate this by picturing the immediate environment around a person as a container. When referring to the container we include everything that a person has been exposed to and use to. His frame of reference; his living space or habitat, his whole being, his environment, his introspective space and the physical being. Both the psychological and the physical forms will create the persons container. We must furthermore realise that the container metaphor we have arrived at is in parallel equilibrium - containing both physical and mental attributes, one is of no value without the other. We provide and cater for people's needs in terms of their psychological, mental, physical as well as their character development, in this metaphor.

An evolving character is one that is constantly attempting to grow and enlarge with newer and more complex reasoning and substance by pushing the boundaries of containment with new experiences. This "container" defines everything that is – "a known environment". This is the persons operating platform, this is his comfort zone, the place in which he or she experiences safety, the most familiarity where he can move and think with ease, where he has the most defined choices and knows the expectations of the environment and the people within it. Within these confines of the contained environment and its perceptual boundaries we all live, work and think. Within, "The container" we are ourselves, and he or she can adjust expectations accordingly, with some real affirmed knowledge of cause and effect from previous encounters and from experience within the contained environment to cope with any change effectively.

The concept of reframing attempts to enlarge this space around a person, by enlarging his frame, we are moving people from the well-known to the un-known- **becoming prepared**. The process of which we are now about to describe. Know and understand, that the larger the container grows, the less predictable the environment becomes. Society historically has attempted to further and further restrict and constrict the containers provided for people, by labelling them. "You are too busy" to do that, too smart to try that, too highly rated to risk or so insignificant in society, that no one will listen. It people that prevent people from expanding their containers, people restrict people, not thoughts, they are merely perceptions. Let us go to the Supermarket and explore this implication further, if your containers label reads "jam", then you belong to the isle where "jams" are kept. In this section and class of existence, "jam" people live in small houses and take the bus to work. In addition, "jam" containers only need to concern themselves with being ready. Now the "sandwich makers" are a higher status of people, they live in big houses, drive expensive German cars and have the "right" to dictate to jam people. All the jam people need to do is sit on the shelf and be ready. In other words just go about your ordinary life and we the Government or your employer will do the rest for you, we will call upon you in the event that we need your particular skill...

This is where the importance and the complexity of increased choices become apparent. In choice lies freedom, the freedom from which revolutions stem from, to choose that which you want and do not want without due or alternative influences imposed on you - like the burden of social class and status. Therefore it stands to reason, the larger the container in which we live, the more choices we will have and inevitably be called upon to make. The larger our containers are, the vaster our knowledge base will have to become to deal with it, and the greater our experience must be to cope as adults. The upside is, we have more personal responsibility, we have more self-worth and gain more experience. It becomes an upward spiral and the container grows and keeps growing. This is the point we want to arrive at, either people spiral upwards and outwards or inwards towards collapse.

The new flexible-container must be large enough a container to allow for some real self-expression, family time, a value system, an integral standards system, a beliefs system, a love and trust system, that will equate inner and outer balance – thus **becoming prepared.**

The Matrix, will define our limitations, we will no longer live with the habit of denial, which will help us to become significant Predators.

We are all adults and we demand to be treated as such, never the less even adults require structure and formality, we must have a boundary system, a reference network, a matrix in which every system belongs to its specific sphere within the personal mental container. To affect a successful paradigm shift then requires some sort of reward. With a strong focus on improving communication and building trust, people need to trust the leadership unequivocally or the tail of the organisation will remain stuck in the door that has been closed on the past forever.

Letting the influence of the "new container" flow, as if introducing a new fresh stream of cold water over barren land is the concept of change. Implementing it is like trying to contain water and directing it all at the same time. This will require a lot of mental legwork, explaining the vision so that everyone buy's in will take time. Crisis management must be catered for because during any change over the company will experience a "rupture effect". Some of the water/change will not reach the intended destinations and blockages in communication could occur, contamination of the water, of what should happen vs. what is happening could set in. We have to be realistic to manage this aspect, one should coach "change managers" to help with facilitation and collaboration of the process. All these eventualities need to be catered for within contingencies.

Someone explained it as grass fire fighting skills and it stuck with me, so one could refer to it as "grass fire fighting skills". Have you ever seen how quickly a grass fire can get out of hand? Well emotions are like that, so prepare by putting in fire brakes, change management culture firstly, change organisational culture secondly, re-engineer systems thirdly, or face a situation where mental stress and physical turmoil could erupt – especially where people's positions become compromised. Evolution is a conscious decision, but that does not mean that everyone will benefit immediately.

People always believe that they are right and are doing well by their own standards in the absence of clear standards and norms; they have "convictions" like blind faith, from their own perspectives, that were enforced by a previous system and set of beliefs. Even the most evil person from their perspective believes, he or she is doing right by their standards and convictions. Otherwise, they would not be doing what they are doing. On the other hand; would they if they only knew better. The answer is a definite yes, just look at our children and the choices that they make because of their containers, their experiences and their scripts as well as perceptions. Therefore, from this we can safely derive that knowledge is power. For adults, it will take more than knowledge to make this transition; it will take empowerment, capacitating and on-going good communication in the form of dialogue. The leader will dictate the speed of change and the fluidity, due to his or her management style.

Are you Ruling or Managing?

Rulers apply rules; on the other hand, managers use effective communication.

A number of strategies and techniques exist in the use of dialogue to reframe inflexible conflicts in leadership style. These include the process of "Trustworthiness & Culture re-engineering"

Reduce tension and manage the de-escalation of hostility: with techniques such as listening.

Perspective taking: techniques such as acknowledging critical short comings, toward better understanding of identity and characterization frames, in order to see oneself more objectively and the other party in a more positive manner.

Establish common ground as a basis for agreement: techniques such as searching for common ground enable reframing around a smaller set of issues, in order to open up communication between parties. Such processes seek to identify desired futures in order to shift the focus from a short-term perspective to a long-term one.

In business, every sales representative uses reframing and visualization when he says, "Picture yourself owning this, it will become the envy of your friends and colleagues."

Shifting the mental gears; by changing – or reframing - the paradigms of managers.

Today, in most companies when your opinion is wanted "it is given to you". This mentality stems from a fundamental belief entrenched in academics literature and schooling pertaining management principles. At this level, management is purely concerned with control and output. This has become a management culture absorbed and entrenched in senior managers; they are the thinkers that design controls and have control, this is managements only purpose. By mastering control, we have mastered management. How far is this removed from our current reality? However, this was true, in the industrial era it might have been; where many workers were getting by, just by the seat of their pants, they lived from hand to mouth, had lords and masters for "managers". Sucking up and kissing the feet of your master was the norm, now we have the handshake. Now we have managers, ("Boss men") that still want to endorse this primitive paradigm. They feel they have earned the right by having the position; the thing about position, is this, with position comes responsibility - it should not give us a sense of accomplishment and power over people. This is also referred to as the "halo effect", a false sense of importance and what management is all about. Nothing could be further removed from the truth about the role and function of management today. The fact of this matter is that no one is indispensable, firstly. Secondly, the truth of the matter is, we have all evolved as people. Now we have the complete opposite reality when dealing with our workforce, they have rights, education, and unions, however the paradigm on managing has not changed; we still have the carrot and stick managers.

Moreover, on the other side of the spectrum, we now have a workforce that just have wants, their basic needs have long since been fulfilled for many at least, they are all thinkers to a certain extent, with highly developed senses of reasoning and understanding, they are all exposed to knowledge and learning, as well as information. This is where the significance comes in today, we now have thinking people. They want their satisfaction on the job, but they find it off the job. Because of this aspect of misalignment of management paradigms and workers just having to perform, perform, perform. We have evolved since those dark ages and have moved into the wisdom era, the age of reasoning and knowledge. The new concept of working and living with abundance has emerged. Nevertheless somehow our own tail is still stuck in the door of control from our distant past; the old blood of overbearing control and rigid management styles of the industrial era is still running thick in our veins and universities.

The on-going conflict between business and stakeholders emerge here as the culprit. We have to identify which core principles to be present for effective managing of stakeholders: (this implies that everyone is managing a problem as a collective, and not just the managers as it is taught academically, stakeholders; all share equal responsibility for the success) this type of managing requires;

1. Forms of recognition for all stakeholders, their role and function must be recognised.
2. Moral minimum standard to be upheld, which places moral principles above the interests of any manager or individual role-player.
3. Valid assumptions of how trust, honesty and loyalty is recognised and rewarded should be infused into the management's relationship with all stakeholders.

It is said that we must re-write the music of management to get rid of all the soured notes; when our infrastructures shifted towards modernisation and globalisation, we forgot to shift our focus on management philosophy accordingly and now everything has ruptured and soured. The significance of this statement is the problem that was created, one cannot solve problems in the same way as what we created them, it requires a new paradigm altogether, we have to revisit our thinking about management and have a total shift of managements paradigms altogether to align our style and management core with the new way.

Our global obliviousness towards fundamental changes in parallel with human development has left us stuck in a grove. Mainly, because we only had to follow one route to success in yester year, today we face the phenomenon of dynamic changes in business and global economy. Today we have to do things in parallel with change and not only focus on our own success as a key measurement of our accomplishment. We need to be proactive and no longer reactive to succeed. The truth of the matter is that success like winning is short lived; it sets like the sun and fades likewise. Therefore, nothing else fails more to motivate us like focusing on success and winning - as criteria to gauge effective and efficient management. Because we fail just by having succeeded, we get to repeat the success cycle, repeatedly. People have been conditioned from school days to view success or winning as the ultimate yardstick and measure of accomplishment. Therefore, we are by implication teaching that someone has to lose, in order for someone else to succeed, just so that they themselves can fail as they reach their objective, in order for someone else in turn to succeed. We all eventually have to become failures at one time or another. No wonder we are all so very tired. It is because of the ghosts from the past we chase. The truth about success is that success is not something we can store for the hard times, and rely on when we need assistance in matters of mortal danger, it is nothing, and then I ask myself why are we chasing it again. If it is not sustainable, it is just not viable. We are not leaving a trail of wisdom and knowledge nor acquiring it by doing so, a legacy to follow, can you hand over success to your son, or daughter - no - we could argue that the fruits could be handed over - yes. That is the point. Success is what we say it is, it is something of our own making and understanding. We are building sand castles, in the wash of the sea if we want to be measured by others standards of success. Success is for a small instance of self-gratification, and a sense of accomplishment, but what is left, just a beach of success, tons of sand. The memories of the sand castle fade likewise, like the quick fix success itself created - fades. If success does not leave behind knowledge, wisdom, understanding, and sustained growth, then it was worthless pursuing it.

Our paradigms should change drastically on how we motivate people to climb the corporate ladder, for it is lonely at the top and you make many enemies on the way there and back. Somehow, "they" forget to tell young wide-eyed executives at university this, by having to sustain a path of win-lose just to get there, just to have arrived today and to have failed tomorrow. Rather change the focus to being prepared, and staying prepared to achieve more, without setting a ceiling on our abilities, for others and ourselves. Be the best at what you are where you are.

Being Prepared - This new (required) paradigm will necessitate radical developments to take place in parallel to the strategies we develop, all along whilst striving for objectives, the one after the other, we need to also create opportunities to enrich people. We help create abundance in this fashion, something that everyone can share in and carry away after the project is done, that you can leave behind as a gift. We must all arrive at the same instance – of becoming prepared -, or we will have failed our purpose and ourselves. Once again, as I said before, we must rather build on things that will last, like the development of knowledge, wisdom and skills, the sound and non-perishable habits that can be passed on. Striving to build a unified corporate culture supported by healthy habits becomes the true measure of achievement, the serving of one and another. Every serving becomes a brick for monumental accomplishments in the future, monuments that will last, that will have spiritual, emotional, and intellectual meaning. This could be aligned to marriage. Therefore every project, every objective, every goal we work with must become another high point for our monuments. For all things materialistic can only go to dust and all things shared become spiritual, and truly ours, it forms bonds that transcends time, for now and forever.

These are the legacies; the true virtues of successes we should strive to leave behind as managers, for others to see and learn from. Life is about the sacrifices we make to get the better and good to grow, to leave as road markers on our own personal quests. In order to keep the legacy of interpersonal relationships strong, we have to inculcate healthy character and habits. The initiator of sacrifice and creator of trust is the king of followers. Worthiness becomes only those worthy of their own sacrifice and trustworthiness, a true measure of success amongst all tiers. This is reframing at best...changing our collective paradigms, our communal thinking, of what constitutes things worth living for, working and dyeing for, in line with what is desired by all as the ultimate guiding principle. That principle is trust; trust builds confidence, which in turn creates much desired passion. We all seek to live, love and work with passion; success does not give us passion. What we focus on more, we create more of, energy goes where attention flows, it attracts people, and eventually sows the same values and principles we live by amongst the ones that get attracted.

There are a few final practical points about reframing to keep in mind. Much of the reframing process is "about changing the verbal representation of an idea" firmly held in culture, so that the collectives essential interests are all still expressed. By following this paradigm, political emotions become neutralised, and position taking starts marginalizing to acceptable norms. We start communalising, forming a team with one purpose and focus. We will eradicate party forming and politics. It becomes a purification of the unwanted cultural elements.

We all want options and alternatives to help us cope...

Enhance the desirability of options and alternatives to have one working culture: Several approaches exist that may enhance the desirability of alternative options when presented to parties with divergent frames on how things should be done and should be managed.

We will never be able to reframe company culture without understanding it as it exist currently. Understanding, is what we seek first, by understanding the other parties frames and pictures first, seeing others perspectives the way they see it, other than our own, creates awareness. We need to find the motivation that drives the culture, the elements that gave birth to it, if we hope to change it. Third-party interveners are often helpful in this regard. Parties, who enter into conflict resolution processes with their own interpretation of the problem and the solution, will accomplish very little, an uneasy truce at best. If we do not get into each other's picture frames, then we will see only the fog of war. How best to resolve conflict on cultural level is still a science that will evade us if we do not see pictures within their owner's frames, and not ours. In addition seeking to reframe other attributes of culture, as losses or gains, this can enhance the openness and creativity of parties to resolve some disputes amicably. Understanding where others are "coming from" is the key attribute towards finding solutions, towards turning the tide; this requires the ability to step outside our own mental frames to perceive the situation through another person's frames – their perspective. In order to find the same sense and significance in what someone else believes in, you need to look at it through their eyes. Once you do that, you will have some ground for redirecting attention towards looking at others alternative views, their mental containment - as labels. This requires the understanding of cognate intelligence. Here is an explanation of this type of cognitive approach to solving frames of reference.

"The man of action must at times trust in the sensitive instinct of judgment, derived from his native intelligence and developed through reflection, which almost unconsciously hit's on the right course". - Clausewitz, On War

Understanding True Intelligence.

DEFINITIONS and UNDERSTANDINGS OF INTELLIGENCE - by David Lazear

Scientific research has called into question almost everything we used to think about human intelligence. Here is some of what they have found . . . we need to take note of this, it will aide us when entering into dialogue about change.

1. ***Intelligence is not fixed at birth!*** In the past, we thought that our intelligence was more or less set at birth by heredity. We thought it could be assessed through different kinds of I.Q. test's, which would tell us how smart we were. The I.Q., we thought, would reveal what an individual's intellectual possibilities were. However, the so-called intelligence tests did not take into account the many different environmental and cultural factors, which affect the development of our intellectual capabilities. Many experts now feel that intelligence has been defined too narrowly. We are all much more than an I.Q!

2. ***Intelligence can be taught, learned and improved!*** Because our intelligence capabilities are part of our physical and mental being at birth, they can be improved and strengthened at any age and at almost any ability level. There are simple things we can do which will strengthen our intelligence skills–much like what we do to improve and expand any skill in our lives. Generally, the more we practice the better we become. We can learn to be more intelligent, in more ways and on more levels of our lives than we ever thought possible before!

3. ***We are smart in many ways not just one***. In addition, what is more, these different kinds of "smarts" are available to us right now! This is what we're talking about when we refer to "multiple intelligences". There are many ways of knowing what we know in our lives. Moreover, there are many things we do to help us understand, and gain knowledge, in order to learn things daily. We were born with this intelligence already in us! There are many examples of people who were not very competent in the values their schools held but who have gone on to make major contributions to our world–

- **Leonard da Vinci** if alive today would likely be put in a class for learning disabled people. He had trouble with reading, writing, speaking and doing arithmetic calculations. Yet he is probably one of the most gifted people who have ever lived—poet, sculpture, musician, painter, architect, geologist, engineer, botanist, philosopher, physiologist, anatomist and astronomer all wrapped up in one person!
- **Henry Ford** had difficulty reading and remembering basic facts. To compensate, he surrounded himself with men who were able to produce the appropriate facts and figures when needed.
- **Hans Christian Anderson**, one of the world's most gifted storytellers, had difficulty reading and writing.
- **Nelson Rockefeller** became an accomplished extemporaneous speaker partly because of his difficulties in reading the printed text of his speeches.
- **Albert Einstein** is one of the most well-known of these who were not considered very smart by the usual intelligence standards but whose scientific contributions may have more far-reaching implications than any other scientist of the past century.

Scientific research has called into question almost everything we used to think about human intelligence. Here is some of what they have found;

- **Visual-Spatial Intelligence - *"Image Smart"*!** If you are strong in this intelligence, you tend to think in images and pictures. You are very aware of objects, shapes, colours, textures and patterns in the environment around you. You probably like to draw, paint and work with clay, coloured markers, construction paper and fabric. You may love to work jigsaw puzzles, read maps and find your way around new places. In addition, you are likely excellent at visualizing, pretending and imagining.
- **Logical-Mathematical Intelligence - *"Logic Smart"*!** If you are strong in this intelligence, you tend to think more abstractly. You like to conduct experiments and to solve puzzles. You love the challenge of a complex problem to solve. You ask many questions and analyse almost everything. You enjoy working with numbers. Moreover, you are probably systematic, organized and always have a logical explanation for what you are doing or thinking at any given time.
- **Bodily-Kinaesthetic Intelligence - *"Body Smart"*!** If you have strength in this area, you like physical movement–dancing, making and inventing things with your hands and role-playing. You can often perform a task much better after watching someone else does it first and then mimicking his or her actions. You may find it difficult to sit still for long periods of time and are quickly bored if you are not actively involved in what is going on around you.
- **Naturalist Intelligence - *"Nature Smart"*!** If this intelligence is one of your strengths, you love the outdoors, animals, plants and almost any natural object. Conditions in nature, such as sunshine, the wind, the changing seasons probably have a strong effect on you and may dramatically change your moods. You tend to have a deep respect for all living beings.
- **Musical-Rhythmic Intelligence - *"Sound Smart"*!** If you are strong in this intelligence, you are probably very aware of all the sounds in your environment. You probably love music and rhythmic patterns. Various sounds, tones and rhythms may have a visible effect on you. In addition, you may be skilled at mimicking sounds, language accents, another's' speech patterns.
- **Verbal-Linguistic Intelligence - *"Word Smart"*!** If this is a strong intelligence for you, you have highly developed skills for reading, speaking and writing. You probably like to read, play word games, tell stories, get into involved discussions with other people, work crossword puzzles, tell jokes and learn new words.
- **Inter-personal Intelligence - *"People Smart"*!** If this way of knowing is more developed in you, you learn through personal interactions. You have many friends. You show empathy for other people and can accept points of view, which differ from your own. You love team activities. In addition, you are probably skilled in conflict resolution.
- **Intra-personal Intelligence - *"Self Smart"*!** If this intelligence is one of your strengths you are self-reflective and tend to be "in touch" with your inner feelings, values and beliefs. You are intuitive. You are likely inwardly motivated and do not need external rewards to keep you going. You are self-confident and have clear goals for yourself. Other people will often come to you for advice and counsel.

The last essential element is self-synthesis:

Self-Synthesis: *"The process of combining the parts to form a whole"* – getting back to balance-synergy equals renewal; balanced renewal is the process of sharpening anyone new dimension of one's life that we have neglected for too long. For instance, will have a spin of effect on all your other aspects of your life.

More on Self- Synthesis.

Self-synthesis is the process of creating oneself.

Our habits influence our ability to live in balance. By improving in one dimension, your ability in other dimensions will be increased proportionally. By raising new energy in one dimension and in turn it raises new energy in the next, energy creates more energy, which will become an upward spiral of continued growth. This principle requires something positive first, then, learning from it, seeing the benefits and committing oneself to doing it again, until it becomes a habit. It is said that - any behaviour reinforced will become a habit over time. Just like smoking and drinking, good or bad habits form from the effect it has on the person and how they relate to it. Alternatively viewed or described as "body hits", a pleasurable reward, that could be deemed passion, deducted from a collective experience. What we use as triggers can be very diverse, exercise, eating, drinking, smoking, sleeping, stress, laughter, music, work, crying, gambling and sex is a drop in the ocean of things that can form spontaneous triggers to perform with passion. The point is that any specific one could become habit forming; consequently, we would like to capitalise on this knowledge by forming many good habits and enforcing them. In order to have a balanced life, we have to have our habits checked. We need balance and trade-offs. People have sublimely consented to all forms of control; we have become co-dependent and not interdependent because of our submission to control. Co-dependency becomes our mental "Berlin wall"; we lose touch with what is really happening, and with what is really important when we blindly just conform. We have workers on the one side sharing common beliefs and management on the other side sharing their belief in control. We sit in waiting, waiting to be controlled; we have subliminally at times been conditioned to accept control as the only way to manage people, in all its forms and mechanisms. We eagerly await word of the next directive, assignment or project and will do very little else, until they arrive, this is the attributes of overbearing control. We have adopted a stance of disservice, indecisiveness, not just to the organisation but also to ourselves, we have become too scared to act. We are just waiting to be told to co-operate and support each other without question, do it now and moan later. This merely enforces weakness throughout, and we all become weak by virtue of our formed co-dependency. Eventually it becomes a corporate habit. It gives us grounds for justification for bad discipline and unsound decision-making. The onset of more bad and weakening behaviour patterns emerge as no one wants responsibility. We have become control dependant in order to work; this then becomes institutionalised, to the very point where no one takes responsibility for anything anymore. The accountability is bounced back and forth. We reach a face off; the one waiting for the other to change their ways, and the concept of co-dependence keeps prevailing. With more control being introduced and more weakness transpiring, we have been stripped to a mere numerical value – the employee pay number- our humanity and value is gone. The real challenges are overlooked due to a lack of knowledge and devotion to task. I have found this to be true in organisations as well as individuals. Their habits dictate their character traits, which flows into their work.

The drive activation "Triggers"; why is it so important for man to discover and to win –to understand the "fit" of a win, in strategy.

"When we ardently seek to win, we become anxious about the results we have yet to discover". We may procrastinate and do nothing to win because we might fear to lose. The effective person, the predator can happily win or lose, without losing their direction or balance at the core, always striving to stay effective. The reason being, they have made a consistent effort to change their paradigms, their views on life; they know what matters and what does not - they have found their equilibrium with inner peace. Predators are - **TOTALLY PREPARED**. When actively seeking a learning experience in everything they do, no matter the result; they do no longer fear losing. Because every endeavour is regarded as a stepping-stone, a learning experience, a test of one's abilities, so win or lose, the effort was worth every second. Because losing and winning to them is one thing, win or lose, it's the experience that counts. For what they want more than winning or losing is to achieve their ultimate goal. They realise that losing is the left foot and winning the right foot, in the walk to personal freedom, so if they keep winning they will be going in circles but if they win, lose, win, lose all the way they are actually progressing. Predators also have a greater awareness of survival and its significance; the higher purpose of man and how to ascertain their destiny; in this they find the power to go on, beyond impossible odds, they are very aware of the spiritual cycles of highs and lows in life. They comprehend the "fit" of winning, they know where they fit in the greater scheme of things, man is both flesh and a living organism and everything in the universe comes from one centre point, the nexus, the core and are interrelated because of this. Ensemble means we are altogether, all from one place and this is characterised by the interdependence it creates, the interrelationship of all things, living and non-living. We are commanded to serve; by serving, we serve our purpose – and fight against idleness. This statement accommodates growth and intellectual development, our own personal freedoms. It has clearly identifiable objectives and lastly it has structure, it supports the architecture of connectivity and allows systems to develop and connect, both within and outside us, giving us boundless energy. We all know and understand that energy is the one thing that we need, to function. Only by serving, do we connect to a system, and establish this connection with one another and the universe from where this energy resides. Man is a social creature - the resembling of humanity, with its creator has brought about social bonds, religion, social structures and rules. To illustrate this belief, everything has a beginning and an end; all things are universally interrelated into cycles of dead and living. The only thing that is not constant is the spiritual spiral we journey on to greatness; this is our freedom and connection to all dimensions, the ever-evolving entity fed by the human spirit's desire to change and grow in all manner and direction – constantly we feel the urge to do something more. We are pushed by an invisible force to carry on regardless. Even animals and plants show this resilience to keep going...

Change is man's making, any change, be it good or bad, ultimately change makes us stronger – regardless of our perception.

Just to illustrate this natural phenomenon.

Research in Australia showed that change is like torture to the brain, if we are not used to it. Let us take yet another practical example to explain this, Piaget – studied biology to understand the theory of knowledge; he had an intense interest in the plant, Sedum, varieties which are common in rock gardens. He also studied snails, in particular Limnaea Stagnalis. Piaget transplanted some Sedum plants in the Savoy Alps in order to see how the plant would react to the change in temperature and cope with cold. The experiment yielded that the plant grew smaller, thicker leaves in order to increase photosynthesis. He also took snail and transplanted them from tranquil still waters to turbulent and rocky shores, the snails reacted by changing their shells from an elongated shaped to a globular shape. One more example of biological adaptation, the coral on the landside of a coral reef where there are no or little currents and torrents from storms, are bigger and thinner with a lot of small sea life. This is where the reef is well protected, but the coral is dull and lifeless, in comparison to the open seaside, where the coral is smaller, thicker and very much alive, with an abundance of bigger sea life. The reason for this is the coral exposed to the open sea is tougher to eat, break and damage. They have had to adapt to the forces of the open ocean and bigger predators in order to survive.

This is a key concept when we plan re-engineering, Radical Revolutionary Strategy is neither here nor there and it is all encompassing, challenging and frightening at times. It forces us to transform ourselves, in order to transform others for the better and greater good, man's adaptiveness to changes is well recorded, we perform to adapt, to step outside the known into the unknown, to do the impossible and to do it well - this is entrenched in us. We should set our seeds according to the soil! - it is said. What this implies is don't try jumping the Grand Canyon if you have not even tried jumping across the fishpond, everything within reason and within your ability and means, our soil is our experience, our ability our means, the seed is your exploration and endeavours and the knowledge that they instilled. They must complement each other, the soil is our wisdom that only comes from having experienced, we must have the nutrients of experience, the experience to be able to nurture and feed the seed, or neither will be able to give birth to the new. The new will only come to be through changes having taken place to make way for it, in order to adapt effectively to any future change, in any dimension of our lives. For if we keep doing what we have always done, how can we expect any change of results?

It is said, that any behaviour positively enforced over a period, minimum 21 days, becomes a habit.

Therefore, we would like to get into the habit of being able to survive complexity and address conflict all in the same instance, by imploring for effective non-perishable strategy... The type of "rock breaking strategy"; that could be used repeatedly with success. Strategy that grows off itself, that will eventually become our strategic habit.

If you have come this far, you have the makings of a true strategist; this was the hard part, now to the fun

We require endorsed principle centred leadership, which can take up the slack and run with it, we also require good administration and we call them change managers. Without structure, there will be chaos, without true leadership there will just be anarchy. Strategy without structure is like an aeroplane without wings. What is required from both leadership and management today is more flexibility and understanding of human nature, in order to create a required strategic balance? The next chapter will address these fundamental principles of organisation forming. We will deal with how leaders must think first and in a later chapter how to build and organise.

Strategic management has become stuck with vanilla flavour only.

The average change management programme is "plain vanilla", textbook and so cliché. Academics have moved into the consulting industry and have produced a wealth of methodologies and a plethora of do's and don'ts for us to buy and sell. Most of them are like two peas in a pod and even quite illogical.

Consultants the world over have cashed in on change management; by writing managerial cookbooks - it is not difficult to get the "plain vanilla" variety wrong when you do it step by step. They all have perfect plans in place. Their sales skills are exceptional, they are well groomed, and well spoken, and come with referrals, and we welcome them because they are selling what we want? Then we get to go into the session – it tastes good, it looks good – so it has to be good. Everyone is all fired up and positive after this session. Returning to work ready to implement the "plain vanilla plan". Management perceives that everyone knows how to get from A to B and knows who is going to be coming along for the journey. Somehow, the intended journey never starts off without hiccups and many unexpected turns, our baggage gets lost, and we arrive without visas...so what went wrong?

They forgot to focus on balancing and understanding the importance of corporate cultural influences: (the way people traditionally get things done) the two opposing parts that form good strategy.

Yin and Yang signifies the good and bad or opposing influences in a life cycle and in this instance the corporate culture. Every plan has good and bad viewpoints and nuts and bolts. However, we have to realise that every strategic journey we embark on has a specific life cycle. What is relevant now, becomes obsolete or irrelevant in a month's time. Consequently, the fact of the matter is there will be successes and failures with every plan. Strategy on the other hand is not just a "plan". It is the "master plan"; the plan of all plans, which combines and comprises of several other plans, and incorporates several divergent strategies, this is the distinction. Many people think that one plan is a strategy, it's not. Plans – the vanilla flavoured ones have one route, whereas Strategy has several routes. Plans have no need to incorporate people or culture; they are referred to as resources. Strategy has all the components, checked, verified, analysed and defined.

Studies have shown that the main culprit – just planning – and not strategizing, enforces the partial adoption and poor usage of new processes within old systems, as well as disregarding the influence of corporate culture that requires re-alignment as well, with any change contemplated. The "vehicles and platforms" we used in the past, don't have the same characteristics when we rebuild them. What we had in the past that worked, we created in the past based on what we did, and what we knew - we cannot cope with the new vision of the future along the same path. Before our plans can take effect, we have to incorporate all the attributes of an existing culture - still stuck in the old ways of doing things. When we refer to culture, we refer to the organisation; its systems, people, infrastructure and design. The facts are that culture directly influences leadership in the same fashion, as we said in the intro everything is connected - either good or bad and leadership influences culture likewise, this we know. Therefore, we need to make sense of it. By focusing on the "corporate environment" firstly and by acknowledging the way they do things now - in the main culture traditionally – and how they utilise technology and systems. The question is where is our emphasis focused on: on structure, strategy, resources or systems. Who has the role of determining the emphasis, which in turn influences both the remaining leadership and the peoples culture that has to decide on the new course of action. Corporate culture will ultimately dictate the influence and determine the type of leadership that will emerge and their mind-set and so will the individual's culture and visa-versa when faced with change.

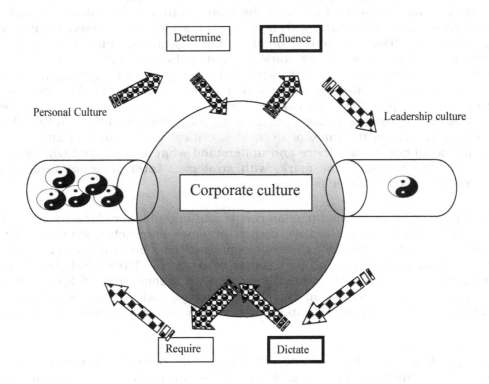

The Forming Elements of Corporate Culture.

An in-depth look at all the aspect that has a cause and effect on culture.

In my mind then when dealing with the issues of corporate culture, the simple truth is this, if we do not embrace the human psyche, its dynamics and how it directly influences culture like it does religion; then we lose sight of how corporate culture becomes a "religious" devoted affair in business. People even at work religiously repeat the same behaviour to get a result. Culture is not regulated by rules, rather by "a way of doing things traditionally as a norm" as cultural groups. The person's culture that he was brought up into creates contrasting ideas about what should be happening versus what is happening and how to bridge the gap – contrasting these ideas against a current reality when seeking a fit. This is the nexus, finding ways to migrate people with systems, and structures. If not viewed within this paradigm, we will stay lost in a sea of who is right and who is wrong; simply because we have no point of reference anymore, the landscape has changed. The corporate environment has become fast passed, with too many opposing forces created as a result of change in contrast with cultural diversity. Strongly held views that prohibit it from becoming one identity and one culture. Because it just cannot keep up with the speed of change. Entrenched culture only becomes unified in its attributes and beliefs, when it gets to migrate with the systems and processes – then it becomes corporate culture, if not it becomes cultural diversity. If we do not see this; then the result is that culture does not identify itself. It becomes an affair of work and reward, with no emotional attachment, a mere transaction between employer and employee. "People's" perception about the organisation influences their culture, this is the one element that dictates how we work in as an individual and as a team, think and act. Just like in natural life, when we lose our identity in a group and as a group, we lose our values, our direction and eventually all hope along with it. Frustration causes low morale and in one breath, we deal from a paradigm of weakness, because we feel threatened – left between two extremes - choosing between the known that does not exist and the unknown that does not exist either. If we have not taken the time, or deemed it critical to explain and embrace the type of spirited organisational culture we desire and understand what forms it and what supports it and influences it, then we will miss the mark, with strategy... **Inter-personal Intelligence** *-being "People Smart"!* Is a good strategic principle.

Coupled to this, the beliefs we hold true as people and organisations, the habits and rituals we practice at work, and the perceptions we preach becomes entrenched elements of yet another culture, a sub culture. All of this will steer our organisations along with us on a collision course with any change that is forced, so people become resistant to change and the more we force it from a management perspective the more fragmented we become into dealing with sub culture. The question is are we structured as an organisation to cope with change by virtue of our culture, if not then in essence we embrace stagnation. No matter how hard we plan or strategise.

The ways available towards forming one culture, that is receptive to change. By finding one direction for any organisation firstly, that is shared by all involved becomes the **"True North"** principle. How we stay on course with it, could become questionable if we are not of one mind on how things need to get done by changing it. Yet, we carry on regardless of consensus on this point, we enforce weakness in our corporate culture by developing scarcity and competitiveness by virtue of our own beliefs of what will work. If this was a marriage, and we treated our spouse and children in the same fashion, do you think they will be smiling. We have all seen what happens - chaos appears rampant, diversified views, styles and a total lack of action and implementation emerge – where change gets bulldozed. How does the organisation see its role and function in this regard, where unity equates to strength, and is the plan also concerned with the alignment of personal beliefs, that influence culture? The second element is "The test is satisfaction", do individuals find satisfaction on the job or from the job – this is the test of a healthy corporate culture. This is the universal question on most business minds today, on how to solve this dilemma of total integration of local and global culture - the new age nexus we desire, but it eludes us even at the smallest scale. We have to start with small steps by questioning our own paradigms on culture by reviewing its importance for our organisation effectiveness and wellbeing; do we still require a homogeneous culture to be successful? If not why bother?

The only way to form healthy relationships is to address culture (a set of beliefs and views) and align them with the corporate values. The third element is intent the bottom line is, if we want culture to form, then we need to address first-things-first; the aspect where every person knows what is expected of him or her in clear terms, they want to see where the organisation is going, and what they are aiming for. People need to feel and know they are significant and safe in this work environment if they do what is expected. They want to know that effort and trust will be rewarded, appreciated and recognised. If the leaders are not secure in this belief themselves, how will it flow to the followers? In order to enable a person to see we must put them in a position to think firstly, in order to act, by themselves and for themselves, they have to be empowered to use their endowments of mind and spirit, this is a give and take situation. Without action, there will be no sense of purpose and meaning, without structure, all is lost.

DIY:

- *Develop a sense of purpose for your organisation,*
- *Live up to this expectation, one day at a time,*
- *Realise that what you do now is a way of achieving your purpose tomorrow, or even the next day.*
- *Become flexible in your approach to life and work.*
- *Ask, "What else can be done?" rather than "why me?" then when one door closes go and knock on the next one, secure in the belief that:*

"When one door closes another always opens"

– Johan Campbell

The truth is "that all human beings" want to be part of something; create that "cult", that something truly exists; nothing motivates faster than the sense and speed of purpose, it creates all the essential elements of strong corporate culture. However, if we have no clear alignment plan, which fuses the man with the purpose, then we have alienated, and have failed human nature itself at the core - the meaning of our existence is to seek purpose – this is the enigma we are all facing in any corporate dealing with diversity. Diversity, needs to be managed and influenced...purposefully, with intent. How can we then want to find fault with man's behaviour in terms of performance deficiency – where we want to measure him - if he has no reference point within the organisation, no "True North", no mental compass. What is the point of reference that we will use to define deficiencies then, if all boils down to a lack of individual and common purpose. If this question has never been raised, then there is still time to address it. Where everything is "pure vanilla" in HR, we are sitting on a time bomb. We are purely overlooking the blatantly obvious, the human factor and how to enhance its character traits to work and how we connect it with enterprise to gain its optimum potential and utilisation. Again, it comes back to the "vehicles and platforms" we created in the past, that cannot cope with the new vision and demands of the future. The plans have not incorporated all the attributes of an existing culture in flux and how to harmonise it to perform as one unit. We have over analysed the basics of human nature and the catalyst behind success. We lack a "true sense of purpose and direction", it is back to the basics. We have to break away from the old management views where management becomes "pure vanilla" from a leadership perspective when the organisation is not perfect, the entrenched belief by the "experts" is that if we all follow methodologies and a plethora of do's and don'ts then we cannot fail, we are in control, it will become perfect again if we just hammer it back into form. This will be the fundamental argument; this system of do and don't not only doesn't work anymore, it has become disabling. Complimented by the denial factor, we, the experts have systems in place, we have strict rules and codes, now no one can get out of line, it works - it's perfect. This is pretty much the norm of yesterday, however today, with this type of business mentality; the CEO's management style becomes the focal point for a success factor. Why then, if all the facts point us in another direction, what then, what is missing from the "vanilla formula"?

Predominantly, we can trace it back to three basic components.

Firstly –

o Poor organisational and strategic planning no continued alignment of the organisation with human "needs" that stand in stark contrast with that of its peoples' inherent "wants", by reinforcing purpose.
o Organisation is no longer just a scientific model of some sort, not just about good leadership and management qualities and skills, but more importantly peoples needs and wants, what is done about this. In other words, we are acting in conflict with the peoples' ideas and beliefs of how things should be done to achieve greater satisfaction on the job and successes – their culture.
o Our perceived business strategy is not our peoples reality, it is our business reality, they are not fused with the strategy that should fuse them with the organisation.

Secondly –

o A total lack of managerial skills are being observed and everything has become systematic, a step-by-step procedural management style - the cook book approach is observed everywhere, no one takes accountability let alone responsibility, we just delegate it away, and cover ourselves. This paradigm does not allow any form of self-governing or decision-making – it lacks self-development and managerial support.

Thirdly –

o We observe a control based leadership style; referred to as a *"defused leadership culture"*, that lends itself strongly to the "go and fetch boy" type of approach, then a *"defused management culture"* it is.

The old "Defused Management Culture" reviewed.

What constitutes a defused management culture? Does this sound familiar? Leaders in these types of companies are always too important – the "Halo effect", or too busy, or just too involved with "serious urgent business" to otherwise care or "listen". Managers become too concerned with their leaders urgent business agenda, satisfying all their needs, and following blindly, so much so that they stop challenging their beliefs, directives or motivation, they just fit in. They get recognition and get better treatment than those that stand "opposed" and are too far sucked up into the leadership's faltering style to give good solid advice anymore. They become the leaders lapdogs, go, Boo-Boo, sit, Boo-Boo and fetch Boo-Boo, good boy. By implication, they create division, with the so-called opposed party's within the organisation, which now belongs to a lower class/ sub-culture, reluctantly they too start duplicating faulted instructions, directives and start incorporating it into their instruction sets by default as a survival mechanism. Which they also filter to fit, to become part of the upper class again. It becomes a new culture of do or die. Just do it, no matter what and then complain later. The reality of the matter is -You never get to complain, the rhetorical patronising line of "if you can't manage then you know what to do" and the attitude is "if we want your opinion we will give it to you". With the end result that people become disabled, switched off, by virtue of this type of management style and culture, they are perceived to be negative and resisting, due to a lack of mutual understanding. This creates the classical problem; the fault-finding mentality, if there is a deficiency or financial deficit it must be because of the lack of control and or supervision. Someone is not doing his or her job, - get the attention away from them - thus a problem exists. The leader commands that it be fixed, without taking the time to understand the underlying – real problem, (his leadership qualities) or he takes a more dramatic approach and calls for the person or persons responsible to be moved, investigated, or fired. They will predominantly focus on solving the "perceived problem", rather than doing some introspection and start solving the real problem. It all started within the system by remote control, that they themselves created, following orders blindly without thinking consequence and ignoring it, or by generating more red tape to tighten the screws to force the management into action by intimidation.

This is called a "defused leadership culture" – the "power trip", the "demigod syndrome" or "halo effect", because they defused the human element of vigour totally by becoming a dictator, by killing the very fundamental requirements for continued performance and growth - the spirit of self-esteem and team work. They are in essence cutting it out like a cancerous tumour, for they do not recognise it as a prevalent and integral part of any system. By virtue of their collective actions, they suffocate the organisations emotional intelligence - a self-perceived ability, to identify, assess, and manage the emotions of one's self, of others, and of groups.

Daniel Goleman devised a model that focuses on a wide array of competencies and skills that drive leadership and performance. Four main categories future;

1. Self-awareness — the ability to gauge and control one's emotions and recognise their impact while using gut feelings to guide decisions.
2. Self-management — this involves controlling one's emotions and impulses and adapting to changing circumstances.
3. Social awareness — the ability to sense, understand, and react to others' emotions while comprehending its impact on others behavior.
4. Relationship management — the ability to inspire, influence, and develop others while managing conflict both internal as well as external.

"Unintentionally" we sometimes destroy our support base and networks, because we distance ourselves from emotional involvement, then a new enterprise culture develops, that of not thinking, just doing, a defused management culture.

In this culture, no one lasts, not even the "dictator", all succumb to stress and pressure. You will find no effective positive management and this is no excuse. The fundamental flaw is the lack of a required understanding of human complexity, this stems from the habitual application of classical business leadership models that are all based on old paradigms of organisational behaviour and study, which has since been phased out by all major companies. The ability to comprehend the usefulness of the required additives of human interaction, that of a "fused culture" is not common; on the contrary, it is very scarce, seldom observed in a "defused culture". To achieve continued revolving growth, requires insight from managers and leaders of what it takes to go beyond the purely obvious, the physical and systematically inclined managerial attributes of systems management, does not have this additive. Mostly statistics and financial statements are all that is required to guide them. In the long-term, it takes more than just this type of academical reasoning and paperwork to control; it takes a required specific strategic insight and emotional intelligence. They are stuck in day-to-day quick fix activity that yields only superficial results, with no long-term prospects. They are no longer in touch with the real-reality of their situation; they live in denial, they are just acting out their roles as mangers and leaders, scraping the bottom daily, patching the tyres. They live and work in total denial of what is happening, inside, outside and around them - and will never be brave enough to admit that they are the architects of the problem. Furthermore, until such time that we, the current leaders, have been assured of the fact that we, ourselves are not at risk of losing control by giving it away. On the contrary, it is only by failing to incorporate the principles of emotional intelligence that we create a fused culture, that we recognise the strategic benefits of this principle of having fused leadership. Without fused culture, where everyone becomes a leader in his /her own right and gets to act with esteem that we feel part of something greater, bigger, an indispensable stakeholder. Without fearing any prejudice, a true team player, desires communal responsibility and managerial support that embraces commitment towards achieving the goals of cultural unity, without fear or favour. If defused cultures become entrenched, it will always create unilateral divisions within the organisation. A total one-sided approach is always clearly visible here, a top down one, regardless of its consequences, "because it works". Yes, but at what cost, all the lifeless human minds lie like beached whales, because their direction finders and their reality do not connect, to guide them. They might even get away with it. Management and leadership that is might even pull off major feats whilst doing so, but the one aspect that suffers is the trust, and bonds that gets destroyed in the process, the stewardship opportunities that are forever lost. Lost is how everyone feels, deeply rooted and entrenched within peoples emotional bank accounts is just emptiness, it constitutes a final overdrawn bank balance. Staff closes their emotional accounts because of this, one after the other, people like banks follow suit and blacklist leaders and managers in their minds that have overdrawn on personal emotional bank accounts, people like banks require interest. It then becomes a bankrupt emotionless roller coaster enterprise, if we don't pay " interest" in our people. Our personal belief systems are crushed by this type of leadership style, to the point where people in the organisation become disillusioned with their perceived reality. They view their efforts to align themselves as being hopeless, they distrust their own abilities and work, because they get treated as inferior - in such a manner that they act and feel like teenagers again, feelings of insecurity in their roles as adults start to come in to conflict with their worth within the organisation it becomes questionable, everything that gives meaning seems diminished or destroyed. People then tend to become either reckless or forceful in their ways, they behave or treat colleagues like teenagers would if they feel neglected, on the other hand they become defensive and suspicious of one and other, because of all this inter personal conflict.

Within this culture, the sheep just following the flock and take on a stance of passive silent resistance, as their only means of defence. If we fail as leaders and managers - to fuse human dynamics together with corporate culture in the near future we will lose our essential driving force. When we lose sight of the driving forces behind enterprise then we lose sight of the element of "people power" in our strategic plans. Leaders have become too calculated in their reaction, they have become just too predictable, too systematically trapped and focused on systems management. They start measuring assets in terms of items and its market value, rather than people potential. In the board room the standard archaic view echo "people are there to work", they are to follow orders and to do as they are told, if they don't like it, then they know what to do, they must leave, period.

How does this approach affect the enterprise as a whole when challenged with change? The standard answer will be that "they are not ready to be tested". The first action item that came up consistently in surveys was failure to train. Without training, we will lack the empowering attributes of emotional intelligence – the desired leadership qualities. How can we expect the desired results, if we don't plant the seeds. In line with this was the aspect personal skills development and qualifications that forced individuals into making haphazard decision making. Behavioural differences in our managements corporate culture affects every aspect of the organisations ability to perform. A lack of skills and knowledge effects our speed, accuracy and results.

The next compounding element is the total lack of coherent management; managers that chop and change, shuffle and move the goals and people around just create chaos. This practice voids people from taking ownership and responsibility of their work. The ability to lead in a coherent fashion becomes vital towards forming synergy between the people and their task. Taking ownership and responsibility of a task, this is no guarantee that they will succeed either. Getting people to take responsibility and ownership, it is not a failsafe, because we are all fully aware of how complex the working environment can become in an instant. Therefore, it has to be quantified; failure to manage coherently is mostly because of the lack of a more subtle element - trust, insufficient skills and the desire to take responsibility. We cannot, for one moment think that just one aspect in the formula will guarantee good results. Consistency creates stability. Secondly, we cannot expect someone, or for that matter anyone to lead or mange if they are not fully capacitated and capable, we have to be consistent in our appointment of managers to follow one criteria for all. This creates entrustment; everyone is at the same level of proficiency. As well as fully entrusted with accountability for their sphere of influence and control span and or the required level of responsibility and everything that goes along with it. This creates balance.

Capacitating requires training, development and guidance, which in turn require clearly defined standards. It does not stop here either, we have to respect the required decision making power that goes along with any position of authority. Delegate this with the tasks and responsibilities and nurture it within a stewardship role. The organisational design should be level, we cannot build on foundations that are not level. Structure follows strategy. This concept requires a uniform culture, fused with peoples requirements and their capability. In other words, we require much more from our structure. The way we plan people and their activities around their capabilities and their responsibilities will deliver the desired results.

By concentrating on the focal points for departure in getting strategies to work. Four major compounding factors emerge to contemplate; most failed attempts at lasting enterprise are a direct result of design. There was just no motivation in the enterprise to rejuvenate itself to "win", let alone arrive at a win-win or no deal situation with the role-players.

The balancing of principles when designing systems

The importance of core principles cannot be overstated when contemplating design; they will act as catalysts within enterprise. This is one of the most critical aspects for leaders and managers that want to achieve effective change. Balance and equilibrium resides on our ability to construct and maintain the "critical value activity chain"- that which links the present with the future. In order to maintain equilibrium, we have to keep momentum; we have to align all the forces. The importance of this process can be better emphasised by looking at a span of oxen, pulling a wagon. We have the older oxen at the front – the leadership, the younger behind – the management and the inexperienced and younger still behind them – the work force. All oxen are of equal size and strength in a balanced span. This creates internal balance, if we disturb this natural logical balance by only feeding our attention to one or two oxen – one or two systems - and we let the rest starve, as a consequence of our designing teams, we can expect to go off the path sooner rather than later. What we focus on we get more of. That which we are focused on, will ultimately determine where we will go. Therefore, our focus needs contemplation. By only focusing on middle management, we starve the leaders and workers. We are in essence disturbing the "natural balance", by losing the cohesion of the span of oxen. This analogy reinforces our belief in the principle of keeping with designing balanced structures. The principles that dictate balance are the custodians of structural integrity, both fiscal and managerial. Once again, and this point can never be over emphasised - that the leadership's executive style - will dictate whether there will be balance or not. Leadership on the other hand can never function alone, or in a vacuum, they have to rely on their management's potential to cope with their style of leadership.

Leadership "Style"

Change management is dictated by culture. By their "style", referring to a particular focus of the core leadership group, what are our leaders inherently focused on and what should they be focused on? Is their aim too high, too low, or too vague? Does the leadership style lean itself towards freely interpreted and comprehended task analysis and execution, or is it systematic? The interoperation hereof is based on perception. The interpretation of the perception will dictate if tasks are strictly spelled out to the letter in instruction sets, that do not allow for alterations. Are these then passed on to management with the tasks having no potential? How much task potential do we want in our designing of systems and structures?

Tasks have to have an element of "Task Potential"

By task "potential", we are referring to the ability of the organisation to deal effectively with the task or product concept formulation; focusing on its enhancement. By implication, we have to ask, could the task-inhibiting factor be filtered, either by our own personal imprinting of our understanding of how things should be done, our interpretation of how directives should be followed as they are passed down from leadership to management and then altimetry unto the workforce. The question of "giving tasks potential", gives rise to two elements; the communication of directives and concepts of management within a system, being mostly top down, it could either enrich the concept or it could protract from it for the same reason. The way and manner in which instruction sets are passed down will determine - and will ultimately directly impact on - the effectiveness of any desired outcome – being the "tasks potential". Moreover, are we failing to manage by managing only with overwhelming emphases on the control aspects of a task – the feeding it in and getting feedback, and how to measure the success thereof, rather than on the desired "tasks and giving it potential"? When our main focus is purely on control and feedback when delegating tasks and or instructions, we are in essence passing down inability; we are crippling any move to improve on the final concept or product. This also sends a message of no "trustworthiness", by this we are directly implying that we do not *trust* you the leader or manager and you are not *worthy* of making decisions on our behalf, totally stripping away any form of initiative, are we leading but failing to lead, by purely following this paradigm. Where is the passion, is passion not what drives us, we are motivated by changing things, and not so much by new things, is the required element to counter this anomaly with built in, creating and growing passion for people to perform is key to sustained flexibility and growth.

The centre of the self

The aspects of leadership style

"Leadership style" has everything to do with the overall effectiveness and wellbeing of an organisation, leaders and their self-groomed style of what it entails to be effective can totally influence the whole organisation, especially if their style becomes somewhat erratic. It is normally just a very fine definitive line between balance and imbalance, which should never be crossed. Sublimely sometimes, out of pure desperation or frustration, out of our innate want to control our environment when it "seems" to become chaotic from a leaders perspective. Where instead we have to surrender the control – contrary to our thinking - to the right people, unconditionally and rather become the parent figure, that gives the direction; this shifts our paradigm from direct control emphasis to guidance and focus within the production lifeline cycle of tasks, "generals" or top down leadership are supposed to be "strategic leaders" and not "operational". People closest to the task knows best. Believe it or not, this very insignificant aspect can have a tremendous effect on morale and self-esteem amongst the rest of the management if disturbed, where "generals start driving tanks" etc. – proverbially speaking. Otherwise, if allowed, all our workers good intentions will be short lived where we are purely focused on control from the top down, we lose sight of our strategic intentions and all the aspects of what strategic means, we will not be leaving a legacy of serving and winning. On the other hand, if we have clear goals, roles and visions in place that are filtered down in time by the "generals", we will arrive on queue when it counts most, we will be capitalising on sustained growth of initiative taking – this creates task potential. This very aspect of relinquished control seems foreign, it drives in against everything we have been taught and believe in. This difference in approach will instead be termed; creating "task potential" and a "cultural management style" that can be copied, mimicked and passed on. This aspect will be dealt with later on, the point is that with daily inputs of this paradigm and strategy we mimic a required synergised new culture, where feedback becomes instantaneous from beginning to end, our awareness of our stewardship and personal role and function becomes divined and clear. We are in effect expelling fears, our own firstly and then that of the people we lead. Job security and satisfaction will only become guaranteed if the relationship between employer and employee is open to scrutiny, feedback, and inputs of a critical nature.

Everyone wants recognition for their competence and achievements – or hear that it has been noticed and appreciated. This does more for confidence than any medal or money, this becomes a significant attribute and influence in building people. If we develop it, the ripple effect spills over into our total productivity and effectiveness, our communication is now open, both horizontal and lateral. When we are clear, we communicate clear directives on where we stand with one another, what is expected and how we will be measured and treated in clear terms – pertaining to reward and penalties. We as peers can align our subordinates by supporting them more with strategic conversation and personal interaction, if you want feedback, make sure you give it like wise. Trustworthiness grows proportionately only when developed in this manner – just like in a marriage, if the communication becomes strained then so follows the relationship. Strategy is all about good strategic communication. We have to trust first to be trusted and only then our own worthiness alike grows into the "expert opinion", all is not lost in the process to ineffectiveness, it becomes the ideal learning curve and bonding experience instead. By virtue of our own thinking of others, we judge them; either as being ineffective or effective by our own standards and perceptions. Especially when we want things done our way, this aspect is only rationalised when we do things hands on and it works and then let go, leaving them with a concept, only then have we unclouded perceptions around effective ways of doing things. However, if we just force it down as an instruction set, it won't transpire at all in the manner you desire. The point is, if you want people to believe in your way is best, then have to have tried it their way first. Then the test is in the results you achieve. They have to be challenged to do it better than your best effort and not be pinned down to that which we believe to be the best.

By conceptualising our own fears, we pass them on and create a very dysfunctional managerial and disillusioned leadership culture, by not wanting to relinquish control out of our own fear of failure, we breed more fear of failure. When we take this approach, we create unbearable amounts of noise; misinterpreted instruction sets within the chain of command and its communication systems, of which the ripple effect cascades downward, which leads to further confusion. The final effect is a total loss of cohesion within the organisation and then mistrust and total chaos engulfs us.

The logical question now is how do we prevent or overcome this "leadership style" vs. "creating task potential" issue? Style is a question of character, which is never a simple one to address either, if we have to look inward; with critical self-analysis we become aware of our own fears of failure, and we recognise that we have shortcomings, and by doing so we have to conquer ourselves first, our fears and our perceptions when in positions of power. What we focus on we get more of, don't we? We are our own worst enemy when it comes to doing this thing called management truthfully. Firstly, our egos are most likely to be blamed, for our vanity and we all hide directly behind the insecurities of our own fragile egos that will not resist for one moment to cover our weakness by resorting to control as the only means to defend ourselves. What we don't realise is that all forms of control are always challenged at some time or point. The other thing with very tight control is that it requires someone to enforce it all the time. Precedents are always created in this manner where we have an abundance of control overloads, eventually the controlled system collapses on itself, because everything is starved, no one wants to move until told to do so, we stand the risk of taking a serious bashing of our fragile ego if we get it wrong when we take the initiative. Whenever we overload with control we tend to create the opposite effect because of our focus.

Although we do need forms of control, the question to ask ourselves is what the true intent is, what value will it have and to what extent do we need control, to what extreme should we have our control. The answer to this is a true mental maturity, the realisation that our fears own us – no more. Other's never judge us based on our fears, rather because of our lack of good behaviour and affirmative action to overcome them, which stems directly from our belief in fear if we choose to harbour it. This aspect of fear and how it shapes us, drives us as managers, and people, opens up an internal portal to focus on our own beliefs and fears and take them for review. Take the time to think about fear and how it inhibits and controls us, before someone else does it for us, this is the pivotal turning point, the fulcrum for our mental departure; we have to overcome ourselves, our fears first, in that we have to work within, from our inner most fear and open up. We have to understand why it is that we have formed this culture and is it aiding us or destroying us, we have to empty our mind of bad influences and make space for new things that can aid as. When we are frustrated, and feel pressured, this is because we do not want to change from one premise to the next. Because, personal culture develops from one's personal scripts and growth experiences that we chose to hold onto, in other words all your trials and tribulations, good and bad right through life to this point, has left imprints that we work from, we have to choose which to keep and which to discard.

Everything we have experienced has culminated to this point, here and now, is the cumulative result of what we have had to endure as an infant, toddler, teenager, youngster and adult. How you have overcome them or not, has to do with your perceptions and the fears that they created, the ones we created around events to protect us – even as teenagers – they still drive our decisions today, with people and relationships pertaining to our own personal reference criteria. Give this some deliberation; we must question our motives and the things that created our fears, before we can change the perception for others and ourselves.

We have to let go of childish inhibitions that want to control every aspect of life, it is not within our power and it is futile. What should be important to us as individuals is how we categorise these aspects, for this alone will determine our outlook on life and our character until we change them. The way in which we perceive our worth and ourselves, if our stature in society is of critical importance to us, we should ponder more on our manifestation of it because this realisation will ultimately define our identity and even our personality.

We should realise that what drives us in business is our character and then our endowments and experiences. Contrary to popular belief it is not hard work to change anything we think, and do, it is just an ambition being satisfied, ambitions change, is it worth the pursuit. Once we have overcome our charter and fine-tuned it, we have to revisit our belief system; this is the final challenge in finding direction with a moral compass. We prioritise our beliefs around four cardinal attributes in this regard and religion will be excluded here.

They are; *love, wealth, family and esteem.* How we prioritise them into our own lives will depend on how we view their order of importance or significance in our corporate environment, it will ultimately also affect who we are and reflect to be and how we interact with others and the organisation we are in.

The influence of people's beliefs on management style.

1. *Love centred first* - the emotional-extroverts, they need to sacrifice themselves, give and be there for everyone who needs a shoulder to cry on, the needy, they have soft hearts, but take big gambles. They are excellent judges of character, they give advice freely and personal guidance in affairs, ranging from marriage to finances and any other subject. Openness and honesty are their greatest virtues; they are risk takers and spend money they do not yet have. Hopeless romantics, fun loving people with a desire to just be accepted. Good hard workers, but they lose interest. They do not like to be scrutinised or taken for granted, very emotional at times.

2. *Wealth centred first* – the unemotional-extrovert, these people slave away, work is their greatest passion and that is the best way to express themselves they believe, although they like to play just as hard. Wealth centred persons are fair judges of character and love people, they seldom give advice freely; they do believe that everyone should decide for himself. They only take calculated risks after having thought things through. They spend money wisely, on things with value, but always seem to have in reserve. Romantic at hart, with a great love of the outdoors. They withdraw and become aggressive when unhappy. They will be balanced between work and family.

3. *Family centred first* – emotional-introvert, these people place an immense value on family and they would rather stay home and stick to their regime of routine. They are honest and loyal, considering themselves to be good judges of character and they tend to give advice freely. They love living on credit, spending more than what they can afford, and risk takers. Very romantic and daydream a lot. Preferring the luxuries of home over any other place. They would rather relax at home than work. When at work they are very meticulous workers that are profusely loyal but tend to complain a lot.

4. *Esteem centred first* – unemotional-introvert. These people tend to take a cognitive approach to life they are analytically minded, seeking recognition and reassurance. They are fair judges of character. They seldom give advice, but when they do, it is restricted to their field of expertise. They will risk if the benefits outweigh the consequences. These people will only spend within their means and are rather practical in matters of the heart. Content with very little and are at ease anywhere, they sulk when not happy and take many remarks personally. Being very social and committed to task, they will work hard to get what they want.

This is not a hard and fast scientifically backed study of human behaviour; it is rather a burden of truth that leaders and managers have to deal with daily.

The element of uniqueness.

We all think and believe we are unique in some way or another. That, which guides the self to make every person unique, becomes our cognitive departure, existence, and role. Uniqueness is not a skill it is an attribute of personality, that we practice to get people to notice us. However, if you want to win people over you have to talk to their thoughts, beliefs and perception; this is where we generate paradigms with other people that we have skills. Although we have a primary characteristic trait, that we sell best, and excel at, we do not operate as a professional just from this one centre; we tend to incorporate other centres as well, depending on our moods and circumstances. We act the way we feel, we feel the way we perceive things to be, and we perceive things the way they are created.

o   When our personal beliefs and culture are challenged, or collide with, then our institutional culture gets directly affected. Something or someone created a perception that influenced us directly. Good or bad, it is all in how we perceive the situation that counts. When bad or negative, then we need to find the faulty scripts and perceptions and rewrite them, replace them, integrate them and enforce them, to become our new character. We first have to win the war internally, before we can cascade the good eternally. In the new millennium, our ability to change our thinking and keep up with change will be the deciding factor in management and its potential to deal with change effectively.
o   The ability to perceive, recognise, understand things for what they are, and not for what we perceive them to be, will require emotional intelligence. This requires action, react to feelings of yourself and those of others, and understand how it affects everyone concerned.
o   The ability to distinguish between various feelings and emotions, created by words, gestures and communication, and how to handle them, shows intelligence.
o   The ability to express and control your feelings appropriately, under stress, and to change the mood, will become an indispensable tool for managers.
o   The ability to listen to others, to have empathy with them and to communicate effectively in terms of emotions and thoughts, and then to change the perception to change the outcome is imperative.
o   The ability to use just the information at hand and make a judgement call, and apply filters in directing your thoughts and actions so that you live effectively, are motivated by a higher order principle – to think before you speak.

These character traits of critically thinking people living with others imbalance in thinking, will have a direct and equally important effect on our "potential" as leaders, to lead and manage effectively others, if we do not change the way we view and integrate our beliefs, then we will create instability. This in itself raises more questions about the importance of character and culture, for they are one to begin with. We cannot separate ourselves from our identity, heritage, beliefs and our culture and I am referring to the ethnic culture here. It also stand to reason that culture also has a great bearing on our personal beliefs, views, perceptions, biases, and yes our personal culture if gone unchecked. In addition, this dilemma requires further explanation. If we have done our calibration and we find that we are not the cause of any deficiency, then the organisations culture is at fault. Therefore, to recap, it is now quite evident that our management style will ultimately and directly influence our organisational culture and vice versa, because of our own culture and beliefs that form our character. If we do not value the importance and significance of our greatest asset, our people's character, their culture, with the diversity it brings, then we will see imbalance in the long term if we do not work towards having one corporate culture. If not then there will be no reference point left to measure right from wrong with –

referring to peoples own culture as reference point for them vs. the company culture. Cultures need to align to work. This in effect, will require leaders to communicate effectively the type of culture they would like to see develop. From a management perspective; we need to keep in mind the significance of collective labour agreements, their aims should include respect for each other and the company, and the company culture. All in order to perform with parity in the work place. This implies that our ability as an organisation, to develop and implement codes of conduct in tandem with the potential of all our stakeholders and our product. To develop ourselves by joining these two aspects, in order to do this we have to relinquish control over all things as leaders and bring our power and knowledge to the people that work for us, to empower all.

How well we handle ourselves and each other in matters concerning labor, clients and colleagues, will become the yardstick for interpersonal growth and culture development.

Not unilateral but lateral in dimension, everyone must benefit, not just a handful of carefully selected people we like that think and do like us. To close the gaps between our resources and their differences internally, to effectively develop a brand name, a product, and a culture collectively, that embraces all the potential of the organisation as a commune, as a whole and its diversity. "Unity is power" however - diversity becomes strength when harnessed. In the words of GWEE LI SUI –"No work is ample and no wall strong if you should slight (make as if it is insignificant) the temple" A man's soul is where his heart is and there you will find his temple. Where he worships his beliefs, so do not make "slight" of this spiritual-intellectual influence on management/leadership and peoples' character. Now we will try to resolve this dilemma and all its attributes by looking at virtues.

The element of enhanced virtue

"**Mitigation**", is the active intentional process of lessening the blows, it is like self-defence for an organisation. This can only be achieved through actively concentrating on virtue enhancements. Aristotle realised this and formulised this concept. Virtue is defined as a means between two extremes, excess and a defect, with respect to a particular action or emotion.

Aristotle defined ten specific virtues.

- **Courage**; is a means between the two extremes of cowardice and foolhardiness, which is based on fear, either giving into it or acting because of it.
- **Temperance**; is a means between the extremes of self-indulgence and insensibility with respect to the desire for pleasures of the body, like eating, drinking and sex.
- **Generosity or liberality**; is a means between the extremes of extravagance and stinginess with respect to the giving away and taking of money, the two extremes are extravagance, who gives away excessively, but is defective in taking in money, where stinginess is excessive in taking in but defective in giving away money.
- **Pride**; is a means between the two extremes of vanity and excessive humility with respect to one's desire to receive great honours or be humbled.
- **Good temperament**; is a means between the two extremes of irritability and apathy with respect to one's proneness to anger or apathy.
- **Truthfulness**; is a means between the two extremes of boastfulness and self-deception, with respect to the way one presents oneself to others in a specific situation.
- **Wittiness**; is a means between the two extremes of being a comedian and being plain rude.
- **Friendliness**; is a means between the two extremes of being overly friendly and being unpleasant, a desire to please others through specific behaviour.
- **Modesty**; is a means between the two extremes of bashfulness and shamefulness with respect to one's susceptibility to shame.
- **Righteous indignation**; is a means between the two extremes of envy and spite, with respect to the pleasure and pain that one feels at the fortunes of others, whether good or bad, whether they have deserved it or not. The spiteful person will rejoice at others misfortunes, whilst the righteous person feels apathy.

Here again we can clearly see how our character will guide us between the two extremes pertaining to how we will apply virtue. Indolence of mind to comprehend this aspect will breed inconsideration to the mere formality of virtue. For virtues are like seed, if they are not watered they will not grow, if we do not embrace them they will fade.

The cornerstones of virtue are firstly honesty, courage and then action, without action, they will have no significance. Nevertheless, there is more to the cornerstones of virtue, we have to incorporate; thoughtfulness, calmness, balance, humility, innocence, personal detachment, seriousness and self-control - when applying the great attribute of virtue to any anomaly.

Moreover, to experience the emotions that give rise to response is by choice, we choose to do good or bad, but it is not always this simple. Emotional triggers in us solicit responses when we become emotionally engaged, when we experience the emotions of fear, anger, hate, pity and pleasure. Individually we arrive at different responses, at the right times, in the right situations towards the right people and for the right reasons...but, this is not always true. Because of imbalance in the subconscious mind where a perception tells us to think and do otherwise, then we sometime arrive at the wrong responses, at the wrong times, towards the wrong people for the wrong reasons.

The reason for this is mainly perceptions we have adopted, that have gone unchallenged. These unchallenged perceptions become our belief and principle centres, our inherited "knowledge". No person was born badly or with bad intentions, it was because of perceptions introduced by "confidants" that we have relinquished certain virtues in life. We have forgotten the attributes that makeup validated virtue. When we only apply our perception, we close off any possibility to affect desirable quality thinking. Therefore, we must always be mindful of the influences of our perception on the outcome of our reaction to stimulus. Perceptions are pure manifestations of the fear of the unknown, so we form opinions without trying to understand and make sense of the other persons paradigms first.

We tend to become judgemental and take up a defensive stance, out of fear. We feel like we are failing, failing to listen with intent, failing to see good intentions and failing to conquer our irrational fear of the unknown. Because of perceptions, we hold on to what we believe, as if they are the only view that matters. We need to realise, that there are many flavours of reality and knowledge out there, not just the "plain vanilla" flavour we like. Although, it is the most popular, other flavours signal a change in vision, perception, culture, thinking and beliefs. The one who has made it his passion to pursue epistemology - the science of knowledge - will always be the one presenting the different flavours. The educated man will know that the logic in the same degree of certainty and demonstration is not possible in ethics as it is in mathematics. For one is just as powerful as 10, in ethics, but not in maths. We need to understand from which paradigm a person is reasoning first, for instance one could refer to one army, as to 10 soldiers. It is just a question of opinion - perception. We need to reason with intent, to create understanding.

Reasoning with intent

These are important lessons in reasoning; they signal the difference of opinions between people on certain subjects. Reasoning with intent; is the difference between arriving at understanding or exiting the debate with defective reasoning. Therefore, logic would imply that reasoning applied to a problem should exit with a solution – however, solutions are not understood the same for everybody. Thus if ten is too much and one is too little, then we could make our difference 5 - practically speaking. What if 10 pounds of meat is too much and one is too little then logically speaking five should be enough... enough for whom? Our frame of reasoning again affects our final perspective on what is true and what is false, because of our own perspective. Where party one is a 260-pound man and he can easily eat ten pounds of meat in a week, referring back to his perception of enough, opposed to party two who is a female six years old. Therefore, the right amount will vary from individual to individual, depending on the reasoning, in this instance based on nutritional need. Therefore, in business, people tend to stick with averages, or inflated biases and our reasoning should take on the same principle and not our personal preferences, this constitutes balanced reasoning.

Finally, consider this; if you do not explain your reasoning, and motivate it, then the people you are communicating with will most surely yield their own version of your reasoning according to their understanding, and their actions may differ greatly from your own expectation. The good of man resides in his choices, and ability to choose, governed by the activities of the mind, which becomes his reasoning. Therefore, in effect a happy man is one who is aware that he has a choice, and of all the elements and flavours of uplifting reasoning. We must consequently consider our actions and interactions to get our intentions across, for it is our interactions that ultimately determine the reasoning of others, and the altering states of existence of successful communication with intent. Symbolising intent gives it meaning.

The new face of "symbolic" leadership

Very few leaders today will achieve icon status, because of their symbolic representation of what constitutes true leadership dynamics. If an organisation becomes threatened because of its cultural deficiencies and inadequacies, then it is ultimately the function of leadership to recognise and change their style. True symbolic managers and leaders place a much higher premium on mutual trust in a relationships with their following, and open communication. A lack of good corporate culture has become the number one dysfunctional attribute in organisations today, where leaders fail to realign the culture with new assumptions, new paradigms and perceptions, to function with true north principle. Within strong corporate cultures, the supporting mechanism is their strong networks they have with staff, open communication - without fear or favour - in a just and unprecedented, unbiased manner, with no divisions, no unilateral cells of preference, only one people.

The symbolic leader becomes the champion and custodian of culture, the hero driven by the ethic of mutualism. They inspire people by distributing responsibility and accountability. They allow people to choose, they communicate with intent. Rather than being seen as the glue and source of identity, they relinquish this, and control to all levels. They see their role and function as direction finder, strategic, as pathfinder, as performing the stewardship role. Charismatic leadership only manifest itself where good virtues are applied. Where all fear has been dealt within a systematic, personal and accountable manner. They have true empathy and a true desire to see others thrive. Symbolic leaders remove all obstacles for their people, they are not driven by self-gratification; on the contrary, it is large sacrifices on their part, forgiveness and understanding, that gets people to trust them and follow them. Self-serving gratification comes at a large expense, it always has to end in a "win – lose" situation. By so doing we have our following adopt these principles, being good or bad, because people mimic idolised position, thus if the leader becomes the idolised position they will mimic his behaviour and habits over time. Symbolised or symbolic leaders run one risk, the risk of attribution.

The cause and effect element of attribution

Cause: Attribution is the primary understanding or perception we have of other people. What attributes do we see in them and what are they lacking from our perspective, as well as certain perceptions we have about peoples culture, religion or race in these positions of symbolic leaders. The cause of coupling attribution stems from; insecurity, apprehension, or a highly competitive thinking of others. We are pack driven, we have to be in control and the higher we are up the hierarchy, the better our chances to compete so we always jockey for position even along these lines, by chopping at the bigger trees base.

- For example, if we apply *Actor- Observer* perspective, then we see others behaviour as a result of their disposition, their character and we see ours as purely situational, or circumstantial. We do not attach ourselves by walking a mile in the shoes of our counterpart; we refuse to believe that we could have acted in the same manner, had we been confronted with the same outlook on life. We judge and reason from a denial perspective, with a belief that things like that cannot and will not happen us.

- The other attribution of **Correspondence Interference** perspective relates back to our interaction and past encounters with a party and the regard and perceptions created by our confidants around certain aspects of this party, we therefore assume too much and we assume any unusual act as a disposition, purely on assumption.
- The attribution of **Positivity – Effect** perspective relates to us seeing and believing that only people we trust and like are positive, anyone else is miserable and negative.
- The attribution of **Fundamental Attribution Error** perspective, we overestimate the importance of dispositional, character factors, we believe that only the characters that are well spoken and slight of mind and thinking have innate potential because of this aspect.
- The attribution of **Co-variation Models** perspective, we look for similarities between us to narrow down attribution in others, so in essence, the more we are alike the more we will think alike, thus he or she is one of us, someone to be trusted. This cannot be true, it will distort our outlook and perception, we will become totally biased, towards others that are not like us.
- The attribution of **Scapegoat Theory** perspective, we like shifting the blame to someone else, because we are in control we cannot be accountable, or held liable for failure.

Effect: we arrive at conclusions that guide our thinking and reactions to such stimulus, based on our current evaluation of situations, without applying filtering - filtering is the conscious thinking about thinking - the application and incorporation of virtues and insight. We have to in effect, unpack the translation of any communication in an unbiased manner, our internal aim is to add value, to form understanding in order to be understood. We can only achieve this state by listening attentively, listening with intent is feeding back to the communicator the elements within his or her reasoning that could lend itself to open interpretation, or be misinterpreted, thus we endeavour to narrow otherwise open interpretation to more specific understanding to form common understanding, to gain clarity. For example;

Symbolised understanding; is a method of getting the point across, a tool where we find concrete objects and symbols that are generally used to describe an aspect, that hold the same universal understanding to explain otherwise abstract ideas or reasoning. This is useful where we have formed cryptic communication and have to explain the value of the objects to someone, who is not knowledgeable about the culture and language difference that comes from interpretation and translation. For instance, the word "lekker" in the Afrikaans language means, tasteful, but it has been adopted into the South African English to mean nice and joyful, thus two different meanings. In the IT industry acronyms or cryptic language are used, that are of no consequence, nor relevance to someone who is not interested in this field. Thus, any culture has symbolic and cryptic specific language interpretations that are of abstract value to someone that is not knowledgeable in this area of expertise, or who does not know the culture. Therefore, we have to use more relevance to the situation, basic concrete general terms to communicate, likewise, our own multi-cultural experiences have formed certain attributes within our reasoning, language and understanding of things and concepts that we have to keep in mind when reasoning; (we will explore this phenomenon again in more detail in the next chapter.)

These language and cultural attributes strongly influence our decision-making capability to the following extent.

- Our **Anchoring and Adjustment Heuristic** bias; influence our estimates from the known to the unknown, we anchor ourselves in what we believe or perceive and know and we only work inside this framework as reference. We do not recognise anything else to be valid.
- Our **Biased Sampling** bias; influences our nature to base our decisions on available small samples of information, from which we draw final conclusions and believe them to be true.
- Our **Bounded Rationality** bias; influences our use of logic in decision-making. We only want to deal with facts and truth; we do not recognise anything else as relevant, because it seems illogical.
- Our **Endowment Effect** bias; influences our perspective on what is important and what is insignificant, we value material things we own, more than relationships, because relationships take time and effort. Material things give us a sense of security and worth.
- Our **Illusionary Correlation** bias; influences our reality, we see relationships where there are none, we see correlation where it is impossible to form.
- Our **Overconfidence Barrier** bias; influences our judgement, we are too confident in our ability to judge and do it regularly and even openly, the subconscious covering up of our own deficiencies, to reflect attention from us.

These are just some examples of our formation of thinking. Where we error in our choices of decision by its influence on our perceived logical deductions, we preach unbiased behaviour but we practice it, we point out weakness, but we very conveniently forget our own dispositions weakness. In effect, we pretend to be someone we are not when thinking this way. Insecurity and vulnerability are personal issues, we all have them, they are our demons, but we all have to overcome them, the more we deal with them, the more we realise their insignificance. People strong in character and conviction have no insecurities, he or she knows that, they are only manifestations of personal insecurity; no one is a potential threat. We all live as equals, we were created equal, we have all been endowed with the same seeds of success and only through our conceptualisation of perceived threats and barriers do we act as if threatened and wounded. These are the fundamental elements of reasoning we have to attune ourselves to in order to break the burden they bestow on us intellectually, and what is more, the mental elements of error will influence and affect our physical dimension.

We are and become that which we think about most, what you sow you shall reap.

If this is true then success is made in the mind first, as a first creation.

This is exactly why this book concentrates on diverse views on thinking. We are training you to think like a maverick, by throwing as many angles at you as possible. The next chapter deals with how to get your thinking across to people, three-dimensional thinking is thinking outside the box, if you are leading and or managing, you will benefit greatly from this type of thinking.

Chapter 6

TRIANGULATION – working with concept thinking

TRIANGULATION

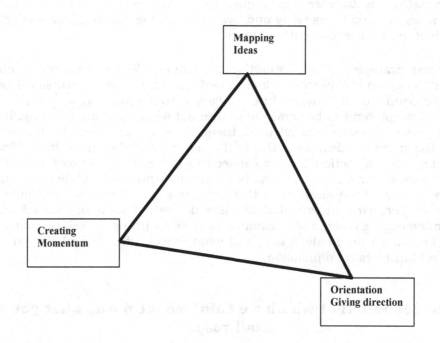

This is the prelude to C.A.P.S. (Concept, Attributes, Perceptions, Systems)

"If you see it, you tend to believe it."

Only those general principles and attitudes that result from a clear and deep understanding of triangulation can provide a comprehensive guide in the form of direction towards going over to action. It is to this that opinions on specific problems should be anchored, we should give it direction. The difficulty is to hold fast to these results in the torrent of events and with new opinions. Often there exists a gap between principles and actual events that cannot always be bridged by a succession of logical deductions, the odd conundrum. Then a measure of self-confidence is needed and a degree of scepticism is helpful. Frequently nothing short of a crucial principle would have sufficed which is not normally part of the immediate thought-process, but dominates it: that principle is in all doubtful cases to stick to one's first opinion on how to solve a problem and then to refuse to change unless forced to do so by a more clear conviction and direction. A strong faith in the overriding truth of tested principles is needed, the vividness of temporary impressions must not make us forget that such truth as they contain is of a lesser value. "By giving priority, in case of doubt, to our earlier convictions, by holding to them stubbornly, our actions acquire that quality of steadiness and consistency, which is termed strength of character. - Clausewitz, On War".

Taking the three steps:

Step one: The "Mapping" of ideas to form concepts:

From time to time, we are faced with huge challenges that require a great deal of contemplation. During times like these is a necessity to take thinking to a higher level, if not then why bother with strategy, what is the point so to speak. Strategic thinking is aimed at organising and structuring means at our disposal to reach a predefined conclusion. When reasoning requires uniqueness and specifics, in the absence of any available logical resolve to a problem, then we resort to formulating a strategy. In this instance, we will use triangulation and mapping – the illustrations of the problem and its attributers – to address the challenge. The word "Map" when used in literal terms refers to a record, chart or diagram - representing the facts. We want to create accurate records of our thinking in the same manner, as we do when drawing geographical maps of terrain. All in order to visualise our thinking by mapping them clearly for others to see. There has to be a need first, that cannot be dealt with via conventional means. It is the same as a woman wanting a wedding dress, we all know the concept, do we however understand the specific requirements? A dress can be bought at any clothing store, a wedding dress – well, I do not think so, it's far too emotional and specific. Surely, every wedding dress has its own uniqueness, the same can be said for ideas becoming strategies. Visualised strategies also requires specifics; the who, the what, where, when and how - are now being connected to the first aspect, that of necessity. Maps connect aspects that are related in a schematic depiction. In addition, you will require your structure, the vehicle to facilitate the process, or to accomplish and compliment the strategies with to be part. By identifying your problem statement graphically, you create focus, so that when you have to explain a particular aspect of the "terrain – map" - your vision, mission, goals and strategies – then it will be layered to form a visual concept. With this concept in place - you will be able to visually follow the law of creation, step by step - which implies everything is created three times.

The law of business creation holds the following;

- In the first instance. It all starts with an idea.
  - Ideas are created in the abstract, the mind, and are not tangible to all.
  - The idea needs to be linked with known concepts, so that people can associate with them.
- In the second creation step. The concept.
  - Deal with the concept in a model form.
  - Create associations with the desired end result in mind
- And the third creation step. The assembling.
  - Deal with finding ways and means to make it reality.
  - Identify the aspects of the idea that will give it form
  - Give it life
  - Ultimately, find the means to bring it into existence.

The law of creation requires creative thinking; it is a process of bringing ideas to life by making it visible to all. Just a side note on ideas, many people have ideas, granted, however, very few materialise because they do not create them. When we sell ideas as plans, it is normally left open to wide interpretation. Then these ideas get lost in translation. Therefore, we wish to narrow it down to a specific concept – and not an open interpretation. We do not want to find ourselves with a situation where someone interprets; "hill", when you are trying to sell "mountain". Through triangulation, we create specific visualised representations of our vision, we define our aims, set our gaols and realise our ideas. The process of levelling perceptions in order to narrow it down to specifics, which require creativity, and form that should emerge some form. From the word go we must focus our strategic communication and focus on specifics, context and content. This is why we choose to follow the "Map" analogy. We will deliberate this first aspect in depth later on. Nevertheless, a map is useless if we do not know which way is North, this requires the ability to orientate oneself -the second aspect is orientation.

Step two: The second significant thing or aspect is, our "Orientation" – OODA – towards strategic conversation

We need to make sure that every person in the group is orientated and focused on one reality – that we all have the same point of reference. That we all work towards the same reference point or goal. How you may ask. We have to deal from one paradigm that includes two elements, the business level and on a personnel level. Especially given the increased reliance upon trusted relationships and networks, both internal and external to achieve strategic goals with. Strategic orientation at business level could be defined as the implicit identification of dominant factors that influencing strategy conception. The in-depth understanding of the changing nature of the strategic environment and the potential impact on the strategy is cardinal to orientated discussion. This type of orientation will directly impact on our ability as a collective to analyse and to find the best solution within the given circumstances – and time. Orientation referrers to factors that influence strategy directly, mostly internal.

Dominant factors that influencing strategy;

- such as the rate of modernisation,
- management characteristics,
- global trends,
- the utilisation and application of technology,
- organisational review;
  - to provide recommendations for changes by using a systematic process aimed at identifying:
    - accountabilities,
    - the required resourcing,
    - the most suitable structure, and
    - the roles that have the accountabilities and responsibilities.
- Key Performance Indicators;
  - Key Performance Indicators (KPI) by definition; are financial and non-financial measures used to help an organisation define and evaluate how successful it is, typically in terms of making progress towards its long-term organizational goals.

These have become the dominant factors. Future strategist need to be able to identify these essential elements in there thinking, before making strategic decisions and preparing plans which reflects their strategic priorities, because strategy and dominant factors are the drivers of performance.

Strategic orientation at conception level could be defined as a strategic mind-set, being blatantly honest and critical about how we feel about the choices and assumptions being dealt with. We have to be able to state our case openly, and critically - whether we are in agreement or not, and be respected for our opinion. There is a tendency when making plans where only the leaders, and professionals get to make a case, and everyone else gets dismissed. We have to work around this aspect, when going strategic, to show by sharing our fears and optimism openly that we are being trustworthy and part of the orientation. Trust - implies more than just being trusted or honest and of good character and inclination. People will only trust someone that is open, and honest almost immediately. It is most surely, what follows from that first interaction, and word of mouth that we will dictate the level of trust furthermore. The sayings that "don't judge a book by its cover" and that "first impressions count" come from entrenched knowledge of the importance of first interactions. The alignment you have to create with others in order to sell, first yourself, by coming across as being stable first and then honest, able, capable and willing sends a message of service, this builds rapport. No ego-trips, no make-believe, no bold and blatant contest for position will win you any favour with first impressions. On the other hand, don't include people that do not care much for detail, that just want things to work, it will derail, or lengthen the process beyond comprehension. Just being focused on the task at hand, the real you, without the mask, without any agenda. Relationships that start from this paradigm, prevail and strengthens over time, anything else is just antics or interactions based on needs and wants. Self-centeredness kills ideas, simply because there are more "I's" in doing thing than "we". This is the orientation we seek with our people that are open minded to others that seem genuinely interested in whatever task requires their attention. We require attitude, a specific mind-set that opens up constructive and critical debate, frication is good for revolution.

Step three: The third aspect is creating "Perpetual Motion", or "Momentum".

Excellent communication is key and pivotal to anything that is strategic. Without it, there will be no action. Communication, in whatever form, is key to successful strategy making and execution. Well this is the part where you will have to sell yourself, before you can sell or start communicating the concept of strategy. Prepare your thoughts, filter them, and plan the strategic communication, before trying to sell concepts. The point is; you cannot sell anything if you cannot sell yourself, or alternatively if you do not have anything to sell as a concept. Even if the concept is you – as a person. Preparation gives you the ability to assess what it is you want to get across, or out there, just like an election campaign gets designed beforehand, to send one message out there. Just the same, you have to gauge what is needed and what will be sold, to satisfy the needs and wants of people and organisations. Then by exchanging your ideas, you will have sold 20% or more of the concept, because it is based on a "truth". These two elements – excellent communication and contemplation - working in tandem create a surge of energy. If we believe in something, we communicate it with passion. The "buy in" has to take place here with you. This starts the move, the momentum. People in general dismiss people and things they do not understand, do not know or trust. Although they will listen, even attentively, will they act? We require the "domino effect", seldom do we realise or reflect on what clinched that deal for us, why did that person respond to us, why did they act exactly the way I wanted them to, well this is exactly it. It just takes a small initial amount of positive energy, created by a personal belief in the concepts and ourselves we sell, conveyed by excellent communication to set in motion a chain of events, just like with dominos falling.

Designing concepts takes a lot of time and planning - to stack the dominoes - our ideas, and their attributes - for the concept to form. Although it only took one decisive small amount of energy to set it all in motion. When we flick over the first domino the rest should follow – only when we creativity designed and contemplate the process from start to finish for ourselves, will we succeed in passing it on to others to see. Only then, will we know when the crucial moment will be, where that "decisive" energy takes over, and we start the first block, and all the others follow, until the last domino falls into place. The deal is done; the concept is sold, just as dominos uses momentum to fall when stacked. If we cannot create enough energy through conviction that our concept is workable, the process will stop half way, or even sooner. In the same way, we have to keep preparing for momentum when selling concepts. This is also a numbers game, the more alliance you can form, the more credibility you have; the better your chances are at succeeding. The more dominoes in a stack – the amount of time and effort we have put into it - the more options we have in reaching the desired result via different routes. In addition, the clearer the concept the faster the breakthrough, and take down of resistance will come about. If you get stonewalled, it's normally due to a lack of concept – we did not give it enough thought - or personal credibility. This aspect is thus two fold. We need a presence, and we need a workable concept.

Alliance, and networks strengthen our credibility, more is better. The more you talk about it and get feedback and support the stronger the influence. If you now have all your managers, or sponsors on board as "team players" with the same game plan, you will no longer need to pull by the nose and kick by the ass – excuse the pun. If this were true, then how can our effort not breed successes when everyone believes in it?

Clarity; be clear about the intentions and expected outcome. As a result, we must strive for a single team effort, where everyone is clear on their own roles and function;

- On what they have to do,
- where – they have to do it,
- how – it should be done,
- when – it should be done
- and who – will be responsible for what.

People want to know how change will impact on them... These are the attributes of a good concept, it included roles and functions.

Authority; We have to be in a position of authority to delegate effectively. When we do, we need to give down clear instruction sets "maps" – action plans and action items - with the responsibility for people to start acting. This will definably necessitate a map – detail. Not a plan as is the norm, we live in the information age, people want details; the significance of a map is that it can be easily interpreted, where a plan could be to open-ended – whereas maps, as you well know, are detailed and accurate representations of the real terrain. Plans on the other hand are just lacking the required precision and are left open to wide interpretation, and a lot of explaining. One sure way of getting ideas to flow is to give people maps, instead of plans – all good but no longer the primary means. They now become second to maps, to leave us to decide on the best course of action, consider the alternatives that are in favour of the concept, thus elevating the thinking of how to approach the task at hand. Show that you understand the task and its difficulty in depth and that you are comfortable with certain assumptions beforehand. This makes you the authority on the strategy.

Modelling the concept perception. We sometimes hear the remark that people are stupid because they do not understand the job function or task at hand – they just don't get it – or "SEE" it – we could, and mostly are mistaken. Everyone has the ability to "see", but not to interoperate things accurately. However, we do not all express ourselves equally well as well when communicating. When passing on tasks it the same way – by saying the same thing differently – we create different realities. We have to realise that not all people are SMART. I refer you back to being "IQ Smart" in the same fashion because we all experience life differently and this aspect governs how we attack our tasks. Don't generalize! Understanding and working with concepts takes time; to understand that we are all programmed differently, thus think and perceive, and reflect on things from different points of view, is critical to the outcome - this reflects maturity. Maturity is the balance between courage and consideration. It has everything to do with our personal and professional credibility, where people are confident in our approaches and intentions, we will gain their support. Thus, the emotional side to our logic in dealing with matters complex will be soothed. No one will become anxious about the outcome. Perception is the one thing we will have to manage throughout. Just like several people standing in a gallery looking at a sculpture from different angles, just the same way we all "see" differently, and perceive differently, we do not all operate with the same operating programmes either. We attack problems and tasks, in the manner they were related to us. We process information differently, like with personal computers operating systems – (Windows vs. Linex on a PC). Most companies merely bulldoze and hammer out the core strategy, sell it to management, email it to the troops, and away they go. No, we need to better understand the intricacy of uniting thought and perception with concepts and choice.

Human nature prevails. We, the unwilling, led by the unknowing, are doing the impossible for the ungrateful. We have done so much, for so long, with so little, we are now qualified to do anything with nothing. - **Mother Teresa.** Enter human nature again - if "I", am still feeling insignificant, as a player, and do not get a platform to voice my opinion and concerns. Then "I" – will be raising my significance, or either withdraw - in mind - but not necessarily myself in person. This is a personal self-worth and self-defence response – to this old practice of exclusion of some people and unilateral implementation of strategies with no resources. This aspect manifests itself in an environment where there is very little mutual trust and respect, and to much competitiveness, things like this is more often observed. Where people have forgotten how to say please and thank you. Mutual trust and respect creates an atmosphere of win-win, without it, everything becomes childlike behaviour and stops to a grinding halt, interdependence needs to be re-cultivated, remember, trust and mutual respect works in parallel.

Share and share alike. Asks yourself this, how many times have you experienced this happening in your lifetime, where you have personally had to exercise mental self-defence, where you just withdraw what you had on offer because you had not been *afforded the opportunity to become part of the "team".* Have you experienced this sense of being purposefully or even maliciously left out in the rain or cold at some stage of your career, by the "key players"? These are the dark emotions, which whelm up inside us like cold wet fog, when we are part of a win-lose lose-win organisation or team. Emotionally we are being bullied. These are the corporate tactics of the unscrupulous, they want us to descend to their level, which is the only place they can weigh us down, where there are no rules, just dog eats dog. What you will find is corpses left everywhere, mummies walking the corridors and on the walls, in the hallways they will have big framed pictures of previous DOG -leaders that were "shot"- and fired, "stabbed" and double-crossed or had short-lived victories against them, figuratively speaking on the "battlefields" of the corporate world. Where everyone just has to get to the top and no matter how many people you have to run down or over, it makes it all "worth it" in the end. This style of corporate governance always caves in, where everyone is competing with everyone else, just looking out for themselves, just wanting to get ahead, they lose sight of the really important things in life and their own goals.

"Invisible influence". On a personal level. Have you not been acknowledged as a key player yet, how does it feel? Just to have to solve the whole mess later on, all by yourself, and on a regular basis. Is this your curse for being proficient, willing and able? If you do decide to exert your worth, knowledge and skill, then everything just gets dumped in your lap, or you get silenced. If this is the case, then you could very well be the one we see sitting around the board-room table in a big corporate environment just nodding his head respectfully, but withdrawing what you had on offer with every passing minute until it reads zero. Why, because we are not getting "a Fair Deal" – or at least in our minds, we struggle with this issue daily – are we playing offence or defence etc. However, these answers are clouded by internal politics, in the race for position, power and favour. This is an age-old tactic to remain in control, as still practiced by some. Corporate ideology plays a key role in how people will offer their service.

On a collective level. The tribe members in Africa get together around a big fire and respectfully talk about "Ubuntu" - "we are right", "the people know". However, what if they don't know the difference between right and wrong, what then?

The belief is that, a person with "Ubuntu" is open and available to others, affirming of others, does not feel threatened that others are able and good, for he or she has a proper self-assurance that comes from knowing that he or she belongs in a greater whole and is diminished when others are humiliated or diminished, when others are tortured or oppressed.
Archbishop Desmond Tutu (1999):

A very nice ideology – but what if the leaders in a corporate environment themselves are morally corrupt, and exploit this belief to their own advantage. Everyone is compelled by virtue of the collective towards supporting their leader right or wrong, this is the nature of human thoughts - in denial of the truth – they would rather join the collective mess than oppose it. Everyone wants to belong, but at what cost? It becomes one emotionally drained roller coaster ride of hit and missed affaires – where we become morally corrupt as people and organisations. We cannot and should not operate "blindly" from such a team paradigm; we have to become the majority, even if it is only a majority of one. Every forest started with one good seed. The fact that the majority agrees with corrupt leaders, only implies that the majority of fools are in agreement - always - for the sake of belonging – even then, we stay collectively responsible. Now no one is directly to blame, this is absurd, this is covering up weakness, this is not true teamwork. Therefore, the point to make here is this. Even if everyone has the same map, and orientation – morally – it is still no guarantee that they will all navigate strategy successfully either. This is why we have to make sure that we orientate them - "ALL of them" - with a sober style of leadership. These are some of the "invisible influences" we have to contemplate and deal with.

Leadership is by choice and orientation and not by designation; leadership is about taking lead and responsibility. Leadership is all about orientation and accountability. Therefore, the true leader will realise that having a plan is no fail safe, we need good morals as well. In addition to having a map, a map of the South Pole for instance will be no good if we find ourselves being in the North Pole. The concept has to fit in with the reality of the given situation, on all levels. Worse still, without a moral compass, and a directionless leader, we will keep going in circles. because the right leg is stronger and the dominant therefore the right leg will take a bigger step when the mind cannot pinpoint a beacon to navigate to, to keep us going straight. Personal trivia will derail us. We need clear direction and directives, clear-headed leaders, with morals - that do not constantly change. It is of no use assuming you are heading "North" just because you have the map and compass orientated like wise. Many of us have defective compasses, and maps that do not fit. The proof is people and originations heading in all the other wind directions - imagine that. Nevertheless, it happens daily, where the leaders make sudden changes in direction, and don't communicate it effectively. Looking back over your shoulder and you are standing all alone and lost. Therefore, it would be expected that we arrive at one central point as a collective if we are all orientated and on the same map, if we all have a compass – good communication, and morals - and we are all leaders in our own right. This would mean that every aspect of reasoning was in synergy. Synergy; simply defined, means the "Whole" is greater than the sum of all its parts. It furthermore implies that all the parts are in constant communication. We have mastered the art of having stable work habits that are conducive to change, and influences. To achieve this we require the "triangulation" of the trust matrix to prevail. If we want the initiative back, we require inventiveness to survive against these odds.

The question that we are addressing here is how to develop our awareness and our ability to change along with change itself, and still be able to find synergy and keep our direction, with all the delicate influence on strategy. Experience is essential ... and failure is indeed the mother of success. But it is also necessary to learn with an open mind from the experience of others: and it is sheer "narrow mindedness" to insist on one's own personal experience in all matters at hand and in its absence, to adhere stubbornly to one's own opinion and reject other people's experience. Is a disaster waiting to happen.

- Mao Tse-tung, Selected Military Writings.

The art of orientation: the "OODA" loop.

The Art of "Orientation" and "Triangulation" finding direction with: The "OODA" loop

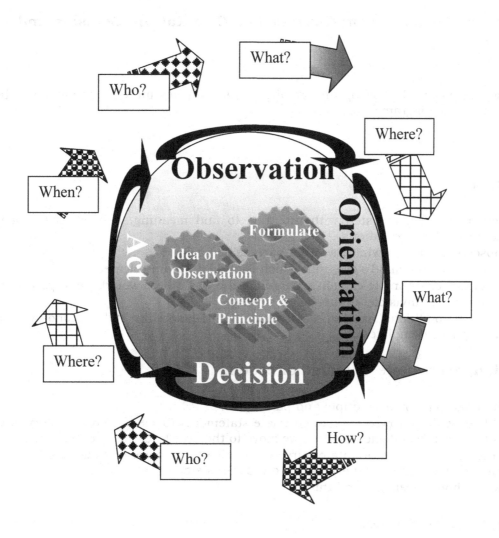

Col John Boyd, USAF (Ret), coined the term and developed the concept of the "OODA Loop" (Observation, Orientation, Decision, Action). Perhaps most importantly, Boyd was instrumental in explaining and disseminating the concept of "cycle time" and "getting inside the adversary's decision cycle".

The Orientation of all things strategic.

The importance of the "OODA" LOOP:

In Military terms it stands for; **Observation, Orientation, Decision and Act.**

In this case, we will be borrowing and re-aligning it to mean more to compliment the deeper understanding of the diagram;

Observation;

- Listen attentively, to listen with intent is to find meaning, a need, the concept, or to understand the expectations.
- To observe, is to "see" what the other party is doing.
- To visualise in the mind's eye, that which is audibly communicated
- Or alternatively trying to explain a paradigm the way others would see or perceives things.
- To take note of "invisible" influence on strategy
- Observing conditions as they exist currently, Leadership style, economy, budges, or whatever is contemplated...

Orientation; to orientate, is to find direction,

- with maps, perceptions, scripts and paradigms.
- As if I see with borrowed eyes, to correlate statements to see if I have the correct version of the other party's statement, before we move to the next level- decision making.
- On the other hand, to orientate ourselves is also to prepare, or to get ready for battle, by finding vantage points and evaluating our options etc.
- How we should feel, act, and think

Decision; to go for it or not,

- we now have to come up with possible solutions,
- we have to realise that for every action there is a equal and opposite reaction
- and we have to plot the course beforehand mentally,
- against the cause and effects of our solutions contemplated and weigh them.
- Decisions create alternatives and options, that create more decisions.
- if we cannot decide or are indecisive, we limit our options and lose the initiative,

- this whole cycle is created to get the intuitive and keep it, we have to act to see what the reaction would be,
- as well as to be open to disagreement, conflict and securitisation.
- Alternatively, we have to restart the process, at any stage that we cannot move forward.

Act; is to

- interact and reach affirmation of the problem statement,
- to anticipate the expectation statement and the alternative statement,
- this will produce the solution statement,
- that needs to be read in and verified by repeating the loop, to bring it to being. (Statements are the actions we take, the original affirmations and testimonies of the concepts, facts and perceptions we based our thinking on).
- Deciding to, fight, flee, or surrender. Is all beneficial, because we acted.
- It is the process of implementing one's alternative, when we observe that the initial assumptions don't work.
- Acting is also implementing by testing your hypothesis.
- The results of acting goes back to observation, and the loop starts again

The underlying art of the OODA loop is to go through this cycle **of OODA** as fast as possible; the one that can move from the one instance to the other the quickest will gain the initiative in the interaction. If you lose the initiative, you lose the control. Your aim is to get to an "advantage" situation as soon as possible. The OODA loop; revolves around **changing** the adversary **mental attitude** and not around killing him. This aspect is based on a deeper understanding of the adversary and his *behaviour* - and how it *could be influenced* - through skilful observation, orientation, decisions, and actions, this equals tactics. The purpose of the loop is to relate a chain of events (dominos) that has to be placed in sequential order before we can act, the longer the time cycle in the loop is, to get from one aspect to the next the bigger the loop, and the longer the time cycle will be. This aspect creates opportunity for the adversary to complete several smaller loops within the same amount of time. Thus taking the initiative, whoever has the smallest loop has the initiative. The one who takes the initiative and keeps it has the power, the other one has to react to him and try and catch up and pass. At every time-out interval, the adversary has to look at the effect his loop had, but you keep changing the outcome, by going through the loop faster without him realizing so he becomes concerned with his inability to solve the situation effectively, the adversary now experiences emotional and intellectual collapse.

The aim is to get the initiative – and be in control. In armed conflicts, the principle of "tactics" is applied, by using military skills such as; out-manoeuvring, flanking, attacking, withdrawing, or any combination thereof. Not excluding, camouflage, deception and espionage tactics etc. – this physical quickness creates "perpetual motion", it produces accelerated speed and freedom of movement, the effect of which generates feelings of confusion, panic, hopelessness and forces desperate actions on the opponents side and destroys his will to fight, as cohesion is lost within the ranks, moral falls. The way it is done is to focus on the strong point, with a concentrated effort and to re-enforce the mission directives with added support. Learning from this, we can take it internal as well. Where the organisation is going through their loop faster than what the workforce can keep up, then it will have the same effect of collapse internally as well.

In corporate life, these same principles are applied daily, but just with more subtlety; we will go into the "Art of War" and battle tactics in another chapter on Mobile warfare.

The communication

Remember what we said about too much information. If one gets too much information, we reach a point called "flooding". Just like a dam overflows when it gets full, wherein this case visual and factual information instead of water flows out of the equation and is lost. Whenever information becomes over whelming, or too much to work with, too much to make sense of, then information becomes totally distorted or complex. Mapping of information, creates order and synergy.

We need to be aware of this aspect when in discussion with someone, not to overstate nor understate the concept.

Language on other hand and cultural attributes strongly influence our decision-making capability to the following extent;

- Our **Anchoring and Adjustment Heuristic** bias; influences our estimates from the known to the unknown, we anchor ourselves in what we believe or perceive and know and we only work inside this framework as reference. We do not recognise anything else to be valid.
- Our **Biased Sampling** bias; influences our nature to base our decisions on only available small samples of information, from which we draw final conclusions and believe them to be true.
- Our **Bounded Rationality** bias; influences our use of logic in decision-making. We only want to deal with facts and truth; we do not recognise anything else as relevant, because it seems illogical.
- Our **Endowment Effect** bias; influences our perspective on what is important and what is insignificant, we value material things we own, more than relationships, because relationships take time and effort. Material things give us a sense of security and worth.
- Our **Illusionary Correlation** bias; influences our reality, we see relationships where there are none, we see correlation where it is impossible to form.
- Our **Overconfidence Barrier** bias; influences our judgement, we are too confident in our ability to judge and do it regularly and even openly, the subconscious covering up of our own deficiencies, to reflect attention from us.

Remember, "The Amateur sells pre- fabricated products as solutions the Professional sell solutions as tailor-made products". In order to sell solutions you will have to stay in observation mode for as long as it takes, repeating a couple of loops before starting your loop (OODA), toward finding the solution that is required. Ask the right questions, to get the right answers, what is it that the other person envisages the solution to be, diagnose before you prescribe, listen before you speak, seek to understand before you seek to be understood. By asking yourself what is the question that he or she is trying to solve here?

What are the right questions to ask, well, all the right questions start with:

- Who?
- When?
- What?
- Where?
- How?

Focusing on the "Map idea" again and incorporating these aspect, but now in more detail -.

Before you venture on to new battlefields, – business ventures -fix, repair and prepare your war machine. Map the habitat, start with the physical and most obvious first. The "hills" will constitute – obstacles and strategic events that need to be catered for by the unit (I prefer to use the term unit, it could signify small, big, or medium in size and does not exclude any venture). The climate - the things that could influence negatively or positively on your management style as a leader, yourself, your unit, and your concept. Visualise your "rivers", ", resources", ", suppliers" the "grassland areas": the "assembly lines", the "production facility". The point is to visualize the environment and find the symbols that best describe, relate, or can best be associated with the vision you are carrying over graphically. Then we want to speak symbolically so that people are all orientated towards the vision.

Don't do things on assumption:

Design is done in a three dimensional fashion, top down and bottom up and from horizon to horizon. Become aware of thing at grassroots level first. It has to be done with people in mind and people in the know, because managers tend to stay on the main routes only, whilst others go on assumption based on past and previous experiences. The old trusted way things were done, but how is it done today, now? No more old school mentality. Ask the new guy, the janitor, the doorkeeper what they think, you will or could be astonished at the insight and hindsight they may come across with being at grass roots level daily. This type of 360 degree input strategy, will give you a real-time three-dimensional display of the current environment. The best top ten companies in the world kill their best selling product only to have to force themselves to reinvent it every year with a bigger and brighter logo, packaging etc. You have to take on an attitude that the best is only the best when in stays effective. On Efficiency; the moment anything is born it starts to become defective, the same with ideas and concepts. It is always amazing to see how problems and key performance areas jump out at you once you visualize the management habitat and evaluate the actual product it created in retrospect. This brings about the concept of reverse engineering. It is "Back to Basics".

Fundamentals are the key to success. A massive paradigm shift needs to take place. - Stephen R Covey has a very insightful way of describing this metaphor: he says – all things are created twice, "begin with the end in mind" it is based on the principle that all things are created twice. There are mental or first creations and a physical or second creation to all things...you work with ideas, you work with your mind until you get a clear image of what you want to build. Then you reduce it to a blueprint and develop construction plans.... the carpenters rule is "measure twice cut once" (from his book the 7 habits of highly effective people, powerful lessons in personal change 1989.) - Stephen R Covey.

Reverse Engineering: relies on our creative thinking to project images from the future to the here and now.

Our ability to explore and discover: is one of man's greatest attributes, from childhood we entered the realm of expedition, of life and all it has to offer, we were all little Livingston's then, and many of those encounters gave us tools and knowledge that still hold true for us. We used all our senses to derive answers for our newfound concepts. The collective assumption of what we had discovered from several encounters whilst exploring on our journeys through life, has left us with some assumptions. The question is now are they still there, are they still accurate and are they still sound assumptions. It all depends where you are reasoning from...

"What is the aim or purpose of strategy? To overall improve our ability to shape and adapt to unfolding circumstances, so that we (as individuals or as groups or as culture or as a nation-state) can survive on our own terms".
– John R Boyed.

Nevertheless, what we have to realise is that for every good deed we strive for, for every change we strive for, there will be an equal and opposite energy, school of thought and paradigm opposing it. Mainly because we assume a lot, and from that we derive a lot. We will not experience any growth if we do not work at testing our assumptions. The golden triangle – mapping – orientation – creation - is the one side to an opposing other side – leadership – ideology – and communication that works against itself. For every force, there is an equal and opposite force, this is a natural law, and thinking is powerful.

Lesson: "What you vividly imagine, ardently desire, you will evidently achieve if you just give it enough consideration." When in doubt I find that retracing my steps, back to the known ground, it does not take as many steps, backward, as it does finding the path in the dark, without a clear course and getting lost eventually, because I had no map. This is why reverse engineering is so powerful; it has map. With reference points – the ability to pinpoint your current location, the ability to find yourself with orientation. In summary, it is tough to effect meaningful lasting change and to be effective. Positive attitudes conquer all. Staying positive however is hard, especially if one suffers mentally draining and spiritually dampening experiences consecutively and consistently. Getting up after a hard fall and mounting your horse takes a lot of courage. To define this required courage, so that it makes sense for not everyone is simple, we all perceive strength differently. The truth is, that we have to let go; we have to let go of our urgency addiction, our need for instant gratification and our need for control. Nevertheless, we believe that the very basics of this fundamental principle are the creation of unity of mind-set. We have entertained the crux of the value alignment model, the golden triangle and will ponder on this aspect some more-and-more with every chapter henceforth to give it meaning, the one thing that we miss is the concept of instant gratification that spoils this opportunity and we are all urgency addicted and hate waiting for good things to happen. The thing about being urgency addicted is this, instant cash, instant soup, instant food, have all got one thing in common, they only last for an instant, and then the gratification is also gone. The only things worth living for are the ones that are lasting, but the thing with them all is that they take time, effort and a deep desire to become more.

A leader will emerge within you by becoming the thinker and not just the dreamer; you will become that which you always sought – living with a higher sense of purpose. Talking about finding direction and making sense in life and the stuff we always want answered. Well, my philosophy is simple, it is all about choices and every day you are given and driven by choices. Choices belong to a hierarchy within our needs pyramid, most of them are guided by what we want rather than by what we need. Order must prevail, if we just get all the wants, our needs will have to be sacrificed. People need order, they need rules, it gives them a sense of security and fairness. Everything has a place, a time and a purpose in our hectic socially structured lives, again this is by choice, if we choose it, then we live it. In other words, our lives are only the sum of our own choices; if we choose hectic lifestyles, we will have hectic ones. This is the only way we can successfully affect balance, by choice, nothing in our lives will change if we do not choose it to be so. How we choose and what we choose will affect us. Therefore, we need to make decisions about our choices, based on our daily situations, things change fast, and new emergence impact on us unexpectedly. The complexity this creates within ourselves, trying to establish order and overcome panic, relates back to our order of merit in prioritising things of importance in our lives first vs. other things we have no control over. What we think about we attract. How the one affects the other through choices and deliberation dictate what becomes of us. This aspect will mostly certainly differ within every situation according to our programming, mood, frame of reference and experiences. However, the fundamental role that human emotion, intelligence, thinking and choice has on every aspect of strategy has been covered extensively now, we are just redressing it here, mainly because it has seldom been considered or covered as part of the strategic thinking process. From here on out we will wrap it up and only deal with the attributes of strategy itself. Chapter seven deals with the "Self" – and will conclude the section on how we as people, managers and leaders impact on strategy as people, from our paradigms. This becomes the flipside of the golden triangle of strategy.

The flipside of the Golden Triangle:

We should not disregard, neither over emphasise the real importance and value of a good strategic mind. The psychological state of our mind and our emotional wellbeing, as well as our physical demeanour is all an essential and integral part of our success formula.

The Physical body vs. Strategic momentum: In life, good health is key to our overall performance. Man viewed as multifaceted "machine", with a mental and physical union; whichever way it has a direct impact on our parts to be functioning in balance, in order to function at our optimum level of proficiency. People that say they are trying are in fact lying, about them trying, they do not have the will to think, that is why they say, "I will try". In high stress situations, we sense and feel pressure. The body, soul and mind take equal amounts of pressure strain and stress that drain our will to achieve greater things and consequently think. We are only as strong as our weakest point. This aspect will not affect us all unilaterally - in the same manner as it were - everybody has his or her own unique threshold. Personal and professional diversity is what separates the men from the boys, the winners from the losers, the ability to wilfully do something or choose not to. This character trait that divides the successful from the not so successful is driven by ones willpower. This is the aspect that creates and sustains our momentum in life, to drive others and ourselves onwards, forward, only with strong conviction do we breed strong willpower and people. Willpower creates momentum.

Our Mind vs. Our Mapping – The Growing of willpower comes from an ardent belief in success, like evolution, where exploring and learning is viewed as the keys to unlocking this. It too is a process, from being a sheep just following the herd, then following the norm, then becoming a predator, and then becoming vigilant takes powerful surges of mental and physical energy. Recalibrating the mind-set during induction into radical strategy takes time likewise; you have to test the new theories and bring them into effect one-by-one, to see what will work for you and them. Radical strategy is about an awakening, utilising our total awareness, to new possibility by getting people to think differently about challenges, and therefore effectively; it is a culture of self-realisation. Thereby ascertaining freedom and gaining more responsibility to serve. Change comes from within, bringing a new dimension to the table that you for one believe in, a changed mind-set, with a new map, and a working compass – like that of a predator. We have to embark on the process of reengineering ourselves first, we have to become hungry, blood thirsty, by viewing, every concept, project and attribute we require to change. The focal point for thinking - from the other side of the thinking spectrum. Many books express our desires for change by saying and claiming that "from this day forward you and I will become a changed man", by just thinking positive - do we ever. No, we have to work towards the creation of the new, by changing the way we think, about innovation, abundance, and draw upon the internal as well as external universe. When we think from the ideal to the now situation, then we create twice, firstly by changing our thinking and then by charting the way for doing it. The more we think reverse engineering the more we act in reverse engineering mode and the more we will arrive at the foreseeable. Again; "What you vividly imagine, ardently desire you will evidently achieve". To imagine it first, we have to be able to visualise our concepts, this is called mapping. Mapping concepts so that the mind can get a firm grasp on them, you have to see it to believe it, to describe it, to feel it, to achieve it.

Spiritual vs. Orientation - in our normal day-to-day life we mostly affect our choices based on the situations or people at hand. We have a good feel for the concepts they emanate. When in future mode we lack the same principle.

Daily we make our choices based on:

- "The things we have to do",
- "The things we need to do",
- "The things we still can do" and then,
- "The things we still want to do".

The Radical Revolutionary Strategic Management Matrix For Predators

In every day-life most of us just live and hope it all will get better, sometimes things do, and sometimes they don't, this is not enough for strategy formulation. Day to day life is about the current reality, it does not change much, whereas the future changes like seasons, in tandem with what we think and do. Our thoughts and actions in the past, dated the current situation, and season we are in. Instead of just trying every day, rather be connected and start doing things in a planned predetermined fashion, do not ever become distant from your future, especially from those you need to build trust and a credit with, those that need to come along. We are and always have been created as pack animals, herd animals, we belong to preconceived structures, and guiding principles. Structures and principles dictate how we act and think, like being grateful for what we have, and showing gratitude.

Life is about attitude; in all spheres of life, an area of control or influence, visualise what you want to materialise. Visualise your destiny, that desired end result. You have to choose it, to see it materialise, to get it. This is still not enough, you need one more element, to be emotionally attached to the associations you build with people, and things, even your future, the feeling of things. With that statement, I would like to ask the question now, how does one seek one's purpose without feeling?

All religions have some dimension of commonality pertaining to the essence of things and how they make us feel, believing in providence and predestination – creates feelings. If this is still the case then why are we still fighting it so vigorously? Why do we try so hard to plan our future into the future with the greatest of detail, but we just don't feel it? We all worry about the future in greatest of detail; that's a feeling, however its negative, what's going to happen to me, my children, to the extent where we lose sleep over it, lose hope and lose our self-control and value. By endeavouring to be livening in the future, we have to conjure up all the worst-case scenarios until our minds become so busy that we cannot focus on the current reality anymore. It just all feels wrong. We tend to lose our "focus" on what is truly important and in which direction we should be travelling to find "it", because we lose our emotions, the feelings of joy, and the excitement that great expectations create. Mainly because of our internal longing to be somewhere or with someone in the future, the important questions and choices we make today, will predict where we will arrive in the future. Be it physically or mentally, we have to suffer mental transformation by gaining new insight, to create the required tested insight. When we have required insight – the knowledge required – then it should generate positive feelings, feelings create moods, and mood sets the stage for action or procrastination. This aspect in effect complicates our lives more than anything, just a little thing like a feeling, could create unnecessary friction, or emotion. Life is simple, people make things complicated (because they need to feel) and it is people themselves that have this tendency to want to complicate things because of the way they feel about them – we tend to only see and concentrate on the negative, where we see no strategy. What is so hard, if it is so simple? For some, it is the big things in life, for others the small, that gives them joy. Joy emits when they just take care of their spouse and children and on the other hand, that which they have been given to take care of, it might just be a dog, and everything else then seems so insignificant to them. Well If this is true in your life, then this is what you will always have, because this is your desire, your dream. The same with strategy, it is not difficult. It is feelings colliding with facts that make it complicated. The principle here is the law of desirability; it holds that we attract what we feel for and think about, the things we want and desire, we more regally entertain. The *desirability* of a strategist, is educating people, to rid them of mental impoverishment before strategising becomes the main aim. You have to sell a "political agenda" before we get to strategise. Some believe that we have been "politically" brainwashed in the past few decades, and people need to see it to believe it. We have to move from unidimensional to multidimensional thinking again. Cultural changes the world over is a good example of how powerful „politics" have become. It deals with primarily changes of thinking imposed on a race or group through politics. Politics exist in the work place as well. Politics have penetrated cultures and lifestyle through our emotions, and we have changed, not just based on facts and beliefs, but because of emotions, all created by politics. Political agendas are strong in unidimensional thinking – the – "we are one", and - "one for all and all for one" - ideology. All strategically conceived aims promoted by thinking only. In the cultural sphere of politics, the socialist revolution promoted socialist ideology along this vine as a prelude to revolution, transforming Russia from communist to capitalist. The ultimate goal was the implementation of "correct thinking", you have to think like us to be like us or more especially, create the understanding of how to be us. The underlying objective was the creation of communism, the promised kingdom, and to guarantee the state of wellbeing and the people of happiness. Now the symbols have changed. Good strategists know the value of politics and use it.

We are multidimensional in our thinking, choices and emotions, and therefore truly vulnerable as a result, if we do not understand strategy in all its forms, it could be the end of us when we are couched into "unidimensional thinking". Unidimensional thinking, has only one person thinking and the rest following blindly. Each one of these segments, the physical, mental or spiritual can steer us at any given time, to pursue our desires. All people have one thing in common, they desire things. Some desire earthly things, and prosperity, or all things on an economic plane – then some physical pleasure, and then some spiritual – it is all good. However it has to coincide with the ascertaining of significance, through freethinking, there has to be a point to it, all of it, it has to feel good. However, freedom to think does not always and necessarily entail freethinking either. Freethinking means that the human being is able to progress from facts to generalisations, or vice versa – to descend from the greatest abstractions to the most specific realities. In order to avoid disturbing the process, of thinking, the thinking person has to treat many a generalised idea or theory with scepticism, and develop from it concrete examples of events, as an appropriate means of thinking without ignoring or despising philosophy. Experience creates meaning, derived as knowledge from it, particularly from or through sensory observation, and not derived from the application of logic; nor should s/he prefer empirical facts to abstractions. Therefore, just because we are intertwined, and what we desire will influence our moods and our mental stability, as will it others; we have to stay open minded. We have to consider how we choose, between the physical, our thinking and the spiritual side, pertaining to our desires and the consequences thereof. Our actions and focus in pursuit of our desires will attract what we will have in our lives, how we will feel think and act accordingly. Our ideas, our views and our interactions in relationships on many levels are being challenged by this merging multi-dimensional shift of consciousness – we have become conscious of our ability to think about thinking. Even our religious beliefs and convictions define how we act and inter act, feel and react, as well as how we make decisions, and this is how others perceive us, by the way we think, and act. Therefore, stay close to personal truth and endeavour to remain balanced in all spheres always: do not try to rationalise everything that you get criticised for. For instance, when you are told that you are overworking yourself or enjoying too much of a physical pleasure, it is more often than not - the truth. Change your view; look outside in it could change the total perspective on your outlook. The time you spend slaving away at rationalising is lost. Never ever, let the main focus in your life become the only driving force in your life, namely work or the pursuit of desires. Life is just too short to just spend all your time and energy in one dimension, everything we want we will obtain, if we seek it in all dimensions. How we choose to use our multidimensional abilities, is the key to happiness. Furthermore, certain things should just be left to take their own natural course. This does not imply that we have to work ourselves to death or just let things slide, no, our actions and thoughts should create wealth. Whatever we choose wealth to be should make us content. True wealth equals happiness. Find inner joy first then the outer things will manifest, and we will all be wealthy in one way or the other. In western terms, "wealth' equals "capital"... The true meaning of wealth creation should be aligned with a total package, that includes good relationships with family, friends, a hobby, health, and spiritual gifts, not one dimension should take preference to the point where it becomes disproportionate. The titles and fame, will never bring you the things that bring long lasting love, fun, or true satisfaction. We need to recharge our willpower daily to carry on, and it is only trough spiritual interaction that we do. Spiritual things are only to be found in the hearts of loved ones, and the things that make us feel good about who we are and what we do. Live and work with joy, it creates new energy. The key to true success that is lasting is ascertaining balance, balance between what you wish for and what you work for. There must be a correlation between the two, they must not contradict each other. Yes, it is very "Noble" to be called a "Workaholic". However, give to yourself to experience fullness, so that you can give to others with delight. Repairing a relationship is like trying to repair a broken ship, the longer you wait the more water it takes on until it eventually sinks. You cannot function at optimum levels if you are letting your mind run around looking for the rest of the "101 Dalmatians" type of scenario. By desperately trying to get all those puppies into one basket so that you can find some sort of rest and inner peace, takes time and organisation. What are the chances? We cannot control the happiness or anger of other people, we cannot ask of others to create our happiness like wise. Emotions control our inner mind, that in turn controls our inner peace and happiness. If you are upset with someone else, it does nothing to them – in the same way that it influences you. In addition, such is life. However, if we surrender the future and the day-to-day stuff, then we only have to focus on getting 12 puppies, strategic ones, into the basket, they go in one by one, in our time spent doing so it will be 100 times more productive and rewarding, this reduces stress, this is the point we would like to make. Rearrange you busy mind to focus on what really and truly matters, as would a predator, focuses on the blood spoor, and the kill – and do not try to catch the whole heard in one go - yes? This could work for you – "you never know", let's explore this maxim.

Lesson on assumption and feelings:

"You never know" – a Chinese parable

Long ago, near China's northern borders lived a man well versed in the practices of Taoism. His horse, for no reason at all, got into the territory of the northern tribes. Everyone sympathised with him.

"Perhaps this will soon turn out to be a blessing," said his father. "You never know" After a few months, his animal came back, leading a fine horse from the north. Everyone congratulated him. "Perhaps this will soon turn out to be a cause of misfortune," said his father. "You never know" Since he was well-off and kept good horses his son became fond of riding and eventually broke his thighbone falling from a horse. Everyone commiserated with him. "Perhaps this will soon turn out to be a blessing," said his father. "You never know"

One year later, the northern tribes started a big invasion of the border regions. All able-bodied young men took up arms and fought against the invaders and as a result, around the border nine out of ten men died. This man's son did not join in the fighting because he was crippled and so both the boy and his father survived. Life takes many unexpected turns, therefore serving and surviving takes from our physical, mental and spiritual energy. The law of desirability; holds that we attract what we feel for and think about, the things we want and desire, we more regally entertain. Never in the history of the world or the consciousness of man, has a time been more exciting to entertain that which we desire. Embrace the multi-dimensional shift of consciousness, embrace the changes it brings, welcome the opportunity to experience your life from expanded views by being open-minded and receptive, you just might like what you see. There is no difference when we enter into strategy. I like radical change – but believe me it never takes place without resistance. "You never know", how life will turn, I have lost some friends and colleagues over expanded views. I assure you it has always paid huge dividends well worth the sacrifices made – even to them that stood opposed. Nevertheless, it was always mutually beneficial, never vindictive. There is a time to be a sheep and then there comes a time to move on and become more, get your mind around this aspect of change, change is good and it is part of life. The hard reality of this sector where we implement continuous change is this, very few tend to enjoy the ride. If you are playing it safe, then you are taking short cuts and many of us like playing it safe all the time, it gives us a sense of security, mark my words it will catch up with you eventually and then change will seem like the end to you. Rather save yourself the embarrassment later, of being forced to change. Rather let someone else take your place – in the comfort zone - because you are in a comfort zone when we procrastinate, give it up, move on and give it to someone else. Get out of your comfort zone and you will experience pure joy again. You will be able to label the "New Stuff" yours, fun and exciting. Rightfully so, you are now the architect, that will be getting rewards you never imagined. Just by stepping outside of the "fish bowl" – that office, where you spend half your life – rather go and meet people, see people – network – share your ideas, the strongest force is the one that comes from the source of many. What this implies is sell your vision, talk the talk and then walk the walk. Exchange views, do research and find truth and you will find your direction? It beats the "Bowl" any day, where everyone can watch you like a gold fish. Everyone knows exactly what you are up to, the walls have ears you know. Jump into the sea of knowledge, at the chance of embracing others in the same world, taste new waters of wisdom, the world and the knowledge of management is vast and daily someone somewhere is pioneering something new where you could add value, "you never know". I have learned and grown much by following this paradigm.

William Hastie said: "History informs us of past mistakes from which we can learn without repeating them. It also inspires us and gives confidence and hope bred of victories already won."

Many, no thousands of books exist on the topic of "designing" good strategy.

" He who rejects change is the architect of decay. The only human institution which rejects progress is the cemetery." ~ Harold Wilson.

"Excellences is an art won by training and habitation. We do not act rightly because we have virtue or excellence, but rather we have acted rightly. We are what we repeatedly do. Excellence, then, is not an act but a habit." ~Aristotle.

This chapter deals with those required parts. Having good strategic focus is not good enough anymore, we must have 20/20 vision. This perspective will be enhanced, with critical thinking, and concept thinking in the following chapters. Creation is a strategic concept; the building blocks for strategy, derived from many sources, then finding the right relationship to make a total concept this is the key to radical strategy...

 Finding the right strategic fit, is both essential and critical. In order to clear our preconceived views of how to initiate strategy; by only going through a process of putting ideas on paper, disseminating it, and then waiting for the results, is out dated. Strategy conception today relies on our ability for recognising the relationship of parts that form a total concept. What we see, is how we see strategy, and this is what others will see, when we show them.

For instance -how do we see;

- Control vs. Destiny – where does control stop and destiny start?
- Choice vs. Change – how much choice do we have in change?
- Failure vs. Success – is failure a prerequisite to success?
- Balance vs. Self-Worth – does personal balance require worth?
- Production vs. Capacity – is production related to capacity?

These hidden elements of perception cause flaws, they are our blind spots, even with seemingly perfect strategy, and well schooled and trained strategic veterans, we have seen them not checking their blind spots. Veterans conversed in the theories of good business and strategy, even they still make bad strategic decisions, because they don't have 20/20 view. While in some instances ignorance and pride sometimes also plays a role, the cognitive itself -how we think-is sited as the culprit. Insights from behavioural science help explain why we don't always think rationally and how our logical flaws can lead to serious flaws and bad strategic decisions.

Control vs. destiny: The first significant step in preparing strategy is to understand the significance of control variables and its attributes affects strategy. Strategy does not exist and function in a vacuum, it relies on its habitat to flourish. The "habitat" has both a direct as well as indirect impact on the excelling or inhibiting effect on the people that are now responsible to perform tasks to get the strategy to work. The potential of our strategy to succeed will depend on our systems and methods of intervention and control alignment. If not aligned we will lose control as we pick up speed, to the point where strategy fails. Either because we strangle it, or let it run wild, because of our control mechanism. The second aspect is; the ability to embrace change as something good and both essential. The third one is, a required ability to see relationships in their duality; for what they truly are and not only for what we perceive them to be.

Where others only see complexity and chaos with global changes coming about today, true strategist will seek and find alternatives by looking and studying relationships, their parts; this is our goal as strategist, to gain above average insight on how to solve chaos. By firstly studying the relationships formed by parts, their attributes and the identifiable elements that provoke instability, that ultimately leads to chaos. Having succeeded at strategy once or twice does not necessarily guarantee repeated success, thus it relates back to the continuous sharpening of the strategic blade, the strategic mind must be filled with unambiguous practice of the tools of the trade to form the traits and habits of success.

Only those who choose to accept that continuous transformation of perception and ideology is an integral part of staying abreast of developments, and on the cutting edge of innovation, will master the overall resilience of the strategic mind and therefore master strategy. Our personality, the very self, our ego, has everything to do with our effectiveness as strategist, and our leadership abilities, it becomes the total sum of us. The way we influence the growth path, and outcome of events resides in our mind-set, because we leave our signature on every aspect of strategy we conceive. Strategic change in thinking is therefore crucial and never ending, but only effective if we can change people's strategic habits along with it. By only changing ours and our own way of thinking along without affecting others is senseless. By aligning our perceptions of how things "should get done", and what the outcome "must be", with how things "are being done and what we could expect things to be" if we let them. Change then becomes a strategy in itself, where we view strategy not just as a mere calculation, but it has to be encompassing all essentials. Strategy is therefore only effective if the changes we made were effective if it becomes interrelated; it has to connect the abilities of people and our choices as leaders on where we are going and how we are going to get there, into one working relationship. This then implies that any transform must effect a chain of events, with elements and attributes, to the extent that each relationship benefits. At each level, we need to address the complexity of constants and variables that will come into play. Just like DNA strands, it all has to fit, connect and gel, to achieve both internal and external balance. In other words, the "resolution" has to fit in with the prevailing circumstance, to become the ultimate "solution" to the problem as it was created. The solution must not just work, but work for all, it must not create new friction. If no amicable results were achieved in this union and formation of parts forming relationships, forming a chain of activity, then it was not the right choice. One strategy must encompass all the attributes of a problem, we tend to devise too many strategies and then they compete with each other, in terms of resources, capital and time. By choosing right, we avoid a lot of unnecessary resulting chaos, and uncertainty, and mostly consequential choices are a result of haphazard thinking - bad personal strategic habits – where we want quick fixes.

Habits, becomes our nature, therefore we have to refer from using too much of our own choices and influences initially, and get to grips with the perceptions of others first. Strategic excellence requires from strategist to recognise the elements that becomes the strategic cocktails ingredients, as they exist in minds firstly, then in practice, before we seek a resolve. The constants- the things we cannot change – and the variables – the things we can change must be sorted. Furthermore, being able to differentiate the facts from personal perceptions, and our own input takes time, and then marrying the goal into one union is a delicate path of assembling. The strategist job is to find alternate relationships, workable alternatives, and then create new relationships with them, that become one successful union – and strong strategy. The purpose of strategy is to solve as many problems as possible with one great effort, and to get normality, and sustainability as a result. This will require change.

Therefore, **change is** in two fold – **two required parts**, the one-part is the *constants* and the other part is the *variables* - thus circumstantial in nature. We have to cluster our thinking into those parts we can control, and those parts that are left to destiny. Furthermore, to this, we have to recognise and find the opposing forces, those forces that work with and against us as a person, a group, and a sector. All the - constants and variables, have to be identified. The minds power to effect changes is unlimited, based on the fact that we only use 5% of it, only by our own choice do we impose limitations on what we see as achievable, or what we deny ourselves to see – yes we limit our potential because of insecurities, and perceptions, we even dampen our own potential because we choose to follow denial. This creates an energy that we project, if you think a thing can be done or not, then you are right, either way. Everything in life exists because of energy, energy existing in two opposing states; positive and negative, taking turns. The universe is a continuum of interrelated systems of energy that affect one another. We observe that some events take place at random - both termed good and bad – and others as planned. Whichever way, they are still controlling and influencing us with the energy they emit; like ripples in a pond – call it the result of choices (by whomever) and changes (of whatever nature), they are all interrelated. These instances often change or redefine, and even influence our next course of action/s for us. Therefore change has two parts, the one part being that which we can **control** (seen as positive) – the controllable - and the other that which we "cannot"(seen as negative) – call it **destiny**. To deal with this aspect on a strategic landscape we need to acquire "strategic currency".

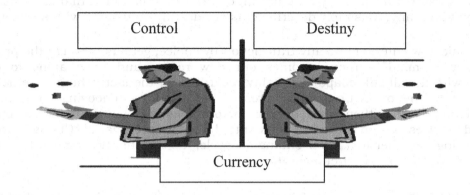

Acquiring the secrets of strategic "currency"; the ability to make relevant strategic choices in the face of positive and negative energy – and dealing with this complexity. In order to affect feasible change – we require this insight to negotiate strategy well.

We have to realise that the distinction between "Choice and Change" are two parts of one coin - a conundrum; the economics of decision making that influences our reality. Just as with real currency, we get more done with strong currency, than with weak. Strong and weak currencies, translate directly into negative growth and positive growth, such is the nature of "strategic currency" and strategy. It is either strong or weak, depended on our choices and the changes we envisage – and our (personal) strategic thinking habit. Whether or not "choice" falls inside or outside our control span (how much say we think we have) in the matter of choice? The fact of the matter is, the power of choice is from within, what we choose becomes our focus, which becomes our destiny. Our ability to choose well; will reveal our inherent strength or otherwise weakness. By choosing right we expand our sphere of influence, by choosing wrong we contract in significance. Simply put, the strength of choice is the fulcrum, the key to change, influenced by the options and opinions that we exercise or entertained that go along with choosing, the more options we have to negotiate, the stronger strategy becomes, and so also the speed of changes we desire. Furthermore, the closer we are to choices we have to make – the better we understand what is at stake – the greater our sphere of influence. Our knowledge, experience, skill and understanding boosts us - the stronger our influence becomes, and the more energy we radiate. However, the further away from our sphere of influence, the weaker it gets. This is the power of control span, you either are close to the core of the problem and understand its nature in full or you are at the other end of the spectrum, perceiving it. Strange thing with all things related to choices on the type of control we wish to have over it; it tends to take a natural course, it follows like a river, with the path of least resistance, called potential, it either has a potential to go very wrong or develop into something great. Whatever the mind can conceive, it has the ability to achieve it is said. Therefore, if we think it won't work then it will not. Influence therefore becomes an energy, that can derail or hamper our strategic path, dictated by our ability to conceive it as real, if we cannot see things clearly, then we perceive it as danger, then chances are we revert to the default, and set ourselves up to fail, and leave the outcome to destiny so to speak. Destiny in this regard is seen as the natural phenomenon's that occur like seasons, it influences people, their moods, markets, trade... everything has an order, a rhythm a flux, that requires choices, and where we don't have any, we simply describe it as our destiny, and same with strategy.

It is very ironic how entering into any transaction by choice, gets us to weigh the pros and cons - "this currency of mind" - then becomes our new reality and how failing to do anything constructive with it, will still shape our reality regardless of the fact, whether we acted or not. If we do not seize the opportunities life presents of "trade" – choosing to think about the consequences and plan - then someone else, or our "destiny" will do it for us. Life and living requires and revolves around these two constants, before we act, that of "Changes and Choices" – the one following the other in a never-ending life cycle, as the only two constants to our progress and growth, the rest is purely circumstantial.

To explain this. Just like a coin does not change physical form. Although it changes hands and buys stuff. The same with self, we do not change physical form as our worth increases, but our mental energy becomes our potential wealth. Life itself is a process of continued metamorphosis of forms of energy, in other words change. We start out as a form and as we grow so grows our worth. From what was, to what is, to what will be, or towards what we want by choice. We have to embrace change as a set process, unavoidable if we want to progress, just as time and season's changes. If we want summer, we first have to make way for autumn, winter and spring. We have to realise that every change, will bring about a succession of changes before it reaches its ultimate destination. The journey has equal and opposite effects on us, that will evoke a cause, for a response. We have to contemplate this always when making a choice, especially a strategic one, and check that our assumptions are not flawed, out dated, or irrelevant. Because very action creates a response, and a equal and opposite reaction, this has to be contemplated and not left to chance or destiny.

Strategic planning is all about contemplating all the variables, influences, drivers and all the seasons required to make it through a year. It is about summoning the strength, or collectives, wisdom, power and knowledge, of all our past choices and what they were based on to create a new future. By planning with both some amount of certainty and uncertainty for the worst, and thinking beyond the initial limitations of our choosing. Then – only by choosing right do we start a habit of giving rise to the changes we wish to see, by being able to predict the next course of events, because we have steered this path before successfully. We have to realise that all choices about change - alone is worthless if we don't have the experience it created, it is how we plan to realise a specific goal and the choices that go into the planning, that must create the focus we require to see the relationships forming - that makes it become valuable. It may necessitate a continued metamorphosis of beliefs and views as the plan starts transpiring, changing the way we plan – utilising our potential; our skills and knowledge as products of our own growth -, before we arrive at the desired state – with our strategy. The point is strategy is not cast in stone, it has to be resilient and adaptable.

Moreover, we have to realise that we will have changed nothing; if we do not change anything significantly enough to effect radical changes. Planning is only one part, nothing significant will happen in our lives if not by choice and incident. Either way; the point to make here is this, this sword cuts both ways; **change** comes about by choice or incident, and **choice** comes about by an incident that forces us to change. Whichever way the coin drops, heads or tail; it will always have an emotionally inspiring energy that it brings with it, or cause a disrupting emotional effect on our inner balance when dealing with this aspect – everything we are affects everything we do.

Therefore, it is either physically and or both mentally inspiring and draining when we have to conceive strategy, we experience mental emancipation or numbness and we become emotionally charged or disabled when dealing with the two extremes of choice and change. Strategy is about finding the two opposing parts that form the one whole; everything in life has two equal, but opposing parts that can be united in balance. We tend to perceive feelings in either direction daily by dealing with this aspect.

Mostly we don't know what to do if we cannot see the distinction between two parts forming one, or show balance when the coin falls wrong, we become a ruptured being, we experience total loss of energy; spiritually, physically and mentally it taps into all our resources of energy. Our circumstances can at times take us down the rapids of depression and despair, we see no way out, and we then lose control. Then we tend to follow path of most resistance, because we don't focus on potential, we focus on the negative, when we are down and out. I for one have never heard or seen anyone on treatment for being high on life, for succeeding, etc.; however the contrary is very true.

The self. Then why can the "SELF" not handle the opposing part of the whole? If we are the architects of strategy then our input must be filtered, so that we do not get any negative or harmful ideas to flow as a consequence of our emotion state and wellbeing. When the self, becomes ruptured, where things are not going well, then internal forces causes a loss of energy, thus resulting in imbalances throughout the system. Internal balance can only be restored once we have prepared ourselves for this instability, we will not always work in environments that are pleasant, and conducive to team work, some may be hostile and very negative, also the result of emotional rupturing, a required process by the way, it dislodges us from our beliefs that brought us to this juncture, it forces us to changing how we use to see things, by making them negative things. We prepare feverously to win and achieve, constantly, but we very seldom prepare to fail, like wise we don't plan for exit strategies. Strategy and human habits follow the same direction. Think of it in terms of a metamorphosis gone wrong. Things taking place in a space that is too small, that only has room for one form of energy, either positive or negative. Where positive energy, is seen to be the soul of strategy. Where any being refuses to be transfer from the one to the next form, it resist because of its perception, it has to be torn from the old creature and be transferred to the new, a very violent emotional process. Just like moving into a new house, we are very eager and excited, and then with time it wears off as reality sets in, then, at first, we feel very unsettled but as time passes, it grows on us. This is where we have to concentrate more time on, the soul of strategy, the spiritual side, we need to prepare it for the move, the negativity, and give it time to come to grips with change and a new reality. Only through total preparation in either direction of the spectrum will we succeed at strategy. Strategy like self, aims to follow the path of least resistance – the required routine, where it can exercise choice. This requires total preparation.

"Total preparation", the bank account for strong strategic currency:

Life is like rowing a canoe. If good times can be compared to flat lakes, and rapids like torrent times. Then being in a canoe on a flat lake for all your life and then out of nowhere a huge waterfall appears will spell sure disaster. Out of the mist, we hear the terrifying rumble, the waters of the lake is speeding up and no matter how hard we try, it just pulls us in and you fall over the side of it. The warning signs were all there, but we chose to ignore it, we did not take the time spiritually and mentally to prepare, then during the fall, we experience this huge mental numbness. If we have never experienced such events, it will be unsettling and we could drown in our despair or rise above the event and carry on depending on our preparation.

The point is this; life presents us with multiple choices daily, and occasionally with imminent disaster. We handle each event differently. Yet we expect by some miracle that everyone will act as excepted when we dish out our strategy. Yet, we are all different, some of us like to travel at night, others at day, but both tend to steer away from those situations that require major change in their set routine. Our preferences dictate our habits that prescribe how we choose the path of least resistance. Because of our routine minded nature, we avoid things that will be out of the ordinary, we are creatures of habit. Instead of opting for change, we choose routine; it gives us a sense of security. In a world where sacrifice wears an overall and effort pushes the wheelbarrow – nothing is routine anymore. Many run at the site of sacrifice and effort, for it implies work for sure, hard work, and sacrifice on our part, and the break with our favourite routine. We immediately start resisting, a great desire fill us to escape, a temptation to bail out, and give up and run. Keeping your head whilst others around you are losing theirs in circumstance like these, is no joke. We do not want to undergo these experiences; we had rather put it off, either out of fear or stupidity. By implication, we rob ourselves of the learning experience it would have created. The truth is that in some instances, change requires from us, to change our habits, perceptions and in some instance even our routine, just to get us through a season. We do this naturally with our clothing, as seasons change, but boy is it difficult to get our minds around this paradigm, to adapt to it when it comes to strategy.

We want to stay on the calm lake, where things are simple, where we can go about our daily routines and the lake will always be there when we get back. Although some of us have chosen to go down the odd stream here and there - to improve on our fitness, some have gone on a diet, read a good book, took some time out. These are the trips over the small waterfalls, because of a heightened sense for adventurous nature. Thereby gaining more experience and knowledge and only they learn how to make small emergency repairs along the riverbank. The sealing of small ruptures, by having taken the time out; some call it leave, family time, or a night out, that could have lead to imbalance if not, because we were taking on too much water – responsibilities – that adds weight to our canoe. These habits form pearls of wisdom - by having chosen to do so, sometimes we are so close to the wall that we do not see the door – we only ascertain new skills and energy to balance our hectic lives with when we take time to stand down. When these people have to face the big events in life, the huge waterfall, they have prior essential knowledge to navigate the fall, they also have a support system to fall back on; they have formed a required skill of repair and maintenance – a essential habit – recalibrating balance by living a diversified life of equal portions. This in itself is no guarantee that they, themselves, will survive every fall. The significance of this aspect is, that strategy follows us first and not us it, only when the task of formulating a strategy is finished, do the roles change. The better we are prepared, the more enhanced our strategies will be. Conversely, this natural balance and our hopes and dreams, can only be restored after having survived the huge waterfalls of epic change in life. It is no good having dreams and hopes only, if you cannot effectively steer your canoe on the lakes, streams and rivers of circumstances, and whatever it conceals below - towards the ocean of eternal life. One needs to become radically minded to push the limits of our mental and social containment, in order to see all things as inter related - in order to prevail. Both as an individual and with strategy. We need to explore more, understand more, sacrifice more and dare more, both emotionally and spiritually, we have to get the overalls on and push the wheelbarrow. This builds lasting character trait's and experience, creating the required insight required for strategy, experience. To be a bit more radically minded is to be more effective. We have to realise that neither our results, nor our self-worth can help us to survive the huge falls in life. Only by choice do we prevail against incredible odds, by building on our mental resilience to deal with change effectively, we are in fact creating a "can do attitude". Growth in all aspects of the word goes along with experiences; they are in tandem with one and other. Without taking the radical leaps in life, we will have to make peace with our inevitable reality, because we chose never to gamble, or take a chance. We have to ask ourselves; is it worth it to be angry, to fight, to plot revenge, to give people a piece of our mind all the time, are we not just wasting precious energy by having our focus on all the wrong things. We spend so much of our valuable time engaged in activities that are of no value in our lives and many do immeasurable harm, the same with strategy, it follows us, our thinking, our habits, and our beliefs.

We are often so busy worrying about stuff that has not even happened yet, getting angry at others because they don't want to play our game, planning revenge that we have no time left to actually do anything else that is productive. There is only one question to ask if you are here. "Can I do anything about it?" If the answer is yes then do it, if the answer is no, then all the worry, anger and revenge in the world won't help – will it. Thinking like this is like chewing gum for the mind; it keeps you busy, the flavour of the moment feeds the fragile ego and we feel in control for a while, then it fades as reality sinks in, it gets you nowhere. ***Is it worth it?***

Getting the required natural mental balance back to succeed at strategy is pivotal to success.

It is said; that what we focus on we get more off, if we focus on bliss, we get more of it, therefore, energy flows where attention goes, what are you focusing on – not think or planning – but focusing on, will determine what you will get. The plan/ strategy could be focusing on going left, but we subconsciously are focusing on going right. This process equates to rowing, we require a force on both sides of us, the left paddle is to the right; opposed but the same, both required for rowing, steering and balance. If the left paddle on the ore is **change,** and the right is **choice**, then this equals two strokes on our journey towards progress and personal growth. Although, by only experiencing and exercising **choice**, thus rowing with the right paddle or on the right side only, we will find ourselves going around in circles. Just making choices and thus achieve nothing meaningful, just choosing something won't make it happen, as only one paddle will be rowing. We will still achieve movement by choosing it, if our burden is heavy we might just lose balance in the process and topple over, or allow circumstances to take us - the currents - will then determine our destination. If it chooses you and takes you, you will then be thrown over many waterfalls without choice and you might not fall into the next lake, for on this river of life you could find yourself in rapid after rapid, such is nature and such is life. Until you desire change and choose it. Balance will return the moment that we "choose" and "change", when we row with the "left" and the "right" paddle again, now we could also take control and steer our course and break free of the currents. The lesson taught here is this. By failing to choose change, our circumstance will become our master and you its servant. Only by choice do we gain momentum. By changing a habit that forced us only to row with a left paddle, and move on with our lives the way we want it to, the left and the right paddle, choice and change, creates the motion required to experience control and establish balance in the self – the canoe - on the waters of life.

On Failure – Failure becomes our personal fertiliser:

Just like natural fertiliser, failure stinks, but without learning from it, the fruits of our labour and crop will be small, colourless and tasteless. Only with fertiliser can we achieve excellence and quality, colour and a great tasting crop. We will have to experience failure then from time to time as a required process, except it as if a required ingredient to success, for it truly is, as we except and experience life and death. Yes, it's all right to grieve and cry and be angry at failure like death, it is this experience that makes us appreciate life and success. The failure teaches us valuable lessons, that become our fertiliser, if and when we use those lessons, a required process in personal growth. The same with success, if we do not choose it, we stand to lose it to someone else. In conclusion; failure we do not want and we do not want to choose to fail. Failure is no longer an obstacle to success; it is the fertiliser; it forces us to reconsider and evaluate our assumptions and options. The same as the canoeist who has to leave the river at times during the race. In order to find a better view of the self and our situation - the canoe -, to repair the damage incurred, to get some rest. Then with the dawn of a new day we see a path that we can walk, by holding this canoe, the self, above our head, we let the water of circumstances flow out, that which makes us heavy, it is the only way. We can then negotiate the obstacle with a lighter self on the other end. This becomes significant in that sometimes we cannot rely on the self alone to continue the journey; we have to rely on the spirit, the canoeist, the canoe, the ore and the paddles as parts creating one whole to get us around the obstacles, the pit stops in life.

How do you measure yourself, your worth and that of others; what is worth living for and what is worth dying for, what is worth changing for, what is my worth?

The human mind is all complex, in parts, the physical and the spiritual, same as with strategy, the physical and the unseen, forming one whole. It is with this insight that we need to know more about the significance of parts in order to understand the potential of any whole. Could it be that our attributes are the parts forming us, either good or bad and not us as a whole it? The true measure of one's worth is then locked up in our parts: our attributes, one's determination, beliefs, experiences, faith, and choice - our "currency" and knowledge to name but a few. In our quest to enhance the self in order to become, like some eternal force pulling us in all directions simultaneously at times it seems, driving us. We want many things daily, for ourselves and others, but the wanting never seems to stop. We keep wanting, and wanting more, nothing ever seems perfect. The cup never seems to fill and our thirst of wanting more never seems to be quenched. When we have tried just about every flavour life has on offer in pursuit of our wants, with knowledge -, self-indulgence -, food -, money - and career changes – all the flavours, to name but a few. Yet, our path towards finding that undefined want, it never stops, no matter how many direction changes we take in pursuit thereof, we still end up wanting something more, but what is it? We always seem to arrive right back where we started initially, having more ,but just not having enough, just having to do it all over again, wanting perfection and contentment, joy, fun, whatever drives our desires, just maybe, this time around it might just happen or so it seems. Contentment is always a short-lived victory, no one is ever perfectly content with what they have, are or strive to get, wanting becomes a driving force behind everything we do. Only once we have learned to master patience and sacrifice, only then it seems do we form the understanding of what wanting constitutes. It is a constant process of changing needs, taking us back to the principle of the "law of the harvest". We need to toil and put in the fertiliser, the time require to perform a task, planting the seeds and then we have to wait for the fruit – it is a never-ending process driven by wants. All essential elements and attributes of mind, and our strategic human nature. It forces us to use the mind in creative and constructive ways, and in doing so we gain insight, we develop tools and skills. Through the experience of our trails and error they emerge, so do our strengths and weakness. This is how we get to know our strengths and weakness. It is this aspect of becoming more, that drives us and realising that knowing becomes a process of meaningful deliberation, that develops the self. Some call it faith, or a belief system, it gives us a required spiritual strength, we seek; in order to overcome and master oneself, and to manipulate our habitat to our benefit.

The one thing that gets us to move, is fear. We fear ourselves more than what we fear death for it is the power of the mind that dictates man's future, his actions and his thoughts. It is fear then that drives us. Consequently, the gift of living we deny ourselves at times, as if we are going to cheat death by not embracing change, out of fear. Fear drives us to live a life with unfounded self-imposed limitations; we try to keep ourselves from what we do not understand. However, time and time again, it is just those fears, that keep us stuck that once overcome, only then may we experience greater understanding and achieve balance and the things we desire. We will only realise the benefit of riding rapids if we have experienced the ability to spiral above circumstances for ourselves and evolved by having done so, because of an earnest desire to concur fear. By accurately pointing out to others their mistakes, we err ourselves in that we do this on assumption, based on our own fears. Without understanding why, we keep everyone on the lakes, because it is safe. Thus far, we do not want to change ourselves, so we seek other to change our reality for us, to make the difference, on our behalf. If this is our dilemma, then we are purely focused on the negative; and the media enforces this negative paradigm for us daily, we get robbed by virtue of what other perceive the world and our situation to be. This point is relevant with strategy, addressing people's fears. Who will know what lies beyond that waterfall if someone does not cross it? If the media tells us that we will drop of the end of the world and big monsters await us on the other side. Do you think Christopher Columbus did not contemplate this and never the less took a chance. If it was not for men like him, would we all still be living in fear? We have to do this for us. However, have we ever played the part of the "Radical tour agent" and started to focus on doing the positives for ourselves, becoming the pioneer, the "rapids tour guide", it helps to empower us. Nevertheless, we cannot do this without having attempted the plunge, the change, the things we debate for hours to no end and dream about, without going over to the required action, gripped by fear. We cannot teach people balanced understanding and reasoning if we ourselves have not mastered the concept, this type of mental vision requires experiences. To explain this;

Understand first and then being understood also creates balance:

We first have to understand the nature of water – life – and then the many forms it takes on, before we can rescue others. For this very reason, we should neither impose on our self, nor others any mentally-incapacitating roadblocks - by enforcing perceptions. People, in general only change or create habits by having to do things for themselves and having gone through the experience, only then do they form the desired character. Get them to ride the small streams; this is referred to as building capacity.

We teach the importance of this principle of building skills and capacity to new parents, yet in business, we block the same principle out – we turn the emphasis from teamwork to power play. What you resist will persist. With strict orders, with; "do this" and "do that" – for adults? The old classic saying comes to mind; "my way or the high way my friend". By posting warning signs all over the – lake -, "rapids this way stay clear". We need to give control, to the leaders of tomorrow, give them the freedom to make decisions, to do things for themselves, to choose, once we have schooled them well in the ways of the river, the lake and the streams, we have to let go.

We have all made mistakes coming down the stream of life and we are bound to make some more. The importance of balance only becomes apparent once we have lost it. By losing one's balance then regaining it in an instant, only comes from learning co-ordination and reflex for oneself, thus forming the habit of balance. Once the habit is formed the learning will become absolute at some stage of our lives and become reflex, it is humanly impossible to go through life not having made any mistakes this we know. Learning, listening and observing how things ought to be done, is a very natural phenomenon, but this does not pass on the skill and part of the process of ascertaining intellectual growth, balance and forming good habits like – resilience – it only comes from having almost drowned.

Only by doing things for ourselves do we gain any meaningful experience from it, which in turn builds confidence and character, ultimately forming once again the healthy social required habit. This is how we develop life skills, job skills and ultimately leadership skills, these aspect forms equipment with which we negotiate obstacles with, the starting blocks in the race towards building capacity and competency, all the desired aspects that are very crucial yet essential for any growth.

Understanding how significant change comes about.

In order to achieve, effective changes in one's life, you first have to start from the self then. You firstly require time and then practice, patience and good guidance to master skills. Change through our knowledge gained is only the underlying aspect of any potential growth. How we utilise this knowledge is how we are defined in the end. The answer then is not just acquiring knowledge, by training people but how we breed a core of competence by guiding them, towards wisdom and balance. It is only when this holistic change becomes into effective that habits start forming and culture develops, this then becomes an effective change. Starting with "The law of the harvest", it has to prevail in order for growth to become continual and fear to dissipate. When we seek this natural foundation through habit, then we are laying solid foundations. We realise, that we cannot change the outcome of all things in life, but if we repeatedly do what has been repeatedly done in the old self, by repeating it, the results will stay the same because of a defective and out dated habits remerging.

In nature; **The law of the harvest** dictates that we prepare the soil, long before the crop and that we put in place all the nutrients and essential elements into the soil, that will give the seed the desired character to yield the desired crop. We have to repeat this cycle every three or four years, it does not stop with the first successful crop. Therefore, only through investing more "time" and much more "effort" will one reap good crops on a regular basis. Learning to listen to the winds of change more and less to the folk law... However, measuring twice and good planning is the art of building. This is the strategic way. Yes, sometimes you will need to cut through personal agendas, but the risks are small compared to the learning curve we all will experience by having done things for ourselves, we don't do anyone any favours by dragging them along.

Become a rapids tour guide. This way you are in the thick of things, and others get to do it for themselves with your guidance. Following you as a result of following this paradigm it will cascade outwards, anyone in contact with the new self will be following suit and soon everyone will become a tour guide and apprentice. Thus, producing a better skilled labour force and consequently also leaders, and creating the ultimate human crop that flourishes on teamwork. Like crops, the whole plant has to be healthy and strong, just like teams, before the fruits of mind and labour will be. Leaders are at least trying and succeeding at the same token today by dragging people along with – things like affirmative action, short term it does wonders for politics, in the long run we are setting some people up for a lifetime of failure and so to organisations, because trying is like dying, it is futile. You either do a thing right or you don't. Affirmative action is the escape goat for a lack of proper training and skills development. We have to choose it, to succeed in it, we cannot push someone towards success, we have to be realistic in our expectations as well, not every person has the same ability or desire to succeed and some will always just be sheep – because of their habits not changing. We have to change the perception, to change the habit, by virtue of having been sheep for so long, they become very content on just following the folk. They lack the aspiration, and get robbed of it, it's all easy come easy go.

Coping with change: Man himself cannot hope to cope with change if he does not have within himself found his personal reality yet, this personal reality is what forms his foundation for people to aspire to greatness, what we think about, we become and want more of. If we cannot teach life skills, to strengthen foundations, we will find ourselves with many homeless and mindless people. The same applies with a lack of good emotional, spiritual, physical as well as moral foundation or bank account. We can never just want to build our lives on one aspect as our creation, liken the outer or inner walls of a building, the same will apply to our organisations foundation and when designing a strategic plan. We should start with a solid foundation; we need to incorporate as many good aspects into our foundations as possible. So that we are assured that, our life's work will not crumble before our eyes eventually when we have completed our work by putting on the roof, of retirement. Just, because we have failed to apply the required wisdom of building on sound principles. Strategies don't fail because they were all ill-conceived, but because we apply flawed reasoning, and prepare people poorly to carry on after the expertise of the day retire. The key to surviving change and having stability within organisations, is to keep the initial efforts going. The same with finding the balance within our characters structure, that which is within us. The foundation will be our spiritual life, our religious beliefs and our mental well-being. These could be termed, our inner walls, that will be our moral and ethical and spiritual structure and the wisdom and knowledge our outer walls, our physical, character and trait's and maintaining it, like we do o house or building. Remember strategy is the building's design specifications, once done, it has no or little relevance, the building is there. How we maintain, expand and look after it is the second challenge. We can only find and maintain balance if we build on a level and strong foundation. This will only come about once we have totally grasped the concept of purposeful living, like the bricks in a building, if only one becomes dysfunctional, and brakes, it has to be replaced immediately, by same or similar, to keep serving its purpose .

Our purpose; As man, we all have a purpose, this we know and in the back of our minds this aspect has dawned upon us on several occasions, it surfaces into our conscience and floats out the same way it came in. We try desperately to come to terms with it, grab hold of it, in order to understand our existence and its purpose. Forever, trying to figure it out, to make sense of it, we have this unexplained euphoria of achieving greatness or something of that nature. How do we make sense of this, the only logical explanation is that we were predestined to be. The question is what? The answer is not always pleasing, but it relates to finding yourself, before you will find others, before you will find your destiny. We don't need to figure out everything in life, this is not our destiny or our purpose, for all knowledge will come to pass it is said, that is our preoccupation, with worldly beliefs, our purpose is not to find power, this is a personal quest. Destiny and finding destiny is not the categorizing of everything and everyone around us in order to see where we fit into the greater picture and social pyramid, either to accommodate the so-called reality of capitalistic living standards and be measured by our class, as it is the worldly belief. No, destiny is just not that, it is a divine prerequisite, one of the moral and ethical value and fibre. It all begins with a deeply rooted desire to find one's purpose, purposefully. A belief that we do not have to live in fear, there is more than enough fear. Instead we need to choose to live with an infinite nature, with abundance. This will only come about by starting with oneself, from the inside out so to speak, building on character as foundation. By realising that one needs to abolish worldly beliefs first, a pure character is formed from an empty character willing to find the required filling, test and experience all things in life and then surrendering the bad things and habits. By only holding on to the good habits, it is then that we realise that not all things material are worthy of our primary quest or pursuit. They merely make life more comfortable and brighten up our sense of worth and spirit. Man is an emotionally charged being, therefore spiritually guided; consequently, it makes sense to pursue those things spiritual more often than not. He strives for joy and companionship to recharge this emotional-spiritual power and source at the centre of his existence; hence, we need to build our lives around spiritual principles as well, that of purity, integrity, love and service to all fellow man. In the following chapters, we will go into explicit detail and cover a diversity of aspects to form the true self and to build on a solid foundation of the self, that will be able to take the heavy burden of the roof of retirement and destiny. Yes incredibly difficult this thing, called "true balance", it requires sober insight, intent, a purpose. The issues that life throws in our laps, including dealing with perception, political agendas, character conflict, beliefs and social politics that somehow always gets the proverbial finger in the pie and messes up a great deal of good intentions, it's not easy. Therefore as a strategist, you need to trust and have true faith in yourself and your beliefs. For they will be tested, if they are not deeply rooted, into a solid foundation, they will be pulled out by the slightest jolt. Leaving you uncertain, we need to be certain, because we are charting the way past the waterfall for others, into the fear and come back as victors.

Some words to reflect on pertaining to the perception of self-worth, if you find that others do not rate your abilities as highly as what you do yourself, do not be too sure that they are not wrong. If you allow yourself to think this, you may easily fall into the belief that there is a conspiracy to prevent the recognition of your merit and this belief is pretty sure to be the source of an unhappy life.~ Bertrand Arthur William Russell

Measuring people and their production:

Growing pains: in practice

So there will be no panacea or universal cure – for good common sense. Therefore, as administrators of strategic affairs, beware of the measures used to gauge production, diversity and progress when pushed for "production figures".

How do we measure production and should we?

The rule is: Measure Personal Capacity rather than Productivity:

Taking into account that every man will have his own personal rating of his inflated worth and growth towards mastering the fundamentals of any subject or skill, some people are over confidant in what they are capable of. Tolerance in the refinement of taught techniques is a cycle; it cannot become a hastened process. Becoming a formidable manager and leader takes much more consideration, especially to assemble a team. In this instance, the "team formation" becomes a time consuming business altogether, we have to deal with all kinds of fear.

We can do a lot of things right, but when we keep doing the right thing, we tend to become that which we strive for – a formidable and capable team. This should be the measurable benchmark to strive for when gauging productivity, creating teams that will stand up to the test of real life. In order to turn out functioning teams fully trained and equipped and not just a measure of the individual's performance in terms of **"Productivity"**, this is a team sport for crying out loud. In addition, teams belong to systems; both have to be strong, flexible and compatible in order to produce. Teams are only as good as what the system is "fair and supportive". We mostly focus on judging individual production and adding the ingredient of personality – whether we like them or not - to equate to the sum of his or her ability. Ability is judged on effective communication, appearance and work rate. Administrators just want to know "How many "golden eggs" does this "goose" lay?" Where does experience ever come in, as an assets, does the experience not count anymore? Don't do this, don't measure people like this, you will kill intuitive and eventually the enterprising spirit of the individual and even the team. If you pit people against each other based on a warped system or base line, then you are in essence directly creating rivalry and polarisation, do not let your people compete with one and other, in respect of likeness. Having "best employee of the month" based on we like you best, well there is a killer for sure. Rather revert to recognising production as a team result and effort and by rewarding team loyalty.

It will do wonders for the system and working environment. The motivation is that not everyone is performing at his or her optimum level every day, it is impossible, however their input at critical times become invaluable to the team effort. Without it, the team will suffer. Current trends are to push the ones that seem to keep laying the golden eggs harder, yes, we punish performance, by hanging a reef around their necks, they never get the opportunity to pass on their skills because they would rather work for the reward. The harder workers and the one's with drive and ambition is exploited, the lazy ones just drift along, what have we achieved in hindsight - is one person having to pull the teams weight. Management just pushes them harder, if he can do it so can you, and harder, day after day. The effect is, well to say the least very predictable. Quality drops, work rate drops and overall the units become demoralised, when if prolonged stress and burn out will set in, you champion will burn out and the team will be useless and battle tired.

Learn to say "NO" and mean it, because if we form opinions about people that are not like us and label them or put them into little boxes, then they behave like wise. Then this becomes a cancer, a stigma and people eventually start behaving according to the label they carry - habitually. This is not conducive to success or harmony in a team environment; you turn everyone around you into a label - either a "lazy or hard worker" – you will soon end up with, why is no one working today? Well the "driver", the "BOSS" did not come in today to tell us what to do -sir. - Scenario.

Let's first look at gauging real worth; by looking at the aspects of real production, real ability and real capacity. The two terms production and capacity sums up the approach.

- **Personal Capacity;** Refers to the persons work rate, the person's ability, to perform the task or required function. How resilient is this person, how motivated and confidant.
- **Production;** The completion of a task, the success rate and quality obtained at completion as well as the quantity achieved (Does he or she perform and effect positive feedback within a group, find self-motivation and positive reframing easy, is he or she effective at what they are appointed to do). If not then they don't belong to the group.
- **Production capacity;** reflects on the effectiveness of the individual to perform a required function within a group, do they fit. In a group scenario, or single-handedly, with or without guidance and or assistance can the person rise to the desired level of production? Still achieve the standards and quality expected of production. What is the gap? Does the person only require more training, guidance, or is it case of refresher training and or practice that are merely required. Otherwise is he out of his league playing tennis with a golf club scenario, just too junior to be competitive in this group?

Production and Production Capacity measured:

Production should form the basis of your performance management evaluation style. We have to calculate the deviation, in order to ascertain the deficit from our set benchmarks. For all of these are measurable. Where **production capacity,** is linked to action items that can be re-aligned, or delegated as well as refreshed and or calibrated, but cannot be measured, only monitored. Production Capacity with reference to conflicting tasks and schedules that disturbs the groups synergy. Production Capacity relates to system affecting synergy and open communication, by virtue of having an unsynchronised working environment, effort is lost in translation over things that take priority. Do priorities change daily?, if so how and why? The effect is work comes to a standstill because of production lines getting materials late, systems that lock up, or lacking essential resources because they are over stretched, or none existing. The other indicator is poor managerial skills, reverting to the practicing of crisis management behaviour. All these aspects and more impact on groups that require a whole team to function properly, the classic symptoms are too many meetings and tasks overlapping, shifting the emphasis daily and in short just pure bad organisation and prioritisation.

Personal Capacity: This refers to the individual's production capacity and that of the manager, both seen as working together as a team. Where managers do not have the required capacity to lead and manage at the same time, things go wrong. We all know this requirement, but we seem to forget to change into this gear of thought when being grilled by Top management who always seems to "over analysing productivity" as a consequence of labour and not management and want to know who is not pulling his or her weight. Unit performance standards, is always a very thorny issue. How should it be measured? Well if they were not there, how would it affect the reality at hand? Always ask this question when confronted with differences between unit productions, because different environments and specialities, have different impacts on production scores. In Police circles - they never need an armoured vehicle and a riot squad until a riot breaks out, then they have far too few. Same thing goes for bomb and narcotic detection dogs. Still we have people who bitch and moan about the amount of time and money that goes into training them and sustaining them, or don't, until a "gun" goes off at a school, or they experiences a sudden drug problem, well who do they call then? – go figure. The same principle applies. The long and the short of it, it's an essential tool only when crisis strikes, do we need it and the answer to this will dictate the response. Especially if it can or will save lives, so it comes back to production thresholds, has this unit reached its threshold? Two, are they expected to perform other functions on top of their core functions that impact on their proficiency, or are they properly supported in terms of logistics and have they been properly retrained and rewarded.

The next conundrum. Did the system perform or the man, or teams, where do we gauge the production? Who did the work? – Always start the analysis with the team, then the man and then the system. Therefore, we have to think quickly and motivate a drop in performance and productivity. Well it all relates right back to the opening statement – **ABILITY**.

I will take you back to *Ability* because ability and **Capacity** should be viewed as one enabling aspect throughout and stems directly from the training received. Your training and practice sessions should be dynamic yet simple enough to enhance the underlying talent of man to surface with each training cycle. Never separating the two's development curves, each are of equal importance in terms of the development of teams. **"Production and Capacity"** vs. time well spent training – which by the way will always be a point of heated argument any way. We cannot expect good production without assembling the components required, namely the human capital collectively responsible for the final product.

As a "COMMANDER" of sorts, you are only AS STRONG AS YOUR PEOPLE, are wise, trained, willing and able - in relation to - a chain only being as strong as the weakest link. You have to un-label, the labelled; you have to be both a leader and a manager today to be effective. When we enter enterprise, then it's no longer the canoe, but a battleship, filled with many selves, creating the ship. Managers manage systems, yes granted a requirement, but for whom? Ask this; for whose benefit? Let me explain; we can do our jobs without tons of required paperwork – yes, but management can't. If we unpack this aspect of management generating tons of paperwork – then it relates to the generation of paper work to keep control and gauge production, and to follow sets of rules and very little else.

This aspect alone impacts on production, - it starts to slow down the system eventually - if the management becomes over bearing with analysing production, with too much paper work, too many orders, too many directives and too little trust, support and time. Then management has lost focus of their core business and that is to enable...let's close on that note and move on to the next chapter and start exploring alternatives in this regard.

The next chapter will start the foundation work for making radical strategy work...by explaining it with principles.

Becoming "Radical" with Strategic Management Principles.

By looking at new approaches to organisation.

Attempting to carry out a new Radical strategy and adding it to an old organisational structure is the same as trying to get back into your favourite old shoes, from ten years back. It's the same with any old organisational structure; it is unwise!

Are we future focused organisations, or just watching the bottom line? The fundamental principles of revolutionary radical strategic management embodies this concept of holistic change. By breaking the shapes of everything that you have come to know about business and learning from it, taking what works and attempt to enhance it, and redesigning the rest to work in collaboration of the main effort. To purely revisit the old tested and tried methods and models, to adapt them to the new millennium is only a partial fail safe. Why, just look at our kids, they are getting smarter with every generation and mature equally fast, they think more rational and can deal with more complexity and issues at ever younger ages. Therefore, it stands to reason that every generation is evolving faster than the system are, the tail – the new recruits - are moving along with the animal, up the spiral, but gets stuck.

Every generation has increased intelligence and maturity, greater than the level of its predecessor; we are becoming smarter as a race. Technology is leaping us forward in parallel and is taking us with it. The global context is changing every five years; encroaching and tightening the time spiral on us, we have become global villagers. We can see in real time what was happening in Baghdad. September 11th affected the global economy; the world is becoming a much smaller place. The question that comes to mind is this, how can we still want to function within the confines of the old business models, with just one specific business model that worked five years back? Against this backdrop, it is pure madness, especially if we contemplate the rate of change and innovation. We will have to start taking multidimensional approaches in business, which was never the case, or of any consequence say ten or even five years back – like factoring in how many employees will be lost to Aids in a year for instance. In addition, how would that affect our reality?

What is our aids policy – do we even have one? Will the economy of the country have enough skilled labour to support our organisation at around 2015? If current trends in worker migration prevail where workers work for the highest bidder and are anything to go by – will we have enough expertise locally available. Will the shortage of fossil fuel become a factor in organisational systems design, and its dependence on it; do we have to look at alternative means of energy to power our organisation in the future with restrictions coming into effect to clamp down on global warming, etc. How will the economic boom in say China impact on our business principles and product? Then there is also the question of environmental design, the safety of our employees, crime is statistically increasing globally as recession has set in. Health is decreasing due to stress, new strains of old viruses are emerging and affecting international travel. More woman are coming into senior management positions, what do we do with their children. Will kids at the company's day care become a norm rather than the exception. Will their transport to school, and home be covered by the organisation. With more emerging liberal labour legislation, will the company be forking out more for social responsibility, and will they have better relations with their unions to avert any strike action that could become crippling. etc. All these seemingly trivial anomalies from the past have now become real considerations when pushing to maximise the workforces efforts. Will we make some sort of provision for these attributes to align with our strategy in the near future. The future aim of strategist will be to hold onto your skilled labour what you have, with everything you have. Our ability to accurately forecast and assemble radical and encompassing strategy will become our only hope. Large corporate companies will only survive through their ability to hold on to skilled and trained "healthy" labour, with effective strategic intent.

The emancipation of labour rights and privileges will become the new frontier and challenge for corporate companies on the strategic landscape, we won't feel it now, but during recessions, fewer and fewer people get the opportunity to get trained, or get an academic qualification. Therefore, the pool of intellectual capital has shrunk likewise, and the effects will only be visible in the years to come. This new field called human capital or human asset management, will surely emerge as an crucial element on the strategic landscape. By building this aspect into our strategy now, the corporate environmental designs we contemplate will make space for the likes of corporate safe housing developments for employees, with private schools, sport, gym, horse riding, golf course and transport to and from work etc. The supply pool will not be able to keep up with the demand. Global trends seem to be a good yardstick of this new approach towards genuinely looking after employees as if they are all family and worth their weight in gold. If it so happens in the States and Europe it is bound to happen in other emerging third world countries as well and other places around the world. China is already looking at getting more foreigners in to perform certain specialised functions. This will in essence "privatise" the skilled labour force for the top echelon, especially those that are artisans, or skilled in specific scarcity fields of expertise. I predict that this will become a trend, where the highest bidder will be the only ones having specific skilled labour working for them. Skills will become a commodity within the next five to ten years. All due to the influences of aids, hunger and war in Africa causing global spin off effects, even as far afield as in first World countries, where they will feel the effect. If we are oblivious to these approaches and styles of lateral thinking, we will not survive the near future let alone the distant.

We have to "think wider" than the norm. Thinking wider means flattening the organisational structure, so that we can use the money to keep specialised labour and pay incentives that are competitive, with fewer managers and more specialists in the hierarchy of companies, in order to have the best schooled and skilled labour available as the availability of able-bodied workers will shrink dramatically, due to illness, age and globalisation.

The traditional roles and functions of leaders and managers will also have to change, from master and servant roles, to more co-operative team managers and flatter structures. Where managers become co-ordinators, CEO's become father figures and are only concerned with the wellbeing and support of staff, and stretching the budget. This aspect requires a completely new paradigm shift, from the conventional to the foreseeable. It will have to incorporate all the following business models and not just one:

- Functional organisational structure - but with specialisation
- Geographic organisational structure – with specific decentralisation
- Decentralised business divisions – due to nature of task
- Strategic business unit's – with project teams
- Matrix structures – as frame work

"PROS" Of traditional approaches to organisation

Hierarchical structures make good strategic sense when and where:

- Activities can be divided into simple, repeatable tasks & efficiently performed in mass quantity.
- Important benefit's too deeper functional expertise exists.
- Customer needs are standardised.

"CONS" Of traditional approaches to organisation

Hierarchical structures can be a liability where and when:

- Customer preferences start shifting from standardised to customised products.
- Product's life-cycles start growing shorter.
- Flexible manufacturing starts replacing mass production.
- Customers want to be treated as individuals – and demand service orientated organisations.
- Pace of technological change causes accelerating markets, profit margins shrink.

Other - Major drawbacks;

- Lack of responsive customer service or customer service ethic.
- Slow to adapt to changing conditions, with it can wait until tomorrow attitudes.
- Model one: World standards in corporate environmental design; leading companies have adopted the following principles to keep and gain market share.

Success in fast-changing here today gone tomorrow, global markets depends on:

- Quick response to shifting customer preferences.
- Short design-to-market cycles, with quality, and value for money as the main emphasis.
- First-time out quality. – Branding is no longer an issue – price is.
- Custom order turnaround time & multi-version production.
- Personalised customer service for targeted market segment, as well as product back up and support in your native language.
- Accurate order filling & expedited delivery services.
- Rapid assimilation and integration of new technologies.
- Creativity & innovativeness, keeps rolling over.
- Speedy reaction to competitive developments.

Corporation building revolves around a revolution in organisation-building blocks.

- Leaner, flatter, decentralised smaller structures. Alternatively, large centralised operations.
- Reengineering of the work processes to decrease fragmentation across functional and production lines.
- Process teams & cross-functional work groups – expanded job function, multi skilled.
- Lean staffing - where support functions are mostly outsourced.

- Partnerships with key suppliers & outsourcing – no more businesses within businesses (we either build cars or sell cars, not both.)
- Empowerment of all staff – career path training
- Across the board electronic information systems
- Accountability for consecutive and consistent results – rather than increased production.

Model two:

Splitting the functions to create functionality:

The author Dr. John Sample-PhD made it available for redistribution, so it's in its original state, an essential read. **The Mager pipe:** "Based on Mager & Pipe's" (Robert Frank Mager and Peter Pipe) Analysis of performance enhancement, by identifying first -Performance Problems" this system will allow effective management of any organisation.

Method two: Using Subject Matter Experts to Identify High Liability Tasks

In more pristine times, the primary reason for requiring and providing effective instruction was to increase the probability of correct and consistent performance on the job. Corporate executives and their performance improvement managers are now becoming concerned for a second reason. This second reason for instruction involves avoiding or limiting civil liability for failure to train to standard for a business or governmental entity (Sample, 1993, 1995). Given this second reason, instruction becomes -- in and of itself -- a defence to a suit alleging failure to instruct or train to standard. The second reason probably would not exist, or would be minimal, if the first reason were attended to more effectively. Unfortunately, it is the second reason that gets the attention of Corporate Coe's and governmental executives.

Framework for Identifying High Liability Tasks

There are several approaches for determining the likelihood of organisational liability for failure to instruct to standard. The most traditional approach is to monitor civil (and sometimes criminal) case law for precedent cases that guide the legal system in their deliberations and findings. Such an approach is largely reactive since the performance improvement manager must rely upon advice from legal counsel to keep him or her informed about cases that have already been decided.

- A second approach uses existing statutes and regulations to guide strategies and instructional programmes for compliance. Examples include EEO, OSHA, Nuclear Regulatory Commission and most recently, the Americans for Disability Act. This approach has the advantage of technical assistance from the regulating agency (Ledvinka & Scarpello, 1991). Although too much assistance can become unwelcome, at least there is a source of legal and technical information for designers of training programmes!
- A third approach is more proactive in nature and when combined with the first two approaches, we will ensure the identification of potential high liability tasks. This approach uses a validated task inventory, routinely maintained risk-management and personnel records and subject matter experts (SME's) to identify high liability tasks. Although the context for this article is a mid-sized sheriff's department, the process may be easily modified for business and industry.

Identifying High Liability Tasks - A Law Enforcement Example

Most task analysis efforts result in a list of tasks and the identification of knowledge, skills and attitudes (KSA's) necessary for selecting, training and supervising personnel to standard (Swanson, 1994). The conventional wisdom in law enforcement today is to group potential high liability into several general areas: driving, first responder/first aid, the use of force, firearms and sometimes civil rights issues (Berringer, 1987). These broad areas serve to put administrators, supervisors and training personnel on general notice about potential liability. What has been lacking is a specific process for the identification of tasks within those broad areas that carry potential high-liability. Given the above framework, the first step was to develop an inventory of tasks performed by sworn personnel in the sheriff's department. The second step, the needs assessment, was to analyse routinely kept risk-management and personnel records for tasks associated with the following: auto accidents, workers compensation claims, professional liability and internal affairs complaints. The third step was to have subject matter experts (SME's) review the results of the needs assessment to determine which tasks have the most potential for high liability.

Step 1 - Development of Task Inventory

The task inventory used in this study was generated from the "Job and Task Analysis of Florida Law Enforcement Officers". The original task list of 528 items was updated by eighteen representatives of the department. This group identified an additional 22 tasks performed by sworn personnel in the department.

An inventory consisting of 550 tasks and eleven demographic variables (sex, assignment, etc.) was distributed to sworn deputy sheriffs and their sergeants. Each "Law Enforcement Task Inventory" included a mark-sensitive optical scanning scoring form. Instructions for completing the task survey were also included and the respondents were given two weeks to complete the assignment. Each booklet and scoring form was assigned a number that corresponded to the deputies' identification number. Each deputy was to determine if he or she had performed each task during the past year and if so, to then use a 5-point scale to estimate "relative time spent" on the task (1 = very much below average; 5 = very much above average). One hundred fifty-four (92%) task surveys were returned to the personnel unit for processing. The optical scanning forms were scored by the testing and evaluation centre at a major state university. Statistical analysis was provided by the computing centre at Florida State University.

Step 2 - Needs Assessment and Data Analysis

The author and a representative of the staff services unit of the sheriff's department reviewed incident reports to determine what specific tasks were being performed at the time the incident occurred. In this context, incident means any single occurrence of an automobile accident, professional liability claim, internal affairs / citizen complaint, or workers compensation claim. A summary report was written for each of these areas. In many instances, multiple tasks were performed during each incident. Both analysts had to agree that one or more tasks were performed before a task(s) was assigned to a specific incident. Incidents were determined for an eighteen-month period.

Step 3 - Use of Subject Matter Experts (SME's)

Subject matter experts (SME's) are those individuals who have specialized expertise and whose judgment and professional opinion will withstand rigorous scrutiny. In a law enforcement context, SME's must have the experience and ability to provide creditable testimony and to withstand cross-examination if they were ever required to testify in their area of expertise. SME's must be chosen carefully for a department's future liability may turn on their expertise. It was recommended that the sheriff's department use external and internal SME's for the required type of expertise. In this regard, the use of SME's is similar to using external observers for assessment centre activities.

In this instance, the sheriff requested the assistance of seven internal and external subject matter experts. The SME's for this project represented driving, firearms, first responder/first aid, defensive tactics and general law enforcement administration. Included, as SME's was a representative of the state sheriff's association and an attorney from the insurance company that represented the department. They did not receive any compensation for their assistance. The SME's met for a half-day to assist the department in identifying tasks with high-liability potential. As a group, the SME's reviewed the summaries of the automobile accidents, internal affairs complaints, professional liability and workers compensation claims. The next objective for the SME's was to determine a practical definition of high liability tasks. After lengthy discussion, the SME's agreed upon the following working definition. A high-liability task . . .

- Results in claims involving death or significant injury to members of the public or deputies, or
- Results in a loss (settlement or judgment) of $50,000 or more, or
- Results in multiple incidents of the same task or deputy, each incident $5,000 or more loss, or

A combination of the above.

Having reviewed the report summaries and given the above definition, the seven SME's were instructed to review the task inventory to determine potential high liability tasks for the department. Working independently, each SME used their experienced judgment to determine tasks with potential high liability. For tasks of their choice, the SME's assigned an "H" (for High), an "M" (for moderate), or "AL" (for low) potential liability.

The SME's were also instructed to determine potentially high liability tasks using an alternative method, nominal group technique (Martinko & Gepson, 1983; Moore, 1987). This approach to group decision-making requires that subject matter experts identify high liability tasks and silently vote to determine a priority ranking. In this instance, each of the seven SME's were instructed to assign ten votes to the ten tasks having the potential for the highest liability. The task with the highest liability received ten votes, the next highest liability task received nine votes and so on. Triangulation: Task List, Needs Analysis, Subject Matter Experts.

The following list of tasks is the consensus of subject matter experts from the above-described procedures for determining high liability tasks for the sheriff's department.

The rank order in the left-hand margin is the result of the SME's assessing each task in terms of High liability potential.

The second list of rankings represents the rank order from the nominal group technique (NGT).

Table 1: Ranking Of High-Liability Tasks By Subject Matter Experts

RANK	NGT RANK	TASK DESCRIPTION
1	4	Purchase vehicles or vessels
2	2	Apprehend suspects
3	3	Control disorderly or irate persons
4	1	Make Arrest
5		Confront or monitor groups
6	6	Conduct felony stop
7	7	Administer first aid
8		Rescue trapped persons
9		Act or respond to extortionist or kidnapper
10		Use animals to control crowds
11		Conduct traffic stop
12		Detain suspect vehicle or vessel
13		Participate in the execution of arrest warrants
14		Protect victim or other threatened person
15		Seize or confiscate illegal apparatus (such as distillery, traps, drug equipment or gambling devices)
16		Guard prisoners outside of jail
17	8	Search for explosives related to bomb threats
18		Use animals to detect or apprehend intruders
19		Transports ill or injured persons from remote area to meet emergency medical team

Note that the NGT method resulted in two additional tasks that were not identified by the first method: (1) Conduct active patrolling of assigned areas and (2) Set up road blocks, each ranked 5th and 9th respectively.

It is of some significance that the two methods essentially resulted in similar rankings. Multiple methodologies are always preferable in applied research of this nature and in this instance, confidence is increased in the validity of the final task list since both methods yielded very similar results (Cascio, 1991).

There is no particular magic to be attributed to the final consensus list of high liability tasks reported in this article. A different group of equally competent subject matter experts could have identified a different mix of high-liability tasks. What is defensible is the process by which the tasks were systematically and rigorously identified. In this instance, the sheriff's department has confidence that a grand jury or civil trial jury would conclude that reasonable steps were taken to identify high liability tasks.

Strategies for Preventing Liability

The results of this applied research project cast the identified high liability tasks into what the courts refer to as foreseeable field incidents that officers could be reasonably expected to experience (Canton v. Harris, 1989). Having identified high liability tasks, the sheriff's department is now on notice to adequately prepare sworn deputy sheriff's and their supervisors to respond competently to situations in which these tasks are required (Sample, 1990). Failure to do so could result in civil liability against the department's insurer and the county. It is important that chief executive officers require extensive written policies, training, supervision and discipline for such foreseeable tasks (Ward, 1988).

Supervision vs. training

The Mager pipe: Supervision vs. training is the best place I know of to begin, with this model. What this is really about is how to address PERFORMANCE problems...which makes it much more than just a supervision or management tool, although this is where it is often applied.

Let us say that we have a: Performance Discrepancy - The difference between what IS happening and what you WANT to happen. If you have one, you must first determine if it is important enough that the current behaviour should be changed. What will it cost? (Time, money, lost work hours, etc.) It may not be important enough to spend the amount of resources needed to fix it. The simplest way to determine this is to make a list of all possible consequences arising from the discrepancy and calculate their cost.

If it IS important enough to proceed, the next step is to determine if there is a: Skill Deficiency - The worker simply does not know how to perform the job. If this is the case, then you need to train or make some change in the job, or bring in a different worker. The decision on which is needed must be carefully considered, since even though I, for instance, am fully capable of grooming a dog, I would not have the slightest idea of what you wanted me to do if you spoke to me in Afrikaans, which I do not understand. I thus have a skill deficiency in literacy for that language. Make certain that there are no hidden issues involved (partial deafness or partial sight loss, other health issues, stress, personal issues [having gone through a divorce, I can certainly relate to that one!] etc.) If the worker COULD perform the skill satisfactorily in the past and there is no noted physical or mental issue, which has happened since that time, you need to determine how often the skill is performed in that workers' job. If this is a skill he has not used in a long time, he probably does not need "training"...what he needs is "practice". (Heaven only knows how much time, effort and money is thrown away putting officers back through training classes when all they really needed was a chance to practice!)

Maybe he is just "rusty" from not needing to perform the skill for a long time.

Fact and Fault finding: IAD- Immediate Action Drill, in a small booklet form: -Maybe he does not even need much practice...it is possible that a "job aid" such as a check list, or written instructions will resolve the issue. This is especially true for skills that are needed infrequently, yet are critical when they are needed...immediate actions are required, but no one experienced is around to advice accordingly. Has this happened, yes, so let's plan for any such eventualities? Check lists are absolute gold when the pressure is on and customers demand action. Instead of supervisors giving incorrect orders thereby corrupting the system so to speak with his own doubts in high stress situations, we anticipate such eventuality and cater for it accordingly. Situations arise where a mistake...and we all make mistakes sometimes...can make a bad situation worse.

Capacity - Again it is possible that the worker is simply not capable of doing the job. Here the "experts" say replace the worker, but you and I know we cannot always do this due to issues beyond our control, if this is the case; we just do the best we can.

Punishment - If there is NO performance deficiency, we must ask, "Is the desired performance "punishing"? That is, does the worker feel like he is being punished for doing his job well? (Let us take three typists in an office. Two are worthless and one is the best you could ask for. They are all being paid the same and supposedly do the same job, but which one are YOU going to take your transcript to for it to be typed well? She has to work like a mule and the other two do almost nothing. That is "performance punishing"), this aspect kills enterprise and creates tension..

Obstacles - Are there obstacles to performing? Perhaps supervisors are not willing to allow subordinates to use newly acquired skills because they are held responsible for other tasks, which the administration values more. Here the problem is above the level of supervisor, since we, both know that if the Boss said, "Do it! And no excuses!" it would be done. (If there is no time and money for new computers and acquiring qualifications, it is because someone up the ladder does not care enough to find the money...not because it is simply not there...but we already know this.)

Does performance even matter? - If it does not matter to the worker, the answer is to "MAKE" it matter. Obviously various reward / punishment – disciplinary action - schemes may be needed. However, the base line should be to reach what is termed a Win/Win situation. For Win/Win to come about and into focus, the organisation needs to change as a whole. In terms of structure and systems thinking. We will deal with systems thinking in a chapter all by itself because it is very involved and needs to be done right. Coming back to structure, old term that " everything flows from the top down" - so " What goes on in the Head will manifest itself in the body". Good or bad decisions, but what is even more significant is that in order to get the focus on "closing winning deals" right. The organisation or unit needs to focus on methods that produce results and not just on results. Systems need to be encompassing and not just functional; the compensation system, information system, training system, the planning system the value system and the synergy system. This will be addressed in "The chapter on Systems Thinking", but just as introduction; concept thinking about how to close the gap between the workforce and the employer has come across in many forms to us, but to summarise some of my favourite authors works; Stephen Covey and Roland de Vries works – to summarize the Win/Win concept;

- Win/Win can only survive if the systems support it.
- People evaluate themselves, by using criteria that they themselves developed.
- By a deeper understanding and alignment of the "vision" and "mission" and "goals" of the organisation, as they were intended to be understood and the product they are supposed to deliver. Within a value system that is aligned with true principles of –"Trust", "Respect" and "Integrity" the abundance theory.
- This has to be an agreement, preferably in writing, a performance contract of sorts, that stipulates the desired outcome and rewards and penalties, as well as the framework in which you may freely operate to achieve the vision, mission and goals.

Clearly defining the role and function of the employee, coupled to the required resources and support he or she will have, should be covered in the interviewing process already. In short, the system must be a fully aligned and capacitating system, if not then it was poorly designed, or the end and the means are unrealistically defined.

Win/Win agreements are tremendously liberating, but as the product of isolated techniques, they won't hold up in all instances, even if you set them up, there is no way to maintain them, without personal integrity and a relationship of trust, called verification and calibration.

Verification and calibration: - The question is, "If your life depended on it could you perform this skill, or demonstrate this knowledge / ability right now?". If the answer is "yes", (and about 80% of the time it will be) then there is usually a supervision problem, or a systems problem somewhere in the chain of production. Sometimes it is at the level of those who "supervise" the supervisors as well as at the first line supervisor level. It is absolutely amazing how many supervisors and managers will not get "nose to nose" with an employee and tell them to shape up or else and back it up with consequences...amazing.

Well we have highlighted the problems and we have alluded to some solutions, but what is the real answer, we would like to call it MQM – Matrix Quality Management. The next chapter is all about the quality of our strategy; no one will buy or sell strategy if it has no quality.

Strategic planning focus; past and future.

Strategic planning in the past has mostly focused on the hard-core attributes of planning, the likes of, "vision", "mission' and "structure'. The softer and more "feminine" human element and attributes have always been left silent. I don't want to get all soft and furry on you, however please read the intro and give it some thought.

It is with human reactivity to stimulus in mind that MQM originated. MQM, primarily focuses on adding the new spice of developing true quality "human capital". The term "human capital", has to some extent just become a buzzword, merely referred to in training circles and when politicising issues for votes and favour with staff. Capacitating people, is the total planned re-alignment and instilment of non-discriminating, apolitical ways, that fits in with the core business of the company or organisation. The rationale behind this is; we have come to the total realisation that strategy is just not strategy, nor useful or as effective, if it does not effectively address all the elements and attributes of diversity and its impact on strategy as a whole. This equates to a professional architect drawing up building plans, only to have unskilled labour build it with inferior skills, equipment and material. However, strategy is aimed at productivity and efficiency, that must deliver on quality. To get quality as an element, we have to focus on human reactivity. TQM (Total quality management) – which focuses mainly on developing mental tools, aligned systems and well equipped teams. These are great starting points that deliver greater results, why? Mainly because it has been given structure, and structure belongs to systems. The question now is how do we combine and integrate our strategy into an existing system with an element of diversity amongst our people. Only by reviving and reengineering the company culture can we elevate to the next level of progress, by incorporating and fusing the last element, the people, we call this process MQM (Matrix quality management).

The focus of such a philosophy;

Thus the focus point has changed, even the paradigm, the importance of healthy living and having quality relationships, comes before wanting to ascertain objectives, where previously it was the other way around. We view this as a relay race, where everyone has to give 100%; we want 100% of their effort, time and willingness to succeed against all odds. If the track is the system and the stick is the product and the running shoes are the tools and winning is the objective, how do we define quality. Do we define it by the outcome or the process? Did we win, or what? If we want to shape behaviour and fuse people, we have to focus on process; its elements and attributes that enhance our outcome, referring to work related performance. Performance comes from good habits being formed. This theory holds that living a quality life, with quality relationships, will result in a better quality person, delivering higher quality in production. I have dedicated a whole chapter to elaborate on the importance of culture. This chapter just explains the new ideology called MQM (Matrix Quality Management).

What is the impact of discarding such a principle versus applying MQM.

We can all associate with the stresses created by modern living and its direct impact on traditional family and corporate life as we know it and it is taking its toll. Without deliberating this too much here are some facts. It has been estimated that stress will become the number three-incapacitation factor of the workforce and thus production in the next decade, next to coronary heart disease and Aids. The reason being, this world has become filled with "urgency addictiveness", everything has to be done now and this puts us in conflict with our other roles and obligations, that are also urgent. We are now using private and family time for the job, so we have to make up in double time to catch up; we never do, so in effect we are literally burning the candle at both ends. The principle of speed and effectiveness is good; however, we have so many people in the system that have no business being there, that only a handful tend to carry the burden and brunt of the total work load, so speed becomes useless, as we get bottlenecked by the incompetent and the ignorant.

We see the symptoms of urgency addictiveness everywhere; deterioration of service delivery, infrastructure decay due to over utilisation and none effective maintenance, sharp criticism on the implementation of government policy, and systems, that still gets implemented no matter what. Competing for favour via unscrupulous means, comparing worth, complaining, tell-tale behaviour and contending for position amongst other things and let's not forget politically inspired protocol. The likes of likes of affirmative action, black economic empowerment and the list goes on. This new tendency to "normalise" society by means of political opinions and involvement has ruptured sound habits and business cultures for good. The tide has turned, the two things that distinguishes organisations and society as well as people is their culture and functional discipline. In effect, politicians have now put a proverbial spanner in the social mechanism of nations as well and it has started to invade the work place, in an attempt to hide the issues of "previously disadvantaged groups" that governments themselves created, and are still creating, with a new social problem for the strategist to deal with. These quick fixes by governments the world over has had major devastating affects in just the past ten years. It has and will have a bigger negative impact in time to come if the paradigm does not change. Because they are still just addressing one side of the coin, where affirmative action is seen as a positive move, but on the reverse and receiving side used to create segregation and polarisation. A great example of how a strategy can go wrong if not addressed from all perspectives. The effect is that in time to come it will have an direct influence on all cultures and end up at the same starting point, having to solve disparities again, by implementing a none affirmative action, it's useless.

The fact of the matter is, it's just no longer healthy to work in highly competitive big corporate markets; it has become the corporate induced ill of the 21st century. This very aspect has embodied the cry for fair and just labour practices to name but one aspect and equal protection by the constitution. Which in itself only pours more fuel on the fire. Nevertheless, as strategist we have to become politically "polite", we have to equip people and organisations to deal with this diversity beyond the scope of simple strategy, and make it part of our strategy. This in itself does not cover the additional emotional trauma inflicted upon us daily because of this corporate driven behaviour, we can all associate with emotional trauma inflicted in the work place and in our personal lives. The undermining behaviour of subordinates, the bullying behaviour of superiors, the death of a family member, a divorce, etc. However, do we disassociate ourselves with these aspects that cause personal stress, by saying this is work related and this is personal and this is political, all in the same way? It's impossible; we remain the same person throughout, and our cultural biases and habits define who we are and how we see, feel, and do things and work. This creates stress, stress that follows you wherever you go.

Deliberating the concept;

Still it seems that we cannot grasp this concept; we choose to see an indirect relationship between production, policy, strategy, corporate culture (or a lack of it) and a private life. In addition, in this modern era and context; do we give any thought to work related trauma as a disease spreading faster than Aids. It has become increasingly prevalent in the last ten years. Work related or work induced stress – pressure and politics - literally makes people sick of working – this is a fact. It is estimated that as much as 25% of all consultations to private physicians are diagnosed as being stress related. In the latest studies done on stress, we see a rise in panic attacks, angina, ulcers, heart attacks and high blood pressure as well as depression to name only a few manifestations of this new age work related disease. Yes, the consequences of work related stress is directly linked to continued prolonged and recurring "bad organisational behaviour". This aspect must be treated very serious; regardless of one's position in the hierarchy, or in the colour spectrum of race, we are all affected. Alternatively, we will all face early ill retirement due to our inability to stay mentally healthy, the more competent people go off sick first, the more work gets redirected, so in effect no one will escape.

This little tale describes this phenomenon, the farm mouse found a hole into the farmer's food store and decided to move in. The farmer became aware of this new uninvited guest and resorted to setting a trap. The mouse got his tail stuck in the trap and was crying out in agony to the farm animals, they all replied in their own way; The Pig -"it's your own bad luck", The Cow - "sorry I am to busy", The Rooster -"can't help you I have an appointment". Then Snake came out of his hiding place hearing the cry, found the mouse and ate him. He was too full to move and hid under the shelf. The next morning the farmer's wife came and stepped on his tail, the snake bit her. She got very ill and the farmer killed the rooster to make chicken soup for his sick wife, he was tending to her night and day, he did not have time to go to the market to trade. He killed the pig so that they could eat. One day his wife woke up all better and she went to milk the cow, the cow had no milk because it was standing on stable and no one milked her for days, and her milk eventually dried up. So they sold the cow. The moral of the story is, help the small and the weak now and respond to cries for help, because somehow, somewhere, it could affect your own destiny.

IPS or "Inter personal stress" can be effectively addressed in the work environment if we implement "Matrix Quality Management" – MQM. With MQM, we install a sense of balance and normality. All our corporate system supports and relies on healthy mental living, which de-escalates unwanted stress. Then it becomes a second force that is harnessed by the organisation and it will inevitably give it the ultimate edge. As an internal capacitating element we will develop exceptional strategy because we address the real issues on productivity, a driving force unequalled by any other schemes. We cannot leave part of our core, that which we are, at the front door anymore, when entering the organisation, we enter as a whole person with a whole healthy composition. Culture is the fulcrum, around which peoples core values evolves and function. It creates FORCE -The very life force we are all related too.

FORCE implies:

F - *Fear,* is the greatest motivator, fear of rejection, failure, ridicule, etc. To effectively manage fear then is to teach balance, we only ascertain balance in cultural diversity by continued adaptation, by improvising and what follows is our ability to overcome our issues, most of our fears are self-imposed and realised, they are only our own and universal.

We have to give and teach people life skills first, before we teach them job skills and reaching objectives.

O – *Orientation,* is seen as our ability to effectively orientate ourselves and everyone else, it requires direction and a sense of purpose. You can give direction all you want, the only thing that gets people to do things consistently however, is a sense of true purpose, coupled to a clear directive and then only direction. People need to do meaningful and fulfilling jobs, in order for them to first feel, and then become part of the greater scheme of things, this is true human behaviour and not a phenomenon, therefore, any foreseeable paradigm, on the migration of performance evaluation and fulfilling certain prerequisite, requires these few aspects to be present when contemplating effective changes in direction.

We have to show clear direction and purpose in everything we do or say.

R – *Religion,* we have to form a work religion, a culture of "can doers" and incorporated it into the global corporate culture, of risk takers, people that have enough confidence and authority to act. Many of us have the confidence in our conviction to act, but we do not have the authority to do so, with the effect that things stand over, for authorisation.

We have to except and expect diversity and learn to embrace it, without having to sacrifice our own beliefs. Coercion breaks cohesion, we have to change our paradigms, from methodology addiction, to initiative development, don't wait to be told what to do, do it if it is the right thing to do, change the paradigm from; "I intend doing it" but I am waiting for authorisation – to "I can do" it – type of paradigms.

C – Building *Cohesion,* by fostering stronger relationships of trust and mutual support and likewise behaviour, we will only find "the way" if we follow the directions to our goals with a combined sense of purpose. We don't have to wait to be told to serve, we are intent on doing it, so why do we change our mind-set at the front door, when we enter the organisation, then adults start behaving like children, waiting for mom or dad to say it's okay.

E – Evoke *Extremism,* we have to become more radical in the ways we do things, solve problems and get results. What this implies is, if it works; let it work, what works for the one, won't necessarily work for the other, so create or find a way that works for you, then find the middle ground. We tend to want to generalise everything in terms of standardisation. We require freedom of movement and thinking, as well as space to exercise some creativity too go over to action. Standardisation cripples this. We have to look at the total human in all its parts that have unique requirements and how this may or may not impact on our strategy. We also recognise that there are several methods to counter stress. For instance by designing and building quality working environments with climate control, natural and artificial light and heating / cooling, with comfortable orthopaedic endorsed chairs and design.

Implementing such a philosophy:

Firstly, we will need to come up with a concept of what we deem to be MQM for ourselves within our industry and means, and reflect it in the vision and mission statements we create. We require a constitution of sorts, that protects our own quality statement, that defines the framework within which we would like to see our organisation flourish, and ourselves as individuals. Called our statement of "intent". This is not a nice guy approach towards solving real world issues, if you "intend" doing it, then you "intend" it done, and we can hold you accountable, it's a promise to be your best and give your best.

Secondly, instil enthusiasm and commitment to task, by developing open trust and real openness in communication channels. We have to be able to tell someone to their face what we think of their work ethic. This will be encouraged to create parity in the work place. We want mature interaction, anyone putting a concept or viewpoint on the table must be willing and able, to defend that statement. Being able to raise your voice, your opinion and defend and motivate your thinking, is liberating, this should and will become a principle. In addition, on the vision and mission allow the collective to carve the framework scripts, the principles that they will embrace, endorse and enforce by merely doing the right things – with leadership and then by doing the thing right – with stewardship. This will take time and conviction. This in itself does not constitute the total solution to the question of efficiency and effectiveness either. It only gives you depth in terms of foundation to launch strategy from, the likes of which you never had, more and more people and organisations want their worth to be noted, this is the start of such a religion. The religion of creating worth by designing a culture that truly embraces it. The way to find it is only limited by our two opposing forces from within, our "will" and from outside our "fear". Give any man a reason to succeed and he will, it's a question of what can I do under these circumstances that will make a difference in such a man's life, that will have impact, that will make his efforts count. It is only once we realise that when we harness peoples potential in full, by allowing initiative to flow freely that we will find their worth. The formation of a culture of this kind stems from the formation of what is defined as success by all concerned, we mimic successful people, cultures, and symbols, the norming and forming of culture needs to become a team effort. People need to feel quality, to experience quality, to start believing in quality again; to start living with quality…and it is hard work.

Strive to achieve the transformation with little steps, each day by having time set aside for active group sessions and discussions at various levels to define quality, in terms of systems, procedures, time management, resources. Keep your management and people involved in corporation and relationship building and then change the control towards focussing on strategy. Everyone has to become a strategist, implementer's of principles; the greatest challenge is the reward structure that truly motivates, in order for people to do the sacrificial things it takes to make strategy work. Therefore, it stands to reason, if it is from the people, for the people, by the people, who will oppose it, who then will question it and not be able to understand its significance. Reward structures must be creative; using the full range of reward and yes punishment mechanisms – no, no more carrot and stick, it just does not produce the offspring we desire from such a process. However, positive reinforcement should outweigh negative reinforcement to promote a healthy work environment. "Punishment" should also have a measure of retraining and reframing, in other words a positive element.

Create a unilateral Quality-ORIENTED reward system:

- Define jobs in terms of the quality to be accomplished and not quantity.
- Stress "achievement of objectives and millstones" not "just hard work and activities"
- Track actual achievement vs. targeted performance via a system that is fair and not just by a thumb suck.
- Use performance targets in strategic plans as basis for incentive compensation, with pre-determined rewards – for ascertaining long-term objectives on time.
- Have SEVERAL performance measures, as milestones to determine actual performance.

Define; "Doing a good job" – be specific with what you require by saying exactly what it means achieving pre-agreed-upon performance contracts, it means teamwork, it means quality. In addition, have a "definition" for each of these aspects that should be clear enough for anyone to grasp. Be very specific on:

- The *desired results* that you would like to see.
- The *specific guidelines* to be followed towards achieving such results.
- The resources *available* i.e. financial, technical and otherwise.
- The *accountability & responsibility level*, the standards that need to be incorporated and conformed to.
- The *consequences* of performance and non-performance or poor performance.

Guard against "Performance Bias";

- "No excuses for a drop in standards" standard must prevail, you must manage yourself – with complications seek immediate remedial action, first in report form, from each individual party concerned in the team. Analyse and find common ground before acting, sticking plasters on problems tend to back fire. Accountable management, seek answers concurrent and in consultation with the effected group. Top management should be held accountable 70% of the time whilst the rest only 30%.
- Time out, time due, commuting time to leave, with the potential to buy it out later, is another reward for good work.

- Alternatively, a good team building exercise, friction brings about stress and every person has a friction and stress threshold. Once crossed all rational barriers are broken down and respect is buried in the sand like an ostrich head. This is the ostrich syndrome, people ignore each other if there is friction, they take sides and form groups, then the gossip starts flowing and it all falls apart. The saying of to mush "familiarity breeds content" comes to mind here – the point I am trying to make, is that we require truly professional clinical leaders, one has to be formal and fair, by having formal rules of interaction, formality must prevail, no casual chit chat, let's all go fishing all the time atmosphere.
- Relationships are ruined by professional jealousy and everything eventually turns to a boiling point and infighting occurs, the organisation suffers eventually. Therefore, professionalism must prevail as an aspect of quality relationships, to be hands on and take control; never allow unhealthy competition and groups to form to infringe on discipline.
- One cannot reward "trying hard". Trying is only part of it, but achieving is all of it. Most people try all their lives, but they never get to a point where they actually succeed. This is a mental block that requires a paradigm adjustment.
- Performance across the board and not just reaching targets "pays off". This aspect must be a major, and not just a minor piece of the total compensation package. Most importantly, any incentive plan should extend to all managers and employees and not be coupled to salary scale, or position. In addition, it could come from profit sharing. This one aspect needs to be budgets for to prevail.
- The reward and incentives system should be administered by a custodian group made up of union members and must focus on being representative of labour and management. Where possible of course, with scrupulous care and fairness and without prejudice to be effective. The Reward schema is management's most powerful implementation and change implementation tool, if used clinically it will signal the desired behaviour & performance required. On the backside of what has just been mentioned, there is the issue of equality, very important and in some cases it will even stand in stark contradiction to what is pleaded, contradictory - Reward driven people go all out to achieve and;

Execute strategy effectively.

Meet with the objectives within the strategic plan.

- Beware of pitting people, or lining them up like racehorses and racing them for reward, this is not what we are preaching, you will have to factor in individual ability and workload, amongst other things. However, most important as Carl Rogers taught; " that which is most personal is most general". The more authentic you become the more genuine in your expressions, particularly regarding personal experiences and even self-doubts. The more people can relate to your expressions, the safer it makes them feel to express themselves.
- People start to communicate effectively due to wanting to communicate, in order to be heard. Pockets of trust are built over time and half sentences start to constitute whole conversations as time pass.

- Covey refers to this process as "Building Emotional Bank accounts", "based on trust and mutual respect – and discipline". He speaks of THE DESIRED ATTITUDE: "if a person of your intelligence and competence and commitment disagrees with me, then there must be something to your disagreement that I do not understand and I need to understand it. You have a frame of reference here that I need to look at; we may differ so that we may agree, about something if not compromise.

The second required aspect of MQM -The role of Interdependence and the element of people:

You cannot go it alone all the way is the message. The incorporation of principles, is very significant in that it relates very strongly to how we start focusing. Principles and the necessity thereof, extends to the embracing of value sets, the ultimate goal here is to create the unity of mind, effort and focus, in support of objectives as a collective. The development of a new culture will require a change in perceptions, that will align us with our values, which are mostly inherited time-aged customs, that have become our habits, which is never easy to change and attitudes only change if the reality of things changes. These are the key ingredients of "work culture" forming: or rather sub culture that we want to change or establish here first. For all people belong to a "clan", the persons ethnic culture will always reflect in the way he experiences and perceives his sub culture, influenced by perceptions and attitudes towards interdependence. Interdependence is not mutualism in this sense; it is a culture of thinking, an attitude, a mind-set of shared vision. Where we don't share the same vision, we create drama. The less we share and become like minded, the more we become indifferent, estranged, and move apart. Therefore if we don't share the same ideology, way of thing, doing and getting results, then it creates frustration, inner turmoil and drama. The key is to share a common vision, not just a strategic one, no, it has to deal with how we see priorities. If your vision does not create the same priorities as mine, then we are at odds. Working together but not being totally dependent on each other for both survival and success, is defined not by vision, but how the vision defines priorities. For instance, if the vision is to build a house, then two people will list their own statements of priorities, if it has not been set or predefined- this creates drama. This is the spanner in the works. It is by choice and not necessity, it's about closing ranks, it's about rising above personal differences and still being independent to think critically, and both mutually. It's all by choice. Not having to sacrifice one's thinking or freedom to think, just to be part of the "Unit". This is a minefield of assumptions. Everyone has on opinion. This aspect shows and requires highly evolved levels of adult maturity, in order to think with emotional intelligence, thus forming a new culture and doctrine. Cultural diversity is also the reason why this book starts from the premise of human emotional reactivity to stimulus. It is a higher level of co-existence, where we have to adapt or die. By setting a premise for fostering mature relations and interaction, by understanding what makes people think, how they think and why they react the way they do. We create a framework for collaboration and coexistence when we understand what it involves. Without such a frame work there will be turmoil and continued drama. We pride ourselves that we are more intelligent, resourceful and smart, by being able to change personal paradigms in business. However, the next step is to lessen the drama. We can keep changing all the other things, all to no avail, no matter how smart a scheme, because it deals with people, this is the embodiment of the culture and the principle of interdependence. This relationship that exist between people and people, where we judge a book by its cover, that everything is fusing towards one universal point, are we right or wrong, then we are going back to the beginning. We all know -Independence means to be self-sufficient and not having to answer to anybody and dependant means the exact opposite. Whether or not we would like to admit it, or not, we are all dependent, in one way or another and at anyone stage of our lives. We will become depend again; we all have to answer to one another and a higher authority – that is a dependency – any relationship is based on needs, wants and beliefs. We are also all independent; in terms of our choice of relationships, of movement and whatever else. The underlying key is to acknowledge this, this diversity in man's nature that we all have in common – and is a principle and a given. Through conceptualisation we form a deeper understanding of what is essential on a bigger scale of things, in this dynamic essence of living and being man – unique yet the same. This change takes place from the one opposite to the next, in our favour and then against us. The realisation that life is a pendulum of independence today, that can change to dependence tomorrow and so on. Your support today can turn to hostility tomorrow, just because a perception changed, then the very next day take a natural stance again. This is just the way life is, inconsistent yet consistent and complex. The one thing to decide on now is how it will affect me as the individual in this regard, and the unity – or culture - that I belong to currently. Is it interdependent, dependent, independent and how will I benefit from any change in this regard? Whose interest are being served best, if we take the principle and apply it. As a person in an interdependent culture; we think before we act, we measure twice and cut once. We have to hear all views, about the best course of action in prioritising the agenda, and its priorities. As a manager and a leader we seek council before we act, because the best speech you will make in anger today, will be the one you will always be reminded of tomorrow and the next day. Just this thought on having to choose between a preconceived paradigm, to prove a point here. People try to fit all "new things" into their current plans, if it does not fit, it gets rejected. Therefore, we have to design a brand new course of action, on designing action items and how they will take priority, against a measurable. This way we leave room for people to add their opinions, and assumptions, only to be scrutinised interdependently, thus everyone has an ability or chance to change their perception, or plans with change as things changes. Everyone is in the OODA loop; OBSERVATION, ORIANTATION, DECISION, ACT.

On choosing right. Choosing between "pedigree" and "street smart" people as an example. When we need to gauge quality, with the old paradigm of our parents saying get a degree and then a job and you will be set for life, gauged against the current reality, will this measurable be valid? Well in some instances yes, but this paradigm is fast fading away. The reason being less and less people can afford to send their kids off for a higher education. Mainly because this philosophy calls for a great deal of financial assistance and political ideology can stop or advance ones chances here as well. Opposed to the other reality, the guy who had to work to support himself and his family whilst studying part-time, who had to learn by trial and error, who had to adapt and endure hardship all the while and was still expected to cope. Will have better skills to survive today in the flux of markets. We refer to them as "street smart". Big companies now realize the value of textbook versus the self-made man, the street-smart person. The self-made man tends to be coming up trumps more often, so the belief that you are limited in terms of education if you do not have the previously "required" degrees to ascertain the means to move to the next level of management, is fast disappearing. You can become over qualified in this day and age for a position. On this note, you don't need a PhD, or any degree in order to capacitate yourself, to think strategically. Strategy is about **"TAPS"**, Tactics, Accuracy, Power and Speed. This aspect is never taught in any academically inclined university, only in the University of Life. For sure this philosophy does not apply in all fields. However, in strategic terms these elements can be co-opted as SME's (subject matter experts), taking the Henry Ford example for instance. He surrounded himself with SME's. Expanding our personal field of influence outward is easier done within a collective, to force the point home, of interdependence, where everyone drives the priorities shared. Opposed to the other reality of a single entity driving the whole organisation with his/ her own set of priorities. Without this maturity, the system caves in due to professional jealousy and personal agendas - it becomes pure cannibalism – and drama ensues because we don't share one common vision on what takes preference against what is preferred.

The assembling of a council of confidants

In life, the one who has the wider frame of reference, has the bigger sphere of influence, so character and knowledge will let influence prevail. Well yes, this is a tough one; any old timer will tell you the best of battles he had ever thought was with his own – like-minded people. The very people he was fighting for, occasionally coming and doing a Caesar impression on him. Well we all care increasingly more about "Stuff" as we get older and wiser, we do not take everything for granted anymore and we should not. This is also our moral weakness, we take too much for granted, we assume that the weather will be fine, we measure others as we measure ourselves and this is not always a good yardstick to measure others, and priorities by. The young and the restless have a value system unique to their generation, and they see priorities from a different frame, that is still developing and they need a firm hand to guide them. The small little Jackals that can so easily destroy the vineyard with pure unchecked ambition, the young men and woman in the organisation need to be disciplined in order to form them, to appreciate abundance.

"Take us the foxes, the little foxes that spoil the vines: for our vines have tender grapes." referring to the young –

At the time this was written, vineyards had protective walls around them. The purpose of the walls was to keep out the animals that would harm the grapes. *Foxes* are a generic term and include jackals. These animals would not eat the flowers nor the vines, but only the young fruit, the grapes. If the vineyard were not closely watched as the fruit came on, these animals would destroy the fruit of the vine. Because they have different priorities to that of the farmer.

The moral of this story is close your ranks with a few good men, the strongest, the bravest, the boldest, the peacemakers and not the war talkers, for they will eventually become your council and in counselling we seek profound wisdom. Like wine, the older the better. Where war talkers will get you in a mess and turn around and make you the author of it. Remember, if you choose average, or poor performers, you can only expect like-wise results. Things won't change for the sake of change, just because you want it to, it has to come from within – a trait already formed. A leopard does not change his spots, a lazy person needs to rest a lot. Get people with "can do" attitudes, the young and the restless at heart, they still have something to prove, on the upside for them, you will programme them to your likening if you have an open culture in place they will adopt it and they will cost you a fraction of the experienced veteran. However, if you don't, then get the old timers in. This aspect can make or break you as a leader and a manager; the ability to choose the right people for the right job, with the right mind set. If you seek everyone's opinion and approval, be sure you will get it, however, will it have meaning, will it add value, will it give you and them purpose and direction. Your deductions will become superficial if you listen and act and listen some more and act some more. Realise that everyone has his or her own agendas, good and bad. Moreover, do not strike deals with people you seem to like, but work with everyone as if they are indispensable and well liked. Thus in a totally professional manner and only if they are prepared to enter into a vision-drama situation or no deal. The more we share our vision about the vision, and how we will priorities our actions and effort, the less drama we will have. Otherwise it becomes favouritism, it is very natural to be liked, but like with all things in life we change our taste in fashion as time progresses. When making strategy, make the plan, afford everyone an opportunity to tweak it and then set course and act, act, act. Stay with this mentality or go for broke. For if you do not follow this route it will start to boil with uncertainty, the emotions will flare up, division will set in, and it will become a very heated affair, who has your ear and who does not. Strife and unhealthy competition for favour and good will with the "Boss" will soon emerge, mark my words.

The flavour of favouritism.

People will mimic the roles that those that get favour from you play and soon everyone will act accordingly – looking for favour. Do not ever assemble a council of people that think just like you, (fools think alike) it will become a council of fools. Alternatively, seek council from everyone at different stages individually on areas that they excel in – SME's, or they will form a cell of resistance and undermine everything you do or say. Recognise worth and utilise it, before it turns to a form of passive resistance, it sometimes becomes a dogmatic situation whereby they plainly will follow rules to the letter – meticulously, and if it all falls apart – "but you said...." It will become a compromising and demising position for you, if you are not fair, eventually you will be forced to take sides and protect people. Thus diminishing your professional position eventually and inhibiting your potential. In addition, if you allow this favouritism to prevail, it will strip you of your armour, that skin that says you are the though SOB. Never slip on this, there is a very definite line that should never be crossed by a leader, if you allow one step across it that goes un-reprimanded it will sure enough become a rebellion in motion. Because if you signal you can be pushed and pulled, by your confidants and manipulated into compromising, well then you are sure to find yourself in a compromising situation. Someone will defiantly try their luck and if he gets you to move from your fundamental foundation, then you will become their puppet. Remember it is the submissive that has the control and not the dominant one. Moreover, the more they push, the more buttons you reveal to be pushed in an attempt to regain your footing. Soon it will become impossible to steer the course of things back to the norm.

Some wisdom on setting up your council of confidants when you are going it alone:

"If you do not seek out allies and helpers, then you will be isolated and weak."
Sun Tzu, "The Art of War"

Look at this aspect of seeking council more closely in order to understand what seeking council constitutes. It stands to reason, and this we all know, that you need to surround yourself with capable people. This is not always possible and most of us have to work with what we get, or have. In this instance, we only seek council from our senior management or colleagues at the same level in the organisation, let them become your soundboard. Remember they do not have as much to gain, no agenda to work on that will directly involve you, if you fail they fail, as opposed to your group and section which have their own agendas and would all like to impress you and your seniors. If you do not wish to follow this advice then you have already reached a stage of interdependence and mutual professional trust, with your juniors. If not there yet, then you will be a predator seeking advice from the likes of vultures and hyenas on where to hide the carcass from the lion, it just never works out in a very competitive environment. There are steps to work with, from the "norming", to the forming, takes time. Therefore, you will have to draw upon your experience and profiles of the people with the necessary skill and competence to aid you in this regard that you trust. In order to perform the job well, to give it the quality it deserves. Let me explain this aspect of horizontal and vertical council by means of referring to a family as example. People within your subordinate group are seen to be like your "children", certain aspects are important to be discussed with them to get their view point and understanding of it. However, other subjects are only to be discussed with your "wife" and then certain subjects only with "family" and then critical subjects with the "doctor". Among all the ingredients when seeking council, the most important one is trust and trustworthiness which is so fundamental that:

Sun Tzu believed that the moral strength and intellectual faculty of man were a very decisive factor in achieving certain success he simply called it, "The Way".

Mutual trust is now recognised as "the way", to be the underlying factor to any successful interdependent endeavour. This is mostly easier said than done. Because of the fact that the Human resource departments and politicians do most of the recruiting for large agencies, governmental institutions and it becomes a circus. They pick family members and friends – so their agendas are not pure and sober either. On the other hand, the HR person picks someone that he thinks would make a good "warrior" based on his background and perception. The conclusion is this, although council and seeking counselling is a private and personal matter. We must understand that, it is always important to diversify your ways in which you seek council, for every individual will ultimately influence your decision making ability according to his or her reality. If they get called upon more often than others, then they start filtering in personal perceptions. This is a very dangerous alliance and practice, because you are elevating such a person, in stature and in confidence – this will diminish the others in the group. Without regarding the consequences of just having one or two focal points, confidants, from where you get input and feedback from, you are literirally painting yourself into a corner here, by limiting your options and knowledge base due to the limited sphere of influence you tap into. You become very detached from the real reality according to the collective, because you are only concerning yourself with your most favoured confidants reality, which will evidently become your collective reality and alienate the rest. This type of reality and relationship, especially when it is with junior people, normally becomes very warped due to the closing of ranks with one another. By totally confiding and believing in one another's abilities, by segregating yourselves from the rest...alienation creeps in because no one else dares to challenge you and everything starts decaying because of this unhealthy union.

When selecting quality people for strategic positions, contemplate the following:

- What kind of core management team is needed, against the priorities set,
- what is the minimum experience required, or specialisation level needed.
- keep in mind you can outsource, in order to carry out the strategy effectively by utilising SME's,
- or to design it at first, because working "ants" is more desirable, than working with "sheep" when you have to get off to a fast start.
- Profiling and records of accomplishment speak novels about competence and attitude.
- Qualifications are like tools, good to have, but it is not necessarily a good measure of true competence. (Jack of all trades but master of non – principle applies)
- First see if a candidate from the existing management team may be suitable for the position or could be promoted to fill the position.
- Where your core executive need strengthening - due to new skills development requirements, find a solution.
- Promoting from within vs. bringing in skilled management talent from outside or doing both, which will best serve our objective, and priorities best.

Determining the amount of specialisation or diversity that will be required by mixing things up or not, pertaining to backgrounds, experiences, do we need quantity or speciality, know-how, styles of managing and personalities to compliment the group should be looked into and not just competencies. Putting together a strong management team with the right personalities is like playing with a "chemistry" set, you never know what could happen, and getting a person with a mix of skills takes time.

Spin-off's

Building a dynamic group with strong core competency, will deliver flexible strategy, because experience and intellect is required to achieve this.

When it is difficult to out strategise rivals with a superior strategy the we have to look at:

- The next best avenue, strong strategic leadership, to out execute them with -
- Superior strategy implementation! – at every level and stage, becomes the key.

Building core competencies that rivals can't match is one of the best ways to out execute them, or out manoeuvre them, the process of killing your best product and reinventing a better one, take the intuitive and keep it, every quarter review, fine tune, this requires farsighted core competencies to be built in.

The revisiting of our strategic-relevance and setting priorities, by developing core competencies, this will create;

- **capability** -greater proficiency = product development
- **ability** - better quality = value for money
- **capability** - better manufacturing know-how = upping quality
- **ability** - superior cost-cutting skills = more capital
- **capability** - better marketing & merchandising skills = branding
- **ability** - skills capacitating =capability to provide better after-sale service

Ability and **capability** enhancement is the key words here; our ability to respond quickly to any changes in customer needs and being in tune with the customer market segment and its trends, require two aspects, ability and capability. This can be achieved by cross venturing to increase our capability, going into partnerships, like the Sony & Erickson partnership in the cellphone industry. Alternatively, by outsourcing certain aspects of the business to other companies that can build or manufacture the components, or design them at a fraction of the cost or time.

Effective collaboration; is the extreme combination of two opposites, what we know and what we perceive we can achieve. It has two elements; ability –aptitude, and capability – competence. *Ability*, from the Latin, meaning "skilful," is the quality of being able. It refers to competence in doing things. Whereas skill, is something that has already been acquired. It is what we can do now and *in the future*. *Capability* refers to a feature or faculty, to be capable of development, to the facility or potential for an indicated use or deployment. In other words, capability is "future" oriented. It is what we believe we can do somewhere *in the future* with appropriate instruction or joining. It is what we "believe" possible, what we can achieve should we...

Just a word or two on collaborating between powerful entity's: Best explained in a little story.

Partnering With Lions

This fable was originally reported in a Roman civil case, over 1,000 years ago.

The lion approached the wolf and the fox and suggested that they form a partnership for the purpose of hunting game.

The lion explained that each had particular talents that would lend themselves to such a partnership. The fox was wily and could trick the quarry into the open; and the wolf was swift of foot, so that he could direct the quarry to where the lion lay in wait to complete the kill.

After some discussion, the wolf and the fox agreed to enter into a partnership with the lion.

All went as planned and a deer was killed, but when the wolf and the fox tried to share in the kill, the lion challenged them. They stood by, helplessly and watched the lion devour the entire carcass.

Afterward, they asked the lion why he had only left them a few scraps. The lion replied, "All I took was the lion's share."

To this day, we still use the phrase, "the lion's share of the profits". In addition, the fable has a moral: *"When you enter into a partnership with a lion, you must be wary at the commencement of the partnership of how the profit's will be shared at its end".*

Opposition to the truth is inevitable, especially if it takes form of a new idea, but the degree of resistance can be diminished – by giving thought not only to the aim, but to the method of approach. *. B. H. Liddell Hart (1895 –1970)*

Change brings about cause and effect

We have to understand the importance of analysing the cause and effect of business theory. Especially with re-engineering. Especially pertaining to the "what are we – really - getting ourselves into" and is it worth the effort and cost.

First things first: *Re-engineering normally coincides with the realisation that something drastic needs to be done, and it better be sooner rather than later. Where the organisation is losing market share or efficiency for instance, and at the current rate will have to close business if no "critical" intervention takes place. Strategic re-engineering is a "now" for the "future" oriented survival plan, that calls for a totally different approach to better the current situation, both holistic and drastically. It is not a change control principle; where one merely changes controls, policy, managers and/or methods of production. If something does not work change it or buy a new one – type of dogma. With re-engineering the sky is literally the limit, confined to the idea that there is still possibilities available and all is not lost. The only thing that stands between the dream and the outcome is a radical strategy coupled to finances. Finances that will ring fence the limits of one's imagination. The first step will be to identify the capital offset against the projected gains on a time line of implementation to justify such a venture to the investors and or stakeholders.*

We require firstly; effective and proficient people to steer the initial assumptions and theories with. A strong degree of project, strategic and financial management skills and guidance are prerequisite for successful strategic re-engineering. As there are many factors to consider that require diversified informed input, especially on the following:

The total cost of the envisaged re-engineering project for the organisation, from the bottom up, from;

- Allocating ample resources to mission specific components and mission critical activities, by eliminating waste and inefficiency.
- Enabling new strategic initiatives like; automation, specialisation and empowering supportive components, such as software, hardware and tools to aid tasks of aligning policies and procedures to compliment the new systems with.
- Researching and developing, or adopting best practices and mechanisms towards supporting continuous improvement.

- Cost to company; looking at possible re-structuring of remuneration packages and the implementation of proper rewards and incentives schemes, conducive to the organisations overall wellness.
- Legal compliance and new training required; certification, legal compliance, insurance, registering and getting certified.
- Lastly, becoming leaner, by cutting the fat; subsidies, incentives, and bonuses.
- Addressing the question of diversifying;
  - by looking at; general inefficiency – re-profiling of all jobs, outsourcing, rentals, maintenance and service contracts, joint ventures, creating alliances, improving on turn-around times.
  - Proper task evaluation with supportive; job descriptions, structures and the human resource skill level requirements.
  - creating a new corporate identity and culture, with less managers, by incorporating environmental redesigning.

Demographics

The choices are divers and could include dilemmas such as what to do with the current work force vs. a total new work force.

Target markets profiling; the characteristics of a human population or part of it, especially its size, growth, density, distribution, and statistics regarding birth, marriage, disease, and death

Locality

- Moving the entire company and re-settling in another province or country, because it is cheaper, less restrictions, labour is more specialised and skilled etc.
- If cost is no longer a problem, or the option becomes affordable, then we have to look at some degree of intra-industry integration by entering into innovative cooperative agreements with companies from other industries.
- Looking at ways to achieve cash flow improvements.
- Cutting on operational costs by downsizing on none profitable departments.
- Will these aspects when thoroughly contemplated justify our reasons for reengineering?

The fundamental reasons for re-engineering:

- A change in market direction;

    - Migration, where markets are entering a totally new field, or breaking into the market with new product.
    - Contemplating expansion – with down or up scaling; decentralisation, or globalisation - outsourcing – or centralisation - specialising of components of the company
    - Switching to technology with partial or total automation of departmental functions.
    - Amalgamation or separation of companies.

When experiencing; de-escalation of all services levels, stagnation in growth over extended period or its just no longer profitable business.

Understanding the fundamentals.

It is not always a good idea to restructure and re-engineer if the reasons are not mentioned in the five points of priority statements (above) that justify re-engineering.

Reorganisation and re-engineering are two different animals, the first is "politically" driven the second is economically driven, and they have different aims and approaches. It would be a disaster to assume that they are the same. Just to have the two co-inside, especially when it comes to cost and the loss of cohesion, expertise and the loss of corporate culture – that could lead to total invectiveness if re- engineering fails to survive the burden of change.

However, the return on investment is rewarding where and if re-engineering was successful. The model can be duplicated, as tools to any venture capitalist requiring re-engineering strategist, to realign them with new ventures. He will now have a core competency trained up and ready for future alignments. Building dynamic change compatible organisations should form part of the vision of re-engineering, as nothing stays constant, except change.

MQM & Re-engineering philosophy.

Re-engineering and MQM (Matrix Quality Management) seeks one-time quantum gains;

- both in capital in order of 30 to 50% or more opposed to marginal gains, as well as;
- MQM seeks on-going incremental and sustainable improvement of human capital, by continued building of resilience, to cope with change and still keeping with quality enhancement. It becomes a culture building project, to enhance both corporate, strategic and the functional discipline of people. In order to keep turning up with quality solutions, that are holistic in design and approach. The offset is increments in salary, promotion and incentives.
- Re-engineering and MQM are not mutually exclusive, they are inclusive.
- First, re-engineering is used to produce a good basic design yielding dramatic improvements;
- based on utilising superior recourses and technology.
- incorporation of skilled and professional labour and building out from there,
- the basic design is used over and over, it was intentionally symmetrical and flat, so that it could be expanded into any direction at any given stage – the business design matrix.

Then, MQM is used mainly to perfect processes

- by removing red tape and gradually improving efficiency and eliminating waste.
- MQM looks for the "error programming" caused by human intervention or dysfunctional or out-dated systems.
- The result is aimed at clearing bottlenecks.
- Every system component is designed to focus on quality from cradle to grave, speed and accuracy is paramount.
- This implies that if it is not to specification it simply does not get passed on to the next level.
- Minimum standards, and best practices are applied/ adopted and implemented...

The Matrix refers to a well-designed and organised framework within which every aspect of re-engineering is quality tested first, before interconnecting with the next level of business design, at systems level, at any junction.

The matrix is designed to bring about an atmosphere of co-operative design of business structures to achieve goals. With the business matrix as map, or design reference.

It is not a "Hippie colony" of sorts. It is an adult intellectual playground. Also referred to as "assertive", "as long as it is quality it is good- and our strategy". Where the basic principles of the constitution we formed beforehand starts governing everything.

Then it is no longer just a matter of designing systems with very few "laws", and flaws, its holistic, and "red tape" no longer prevail, but rather systems with the least flaws.

Rather a greater emphasis on the "Ethic" and "Moral" values, internalised, to ask of the people to give it their best and was it quality. With a strong emphasis on work ethic; which is vigorously enforced by penalising bad "the behaviour" of people rather than bad behaviour of systems – systems are hard to change, people can be changed faster, but the systems need to be flexible to take up the speed – and be more effective, bad quality and low work rates are attributes of work ethic and badly designed systems co-existing.

Colleagues that live with the knowing that performance and loyalty will be rewarded, not just with lip-service but also with remuneration, promotion, and everyone is on a personal performance contract of his own making. This is no longer a company with driftwood; everyone is "green and growing".

Re- engineering starts with reverse engineering, by looking at things in hindsight, is said to be an exact science. Therefore we first seek our own deficiencies before attempting to change anything.

The Art of Reverse Engineering; requires active and decisive methodology combined with skilful leadership and experience to pay dividends, it is the "golden triangle" of design.

Reverse Engineering is the process of going through *the leadership loop*; **(DQQI)Designing, qualifying, quantifying and then identifying.** Leaders come and go, the only thing that remains constant is the current leaders ability to lead effectively, called leadership.

Common mistakes with leaders taking the lead with restructuring;

- **Take an active leading role when heading up restructuring** – people do not like a lot of verity, antics and choices when confronted with humongous amounts of change.
- They seek guidance, stability, understanding and vision - leadership.

Assumptions are very dangerous at this stage, it might cause a lot of contention later on as well, and when your group sees you generalising, assuming and being easily influenced and swayed, they follow suit.

Beware; you are setting yourself up for failure and your team, if you are not concise and clear. They, your team, your managers, colleagues will assume that assumptions would be in order with you and are acceptable as a practiced principle, the first thing that pops up in their mind is, if it's good enough by the Boss's standards – we can tap dance and he will be happy- kind of mentality.

Leaders dictate the level at which follower's will have to think:

- here they need to think critically, and their assumptions need to be verified – because they become catalyst for thinking, and steer the direction of change and design.
- leaders tell people how to judge them and themselves and by which standards they are held accountable.

If you do not allow participation with the **"Design",** and fluidness of ideas to flow, remember slow is fast, and then you will be not be off to a fast demise;

- Measure twice cut once – is a carpenters law
- Take the time needed to get the full picture across, of what is at stake.
- Then only start **"Qualifying"** peoples arguments;
  - o Test assumptions; statistics, everything you will use, needs to be verified
  - o so that they make sense when contemplated as possible solutions to all,
  - o before grabbing the first fix, and running with it - you will kill enterprise someone said – if you merely grab at straws.

The same is true for the opposite, some individuals always want to be right and want to be heard and normally they are, so everyone stops challenging him or her and goes with the flow, eventually, and stop thinking problems through.

"Qualifying" becomes a big danger area, never stop challenging authenticity, authority, originality and correctness.

If you do, it will enter into every hypothesis and corrupt your model at some stage or another.

It will be more readily expectable and advised if it can be factually backed when designing the concepts identified as solutions.

With **"Identify"** - either academically and/or scientifically it should be backed by sound reasoning.

Having such a filter for modelling plan, or design backed up with factual correctness and practical insight and creditability leads to perfection.

We have to filter, to eliminate future waste, and be open to be scrutinised.

Reality check;

We have to fit the model with our reality. It, the model must be in harmony with the market you are venturing into, the problem you have to solve, the challenges you have to address, towards being on par with other leaders in the field.

By taking the visible role you are endorsing the concept and enforcing confidence. It never pays to take up a low-key, behind the scenes role. When redesigning or engineering major change.

Great change does not come about by making great decisions on the premise of pure consensus, neither nor authoritatively, it dictates the following elements to be present before it will be implemented;

- **Trust**
- Transparency in communication and good old fashioned common-sense.
- It needs to make sense to change and there has to be a quantifiable and untreatable reason to do so.
- People in general do not prefer change much, just as changing for the sake of changing is not acceptable reasoning either, it has to be essential.
- The vision for change has to be shared and understood.

Be personally involved in the conception phase;

- **"Designing"**- it, steer, guide and co-ordinate. Nevertheless, never ever hand over, if it can be avoided. Several reasons come to mind; in matters very complex where millions of dollars or jobs are at stake and the stakes are high. Remember -the leader/s stay and remain fully accountable.
- **"Qualifying"**- check and recheck everything for yourself before signing off on it, whatever it may be. However, the core reasons will be and remain ultimately at the door of accountability, the rest of the team is merely responsible for the implementation.
- Moreover, where and when delegating, **"Quantifying"**- do it within the framework of accountability and make sure to state the cause and effect law clearly, as well as the recourse available to the function, should the assignee fail.
- By implementing strict criteria and guidelines as well as all the details, before handing over, we steer towards specifics, **"Identifying"**- the desired outcome required.

Factors to consider when distributing and delegating tasks:

- The persons level of experience and accumulated knowledge about the subject or task.
- Whether the person is new to the job or seasoned at what he is about to tackle.
- The persons network of personal relationships; his or her support group - the type of friends he keeps and in what regard do they keep him or her.
- The persons own diagnostic, administrative, interpersonal and problem-solving skills.
- The level of trust and the confidence with which the person performs his task.
- The type of leadership style and manager the person is most comfortable with, as well as working environment.

Managers conclusions about the role he/she should play in light of what has to be done, as well as the persons mutual respect attitude (does he respect his supervisor or tolerate him). Discipline - is to moral as important as water is to sustaining life, you cannot slack on discipline and ethical formal code ever. Once you allow subordinates to cross the formal lines of respect and discipline, it starts impacting on all aspects of group dynamic. –e.g., why can Kevin come late? Why does Lucy get time off? Why can he go out to lunch with the boss and not me the supervisor, etc.- keep it tight. Mutual respect when interacting with other interdepartmental colleagues, the principle of "bad planning or a lack of it does not constitute an emergency on my side", hold truth, don't bully your way through other departments if you did not plan for contingencies.

The three simple steps to building a dynamic organisation:

- Start by selecting proficient and competent people for key positions.
- Constantly keep developing skills, core competencies and competitive capabilities with current staff, through continuous career path training.
- Keep revising strategy, systems and resources, until it reaches the optimum level, or as required and look at supportive organisational structures every so often, not just annually. Their growth is not always in parallel with the core system, and could be hampered by the fastest or slowest movers.

The four rules for creating core competence:

1. It has to be a unilateral process, embarked on by all departments in tandem, that tie up at one point – a shared effort and vision.
2. Different requirements typically emerge from different managers, especially middle management, even in the same groups and departments that could identify a short fall or blind spot, act speedily.
3. Gaining the competitive advantage requires specialisation, keep it current and effective, by developing core competence, by concentrating more effort and capital than rivals on creating or strengthening core competencies, and maintain perishable skills.
4. The scope and level of competency required, needs to be broad and flexible in order to react to changes in markets and customers' needs.

Building capacity amongst managers is a time consuming effort, even more so with general staff. This specific initiative is an exercise best orchestrated by the senior managers who, has to be re-programmed in the new doctrine before it is rolled out. In order for them to understand how the firm's core competence are interrelate and changing, they need to experience it first-hand. This fostering and building of inroads of understanding of what is transpiring at grass roots level, as well as between departments and institutions are of the greatest and utmost importance. No one can exist in a vacuum without guidelines, information, and communication, especially when dealing with all aspects of interaction. MOU's clearly define the understanding and the grounds on which it was made, we deal with the problem of "referral – it is not my problem – so who's problem is it then" to connect, we need a reference point, and systems that are aligned. In short, it is the same as a constitution and mutually binding to all.

The value and effect of building core competency

- It enhances the propensity for achieving the competitive advantage, as a shared ideology.
- It becomes the vehicles paving the way to above-average performance over the, short, medium and long run.
- It greatly improves chances for overall improvement and long-term survival, by escalating chance of success, and the better "we" get at succeeding the better "you" succeed.

The overall organisational scheme is one of the central tasks of organisation-building and effective strategy implementation! Strategy without competence is worthless. The strategic relevance of good, and pertinent training can never be overstated, and the refreshing of "perishable skills" all coincide to gain a lasting competence for redesign to be effective. The lack of competence is a complication of "diseases". We need creative entrepreneurial minds, they don't always come off the shelf, an management oversight. By only applying a remedy to one area, by fixing it, you will provoke another; and that which removes the one ill symptom produces others. Everything interacts, and relates. Training is not the alpha and omega, but a good place to start immunising for future problems...structure follows strategy, so too must our training, follow the strategy, to support the structure. Training in a dynamic environment that becomes *expensive*, due to its repetitive and reoccurring nature, people tend to be promoted in a short time, or resign to go onto greener pastures, once deemed competent or qualified. With them they take all the essential experience gained, do we fill the voids created effectively? We need to be able to hold onto intellectual capital or build "revolving capital" with new people filling vacant positions. Not just by looking at a job description, to secure a match. We need to look at the levels of competence and experience required as well. The significance of training goes beyond skills development. Training is the key *attitude adjustment* tool; because it changes aptitude and aptitude changes mental altitude, that changes perceptions. Training in itself should be the vehicle, through which the *organisation evolves* into the new animal, where we breed the culture we desire, with constant evolution, refresher courses and follow up courses and building on success stories. Training has to be on going, and a career path orientated affair to add value. A lot said, but the one thing found is that very few companies actually invest in career path orientated training that is structured, and in line with the strategies of the company and its core business. Training is done on a "we have this, do you want some of it basis". No, in order to be *adding true value* to the development of people, training needs to be strategic and aligned, it has to be structured and relevant. Courses are normally dished up at the *drop of a hat*, where shortcomings have been identified, and what is worse, most companies draw from what is marketed, and don't bother to see if it is relevant and if it will add value. Nothing wrong with this type of "add in training", however caution on the side of relevance, people want to learn how the job should get done, as prescribed by their seniors, rather than by some "textbook mechanic". If it is not conducive to *personal and strategic development* in the long run, it could rob others from a training opportunity that is still required, because money are now being wasted.

Challenges of disparity, not everyone is schooled equally, in the same subjects and at the same level. Thus, certain disparities develop over time. Find ways to close the gap;

- Therefore it should be imperative that *career path orientated training be rewarded*, with relevant subjects that should be compulsorily, standardised and institutionalised – this add-in could be viewed as merit points towards applying for new positions, an increase or promotions.
- On promotion, with a career path planned beforehand, revised annually and supportive of the matrix structuring, there will be a *clearer benchmark and criteria for promotion*, a specific study path for every position within the organisation.
- Some positions at junior level should be created with systematic advancement in mind. This implies levels of remuneration within the same post, maybe four levels of remuneration. In order to go to the next level one requires a specific qualification and when you get it, you get an automatic increase upon delivering a *recognised prescribed qualification*. This will encourage staff to school themselves and capacitate your workforce.
- Most if not all basic training and qualifications, should be focused on the *developing of core business skills*, and not nice to haves, that the trainee can master in a very short space of time, even in his own time.
- At junior level, courses should be short, snap on courses e.g. phone etiquette - will directly influence his specific work quality – we can add value. Every successful pass of a snap on course, gives the employee points, when interviewing, these *points will count towards a qualification course*.
- All courses should be designed to be scored, a weighted score is added to each skill and qualification and study fields should branch out into other fields and be bridgeable into other positions with accumulated credit points. Therefore, if the employee wants to switch departments, *his training, experience and qualifications will carry weight*. Otherwise what is the point of getting qualifications in the rat race, if only the favoured ones get promoted.
- All prior learning is scored as well. In addition, any specific higher learning is scored as well. The last aspect is also year's service and experience; taken into account and scored likewise. This brings about "fair" competition when rallying for promotion. The organisation can determine that only people with a score of "x" need apply. Then only on the short-listing does work ethic come into play and experience.
- *Training is a strategy-critical activity* and must form part of any core business, where technical expertise is changing or advancing rapidly. Mostly failure to train result in failure to achieve.

Strategy implementers ensure training functions are;

- Adequately funded and accredited with training facilities that are up and running.
- All training is structured towards achieving value, and symmetry – we need to be able to gauge our competence. Where people resign, get promoted, get transferred etc. We need to be able to measure our intellectual weight loss or gain so to speak, to keep a healthy balance.
- Only where effective training programmes are up to standard, budgeted for, affordable, deliver on benchmarks set, accessible and in place – do we find structured development. That supports the requirements of the strategy, its goals and vision.

Structure has to follow strategy or does it, are they not interrelated?

I do understand that a lot of you who will be reading this book are quite conversant with business and the maxim of "structure following strategy", nevertheless, I urge you to read this section to refresh your perspective on what you know, and urge you to do it with an open mind. This is a very compact overview of considerations to be followed. The idea is to reinforce the importance of sound business principles here and how systems thinking will interlink, the formal approaches to business with re-engineering.

By structure we are referring to the organisational structure depicted as a chart.

Here we have three distinct but related things that are true of all.

Its aim;

- *the division of labour in the organisation*: dividing work into traditional tasks or roles such as
    - operations,
    - logistics
    - transportation,
    - and training,
    - and defining them into units, e.g.,
    - branches, departments, administrative units
    - or divisions according to a uniform criteria in terms of; mission, function, unit size and/or region.

The distribution of authority and responsibility to individuals within the organization, being made responsible for a branch or division or sub section. This is the organisation's responsibility structure. Coupled to a name, designation or rank. Call it the reporting structure.

the organisation's system of measuring and evaluating performance, how it organises information, inputs, outputs and costs. This is the organisation's financial and (MIS) management information system flow diagram or structure. These attributes are normally centralised, to form the support structures.

Strategy should determine structure. Therefore strategy informs us, or should, of what will be required. Strategy should also define the means to realise the purposes of the strategy, and not just the vision. Through the identification of forces that interact and act against the strategy, project, plans, budgets, research, policies, legislation, etc...are not always clear. It should at least define the organisations goals and its mission statements realistically, and factually against the internal and external forces experienced. All in relation to its environment and what it hopes to achieve.

Different designs for different purposes are available;

- Single-mission organisations should be organised along functional lines
- Multi-mission organisations should be organised along mission lines;
- Multi-function organisations should be organized along matrix lines.
- Where a matrix organisations are normally large enough to justify an extensive division of labour.

What is an organisation chart?

It is a depiction of how functions will be divided, both line and staff functions - The functions of a department can be defined as a line or a staff function. The functions which have a direct responsibility of achieving the targets for production (or sales) are referred to as line functions. The staff functions are those which do not participate directly in the activity but aid, or support line functions to achieve their targets. Every organisation thus have both a formal – line - and an informal – staff - organisational structure.

Examples of organisational structures are:

- Hierarchical structure (typical for the small, entrepreneurial organisation)
- Line-staff structure
- Functional or Departmental structure (based on function, products/service, customer type, geographic region)
- Matrix structure (dual reporting lines)

The application of organisational charts.

- Defining the roles, salary scale and level of responsibility of all personnel within the organisation.
- Establishing a hierarchical structure of authority, powers vested and, hence, decision-making authority.
- Establish a chain of command with specific rules and regulations relating to reporting procedures and accountability methods.

- Establishing control mechanisms, such as the degree of centralisation and the span of control over people and resources.
- Establishing strategies for co-ordination of work practices with other structures.
- Establishing decision-making processes pertaining to budgets awarded.
- Establishing specific operational functions and tasks.

Limitations of organisational charts.

It is only a snap shot of how labour distribution into functional units should or could look. It does not address organisations changes, and specifics.

It does not help much to understand what actually happens within the operations side of the organisation. In reality, organisation keep changing internally, with promotions, and staff movement that follow its own route.

Traditional organisation charts are static, and cannot cope with changing elements.

We have to understand the importance of any changes, in design of the organisation, as it has both cause and effect. With re-engineering the aim is to check what works and make it better, faster, and simpler pertaining to;

- *arriving at one winning combination that works for the organisation,*
- *with clear roles for employees, both in terms of accountability and responsibility, as well as where they will belong in the system.*
- *With a compelling vision of change in direction, where everyone believes that it will be beneficial to all, because they were made part and parcel of the changes contemplated, had input and could criticise the contemplated restructuring.*

More points to consider when looking at designing a structure from the ground up, or re-engineering. We need to start looking at the principles of structural design, and what it implies in a collective, when we say – "Structure follows strategy".

Mostly restructuring coincides with sudden changes in direction and strategy, that requires a revalidation of our current structure. Is it still effective? Or, do we have to change the "boat we are sailing in". When having to contemplate a completely new structure to facilitate the changes contemplated.

These aspects may require you to consider the following givens:

- Contemplating any changes in strategic direction has risks. Using the same structure, or a completely new design, either way, it will impact directly on the structure, we need to find out where and how, and by how much.
- Alternatively, when streamlining. Here we only consider components of structure; only a branch or a unit will be effected, even so, we need to gauge to what extent will it impact on the rest.
- The true detail of the effect will only emerge, once the amendments as needed to support the changing strategy, are enacted. Only when in motion, can we see the affect of what was designed.
- with any radical strategy it is conceded that any change will have repercussions we could not have seen or perceived; we need to gauge to what effect, and ready ourselves with alternatives and options.
- Therefore the ripple effect of change needs to be absorbed effectively.
- Alternatively, it should even be contemplated to alter the complete structure with a new structure, for successful transition to full implementation.
- Whilst looking at transition options, consider research done in this regard.

Research results into structure indicate that:

- Organisational structures affects performance directly and tampering with it causes chaos.
- Changing anything on an existing structure affects the global structure at some point.
- Mainly because structures form invisible connections, and relationships over time through people. Mainly at operational level not seen on the design. Where they become reliant on each other for certain aspects.
- Therefore - Any changes, if not carefully handled, could disturb the balance within the rest of the structure.
- Structural size, will impact on scaling; that merits reassessment whenever strategy changes take effect.

Scaling up or down

The bigger the structure the more complex the systems and level of co-ordination required to reassemble the connections necessary, the more room for error and the more prone the organisation is towards losing its unit culture to perform, new mangers, systems, offices etc., takes time to gel, and reach optimum output again.

The smaller the structure, the simpler the systems required, the less impact on unit culture is observed and the less error.

Matrix management structures was developed because of this phenomenon to replicate the principles of small into big, without having to break up units, with restructuring of organisation. Business units stay as they are, it's just their reporting lines that differ.

New strategy likely entails different skills requirements and key activities to come into play, it all takes time and effort to complete, to get it to the ready, and then operational.

How work is structured is a means to an end and not an end in itself, how we ask the questions to solve our dilemmas with, will determine the answers to the means we arrive within itself.

1. Who is needed, the level of skill and competence, as well as level of accountability?

2. What are the results we wish to see, and how will we measure it?

3. What will the cost be in terms of options x, y, and z?

4. What standards and safeguards will we adopt, what is the feasibility?

5. What are the risks, rewards and possible penalties involved?

6. For what period of time will we be needing this structure, and is it the best when gauged against our evolution and growth path?

Structure is seen as a vehicle for:

- Combining essential elements of business in graphical form.
- Facilitating the expression of the execution of any strategy
- Structures assist in identifying required "stuff" and putting it in the right place;
    - Recourses
    - Communication,
    - Logistics
    - Support
    - Infrastructure
    - Legal requirements
- There is also "structure", within structure, within structure, that gives things structure.
- Administrative structure - The setting of performance targets and standards, and systems.
- Training and development structure - Capacitating some people at some levels, (is only a partial fail safe).
- Managerial structure - We need to go deeper, we need to look at control spans in new structures
- Communication and technologies structure - New lines and forms of communication, or technologies

- Resources structure - Resources, infrastructure, and labour requirements.
- Confinement structure - Restrictions, labour unions, climate, legal, geographical, cultural etc.
- Command and control structure - Elements which requires greater levels of autonomy or dependence – decision making, - within the command and control structure.
- "Harnessing" individual efforts to become one effort, to achieve the goals autonomously requires heightened skills from managers and better resource development and utilisation.
- Overall "command and control" or co-ordinating of performance and tasks of diverse nature, requires a communication structure, every element of structure with in structure requires a supportive structure and resources.

Giving strategy structure promotes the critical, intellectual, scientific, academic and rational aspect of strategy. It highlights effective thinking, planning and implementation at each stage with well-co-ordinated efforts, broken up into segments that can be gauged and fine-tuned; through short, medium and long term goals.

The benefits of structuring our strategy

Mission critical processes can be clustered or decentralised: better work distribution. Thus reducing fragmentation or duplication of required processes that have to run in tandem, to get to completion in time.

- Better centralising and sorting of tasks that belong together under one administrator.
- Or alternatively decentralising units to be closer to the end of line, to speed up things.

The ability to chop and change by applying traditional models that segregate management elements into work groups. Cuts out bureaucratic and autocratic thinking – therefore addressing management styles and models that differ from the one to the next department.

It could also involve;

Compressing formerly separated tasks into one function and not just a department, performed and overseen by a group and not just a single person in charge of;

- Performance enhancement with all the resources at the groups disposal, and even some automation, or total.
- Integrating tasks that are sorted into talent pools, specialising in specifics, where we have specialist concentrating on this aspect only.
- Organising team activities that spawn the development of better core competency that supports the whole structure in specific activities.

- Reorganizing and adjusting workers to function in colonies rather than departments to link up and deliver team results.

It provides;

Diverse and improved new organisational design options, strong with strong, weak with weak and then cross politicisations once the competence has been reached. Enhancing the potential outcome with;

- Instant dramatic gains in productivity and organisational creativity.
- Flattened organisation structure equals expedited decision making – no longer is strategic emphasis at the top but now it resides with the middle management, even more so at operational level.
- Financial overheads are cut by reducing the amount of executive posts, we no longer have "Fat Cats" that drain the financial gains with huge salaries and perks that push strategy implementation, to get the bonus, this money is now utilised to improve systems and resources with.
- Responsibility and decision-making is thereby automated and done with authority and confidence, it pushes up customer confidence, because the frontline is fighting the good fight with the mandate and resources to do it with.
- Improved personalised interaction with customers, sharing of the corporate culture and vision is now tied up at all levels due a sense of belonging to the process, this creates responsibility and authority.
- Strategy-critical processes are unilaterally driven, no longer top down;
- Processes becomes unified and synchronised at the floor level,
- Performed much quicker and at a lower cost,
- More responsive to customer expectations, changes and deadlines.
- Strategy becomes the plan of the organisation and no longer just a person.

Strategy is the determination of the direction of the main blow – The plan of strategy is the plan of the organisation of the decisive blow in the direction in which the blow can most quickly give the maximum results. In other words, to define the direction of the main blow means to predetermine the nature of operations in the whole period of war, to determine nine-tenths of the fate of the entire war. In this is the main task of strategy. Joseph Stalin, quoted in Garthoff, Soviet Military Doctrine, 1953

The Process of restructuring in a collective format called re-engineering.

First we have to understand the nature of strategy when dealing with re-engineering and restructuring: For Strategy here becomes twofold, in two parts, the one part is the natural element. The traditional - Industrial Organisational approach - the models, the targets, project planning and methodology, the things that most strategist are well conversed with. Despite the fact that it is humans that drive the efforts. Therefore, the second part is the human element that we now incorporate in matrix thinking. The "sociological approach" – dealing with all things related to human nature as a whole.

Here is the twist; many strategists only or merely function from the one paradigm, one school of thought that leads to one single strategic concept – this is the norm. However do we still see this as being fundamentally right, no, it can't be, because we don't seem to get the required results. The world has emancipated, only when strategy succeeds in forming several strategies as a result of the type of thinking applied from having one core strategy, that encompass all other, then do the process of fusing both parts to form one total concept, become a "Radical Strategy".

Radical strategy holds the belief that everything in strategy has two opposing parts that one has to fuse seamlessly with the other to become a whole – before it becomes true radical strategy.

We tend to spend too much time and money on crafting one perfect strategy on paper and too little on the challenges of implementation, the fitting of such strategy into the human domain. Even with radical strategy, we always keep in mind the critical element of *how the organisation does things traditionally* and depart from this focal point to enhance and capitalise on that, as an innate strength. For it is a strength derived from habitual traits that we wish to harness. This aspect is echoed in the diversity of managerial activity, there is always more than one way available to solve any problem and the art is to find that one way that will fit best.

Consequently, with radical strategy, we recognise this element and implement it with the "wave breaking" effect. This ideology stems from watching waves break on a beach. They come in small, and big layers, one following the other. Likewise, multiple waves of initiatives and not just resorting is used. We don't settle with just one "Best Plan" as is the norm, no, we complement each initiative and plan with several smaller strategies, to see which one takes us, further, faster, with the least resistance and then only do we formulate it into one strategy. A master strategy that compliments each defined objective, towards the main directive. By dually throwing expertise, money, or resources at problems, we do not create waves, instead we create ripples. Ripples require consensus, too many "Chiefs and too little Indians", it always becomes a factor; everyone believes that they can do it, and do it better.

The point is; we require a total more holistic approach towards solving problems, a total paradigm shift in business design is required today if we want to truly succeed and not just survive. We have become somewhat ineffective due to our eroded reality – of the BEST plan, and stereotype thinking - that we hold onto for dear life. These stereo types still use the "think outside the box" saying, then I know for sure they don't know how to think or solve problems effectively. Today there is just too much change, to little time, and resources, to just choose one plan, and then gamble with one strategy. When in fact we only need to run with tailor made changes, and versions of structure and strategy that exist, that can evolve on its own. We need one "Master Strategy" and "Master structure" that can be hooked onto, like a relay race, the rest can plan the second wave, pending the results of the first, that will take us beyond the break point of the first, then the third wave, and so on and so forth. Should the first wave not succeed the second one will, in this fashion we learn from our mistakes, if not, we can back step or move to the third, but one will eventually succeed. It is a question of proper co- ordination, and using diversified efforts and structuring of resources and activities all lined up in tandem. Things are no longer seen to belong to silos. We must be mindful of the fact, that it is people who craft strategy and not organisations. It is also these people who will or will not effectively implement them, therefore, never risk everything on one endeavour when it becomes foreign to the labour force, one person and one paradigm might let you down; follow multiple routes, or waves of "attack". If we all know and understand the goals, then the main objective becomes clearer.

Step one; Plan - *"The plan of strategy is the plan of your people, and not the organisation".*

The very people that will have to execute the plan, will be the factor of strength we require. Everyone can prove they are strong or intelligent once. Strength and Intelligence on its own can be very impressive, the real question is can they prove it again and again, consistency counts where situations change rapidly, when consistency is observed right through, that's when it becomes real, then we have delivered, and we have real strength.

Formulating the strategic plan. Firstly we set objectives. Objectives are seen as the direction our goals will follow to reach the final objective. It could be seen as planning a journey, to a final destination, along that journey we will have to follow many roads, stop at places to sleep over, refuel, eat, take a body break etc....and then arrive at our final destination. Objectives could be seen as the towns we pass through, goals as the road we travel on. We will start engineering our plans with the end in mind – the final objective. Objectives are broken up into "GOALS". Goals are multi-facetted, they have many attributes; physical, mental, symbolic and unseen in nature. A goal is not smart, it is complex, with complex attributes, thus a goal is in fact many elements made up of smaller attributes. Thus, the final goal will become several goals, in order to achieve the main goals, to achieve the objectives, to reach the final objective. We need to reverse engineer our goals. If all things are created thrice, or three times. Then we need to; identify, quantify and qualify each step first. Firstly the abstract, *in the mind* and then from the abstract – to the concrete *on paper* and then into its physical or *final form, that fits with our reality*. This is the very reason many fail; they fail by only seeing the physical perspective, the final picture. Without fitting it in with their reality. This is far removed from the reality of its creation, of what things were before they became the sum total – the essential elements required and combined to form the final envision - objective. Therefore, we have to dissect goals into elements and attributes. We have to split them.

Everything, has two parts, one in contrast to the other, the one cannot exist without the other, when combined it comes into balances and becomes an _element_ or an _attribute that make up a system that constitutes a goal, and several goals an objective, and several objectives the main objective_. Let me explain by _identifying_ the essentials of goals.

Attributes are - something described as having particular qualities – belonging to the bigger whole forming _elements_ –

Elements are -the basic and most important things that define _parts/ concepts_ – that in turn form part of a system or concept.

Concepts and Systems are -a combination of related _parts/ smaller concepts_ – small and big - organised into a complex whole that serves a specific purpose.

Address the nature of all things as they exist, because they originate from those opposites of the spectrum themselves.

The characteristics of radical strategy:

Understand the uniqueness and necessity of the "newness" - a new concept. Then dismantle, re-assemble and afterwards simplify the process first. Find the best fit by looking at opposing parts that will form one whole, joining with the system you have; i.e.

Determine which parts of processes need to be automated, outsourced, or eradicated.

Evaluate each activity on its own merit, in terms of "CAPS"; **_Concept, Attributes, Perception and System_** - determine if it is strategy-critical or not. This way you will know where the critical path in the organisation resides and with whom.

Weigh up the pros and cons of outsourcing, economically and both organisationally as well as strategically.

Design the structure for performing the remainder of activities, as supporting add-ons.

Work out the total cost of the project -linking budgets to sub- projects etc.

Crafting strategy-supportive policies and procedures that are utilised unilaterally, in other words just one master policy, from where all else will flow.

Analyse and devise your own mission specific sets of: Best Practices (BP's), Standard Operating Procedures (SOP's), communication systems requirements, software and whatever will be required that will fit. Why do we say this? Because someone will sell you a Porch, when in fact you only need a tractor to do the job with. We tend to go to extremes, and it is mostly not a necessity, it's just a nice to have.

This will then give you the nine competencies required to steer goals and objectives with;

- The "scale and scope" of the goal
- Creating "Team Spirit"
- Defining what is "Customer Excellence"
- Addressing "Poor work rate" and "Absenteeism"
- Creating structured "Communication"
- Specifying what is; "Compliance and Quality"
- Identifying what is required from "Training and development"
- Show how and where to start "Aligning departmental strategy with company strategy"
- Setting benchmarks for "Achievement of key measurement factors"

Step two: Strategy **implementation** needs to concentrate on fundamentals first and bells and whistles later.

Evaluate optimum performance levels for each unit; then set the benchmarks and determine what will be required to reach them with goal setting, before thinking of designing the systems and structure. Remember, the system is only as strong, fast, and productive as the bottlenecks are wide, the goals are realistic, people are competent, and processes are aligned. We tend to jump to systems design before we clearly understand what we require at grassroots level. No one, and i mean no one, can design outside their means and capacity, or that of the environment that the structure will have to reside in. Although we can think and plan in this manner, it is not the way to go. The idea is to work with every aspect of the matrix, at the smallest level first, by reverse engineering it, this implies, from the most prominent form, the current reality, to where we need it to be, to be both effective and efficient, and to fit in with our projects parameters. Only with full informative, supportive and argumentative deductions, will we arrive at the ideal state of any objective. On the flip side of this reasoning, we have to remember that we can never afford something until our very livelihood depends on it, then it is normally just too late. This principle needs to prevail here as well. We have to make sure that mission and strategy complement each other, and that the structure is strong, and effective...

Spend more time on aligning and planning goals , than what you do on objectives. The objectives can look great, but without the necessary support, they could collapse. Goals are the foundation, if they are weak so will be the objectives.

~ 198 ~

Screen requests for new capital projects and bigger operating budgets carefully, it could become totally irrelevant in the months to come. Be future oriented whilst also focusing on basic requirements as well.

Be committed and willing to shift resources to support new strategic priorities on the critical path with, endeavour to prevail under pressure. Act and act fast when doing things right. Don't let pressure overwhelm you, and force on you to perform crisis management.

Make a persuasive case to fellow superiors and supervisors, on what resources are really needed, by targeting strategic line functions and clusters first. Administrative functions, that generate statistical data, document processes, and give us information, is the norm. These are the core competencies of the organisation that feeds the critical path of core business. This is where you make money; the rest is just bells and whistles, as far as you are concerned. The point is get the basics in place first and see that it runs well, before adding anything else.

New strategies often call for significant budget reallocations and or cuts.

Downsizing in some areas and upsizing in others will require careful review.

Terminating all activities that are no longer justified, is a process of elimination, be prepared to step back if it impacts negatively on core functions.

Stop or at least streamline the funding of activities that yield no fruit just for the sake of having them, guard against fruitless expenditure. Channel the money where it will yield instant results and dividends first.

A few things to keep in mind, the emphasis have shifted for creating structure.

The goal of strategy is to unite diversified actions into one act, to create harmony and balance through structure designed around systems, in order to reach a predetermined objective. The idea is not to control every aspect, like a drop of water, but rather direct the flow of work, like the attributes of terrain, that steer the course of the river instead. Easier said than done, well gone are the days where strategy and making strategy only belonged to the upper echelons in management. This emphasis have become obsolete, by virtue of our top leaderships inability to cope with the fast changing pace of developments over a very wide and diversified field of interactive developments and components. It's like a Captain of a luxury liner wanting to control every aspect of the ship, whilst navigating icebergs and high seas – maybe that's why the Titanic sank, the Captain must have been in the kitchen arguing with the Chef over the menu – yet some still do business in this fashion.

The key emphasis has shifted from pure leadership models towards supportive hands-on and collaborating networks, whereby everyone has to manage some part of the work. Only then will personnel be able to carry out their role and functions both *efficiently* and *effectively*, if we give them control, all in line with the strategic intent. Staff is now also focused on medium and long-term objectives as well and not just daily routine. Delegating up as well as down, this is still a weird concept, try it sometime, it works. We ride the golden jingle of feedback; "feedback is the breakfast of champions" someone said. However, what if you were constantly involved and asking where you can give support, would you still require as much feedback? No, you will be living and working with your finger on the pulse, beat by beat. Strategy is fluent, it's not at all about doing "the right things" only, rather it has become a situation of doing "the thing right". Before worrying about how fast your train is going, "think" about whether it's going in the right direction. First time out, this style blends efficiency and effectiveness seamlessly to form an effective strategic style. We first think and then act, again, this points us to the two opposing parts – doing "the right things" – *Effectiveness* - and doing "the thing right" – *Efficiency* - becoming one, through the integration of several paradigms. We realise now that parts influence each other equally, so strategy also follows from structure, and from structure follows revised strategy. The one is the habitat and the other the habits of people. Self-awareness and self-control allows for more freedom than rules and regulations imposed by others, things have to belong to be effective when combined to form unity. Just like a goldfish won't make it in the desert and a camel won't make it in a fish tank, the relationships we design needs to be mutually accommodating.

This brings us to the concept of Asymmetrical Strategy.

Asymmetrical Strategy; also known as the "David and Goliath strategy": Describes a specific field of strategy aimed at conflict between a strong and weak opponent. It could be seen as unorthodox; or lacking equality, balance, or harmony with the strategic norms of conventional strategy. The concept revolves around a weaker or disadvantaged opponent effectively utilising some special form of strength or advantage, that he can perform consistently well. By exploiting a – gap - in terms of ability, or skill against the stronger opponent. The innate advantage is used to create a shockwave in the environment; either by disruption, distraction or to impede the opposition via unorthodox means.

The aim is to get advantage or leverage by using a small amount of effort to create a disproportionately large effect.

This chapter was created to focus on the holistic application of applied intelligence, training and technology to defeat both current and future asymmetric threats with. By example; the threat is the equivalent of venom injected into a human being by a venomous spider. Where there is a "gap", there is an opportunity. With the effect, that the target experiences a loss of sight, lameness, disorientation and eventually total paralysis as the venom passes through his system. Something so small, so seemingly insignificant, that can cause such a mighty effect, should make us think about our own capability gaps. Things, seemingly small, and trivial, that could reverberate through the total system and affects it in a big way. We have to see if we have such capacities, and or weakness, that could be targeted or used to our advantage in our strategy or structure.

Clients expect their service providers to pay the same attention to customer care, innovation and even previously insignificant issues such as corporate social responsibility and diversity, as they do.

The time has never been riper for emerging firms that are prepared to think and act in unorthodox way to develop models that closer meet their; clients, business partners, and labours needs and to take business away from the mainstream players, and visa-versa. In business strategy, the term asymmetric strategy would do just as well, if we consider such attributes as both threats and opportunity. The challenge for the currently dominant firms, of course, is to make sure that they learn and evolve fast enough to be able to ward off this threat, by adopting the asymmetrical strategies in closing/ opening gaps, that is now also termed **two-sided markets**, also called **two-sided networks** in business circles.

For example; where with traditional business models, for instance where a retailer use to act only as a hub for food, and goods distribution within the food supply chain. The emphasis have shifted globally today, from the traditional positional strategy: where the retailer seeks to establish and maintain a strategic position within a value chain, and only sell specific goods – and not services as well - related to his enterprise, like the traditional greengrocer. Business strategies have now diversified by utilising asymmetrical elements, and thus we see more partnerships between upstream and downstream. It is no longer just a question of supply and demand, economics of scale and the economics of scope. It's about the survival of the fittest, and the ones with the best supporting networks, services, products, strategies and structures and right priced goods combined.

Furthermore, the emphasis has shifted from a value-chain perspective to a service-oriented perspective, we can see more and more retailers providing a multitude of services as opposed to just the traditional goods, downwards as well as upwards. Companies have diversified, specialised and outsourced. With the incorporation of niche market goods and services, such as online ordering, deliveries, catering etc... This implies; business within business, goods within goods, and networks within networks. Their objectives have split, and mirrored. Having your own contracted suppliers, farms, and manufacturing plants producing the exact products to specification as needed, when needed by them, and delivered where they need them. They have adopted an in-time approach rather than an on-time. Goods are aimed at wants -what the markets desire, and to specification. Services are incorporated, at many levels, deliveries, readymade products; cooked TV dinners, baby food, or to caterers required quantity and specification. This business model is intersecting at various points in the market segment as one entity. This is only possible where the strategy and the structure is flexible. This takes us from a **positional strategy** to a **relational strategy**. No longer just focused on the **economies of scale** and scope of business, the relational strategy use to emphasises how **economies of social norms were changing,** it did not influence trade, versus economics being the only driver, sales are now generated in relation to two kinds of demand context. How to balance the exploitation of each of these forms of capability gaps - and still gain market share, has become the challenge.

How do we apply it in business, well it equates to superiority in:

- Thinking – paradigm shifts towards the unorthodox.
- Planning – using an outside influence to disable / enable an inside influence.
- Focusing on better timing and more co-ordinated effort- using conventional and unconventional means in combinations to eliminate waste and capitalises on efficiency.
- Execution – aggressive and bold in nature, with the interlocking of both conventional means and unorthodox means to achieve the objective.
- Thinking: The first criteria will be to seek and exploit weakness – both internal and external, our competition. When we are weak we are competing against our self, when strong we start competing against others. This is the distinction in the thinking and making of strategy.

Contemplating the influences on strategy; in terms of the following criteria – both internal as well as external;

- The level of skill, experience and ability involved in assembling systems, structure and strategy.
- look at the attributes required; the finances, marketing, production, pricing and distribution – with the emphasis on turnaround times and capacity etc.

Lastly, the perceptions created surrounding the company, leadership, employees as well as their product.

- **Planning:** The second will be to initiate low-key activities, which will not spark full out confrontation or raise suspicion. The testing of the soft spots in the armour to confirm the initial assumptions of identified points of weakness.
- Weakness manifests itself at three levels:
- **The Culture:** The profiling of the corporate culture and its weakness; such as preparation, controls, policy, training, the way they get things done, is it systematic, dogmatic or autonomously, or chaotically done etc.
- **The Structure:** Is this an interlocking or disseminated structure and how is it commanded and controlled. How do they use technology and how do they communicate. Again, what are their time frames like?
- **The Strategy:** Does it change much, is it comprehensive, was it implemented successfully. How do they treat people, how do they motivate people and what are their biases and preferences.
- **Timing and co-ordinated effort:** The third will be to cover strategies, to mask them, like a Trojan horse. So that the address of the aggressor is not known until, the conventional strategic waves can form and come into effect.

Then the interlocking between conventional and asymmetrical strategy will escalate into one act.

This final act will be defined by the corporate culture, be it either liberal or conservative.

The term-defused decision-making comes to mind, it hampers the formulation of any coherent strategy and this problem is particularly acute where systems function chaotically. With asymmetrical strategy, we have to think and act as a collective, the objective must serve the cultural as well as strategic intent of the whole system and its sub systems, and be related to processes or else it will fail. Asymmetrical strategy is highly dependent on collaboration, the sharing of power, skill and resources to achieve one common objective with which everyone can identify with. It deals with company politics, so it stands to reason that if the company politics and agendas are not behind the move to implement asymmetrical strategy it will not survive. Strategist has to be mindful of multiple influences over the direction of policy influencing strategy and corporate culture in this regard before contemplating any such strategy. Bureaucratic leadership styles play an important role in influencing the corporate style of strategy, and therefore the structure, tensions exists between leadership that are not visible on the surface at the strategic level, that want their slice of the pie.

Everyone wants flexibility in setting objectives for formulating the structure, so as to avoid limiting their options and credibility on the strategic landscape, for it changes rapidly, we have to have their inputs. They don't want to be remembered as being part of the companies "Water Gate Scandal" it looks bad, so to avoid limiting their options in conflict they distance themselves from any unorthodox strategy. We need to be mindful that this aspect in itself could become the opposition's target, or soft spot, that they can exploit in their own asymmetrical fashion. The question now is, do we have enough structural integrity to trust in our structure, and to implement such strategies. Transparency and openness can become the corporate weakness and target of the opposition. The question should rather be, if your survival depended on it would you use it, if yes, then the next question will be to what extent. With reference to an asymmetrical defence system, or attack system, or both scenarios using asymmetrical strategy as a means to an end to both attack and defend our structure with. These are but a few moral and ethical dilemmas shared in raising unorthodox strategy. The answer is to organise our structure more in terms of networks rather than hierarchies on the surface. This will protect our structural integrity; the next step is to step off from the platform of traditional business models - the pyramid shaped structure - and enter into the network system, or systems thinking model, as the new alternative, now referred to as the Matrix. This in itself creates problems, for networks rely heavily on infrastructure and technology, especially information technology.

Execution: conventional strategy and conventional structures, like conventional armies are still the only proven method. Our only security is that we are mindful and prepared. The usefulness of asymmetrical strategy, and systems thinking is limited in terms of its ambiguous nature, but it's good to know that it can serve a purpose in the right theatre of operations, should the circumstances arise. The idea is not to attack the opposition but its culture, structure and strategy, whilst protecting our own. This brings us to systems thinking, which system is best suited to fulfil our needs. If we understand systems we can strengthen our structures.

" Subduing the enemies army without fighting is the true pinnacle of excellence" – Sun Tzu, On the Art of War

REFRAMING the way towards change, Systems Thinking, the way toward structure.

By; Robert L. Sandidge & Anne C. Ward

(Chapter 11 from Quality Performance in Human Services Copyright 1999 - Brookes Publishing)

REFRAMING AND SYSTEMS THINKING - Systems thinking as described by Senge:

Business and other human endeavours are ... systems. They ... are bound by invisible fabrics of interrelated actions, which often take years to fully play out their effects on each other. Since we are part of that lacework ourselves, it's doubly hard to see the whole pattern of change. ... System thinking is a conceptual framework, a body of knowledge and tools that has been developed over the past fifty years, to make the full patterns clearer and to help us see how to change them effectively. (1990, p. 7).

"Senge" introduced a tool for diagramming systems that shows cause and effect, as a way to "see" what is actually happening graphically (i.e., how the elements of a system are related). This allows us to "step back" and see the situation portrayed outside of ourselves so that we can more objectively move things around, play with the variables, make predictions. Any method we use that gives us more objectivity will help us to get out of our frames of meaning and, therefore, to have more choices with which to experiment.

We invite consultants into our organisations in the hope that they will help us "see" our situation in new ways. Consultants can do this precisely because they are not deeply or historically involved in the organisation. They tend to see in terms of patterns and perceptions. Because they are detached from the organisation culture, consultants are often able to discuss organisational patterns in objective terms. This, in turn, can teach the members of the organisation to reframe their thinking into more objective language. An experienced consultant is also likely to have seen and worked with similar organisational patterns before and we expect him or her to help the organisation change "frames" with confidence.

Systems thinking is not about designing silos or islands that are created to function independently - separately – no, they should be directly aligned, it has to form a matrix of inter-connectivity – co-existence- like a vehicle and all its parts.

Systems thinking

What is a system?

By Definition; **It is a complete predictable cycle with recurring sub cycles, interlocking with networks, structures, and processes occurring in set sequences, that serves a specific purpose.**

The Systems Map:

The Radical Revolutionary Strategic Management Matrix For Predators

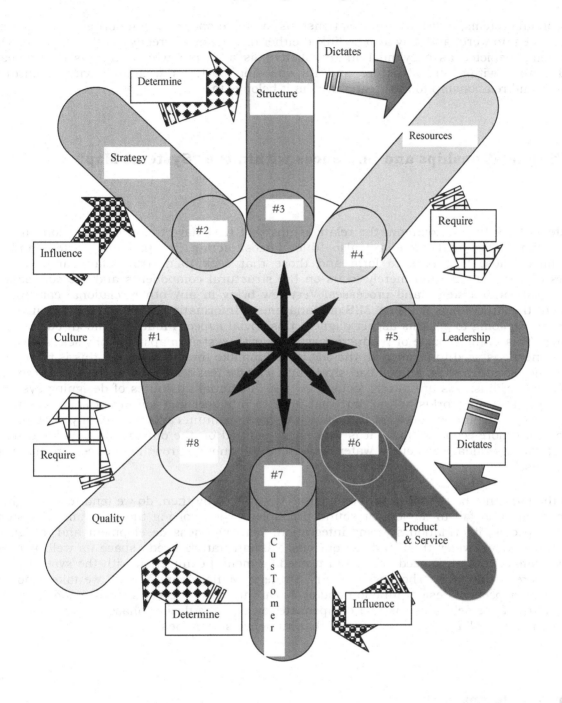

It may also be an artificial construction created to represent or explain an actual natural occurrence. Systems are unique entities, that have set boundaries and capability. Systems consists of subsystems, and have interrelationships to create specific inputs or outputs, required by other system to work, and may also be linked either directly or indirectly to other systems. One such system, (depicted as a cylinder in the sketch), is an input which satisfies or creates a required output within the structure and its opposing part, as well as having a cardinal importance and relationship to the greater system it belongs to...

Revisiting relationships and influences within the "Systems Map".

All systems have this in common; the relationships that they have to form to function, and we have to acknowledge that there are also "duel forces" acting in upon any system and its relationships. Those that seek to form and those that seek to destroy. Many architects or designers of systems only and merely focus on the structural components and the connections they have with sub systems and processes. Very few bring in any other relational concepts to compliment the subsystems with, i.e. MIS or Management Information Systems. Very few invest in the how are we going to get this aspect aligned, this trivial aspect influences mood, culture and work rates. This is the flipside of productive systems with system maps, the physical as well as mental connections need to be aligned; the one is nothing like the other. Maybe this is the reason why we suffer so much work related bad stress and why we feel dead tired at the end of the day. The architects of business are purely focused on the functional attributes of designing systems. Two concepts that are worlds apart , but that have to intersect and joining at some point, the first; if you buy a plant and you want it to grow it to the maximum capacity, would you plant it in a smaller pot (more economical), that is very nicely painted on the outside, or would you use a bigger pot with a drainage system, a watering system and enough growth enhancement material, in a "hothouse".

Would the latter not be the most obvious choice? It would. Why then, do we tend to lose sight of our own reality and fail to implement sound principles, when solving the problems of systems design and people, information systems integration. With business development and design we have to think wider, wider than just the obvious. Human nature needs space as well, it needs regulated climate control, it needs light and it needs a mental connection with the system... The difference here is that with "The Revolutionary Strategic Management Matrix" we take a holistic approach, all aspects of design, function and cycles are unpacked, every aspect to add value. We incorporate the force field analysis and compensate for it in the design phase already. Keep this aspect in mind, we will refer to this as forces that influence system design.

The force field analysis;

"Redesign with an environmental analysis in mind, that of force fields", we need to create systems protected from imbalance, to create a force field we require insight into the forces that impact on systems.

The four forces that influence balance and that drives systems;

The Radical Revolutionary Strategic Management Matrix For Predators

1. **_Determine_:** is an dual force, a driver, it is both external and internal; this "force" is a given and does not change, if the preceding force influencing it does not change, its sole purpose is to determine what will follow, it will keep influencing the two subsystems it joins.

2. **_Influence_:** is an dual force, a fuel, it is both external and internal, the sister of "determine", a force that we can change and that we do have control over, we seldom do any critical evaluation on it, strangely, we mostly try to change the outer forces that are all constants and out of our control, but the ones we create internally, we leave to their own devices and nature. Internal influences are a very strong force that can be used to alter and counter external forces.

3. **_Require_:** is an internal self-destructive force, and has to be replenished, (people require things to be consistent, and so do systems) before they will perform, and so do managers. Require it is the brother of "dictate", if this force is not lead by a strong relationship and structure to guide it, it will deteriorate, the preceding relationship will suffer, in a destructive manner, it needs to be lead and guided in a consistent manner. If not, it leaves a path of destruction between links, and can become crippling. Consistency counts where situations change rapidly, when consistency is observed right through, that's when it becomes real, then we have delivered, and we have real strength.

4. **_Dictate_**: is and internal force, the other half to "require" and opposes it, it is also an adamant force; for once it is created, it seldom changes without being destroyed or replaced by a new dictator.

This is the one aspect of radical strategy; the strategic management matrix sets itself apart from current trends in design, it realizes that there are forces within the business matrix that need to be in balance in order for the systems to work.

Taking stock of the opposing or destructive forces of systems, by seeing and understanding the relationships of systems we can determine key performance areas: To explain this, when leadership is not effective. Look at its opposing force or relation, culture, 80% of the time it will be culture in this example that will be the place to start towards finding real answers and visa-versa. The same is true for the rest.

Culture directly effects	⟷	Leadership
Strategy directly effects	⟷	Product & Service
Structure indirectly effects	⟷	Customer
Resources indirectly effect	⟷	Quality

(The numbering of the Silo's are indicated as #1 - #8 and spans two chapters, 12 and Chapter 13, *refer to the systems map at the start of this chapter,*)

Critical aspects of system design; unpacking the sub-systems and forces in the system map:

 # 1 – Culture; within culture we find organisational culture and its history, the founding principles on which the organisation was built, what the organisation stands for, strives for, hopes for, we find an ethnic culture, a religious culture, an ethics culture. Then we find sub-cultures inspired by, gender, age, value systems, social status unionism, and lastly a recreational culture or a lack thereof. All these aspects determine the core energy of the organisation. From this energy and diversity we look for, innovation, creativity, leadership, agility and flexibility. We also want to grow an ergonomic working relationship that will lean itself towards, participative management and the need for CRITICAL THINKING and thinkers, to develop synergy of vision, mission, goals and team spirit.

Referred to as the organisational culture, the sum of all the cultures of the enterprise thrown together to form a corporate "VIBE" – or culture. Although it is a sub part of the bigger system, it is a key performance area. A very important part of the system, the human element and its dynamic in a system, this aspect can never be underestimated. If there is no discipline, either;

- personal -
- functional –
- and or operational- discipline, then things crumble...

If hierarchy, clashes with culture, then mutual respect disappears from the corporate identity. We will also see disparity in work ethics, or a lack there off. Corporate culture influences the centre point of gravity, which could bring the organisation down if not sound or remedied.

It is not by chance that "Culture" and corporate identity was named as the number one attribute of success for any company, yes "number one", for it is and should be the first aspect when designing a system to be given a critical review. If this one aspect is flawed at the route, then in essence people do not have the same levels of maturity in mind to see the bigger picture, it revolves around me, me, me. Any sense of work ethic disappears, the proverbial "dry wood" this should be sorted out first, otherwise it will develop, cracks in the foundation and "bad blood" in the management caucus during the transition phase, because everyone is in this race for himself and I assure you it will carry through into the "new" system. So the old saying of garbage in, garbage out, will it holds more truth here that what you could ever imagine. The whole system and systems approach will forever keep struggling to get on to its feet, if the fulcrum it revolves around is weak, namely their "corporate culture". The point to make here is, you can have the best of the best of all things available, however, if you do not have a sound corporate culture, it will all boil down to failure. In order to change organisational culture for the better, you need to make a concerted effort to get to understand what every manager believes in, in every unit. This belief or paradigm will influence the type of culture that cascades from the top, if the top people have bad culture, get rid of them and fast, or influence their perception curvature. Curvature refers to their personal horizons, how they see their people, in relation to dealing with them and how they perceive themselves and view their reality of the organisation, especially at that point where things become future orientated and driven by their own inputs. This creates a curvature; this curvature will curve towards right or wrong, this is what you want to tap into. Influences from managers, on strategy and systems design stem from a culture, a belief, and values system they hold onto. This is the point where managers steer the course of corporate curvature. This is where the organisation looks at the horizon that reflects their future as "they" perceive it, influenced by the current way management is dealing with labour, managing resources and resolving or creating issues. Curvature is best explained as a rainbow, where every manager has an equal influence when in harmony – in other words doing what they should be doing – they are "in-line with company politics and ethics, however, if they are not in harmony they curve over each other, the influence of which creates a mixed up kaleidoscope, thus changing the colour in the spectrum they are influencing, they impede the way that other mangers operate, this becomes a way of distorting others curvature. This relates to circumstances that influence people to veer left or right from the required norm, by having to follow the curvature of the influencing manager that is out of synchronisation.

These are the elements of "curvatures" bending, things that dictate how well we (as an organisation or as a person) will be able to:

- Deal with the anxiety of events that fall *outside one's curvature of controlled Influence*. Curvature bending is mostly attributed to uncertainty; this makes and causes people to feel out of control, they lose their sense of direction and or become anxious. They feel like a tree that has been uprooted by this strong wind of change, very helpless. If management fails to intervene, then it spirals out of control.
- Imminent change of an uncertain nature falls *outside the curvature of the norm and standard people were used to, things are now introduced that are no longer routine and known*, we hear many managers say; "get them out of their comfort zones", well here's the truth. Studies have shown that comfort zones are the most productive sites and platforms for people to flourish in. If management and leaders are doing their intended jobs well, then this should not be a cause for concern, all this kind of talk just conjures up images of "Armageddon". Beware of this aspect and keep people well informed, well supported and updated.
- Threatening behaviour by management; where people are forced to go *outside their own curvature of existence; by management imposing on family values and commitments;* thus implying a possible lifestyle change, where they have to make the choice, between more time at work, and less time at home. Where a change in management style causes an actual change that affects their family life and or level of remuneration, all this pulls both at internal and external cohesion. Forcing more time at work and deductions, or scrapping of incentives this breaks morale, and team spirit.
- Attacks on status and or prestige, will bend the persons character. Things that go *outside the character curvature,* so the person gets forced to go against his character, religious beliefs and or principles. Managers attacking peoples prestige and status, these are tags that people worked hard for and whereby other associate them with the organisation and its structures. Never degrade prestige, or prestigious titles, ranks, rewards and incentives ext.
- A lack of motivation and interest is normally due to depression. Depression and stress are manifestations of disorder within the organisation and or private life, when combined, people feel squashed by their circumstances. A total move *outside the reality curvature* occurs, that sets in and causes disillusionment, which is passed on to fellow members in

the team and family unit. It tends to spread like wildfire; don't keep people in the dark. Don't let them hang out in the wind either with empty promises. Never take all the work away from someone that was dedicated and hardworking and now ask him to do the training, or recruiting if it was not his passion. We kill work passion and ethic by splitting up work that belongs together, because it makes sense, but the cause and effect their off never gets focused on. Only the short term results that are obvious and cannot be argued stand as grounds for conformation of this "vindictive" move – defended as a "Strategic move by management" because we do things without consultation and mediation as management because we "can", thus crushing the futures of people, they have set themselves up to get to their horizon, now it is no longer there. Be sensitive to old "covenants", they have prevailed for years, and age differences, because of the way they function. People at grass roots, referring to middle management should be given the benefit of the doubt and only by proper orientation and consultation should their suggestions be swayed, in addition, other untested ideas implemented.

- Where new systems, merge with new people, with new ideology, tempers and competition seem to be as fresh as well. Because the new clashing with the old and managers go *outside the ambit of good norms and management values curvature*. It all has to do with "newness", where we size up the competition and seek out alliances. Some people value, values, so you need to bring in a value system that is accepted by all concerned. Others value prestige and will do whatever it takes to get it. New managers have the tendency to hide their inability by threatening and screaming and bullying. The fundamental principle of change mangers is mutual respect and empathy and a deep understanding of corporate culture. You attract more bees with honey, than with fire... What ultimately guides groups best is consistent, and good leadership, good command, and control. Someone willing to take critical and crucial decisions of his or her own accord – someone that can create momentum, without creating too much friction... This cannot be done by making stars rise and fall. The defining of true success resides in well-defined common goals that is challenging, if there is no challenge then the goals becomes obsolete. Challenges create excitement and in turn enthusiasm, success is not just measured in monetary terms, or by statistics, but in the ability to overcome as a unit. When creating this condition, there will only be a few that would still want to lead and lead well, call this the grinding process where we sift the weak from the strong, where only the strong of mind and the resilient of character will emerge as victors – and become leaders themselves, because they show resilience. Remember – people make people become stars, managers model them and not the other way around. Power depends on balance and support; so look at what is holding you up and remember that which holds you up, can also pull you down. Managers need to instil abundance, by advocating the rule; "You are only truly successful when you do what you do well consecutively, mainly because you are doing it by choice and through conviction, with the knowledge that what you do has meaning and importance to yourself and others and you can feel the significance and satisfaction by the amount of positive feedback you get and gratitude." This covers section one on culture; we will still dig deeper into this aspect, however for now we need to understand that the way we design our frame of mind, will impact on the culture directly, which is the flipside to strategy. The point made here is that it is not just the function of strategy to plan but also to regulate corporate culture.

2 – Strategy;

A strategy *is defined as a long term plan of action, broken up into a short, medium and long term components, designed to deliver on the promise made in the "vision", to give essence to the "mission" and to ultimately achieve a particular "goal/ objective".*

Strategy implies a comprehensive elaborate oversight of initiatives that should incorporate many different elements, such as:

- The "environmental scan" of the structure, resources and its optimum utilisation
- The strength and weakness of corporate "paradigms"
- The Freedom of mind – tolerances
- The Stratagem – the way they traditionally do things best
- The flexibility and trust level in the organisation
- The initiative and risk taking mentality

Yes, back to basics – everything must relate back to reality and fit. If not it does not belong. Often the makings of a good leader and what separates him from the mediocre, is found in his ability to hit on the right strategy, more often than not and make it work. With consistency comes balance. This aspect resides within the amount of freedom allowed, "Freedom of mind" – leads to creativity, freedom of thinking and expression creates innovation, these attributes are the keys to unlocking sober strategy with.

Stratagem – is described as; the clever use of a scheme that is designed to deceive others or achieve something.

Sun Tzu said: In the practical art of war, the best thing of all is to take the enemy's country whole and intact; to shatter and destroy it is not so good. Therefore, it is better to recapture an army (workforce) entirely than to destroy it – unity is strength is the message. Hence, to fight and conquer in all your battles is not supreme excellence; supreme excellence consists in breaking the enemy's resistance without fighting. Stratagem by extension can refer to any action designed for obtaining an advantage. In other words, the two terms strategy and stratagem are complimentary with the strategy defining the "bigger picture" or overall objectives and goals, while tactics are the specific logical breakdown of practical considerations towards creating actions, action items or plans steer the course of the greater strategy. Therefore, tactics determine the method that will be best suited to achieve the aims - to reach the end goal and strategy defines the parameters in which such tactics may be implemented and to what extent they may be used – the boundaries, also referred to as the rules of engagement. However, put this into a business context and generally, the two are purposely detached. It is often cited that a company has an overall strategy – great – however the action required to achieve the scheme resides in the distribution of tasks or work that becomes the "tactical solution" to deal with a specific problem. The implication here is that this solution is somehow a distraction from the strategy when it should actually be a contributor to its progression.

This may seem a very subtle distinction, although the notion that tactics are seen as entirely separate from strategy can be destructive to the overall development of the organisation. Nothing should ever be taken as if fixed and or immovable. The approach of "you cannot manage that which you cannot measure" must surface in this deduction. Well it stands to reason that you cannot measure that, which you cannot see, nor can you measure it if it keeps moving, so in essence you are only managing the "stuff" that can measured. Acceptance that all tactical solutions should be flexible and agile, therefore there exist no measurement for a necessary required flexibility within the dynamics of an overall strategy. Managers cannot factor in the weather, and supplies always being on time, support being available, illness occurring at critical time and family responsibility that have to be attended to, within a strategy. Not even under perfect conditions will one be able to factor in every eventuality, calculate every margin and probability, the probabilities are too vast. This agility or flexibility will make a strategy relevant to the world around it. Examine how your organisation develops strategic plans, action plans, stratagems and other supportive aspects, like budgeting etc. in this context.

The important aspect of any strategy is the concept of recognising opposing forces, Sun-Tzu talks about a "*cheng* and *ch'I*" - deception and surprise, strength and weakness, symmetry and asymmetries

Now for the creating/ creative forces:

- *Variety*
- *Rapidity*
- *Harmony*
- *Initiative*

Chapter 13 will focus on the rest of the systems that will incorporate these forces to balance the anomaly, as a degree of effectiveness, however, from a different perspective. We will see how systems become interdependent and create harmony, with initiative taking and risk taking, we will create rapidity and variety.

The importance of creating the VISION AND MISSION - statement

This is the orientation mechanism, the fighting creed, the moral builder towards finding the target and killing it / nailing or achieving it, it becomes our target.

"Targets", could be defined as being either politically motivated agendas, or economically inspired goals. That is then formulated into a "battle plan" for business, a business plan or map, the synergising ratification principle. Identification of the organisation's vision and mission is the first step towards any strategic planning process.

The creative forces in strategy; Col. John R. Boyd (1927–1997)

- Variety
- Rapidity
- Harmony
- Initiative

Strategy is based on the relationship among, variety, rapidity, harmony and initiative focused on attaining a specified objective. Rapidity of action is required to maintain or regain initiative. Variety provides unpredictability, eliminating the potential for a foe to predict actions and plan to defeat them. Harmony is the symbiotic relationship between the environment and those operating in it. Initiative is taking charge of your destiny and is required to master circumstances rather than be mastered by them. Exploiting these qualities relative to an opponent on microscopic (individual) and macroscopic (organizational) levels will increase the likelihood an individual or organization will achieve a desired end state. Variety, rapidity, harmony and initiative are linked to the notion of competition in time

Performing a Reconnaissance exercise.

"Now the general who wins a battle makes many calculations in his temple before the battle is fought."- Sun-Tzu

In modern day also referred to as the ENVIRONMENTAL SCAN

Influences both economic, social, cultural, demographic, political, legal, technological and international factors needs to be taken into account. Pertaining to the specific industry sector contemplated, should be probed for inconsistencies and internal organisational factors that need re- engineering to be effective. Do we use perception and information, or do we use business intelligence in our business assumptions.

"Hence, it is only the enlightened and wise general who will use the highest intelligence of the army for purposes of spying and thereby they achieve great results. Spies are the most important asset, because on them depends an army's ability to march"- Sun-Tzu

Why do we need a new strategy? Mainly it is because we are just not performing, a performance gap has appeared.

Gauging performance ratings –by performing a GAP ANALYSIS

Organisations evaluate the difference between their current position and desired future position in the market through a "gap analysis" or between the desired output and current output. As a result, a unit can develop specific strategies to enforce specific outcomes, to close the performance GAP with, or employ specific strategies to win over markets and allocate resources to close the gap, within the projections made.

"Hence the saying: If you know the enemy and know yourself, your victory will not stand in doubt; if you know Heaven and know Earth, you may make your victory complete." - Sun-Tzu

Striving for excellence and quality by - Applying BENCHMARKING

Quarterly evaluations of the companies operational profit margins and production, practices and performance coefficients against predetermined benchmarks, as well as others in the same industry, becomes useful for identifying and adopting "best" practices and standards. Through an on-going systematic benchmarking process, companies find a reference point for setting their own goals and targets. Systems development and project development as well as research and development, should complement such practices.

"According as circumstances are favourable, one should modify one's plans" - *Sun-Tzu*

Core concerns or STRATEGIC ISSUES

The only way to track strategic issues is by breaking them up, into workable parts and then turning them into either action items, or projects, that is time phased and locked into action. Strategic issues are the fundamental core issues the organisations need to address before they become liabilities or obstacles in the way of achieving its mission and realising the vision.

Sun Tzu said: **"The control of a large force is the same principle as the control of a few men: it is merely a question of dividing their numbers."**

Change mangers leading - STRATEGIC PROGRAMMING

To address strategic issues and development as well as training, necessitates deliberate strategies, mission specific and outcome based action items and initiatives for achieving specific mission goals. Companies need to align themselves with the process of setting up effective strategic goals, action plans and tactics during the strategic planning phase, the selling the concepts and buy-in will only take place if it is preceded by a programming phase. Where everyone gets charged with specific duties and functions, so that it does not become a "catch the ball and run with it situation" Strategic goals are the milestones that companies aim to achieve.

The system of setting SMART goals is essential to setting meaningful goals. Smart goals are **s**pecific, **m**easurable, **a**greed upon, **r**ealistic and **t**ime/cost bound goals. The Action plans define how we get to where we want to go the steps required to reach our strategic goals. Tactics are specific actions used daily to influence the outcome of the strategic goals towards implementing or achieving the strategic intentions, plans, or agendas.

"While heading the profit of my counsel, avail yourself also of any helpful circumstances over and beyond the ordinary rules." - *Sun Tzu*

Research and development - EMERGENT STRATEGIES

Hap hazards, crisis-management, unpredicted, unintended, unforeseen events frequently occur that cannot be addressed effectively by existing contingencies, nor do they align themselves with any current strategy. This type of anomaly falls within the dominion of "Emergent strategy" it is "a pattern, a consistency of behaviour over time", "a realized pattern [that] was not expressly intended" in the original planning of strategy. Of which the matter or crisis fell outside the ambit of rational at the time the strategy was formulated. It may results from a series of actions converging into a consistent pattern (Mintzberg, 1994, p. 23-25).

"It is a matter of life and death, a road either to safety or to ruin. Hence, it is a subject of inquiry, which can on no account be neglected" - *Sun Tzu*

Hypothesis or facts? - EVALUATION OF STRATEGY

Periodic evaluations of strategies, tactics and action plans are essential to assessing success, we are all well aware of this, but do we evaluate and base everything on hypothetical assumptions, on expert opinion or do we test them against history and factual matter. The methods employed will determine the reliability of the data that is read in as conclusive. The organisation should measure current performance against previously set expectations and consider any changes or events that may have influenced the desired course of actions. As well as question and take into account the methods used to ascertain the results.

Sun Tzu said: *"The good fighters of old first put themselves beyond the possibility of defeat and then waited for an opportunity of defeating the enemy.*

In hind sight an exact science - REVIEWING OF THE STRATEGIC PLAN

After assessing the progress reports of the strategic planning committee, the directors and investors needs to review the strategic plan, make recommendations and call for alterations to effect the necessary changes, or it needs to adjust its course based on these evaluations. By closing the business, or combining it with another business. The revised plan must take into consideration emergent strategies and changes in political and global markets that could have affected the organisation's intended course. Only then does the management structures need to be probed for inconsistency and low profitability.

"Thus it may be known that the leader of armies is the arbiter of the peoples fate, the man on whom it depends whether the nation shall be in peace or in peril." - Sun Tzu

To be or not to be - STRATEGIC THINKING

Strategic thinking has everything to do with maturity of thoughts and has absolutely nothing to do with age, or background, for it can be taught and learned, people in the organisation routinely make this mistake, thinking that only the old and the academics and scholarly can make informed strategic decisions. Their decisions are based on intellectual knowledge and prior learning and mainly have outlived the authors and sell by dates of their knowledge, but never vocational and practical knowledge, mainly all assumptions within the framework of the organisations strategic vision and mission should be tested against the practice and practicality. Strategic thinking, involves much more to be highly effective than just looking at a wide arraying universe of options and possibility. Through a process of opening up Radical and Revolutionary fronts of thinking, by engaging all the staff in a brain storming session, to arrive at a range of alternatives from people in the practice. No longer just the traditional "white coats" – the management only- versus the "overalls" - the workforce - mentality type of culture". Rather identify the best fit between the two, practical vs. theoretical.

"Hence, when able to attack, we must seem unable; when using our forces, we must seem inactive; when we are near, we must make the enemy believe we are far away; when far away, we must make him believe we are near" -
Sun Tzu

Now employing – *MILITARY STYLED* STRATEGIC INTENT.

Strategic intent is what links people to strategy, this aspect literally connect the dots...with creative forces.

- Variety
- Rapidity
- Harmony
- Initiative

This is where the three levels come together; you must also understand the conflict, have situational awareness and properly define the strategic problems for both you and your workforce clearly. *The real intent is always your focus on perception. Effective strategy works on three levels, the moral, mental and physical.* We are at risk to others physically. But, according to Boyd, we defeat ourselves mentally and morally when we let ourselves become mentally confused or weaken by our moral standards. Integrity really is central and aligned to perception. Moral conviction is a necessity, and encoded by shared vision and values. The greatest danger and the easiest way to lose is to lose the trust that is the basis for social cohesion and our corporate culture.

The moral fabric of society unravels if there is no trust. With trust, you gain respect, loyalty, and common purpose. Without trust, you need detailed orders to run things. All centralized command and control systems are based on mistrust. The way to maintain moral authority is by deed, not word alone. For things to work , and work properly we need to understand their distinctions clearly.

- The top management, our specialist or contractors, engineers, architects, become the "path-builders", and they - require variety
- The management the "path-minders" – they require rapidity
- The last level the work force "the path followers" - requires harmony between all levels, before they will use initiative.

To the first group it gives a sense of direction, strategic intent implies a vision, the "Promised Land". To the second group it signifies a mission statement, a task , a challenge, a sense of finding ways to succeed against great odds, the promise of exploration and innovation that will lead to invention. To the last group it signifies goals, a sense of destiny, purpose, unity, and inherently worthwhile.

To be great at making strategy work is to excel at implementing strategic intent and this requires three very basic but important steps before we launch into strategy and change.

Defining vision; mission and goals clearly - hang them everywhere so that they are emotionally linked to every level as mentioned above. Level after level will have to come up with supporting visions, missions and gaols for their respective divisions.

Set challenges, to every level and communicate them well; people have to "see", in order to follow. Without a "map" of where you want to go, people tend to chart their own course and end up on their own mission. Consequently, hand out maps, have seminars, successful people do whatever it takes, they make a serious effort to communicate these aspects very well. That way you will not have to retrace your steps and stop all the time to get and keep the "caravan of prosperity" going through the "desert" of uncertainty.

Empowerment of your strategic intent;

Finding potential; the greatest wealth of unused potential is to be found in a graveyard, someone once said. Well we have many corporations that are dead at the roots as well. Therefore, the carpenters' law of measure twice cut once is a good yardstick here. When formulating your strategy, make sure you always have a "strategic intent committee" of "builders" that are identifiable candidates as future leaders within the company to come in at various stages in the development process, to give inputs, critique and perform realignment assignments. This builds the critical element of trust. As well as give feedback to labour in general, that focuses perceptions. This is the first measure;

The second measure is to formulate the strategy in stages and at the end of each stage to have a presentation to level the strategic horizon again – so that everyone can see where we are going with this. The second measure or wave; Start up small process, get "people power" going, it is hard to get people into motion. However, if you have a "Need for Speed" then all you have to do is create the catalyst for speeding up processes; "NFS" – Norm, Form and brain Storm. To get that required speed going in the thought-processing department...in order to "Norm, Form and Storm". One needs to actively invite participation at all levels right through. Nevertheless, you have to "Norm" first. Norming strikes at aligning peoples curvatures, getting people out of each other's way, this normalises the situation towards open debate; by pushing people into a specific direction and this requires leadership skills.

Thirdly. Aligning curvature. As we discussed previously. Negative curvature creates connotations that stem participation. In addition, clearly explain the need for participation to formulate the scheme. By focusing the points/point for discussion and debate, by drawing up of action items. Keep things and communication structured. The forming of committees and groups may or may not be necessary to keep the continuity and harmony. Now we can start Storming, brain storming, not open debate that deducts from the effort, by interacting with one and other we break down barriers and form working relations. With continued interaction, we build relationships of respect and open judgment and participation. Storming helps eradicate unwanted perceptions by nipping it in the butt and getting it back in context. So if you have a lack of progress, you have to revisit your patterns that create success, the preludes to the big change. Now we will look at *patterns* that create *success*.

Colonel Boyd's Patterns of Success:

Goal

Diminish adversaries' freedom of action while improving our freedom of action, so that our adversary cannot cope, while we can cope, with events/efforts as they unfold.

Plan

Probe and test adversary to unmask strengths, weaknesses, manoeuvres and intentions

Select initiative (or response) that is least expected

Move along paths of least resistance (to reinforce and exploit success)

Exploit, rather than disrupt or destroy, those differences, fractions, obsessions, etc., of adversary organism that interfere with his ability to cope with unfolding circumstances.

Subvert, disorient, disrupt, overload, or seize adversary's vulnerable, yet critical connections, centres and activities that provide cohesion and permit coherent observation orientation decision action in order to dismember organism and isolate remnants for absorption or mop-up.

Action

Observe, orient, decide, then act more inconspicuously, more quickly and with more irregularity as basis to keep or gain initiative, as well as shape and shift main effort; to repeatedly and unexpectedly penetrate vulnerabilities and weaknesses exposed by that effort or other effort(s) that tie-up, divert, or drain away adversary attention (and strength) elsewhere.

Support

Superior mobile communications

To maintain cohesion of overall effort and sustain appropriate pace of operations within available resources

Only essential logistics

Command

Decentralise - in a tactical sense - encourages lower-level commanders to shape, direct and take the sudden/sharp actions necessary to quickly exploit opportunities as they present themselves.

Centralise - in a strategic sense - to establish aims, match ambitions with means/talent, sketch flexible plans, allocate resources and shape the focus of an overall effort.

As organisations and their scope are far and in-between on the strategic scale, it is difficult to give an overview of how to incorporate this model for each, in a for and against argument, it has to be a deductive process, pertaining to situational appropriateness.

Back to the systems model and how to integrate the aforementioned.

3 – Structure; we all have been taught that structure follows strategy, nevertheless, do we implement this principle once the strategy is in place. No, we tend to stick and get stuck in the same structure we had the year before, maybe with some additions and small changes. So, are we being strategic, by just changing the strategy every year? The main reason why structure has to follow strategy is this. When we think progress we are in essence also thinking change, so it stands to reason that with new developments in the markets and new technology emerging we will have to incorporate as much as possible, and refine are processes. Changes in strategy may necessitate a parallel change in structure, it may even necessitate a totally new structure/s, or better support for current structures. Structure; thus affect performance directly and skills development needs, may need to change because of the implementation of new technology, or machinery etc. How we structure, or not, will dictate how we work and what form our processes and control spans will take on. Referring back to our subject matter experts and studies done, input design wise will also inevitably determine our output. The other very important aspect that sometimes get discarded, is that structures will also guide us when we have to budget effectively, for pay, overtime, expenses, equipment, ext.

The Radical Revolutionary Strategic Management Matrix For Predators

The real significance of an organisational structure is whether it was planned because of a thorough work case study, with job description and technology requirements factored in, as well as human resource equivalents, in terms of qualifications and other requirements. The question is was this incorporated? However we know that most of them are purely a thumb suck, slap it on paper, best guesses in my opinion, get it over with exercise. Where the opposite should be true, where the characteristic of proper strategic planned organisational structures (organic structures) should originate from a proper "work case study". This is the fundamental aspect that distinguishes it from the norm, the fulcrum to success is in our alignment of the two aspects. Planed structure, aligned with a planned strategy, is created bottom up and not top down, via a matrix approach. It must be totally goal orientated firstly, secondly it should be future focused in design and must have depth and weight in terms of being fully capacitated. Let us just linger on this last statement and unpack it, to add value.

"Matrix Organic Structures"; come with a specific job description that addresses a needs analysis of the post, in terms of skills required, equipment required and qualifications required to make it work to its full capacity. Then for extra edge, a financial impact report of this post coupled to current market trends and best practices, should be generated first to support the creation of this new position with all it entails. It furthermore incorporates a human resource study with a fully integrated career path for the incumbent, with study fields required for promotion, plus incentives for making this grade. It clearly stipulates how performance will be measured for this post, the positions is graded in terms of importance, and the performance incentives scheme coupled to this position. Consequently, whoever gets appointed knows exactly what the "job" is, where he or she will be going in the future, how to get there, what to expect for hard work and how to achieve it. Structures need to be made all inclusive, you will find exactly what the job will demand and the support that this position could expect. "Matrix Organic Structures" are, structurally sound and flexible, in that they are designed with processes in mind, to impact on the culture of performance management and company success patterns. They are also totally strategically aligned with the goals and principles of the organisation, and aligned to support the core functions and additional functions, thus flexible enough in design and nature termed "Matrix Organic Structures". They are mission specifically designed with people in mind and the jobs that they will do, and the requirements that it will have, both financially and logistically. Furthermore, we tend to mostly find only the opposite today. "Mechanization structures", "based on the old Portland Cement Factory models." Old out-dated structures, created top down, to see who will have the biggest department. With no links to attributes, and elements of design and concept. It has to look like a pyramid, then it's all good. They are the most obvious to transpire, that just focuses on rank and file (positions and how much they will earn and what they will do), nothing mentioned against performance measurement and targets, even in large corporate environments we still find this today.

Briefly explained, "mechanistic" or – bureaucratic - structures are characterised by such attributes as a centralised decision making body, that branches out into departments and then units. Filled with people, and how much we need to pay them. With very strict adherence to formally prescribed rules codes and procedures. A legacy we inherited, with very obvious characteristics of an age and era long gone – but to a large extent still being practiced. This company will typically have a procedures manual, or a force procedure manual, standard operating procedures for everything, including taking time off etc. With tight control on people and protocol, but very little emphasis on administration and information flows, and systems to support them, a typical example is the classification of documentation - documents marked as confidential. With a magnitude of files, stacked in filing cabinets, under desks and in storerooms, but with no system in place, once it gets filled it is lost, to everyone but the person or persons that stuck the information into draws. I ask myself, in this day and age of information technology, how can any company say they are effective if they cannot even handle information effectively, granted some data needs to go on file, but they could also be duplicated electronically. We will also find a very low level of effectiveness, trust, and co-operation, with lots of "it's not my job, sorry I can't help you", due to the bureaucracy and a lot of red tape.

The top command/management structures hold all the decision making power, with carefully constructed reporting lines, that does not support the so called "open door policy" with very little specialisation within the organisation. When decentralised, the same scenario is duplicated, even operationally; operational decision-making is enforced, from the top down – in other words no one dares make decisions without getting an okay. Furthermore, the same top level management makes it their business to meddle in, to make constant changes, all over the organisational spectrum, they do not just micromanage they control, the organisational adaptive-ness and flexibility of ideas and purpose of management is strapped to the armchair of the CEO. Moreover, if he is not driving on the day, then no one is. Even the support systems, applications and suppliers are tied up in their bureaucracy, with extended time frames for tenders and procurement, it never opens up to free communications and a de-emphasis on initiative taking is apparent. No one dares make a decision, if is not taken up by all line managers throughout the organisation to top management and approved politically, then it does not exist. Everything is operated on and around very formal rules and informal procedures, a remote controlled organisation, a typical characteristic of many a mechanically structured culture – its formalness. Importantly, and to be noted, this structural design has been theoretically tied into the existence of a particular strategy that has been inherited and has remained unchanged for years.

"In comparison with mechanistic organisational structures, the "Matrix Organic Structures" are more likely to spawn autonomous strategic initiatives." In other words, organic structures provide a facilitative context and platform for emergent strategies and change. Because everyone is a partner in the business of organisational management, a stake holder, everyone has a say. "Emergent Strategies will tend to be more deliberate and tightly coupled to the organisations managements vision, opposed to centrally mechanically controlled organisations will have more loosely coupled ones."

Back to - Mechanistic structures –, why do we need to change the way they work? Let's look at the cost, they deliberately restrict managerial discretion and decision making power, which in effect stifles initiative, where organic structures are aimed at the opposite, to eradicate operational and strategic uncertainty wherever possible, which suggests that they will favour the creation of planned strategies to flatten the structures.

Risk taking is restricted to the zero margins, resulting in low imitative taking although they call for it, the truth is that without risk you cannot have a flow of initiative, moreover, mechanistic structures that emphasize control systems and processes, which are necessary to ensure planned strategies intent (Mintzberg, 1979). Although rigidness and adherence to plans will not necessarily promote high performance, when planned strategies are carefully controlled and monitored during their implementation, there will be a greater chance that the firm will succeed in what it is trying to accomplish – this belief has become obsolete due to the current flux in society. Thus, if the planned strategies have "some" measure of merit (that is if, they are not typically "bad" strategies, which is reminiscent of this culture), these strategies should prove most effective when carried out in mechanistically structured organisations where the work culture is sound, but it very seldom is today, due to unionism and political influences. The measure is, do they deliver the required margins required to be competitive, or are they to slow and too rigid to counter strategies made in real time, then they fall outside the "OODA" loop. (More on the OODA loop later)

More effective ways of merging the organisational structure with strategy:

Start by "Specific Individualised Design –SID- of each post and its criteria", keep in mind that flatter is better, faster and cheaper. Split functional attributes to close match categories; decide how many categories or horizontal tiers of organisation you will be able to sustain, or want e.g. Logistics, finances, operations, production and distribution for instance. Arrange the internal unit structures around tasks and activities most critical to success of a firm and its strategy like the trunk of a tree, thus going horizontally only when the first process is finalised. Close matching of structure to strategy requires making strategy-critical activities and organisation units the main building blocks, and focus of design, in the organisational structure first. By pinpointing the core activities and key tasks critical to successful strategy execution and operational effectiveness, by bunching them together.

Remember, strategy is never simple, it is complex, however, the more complex the strategy the more simple its execution. This gives way to the requirements;

- *Rapidity* - rapidity of action or reaction is required to maintain or regain initiative
- *Variety* - variety is required so one is not predictable, so no recognisable pattern develops that an enemy may recognise and use to defeat you.
- *Harmony* - the fit with the environment and others operating in it.
- *Initiative* - taking charge of your own destiny: required if one is to master their circumstances instead of being mastered by them.

Further Guidelines for implementation:

- Defining mission critical activities along the following guidelines:
- This may vary according to;
- Particulars of a firm's strategy
- Value chain make-up
- Competitive requirements

Identifying a firm's strategy-critical activities by micro probing functions, systems and policies first. The fundamentals are;

- What functions have to be performed extra well and on time to achieve sustainable competitive advantage?
- In what value-chain activities would mal-performance endanger success?

By grouping strategy critical activities into department unit's.

Make strategy-critical activities the main building blocks in the organisational structure

Assign managers of these activities; a visible, influential position in the organisational pecking order

Group related value-chain supporting activity and MQM (Matrix Quality Management) activities under co-ordinating authority of a single executive.

Watch out for work process fragmentation, make sure of inter connectivity and process monitoring. A simple practical example is by implementing tracking systems, to track anything and everything, from communication, correspondence and service as well as production and clients, from the cradle to the grave, so to speak via one system and design. Be it by electronic logging. This system is used by emergency call centres it flags calls, emails and clients visiting if they are not serviced within a predetermined period. Email schedulers and reminders with pop-ups reminding the concerned parties of deadlines, meetings and schedules as well as clients and colleagues birthdays, etc. Correspondence is done in record time if serviced on one platform.

The Third objective of MQM is to implement systems that run concurrent and complement each other at the same time forming a matrix of cross referencing and checking on critical activities, so that nothing disappears through the cracks and that all services conforms to the MQM and strategy. Remember everything is done with quality in mind, it can also just be a perception of quality that is specifically generated by the use of aesthetics, nice furniture, dress code, décor and or packaging to serve as a safety net should the customer not get the service intended. Only by fulfilling customer expectations and orders accurately and promptly do we provide quality. The process should always leave the customer satisfied and with an impressionable experience of professional quality and service. In keeping with traditional functionally-organised structures, the pieces of strategically-relevant activities often end up scattered across many departments, so people end up getting referred and transferred when following up queries, this frustrates people and your customers. Have a customer service desk, with trained staff that can do the tracing and running around.

Consequently and in one sentence; guard against organisational designs that cause fragmentation and waste. The reasons are more than justifiable of the argument:

Too many hands-on systems can lengthen completion time and could influence quality.

With the fragmentation of activities - accountability gets scattered to the wind as well, which makes tracking and pinpointing of points of system failure hard to identify, at times even impossible. It also brings about a culture of shifting the blame. If unavoidable make sure that it falls within the ambit of one division or department or have proper signoff and pass on sets of checks and balances in place. Kiazan – is the principle of giving workers the responsibility to "fix it", to minimise waste of time, effort, where the worker must try and fix it and identify ways of improving broken links in systems by creatively coming up with solutions to problems they experience.

Co-ordinate fragmented pieces to avoid increasing overhead costs –waste, cut it out if it is not critically important to the process.

However, I understand that some organisations operate strictly along the lines of fragmentation, or decentralisation, it may be necessary. This then requires well trained and capacitated first line supervisors, that have the say – responsibility and accountability – or it just won't work. They require a very high level of trust in them; call it autonomy to act.

Keys to good decentralised organisation design

- Have fundamental report as well as command and control procedure frame works, not rules, within which decision-making may take place freely.
- Have daily one on one conversations and or communications, to keep track of happenings.
- Inspections and audit's need to be kept regular.

- Do not rotate core command groups or structures if at all possible.
- Maximize how support activities contribute to the overall performance of primary activities and
- Contain costs of support activities
- "Understanding key relationships of strategic significance "
- The answer is in -how to structure reporting relationships – to get quality feedback.
- Identify where close cross-functional co-ordination is of critical importance; identify possible clusters based upon geographical location.
- Strategic relationships to look for are those that;
- Would link units together via natural boundaries or borders firstly.

Secondly concentrating on the calibre of performance of one work unit to another and or which ones could be amalgamated effectively to create a new core competency.

Organisational designs that fragment strategic activities must be avoided, this implies that the service and operational legs can be physically removed and decentralised. As long as the management of all aspects are centralised and fall under one co-ordinator. Breaking this chain by removing one aspect, for instance training could prove to have disastrous consequences in the long term. In other words the co-ordinator must be a full function. Although training could be an in house affair or outsourced the relevance of the training should be gauged and monitored by the relevant co-ordinator, to ensure skills building and core competency level engineering by assembling his own specialised teams, trained to face the challenges of the functions the team/division/department is required to perform...

Understanding how the differences in organisational design will affect management styles and approaches.

- Centralised organisation - Top executives retain authority for most decisions
- Decentralised organisation - Employees empowered to exercise best judgment

Centralizing strategy-implementing authority at the corporate level has merit when related activities of related businesses need to be tightly co-ordinated

Determining the amount of authority or level of decision making power and autonomy required

Decentralised structures have

- Fewer management layers
- Shorter response times
- Greater employee involvement – taking ownership and solving problems

The trend towards leaner structures by stressing employee empowerment is based on two principles;

- Decision-making authority pushed down to lowest possible level. Employees empowered to exercise judgment on job-related matters.
- Outsourcing non-critical STRATEGIC ACTIVITIES allows firm to concentrate resources on value-chain activities where it can create unique value, can be best in industry, or in the world, needs strategic control.
- Outsourcing of value-chain activities makes better strategic sense whenever;

- They can be performed at lower cost and/or with higher value-added by outsiders
- Outsourcing of non-crucial support activities helps;
- Decrease internal bureaucracies
- Flatten organisation structure
- Provide heightened strategic focus
- Decrease competitive response times

4 – **Resources;** constitutes anything that relates to a "means" to achieve a goal and other things that an entity can use to produce goods and services with, to make its wealth grow. Resources may be renewable or non-renewable. With daily innovation in business and technology, the dynamic environment of the market place changes face every six months. To keep up the pace many large organisations have invested in projects and strategic management components within the business, also labelled research and development departments. Charged with strategic planning and research. This is where the re-engineering of structures, technology platforms and resource-allocation decision are made or rather planed and organised in a scientific manner. All its findings, researched and factual anomalies, are tested, hypothesis tailor made and no longer rely merely on thumb sucking and better guessing. Senior management is consulted to guide and lead, they have taken up office with the likes of the human resource department and no longer just act on an expert opinion when needed only basis, a new core competency have been entrenched in the organisation.

The Revolutionary Radical Strategic dynamic is born here, this is the place where the future orientated lives, looking into the future with new eyes, looking wider, looking at resources in new meaningful ways. The resource application matrix design takes into account and incorporates the following; past experiences, history of the organisation and movements in the markets, local and globally, looking for trends and reoccurring manifestations, that shootout. This was a managerial function previously that did not exist, or that did not pose any significant relevance, the constant evolution of resources, raw materials and the cost and quality involved in gaining better strategic orientation within the organisation, with constant re-aligning with key performance areas of the organisation, its values, mission, vision and goals. The team makes sure that it is entrenched in every matrix it designs as a standard seal of quality.

This gives an assurance that, the plan is fully comprehensive and flexible, every aspect of it well researched and rehearsed - tested. Every fact, every assumption is traceable. It has done its test runs, by employing subject matter experts to evaluate the content and context of the jobs, the distribution of work and job descriptions, pre-defining the resources, training and aspects required to compliment the envisaged function with, a total holistic approach to design, it employed human resource work study's to refine and compliment the matrix design. It has backup strategies in place should the situation change.

This is matrix thinking and design and it has two layers (1) the basic allocation matrix; and (2) the contingency matrix. The basic allocation matrix is the choice that seems most prevalent to the decisions that have to be taken to effect successful changes; it also encapsulates the level of funding by considering the budget and legal restraints. The amount of spending, the support systems and office equipment, the transportation, the information technology and all and any other requirements of the unit to perform and function, it is all encapsulated within the matrix. It is a fully comprehensive study with cause and effect strategies to counter and balance any eventuality perceived as potentially threatening. It goes on, it shows the merit on which resource have been allocated, within the budget, it shows projections for growth.

There are two contingency mechanisms built into every matrix design: firstly a standard priority ranking system of items excluded from the business plan, showing which items to be funded first as new money and finances become available with growth and expansion in mind, thus in order of importance and priority, a parallel growth program is pre-defined, if and when more resources should become available. The project can merely continue on a preconceived template. It also draws a prospectus, to show which projects are key performance areas for growth and which are capital hungry, that are of vital strategic importance. How would this approach influence the reality of the current situation, well exponentially, it increases the effectiveness in decision-making and budgeting. Secondly, a standard de-escalating and contra escalating of projects capital projects and expenditure is graphically illustrated, with a cause and effect diagram pointing out exactly what is at risk or open for gain as "Key Performance Areas".

- 5 Leadership; the difference between a leader and a manager is the one is a "path finder" the other a "path minder", the second difference is managers seek to control, leaders seek to serve, how we do this is by choice. Achievement, and happiness should not be inhibited by our ability to control everything in life, as this is futile. Whilst we do control the consequences of our choices to a certain extent, given the fact that we can choose, it is mostly universal laws or principles that do govern our conduct. Thus, we are not in control of our lives as much as what principles are. We suggest that this idea provides key insight into the frustration people have with the traditional models of control and time – The "time management approach in life" – vs. the new paradigm of -First things first - Stephen R Covey).

Why Principles then?

- Principles are flexible
- Principles form part of adulthood
- Principles are taught from childhood
- Principles are adaptable to any situation
- Principles are simple yet effective tools
- Principles become a way of life
- Principles build character
- Principles are universal truths

"A successful man is one who can lay a firm foundation with the bricks that others throw at him". Donald Kendall "

"Success is more attitude than aptitude." Unknown

So where does that leave us?

I would like to think that there is just a little bit more to success than meets the eye. My version of success is that it has everything to do with the instincts and the aptitude of a man or woman, this is why I had "predator in the title". Be like the wolf, adaptable, smart and cunning, yet out of reach from harm's way. Know that your survival depends on the pack; your status in the pack will be determined by your ability to hunt and lead. Leadership has three characteristics: fuel, thought and forecast.

Leaders must have fuel; - we are looking for attributes that cannot be bought like expertise and experience – fuel. Fuel is a liquid, which can go through fine cracks, when it seems to meet a wall of resistance. Fuel can change form to a gas, which makes it unpredictable, fuel can create heat and cold, which makes it interchangeable. It is highly flammable and combustible when pressurised, which gives it power. It is expensive which makes it valuable. A great source of energy that can give light, initiate movement and give comforts, which makes it a scarce commodity – Leadership Fuel.

Furthermore, leaders have to be resilient, and critically minded, apply thought; they have to consider and pre-empt, each move, they have to contemplate each action, they deliberate every strategy, they pay attention to detail, they reflect opinions, they foster ideas, they serve, they give, they are sources of inspiration and guidance – an iconic status.

Real leaders have the ability to forecast; they can predict a course of action, from their own experiences, they can calculate risk, they can lead projects, anticipate resistance, foretell with certainty an outcome and they will be right. Nevertheless, this is not the aspects that makes them great, their consistency is what makes leaders great, by virtue of their transformation abilities; **the four "I's"**

Individualised consideration; The leader cares about his people, the individual and their growth and development. The leader knows his people, their abilities and capitalizes on them, enforces them and credit's them. He makes sure that the individual knows his worth and work. He understands human dynamics.

Intellectual stimulation; The leader prompts intellectually challenging critical problem solving, by looking at old problems in new meaningful ways, by changing paradigms and allowing intellectually stimulating conversation in the work place. His people are stimulated into a cycle of constant learning and experiencing personal growth and content.

Inspirational motivation; They inspire others by communicating high expectations, using symbols to focus efforts, thus expressing important principles in simple ways. The true leader is able to convince others that they can and will achieve the extraordinary.

Idealised influence; Transformation leaders are charismatic, they provide vision, mission and goal and they instil pride, trust and gain respect by doing so. They are role models they live what they preach. People easily identify with them, because of their noble way, their blatant openness. Leadership is about the attitude; it's about growing and knowing.

The aforementioned is good, however - we are living in a fast passed life, – and so it lacks truth: The bottom line is our individual human nature, our character; we can choose to lead or to be lead, either way, we have control. We all seek to control, to keep our inner balance and sense of purpose alive, just by thinking we are in control is at times enough to fuel our aspirations.

Any effort to be in control by being out of control, or to refuse to take control, or to influence a relationship, is in fact just that – a form of control. Call it passive forms of control, much stronger than the physical. You hereby also control, he who controls at a lower level of set control, controls. In today's society it is all about who controls what, where, when and how. There is just no escape from it, the control dynamic surrounds us; with rules, laws, ethics, and codes that dictate how we should act, when we are working with people. Those who say they are not in control, has the most – control that is, at times and they seem to be working and moving in the background. We have all experienced this, where the tables get turned on us and we feel left out, resilience and following principles are your only weapon.

6 – Product and service; the one without the other is like rain without the clouds, it just does not happen. You need a product and a vehicle to deliver it with- service- the two core ingredients to effecting business.

On product and service: Leadership dictate products and service. Customers dictate what they deem to be quality, quality diminishes waste. Markets dictate price. Therefore, the principle of everything flows from the top, well, if the leadership does not place a great emphasis on customer satisfaction and client service, then they are not quality orientated and in general service in such an environment will be dictated by directives as perceived by management as being effective. In instances like this the product, no matter how good will suffer as a result of this internal influence, that's why I took a long road here, the planning and mechanisation of the thought processes need to be synergised to arrive at a key concept of the two key elements to business. The trick is in how to get product and service merging with skills and resources, to create space and ensure quality. Very few see the necessity for creating "space", they understand the requirement for quality, however they fail to prepare space – all companies require space for improvement, in many directions. This is also referred to as capacity planning.

Now capacity planning is fundamental to production and inventory planning and control, but those of us who worked in factories tend to equate capacity with labour hours or machine hours and production output. Therefore the concept of "space" in business is an opinionated matter, rather than a differentiated one. We rarely think about the importance of "space" as being a multidimensional principle, rather in terms of cubic volume as an end state to capacity constraint as one example of the essence of space. Yet our fellow practitioners who work from the logistics focus know full-well that constricted space is the real "space" issue or capacity constraint. This goes further, keeping with inventory turning as an example, by understanding customer demand in real time, we can effectively collaborating with suppliers for delivery – clearly an opinionated verdict, equated from experience, type of business in question and culture.

Creating true space, is a strategic enigma, it revolves around multidimensional aspects concerned with combining plans, ideas and perceptions into a workable solution within the confines of space. Where we have to fit in, expertise, logistics, infrastructure and needs, horizontally and vertically we have to look at resources, manpower, suppliers and customers. From these two the diagonal building block develops to form the Matrix, the space effectively utilised to compete in a world where we are fast running out of space... Preparation to compete and to defend space should form part of any business strategy. We need to plan, and create space, for growth, and all things critical for survival.

"Failing to prepare is preparing for failure." - *John Wooden*

 # 7 – The Customer; this book is about strategy and not about sales skills, but the one thing that will definably effect the customer that can be strategically catered for, is the following:

Becoming customer focused relies heavily on the managements orientation and direction towards team building and spirit. The management's support and the lateral reinforcing of the importance of relationship building, honesty, ethics, service ethic and "esprit de core" is paramount.

Customer loyalty and satisfaction is the key to making it. Rendering better skilled assistance, with after sales service and enforcing your guarantee of service...breeds satisfaction. People understand that products can fail, but service..? Scrutinise your bottom-line and margins, both lower and upper limits to determine trends and out-shooters, to see which products are moving really well and ask yourself why and which are crystallising in the box. Also, examine performance levels relative to the facts and not mere perception. Remember, "You" are always in competition with yourself first. Only when you can compete with yourself and your own best, then are you ready to dance with the opposition at their best. Gauge your performance against your own logistics and staff ratio's with that of the competitions contingent, their delivery and turnaround times. Any aspect of your business you can improve on is an advantage that creates space, as long as you do your comparison on current trends, that will have an direct effect on quality, or service, or the product, this is time well spent and is a good investment. Don't copy everything that works to the letter, it might not work for you. On the other hand, do not guarantee something you cannot deliver on! Take seriously your customers comments, concerns and questions, as well as suggestions about your product or service. In addition to responding promptly to complaints, queries, or questions, actively solicit your customers' opinion about your product or service – whilst you are rendering it. Encourage them to be honest – by giving an incentive! Provide the platforms for such interactive interaction, have forms or surveys on your website for them to use to evaluate your product or service with. By satisfying people needs, you create more needs and in tern it creates more business.

 # 8 – Quality; the concept of quality needs to be clearly defined, because it holds many interpretations. Quality is defined here as having the ability to work beyond the set standards and goals for quality we had set ourselves as a point for departure. By exceeding the set initial projected targets, those targets becomes the lowest limit benchmarked as we approach, or work towards them to in effect outperform yourself quarterly. By setting higher margins for yourself once attained, and using the previous benchmark as the lower limit. In other words we manufacture change, constantly evolving to improve on the quality factor. This mind-set demands that organisations built on the matrix value system of MQM, that of constant change and improvement at all levels, not just sustainability as our focal point. The matrix thrives on networking and not hierarchy to get things done, the system and levers of the matrix rely on close knit interdependency, with partnerships both internal as well as external. These networks eliminate waste and time cycles are shortened significantly, which in turn delivers greater speed and quality, in-between processes. Thus reducing inventory and cost, by incorporating a standard of advanced utilisation of technology to serves as back bone.

You will need to survey your intended market and find out from them what will constitute;

- quality service,
- quality product
- quality customer care.

Dig into your marketplace; Do proper surveys on trends, both local, national and international. Find the "catalyst" the triggers, to motivators, that is moving people towards a product or service. These aspects that customers prefer over others. Learn about preferences and cultural diversity and how this impacts on product preferences, matrix thinking, seeks direction, not from the top executives, but from their leading clients. Get to know if it is price or quality that will motivate the buyer. Determine the benchmark for quality service or quality product or both in your field. Here there is a stark contrast, from Western, the Eastern to African trends, for instance the Southern markets traditionally go for a balance between quality and high volume. The European market is set on high quality brand name products, and the East has started to mix it all up – this is an assumption based on the authority we used to get this info. The question is, is this factually correct, is it credible, a tabloid, a study, etc. So find a credible source before projecting where your market will be, local, national, or international, as it will heavily influence your understanding of what is important to your perceived customers from some ones perspectives, studying quality preferences trends is not just a question of a best guess. I.E. In the motor vehicle industry by way of example, they have adopted a trend to do after sales marketing surveys of all new products sold, to get an idea of what satisfies the need of the customer , what was his or her moving influence in purchasing the product and which other products were rated second and third on their list...

Adopting quality standards and strategies from established leaders in the market will put your foot in the door, for they may have already spent millions on market research and benefited from the exercise.

They may have also opened up a void that could be filled by abandoning certain products, or services with their new strategy, thereby creating markets for prospecting, or niche goods. Adopting and adapting good ideas is a key facilitative strategy towards surviving any venture. While no company is perfect, many do the right thing and yet others seem to be getting the right things done. So whose strategy should be copied as point of departure? Wrong approach, the question should in fact be whose strategy will be able to guarantee change that will ensure market share, or have a higher propensity towards sustaining current business and growth.

Practice what you preach with MQM. By setting rigid, but achievable quality challenges for product, production, and service delivery.

It should close match your other quality performance value chain activity and initiatives. Companies like Coca-Cola have adopted the strategy of " killing their best product" by re-engineering their products "face" to fit in with the current trends, packaging and theme and they have been around for ages, targeting new markets every year with new strategies, pushing market confidence with continued media bombardment of theme and appropriateness to lifestyle.

MQM strives to create a worker-friendly physical environment.

Be sure, work areas are conducive to work, uncluttered and clean. Because people produce best when they feel best, when they are comfortable, then it becomes a comfort zone. The home away from home. Soliciting employees' suggestions on how to improve production, service or a component of the business is an essential part of an efficient work area. Contrary to popular belief the person closest to the task will know best, how and where to improve - give it a try. Your employees know how to improve quality. Create an environment in which they feel comfortable sharing their ideas and you will prosper from the results.

Commuting MQM to Establish "quality" partnerships with your suppliers.

A supplier agrees to meet your MQM standards for quality and service and in return, you agree to give him a sole supplier mandate. As a result, they not only ensure better supplies but also streamline their own procedures by reducing the hassle of dealing with multiple suppliers.

Provide education on quality and MQM:

If your employees know what quality constitutes and how important it is to the overall success of the enterprise. Then you provide opportunities for them to learn how quality can be improved. They then become independent quality innovators.

Corruption and theft, safe guarding the MQM system; Corruption and theft is the number one internal influence that creates disease in corporate environments today, make sure that you have strict measures in place to safeguard against this practice – need I say more.

Chapter 14: Developing a Business plan that includes principles of War

The whole idea behind formulating a business strategy

The whole idea of formulating a business strategy that utilises principles of WAR, is to create focus on what really matters when planning strategy. This idea is nothing new. However, in order to relieve stress, and the frustrations that comes along with business design, we need to take note of some facts, that influence us, and how to handle them. More so, to identify, for "designers" the essential elements of information required at any start up. Many of us can relate to the frustration of dealing with government departments, a company, a university and so on, that thrives on bureaucracy, and how darn difficult they can make simple things. Especially when the pressure is on, and you need to get things done now. Same applies inter departmentally. Even in our own business environments, the smallest of things tend to jam the total system, simple tasks take longer than expected, things go wrong, and people blame the system and controls. When things go pear-shaped, people assume that it's due to inadequate organisation and control, and this needs review, this is not always the case. Sometimes we have just too much intervention, managers and directors must allow subordinates to develop their own methods and systems, use their own expertise, and their intimate knowledge of their equipment. By fostering greater familiarity with their own area of operations confidence grows in parallel. The only constraint is that they must act within the framework of the business plan, and its intent to ensure unity of effort. In this way, clearly identified objectives and goals get realised, faster, where the core functions of your business gets addressed first. The last and final step is solving the aspect of how to best utilise and hold onto this competence, as well as to expand it to its paramount extent.

This is why we turn to War like strategies, seeking the prevention of formulating to many diversified strategies that create *friction*; Clausewitz wrote in war, friction is an "unseen, all-pervading" element. This aspect resides in the cohesion of opinions, where unity is strength, only then do unified solutions emerge. Friedman noted: "Only a crisis—actual or perceived—produces real change. When that crisis occurs, the actions that are taken depend on the ideas that are lying around." Where we have people that work as a collective we find progress, where we don't find cohesion we find chaos, cohesion shows functional discipline is intact – people respect each other and become interdependent. These aspects need to be in place to fight the effect of "Friction". Business is just war on another battlefield. It's about how everything can and will go wrong, how things generally don't go to plan, and how simple things are difficult to do.

Business plans, serves as reminders of our rallying points, objectives, and goals, when we lose cohesion due to friction, or reminds us of our vision in the face of battle.

Strategy is not a lengthy action plan; it is the continuum of ideas that bring about the evolution of a central idea, through gauging continually changing circumstances, and adapting constantly.

Even in theory, any war should end in extremes – or last for short duration, a single decisive battle, or total destruction. However, in practice, friction ensues, that ensures that war is prolonged. Friction confuses issues, creates the fog of war, and as a result, objectives and goals fails to result in some or all of the objectives set. The idea that our "system of systems" will provide us a decisive advantage, is also failing us. How many times have you heard someone say, "we need to put in place a system to fix that" or "we need more controls"? Clausewitz wrote that for a theory to apply to war, it must apply to all previous historical examples of war. If the theory cannot account for something that has already happened, then it is a flawed theory. Actually, adding more systems and controls is the last thing you need. It makes things more complicated. It increases the chance that things will go wrong again, and again. We have to strive for one system that incorporates all. If not, then fragmentation gives friction more room in which to play. Clausewitz wrote that great commanders understand friction and its effects. They know how to cope with friction, through courage, composure, determination and grit. They are realistic about what can and can't be achieved in the face of friction. They keep things simple.

The theatre of war is all about dealing with friction and keeping things simple.

Friction is **generated** and magnified by menace, ambiguity, deception, rapidity, uncertainty, and mistrust.

Friction is **diminished** by implicit understanding, trust, co-operation, simplicity, and focus.

In this sense, to much variety and rapidity tend to magnify friction, we require simplicity, while the presence of harmony and initiative tend to diminish friction.

The Duality

Variety and rapidity without harmony and initiative to lead or guide it, leads to confusion, disorder and ultimately to total chaos.

However, harmony and initiative without variety and rapidity lead to rigid uniformity, predictability and ultimately to non-adaptability.

We require balance...

The Conundrum

How do we generate harmony and initiative so that we can exploit variety and rapidity?

The challenge

We must uncover and strike a balance between two extremes, that of interactions that foster harmony and initiative yet not destroy variety and rapidity in the process.

The Army Field Manual...Has one main Objective.

Direct every military operation towards a clearly defined, decisive, and attainable objective, supported by secondary objectives. Prepare clear, uncomplicated plans and clear, and concise orders to ensure thorough understanding

These aspects comes about only with investing time in building capacity and expertise with a group, that keep these factors in mind when devising strategy. The enhancement of the workforce and rewarding of effort builds moral, another required element, and last but not the least it creates a structure that regulates all aspects internally. The capacity to understand and define objectives and how to achieve them creates focus. Focus drives cohesion, within the limitations of situational appropriateness. Situational appropriateness is a concept of war and requires insight that comes from expertise and experience gained only by having practiced principles of war. However without structure to facilitated relationship building, from where networks emerge, we will also have no synergy. Principles of war; should feature high on the strategic agenda. The ability to recognise new opportunities lies within a collective and not just individuals and their great ideas. The ability to achieve beyond expectation, resides in assembling expertise; with some research, development of skill, and competency. Backed up by solid planning and structure. The transferring of people who have skills to share, will grow more diversity. People, start forming new bonds through interaction and recreational activities, it has a "pollination effect". Boundaries are moved and shifted in this fashion, people have to come out of their comfort zones, that previously existed by having only followed one set paradigm. When following a totally new paradigm, we teach people the power of change, as we are experiencing it first hand for ourselves. Especially continued organised change. Generals, only become experts at what they do, by having done it several ways successfully, however, they do realise that passing on this knowledge to a collective, builds a stronger army. Generals, start planning with "table" and "paper" exercises, their prelude to battle. Here soldiers start developing an aptitude for problem solving as a collective, rather than finger pointing to who should solve it. This evolves into strategic discussion, because they are focused on winning, and on applying principles, this trait should be in place, this required aptitude for creatively solving common problems in and as a collective, stems from their ability that only evolved during "war time"... This makes us ready for "war", where we find one common purpose as a collective and strive ardently to achieve it. All this has to do with preparing strategically for poised success; however in order to gain momentum, it requires a real plan – the business plan.

The driving forces behind business plans

The intent of any scheme must be summarised within a business plan. The purpose of the business plan is to sell all the aforementioned aspects as rational and methodical deductions, a well-conceived and thought through strategy. In other words it has to make sense to people, before it can make business sense.

On the aspect of trust – just assuming everyone is as willing and able as you are to commit. The fact of the matter is, trust has destroyed more people and countries that cunning has ever accomplished. Hope is coupled to trust, and in turn has kept more people prisoner in their own belief that great things will happen to good and honest people. Wrong, cunning and scheming minds seek to exploit this very characteristic daily for their own gain. Therefore, "you" are part and parcel of the plan, and everything and everyone coupled to you, will have an effect on you – and therefore the plan. Good and great plans have failed because they failed to check the operatives, and leaders capacity to cope with extreme amounts of pressure and friction. This point deals with one's immediate circle of influence. However brilliant we are, we are only as strong as what we are sure, and understandable.

Make sure that your family knows what will be at stake, in terms of time, effort and late nights, long trips and having to survive seasons of change as a family unit. This extends to your personal wellbeing, marriage, children, other commitments and tasks as parent and even your immediate family. In other words get your house in order first, then make sure that your partner/ if any, are in the same state of affairs, if not you will have your back against the girding wheal.

Studies have shown that the best business plans, and businesses have failed in practice, due a few uncommon "small" matters; such as;

- Personal issues at home or with partners – distraction and emotional baggage.

- Parental responsibilities.
- Problems with health and or injury.
- Addiction – in any form.

Assuming that there is no competition; everyone is competing, if not for clients, then for resources, or market share, you can never have a business without having competition.

Assuming that patent rights, sole supplier mandates and contracts will protect you – it won't.

"One man" business are the riskiest to have and or to invest in, especially if it involves skill, expertise or talent, if you were removed from the equation, would the business still be able to exist, this aspect even extends to bigger business, where no one is in reserve – competent to take over for a short or extended time, or second in command of all aspects of the business.

Aiming too small; you do too little business to make ends meet, or too big; you spend too much on overheads and resources and earn too little to cover the expenses – without having the support to back it up.

Having partners that have already made it big, that don't take it serious, or that have too many commitments to for fill.

Putting critical issues off – until; we have the money, time, or space...etc.

Impulsiveness -banking on promises made or relying on others to get the thing to work – to cover expenses in time – borrowing from Peter to pay Paul – type of situation. This equates to poor cash flow measures and risk management. The fundamental principle is to convert services or goods into cash in record time. To have alternatives available. A deal is not a deal until all the money is in the bank – it is said.

Underestimating the influences on the type of business – not enough time spent contemplating all aspects, too eager to start.

The concept of preparing for battle starts with preparing the self-first, and then the "battle plan". Just like soldiers have to be fit, healthy and well trained, the same applies.

In the military, this aspect where "top management" entrusts the "commanders with formulating the plan". Where they (the leaders) have set the objectives and leave the detail of the scheme to the experts, this type of thinking sets the stage for formative interaction. We no longer drill into place strategic plans as top management, and fill in the detail as we go along, and still expect that it will work. The days of top down is gone for good, we have to think lateral and plan agile, by utilising our core of expertise – strategic planning has become a specialised field. We need people that can see, and plan beyond the obvious horizon.

Real strategic planning

Real strategic planning takes us beyond the objectives we have set. The plan for the first battle must be the prelude to the next, forming a continuum of initiatives and combining them. This first step sets the stage; it becomes the organic part of the plan for the whole campaign, our point of departure. Without a good plan for the whole campaign, it is absolutely impossible to fight a really good first "battle". Hence, before fighting the first battle, one must have a general idea of how the second, third, fourth and even final battle will be fought and consider what changes will ensue in the enemy's situation as a whole if we win, or lose, each of the succeeding battles. Although the result may not - and, in fact, definitely will not - turn out exactly as we expect, we must think out everything carefully and realistically in the light of the general situation on both sides. Without a grasp of the situation as a whole, it is impossible to make any really good move on the chessboard. - **Mao Tse-tung, Selected Military Writings.**

This is why we only formulate a business plan, after we have reviewed all the options availed, and then only assemble the grand plan, called our "grand strategy". We depart only with unambiguous intent and arrive at an ultimate conclusion, in terms of drafting a desired simple business plan. Our selling point and motivation will be tested against the assumptions and arguments derived from our research. Let's look at war and get even more flesh into our business plan and selling angle. Remember, the strategy could be excellent, but if you cannot sell it, it is dead.

The Three Types of Warfare

Boyd thought it was relevant to firstly identify the differences between the three major types of warfare; (as a business we have to decide what type of strategy will work best) so that one can understand the complexity of war (business strategy) and what it entails. Only then could a decision be made to change ones fighting mind-set and culture. Subsequently, to understand the three types of war doctrines, we will refer to this as strategies for this purpose and illustration and see how we can relate to it, and from it towards forming a solid business strategy, also referred to as the approach we will take. The vehicles to get the plan into being, from the three concepts of war.

Boyd, suggested three types of warfare:

Attrition, as practiced by the Emperor Napoleon and World War I, by the Allies during World War II; the three distinct and requisite qualities of *attrition warfare* are: firepower, mobility and protection. It is imperative to keep these qualities in balance, yet force an adversary's out of balance. So we may say, or are lead to believe that if fire power relates back to the American and

Asian connotation of flooding markets with cheap affordable consumer goods, where the French would be an opposing market, dedicated to Luxury items and branding of high cost, high fashion, high quality. Mobility would be the available market segments that you can compete in and protection would be in protecting market segment, copyrights and patents ext.

Manoeuvre, as practiced by the Mongols, 'General Bonaparte,' Hitler's; *manoeuvre warfare*, the only answer to a big force, is manoeuvrability, the application of this approach to business, is one key word, getting the initiative and running with it. It is the ability to grab by the nose and kick the behind. By misleading and being agile, in mind, creativity and leadership. Described and used to conduct manoeuvre warfare are "ambiguity," "deception", "novelty"", fast transient manoeuvres" and "effort". *Fast transient manoeuvres* are the result of being able to cycle through the OODA loop faster than an adversary. Command and control was to manoeuvre a key element of success.

Moral, as practiced by the Mongols, most guerrilla leaders (revolutionary leaders) and Sun Tzu. Boyd concluded there were three positive counters: *initiative* or the internal drive to think and take action without being urged; this has been discussed in length in chapters 1 to 5, *adaptability* or the power to adjust, also known as the resilience factor or change in order to cope with new or unforeseen circumstances; and acting in *harmony* or a co-ordinated manner, to achieve the main goal. By creating the intentional interaction of apparently disconnected events, to achieve the ultimate goal. Strategies in turn are guided by policy and procedure, called doctrine.

Institutionalising the strategic intent

Strategy relies on policy and procedure to fit, to be effective, and to be in line with how people traditionally do their work to be effective, it needs to be institutionalised.

Searching out, redesigning and adopting of "best practices" is integral to effective implementation.

Benchmarking has spawned new approaches to improving strategy execution;

- Re-engineering of the whole, partial or just a sector of the organisation, could spawn instant grown in capital gains,
- Continuous quality improvement programmes,

- Institutionalising the scripts of Matrix Quality Management – MQM,
- Quality improvement programmes are tools for implementing strategies keyed at;
- Defect-free manufacturing'
- Superior product quality, design and price structuring,
- Superior after-sales service,
- Total customer satisfaction, every customer gets quality service or no service – the motto. We have a 100% guarantee of quality,
- Expedited quality service delivery with a touch of class and professionalism.

Identifying and implementing your own refined and tailor made best practices is a quest for quality and mitigating waste, not a means to an end; it is an continuous exercise in doing things right by doing the right things over and over and still trying to refine and perfect the idea on a daily basis in a world-class manner! – This is the process of "Adapt, Improvise and Overcome", all in order to reach the objective of the strategy, by whatever means available. This is striving for excellence.

Understanding how policies and procedures can enhance strategy implementation.

- It should provide a top-down "guidance" regarding expected behaviours and performance.
- Help align processes and legal aspects with strategy
- Help enforce consistency and uniformity in logistical functions. Be a criteria like a road map to explain how process flow and inter act with one and other as well as defining who has to do what, where, when and how and who will be the contact or responsible person. What documentation will be required and how it should be sent, or processed etc. it should in short be an operating manual of the system and not a way to have control of a component thereof. Very important for decentralised co-ordination in performance of strategy-critical activities in geographically scattered operating unit's
- Serve as powerful lever for changing corporate culture to produce stronger fit with a new strategy

Role and function of strategy supportive attributes - policy and procedure:

- The Role of new policies in implementing strategy. Many top notch business people still get this all wrong, they marry the two, policy and procedure are not one. They are two totally differ attributes of one process.
- Policy's role is to informs us, and gives us options, whereas procedure channels these actions, into a required specific response, that governs our behaviours and decisions in directions to promote strategy execution...
- It counteract tendencies of people to resist chosen strategy...by giving them no choice –

Policy make sure of that – e.g. you will clock in at 08h00 – this is the policy.

Now the **procedure**, is as you get to the gate swipe your card, and then again at the office door – this is a procedure – the how we do things,

The why we do them is policy.

Too much policy can be as stifling as wrong policy or as chaotic as no policy, the importance of policy is it must be conservative with wording and must be as short and simple as possible. It must streamline actions and not be an obstacle, it is there to counter presidents set. Remember in the absence of police we follow the presidents set. Or norm.

Sometimes, *THE BEST POLICY* is just a total willingness to "empower" employees

Modelling a business plan

There is no template available that can be tuned and moulded that will constitute a great business plan for every type of venture, the specifics of the business plan required and the requirements to be presented will be dictated by the situational appropriateness. However the following points are considered to be standard practise in a business plan. A business plan is best described as a formal statement of intent, which includes a set of objectives, the reasons why they are believed attainable and the strategy for reaching those objectives. It may also contain background information about the organization or team attempting to reach those goals.

The four fundamentals of most business plans:

The Financial framework; how much capital and operational financing will be required to get the concept started? How long will it take the concept to mature, to become self-sustaining, or become profitable, will be depicted as phases or stages. Addendums which reflect calculations, to be attached;

- Costing analysis
- Capital budget
- Operational budget
- Grants, investors, partnerships and sponsors contributions
- Loan terms and lease agreements
- Salary structure

The risks involved; how real are they and how damaging are they should they occur during the early stages of development, what would be the "margin of success" if such an anomaly occurred, how damaging would it be. Will any insurance cover such risk and to what extent and at what price, or who will carry the financial risks involved?

- A proper risk assessment profile in terms of a SWOT analysis
- Distribution of wealth, risk, responsibility and accountability profile
- Managements track record and composition and financial status
- Guarantees and contractual obligations

Forecasting; analysing other similar concepts and markets, using statistical data in, forecasts, projections and statistics, to forecast probable success...and surety of results. Referred to as the competitive analysis.

Will include the;

- Financial plan
- Operational plan or project plan (time phase plan, with resource allocations and budgets.)
- And the marketing plan
- Strategic role out plan (the who has to do; what, where, when how and how much.)

Contemplating the critical success influences; on the type of business model selected, also referred to as, business assumptions made, complimented by a description of what is envisaged as an intro, or overview, describing amongst other things the process and assumptions made whilst;

- Contemplating the type of model to build from and the motivation behind it complimented by a CAPS analysis;
  - o The mapping and modelling, of a comprehensive business plan and visualisation if need be – with power point presentation, scale or CAD models and sketches, of proposals and prototypes etc. Referred to as the sales pitch, nothing sell itself, it requires a catalyst.
  - o Looking at geographical vulnerabilities and advantages; mortgage rates and rental rates, complimented with a GAP Analyses.
  - o A critical overview of the strategic positioning of the firm, pertaining to;
  - o Transportation and infrastructure requirements;
  - o Labour availability in that area and the going rates.
  - o Preparing a proposal for financial backing and or possible partnerships. By analysing trends and new markets.
  - o The level of technology and or specialisation required.
  - o Additional resources required
  - o Clearly identifying the specific need that will be satisfied in the market place – the feasibility study.
  - o Legislative compliance.
  - o Standards that will be adopted.
  - o Mapping the influences.
  - o Mapping the influences to get a better understanding of what is at stake is a good idea.

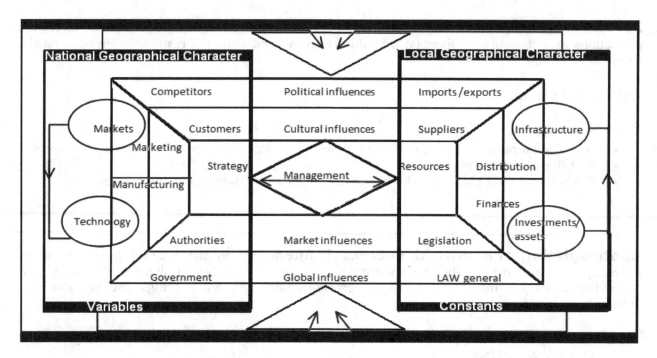

Matrix Strategy connects the Matrix of influences on strategy, with critical thinking; map every aspect to see the connections and relations we have to contemplate... The middle right angle shows the cardinal relationship between two elements and how they connect; management connects resources with strategy and visa-versa. However their relationship is directly influenced by; Cultural influences, political influences, market influences and global influences, this include constants and variables that has to be factored in applicable to the business, as well as, the local geographical and national geographical character. The middle right angle in the centre depicts the internal environment and how the immediate and external environment in turn will impact, with their respective influences, referring to the bigger right angles. Then we also take note of the key anomalies that might impact on our design, the spheres, markets determine the type of technology required and influence it, in terms of the technological advances made in the region, or continent. Silicon Valley is a good example, of regional clustering; it has become a hub for information technology, where determining situational and geographical positioning, in the vertical right angle, we have to factor in all the anomalies that go hand in hand with the geographical positioning of a company. You don't want to build a company specialising in "IT" in Alaska and you don't want to build a fishing industry in Silicon Valley – now do you... The companies geographical positioning will also be determined by the investment you will make in capital, in the region, the investment of business is directly coupled to the availability and suitability of infrastructure, to compliment the type of business contemplated.

The "Business PROSPECTUS"

Is a formal written document that provides a **business** plan and objective for a proposed **business** or an investment opportunity.

The basics of a business plan;

Index

- Executive Summary
- Founders vision
- Company mission statement
- Company Strategic Positioning
- CAPS analysis
  - The *concept* is that of...
  - The key *attributes* of the company that gives it a competitive edge is...
  - The public *perception* in general is that...
  - The *systems* that support the demand...
- Gap analysis
- Finding ingenuous ways of closing the gap, between small vs. big established enterprise competing, has resulted in opportunities that emulated after a SWOT analysis of the environment and business contemplated, that eliminated this threat, by adopting a radical approach to doing business.
- Company Objectives
  - Short
  - Medium
  - and long term objectives
- Company Summary
  - Composition
  - Location
  - Expertise
  - Products and Services
  - Niche product range
  - Sole import mandates and rights
  - Target Market identification and Marketing Analysis
    - our competitive advantage and competitors
    - our market niche
    - our dependencies
    - our pricing objectives
    - our ability to deliver

Strategy and Implementation

- How will you do this within the framework of what you have...you could include; SWOT, MQM, SWAT, TAPS, OODA any of these principles...
- Organisation and Management
- Strategic Alignment with market
- Financials

How we talk strategy, is how we will construct it...We require critical thinking more that intellectual babbling, this brings us to the next chapter, how do we present strategy to the masses...we need to be more colourful in our comunication.

Chapter 15:

All about Thinking; The quiet mind and "Critical thinking".

What is strategic thinking really?

This chapter gives insight into the way strategist must think, and comprehend thought. The word "critical" was derived from two Greek word: "kriticos" - meaning discerning judgment- and "kriterion" - meaning standards or criteria.

Critical thinking ensures that you use the best thinking you are capable of and apply a criteria, in any set of circumstances -which interrogates information with the interpretative intuition, to arrive at intelligence, through the gift of critical thinking we attain the "gift" of focused interpretation. Critical thinking seeks ways of understanding the mind and awakening the intellect so that such deformation of thought created by our surroundings are rationalised, and that the capacity of humans to reason can be nurtured and developed by reframing as well as the imprinting of new paradigms; in order to see the bigger picture, to make sense of chaos and friction.

In this chapter we will look at snapshots of things we have to think about, during a project, or encounter, that will or could influence our thinking and ability to steer the right course with strategy.

Applying critical thinking that relates to the critical decision making processes.

Critical thinking makes one aware of one's own fallibility and corrupted thinking by:

Informing us firstly to be guarded against adopting an ego-sensitive approach. When starting any strategic conversation – we need to think about our own mindset first and the manner in which we will address the crowd, or people concerned, what is our aim, and what will be a desired outcome. We don't start with dominance and ego centric talk: The "I will do it my way", or I don't need anyone, and I will do it by myself" stance, if no one cares to help me. Departures like this - can and will - indeed impact on a required sober departure and stance. Business strategy and etiquette require one to be critical and near perfect.

Recalling previous beliefs; we all tend to use old paradigms, that one once held strongly onto but are now rejected widely. The door to the future is to revisit the past, not to repeat it, don't think in the same fashion, so that you may not plan in the same direction, if you have failed before.

Realizing that everyone still has numerous blind spots, despite their prestige, accomplishments and fame, we need to network the plan to make sure it is well conceived and designed by all not just some, and that it will emerge without blind spots.

Accepting that everyone has some sort of subconscious biases, that hold them to a certain culture of truth and accordingly business assumptions, questioning any judgments and assumptions raised, will be for the best.

"The Quiet Mind" as power tool in corporate "Strategy".

Strategy is not a model, a drawing, or case study, that one can take off the shelf and fit in with your environment and hope it will work. We can learn from it though, granted, however case studies are history, and in many instance we don't want history to repeat itself. Strategy today has changed its face, it has to be both in time – and no longer just on time - and in step with the current reality, that is forever changing, it has to fit in, within the habitat that we find ourselves in. Therefore I opted to give tools and tips to strategists in this chapter that will protect, aid and guide them. In order to make use of the many attributes that are well within our sphere of influence, that we can take control over, that will facilitate this type of critical thinking. All, in line with the current, without having to rise to the level of the great CEO's, just to make strategy that works, all credit to them, but we are not all in idealised positions. Strategy today are made by common men with intellect, at grass roots level, even the smallest business requires a strategy. We only have our minds at times and no other high priced and specialised resources, to utilise as additional strategic tools. This chapter covers many attributes that we can use to be more effective in communicating our goals and objectives, that does not cost an arm or a leg, most of it is just "common sense".

Strategy is just not possible without the agility of mind and in turn, the agility of mind requires stretching and exercising ones mental limbs to become agile minded, and think in different ways so to speak. Do we ever consider using all our senses to think? To elaborate on this concept we need to switch gears, to go up some levels in thinking and consider this against our own perception and mental capacity, as well as thinking technique. How powerful is your mind? Thinking has nothing in common with the power of the mind, strangely enough, it is a learned response, we are taught to think, and it could be learned. The average mind, has the ability to think at around 3800 words more or less per minute – that is six typed A4 pages of information, one can speak at around 480 words per minute, but normal conversation takes place around the 200 words per minute mark. Therefore, the speed at which we think is only hampered by the speed at which we can project our thought, and the way we structure our thought, into conversation.

The best-recorded memory was that of Shereshevsky, he never forgot anything in his life; he could read anything just once and recall it years later. The point to make here is this, he practiced thinking and memory. He had too much information stored in his brain at the end of the day, due to his process used to assimilate information, and had to be taught how to get rid of it. We will get back to this principle of a busy mind, so he was told to write it down, the information and then burn it. We take notes in meeting of important things that we need to remember – and then we work from them - file them or discard them, so in essence we are programmed to be lazy, to forget information.

Words become our medium, that creates a perspective; either of what we communicate to imply or hear and understand. Then assimilation and dissemination of information is influenced by the amount, quality, and degree of difficulty we are facing in trying to understand it, or relay it. Then there is noise, things that distract, impede, or hinder conversation. The more detail, the better the chances are that we are going to get lost, or loose cohesion with our audience. Information is best received in "bite size" chunks. On this point of trying to make sense of bulk loads of information, instead of committing every thought into our own words and later on back at the office trying to paste all the details together, try to do this, rather get the other party to submit a "statement of intent" and then work from that. Memory is only as good as what the person is intuitive and receptive. We all deal with information differently, and we have biases against certain information, that subconsciously block, or absorb it for us. Here is why – he - Shereshevsky, remembered names as colours, numbers as smells, places as living portrait's – making them concrete objects – so let's just stop here for a minute. Ask yourself this, how much detail goes into this aspect of giving names colour, giving numbers scent, what level of thought processes has been developed by this individual to memorise and file information as if a dream. Do we think this hard, and attempt to memorise information this critically. No, we deal with way too much on a daily basis. However, we can all learn from it and use it.

By dreaming, we are merely referring to the "pasteurising of data", removing non-essential words and breaking it down into single elements that form a silent movie. Building a story line, from the data that can be recalled, all in the same instance. Let's just say for arguments sake; that he had a fish and his fish was named "Number one". He tells you about number "one" and what he does all day. However - in his mind - he sees a strawberry, he smells it, he tastes it and he tells you this is "number one", you and me looking from our side into the fish tank through our minds eye, we only see a red fish of sorts, called "one" in our minds eye – presumably just swimming. From his side of the fish tank in his mind's eye he sees a red coloured fish, he sees a strawberry "flavour" swimming in the clean fish tank with a lot of other species of fish, but this one is significant to him, he has a profuse mental and emotional bond with this fish.

He also relates the whole fish back to a strawberry, the colour, the texture of the fruit being similar to that of the fish, the feel of the strawberry, feeling the same as that of the fish when you hold it in your hand, the green leaves feel like the fins. Without the continued use of imagination, we stand to lose the excitement of much possibilities in life.

So, are we in essence "seeing" the same thing? Therefore, it is most important to understand the "viewpoints of everyone" (how people relate to life) from their own unique internal mental perspective. We tend to presume too much about others and their views, we judge a book by its cover – this proves that some people, perceive life with their senses and their environment strongly influences them. Strategist are architects, annalist, and require critical thinking, they need to tap into the mind's eye, to see creation from the same viewpoints in relation to anyone person expressing himself. This is the core factor of having a quite mind, which is agile. It enables us to see past perception and to be able to distinguish between perception and reality, to make sense of thought throughout the spectrum.

The lessons learned here is listening without prejudice; some call it empathetic listening. By writing things down, asking questions for clarity and ignoring not the data, or facts in the reasoning. If we listen this way, we should be able to explain the communication better than what the first person communicating it to us did. If you can achieve this and the response is yes-yes-yes from the other parties, then we are communicating and thinking critically. However, in a perfect world we find something different, we have time constraints, deadlines and what if the person is saying, or implying something we are not liking, do we still listen critically? Keep on reading and test your critical thinking skills. Were you able to follow, or do you have to re-read this section? What was the intended message conveyed here? Successful listening or listening with intent is key to communication and understanding, strategy is all about finding the true intent. Nevertheless, what do we do instead, we make our communications abstract – our thoughts that are not meant to be abstract become just that - abstract, have we ever considered giving our conversation some form, with association. People have difficulty relating to us when they do not see what we are saying – the memory is like a hologram, it relates to forms and shapes and colour in the one part of the brain and finds meaning in the other where it gets attributes.

The brain needs to make sense of information, in order to use it. Consequently it needs to appeal to more than just one of the senses to bring information into association to any references we, may or may not have alluded to. For example, any memory relating to the previous example "the number one", "the colour red", "fish" and "strawberries" will differ from one person to the next. We have all have different attribution to things that are mentioned in passing conversation. Things need to be placed in context, to be framed so that we are all on the same page, in order for things to be implicitly understood as it is intended. We need to decode the significance and the relationship that transpired here, first, the number one had its significance, - it could have meant to be referring to a single digit, or firstly, and so on. In this instance, the red bright fish was a projection of himself. He was always told that he was number one and very bright – red was his favourite colour, he ended up alone and whilst alone he ate strawberries watching and studying this one fish. Have we ever considered the coded message that he was projecting. No, we assumed the reasoning was objective rather that subjective, and that all people reason and relate to us in this fashion. This is an important aspect of conversation, the facts it seemed was in the literal conversation – him talking about a fish. However, what if he was not talking about a fish, what if he was talking about himself and the things he enjoys, strawberries, his fish and him being alone?

The lesson here is people are emotional beings and therefore complex. This aspect can at times be a springboard to communicate suppressed emotional feelings, like anger (frustration) to an open audience in code. Our emotional state plays such a vital part to our thinking, it actually dominates it, we move from the one to the next feeling in just one sentence, from love to hate, from joy to jealousy. Carl Jung, a psychologist suggested that we never stop dreaming and feeling, dreaming is an emotionally activated and driven activity expressing subconscious thoughts and he compared daydreaming to being unable to see the stars as one would during the night, hence you need to dream and force your imagination to work, to make abstracts visible as pictures in order to improve your memory. If and when we want to become a formidable strategic opponent, we need to learn how to carry ourselves, mentally, spiritually and physically, both inside and outside the unit and organisation. By pointing out some scenarios that will make us aware of the levels of dexterity of thought. That could impact on logic.

We will need to apply logic when it counts most, when others see no reason to carry on, and reason itself fails, and emotion and chaos creeps in. At this point strategist are called in, where others see no solution and sees no point to carry on. What do we do? This is the dynamics of group culture, human behaviour and corporate ego tactics. We can only cross this obstacle once we grasp a thing or two about common-sense, that contrarily to believe, about common-sense prevailing everywhere, well here is the truth about common-sense. There is nothing common about common-sense at all, for common sense is not at all that common, on the contrary, it is rare, very rare and seldom applied or observed by most of us, where an abundance of emotion is present. People in general want to over analyse everything these days, or marginalize, and they become overly sensitive to criticism. We have become too opinionated, just by justifying our own thinking and actions regardless of common sense we can live with the consequences, as long as we "win", everything is triggered by unadulterated childish emotion.

We have become a global society of emotionally reactive beings, which has gone mentally, numb and as long as you can justify your actions within your mind, then you are right, then everything is okay, even immoral action. We will need to apply logic when it counts most. People in general have adopted the approach of keeping to themselves and being humbled, we have also become very trusting and recluse. Just let CNN and BBC tells us how things are today, let the government dictate what is good for us and let the politicians make us feel guilty about our culture etc. Fine, however, whilst in strategic mode, we need to actively concentrate on blocking out these worldviews and focus on finding the common problems, with "common sense" and our own emotional reactivity to our environment should be filtered. The most important aspect to an agile mind is, a holistic observance of influences and how they are created – looking outside the norm, listening for the underlying, looking at things from as many viewpoints and perspectives as humanly possible with a calm composure. We have to step back, and look at the bigger picture, to find the door and windows in the wall. For the rest have their noses up against the wall, they have no peripheral vision left, we need to guide them.

Without seeming paranoid, solving a mathematical problem takes concentration; this includes listening with intent and developing an acute observation for all things relevant to the outcome. This list could include "small things, and dynamics, like internal bickering, conflicting operational deployments, clashing egos and personal agendas... When in fact, our only focus is as a norm only on; analysing data in depth and turning information into intelligence by testing and validating the source. Not good enough anymore, in order to work with unequivocal data, we have to take all the inputs. Before accepting anything, as factual data, or as the intended message, we have to filter the communication, and the mediums who send them, as well as receive them. We have to decode the inputs, to see if it is coded – does it mean what is literary read into it, or does it have another innate meaning as well. Most conversation is scrambled, with emotional undertones when we are in stress. The there is also the political and even personal dilemmas. Finding the solutions to everyday problems could prove quite challenging, where it is more about what is not expressed, that what is tangible. The systems, and procedure could work fine, it might be the people that have issues with each other that cause bottle necks, and friction. It could almost border on paranoia if someone does not understand the methodology behind it, at times and for some people, adding spiritual influences are not uncommon either, which gives that type of conversation added underlying intent. We get emotional about small things like the first rain, why not about conflicting views in business, and then act out.

Initial contact with a problem is like clearing the **fog of war**, clearing as we go through the data or communication at hand and making sense of it as it appears. We have to strive for the unequivocal, to find the route cause in its purest form; it must be pure, indisputable, untarnished. This process of filtering noise out can be made very simple and streamlined when on a fact finding analysis, just by asking the other party to submit his ideas or proposals in written form. As a written statement of intent, clearly defining problems and desired outcome. On the other hand, by drawing a sketch or picture of what he sees so that we may relate to it better.

On the back side of this, "logical strategic reasoning goes beyond thinking" we need to see, experience and feel the situation as it exists - to guide one as well - no one would need you if; "they" had all these abilities and tools, now would they. Therefore, be humble in your approach. Never be over confidant, one must develop a very strong report before we can imagine what the problems are, to project images as they could or would appear in the future, just like a movie producer. Especially if you get guidelines from top management to follow, that would equate to you being able to see through their eyes. Which is impossible, but by referencing the "design" against current available or "tangible" models, one should get a better idea of what is expected. It is almost the same visualisation process that a – CAD - Computer Aided Design software programme would produce after being fed all this type of data, but in this instance only in the mind.

This is why the following chapter deals with this fascinating aspect of strategy and how it originates in the mind, and the things that distort its creation. By covering some influences that directly attributed to memory and the workings of the mind, and then relating it to common workplace attributes. In order to facilitate further discussion on topics seldom introduced into strategy before and especially strategic management, we need to give people tools for reasoning critically in a world that finds itself in constant flux. Strategy and people are linked by the hip, if we understand both, we will see, plan and communicate better. To do this we need to understand more about the mind as a critical tool in strategy and how to direct it to find people and solutions.

Standardised reference points

People want and opt for standardised sets of instruction on strategy, so that they can make sense of it. When in fact, the truth of the matter is, in plain words, it is just not possible, due to the evolutionary process and time spirals effect. More on this later, let us finish on the mind and move towards more practical subjects.

The last aspect is memory.

The importance of Perspective memory; a type of memory that allows us to plan into the future, in the way we perceive it, see it, believe and or imagine it to be. However in order to plan one must be able to transport oneself to a place and time in our minds that does not exist yet. Where the difficulty is that we need to take others to this same place. Perspective memory is also the weakest of all our types of memory, not so surprisingly, because we have not yet been able to travel in time, and very seldom dream about the future in great detail. Thus how do we steer around this innate obstacle? Through applying techniques such as explained visualisation and tracing.

Now on to applying critical thinking in the Pandora's box of corporate affairs, and all it has to offer

It is said that -**By studying our past, we may predict the future**. How about, by studying humans, we may create better strategy.

First.

The term **"history repeats itself"** comes to mind. By doing what we have always been doing, we are inevitably be charting the same course that we were on yesterday, for today and unavoidably tomorrow, and we are guaranteed the same results Therefore, it stands to reason that the river when in flood will more likely take the same course it did last year and the previous year, if nothing in its path has changed. From experience of studying the "history" of (in this case rivers), in every case we need to find within the subject matter its history, commonalities and distinguishing attributes that guides it. Our memory of our history is also in our DNA and will affect us the same way it did our strings of ancestors as brethren, thus brothers have certain commonality in the way they think, do and act, the same with a nations under one language, and culture. Much communality in thinking and doing is observed when studying peoples habitats. Our living, working and social environment dictates how we can, must, or will think, and therefore act.

The reason for isolating language here is that culture is imbedded in "ethnic" language. This is another important aspect, attributes and implicit meanings of words can change from culture to culture and can mutate into new meanings if the environment changes. English in England and English in Africa is not the same thing. Nor does it have the exact same meaning when words are used. The English language does not imply culture in Africa, it only refers to a medium of communication. The same with linguistic interpretation, from one language to the other, referring to words and what their intended meaning was before having been translated. Consequently, be very aware when adopting word templates to explain yourself, or in reverse, to interpret things, as having its intended meaning. Be aware that their attributes might be adversely affected by the new environment you are trying to introduce it into, because of cultural, ethical, moral, linguistic ambiguity and cultural differences etc.

Religion and Culture is one of the most significant aspects influencing interpretation, it will always relate to certain aspects being connected in a certain mannerism, as we have "African time" in Africa, which does not refer to an Africa time zones, rather to the way they keep time, or the absence of it. These aspects will dictate certain viewpoints in strategy, like superstition or insensitivity towards keeping time.

The second aspect is "Nothing is as it seems"

This aspect sets the mediocre apart from the brilliant. I always say we have too many experts around, everyone that is well read has an opinion and all of a sudden they become experts. In Africa, this is especially true, where young academically minded want to make a mark and be recognised the minute they step out of university, college and school, they will demand to be heard and express their point of view freely. Because that's the way, they got attention at school and at University, by talking. Now they are asked to listen and do what is expected contrary to their beliefs and expectations, no never they think, so they try and be clever - can this be allowed within strategy and strategic think tanks? - in politics maybe.

This is the danger point where seasoned meets fresh, the "Bermuda triangle" of strategy where every good idea will disappear if you are not attuned to social dynamics, because of new ways and streams of thinking, especially for the young minds although brilliant, they are not seasoned in practice. They have yet to get another essential degree in the university of life – experience. Where things are tested in practice, where everything can be lost in one breath, or twisted out of context by one word uttered, and taken out of context. Be wary when building a strategic think tank/team, have the young minds separated, or in reserve so to speak, from the old school; married people with children who see life differently from school levers and young academics, freshly qualified etc. It all has to do with group dynamics and the level of personal maturity and thinking. Within any culture, including organisational culture, there are time honoured customs, traditions and methods as well as doctrines and even unwritten laws to subscribe to, same as in corporations whether we want to know it or not. We may decide to respect them and their guardians, the path finder's when no one else was around and they are the reason for the companies existence. Subsequently it never hurts to give credit where it is due as well as respect, so respect and empathy go a long way when mixing group dynamics. In addition, not lecturing the young either, myself, I have always been the one to challenge the system and push the proverbial boundaries to see if they could be expanded. By expanding boundaries we create space for new ideas and practices, this is not necessarily a bad thing, but needs guidance. Before becoming a scientist, become an ardent patriot first.

Perception modelling, and how it shapes our strategy

Explained perception and deductive visualisation. We have more group dynamics than what we care to think about in strategic circles, that leads to perception modelling. The challenge is to get them visualised into one concept. We have for instance, the secretaries, the credit controllers the sales jocks and then top management in their own respective corners – with their own perceptions. Even though they belong to one organisation, they also subscribe to an unwritten code of conduct when being forced to choose. Making a choice that will dictate taking sides, especially sides on radical matters; leads to open confrontation within management circles that are territorial, because you are bound to step on some ones toes, or draw someone into doing more work. Let us just jump back to military tactics, where we explore again, the idea; "that nothing is what it seems". Ideas get used in business every day and form part of group dynamics that work, that requires no strategy. Then we call them tactics. We have covered a lot of ground on communication, and the influences, that lead to deception. People use words and ideas to manoeuvring, camouflage as a n army would in warfare. Perception and thinking, all this makes up the props for error and friction. Where it is blatantly obvious that these tactics have been used repeatedly to elude, entice and unbalance the efforts against them. Let's just recap on them –"You cannot fight that which you cannot see" and "you will not see that which you do not expect". Therefore, in military terms, you have to be vigilant and aware of the tactics that is being employed inside and outside your unit and organisation, because they all become influences on strategy. Do not except everything as the truth, as implicit, as factual or that every spoken word is used to imply its understood meaning, as commonly used, or intended, or as it seems, always be wary of the principle of nothing is as it seems initially.

On to alliances.

Alliances within the corporate world are deeply rooted and this is sometimes very cleverly done, you will find that opposites attract, same as with management having to adopt your new concepts, or strategies. If you did not involve them actively from the word go, it will be a hard sale to make without sponsors. Sponsors are individuals that have standing, that like and support your strategy. Without sponsors and co-operation no new radical strategy will fly, any hard core old timer will tell you that if "they" let it, then their own plans might have to take a dive, be scaled down, or be put on hold. For whatever reason, so it might very well be a great strategy, but the timing might be off and it is always about the money, or agendas, or whether you are competing internally and externally with. It also has to be born in mind that the very sponsor could hijack the proposed strategy and rubber stamp it as his own. Alternatively, worse still sell it as the goose laying the golden eggs whilst it is just a concept, when in trouble to divert the focus from him or her. More aspects of human and corporate nature to be weary of, when to play your cards and sell your ideas will only be dictated by the situation and environment you find yourself in. Then it is right back to whose personal agendas will be better served or not. Unequivocally, I say yes most certainly. Usually, no matter how subtle or hard-core the intentions come across. Agendas being served in or by the process or not is a means to progress, it could be at the expense of someone or group, or it could be structured to be a win-win or no deal situation, either way, this will depend on the maturity of the relationship, how much is at stake and the nature of the deal.

Therefore, the playing field is never what it seems – level.

Don't be naive, win small battles, get good people and build relationships based on trust and then win the war. Take note that "collateral-damage" will sometimes be unavoidable and win-win deals might not always be possible, this is also a reality of man and the rules of nature itself. Some must die so that others may live. Take every change in steps, never assume and always keep group dynamics and interests in mind, even within your own core, keep things in check. This is the plan outside the plan, the vehicle to delivering the strategy as a product, this vehicle will consist of internal influences and how else you can sway them and comprehend them. Only by mastering the internal influence will you be manipulating the external and vice versa. If you want to do the opposite, you will find external influences to counter internal influences. Lawyers call this a process of deliberation. (Thinking about thinking, and what needs to be said, by whom and exactly how to say it, and to whom, where, when and what the message must achieve).

The third point, **deciding on the most appropriate course of action,** we like to call it finding the bulls-eye. Seeking the centre point of gravity in military terms, where the joint needs to be severed, to have the greatest effect. On the other hand, the goal must be clearly defined before we will move towards it – in other words, we want to be able to understand it clearly – the GOAL. The reason for this is that we want to be in a position to reverse engineer from it, from the future state to the current state. We want that bulls eye to be bright red, clear as daylight. Many projects have failed because the architects thought they knew what the goal was, but by assuming to much, they missed it by a mile. Just like one would build a model aeroplane for a future competition. Only to arrive and find that they are all flying classic prop models and you arrive with a F16 jet plane.

Deduce specific elements and attributes first, before attempting design.

Take everything in step, strategy is about specifics, being simplified into a uncomplicated understandable plan, and not the other way around. When designing model planes for instance. We will design every aspect of the plane in detail in the mind and then break it down into its smallest parts. Let's just take the wheels of the plane for instance – what type of rim will we need and what is readily available, what is most reliable vs. costly. Covey said that everything is designed twice, first in the mind where we become mindful – aware of the requirements, and then on paper - where we become specific. What research has been done of late in this field? Then assimilate an options list. (For wheels in this case).

This can be viewed as the mental dismantling of a product, into its smallest parts and giving time for deliberation to it as it exists as parts firstly, understanding the reason and relevance of each part within a component that will form the sub-system and in turn become a whole system, creates clarity, which in turn will form the final product. Every design has needs, needs to be seen to be understood. This will translate into -how highly does it rate within the totality of the system set-up, how critical are wheels to planes? The wheels would rate ten out of ten, for instance. Let's take this argument in steps. The attributes that form a plane must consist of at least four attributes to become a concept, (CAPS) this we have learned from forming concepts, in the chapter on "CAPS". Therefore we need a frame, we need propulsion, we need undercarriage and we will need wings. This put together will make-up the key core components or concept of "the plane". The frame and the wings will give it structure that will resemble an aircraft, the propulsion system will move it and the undercarriage will steer it on the ground and cushion its landing.

This is the core components of an aircraft, that form the subsystems or attributes of aircraft systems, then we realise the required support-systems and rate them in this fashion as well. Why rate them? Well later on during a project, perhaps when the plan is being implemented and the team leaders want to cut funds this will assist you, as you do not have to re-run every aspect to know what their priority will be within the complexities and relationships of every component completing a large-scale system etc. Also in terms of quality, safety and impact on the crucial elements and core components necessary for functioning correctly, we have options and knowledge now, that we otherwise would not have had, if not for this process of reverse engineering of concepts. Therefore, if you have weakness, you need to know where it is, to mask it, or to work on it. If you have strength, you need to know to what degree and harness it. This is critical thinking, it dissects everything to its roots – before becoming a plan.

Strategy requires four points of rationalisation; when putting strategy together we require four dimensional mental engineering; *initiative, good timing, reserved time and a quiet mind* to keep it growing towards our final objective, not more plans...

1. **Firstly *initiative***, do we have it on our side or not. Initiative to strategy is as crucial as water is to fish, without it, strategy just becomes uncoordinated tactics and plans. In the movie "Black Hawk Down" the US special forces dropped some 100 men into Mogadishu, everything went well and as planned, until one Black Hawk Helicopter was shot down, then only did they realise they lost the element of *surprise, mobility and cohesion* – together this makes up "initiative". As explanation; the reason being the coalition forces had to be broken up, to save the lives on the hawks. They had an aircraft downed by a RPG – rocket propelled grenade - that impacted on their mobility, for one; that vehicle (Helicopter) could no longer perform its intended purpose within the systems function, two, this dictated immediate remedial action, that was not planned for and the Somali's blocked off all the roads to the site as well as turned the whole place into a War zone. They did not go back to the drawing board and redesigned their battle plan. If hindsight is an exact science; firstly, they should have aborted the mission at the very first site of "smoke" – they did not pay much attention to the fact that tyres were burning in the city upon their arrival, this in fact was the militias way of signalling an imminent attack. They relied too heavily on the element of surprise, tactics and strategy as well as their technologically advanced weaponry, the moment the smoke started they had lost an aspect of initiative, a sub system to their strategy, by only having lost one attribute of their initiative, surprise, it activated the entire militia. The result; the odds shifted, from 100 against 200, to 100 against a 120 000. Lessons learned; always expect the unexpected, plan beyond every eventuality, study the culture very well, know how they traditionally do things and "communicate", then know your vulnerabilities and mask them, and always have a good reserve. Our plans need to match the environment we are working in. If it fails on certain aspects, regain the initiative as soon as possible. Until you have gained the initiative, you will have to rely heavily on tactics or lose. It was their tactics that saved them and not their strategy - planning.

2. ***Secondly- Timing*** – is everything and has to do with the detail we go into when planning influences on time, we can't "make time", we can make a sandwich though, however we can allocate time, by having the gift of being able to see the "gap" as it opens up, being able to see, or identify - windows of opportunity more clearly than others - helps but mostly it comes with experience or from mathematical calculations. Sometimes, we have to do nothing, even though everything is in our favour because we have time, just to test how eager the opponent is to seek out battle (opportunity) or not. At other times, we don't have time and we just have to jump in and swim and see where we end up. In addition, see where the currents of circumstances take us, taking spur of the moment actions and decisions is risky, however, risk is at times inevitable and the only way to get initiative back, and beats not having taken the opportunity. Yes, very philosophically put, the point is that human nature is not static, time itself is not static, time dictates the situational appropriateness, towards taking risk and situations dictate actions that impact on time. No matter how good the plan, it also has to rely on tactics and timing, to pull it off. Timely tactics can save time and eliminate waste, it can close the gaps. Caution; rapidity of action, is not always a fail-safe. Therefore, human nature changes as time changes, as conditions change, as perception changes. In the event where "renewal" is advocated and "more" change is imminent, our reaction needs to fit in with the times we

are living and working in, within the current system and the modes of existence. Most importantly, it has to complement and enhance time spirals, or it just won't work or fit. When looking at the school of "Spiral and time dynamics" we get back to the fundamental needs for survival, critical thinking. *As Graves puts it" the psychology of the mature human being is an unfolding, emergent, oscillating, spiralling process marked by progressive subordination of older systems giving rise to and influencing newer, higher order system as man's existential problems change"*. **Strategic survival depends on the psychology used when thinking critically.** In other words; we have to study the characteristics and temperament of associated behaviour of a person or persons in a group, and their traits exhibited by those engaged in specific activity, how they get things done traditionally is more important than the plan to steer and guide them. How we influence and steer traditional methods, with our strategy and utilise time today by being critically minded, will determine if we will succeed in the future, and survive.

3. ***Thirdly –Reserve some time*** – always have a reserve, or a plan B or even C. Never assume anything. For life, itself is fluid and just like with life everything changes constantly, the only thing in fact that is constant in life is change itself. People, concepts, ideas, plans and alliances, can change in the wink of an eye. This type of dexterity in thinking let's us "see" things outside the norm, let's us rethink our thinking, so we are thinking about thinking whilst we are thinking and set time aside to do it in. By analysing, interrogating and researching our assumptions and only then we try and making sense of the subject at hand. Becomes a process within a process. Only by making abstracts concrete – do they become concepts. Forming concepts, takes careful deliberation, that in turn takes time, strategy is never just about running on pure hypothesis and psychology only, we get to see a lot of that lately, people will tell you they know this, because of x, y or z whilst you clearly know it cannot be. Thus dealing with perception, or not, is the question and at the same time applying the agility to step away from yourself and start to analyse yourself critically, openly, and honestly requires time. Only then will you experience freedom of thinking – for oneself, blocking out the propaganda and false believes, spiralling towards a higher sense of living and thinking – with a quite mind. It all takes time to be still, calm and collected – to rethink the thinking that brought us the answer, before we implement.

4. **Fourthly – *a Quiet mind.*** One cannot come to any rational conclusion to any matter if you do not have a quiet mind. To have a quieter mind one needs to understand how the mind works first and we have run over this in many chapters. However, if you do not give into it, the part where we have to let go, by purely letting go of everything and realising that we cannot go through walls, we cannot want to control every aspect of life and living, we are not Gods. Switch it off when it gets to hectic; the old people spoke of sleeping on it. If you keep re-thinking, one aspect over and over and over it will grow like a snowball rolling from a mountainside and become so complex that your mind will become "consumed with it, from within". It's like someone walking into a library and taking several books from several categories and simultaneously trying to read them all, whilst looking for more and leaving all those books in the isles. Somewhere the brain gets blocked, the Nero-transmitters get over crowded like librarians stumbling over books in the isles.

Have a calm collective centre

The point is this, quiet down your mind, before starting to think, this is essential in order to think clear and critical. For in life, it is not the one with all the answers that have a tacit resilient mind, it is the one who asks the right questions, fully well knowing the answers to them as being unequivocally correct and he is just testing them again, to see that they still fit, and then gives the resolve. However, answers will not always be readily available from the one with all the expertise. This shows true intellect and agility of mind by trying to understand the complexity of the process that leads to choices available, hitting at the right one requires detail, that yielded positive feedback and the questions asked that lead to the right answers. Resolve, only follows from understanding the complexity and not the other way around. The ability to prioritise is the intellectual distinction, between being in control and being at the mercy of it.

When it comes to organising our thoughts, there is this need for doing something - the "things concept" - I am sure we all have *things that need doing*. How we prioritise them, will give rise to better functionality. We have to start with the things;

- *That we have to do* - or have to tend to as a matter of urgency.
- Then there are the things *"we still need to do"* but not necessarily today,
- Then there are the things we *still can do* – if we feel like it,
- and lastly the things we *still want to do*, but never had time or money for.

Some of us get our priorities all mixed up because we fail to prioritise, thus causing conflict within ourselves and for ourselves and with those around us, because we have no system to think with. Strategist have to be able to prioritise, our ability to prioritise the things we want to do give us great pleasure and we crave pleasure, so if you want to experience a calm mind you need to give thought to the hierarchies and natural order of "things" as they exist.

Plan your "things to do list"; every sector of your life needs to be in perfect balance for the *mind* to be agile and critically focussed. Don't fight battles you can't win. For all things need doing it is said, it is just a question of when and by whom. In this regard, the mind is connected in very much the same way that small threads or cable connects telephone poles to each other. Therefore, if you become unbalanced in one sphere of life it will evidently pull down the rest, resulting in collapse.

The opposite is also true as well, if you become an over achiever in one sphere – say your work it will pull up the rest of the poles. Where everything reaches a natural breaking point if not balanced and "snaps" - so yes- stress dislodges your natural cohesion, and ability to think clear. By being over worked, all workaholics are in the same basket, call it acute chronic work disorder – the imminent pending disaster that leads to – chronic fatigue disorder – you can't rest, you go to work to "rest" if you are not at work, if you are not behind your desk or Laptop, you can't escape. Things agitate you; you get frustrated by trivia etc. If this is true, then "You" are facing burn out, you are taking "things" too seriously. You have become addicted to a having unresolved "things", that create a busy mind.

Then we still have corporate War Games – people will bring baggage.

Is someone on your case, or you on theirs? The corporate games we play cause frustration. Frustration causes friction, and it surfaces as conflict. Frustration starts with unresolved issues, i want something, or want it done. The other parties signs off on our demands, we feel that they disregard us, it and we get mad. Beware of signing and encrypting our own communications, we all have one or two unique words we use, like "whatever", when we are no longer interested, this is signing; you are leaving a signature that says it's John, or Kevin's work. Mostly we encode and project our communications when we are in battle mode as well, we say and do things we don't mean. We have to reframe and compose – subliminally – seeking to de-code and re-frame the information at hand before purely acting. Stop and walk a mile in the persons (mind) shoes and get to understand their frustration...

Now, let us take this aspect to a more practical level. Newton's third law of thermodynamics eloquently illustrates this principle, "For every force there is an equal and opposite force". What this implies is, when in negotiations, and being smart is not good enough, strategy and tactics will be not be your sword, composure and restraint will. Subsequently, if someone comes out guns blazing do not retaliate, remember Newton's law. Instead, what you should do is listen, decode and acknowledge what the other party has just said and elaborate on it, show that you understand the frustration, walk a mile in his shoes and show that you fully comprehend, show partial agreement with their stance and then subtly insert your own views. The term a leopard does not change its spots, is so true, some know how to play this game – look for signing – that will tell you who has influenced this person or party. If you are at a loss, give them "the porky pine". By returning the argument to them and asking them how they would like to see it solved to their satisfaction. For instance, just turn the table, or put the boot on the other foot, reverse the roles so to speak and see if that changes the perspective views and or arguments. If they are set in their ways they are set, some people just do not and will not see the light – by playing the porky pine, they will tell you exactly what they want or need, and if they can be trusted or not. Why do people play war games? Because the implicit trust culture is gone, or eroding.

The implicit trust component is gone

People poison people – well not everyone is noble and trustworthy, so what about them?

When you are fighting with your back against the wall the rules change; and your battle focus should to, for in the corporate world as in war the principles stay the same. It is always the survival of the fittest, the fastest and the most agile minded. We move from fighting by the rules to self-preservation and fighting outside the rules in various stages of our lives, some daily.

Many books do not cover this type of deeply emotional sparked battles that take place within our own circles of organisation between managers and subordinates. friction can seriously tap into our emotional and spiritual strength to go forward with our strategy, they sap our will to achieve.

Evil men (and woman) do exist and we need to acknowledge this. They will always walk amongst us, like vulture's circling and waiting their turn to feast in our demise, even if it is just an ego attack that left you scarred. Like wolf in sheep skins they befriend you and then they suck you dry like a leach.

Opportunist are everywhere; they want something and they are out to get it at whatever cost. Opportunity presents itself daily, for them to Hi-jack and take credit for other peoples hard work, input and advice. They will never acknowledge that they learned from people like you and because of you they are where they are today. However, they will never be you, because of the evil ways they follow. Yes its pure evil, when men exploit men, just for personal gain. Once evil minded always evil I say, they can walk the good path, sing praises and even worship with us but what sets them apart is this. Their scripts, they refer back to when under threat and then they show their true colours and speak their whole harts contents, when down and out on truth. Like a wounded animal, they strike out when confronted, and tell you what's wrong with you...your attitude and behaviour is the problem. Life is always according to them, and their beliefs, and they make everything about everyone else, never them.

By observing peoples battle scripts in confrontation situations, we can learn much about their deep routed character traits, that gets emotionally fuelled and loses control when fighting. Then the perfect slayer tends to drop, their guard tends to drop, they reveal the real wolf inside the sheep's skin fly's off. You are that which you were born from and commit your life's work too, your life lived becomes imprinted and reflects in your ways. No matter how hard you try, if you are criminally inclined, your thoughts will manifest that which you think and it will translate into your actions. Same goes for emotionally scared and wounded people. The workplace is their only playground, here they are the Conquistadores of old.

The new generation of global conquistadores vs. the paradigm of tomorrow's leaders.

The stark truth about new emerging leaders. The "Moral Component" in business is losing ground; although we spend a great deal talking about it, promulgating it into law and constitution, company code of ethics, it just seems lost in translation and interpretation, to those who hold it dear.

True ethical conduct, requires three fundamental elements to be present, in order for people to thrive: There must be;

- *an inner driving force*; a form of personal self-motivation that transcend the self and fill others.
- *real skill*, (also people skills)
- *expertise.*

Combined it should translate into *effective leadership* attained in that order. That should translate into effective management. We gather that things flow from within, and that which is within flows from the top, both good and bad. What we think about we create. Our input becomes more significant the higher up we move in the management hierarchy, and forms part of the greater value chain of interaction. Today we have to have the –rules- for management in place, it is somehow expected, both from the character of those placed in authority and those serving, they have to be righteous and honourable as they have to be wise. Because the rules say they have to be...

However, in today's world we find the complete opposite in practice, today the one in authority no longer seems or needs to possess the skill and character traits that is/ was required of their positions in the past, or so it seems. Judging by the poor quality of management appointees and the decisions they take, or just omit taking, due to the stance taken in national politics. This effect will become global and soon, this relates to the so-called realignment of the "social equality status" that has to be balanced. We are moving towards globalisation and this issue becomes a challenge that will hurt, or kill enterprise if you don't have a better moral strategy to counter and facilitate such legal required integration with. On the surface, the intention is good. Do you still not know what I am talking about. The new age practice of "affirmative action", "black economic empowerment", "land re-distribution", and the like. It is a new dawn, in Africans history that has spread out globally, that is corrupt and flawed. Because, expertise and human capital will become an enormously scares commodity real soon, and it won't be based on ethnicity, where corporate firms will head hunt the best, ahead of the rest. In business, there is no fairness, here we have follow sound tested principles for promotion and incentive criteria or suffer the consequences in the long run. There is just no time or place for window dressing, and trial and error. Especially when there is no pot of unlimited funds to pay under performers more with, if the strings aren't tight, then the notes become sour, and corruption becomes rife. Business requires one thing to prevail in order to succeed. Business doctrine dictates the soundness of norms and ethics, that should transfer into the management of accountable and responsible people, calling themselves managers. These effects of political interference amongst other things on the list that governments throw into the works, are not thought through properly and hastened into effect, creating chaos; like their encroaching economic strategies that just don't work, especially now that all governments are calling for more and decisive forms of "affirmative action", all across the globe, this is now evident in all governments and presidential speeches on business economics and trade reforms and agreements. We hear the buzz word everywhere and now it is even legislate it into effect, with heavy penalties on firms that do not apply it. Affirmative appointee quotas forces people into positions that they don't have the motivation, skill or experience to perform the required task. By just judging from current trends in Africa, Zimbabwe and South Africa especially, we can see how this practice has come full circle to bite the inventors in the proverbial back side. Big para-statels are failing with devastating effects. Unemployment, hunger and crime is rising, so is the lack of service delivery, and both aspects act in on the economy, and we see that service delivery at all levels are crumbling – why? Government and local governments inability to spend funds on infrastructure, maintenance and good strategy – just opens the doors to corruption. Where there is no common vision, there is just common chaos. BEE or Black Economic Empowerment - what a paradox in terms. Is this still Democracy, or do I detect a hint of Communism here. The point to make is that it is a process, the law of the harvest and of grooming of people for future posts – is not a quick fix and get rich program like it exists currently, that gets exploited by the powerful few. Affirmative action and equity has done nothing for the masses of unemployed and impoverished, the rich look after their own - this is not democracy or free enterprise by any standard, because it is regulated into extinction, this is unethical, period.

Moral, bound together with its required attributes; of personal motivation, skill and expertise, produces the will to succeed and "fight" the good fight, even against great odds, without it one lacks the required will and desire to take on the bigger tasks that are required of senior managers. Values, are formed by people who understand the principles of value; "Selfless Commitment, Courage, Discipline, Integrity, Loyalty and Respect for Others". Labour no longer come from societies which share broadly these common roots and horizons based on traditional geographical. Usually it was religious ethics and morals only that painted the landscape. Now however, traditionalism; stemming from tribal cultural beliefs intertwined with religion and dogma, that puts a different interpretation on ethics as excepted norms due to the introduction of other/mixed cultural influences. Call it a new Africanised morality, where "an injury to one is an injury to all" mentality originated. These influence amongst others, has changed morality the way we know it in the West, it has changed values and systems for "good". The academical traditional western and eastern styles or aspects of management is now widely regarded as being much to authoritarian. Inadvertently oppressive to the very people that it is set to protect and uplift, we are made to understand and believe different, but the result speak for themselves. The new era of metro sexual, and contemporary morality puts a higher premium on individual rights than on their duty to society; we are no longer duty bound. Notions of duty or obligation are much less apparent, it's just the rights of others that matter. Human Rights have taken over from morality. Where people have rights they must have rules, the more rights the more rules, the more nothing gets done, everyone is just too afraid they will violate a right.

Subsequently, so has the emphasis on attaining material things; material things have become the benchmark of success; we want status; cars, houses and international brand names and rewards. All of this plays an ever greater part in the lifestyles of this new migrating generation, and their value system. They don't just seek remuneration, they demand it, and they keep demanding even more, it is their right you understand and in return for their labour, which they withhold when they feel they are not treated "fairly". The rise of the importance of the individual and their rights, have removed us from a natural order, that of pack status. Giving way to unchecked freedoms in society, crimes against morality and ethics are committed daily, it has become the fulcrum for shifting interaction to a more personal level and the associated stress it brings on due to this thinking, and society spirals out of control. We have societies in turmoil, with labour unions giving themselves more power and rights that what the law intended. The state has created an animal that dictates effects on economic trends, that they can't control, labour unions see themselves as the custodians of people's rights, rather than taking care of their responsibilities morally, especially towards being accountable for the process of building an strong enterprise, as a key role-player as well. They remove themselves from this paradigm, because it will dissolve their power and political footing, they would rather refer to intimidation and threatening tactics and behaviour against the employer and now even government and keep them responsible for their situation. Rational thinking is not their strong suit either or so it seems, military element gets their power from the people they intimidate and organise into groups, being called "the working class", these individuals don't realise it, but they have a profound impact on the success of the company. If only they would change their outlook, their paradigm, with implicit implications for the individual employers concerned as well as the company. This new "Human rights" generation of workforces, just questions things all the time. Every move and motive they don't understand as being strategically significant, results in an attack on the management, they even attack established structures, authority and traditional principles of conduct and any authority is questioned. More often than not, so that idealistic freedom at any cost can be lived. The sad truth is that without rules, morals and authority no freedom is ever prevalent, no one trusts the next one to do right by them or their standards in this context. Hence, even those who get promoted do not necessarily share common standards and values as practiced by the firm. They take their own value system with them up the food chain if unchecked.

The answer to this is the growing of corporate morale, moral resides in the growing of functional unions – striving for interdependence. It is a state of mind that believes in the greater good and understood to be fair. It is that intangible force which moves people to endure and succeed with inherent courage in the face of hardship, overcoming battle fatigue and challenges that makes one rise ever higher above the expected. It makes each individual in a group feed from each other's strength and diversity, without counting the cost to them, all in favour of achieving one common purpose – hands up. It makes people feel that they are part of something great as a collective, no longer a us and them situation...where we label people – black or white and so on... The creating of high moral, it is not hard, however sustaining it is. It requires strong mental, spiritual and ethical foundation, as well as material things to keep the spirit high, the true intellectual distinction, is how to create and maintain it. Only spiritual foundations can stand real strain....the spiritual basis of morale is not so much within ones religion, as it is in the culture formed around an ardent belief in an honourable or valid cause. The distinction between dependence and interdependence. We feel better that what we at times understand things. People still needs to feel significant, if you want them to perform, they must feel they really matter. This aspect has a direct bearing on the results expected in building functional societies. Furthermore, people are also swayed by reason as well as by emotion. Morale must, therefore, have its intellectual foundations. First, the person must believe that the objective he aims at is not out of reach, but truly attainable. He must be confident that the organisation, to which he belongs, is efficient, effective and he can trust them to do right by him – they are ethical. Above all he must have confidence in his leaders' ability. By every means possible and within his power the leader must gain and keep this confidence, not only by his decisiveness in taking action, but also in his calmness during crisis. Leaders need to be criticised more, they also need to be judged in the way they delegates tasks, by allotting tasks to the right people, that are well within their capabilities and thus building up a tradition of trust. This leader knows his people; he cares and knows how to use them effectively. He is busy, with the business of people and growing moral, by doing so. Leadership training will be the next frontier, without interdependence one can create nothing new, slowing down the education process of the new generation delays the advancement of the whole organisation. To expect victory and successes in a scheme, without a proficient leader component, is as good as listening for thunder, where there is no lightning. People need to see it to believe it.

The need for leaders that can effectively command and control arises from a need for, discipline and structure, people require both to feel safe. Where structure will create routine, the size and complexity of the task will dictate the level of proficiency required from the leader, a leader weak in judgement, will most certainly be strong in prejudice. The larger and more sophisticated a work force becomes, the greater the difficulties in preserving its cohesion and moral. Thus the importance of the function of "Command" and "Control" resides in the level of responsibility of an individual leader, delegated to the lowest rank. He has to have some form of authority, responsibility and accountability. Authority involves the right and freedom to use the "power of command" and ultimately, to enforce discipline...and to keep moral.

Miscommunication

Miscommunication: I am sure we all can attest to this, that most boardroom fights were about miscommunication – or an intense obsession with the self, either the ego or the femininity was at risk – or an unfounded sense of self-preservation and self-realisation. Mostly from people that do not feel secure in their role, or threatened by the crowd that they find themselves with. Mostly they feel threatened by a person like – you - that is in control.

The point I am trying to make here is this, be flexible in your "critical" thinking and agile mindedness. People are sensitive to criticism. No-where in life is being right everything when dealing with people. Know when it is good and when it is bad to be right, or when it is just pure stupidity, study human nature. People are like water, shades of blue, grey, black, white and every other shade in between. It all depends on what colour "earth" they flow over, this will ultimately determine their colour.

What this implies is our emotional and cognitive state will determine our colour – our way of seeing, feeling, listening and comprehending things. Beware your emotional state, it influence your cognitive. It is true that the strongest poison makes the best medicine. The knack of moving a man's mind lies in your ability to understand, before being understood, the strongest weapon of all is a mind in which loyalty and devotion to duty act in union. Nevertheless, how you handle yourself under trying times will determine if the shoe will stay on the foot or not and if not, will it change feet? Who will be kicking your backside if you get things wrong?

Encryption: Is Camouflaging the real intent.

The danger in corporate games is that it always gets personal; people exploit your good points and turn them into vulnerabilities. Never cross the line towards getting openly personal, it will get you emotional and the best speech you will always live to regret was the one you made in anger and with great emotion. The fight could also have originated from gossip and professional jealousy. Nip this in the butt, by getting up close and personal, do not leave it to fester, it will.

If it is not pure "STUPIDITY" then it is camouflaging the real intent, contrary to corporate belief, no one is really that stupid to make such a decision, to seem to be stupid, is strategy at times. So yes, the devious nature of man has a great many tricks it can play that one must be aware of when entering the GAME. Strategic thinking and direction it seems is about agendas, served in the process or not. It's about ego's, about self-actualisation and maliciousness it has a lot to do with human nature and how the mind works, one needs to focus on this dimension just like a fighter pilot watches his six in battle. It is mostly, your own kind, which will cannibalise you first or shoot/stab you in the back, "accidentally" by the way if you start to excel at strategy and become known as proficient, just so that they can get ahead. If not checked it could wreck a perfectly good man with a perfectly good plan in seconds.

Guard against forming unholy alliances

Unholy alliances, seek them out, they breed like cancer. One classical example is where top management and grass roots level people are so deeply befriended that their relationships spill over into their private lives and eventually effect their judgement. It becomes an unholy dependence, like the crocodile and the tickbird, that cleans the crocks teeth. With the difference the tickbird sticks to his-own kind once the job is done in nature, this alliance should not go beyond business. There is a distinction between being friendly and friends, a very fine line...

The one has the power and status the other the ability to travel and brings word (gossip) from the rest of the "kingdom". This leads to knit picking and power trips and let's not forget favouritism.

Someone told me once that some managers hide their inability by deliberately creating chaos, a classical example is the new manager that walks in and turns everything on its head - who kicks the anthill. They deliberately destroy "comfort zones", with the lame excuse that everyone deserves to have a chance, and must work harder. Then he walks off to enjoy the "picnic basket" the company puts out for everyone's benefit, and has it all to himself. While the "ants" hasten to repair their "comfort zone". The new boy has his own party. Nevertheless, no one notices because everyone is so busy re-building the nest that they have no desire for fun.

In situations like this, people perceive their livelihood is at stake, or so it is perceived, they have to perform to survive or else?

Does this sound familiar? It becomes a haphazard management style filled with conflicting diaries and conflicting interest, pure crisis management. The trust factor is so low because competition is the measure by which everyone gets ahead and measured. Only the favourites will get attention. This is just a classic example of how not to run an organisation.

The emergence of the flexible work ethic can only be accomplished when all the minds in it are agile; we have to practice and believe that there is something more out there. That our lives on earth are meant to be meaningful and that virtues still has a place alongside honesty and integrity in the work place. The only way to achieve this is to create the abundance theory – to believe that everyone will get his fair share. Now the question always arises what is a fair share. Well from where I am standing, it will be the time plus the effort and commitment to task, that leads to performance, which will determine the size of the share.

The reason I did not state productivity, or time and effort only, is this. I have seen many people in my lifetime and I am sure most of us have, spent seven days at work but they never seem to get the job done. I have seen people work all day without a lunch break and still their in-tray is just getting bigger. However, commitment to task is more of a crucial issue towards reaching success, this is also, where the high morale issue will surface and the "extra mile" people will come from. For anyone that is committed and spending more time and effort will evidently achieve greater success over the aforementioned aspects, not as individuals but as groups.

A dynamic working environment is just that dynamic, it reaches out to other people, as a pack of wolves would, working together. The old, the young, the strong and the weak, and such is the strategic and project managing environment. The reason is this; they do not or should at least not adopt a nine to five workday approach. The leader delegates a portion of work to be done to team leaders with a deadline. Time and date – so, this team makes up their own working hours and they work to get the job done. The reward is Thursday and Friday they have of, to spend any which way they can, why, because they work to finish the work and not the day, at the end of each project commission is paid based on quality and quantity as well as accuracy.

What is more? The only thing that should get measured on production should be a machine in my opinion. If we treat humans with a little bit more respect and give them a little bit more credit for being adults. We might just get them to work when they want as long as they want – this sounds strange, but let me explain. If you feel like work and the work is both challenging, interesting and rewarding enough, then you will emerge yourself in it. Although, if you are tired and had a hard night with very little sleep, maybe because of the new baby in the house, would you not just like to switch your day and night, and that way you can get rest and your job done. Think about this, why is it always essential for us to work an eight-hour day, or a twelve-hour day. If we can pull together, work two seven-day weeks of ten hours each and one week half day and have one whole week a month to ourselves. Granted not always practical, or achievable, will you not take the latter option? I am sure we all will, then we will have no excuse to not get in family time, or take the wife to the movies, go on leave etc. In return we can expect a quality product on time every time because our work force can arrange their jobs around their lives and not the other way around. The source of all great creation is passion; loyalty stands out not in a good situation but in a difficult one. Of course, we realise that this will not always be possible in every unit or company but it could be an option. Because we have entered, into a win-win or no deal agreement and not a suck them dry and step on them to see if there is anything left scenario. These are the stepping-stones of radical strategy; they tend towards wanting to re-form society in un-comprehended ways, to be human friendly by charging and challenging the conventional to look at more lucrative options, that could be viable, if we apply our minds as a collective. The other factor that plays games with how we operate is our programming.

Our individual programming surfaces in our habits

We have all been programmed in one-way or another to act, respond and operate in any given situation. Let's look at our programming, for it will affect our flexibility of mind. The term NLP. John Grinder and Richard Bandler developed Neuro Linguistic Programming. "Nero" simply refers to the brain and how it absorbs information and stores it through the senses. Linguistic refers to the language used to transmit or receive such information, as well as feelings, emotions and sensory up take. Programming refers to our, well programming, our habits, patterns, programmes, strategies and ways we express ourselves and behave in various situations. You have scripts and or habits that serve you very well, but you also have programming that does not, mostly resulting in unwanted outcome. Without consciously being aware of our programming, we have to rely on others to point out to us that certain programmes, habits are not conducive to our success for instance. This can negatively affect our, social and physiological effectiveness and balance should it be repeated; they become our hang-ups and mental handbrakes, your too fat – physical, your too slow – mental, your too forward, you're too this or that... In order to be fully effective one needs to actively seek out bad programming and correct it, actively. The only person that's allowed these scripts or patterns to develop was you, so it stands to reason that only you can take care of yourself. It might require some assistance from a professional, like a psychologist, psychiatrist, or a life coach to guide you, but why should that be a programme to fight against? – Ha, perceptions, only mad and sick people see psychologists, right! Wrong - we go to the general practitioner with something as simple as a common cold, why not look after your mental health in the same fashion. Take it from me it is well worth your while.

Systems' thinking, a whole new paradigm

Systems' thinking is a military principle; the military machine in context is a setting that changes slowly. The organisation is strict and has a command structure that is hierarchical. This means that all procedures are well defined for each level and rehearsed, uncertainty is minimized by simulation training and scenario training to exclude errors when giving orders and to be capacitated and confidant to command effectively. This command structure is based on the fact that misinterpretation of definitions can result in casualties. Thus uniform training is done for officers, to command and control, on the systems available and designed for this. The training that occurs and course materials that are developed are based on this strict form of communication and they use the same predefined definitions to make terminology as consistent as possible. From the air force, the navy to the logistical personnel they all have one culture and language. Courses and learning resources are highly specialized and localized. Carl Von Clausewitz thoroughly embraced the value of critical thinking in his writings concerning military genius. Clausewitz advised; "What we must do is to survey all those gifts of mind and temperament that in combination bear on military activity". *Learn to be fixed-sated on the outcome and to be more flexible on the process.*

Teaching people:

A man expresses himself with as much as he knows. Self-expression that adds value, is the ultimate quest between doing what the two extremes of personality prescribes to, what the ego needs and the hart desires. This power does not come from being right, but from being real. Therefore, studying people; their history, strategy, management, self-control and virtue, are but some of the things that will give you the edge you seek. Mostly strategically and in terms of quality training that is outcome based or should be. In other words, we give people specific training to develop a certain skill, and develop them into a certain direction. Consequently, the training of your people will constitute a large investment in people capital, by improving a skill or teaching new ones. A very important principle of training is the spin off effect it should have, by keeping minds occupied with new emerging knowledge, people experience a great awe of personal growth when trained properly. "The company cares and so should I". It serves yet another purpose; it serves as an intellectual tool to teach people to relieve and manage stress and to exchange views more freely, to reinforce old alliances and to foster new ones. It should be focused on the requirements of effective and sound relationship building. Which would otherwise, not have been possible if it was not for training. The mind shifts gears when one is in training, it is in "absorb mode", open to suggestion and introspection, the titles are stripped away and people become people again. The playing field is levelled, no rank and file, no structure, just a lot of adults soaking up knowledge and expanding and learning from it. This would otherwise not have been the case under normal day-to-day working conditions. Do you see the importance of training? Foresight becomes the beacon to hope, hindsight becomes the measure by which to achieve it, it must be part and parcel of any good strategy to teach the company doctrine, to enforce the principled and balanced requirement of living, a very good place to start effectively in changing perceptions and affecting change, is training, and an even better place to start is always with middle management. The only way to measure the value of something new is to use a new yardstick, with new mindsets. The effect it has is that it pushes the top management to perform and review their own paradigm and it spurs lower management on to come out with new ideas and concepts.

How are we known apart?

This is where you will shape your future. By compiling a comprehensive-Business plan," THE MAP" with a structure that will show your ideal deployment strategy, coupled to a specialised job description for each section or unit. A word on Specialisation; it is not necessarily a bad thing but do not implement it unilaterally, strict criteria must always form an entry criteria for specialisation. A word of caution here, the thing with specialised job descriptions is this. It can get very tricky; it could have the equal and opposite effect and leave you with catch 22 situations if you are not aware. For example; if a person, a new recruit for instance, makes the training and all the evaluation - passes a probation period - and now he or she starts showing their true colour, does he or she perform up to standard at all, – what now? You cannot just send them back now, or fire, the point is being sure, that what you hire is what you require. Be on top of your recruitment game. Trust produces loyalty, mistrust leads to betrayal, other supervisors and companies will hold on to good people for dear life, so, if someone is passed on to you with a smile – watch out!

Col W. Michael Guillot

"Any complex activity, if it is to be carried on with any degree of virtuosity, calls for appropriate gifts of intellect and temperament

...Genius consists in a harmonious combination of elements, in which one or the other ability may predominate, but none may be in conflict with the rest."

The strategic environment is volatile, uncertain, complex and ambiguous (VUCA).

Additionally, that writing introduced the concept of strategic competency. We will discuss the most important essential skill for Strategic Leaders: critical thinking. It is hard to imagine a Strategic leader today who does not think critically or at least uses the concept in making decisions. Critical thinking helps the strategic leader master the challenges of the strategic environment. It helps one understand how to bring stability to a volatile world. Critical thinking leads to more certainty and confidence in an uncertain future. This skill helps simplify complex scenarios and brings clarity to the ambiguous lens. Critical thinking is the kind of mental attitude required for success in the strategic environment. In essence, critical thinking is about learning how to think and how to judge and improve the quality of thinking—yours another's. Lest you feel you are already a great critical thinker, consider this, in a recent study supported by the Kellogg Foundation, only four percent of the U.S. organisational population was considered highly competent in strategic thinking. When it comes to thinking itself, there are still a number of myths to contend with for instance:

- -Thinking is natural and you don't have to think about it to do it well - you do!
- -Thinking skills and intelligence are synonymous – they aren't!
- -Bright people should just know how to think well together – they don't!

  The grand master of military strategy and leadership, Carl Von Clausewitz, thoroughly embraced the value of critical thinking in his writings concerning military genius. Clausewitz advised, "What we must do is to survey all those gifts of mind and temperament that in combination bear on military activity". Also consider the challenge presented to all the military departments by Secretary of Defence Rumsfeld when he called for leaders who were proactive, more like venture capitalists and deal with uncertainty—those unknown, unknowns. Critical thinking is required to address this kind of challenge. To understand the concept of critical thinking, first one must try to define it—what it is and what it is not. Next, the perspective critical thinker must study the topic to develop critical thinking skills. This will present a very useful construct or model for learning how to think critically and how to use critical thinking. Finally, we will consider the challenge of engaging non-critical thinking societies. *Average intelligence may recognise the truth occasionally and exceptional courage may now and then retrieve a blunder; but usually intellectual inadequacy will be shown up by indifferent achievement.*

The model depicts the cycle of critical thinking.

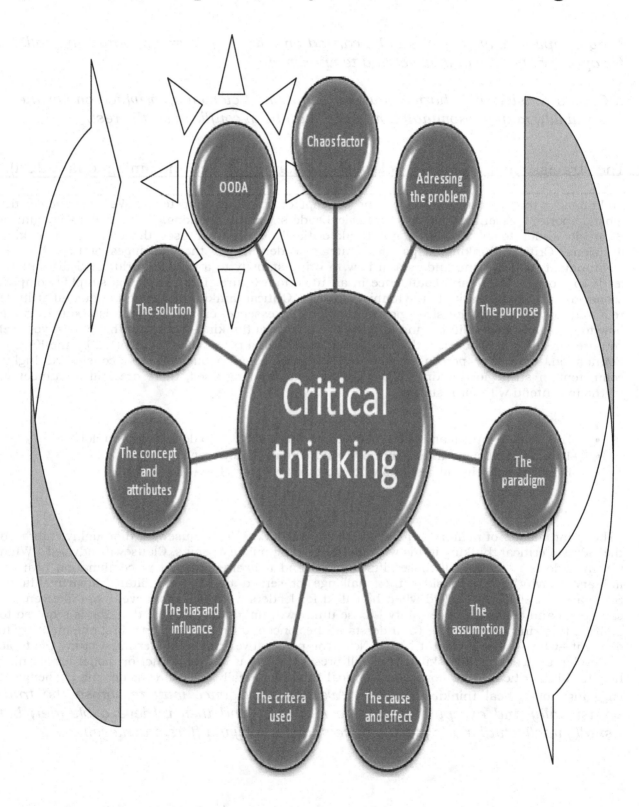

WHAT IS CRITICAL THINKING really?

There is only one thing harder than learning to think critically—trying to define the concept in a comprehensive way. To arrive at a comprehensive definition, one must consider the origins of critical thinking, some misconceptions about critical thinking and some of the attributes of critical thinking.

We can trace the origins of critical thinking back to the early Greek philosophers. The word itself comes from two Greek words: Kriticos, meaning discerning judgment and criterion, meaning standard. Among the philosophers most closely associated with critical thinking was Socrates who strived to find meaning and truth through serious questioning. In his day, Socrates embodied the ideas of kriticos and criterion, two ideas we will consider later when we address a modern construct for critical thinking. He developed the art of Socratic questioning to reach a more profound logic, understanding and reflective thought. In essence Socrates' method was the quest for reason and wisdom. Many years after Socrates, Clausewitz too tried to define critical thinking. As mentioned earlier, Clausewitz called his brand of critical thinking.

"Genius." In his definition, Clausewitz stated, "Genius consists in a harmonious combination of elements, in which one or the other ability may predominate, but none may be in conflict with the rest." He further defines critical thinking as "strength of mind" and as "...the ability to keep one's head at times of exceptional stress and violent emotion." While we have no evidence Clausewitz studied Socrates, there seems to be little doubt Clausewitz understood critical thinking and helped solidify the importance of critical thinking to strategic leaders.

Even with the clear writings of Socrates and Clausewitz, there are still miss-conceptions about what constitutes critical thinking. Many people often use the term 'critical thinking' without understanding the concept, the meaning, or how to apply it. Others progress to a stage sociologist Dr. Richard Paul, calls *activated ignorance* that is, taking into the mind and actively using information that is false though mistakenly thinking it is true.

Another misconception involves the term 'critical thinking' itself. Critical thinking is not being a critic or a cynic. Being a critic or cynic is not critical thinking at all, but many times this is the common practice. Some people even confuse critical thinking with having a critical spirit. This does not mean being negative or hypercritical of everything or every issue.

Exploring the attributes of a critical thinker will help lead to a common definition. Critical thinking can be termed *robust thinking* because it involves many different attributes. Most importantly critical thinking is a *state of mind* whose goal is better thinking. The attribute is being repetitively cognizant of one's thought process. The term 'meta-cognition' has been used to describe this state of being—essentially 'thinking about thinking.' The mark of a good critical thinker then is the ability to continually monitor thought patterns for emotional, analytic and psychological biases.

Another critical thinking attribute is a questioning or inquisitive attitude. Critical thinkers always ask questions to learn more and arrive at greater depth of understanding. Critical thinkers are not threatened by receiving contradictory information. Information, which does not, matched with what is already understood and accepted. Additionally they are comfortable working with ideas and thinking of things in different ways. Finally critical thinkers like to hold their thinking to high standards of objectivity.

Taken together, these attributes give critical thinking its robust qualities. Although defining critical thinking is still difficult, Dr. Richard Paul, the foremost scholar of critical thinking uses the following definition:

Critical Thinking:

- Disciplined, self-directed thinking that exemplifies the perfections of thinking appropriate to a specific mode or domain of thinking;
- Thinking that displays mastery of intellectual skills and abilities;
- The art of thinking about one's thinking while thinking, to make one's thinking better: more clear, more accurate, or more defensible;
- Thinking that is fully aware of and continually guards against the natural human tendency to self-deceive and rationalize to selfishly get what it wants.

A more concise definition of critical thinking is: *the ability to logically assess the quality of one's thinking and the thinking of others to consistently arrives at greater understanding and achieves wise judgments*. There are many other definitions of critical thinking and most are very similar. The key is to recognise that regardless of the definition, critical thinking abilities can be individually developed.

DEVELOPING CRITICAL THINKING

One of the most effective ways to develop this strategic leader skill is by studying the parts of critical thinking—specifically certain elements and standards as one can imagine, there are a number of authors who write about critical thinking including Peter Facione and the late John Boyd. Each presents very compelling explanations and insights into critical thinking. However, Dr. Richard Paul developed a certain comprehensive model for learning critical thinking. The Paul model presents an integrative approach to critical thinking that allows for easier mastery of this essential strategic leader skill. In essence, the Paul model is easier to study, easier to practice and easier to teach. As a future critical thinker, you will have to commit to each of the above actions to reach the level of what Paul terms "Master Thinker".

The Paul model can be presented as two complimentary parts: elements of reasoning and intellectual standards. Before moving to a more detailed explanation of this model, a word of caution. Sometime models tend to discourage certain individuals from learning particular subjects. If this is the case for you, consider this model strictly as a way to learn a new style of thinking. It is not intended as a linear or sequential process.

The model is simply a depiction of how critical thinkers relate thinking abilities to the real world and arrive at reasoned, wise judgments. Using both parts of the model, elements and standards, helps create the mind-matter relationship that is the basis of critical thought.

"Only those general principles and attitudes that result from clear and deep understanding can provide a comprehensive guide to action."

The Elements of Reasoning

In the Paul model there are eight elements of reasoning: purpose, question, information, concept, inference, assumption, point of view and implications. While we will cover each element in this same sequence, please note the elements are arranged in a circular pattern to emphasize their non-linear, complimentary nature. We will return to this mutually supportive arrangement later in the discussion. What follows is an explanation of each element and the standards.

Purpose: Critical thinkers want to assess the purpose of their thinking and their actions. For instance, a critical thinker might ask, is my purpose in line with my goals, values, desires and needs? Many times the non-critical thinker will delude or deceive him or herself about the true purpose of a thought or action. For instance, one may say they want the tough job at the Pentagon because it is exciting and challenging. However, the true purpose may be accepting a position with greater long-term promotion potential.

The critical thinker looks deeper for the essential motive or purpose in each situation attempting to eliminate false purposes. Many examples of false purpose can be found in the media. For example, article titles often obscure the true purpose or intent of the text. Of course deliberate false purposes can also have an effect during war, especially when used as part of an information operations campaign. In the months leading up to Operation Iraqi Freedom, many of the stories concerning the U.S. Army's 4th Division had a much greater purpose than showing morale. As General Tommy Franks indicated, one entire front of the war was devoted to deception—in essence a deliberate false purposes. The key to understanding purpose is—being aware of one's self-deception tendency and cognisant of planned deception operations.

Question: Without a doubt, questioning is the most important element of critical thinking. One can look at critical questioning in three ways: the need to continually use critical questions, the interrelationships of critical questions and the need to ask and answer critical questions at the right time. The critical thinker must seek to identify the primary issue, problem, or question at stake. In essence this is defining the problem. Although this sounds easy enough, things become difficult as scenario's change and events occur which change the central issue.

The astute critical thinker will continually evaluate whether they are trying to answer the right question or solve the right problem. Paul categorizes questions into three types: questions of fact, questions of preference and questions of judgment. For strategic leaders, questions of judgment become the difficult challenges requiring the best in critical thinking.

Whereas questions of fact have one right answer and questions of preference have many answers, questions of judgment require reasoning skills. Using probing questions leads to the deeper understanding required by the complex national security environment. Some examples of questions of judgment with respect to our current conflict might include: what is the best way to fight terrorism, or how can we protect American civil liberties and maintain security? Another timely question of judgment concerns Iraq—how can the U.S. convince Iraqi clerics to support our goals?

Information: In our society there is generally no shortage of information and most often this becomes a problem. Former Harvard professor Francis Aguilar estimates that seventy percent of the information strategists' use comes from outside their organisation and fifty percent is from informal channels. The critical thinker must determine what information is most important and judge the quality of information.

One must consider the biases and filters between incoming information and mental comprehension. Additionally, a critical thinker must see how all the information fit's together and what linkages exist between the information and the entire organisation.

This is a systems thinking approach. Again Paul writes about three ways the mind takes in information: inert information, activated ignorance and activated knowledge. Inert information is useless—nothing more than clutter in the mind. Activated ignorance is dangerous—using false information as truth. Activated knowledge is powerful—truthful information that leads to greater understanding and wise decision-making.

Critical thinkers are generally sceptical of information and as such rely very heavily on the intellectual standards to help evaluate data to create information that leads to knowledge. We will discuss the relationship to standards later but one final point on information deserves attention— a dearth of information. Strategic leaders during wartime conditions often feel as though there is not enough actionable information and this can lead to strategic indecision.

Author Gary Klein calls this paralysis "doubt that threatens to block action." He further states that decision makers often believe a decision can be improved by collecting more information. But, in many instances this delay results in lost opportunities. Military strategist John Boyd considered "rapidity" one of his four parts of strategic thinking. Boyd believed effective organisations avoided getting bogged down in information. They make decisions with the information available at the time. In cases like this, critical thinking is even more important to ensure reasoned, sound judgments.

Concepts: The most powerful element of critical thinking is concepts. A concept is an idea or object that makes some other idea or thing comprehensible. It would be impossible to understand the world without using and understanding concepts. Consider this simple example: the concept of time makes the idea of a watch or calendar possible. We have all read about people who were great conceptual thinkers, people like George Kinnen and Albert Einstein. These men had the ability to think in different dimensions—using known ideas in a different way. One might say conceptual thinking is the seed of "outside the box" thinking. Boyd described this kind of thinking in his concept of "variety." Conceptual thinkers are able to change focus and shift their thinking to see things differently. They remain open to new information and new ideas. These new ideas spring from using multiple concepts.

The Radical Revolutionary Strategic Management Matrix For Predators

The problem with non-critical thinkers is, they are unable to change their concepts. Uncritical thinkers get stuck using the same concepts or use incorrect concepts to interpret the world. They enter a conceptual trap! If one is trapped in a single set of concepts, one can think of things in only one way. Many times the trap is constructed by a person's education, upbringing and belief system. Of course the result at the strategic level can be strategic surprise or strategic disaster.

The United States witnessed an example of this conceptual thinking on September 11, 2001. On that day the concept of 'a missile' or 'bomb' changed and so did our idea of how to protect against such a conceptual shift. Beforehand we were stuck in the conceptual trap that hijacked aircraft are used as hostages for ransom rather than weapons. The attack also demonstrated the power of conceptual traps. CIA Director George Tenet said, none of the warnings indicated terrorists would fly aircraft into buildings—this concept was anathema to our thinking. Even though intelligence activities over a several year period suggested terrorists were interested in pilot training, commercial aircraft and attacks, these small pieces of information individually could not change our conceptual thinking. Conceptual traps require overwhelming, explicit information to dismantle, or strong critical thinking skills to overcome.

The master critical thinker forces minds to think of different ways of employing or integrating the same things or ideas. Strong critical thinkers are strong conceptual thinkers who exhibit the mental agility required to rapidly and comfortably change domains of thinking to critically evaluate and analyse their world.

Inference: An inference is the conscious thought process that draws a conclusion based on the interpretation of assumptions. As the elements go, inferences can be good or bad, true or false, logical or illogical. The key to understanding inferences (conclusions) is evaluating the underlying assumptions and applying good judgment in arriving at the correct conclusion. In the aftermath of the terrorist attacks of 2004 in Spain, many leaders drew conclusions (inferences), which were false. In this case the incorrect inference was the separatist group ETA was responsible for the carnage. Hence we have the saying "jumping to conclusions" and critical thinkers resist this urge. First they carefully evaluate and interpret the available information then assess the validity of the underlying assumptions. This kind of deliberate analysis and evaluation leads to a more reasoned, informed, conclusion.

Assumption: Just as it would be impossible to understand the world without concepts, it would be paralysing to live without assumptions. An assumption can be either an explicit conscious statement of belief or more likely a subconscious belief taken for granted. Authors Neil Brown and Stuart Keeley divide assumptions into two categories: value based and descriptive. Value based assumptions are based on how one believes the world should be—the concept of 'ought.' Descriptive assumptions are more explicit and describe the world as it actually is. Many times this contrast in assumptions creates conflict for the critical thinker—a conflict that will be addressed more thoroughly later. We have all used conscious assumptions to help drive planning when there is a dearth of factual information.

This is a perfectly logical and reasonable approach to thinking. However, the assumptions we make with our subconscious mind are not always thought out or evaluated for validity. Using the Spanish example from before, the underlying assumption was, all terrorism in Spain is cause by ETA. One can easily see how faulty, subconscious assumptions lead to inaccurate conclusions. Another example of this was the 1995 bombing of the Murrah building in Oklahoma City. Again we see the same impact of faulty assumptions—that terrorism in America is caused by Arabs or Muslims. A similar faulty assumption initially occurred with several anthrax scares in the Washington D.C. area in October 2001. Critical thinkers become keenly aware of their assumptions. Not that we question all the simple assumptions that help us make it through the day, but those assumptions tied to inferences (conclusions) with large implications need careful thought. The master critical thinker attempts to bring the subconscious thoughts and assumptions into a conscious level of understanding so these assumptions can be questioned, analysed, evaluated and either validated, rejected, or updated.

"...Fresh opinions never cease to batter at one's convictions."

Point of View: Being able to see things from another point of view is an essential part of critical thinking closely related to conceptual thinking. The master critical thinker looks at situations from multiple points of view and different domains of thinking. For instance, critical thinkers may look at terrorism from a security domain, from a political domain, a legal domain, or a combination of the three. The ability to enter other points of view or consider a situation from another domain can be very insightful. Critical thinkers first recognise their own point of view then acknowledge other points of view and note the contrast.

Strategist Boyd would consider this kind of thinking as *"variety"* and *"harmony"* in that effective organisations invite rather than fear different points of view. Critical thinking organisations operate without letting their point of view distort or exclusively dominate the thought processes. Consultant Peter Linkow calls this kind of strategic thinking *"valuating."* Linkow suggests expert valuators conduct a stakeholder analysis to become sensitive to the interests of others. In essence, this approach requires the critical thinker to deliberately enter another point of view. It will not be easy to initially enter another point of view—it takes extreme mental flexibility and intellectual discipline to eliminate ones biases against doing so.

Critical thinkers do not see opposing points of view as a threat, but rather another belief to be understood and perhaps even adopted. It is worth mentioning that accepting different points of view does not necessarily lead to capricious decision-making. On the contrary, Clausewitz argues just the opposite. He reminds us that new opinions will constantly batter ones convictions and character. But, the critical thinker will not become obstinate as a result. One becomes obstinate, Clausewitz reminds us, *"...as soon as...[he]...resists another point of view not from superior insight or attachment to some higher principle, but because he objects instinctively."* Exploring different points of view will help a critical thinker, especially in strategic leadership situations, understand the environment and clarify ambiguity.

Implications: Implications are what we expect to happen before a decision. Consequences are what actually happen after the decision. Critical thinkers always consider the implications of their beliefs, opinions and actions. In fact according to Paul, master thinkers should think about implications in three ways: possible, probable and inevitable. When thinking about implications, first consider all the reasonable possibilities. In essence this includes everything from the best case to the worse case. At this point one has developed the total expected implication set. It follows that if this set is comprehensive, it will include the consequences of an action. Next the critical thinker should consider which implications are most probable in a scenario. Finally, identify any implications that are inevitable given the situation.

This kind of futures analysis is more than simple guessing. It forces ones thinking to focus on ends. From here the critical thinker can easily compare *possible implications* and *probable implications* with *expectations* of what will solve the problem or address the issue at hand. The critical thinkers expectations become the fourth part of implications: what is a "required" implication given the current problem or scenario.

Relationship of the Elements

By now you may have the opinion the Paul model of critical thinking is a rather linear way of thinking. However, the elements are more complicated than a linear model. For instance, each element of reasoning is linked simultaneously with the other elements. Consider these examples. As new information becomes available to the decision maker, assumptions and inferences may change.

Changes in information will generate new questions, impact point of view, or require new concepts. If we change our assumptions, inferences-conclusions will be affected. Questioning permeates the entire model in that one must use questions to illuminate each of the other elements. For instance, the critical thinker must ask: what is my real purpose, what is the key issue, what is the most relevant information, what are the correct concepts in this case, are my assumptions valid, have I drawn the correct inferences, what points of view matter and what are my desired implications? While this kind of circular thinking is being conducted, one must ultimately come back to both purpose and implications.

The interrelationships between the elements of critical thinking melts into a dynamic system of thought—not a sequential, linear checklist approach. This kind of thinking requires a certain flexibility of the mind and is what this author terms "robust thinking." Just as in robust decision-making, robust thinking constantly updates one's thought process by scanning for new information, checking for personal biases, maintaining conceptual flexibility and sustaining open mindedness.

Intellectual Standards

The elements of reasoning form a framework for critical thinking. Intellectual standards act as a set of principles that help gauge or measure the quality of one's thinking. Paul lists nine intellectual standards critical thinkers use to help raise the quality of thought. These standards include: clarity, accuracy, precision, relevance, breadth, depth, logic, significance and fairness.

Critical thinkers apply the standards to each of the elements of reasoning to create a more reasoned, valid pattern of thinking. As one might expect, some standards are more applicable to certain elements than others with one exception. Paul maintains that clarity is a gateway standard. Each of the elements must be clearly understood for critical thinking to occur. Essentially this is the "meeting of the minds" before serious thinking begins. Clarity does not provide comprehension but it makes comprehension possible. The critical thinker must ensure each element is clearly understood before further thought can proceed with the expectation of reasonable progress or useable results. Once an element is clearly understood, one can apply the remaining standards to achieve a robust level of thinking.

The best way to apply these standards to a particular element is by asking a question related to the standard. For instance, the critical thinker may ask of a particular element, is this accurate? Truthful? How can one verify this? Using the precision standard helps critical thinkers refine information. One question could be, is this precise enough for decision-making? Could this information be more exact? Relevance helps distil the complexity of critical thinking by helping focus one's thinking on the parts of a scenario that relate to the question or decision at hand. As mentioned earlier, normally decision makers are overwhelmed by information, assumptions, points of view and implications. Being able to ask, "How is this relevant" is a step toward simplifying decision-making.

The breadth and depth standard are the two most closely related. Taken together they are complimentary—either something is too narrow or too shallow. The key is to recognise a certain robust harmony between these two standards; for instance, critical thinkers are looking for breadth in point of view, concepts and implications. At the same time, one needs depth in information, concepts, assumptions and questions. In essence, these standards lead to the question; do I have a wide enough view (scan) with sufficient detail on the second and third order effects?

When considering logic as a standard, the simple test is: does this make sense? Another question may apply: does this opinion track with the available proof? Here the inquisitive, sceptical mind is an asset to critical thought. Logic requires one to reflect and reconsider any conditional statement or information.

The significance standard, like relevance, seeks to highlight not only what applies to the situation but also what is most important. Significance will help the critical thinker prioritise information, point of view, concepts and implications. In a sense, significance could be thought of as the first step toward planning effects based operations. Finally, critical thinkers need to consider the issue of fairness. This standard appears the most controversial of the group. Many of you are thinking, who determines what is fair and how does one determine what fair is? Both good questions without a short answer when explaining the standard of fairness. In fact when asking a panel of experts studying critical thinking to evaluate the issue of critical thinking and ethics, the majority concluded that critical thinking is totally unrelated to political correctness, morality, or values. In practice we see this when very skilled professionals use critical thinking to mislead or exploit others.

The issue with this kind of "weak" critical thinking is how easily personal biases and ego creep into the thought processes. Suffice it to say, fairness has as much to do with personal bias and personal motives as ethical decision-making. The thought behind fairness as a standard relates to an individual's propensity for self-deception. So, when gauging the fairness of a decision, the critical thinker must ask, do my selfish interests distort this thinking, or is my decision fair to all concerned? The fairness standard seeks to prevent egocentric thinking. As one's ego enters the thought process, critical thinking becomes poisoned with ulterior motives resulting in sub-optimised decisions. The ego determines the purpose and the central question, selectively chooses information, using only familiar concepts and unquestioned assumptions leading to misdirected conclusions while considering limited points of view resulting in unwarranted implications. If clarity is the gateway standard, fairness is the "gut check" standard for eliminating egocentric bias.

"Come Let Us Reason Together." (Isaiah 19:1)

Critical Thinking: You versus the Situation

Now that we have covered the basics of critical thinking, this section will concentrate on putting this knowledge into perspective by offering a way to use critical thinking. Imagine being able to use critical thinking skills in two dimensions: the inner and the outer. In keeping with our abbreviated definition of critical thinking, remember that critical thinking is useful for monitoring the quality of your thinking, the inner dimension and the quality of other's thinking, the outer dimension. Using the following compendium of questions, one can learn how to use both dimensions. When considering critical thinking to guide the inner dimension of your own thinking ask yourself some of the following questions: What have I said is the purpose of my thinking? What questions do I have about this situation? What do I believe to be the key question or issue needing my decision? What information do I know to be true? What kinds of information do I have too much of? Too little of? What concepts am I using right now? What conclusions have I already drawn? What assumptions underlie these conclusions? Do I need to make any assumptions in this situation? What is my point of view? What other points of view are represented? What implications would I expect see as a result of my critical thinking? What is my desired end state? Does all this seem fair and selfless? Have I checked my reasoning against some intellectual standard?

Now consider the critical thinking required to guide the outer dimension of your thinking. Seek answers to the following questions: What is my true purpose in this situation? Why am I really thinking about this? What questions should I be asking? What questions are required that I have not asked? What questions are forbidden to ask? What information do I really need to know? What information is missing that I would like to know? What other concepts could apply to this situation? What concepts should I be using that would change my thinking? What other conclusions could be drawn from the information available? Are others assumptions available for consideration? What assumptions would radically change my conclusions? Whose point of view is missing from the scenario? From what point of view am I approaching this situation? Are there other domains or points of view that I could or should accept? What are the possible implications from this robust thinking? Which implications are most probable? What implications are inevitable based on this thinking? How do these implications meet or exceed my desired end state? How would I gauge the thinking of others in this thought partnership? Have I applied the standards of thought to this reasoning?

One can see through this short exercise in questioning, how learning critical thinking skills is possible. The key as with any new skill begins with study. This article should be the first issue in your study of critical thinking. There are many more available as mentioned in the notes. Future critical thinkers must also practice the new skill so critical thinking becomes second nature as your default-thinking pattern. The more you practice thinking using the elements and standards, the quicker your thinking will improve. Initially this practice will be difficult especially as one challenges the mind to think in new ways, remain flexible, open to change and confront one's ego. Over time, critical thinking will so dominate the thought process you will begin to recognise uncritical thinking in others. At this point, the practicing critical thinker must attempt to challenge the thinking of others by explaining the concepts of critical thinking in a practical way. Being able to coherently explain, illustrate, or elaborate why certain reasoning is faulty is synonymous with teaching critical thinking. The master critical thinker teaches by demonstrating critical thinking in action.

Engaging Non-Critical Thinkers

Even though much has been written about critical thinking, many questions require further study especially on how to engage non-critical thinking societies. Specifically this challenge includes relating to non-critical thinking societies, reasoning with non-critical thinking societies and changing non-critical thinking societies. To understand non-critical thinking societies, one must appreciate the value of a liberal education. Here the term does not have a negative connotation but rather means being liberated from the control of others thinking. In his book *Critical Thinking*, Richard Paul captures the essence of this phrase by including small outtakes titled "Think for Yourself." What an appropriate way to describe a liberal education. In those societies controlled by warlords, despots and dictators, a liberal education is not universally allowed or even available to the general population. As a result, the population easily becomes harnessed to weak thinking, unquestioning obedience and radicalism. This kind of thinking manifests itself through suicide bombers, fidayeen attacks, child soldiers and fanatical clerics.

Another challenge of relating to non-critical thinking societies is, without the ability to think for themselves, these "think-less" societies become sensitised to basic human decency. Peter Facione in his article "Critical Thinking," describes the process as, refining humane sensibilities that lead to a critical appraisal of what is good and bad in human nature. The lack of humane sensibilities leads to acts of barbarism like those in Rwanda and recently the gruesome killing of contractors in Iraq. Additionally, non-critical thinking societies reject different points of view to the extent they become as Clausewitz mentioned, obstinate. Examples of this include the Islamic idea of apostasy where one who has known the faith and subsequently rejects it is marked for death. Another issue as Facione points out is how easily non-critical thinking societies are exploited both politically and economically. The impact of not understanding the international economic system, legal system, or social system is that these societies lag further behind the rest of the world, live meagre lives, without hope leading to even less critical thinking. Bernard Lewis, author of *The Crisis of Islam*, relates this downward spiral to the concept of frustration felt by many revolutionary Islamists. Facione believes that in time the judicial and economic systems of such a society will collapse. As you can see, there are many challenges in trying to relate to non-critical thinking societies. But, since interaction between different societies is inevitable, how does a critical thinking society reason with a non-critical thinking society?

The question of reasoning with non-critical thinking societies boils down to two issues: what the society respects and patience in reasoning. Both these issues bear on the idea of establishing democracy in non-critical thinking societies. In many non-critical thinking societies, the only thing they respect is power—not culture. Non-critical thinking societies understand violence, not reason. Again we can turn to Clausewitz to shed light on this pint when he posited, "in any primitive warlike race, the warrior spirit is far more common than among civilized people." Perhaps the non-critical thinking societies produce more violence prone cultures but according to Clausewitz, they rarely if ever produce a great commander or military genius because this requires the ability to think critically. At best critical thinking will have limited short-term success dealing with non-critical thinking societies. Without changes, ultimately reasoning with these societies will fail. As Bernard Lewis points out, some of these societies will seek short-term accommodation before turning to violent approaches. Author Roger Scruton writes in his book *The West and the Rest* that the view from many of these societies questions the entire western tradition of reasoning. They equate reasoning as a means to reinforce western values and as a result to accept one is to accept the other. One might ask, without the ability to reason with non-critical thinking societies is it possible to create democracy? Facione posit's "...in such a society, one that does not liberate its citizens by teaching them to think critically for themselves, it would be madness to advocate democratic forms of government." Democracy is hard even under the best of circumstances and while there may be set backs, one can begin the process in non-critical thinking societies but this kind of embryonic democracy will require extreme protection, advice and perhaps a rescue mission or two. Since the quality of any democracy is equal to the quality of the democrats, in a non-critical thinking society, the quality of the democracy may be low for quite a while but a change to "thinking freedom" is essential to nurturing the beginnings of critical thinking. How can a critical thinking society help bring about the changes required in non-critical thinking societies? As discussed earlier, critical thinking can be taught with varying degrees of success within any society. Therefore, one approach should infiltrate the education systems of the subject society. This could be accomplished by direct intervention, with critical thinking teachers, or training for current teachers. Another effective idea is to immediately increase access to books and materials on critical thinking and reasoning skills. In many cases these kinds of works would be the first such editions translated into some languages.

Next, telecommunications can be a tremendous "brain multiplier" if used to provide truthful, unbiased information to the targeted society. What would happen if a certain young democratic nation suddenly inherited one million satellite dishes each with pre-programmed information channels? Certainly, the conceptual thinking required here is not to think about non-critical thinking societies as rejecting western reasoning but rather think of them as an educational challenge. Although the deep creativity necessary to solve this monumental problem is the subject for a subsequent article, the above ideas are readily apparent.

One may argue whether one model is better than the next, but in this case, the elements of reasoning and intellectual standards presented represent the essence of how to think critically. Taken in their entirety, a short collection of questions can lead one to the kind of robust thinking required in today's strategic environment. Critical thinkers today face the challenge of creating the critical thinkers of tomorrow—many in foreign lands who have never known or accepted the power of critical thinking. Robust thinkers must answer the question, how do we accelerate the process of change in a society of critical thinkers over nihilistic decision-making? We are living in the era of 'wars of the haves versus the have-nots' and now more than ever critical thinking seems to be a big part of what is missing from the societies we are trying to democratise. Becoming a critical thinker is an admiral goal requiring a committed effort to learn the concepts, practice the elements and teach the ways. It is critical for military professionals to develop this essential strategic leader skill. Clausewitz recognised the value of critical thinking for strategic leaders when he wrote, "...the human mind is far from uniform. If we then ask what sort of mind is likeliest to display the qualities of military genius, experience and observation will tell us that it is the inquiring rather than the creative mind, the comprehensive rather than the specialized approach, the calm rather than the excitable head to which in war we would choose to entrust the fate of our brothers and children and the safety and honour of our country." – *written by* Col W. Michael Guillot.

| **Chapter 17:** | The Reality of Industrial Espionage and Security |

Vulnerability starts with us, and our strategy...

Words from the wise - We must, on the one hand, strive by all means to prevent the competition from acting on sound principles; on the other hand, a supreme planning effort must take place, to enable our organisation to exploit those principles, in order to facilitate the achievements of our aims and objectives. For this very purpose, every principle, which the competition is likely to apply, must serve as a target for the ingenuity of those who plan – derived from Mao.

The - Strategic Security Management Principle

The aim of this chapter is not to go into detail, but to create a heightened awareness, of the importance of security at several levels, within the organisation. Innovative, state-of-the-art systems possibly will be a good starting foundation, never the less; vigilance will be cheap, but very effective armour. However security is perception and perception becomes reality and how that reality reflects when tested will confirm if the assumptions surrounding the perception was correct, or not, it is only when we get tested, that our security component will give us a true competitive advantage and capabilities, that rivals cannot match, that we can truly say we have become innovative.

Therefore, empowering the organisation and taking it to the next level, is not a mere practice but a principle of critical thinking, when designing a business or revolutionising it. This principle, of getting an advantage and keeping it, by implementing strategic means; constitutes true advantage – it is foresight (being pro-active) that wins out over having to correct mistakes and blind spots in hindsight. The strategic advantages we seek that can be effectively utilised, implemented and applied, requires a great deal of simplicity, in integration, we tend to think that extraordinary measures will be the most likely way to go, this type of thinking normally does not involve the whole organisation, it has to start with individuals, that creates the energy to create the synergy, that cannot be copied or gained by the competition.

In this principle also lies its weakness. If the competition cannot match advantage, they will try to steal it, corrupt it, or sabotage it. Maintaining effective security is a continuous multidimensional task. The challenge of having and maintaining security is in its "joints" – the way it interacts and the point where it interacts with the organisation; we are only as secure as our weakest joint or link. The security of the strategy is paramount first and then the physical elements of what constitutes the business. Keeping an advantage; requires protecting three spheres of business, the intellectual capital, the physical capital and electronic capital. Therefore, it stands to reason that we have three vulnerability levels to protect.

Data security: wherever data travels or resides, be it along formal reporting (meetings and conversations – the grapevine) or electronic. It becomes a target. We have to be security conscious and secure data at all times, to preserve mission critical data and strategies from walking out the proverbial door. On the other hand, we all realise the importance of accurate and timely information, it is both essential and critical to guide strategic action, therefore it has to be protected and both readily available. Prompt feedback on implementation of initiatives, budgets, figures, forecasts and proposals become critical deliverables. In the wrong hands, they can spell sure doom. The question is, how secure and even paranoid do we have to be about our corporate security. Especially in terms of our data, information and systems, as well as backups. If systems are compromised and collapses, so does the organisations core. Will this then become a serious concern, only then?

The term "Cyber terrorism" comes to mind, where any bright-eyed youngster, can study hacking and even break into the FBI, the Banks security, why not yours. During a conference of Hackers in Dallas, a group of youngster was challenged to break into computer networks and computers, to see how effective security was and to see how many they could break into, in a certain amount of time. They were armed with laptops and with wireless Internet connections. Riding around town in a limo, the four of them broke into no less than 36 computers, could read data on 90 % of them and was able to get administrator rights on some network systems and connections all in six hours. This very aspect of security cannot be protected by the likes of mainstream, copy write protection and privacy laws; piracy, hacking, identity theft, viruses and the list goes on. No amount of legislation and law enforcement will stop them. The reason being, that they are objective means reliant on concrete evidence, in courts of law. Opposed to, firewalls and passwords, that is subjective systems that are very difficult to prove in court, where he who alleges must prove, when you do not have the means available and the systems in place how do you prove that you have been had, or the finances to find out who did it, in order to prove it. Only specialised equipment and trained people can fight them in real time. Small to medium sized companies have to rely on commercial software, to protect them. Nevertheless, as time passes so will the concepts and they will mature to the same level as normal evidence. The point is this; systems need to be protected, by whatever means necessary, in order to be relatively safe.

The deliberate integration of several layers of security serves two purposes.

The concept of security itself, is based on layers, a good concept has a minimum of four. In short, as physical means, they are;

- Building security consciousness; the awareness of security and potential threats, attentiveness, self-defences, the carrying of a firearm.
- Inner perimeter security; any form of security applied within the inner perimeter, alarm systems, heat sensors, vibration monitors.
- Restriction of access; of the intermediate perimeter, guard dogs, gates and security lights, passive infrareds, laser beams.
- Perimeter security; high walls, electrified fences, guards and dogs and the likes. This is the concept.

On an electronic level, it differs, but the concept remains the same.

- For instance, encryption, is one of the oldest and still one of the most secure methods of securing data and it is simplicity in its general application.
- This will relate to security consciousness. Password protection is simple, even if all our operating platforms fail to protect us and they get the data, the data is relatively useless. Cradle to grave principle, in layers, we store and protect.
    - point two, physical means - The next method is the fragmentation of data across storage devices,
    - point three, strategic means -intentions. By literally cutting the plan into pieces and giving it out as such for implementation in printed form.
    - point four. The old saying of "don't put all your eggs into one basket" applies to all the above as principle. This will give you more means of security. It is simple yet effective.

Strategy and business plans, as well as operational plans and formulas, are the ingredients that say we are a business, this is the most targeted type of identity theft, our **Information most sought after by competition, covers five areas.**

1. Customer data – email, mailing lists.
2. Supplier's data – contact info, discounts, structures of accounts and contracts.
3. Operations data – concepts, formulas, procedures and any other info.
4. Employee data – remuneration packages, earnings, qualifications, contact numbers etc.
5. Financial performance data – budgets, contracts, tenders, etc.

Accurate and timely information allows strategists and managers to monitor progress and take corrective actions promptly! However, in the wrong hands it could have the equal and opposite effect. Moreover, look at some derivative forms of counter strategy; it is imperative that the strategy be safe guarded against the competitors counter strategies. There are so many examples of this principle of what constitutes safety and security, but to best illustrate this let's go back to:

The Strategic Principles; of Guerrilla Warfare.

This embodies the idea behind the theft, infringement and gain, the criminal mind works from the predator paradigm; "You have to study, the animal, in order to understand it, in order to predict it, in order to kill or capture it."

Terror Attacks Phases: let us look at classical teaching of guerrilla warfare and relate the principles back to our business and corporate environments. The doctrine of the anarchist and people who just do it for fun, are written in the same stone.

You start by gathering intelligence on the target. Any attack, big or small is mostly preceded by an observation phase, also relating back to the "OODA loop".

The gathering of strategic or tactical information consists of the following orientation:

- descriptions of physical attributes,
- routines,
- security and related systems,
- the unravelling of structures within the organisation,
- the, who's who' and who does what, when, where and how?
- by understanding the culture, the head and how they function, it will give you the ability to predict their reactions and next course of action.

This hypothesis is constructed from observation and the intelligence will give you a concept of the target; this can be instant, or deliberate, in other words – opportunity was created due to circumstance – or planned and remember intelligence is tested and confirmed factual-information not just mere speculation on information. To make the hypothesis even sounder we can encapsulate the human element in control of the organisation. By studying his characteristics as if an organism, why I used organism, it gives a better understanding of how relevant this concept can be.

By example; the "rat" cannot fly, he cannot breathe under water, but he can run fast and climb and jump – these are the attributes of a "rats" - personality. Therefore, it stands to reason that we will not expect him to launch an air attack, nor a water attack, although he can swim, but rather he will use his speed and his ability to negotiate obstacles to attack us. Therefore, if we have to attack or defend against him we have to entice him to swim and then drown him, we have to get him to jump and then increase the distance so that he may fall to his death.

This is how analytical the process of profiling becomes; I have just explained it graphically. In addition, all this information is genetically coded and entrenched in our character scripts, our behaviour traits will not change, we are creatures of habit. Our personality dictates our biases towards security. Find the character and you will find its "weaknesses" in the leader, both in his management style; for instance when he is faced with a dilemma, does he act impulsive-autocratic, unemotional, analytic, composed, seeking council or does he stand back and call in the cavalry so to speak, outside help of sorts.

It is said; that by studying the wind, one can determine which direction it will take you. This is the study of concrete things. "Personal signatures" – habit. During World War two, the Allied forces were at a loss when it came to the decryption of German Submarine force movement and communications. They cut all the supply lines. They studied the code in depth, but could not break it in totality. It was designed by one clever German Prof Udo Undeuttsch and later perfected by an Israeli rabbi; Avinoam Sapir who came to the conclusion that every message sent has a "personal signature". We all use buzzwords in our conversation, "bro" "cool" "bud" or some slang in a certain context. With this discovery they could pinpoint the person, sending the message, align this information with the recipients, study the profiles of the division commanders and predict a scenario on a specific front to unfold. Again, personality filters into strategy, to incorporate personal traits.

The Chinese on the other hand believe greatly in the astrologically appropriateness of one's star sign, they have animal star signs and elements that complement those star signs. They would get the birth date of the enemy general and work out the animal sign and his element, (wood, water, fire and earth) – by finding its opposite they could counter him, by disposition of his character traits. Test this principle for yourself, just look up your Chinese animal sign and element and then see how well your attributes are described, your personality, within this context.

The point is this, the trustworthiness and security of data, personnel, communication channels and networks are essential to the overall success of any organisation, in the wrong hands it could mean just the opposite. Users must be assured that information transmitted over the infrastructure will go when and where it is intended to go. Electronic information systems can create new unexpected vulnerabilities. For example, electronic files in bulk can be broken into and copied from remote locations or stored on small flash drives and transported out of the organisation, even to cellular phones Yet, these same systems, if properly designed, can offer greater security than less advanced communications channels.

Just by targeting one aspect of an organisation. For instance, if a company cannot get his product on the shelves in time, or render the service they promised, they won't sell much, or if the production facility can't produce they cannot meet their commitments, if the administration stops, they cannot pay wages or accounts, they cannot collect money, if the managers cant command and control or supervise the whole systems slows down. These are all corporate games to manipulate capitalism, to monopolise and control market segments at any cost or means.

To create syndicates. The need for this insight into radical revolutionary ideas is not to create anarchy or to promote it, but to make leaders aware of dark and sinister minds that manipulate the concepts of war for personal gain in business, even politics for financial gain, for their own personal agendas, be they very dark or based on pure greed. It is always better to step outside the circle of light, our known area of operation, our own references and beliefs and to see thing from where they might originate. If one can see the engineered disorder, one can understand its potential strength and weakness. If one can see the dark, the unknown, feel it, listen to it, then you can and will understand the objective of their thinking, only when we become aware of the existence of pure evil and their masters, do we realise that business is not just about being good at what you do, and making lots of money, it is also about mitigating the potential threats.

THE NEED FOR COUNTER SURVEILLANCE

A "terror attack rarely comes out of the blue" it is usually preceded by a period of surveillance – this can be verified by the September 11th tragedy. Well it is self-explanatory, but how do we counter surveillance of our business. **Start by looking for patterns**, which should not exist inside a stable habitat. This is best explained by monitoring the frequency of occurrence of events that are not considered to be normal. Take the hypothetical example of a major cellphone service provider, which experiences mayor thefts, of large volumes of phones and prepaid cards. As well as failed marketing strategies, somehow the competition just knew what their next move would be, all the time. Therefore, they got in security experts. What they had found reiterates this point of security. They started sweeping the office buildings with electronic equipment for bugs - listening in devices. Even computers and telephones were scanned, to see if anyone is recording meetings, or mining data. They were astonished at what they had found. Their boardrooms were bugged; the cleaner hire company was part of a syndicate that had used artificial plants to hide away listening devices. The CEO's secretary was backing up all her email, to the "public folders" directory – which is available to all to view – she was not "aware" of this. One disgruntled employer copied all of it and sent it on to the competition. They never shredded any documents and the waste paper collectors dropped off all the documents at a home address. They conducted an investigation and found a syndicate selling info to the competitors. Only afterwards, did the company start to implement multiple levels of security, not what you would expect from million dollar organisations now would you. This is what they did. Random security checks were implemented, thus enforcing the perception of – a visible omnipresent and security detail. They installed close-circuited-TV systems throughout the building, even dummy sites and in the general sales area, accounts department and parking area, with a monitoring station. Electronic access was implemented, cards that sign you in at the gate, opens your parking area, opens your office, signs you in and gives you access to the network, etc. Mandatory sign in and identification checks of customer motor vehicles, registrations and personal identity checks for all customers and visitors, became the norm. **The second level** was the tracking of big assignments via satellite tracking, when big assignments came in by containers from the coast; they were escorted by armed guards. All orders were tracked for authentication of the buyer and if it is shipped, it gets protection to the warehouse. All company vehicles have satellite tracking in. **The third level** was the whistle blowers accord, any dealer must report any attempt to get info outside the norm. Therefore, they took a global approach, they are protecting their clients as well and their security protocol has become their biggest sales tool.... This just in short an over view of a medium sized company's awareness level that changed their perception and now they are no longer medium and their opposition is gone, just because of the importance of security, thus protecting its market interests as well, the suppliers and the consumers. With industrial espionage, corruption and so forth lurking in the dark, it is only with vigilance that we survive. They target the obvious, so that nothing will seem to be out of place and that no suspicion can be raised, except if you are focused and vigilant. The next topic is internal awareness. In one study done, it was determined that only 20% of all employees are honest and do not commit crime. The rest 72% will take advantage of your organisation, some by innocent and some by subtle means; taking stationery home for the kids, using company time to do private work, sell information, manuals and take advantage whenever the opportunity arises for personal gain, 8% will actively be taking money, scheming profit's, or be using your company as a vehicle for self-enrichment to further their own business, from within your business. – Just so by the way!

Having support and good networks has become the nexus of serving the corporate world of spider webs filled with intrigue, we deal with the importance of networking in the next chapter, it is not always what you know, but also whom you know that counts.

Chapter 18

Building a Successful Network

The Power of the Social Elite

The greatest power anyone could have in this life does not come from having limitless resources or skill in making strategy. No, it comes from building up clear knowledge of those around you and then forming deliberate relationships with them – called networking.

Networking: involves building relationships with people, not just any relationship, but an "interlocking" one. Interlocking refers to "building relationships and sharing beliefs, principles and knowledge" on things that count vs. counting the things that this union could foster". It is not always a rational relationship; opposites do attract, it's not always based on what you know initially, but rather whom you know that counts. We have to realise that relationships are with people and not with group's and or organisations, but with the individuals themselves belonging to such structures. By only having one or two good relationships within an organisation, we cannot say that we have established a relationship with the organisation as a whole.

The point is, that many people will jump up and say, hay, I have a good relationship with that group or organisation, a very dangerous assumption. Relationships form in many ways, either in a formal or informal manner. It can be arranged, guided or spontaneous.

The other point is that of "Professional courtesy", this in itself does not constitute a relationship either. People think they know someone just because he or she was kind and professional with them; this is a contact, not a relation. Our focus with networking is to create, contacts and then turn them into relations. The only way to make this happen is to make every interaction count, to leave a lasting impression, to convince people in twenty sections flat, that you know what you are talking about.

First impressions do count. The fundamental ingredient is sincerity and professionalism, called credibility or trustworthiness. To start "Interlocking networks" takes up time; we first have to assemble contacts and then engage them on social grounds to get to know them. Volunteer your service and ask nothing in return. Remember you focus is long term, not short or medium; this union should never be based on any agenda, but on sound business principles.

The Radical Revolutionary Strategic Management Matrix For Predators

Most relationships within a network of trust can be faceless, expressionless – even over the phone, email, letters and chartrooms or by referral etc. Based purely on the principle of openness and shared interest, in other words to the point and sincere.

However, the underlying principle is the serving of interest. Every nation and organisation has "Interests", that need to be protected, or expanded or developed and it is people that look for ways to do it, not products or services, they merely compliment, by finding other people that have ways of doing it for themselves.

Everybody is mindful that the other party "wants something", but until you come clean and say what it is exactly, there will be no or little trust. People have to position themselves within networks; it is all about getting the initiative going. All people have "Wants" that are materialised by virtue of looking for networks serving their "interests".

Networking finds this commonality and fuses it, it is the best and most commonly used way, in realising interests and wants.

Based on our individual and innate potential to find things we desire or require – we go through interconnectivity. We have to connect with someone or something. By implication, any medium that we can effectively communicate with, in order to find the resources we require via interaction and networking. We all have networks of support –satisfying that want, friendship, mutualism and interests. We see this in family circles, where some get along, because of shared interest, perception , ideology or whatever, and others just don't see eye to eye. The point is networking is focused on human interaction and gratification, as well as feedback, that creates mutually beneficial emotional and physical transactions and rewards. The key and operative word is action. You cannot sit in one place and want fruitful relationships and transactions to transpire by doing nothing; you need to find a communication medium to start with. Secondly you have to find a message to send and thirdly you require a receiver. This also referred to in strategic terms as the "Mobilisation of Communication". "Mobilisation" implies and requires an action plan; people will act when called upon, for help, advice, service, or to achieve a common goal, to do a favour, or to perform a mutually beneficial act. However, only if you have the pitch well rehearsed and the right audience. Then the act of communicating effectively, comes into play. In other instance the windows of opportunity will open doors. For anyone to be successful then, we will need to acquire consciously the art of negotiation and communication to influence the entry barriers to networking. The barriers to entering networks are;

- Cultural and linguistic barriers
- Fraternity specific communication and terminology
- Technology and acronyms generally used in discussion
- Perception and paradigm of thinking
- Complexity of subject that requires implicit subject knowledge
- Referrals required, or registration and affiliation

There are several ways to build networks:

The radical action network; One way is to apply the opposing forces theory; this theory evokes radical action, to evoke a calculated desired response, often the way to move people is to move them internally first by creating internal influences, by organising external influences that stimulates common interest and networking. Find ways for ordinary people to play a major role in your actions to establish networks, by giving them "power", it strengthens your own position. "Power" could be information, knowledge and skills based. This process identifies you as a leader, with followers.

Entering ***emotionally charged networks;*** requires a catalyst, that creates an emotionally reactive response, to move people because of their convictions, either emotionally, sentimentally, financially, politically, or on other issues of ethnic and moral value, even spiritually. These are the catalyst of emotional networking. Finding the right buttons to push requires firstly understanding of the culture and then being understood. This aspect will get you an audience. The next move is to take to the podium, where it's not about what you know, but how you say it, it's not about who you are, but what you stand for, it's not about where you come from, but where you are going. What it is about is forwarding their "Vision" with your strengths. It has everything to do with class and social structure, you need to fit in mentally, in order to sell them any concept. Networking is all about fitting in, by strengthening ones position. You will only succeed by selling concepts, ideas and notions, based on their version of reality.

The other way of ***breaking into closed networks;*** is by getting a "sponsor", sponsors are influential people, symbols or icons in society, people in positions, family, friends, acquaintances - people with influence, that could invite you in, inside closed and tightly knit circles of trust, you will only get in by sponsorship. This is imperative; people need to know whom you are associated with, especially in networks like this, it's all about who knows who, that referred you. In networks like this it's all about swinging perceptions in your favour. More can be said with a mere perception than with an entire speech.

The political network; emanates from spreading propaganda – or a perception – perceptions work like slogans forming new paradigms. It does not spell out the exact meaning; it just implies something and by implication it gets meaning and becomes a new reality. "Power to the People". This slogan for instance has in its breath a Marxist Leninist connotation that started as a perception and ultimately formed a new political dispensation, Communism, refers to the working class, a carrot and stick method of creating new networks based on social class needs.

Networking with groups; group dynamics is the next aspect, groups can be radically different, but can still be interlocked to evolve around sound fundamental rules of networking, the rules are; forming, storming, "norming" and then performing in the group context. Forming refers to – the group beginning to form due to a common interest shared by creating a concept, a vehicle for them to realise an objective. Members are measuring themselves against others and trying to determine where they fit into this group. Storming refers to – internal discontent as members explore each other's "hidden agendas" and then finds commonality in objective. Norming refers to – the growing interdependence of the group, interaction begins to normalise and then a concept takes form. Performing refers to – the group establishing structures and relationships by working together to achieve the task(s) at hand, to crystallise the concept in order to reach their mutual objective.

One on one networking; is most common, with one-on-one business relations and corporate image, intrigues define their principles and how they will apply it, but within networks that are, more formal. This is the process of "going shopping" – it's not a spur of the moment ½ price sale thing. It is a strategic calculated move to form an alliance in line with their thinking, to affect the outcome of future events. To get access to tender committees, finance committees, grants, sponsorships etc. therefore it is intentionally done. This is the art of having nothing and yet controlling everything by establishing networks. The only way to do this is by developing an "Agenda for Action"- (The virtual business plan – and concept – equates to the strategy of coalition building.)

The purpose of networking is building a successful coalition within networks:

Negotiation: Most people, when they think of negotiation, picture smoke filled rooms. The major difference between formal planned negotiations or the social kind, the on the golf course type of negotiation, as compared to other types, is the need for people skills. Just like in any formal process, planning and negotiation is a much more structured process. In these situations, it is imperative to:

Have a game plan when going out for a coalition; develop an "agenda for action" this implies simply having some guidelines for negotiations with predefined alternatives, should the negotiations meet roadblocks, or experience blind spots. Only core issues must be outlined when selling any idea – detail will follow only once you have sold the concept – keep in mind that ideas need to be flexible. Point out what is in it for them, this aspect should be quite clear and the risk factors involved, this will indicate trustworthiness, the potential high risk areas should be spelled out and how the risk will be managed.

However, it is important to note that this type of negotiation is born out of necessity. Most negotiations you will participate in will involve day-to-day operations of your business, or an informal presentation of a project that could attract attention. In addition, it might spark interest on building long-term relationships and on making deals. To increase your negotiation skills, you need to increase your awareness of what you are doing vs. what they are doing, you have to become the subject matter expert and how they can profit from it and your knowledge. You need to know the market, the pricing structures and the going rates, as well as the competition to be competitive. The best way to do this is to go out and test it first. In short, you need to be on top of your game, not just the strategy you want to sell. Strategy requires an action plan, this is the practice of the trade, described in basic terms, that is both in context and relevant with the current situation.

Learn to use both your intellect as well as your intuition during the negotiation process. Good negotiators are the people who understand how to build key relationships first by latching on, commonality and or directness, sell themselves first. How to identify with what people need and want, mostly people only have a vague idea of what they really need and they want you to give it essence. How to give them what they need and how to get what you want in return, is a skill, an art, having deals done all in a way that seems effortless. It takes many dress rehearsals and practice. This book is about strategy and not sales and marketing, so forgive me for not going into detail on this aspect.

The essentials. The key of coalition building within a network is finding the key to unlock potential by forming a coalition.

Solidifying your newfound coalition – through the implementation of a memorandum of understanding – MOU, is a good way of securing long-term business, as part of your consultation, should you be freelancing as a consultant. In this memorandum you clearly stipulate what, where, when, who and how much it will cost, this union will function around this understanding. Managing differences among coalition members is the key to keeping the union strong, by allowing disagreements in order that agreements may flow from it.

Developing an Agenda for Action: that will develop strong bonds and networks.

Let's stop here and talk about the need for development of oneself. In terms of projecting; write effective business plans and documents, when considering joining forces towards designing any effective new network. Remember everybody wants to be in charge, have the control first, they want to show strength, they don't want to be seen as a corps, so go in for even power sharing and win-win or no deal models, don't go for anything less and be sure to state this. Start by seeking solutions that will fit into "their" current reality, their thinking and culture first, (remember reality is not fluent and changes with every wakening moment and idea, we can only change their reality once we understand it from their perspective and paradigm); therefore, our agenda or plan will start by highlighting their theory that will evolve into a concept. Remember concepts are less flexible; theory is most flexible, if they like the theory then move to the concept, otherwise stick to the theory, until it is sorted to both parties satisfaction.

Theory and **P**ractice are the ideal material to combine human mental activity. For theory reflects and organises practice – and in turn reality; as much as practice manifests and enriches the theory. This aspect is important in more than one way, theory is culture driven, in other words the way they get things done traditionally, where practice is their will to get it done driven by personal convictions, in other words how individuals find the energy to get things done. This will be reflected in their practice or reality.

What is a logical strategic deduction to a problem?

It is the interference of logical deductions by people who are not strategically minded, trying to make sense of it – by relating it in terms of their understanding and ability to communicate complexity. Networks have builders and breakers, which restrains pure strategic logic as an opposing force to understanding strategy in itself. This type of reasoning then corrupts our professional personal view on strategic logic. Where any person wants to understand, or where we want them to understand something. We need to create points of reference first, then enters the strategic equation, it changes the face and facts. In other word strategic logic tells us that if the theory of strategy is strong then so will be the practice, this is most certainly not the case today where only 4% of all managers are proficient at strategy and strategic thinking in the world today. Strategy is just perceived as not being logical anymore. Because logic stems from our individual will and understanding of how to achieve things, it is only our personal uncertainness or reservation, that prevents us from thinking logical. For our logic is clouded by our personal fear of the unknown. However, if we were certain about our conflictions and our strategy, then the solution would have been forthcoming and readily accepted without fear of failure. This aspect is the control aspect when entering networks. With networking and selling strategy, the fear of failure only grabs them if they don't get the logic behind strategy. If we sell strategy we have to be very sure it will work first, and that it is a logical solution, we have to be aware of becoming self-righteous by virtue of our own strategic beliefs and proficiency. Find ways to make things believable. We must not over emphasis our proficiency and the influences of our trusted culture circle enforcing it. With this in mind, it is clear that it is fear, and uncertainty, that either keeps us captive or drives us to pursue the strategic art. The inflexibility of our personal conviction and strategic disbelief, coupled to the practice of rejecting all new knowledge and forms of reasoning, that deprives us of logic. Only people fundamentally different, with something abstract to add, deserves our utmost attention, for they will test our resilience and mind. For some believe that brilliance comes from chaotic minds and are not to be avoided. If this is the case, then it is not strategy that is the problem, but our personal persistence to only follow our own reasoning, to utilise strategy. Strategy itself challenges the normative, that challenges the old faith. and system as well as culture. It is people who fear the changes that strategy creates, for they see themselves losing the comforts of control, status, ritual and worth. This aspect originates from pragmatic programming and character traits. Egocentric thinking, how will this affect me if it is true? It is this type of thinking, which is very common today, which diminishes the concept of good strategy and fruitful networking, as well as coalition building. Therefore, the striving for new certainty and real-truth, resides in the unravelling of chaos, out of chaos comes order, the concept of inner faith and balance, is only held captive by personal fear. Fear, in itself is irrational so how can we try rationalising it for someone else, if it becomes internalised and personal. These are the roadblocks when networking strategy, having to navigate personal issues, that lets us make u turns, and we find ourselves in minefields of mayhem. The next question one needs to ask is this, how much of myself will I give to a network, how open and honest do I have to be, in order to be trusted. What does the one aspect; of openness have to do with the other aspect, trust? For one, openness and trust annihilates scepticism. Scepticism is described as the tendency to express strongly held opinions in a way that suggests they should be accepted without question and then someone starts by questioning them. The result is conflict. I am sure a lot of you can relate to this behaviour, for it is fairly common. Again, it's the old bull fighting for survival and leadership of the pack, with the new bull challenging his dominance scenario. This gives rise to a difference of opinion and creates friction and division, opposing wills that result in suspicion. Reasoning strongly held opinions into context with rationalisation is just not the answer in situations like this, again it's a control issue, give him or her that what they seek, control. Individuals like this practice - coercion - the strict adherence to a literal interpretation of someone's beliefs. They enforced unto someone else, their will, justified as religious and moral. The one with the strongest moral argument or social standing will always win. This disease of ego, denies the relativity of new knowledge, it only believes in a self-scripted truth (mostly that of damnation) for they fail to recognise any other, should one move outside the normative you will find yourself persecuted for being indifferent to the rest. The point is this; we should be doing things out of conviction and not because of it. Because conviction deals merely with a portion of reality in time, and as time changes things change too. Let's draw our conclusions based on knowledge, experience and wisdom that are current and time stamped. Selling strategy is not always easy, but when you ask others that oppose you, to place their ideas on the table, then you get to change the rules and take back the initiative. You get to criticise and ask the right questions and thereby show the weakness and then it is easy to fill them in. Authoritarians are normally good at playing with words, but are not good at thinking strategically; they mostly rely on thinkers to form their perceptions for them. By themselves, they are weak and exploited.

To illustrated this, Han Feizi, as a student, was taught in the Confucian tradition. Because of a problem with stuttering, he did not go the way most wandering philosophers of this age did: making the rounds of kings' courts and making speeches. Instead, he wrote. His book, the Han Feizi, which brought him some prominence during his life and ended up being the main text of the school of Legalism. Han Feizi died because of political intrigue in 233 BC, but Legalism would go on to become the philosophy, which finally managed to unify China.

Legalism holds law as the supreme authority. Stop, what does this have to do with Networking, well everything, one man's beliefs built a whole nations government and structure. There are three components to Legalism: fa (law), shi (legitimacy) and shu (arts of the ruler). Legalism is a political philosophy that does not address higher questions pertaining to the nature and purpose of existence. It is concerned with the most effective way of governing society. The legalist tradition derives from the principle that the best way to control human behaviour is through written law rather than through ritual, custom, or ethics. The two principle sources of Legalist doctrine were the Book of Lord Shang and the Han Fei-tzu.

The Book of Lord Shang teaches that laws are designed to maintain the stability of the state from the people, who are innately selfish and ignorant.

There is no such thing as objective goodness or virtue; it is obedience that is of paramount importance. The Han Fei-tzu advocates a system of laws that enable the ruler to govern efficiently and even ruthlessly. Textbooks apart from law books are useless and rival philosophies such as Moism and Confucianism are dismissed as "vermin". The ruler is to conduct himself with great shrewdness, keeping his ministers and family at a distance and not revealing his intentions. Strong penalties should deter people from committing crime. Legalism is the mortal enemy of healthy self-esteem. No wonder the poor guy got killed, his strategy did not fit in with the current reality. Nevertheless, it was implemented successfully in one of the biggest nations of the world. Therefore, it stands to reason, that one can never have a true faith if one does not test it against all knowledge, living in a stubborn vacuum of ideology robs us of our intrinsic nature to explore our worth. Growth is the process of divulging the fruit's of our exploration, which gives us knowledge and by implementation, we gain wisdom. The point I am trying to make here is this. Do not be set in your ways when trying out new relations and strategy, you will experience resistance. You will come across authoritarians that will take you apart. Realise that forming new networks and coalitions will take time, some are just not meant to be, others will require a total mental make over. The aspect of conflicting personalities will also be experienced, but it is said that the more you practice the better you get. That we can become so unsure of our own programming, that we become in conflict with ourselves is true, we question our very moral fibre and intellectual worth because of interactions with strong willed and charismatic people, therefore, our ethical and principle centres must be stronger when confronted with new ideology. We have to understand others and their radical concepts, in order to grow. We have to evaluate without fear or favour as strategist. However, before we can, we need to find and affirm our own beliefs and anchor them in our faith. Tested and tried wins, when we are ready for new at the core, where it will count most, then our strategic religion will not sway to the tide and break with the force, to become a shattered reality. It is only those that hide behind the relative safety, of ignorance, that creates unsuspecting results – like sheep. Where opposed to the sheep the predators vigilance and cunning, knows what is safe and what is not. His consciousness runs the killing fields of strategy daily with the knowing, that the hunter, can become the hunted. If not knowledgeable of the ever changing landscape of possibility and people ruling it with perception, there will be no safe place.

To illustrate this: In tests done with children at a school, bright kids were ladled in their report cards as deficient learners as part of a study to determine how powerful perception could be, when a new teacher is introduced. The not so bright kids were labelled as bright, even brilliant, in their respective personal profiles that were given to the new teachers to study beforehand. To see what the effect of perception would have on a teacher when applying their trade. The two classes were monitored for a period of one year. The results were remarkable. The bright kids – the really smart ones – labelled as deficient learners had only accomplished average grades. The truly deficient learners had above average grades. In retro analysis, it was found that under close up cross-examination of the teachers and how they taught. That they all had to change their ways in which they taught, in order for them to get "bright" kids to understand the work. This proves that perception is everything, especially when it comes to networking, coalition building and strategy. Therefore, wear a label of professionalism; do not follow in a path of denial and self-doubt it will show, by virtue of our choices and continued programming even in the most sacred of spheres of our life, our religion, we are taught not to doubt. I am very aware of what I read, listen to and how the information is passed on and processed by individuals.

This awareness of "understanding things" are a prerequisite to building good networks, it is a process of learning, learning translates to experience and in turn it translates to wisdom and intimately enlightenment, realise that things are not always as they seem. The enquiring mind has many interesting questions – that merely leads to more and more. That relate to many interesting answers. In addition, that there are more things in heaven than what there are on earth, that should be noted and with concern. This aspect of knowing has brought some of us to a wider insight and understanding of the essence of living, living a life outside the circle of conservative dogmatism and daily routine.

This is the nature of networking, especially strategic networking, where you will find that everyone has an idea of his own, a philosophy, a perception and people share mutually held beliefs and enforce them until it becomes entrenched, even if we are fundamentally different and we stand apart. Universally, many things hold the same truth for everyone. What is a logical strategic deduction to a problem? Solve this dilemma, and find this truth first and then you will be able to sell your strategies to networks, investors and coalitions. Remember the power of perception, is the power of strategy. How we change it and influence, it will determine our gains and losses. This will determine our influence. Pioneers establish dominance by applying a few simple principles that help them influence others.

- *They clearly show the benefits and advantages of their ideas.*
- *They find innovative ways to do and influence others.*
- *They neutralise resistance, preferably in advance* by modelling perception.
- *Listen well to what others are saying, and think critically about it.*
- *Eliminate weak statements from their language, by using concepts.*
- *Create and maintain momentum and rapport.*
- *Keen sense to notice how others respond to change, and address concerns.*
- *Uncover the needs and wants of others, by talking to people.*

Following Patterns

In the very near future, some business economist predict that more business will be applying again, and more intensely the "Principles of War", to keep up with the fast changing strategic landscape and business evolution.

The pattern of evolution and change.

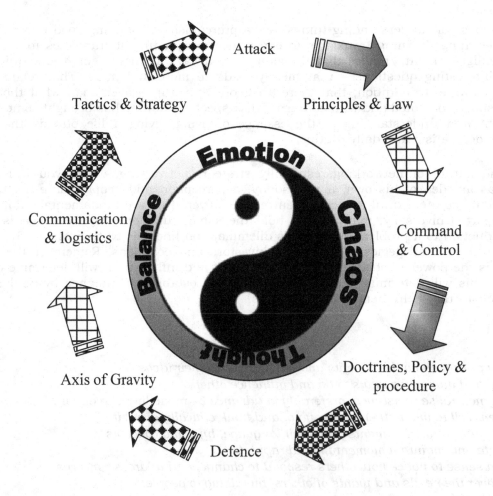

Attack

Tactics & Strategy

Principles & Law

Communication & logistics

Emotion

Chaos

Balance

Thought

Command & Control

Axis of Gravity

Doctrines, Policy & procedure

Defence

We have to start learning from War and what it has on offer, in terms of strategy formulation if we hope to survive in the very near future.

In the very near future, some business economist predict that more business will be applying increasingly more the "Principles of War" - into their business strategy. Reason being; it will become an essential and integral part of how business will be conducted. Principles of War – or, more accurately, principles of war fighting – became the warriors' 'bible,' in every sense of that term. It became the unifying code by which all defined their objective as a union. Principles of War provided direction, doctrine, ideology, and a basis for hope, vision, purpose and salvation – hope for *victory,* and salvation from *defeat.*Those who don't plan strategic, or who plan in a haphazard manner, just won't survive the instability in the economic markets, in the years ahead, as chaos and friction will become a daily phenomenon, that will wreak havoc on cohesion and effort. Just because the world has become a smaller place, with much ambiguity. The speed of change creates both challenges, and opportunities for global markets, that are now fast encroaching on traditional and local markets. Some with well-planned and rehearsed entry strategies are even growing in this unsure climate. Consequently, the lines between local and international markets, are being wiped away slowly but surely. The emphases keeps shifting, from competing for survival and more market share, to staying focused on global as well as local trends. This aspect creates both opportunity and doom, for those who do not realise this. For not only in War does life throw us with a curveball now and again, even in business, thus forcing us to face instant changes never before contemplated. Like large fuel hikes, long power failures and load shedding, natural disasters, global warming, War, migration, and the list goes on. Forcing us to react or go out of business. Where at times a lot rides on just that one decision, plan or strategy. Then, it better be the best we are capable of. Do we find ourselves in this situation, more often than not? Do we have to make decisions that could mean the difference between disaster and success. If so, should we not become totally prepared, and if this is the case focus on our blind spots, and not just on our vision, mission and goals in this regard, and plan accordingly?

Furthermore, far too many companies think that trade and industry laws, governments, well established clients and so forth, will protect them from the effects of globalisation. We can expect to see more stiff competition with huge financial backing and support, entering the local business, and markets in the near future. Even in a down turn economy some companies grow and hit the gaps as they emerge in the market, and filling them. Learning from War and how men perceived it then and now, shows us that one's demise can become the others bread. The history of War draws comparisons to this modern-day corporate business models and trends that we see emerging. Indications are that this aspect of becoming more resilient, is becoming more prevalent, just by utilising the speed of technology and diversification of assets, infrastructure, and resources, companies can now almost move anywhere and be more profitable, if they have the right strategy. Technology today is reliable, portable, and universal, and allows us to reach objectives faster and achieve goals with pin point accuracy. Whilst diversification, combined both on the real world battlefield and in the corporate world, yields the most success, we are still forced to return to make a plan on how to best utilise technology and experience, and make use of "*strategy and tactics*". This very aspect called strategy; defined as the acute study of "things" and defining the governing rules for them could serve us well still, as it did our forefathers studying nature. By taking the time and just going through the selective readings on precepts (a rule, instruction, or principle that guides somebody's actions, especially one that guides moral behaviour) of war and strategy. Then one will realise the relevance of studying actual War doctrines and the philosophy that emerged from it. Philosophy that paved the way to tactics and strategy in War. The only thing that differs is the machine of War and the battlefield, from tanks to delivery trucks and from forests to freeways, apart from that many parallels can be drawn between actual wartime strategy and corporate battles for market segment.

To bring this aspect into a business perspective with assumptions, consider the three grand masters on warfare and see the similarity of their philosophies practiced against the "economics of scale." principle. The **Economies of scale** principle refers to; a reduction in long-run average costs, due to the increase in size of an operating unit. Economics of scale can be internal to a firm (cost reduction due to technological and management factors) or external (a cost reduction due to the effective use of technology in an industry, a drop in inflation, or cheaper labour amounts other things).

In this section we will look how the CEO's of War, "The Three Grand Masters"; **Sun Tzu, Carl von Clausewitz and John Boyd,** all had differing approaches to the philosophy of war. We need to understand that many roads lead to Rome and in strategy likewise, we need to take the route that appeals to our character and strengths.

It has been remarked that; "The three grand masters"; Sun Tzu, Carl von Clausewitz and John Boyd, mastered different ways towards achieving one goal.

Sun Tzu teaches a philosophy on war that is brutally simple.

John Boyd's approach is brutally analytical.

and Carl von Clausewitz philosophy is just plain brutal.

Tzu Sun (544 B.C. - 496 B.C.)

Sun Tzu was born around 544 B.C.E. Almost nothing is known about his life except that he was a Chinese military general who helped the King Ho-lu capture the city of Ying, bringing about the fall of the Ch'u state in 506 B.C.E. From this, Sun Tzu became known throughout the country as a wise and respected leader.

He became renowned for uttering the following truths;

- "All warfare is based on deception,"
- "The supreme art of war is to subdue the enemy without fighting,"
- and "The art of war...is governed by five constant factors...
- The Moral Law; humanity or benevolence;
- Uprightness of mind;
- Self-respect, self-control, or "proper feeling;"
- Wisdom;
- Sincerity or good faith.
- Heaven; signifies night and day, cold and heat, times and seasons.
- Earth; comprises distances, great and small; danger and security; open ground and narrow passes; the chances of life and death.
- The Commander; stands for the virtues of
- Wisdom,
- Sincerity,
- Benevolence- kindness and compassion
- Courage,
- and Strictness.

Method and discipline, are to be understood as the marshalling of the army in its proper subdivisions, the graduations of rank among the officers, the maintenance of roads by which supplies may reach the army and the control of military expenditure.

The understanding the fundamental principles of "War"

The understanding the fundamental principles of "War" will guide us towards accepting the core principles that go into forming the strategies of War. Why do we need to take a few steps back into the past, into Sun Tzu's world? In order to understand the influences that (culture had) Chinese culture in specific - that impacted on Sun Tzu's life and thinking and it lead him in making strategy. Strategy and principles that is still as relevant today as it was then, to understand the importance of organisational culture is to understand forces that influence "War culture" and governing principles that originate from within the organisation.

The importance of understanding and not just contemplating culture and how it influences our guiding principles.

To critically understand; is the human ability to interpret our environment and the prevailing situation with keen observation, to have scripts of the concepts that are visible or unfolding -the ability to predict the course of the river when it starts to rain - to find how this relates to the unique enveloping situation, enhanced by the meaning of this relationship, where the perceived becomes the understood, that becomes reality.

This is the process of critical thinking that starts forming critical understanding – a new way of looking and perceiving, something that escapes the notice of others.

The teachings of - Sun Tzu – took this aspect into account, by applying lateral thinking – creative ways of explaining complexity - that was cognitive - relating to the process of acquiring knowledge by the use of reasoning, intuition, or perception and that made it simple to understand. They dealt with the perceptions of the time; the concepts that peasants understood, the things they had first-hand experience of, that they worked with, these concepts were everyday to them, this connection made it significant in its application. This is what gave these teachings essence. Therefore, concepts that stand in relation to things known and understood, should be used to teach with, to plan with, and to strategise with. Teaching people should be incorporated into all our strategies. People, just don't apply what is known, but what was learned as well; any new hypothesis arrives from fresh knowledge collectively serves as a reference point, towards arriving at the same conclusion with everybody. The time aged wisdom he drew upon, to arrive at the doctrine called "The Art of War" was in essence a simple yet effective approach and this wisdom transferred essential knowledge to common people, that had the need to make sense of strategy, to be taken into account, whenever explaining concepts of a difficult nature. The answers we seek can only be derived from the way people perceived their world influenced from an individual perspective, and their culture. During his time period, teachings were very philosophical in nature, as most people were illiterate and more practical in essence, everything they did related back to the tangible. Symbols were understood to mean something with great impotence. Keep this in mind, I will explain this aspect just now; remember perception is all powerful when devising a strategy, how we define it will be dictated by our own level of proficiency and lateral thinking. However going over to action, requires a violent burst of energy, both mental and even physical. Sharing this world in peace and harmony has never been man's greatest defining attribute, because we are profusely competitive. Only when we throw ourselves into the actual arena do we get a sense of how competitive we are, and do we see how ardently people are set to win, how hard people play and to what extents they will go just to succeed. Transformation is the only way to evolution, mental evolution takes on the same paradigm and sometimes the mind needs to rediscover things for itself, in order to "mature" for life's little battles. The body can be strong, but the mind weak. To be ready for battle, we need to be ready to think, a required level of reasoning and understanding of "concepts" is a prerequisite. This is sometimes termed the process of growing intelligence, the ability to place "things" in the context that relates best to our understanding of what constitutes reality, all these life governing attributes drive men to mental War and back to inner space to contemplate. Such is the nature of thinking and life; it has to suffer death to continue into new life. Things must die, or make space so that others may live, or have space to grow. It is the natural law of evolution and life, depicted within the Yin-Yang diagram

Yin	Yang
Black	White
Cold	Warm
Dark	Light
Empty	Full
Death	Life
Female	Male
Introversion	Extroversion
Moon	Sun
North	South
Passive	Active
Receptive	Creative
Winter	Summer

The Yin-Yang diagram, Also Referred to as "Tao Te Ching". One of the first examples in human history of the age of reasoning, used here to define a moral value system, within a spiritual framework, in an effort towards describing it. This aspect can be seen as the first brain map on strategic thinking, it has cause and effect, influencing balance at the centre.

- Tao meaning – movement, flow ahead, the way or the path – the strategic element of War, " Tao".
- "Te" – is the moral step; "honour" "virtue" or "righteousness". -,
- and "Ching" - as threads following a course of "scripture," "great book," or "doctrine".

Threads can also be seen as the relationship with or between two entities and them coming together forming a union, or entering into one as a concept. Knowing how the people of the time viewed life will give us insight into how they made strategy. This poem is about "The Way". The way to moral living was described in simple terms, straightforward:

The following underline the core principles of the mortal's beliefs in doctrine; in drawing from the simplest forms of life we understand the bigger complexity of it;

- *Force begets force.*
- *One whose needs are simple will find them fulfilled.*
- *Wealth does not enrich the spirit.*
- *Self-interest and self-importance are vain and self-destructive.*
- *Victory in war is not glorious and not to be celebrated, but stems from devastation and is to be mourned.*
- *The harder one tries, the more resistance one will create for oneself.*
- *The more one acts in harmony with the universe (the Mother of the ten thousand things), the more one will achieve, with less effort.*

- *The truly wise make little of their own wisdom—for the more they know, the more they realize how little they know.*
- *When we lose the fundamentals, we supplant them with increasingly inferior values, which we pretend are the true values.*
- *Stupidity leads to force.*
- *The wise are responsible for the foolish.*
- *The honest are responsible for the dishonest.*
- *Glorification of wealth, power and beauty beget crime, envy and shame.*
- *The "feminine" qualities, or "water" qualities, of flexibility and suppleness are superior to "masculine" strength and rigidity.*
- *Everything in its own time and place.*

Accordingly, we seek out wisdom, that creates a set of principles - we can clearly observe that not much has changed since then and now, and all of it still holds firm today. The other aspect is that of creating balance, that is magnified here. Piaget referred to this process as assimilation and accommodation. He viewed it as twin forces that allow individuals to maintain a dynamic cognitive equilibrium. What Boyd refers to as mental images, Piaget calls schemas: mental maps that we construct that aid us in navigating reality. Staying with Sun Tzu and the mental maps that he drew from to create reality, when looking at his belief system, his core values, one can clearly understand how it moved and inspired his thinking. The simple yet effective natural way of describing things to express reality. Let's visit the frames he used and find this golden thread he speaks of, the one thing that everything connects to, termed: **The Ba Qua.**

The Ba Qua – translated ("Ba" –Eight, "Qua" -categories - or code)

In the evolution of all societies, as in business philosophy one will find one trend, once a workable understanding has materialised for accepting things complex it will be developed, in this case the study of nature rendered the Ba Qua.

The next step in evolving this concept was to see how precise this understanding of nature could be formulated and used in strategy. This knowledge became power to be used as the beholder sees fit. Once again, the more fully one understands the detail in things, that which others do not even comprehend, the more predictable the outcome of one's own actions and that of the user will be. Furthermore, the process of making sense of a science or art can most certainly be made to work to the advantage of the one who knows its secrets. This understanding of concepts, formed by units, creating a reference point for themselves and their thinking, creates mutual understanding, and it is this very aspect we strive for in strategy and the purpose of this chapter. The global understanding of all concept/s used and available in the making of strategy is essential. For if we understand history we may predict the future.

Through meticulous observation and study, the Chinese realised that events in nature and even in society were mixtures of Yin and Yang, two opposing forces and not exclusively one force or another. If you read this statement against Sun Tzu's work, it makes perfect sense. It was a unique cultural trait among the Chinese people that they did not dispose of the Yin/Yang theory as flawed when it did not fit every contingency or eventuality they faced. Instead, they accepted the theory of Yin/Yang as a guiding aspect, which deals with the bigger issues from which everything else will logically flow. They have culturally adopted a stance of adapt, improvise and overcome, with Yin/Yang being the departing philosophy, with which they unify and ratify their thinking.

The Chinese started the research of a code to fill the void, it eventually came about to facilitate the extra anomalies of daily life and the inevitable eventualities thereof. Contradictory to modern-day thinking, in all its approaches, the West differs from the East, and so do the South and the North, which deals with theory altogether differently, when a theory is found to be flawed, it will be discredited and discarded in the West. We sometimes forget this aspect.

The West standing is opposed to the stark contrast of Eastern beliefs, where nothing on this earth is new, it is just rediscovered or reborn, new information was a cause for modification and rejuvenation of old theories. Where the East will not discard old theories in totality, just find them a place to fit. Within the new theory, the Yang (male - muscular) influences were represented by a solid line, staked three deep, while the Yin, (female – soft) was represented by a broken line also stacked three deep, implying the one on top of each other. By staggering these bars in varying sequences on top of each other three deep.

The Chinese were able to describe the different degrees of influence as a code and derived certain aspects from the code as if it had a mathematical argument. Strangely enough; and apparently a study was done to find evidence of such a nature within this code, it proved prevalent and accurate, especially when the curvatures of light pattern dynamics were analysed against this code, it was found to be spot on and an accurate representations of computer algorithms and codes...

Exploring -The Chinese world of Opposites:

The Chinese world of opposites has sought to come to a greater understanding of the forces of nature that created and controlled their world, and everything in and around them. This search took them to the frontiers of categorising and analysing events, to create understanding. By looking at those events to see if they could find a common influence, a pattern, as they observed their world through their eyes, and had to make sense of it. They concluded that much of existence could be divided into parts of opposing states yin and yang - as being pairs in one existence. The concept of opposites was born; that heat was the direct opposite of cold, male or female and hard of soft. This concept, presented a way of understanding balance vs. chaos. This conceptualised the theory of cause and effect, which yields the ability to predict phenomena and ultimately the ability to control the outcome.

Extended study affirmed their beliefs in yin-yang and they concluded that placing things into these two categories, was a sound principle, but also studying the inter relationship of these two categories of yin and yang and the significance of their lateral equal but opposite forces and the effects they have on the other. For instance, the seasons changed from Yang forces to Yin in one complete cycle. Likewise, a cooler shady side contrasted the sunny side of a hill.

The other significant thing; Yang and Yin do not just exist as simply opposing forces. This might eliminate each other or cancel each other to balance out. Instead, they concluded that the two forces actually have the propensity to reincarnate each other as they ran through their independent life cycle. Nothing is as it seems, yet everything is constant, yet fluid, hot or cold, it was hot on its way to becoming cold and cold on its way to becoming hot. In modern day, we see that this theory has been extended, it can now be contrasted with the Oscillating Universe theory, which states that the Universe moves inward and outward in repeating creative and destructive cycles. Times of prosperity are not an arrival at some point of the ideal state; instead, it is simply the ascendancy of plenty before the naturally occurring cycle of hardship began.

Likewise, evil and good are not, by implication, two opposing warring forces; they are the outcome of the interchange of all Yin and Yang. The other could destroy neither. Therefore, instead of attempting to eliminate all evil or to create a society of all-good, a balance is sought so that the bad times could be prepared for during the good. That the bad times are sometimes inevitable, so that good may prevail. The result would be a balance of averages.

Sun Tzu did not allow himself to be drawn into over-thinking, and analysing either. All these aspects that life threw at him in a glance and drawing single conclusions of an absolute nature on anyone aspect of combat. Instead, he unpacked it to add value, he broke it down into its simplest forms, yin or yang and got to the very heart of the principles for military success to prevail, time and time again.

The Chinese had learned a lot about the importance of discipline, honour and respect. This came from many wars and they ultimately concluded that in order to justify War one has to remain and achieve balance in all aspects of life, even in war.

Sun Tzu believed that the moral strength and intellectual faculty of man were decisive in war and that if these were properly applied war could be waged with certain success. — *This extract was written by; Brig Gen Samuel B. Griffith, USMC*

Sun Tzu believed in winning, and the ultimate good, but not at any cost, rather he would look for other means and ways to achieve the win. He did not believe in long drawn out campaigns either. His second principle was keeping the initiative; in other words staying in control so that others have to react to you and not you act upon them. Rather you upon them forcing them to stay on the defence, or vulnerable. The last element in his War strategy is not to cause more damage than what is necessary to achieve the win, allowing the enemy to give up and keep face. Let's just look at some of his work:

More on- SUN TZU - ON THE ART OF WAR – principles of strategy:

Translated from the Chinese with introduction and Critical Notes;
BY LIONEL GILES. Snap shots;

Tu Yu says, "not to allow the enemy to cut your communications." In view of Napoleon's dictum, "the secret of War lies in the communications, we could wish that Sun Tzu had done more than skirt the edge of this important subject here. Col. Henderson says: "The line of supply may be said to be as vital to the existence of an army as the heart to the life of a human being. So the commander whose communications are suddenly threatened find s himself in a false position and he will be fortunate if he has not to change all his plans, to split up his force into more or less isolated detachments and to fight with inferior numbers on ground which he has not had time to prepare and where defeat will not be an ordinary failure, but will entail the ruin or surrender of his whole army."

When the common soldiers are too strong and their officers too weak, the result is INSUBORDINATION.

When the officers are too strong and the common soldiers too weak, the result is COLLAPSE. Ts`ao Kung says: "The officers are energetic and want to press on, the common soldiers are feeble and suddenly collapse."

The Radical Revolutionary Strategic Management Matrix For Predators

When the general is weak and without authority; when his orders are not clear and distinct;

Wei Liao Tzu (ch. 4) says: "If the commander gives his orders with decision, the soldiers will not wait to hear them twice; if his moves are made without vacillation, the soldiers will not be in two minds about doing their duty." General Baden-Powell says, italicising the words: "The secret of getting successful work out of your trained men lies in one nutshell--in the clearness of the instructions they receive." . Wu Tzu ch. 3: "the most fatal defect in a military leader is difference; the worst calamities that befall an army arise from hesitation."

The natural formation of the country is the soldier's best ally; a power of estimating the adversary, of controlling the forces of victory and of shrewdly calculating difficulties, dangers and distances, constitutes the test of a great general.

He who knows these things and in fighting puts his knowledge into practice, will win his battles. He who knows them not, nor practices them, will surely be defeated.

If fighting is sure to result in victory, then you must fight, even though the ruler forbid it; if fighting will not result in victory, then you must not fight even at the ruler's bidding.

Regard your soldiers as your children and they will follow you into the deepest valleys; look upon them as your own beloved sons and they will stand by you even unto death.

If, however, you are indulgent, but unable to make your authority felt; kind-hearted, but unable to enforce your commands; and incapable, moreover, of quelling disorder: then your soldiers must be likened to spoilt children; they are useless for any practical purpose.

If we know that the enemy is open to attack and also know that our men are in a condition to attack, but are unaware that the nature of the ground makes fighting impracticable, we have still gone only halfway towards victory.

Hence the experienced soldier, once in motion, is never bewildered; once he has broken camp, he is never at a loss. The reason being, according to Tu Mu, that he has taken his measures so thoroughly as to ensure victory beforehand. "He does not move recklessly," says Chang Yu, "so that when he does move, he makes no mistakes."

Hence the saying: If you know the enemy and know yourself, your victory will not stand in doubt; if you know Heaven and know Earth, you may make your victory complete. Li Ch'uan sums up as follows: "Given a knowledge of three things--the affairs of men, the seasons of heaven and the natural advantages of earth--, victory will invariably crown your battles."

Karl von Clausewitz (1780-1831)

Born into a poor but middle-class family, Clausewitz entered the Prussian Army in 1792. During his formative years in Berlin, Clausewitz learned military science under the guidance of his mentor, Gerhard von Scharnhorst, studied philosophy and literature and developed his basic strategic concepts.

Before Clausewitz left Prussia in 1812 to join the Russian army and resist Napoleon, he prepared an essay on War to leave with the sixteen year-old Prussian Crown Prince Friedrich Wilhelm (later King Friedrich Wilhelm IV, r.1840-1858), whose military tutor he had become in 1810. This essay called "The most important principles of the art of War". Clausewitz's On War is a mammoth piece of work that he wrote to educate the Prussian Crown Prince in the art of War. The work that is difficult to follow, Clausewitz composition stretches over 600 pages of intrigues and contradictions, his concept of throwing the mass against the centre of gravity, creating a hole and punching through it was well used.

The German panzer division utilised the same strategy in world War two. Under Col. Von Mellenthin and Field Marshal Rommel and it was named "Blitzkrieg". Very effective, against the strategic intent of large column advancing, the aim is to find the weakest column and that will be the joint that needs to be broken, like the elbow, if you break the front in one strategic place the rest of the arm will be rendered useless. Niccolo Machiavelli; Clausewitz other mentor described strategy as the planning of a whole campaign and tactics as the planning of a single battle.

In Clausewitz's theory, all military strategy is part of the larger political pattern. All the nation's resources are summoned to the task of attaining the political objective of the War; this is known as the "Grand Strategy". *His* descriptions and ideas on the concept of centres of gravity remains the subject of modern warfare and especially taught in the subject of mobility.

Sun Tzu's; more elegant concept of attacking the enemy's strategy. It is also contrary to Boyd's theory of overpowering the enemy by first outthinking and finally outmanoeuvring him, to Clausewitz, there is no action - no strategy or tactic - that cannot be undone by prompt counteraction. The problem lies in seeing through "the fog of war" and in overcoming its frictions

"War is the continuation of policy (politics) by other means." Alternatively, "It is clear that war is not a mere act of policy but a true political instrument, a continuation of political activity by other means"

Von Clausewitz once observed that battle is riddled with frictions: changing episodes that introduce uncertainty and doubt into the best-laid plans. "Is there any lubricant that will reduce this abrasion?" he asked. "Only one," was his answer. "Combat experience." I have condensed his work to just give us some insight into his teachings.

His –Principles of War

The theory of warfare tries to discover how we may gain a hold of physical forces and material advantages at the decisive point. As this is not always possible, theory also teaches us to calculate moral factors: the likely mistakes of the enemy, the impression created by a daring action, yes, even our own desperation. We should think very frequently of the most dangerous of these situations and familiarise ourselves with it. Only thus shall we reach heroic decisions based on reason, which no critic can ever shake.

Therefore, even when the likelihood of success is against us, we must not think of our undertaking as unreasonable or impossible; for it is always reasonable, if we do not know of anything better to do and if we make the best use of the few means at our disposal. We must never lack calmness and firmness.

"We must never lack the calmness and firmness of conviction."

Mother Teresa was once quoted in this regard as saying; "We, the unwilling, led by the unknowing, are doing the impossible for the ungrateful. We have done so much for so long, with so long, with so little, we are now qualified to do anything with nothing!"

His - Tactics and strategy

War is a combination of many distinct engagements... For only a combination of successful engagements can lead to good results.

I. General Principles for Defence

To keep our troops covered as long as possible. Since we are always open to attack, the enemy, while attacking one section of the front, often seeks to outflank and envelop us at the same time.

A fundamental principle is never to remain completely passive, but to attack the enemy frontally and from the flanks, even while he is attacking us. At those points where we remain passive, we must make use of the art of fortification.

If you remember, the few defensive battles that have ever been won, you will find that the best of them have been conducted in the spirit of the principles voiced here. For it is the study of the history of war which has given us these principles. Just as on the defensive, we should choose as the object of our offensive that section of the enemy's army whose defeat will give us decisive advantages.

The concerted attacks of the divisions and army corps should not be obtained by trying to direct them from a central point, so that they maintain contact and even align themselves on each other, though they may be far apart or even separated by the enemy. This is a faulty method of bringing about co-operation, open to a thousand mischance's. Nothing great can be achieved with it and we are certain to be thoroughly beaten by a strong opponent.

The true method consists in giving each commander of an army corps or a division the main direction of his march and in pointing out the enemy as the objective and victory as the goal.

Each commander of a column, therefore, has the order to attack the enemy wherever he may find him and to do so with all his strength. He must not be made responsible for the success of his attack, for that would lead to indecision. However, he is responsible for seeing that his corps will take part in battle with all its energy and with a spirit of self-sacrifice.

We therefore assure the co-operation of all forces by giving each corps a certain amount of independence, but seeing to it, that each seeks out the enemy and attacks him with all possible self- sacrifice.

STRATEGY

This term means the combination of individual engagements to attain the goal of the campaign or war.

If we know how to fight and how to win, little more knowledge is needed. For it is easy to combine fortunate results. It is merely a matter of experienced judgment that does not depend on special knowledge, as does the direction of battle.

The few principles, therefore, which come up in this connection and which depend primarily on the condition of the respective states and armies, can in their essential parts be very briefly summarized:

General Principles

Warfare has three main objectives:

(a) To conquer and destroy the armed power of the enemy;

(b) To take possession of his material and other sources of strength and

(c) To gain public opinion.

To accomplish the first purpose, we should always direct our principle operation against the main body of the enemy army or at least against an important portion of his forces. For only after defeating these can we pursue the other two objects successfully. In order to seize the enemy's material forces we should direct our operations against the places where most of these resources are concentrated: principle cities, storehouses and large fortresses.

On the way to these objectives, we shall encounter the enemy's main force or at least a considerable part of it. *Public opinion is won through great victories* and the occupation of the enemy's capital.

1. The first and most important rule to observe in order to accomplish these purposes is *to use our entire forces with the utmost energy*. Any moderation shown would leave us short of our aim. Even with everything in our favour, we should be unwise not to make the greatest effort in order to make the result perfectly certain. For such effort can never produce negative results. Suppose the country suffers greatly from this, no lasting disadvantage will arise; for *the greater the effort, the sooner the suffering will cease. The moral impression created by these actions is of infinite importance. They make everyone confident of success, which is the best means for suddenly raising the nation's morale.*
2. The second rule is to concentrate our power as much as possible against that section where the chief blows are to be delivered and to incur disadvantages elsewhere, so that our chances of success may increase at the decisive point. This will compensate for all other disadvantages.
3. *The third rule is never to waste time. Unless important advantages are to be gained from hesitation, it is necessary to set to work at once.* By this speed, a hundred enemy measures are nipped in the bud and public opinion is won most rapidly. *Surprise plays a much greater role in strategy than in tactics. It is the most important element of victory.* Napoleon, Frederick II, Gustavus Adolphus, Caesar, Hannibal and Alexander owe the brightest rays of their fame to their swiftness.

Finally, the fourth rule is to *follow up our successes with the utmost energy*. Only pursuit of the beaten enemy gives the fruit's of victory.

This is referred to as –"TAPS" – Tactics, Accuracy, Power, Speed...

The application of tactics, strategy and principles in times of war – shortened version of Von Clausewitz on war - edited.

Von Clausewitz believed that the principles of the art of war are in themselves extremely simple and quite within the reach of sound common sense. Even though they require greater specialised knowledge in the thing called tactics, rather than in strategy. Extensive knowledge and deep learning are by no means necessary, nor are extraordinary intellectual faculties and or qualifications. If, in addition to good experienced judgment, we need nothing more than cunning or shrewdness. This confirms, that any man or woman, can be strategically minded, and be better that a well-trained tactician.

For a long time the contrary has been maintained, that only schooled and educated men could master strategy, because of false reverence either for the subject or because of the vanity of the authors who have written about it? Only experience makes this conviction in the essence and prerequisite of strategy and tactics stronger. Many men who proved themselves able leaders, and businessmen, yes of the first order, have never had any formal business education.

The conduct of strategy itself is without doubt very difficult. However, the difficulty is not that education and great genius are necessary to understand the basic principles of strategy and tactics. *These principles are within the reach of any well-organised mind and thinking mind, which is unprejudiced and not entirely unfamiliar with the subject.* Even the application of these principles on maps or on paper presents no difficulty and to have devised a good plan of operations is no great masterpiece. The great difficulty is this:

-*To remain faithful to whom you are throughout to the principles and tactics we have laid down for ourselves- and still achieve greatness*

What free will gave to us as thinking, riddles the mind of the strategist with conflict, therefore, he finds himself constantly held back, by conflicting thought is a thinker, and one needs a remarkable strength of mind and soul to overcome this inner resistance to act. Many good ideas have perished because of this friction. It may be impossible to spell out meticulously the causes of this friction; but the main ones are as follows:

1. Generally we are not nearly as well acquainted with the position and measures of the task as we assume in our own plan of operations. The minute we begin carrying out our decision, a thousand doubts arise about the dangers, which might develop if we have been seriously mistaken in our plan. A feeling of uneasiness, which often takes hold of a person about to perform something great, will take possession of us and from this uneasiness to indecision and from there to half measures are small, scarcely visible steps.

2. Not only are we uncertain about the strength of the plan, but also in addition rumour (i.e., all the news which we obtain from outposts, through spies, or by accident) exaggerates his size. The majority of people are timid by nature and that is why they constantly inflate danger. All

influences on the military leader, therefore, combine to give him a false impression of his opponent's strength and from this arises a new source of indecisiveness.

We cannot take this uncertainty too seriously, nor discard it totally, and it is important to be prepared for it from the beginning.

After we have thought out everything carefully, in advance, and have sought and found without being to prejudice the most plausible plan, we must not be ready to abandon it at the slightest provocation. On the contrary, we must be prepared to submit the reports, which reach us to careful criticism; we must compare them with each other and send out for more. In this way, false reports are very often disproved immediately and the first reports confirmed.

In both cases, we gain certainty and can make our decision accordingly. Should this certainty be lacking, we must tell ourselves that nothing is accomplished in life without daring. That the nature of life, certainly does not let us see at all times where we are going; that what is probable will always be probable though at the moment it may not seem so; and finally, that we cannot be readily ruined by a single error, if we have made reasonable preparations.

We must, therefore be confident that the general measures we have adopted will produce the results we expect. Most important in this connection is the trust, which we must have in our lieutenants. Consequently, it is important to choose men on whom we can rely and to put aside all other considerations. If we have made appropriate preparations, taking into account all possible misfortunes, so that we shall not be lost immediately if they occur, we must boldly advance into the shadows of uncertainty. If we wage war with all our strength, our subordinate commanders and even our troops (especially if they are not used to warfare) we will frequently encounter difficulties, which they may declare insurmountable. They find the march too long, the fatigue too great, the provisions inadequate. If we lend our ear to all these DIFFICULTIES, as Frederick II called them, we shall soon succumb completely and instead of acting with force and determination, we shall be reduced to weakness and inactivity.

The influence of a strong-willed leader over his troops, the limitless effort to which his strength of will, not to say his harshness, forced people, was crowned with success. He at least retreated later than anyone else would have. Most of the time, the enemy army is in the same position. However, while we do not see the condition of the enemy, our own is right before our eyes. The latter, therefore, makes a greater impression on ordinary people than the first, since sensuous impressions are stronger for such people than the language of reason.

A general, who with tyrannical authority demands of his troops the most extreme exertions and the greatest privations and an army which in the course of long wars has become hardened to such sacrifices will have a tremendous advantage over their adversaries and will reach their aim much faster in spite of all obstacles. With equally good plans, what a difference of result!

We cannot stress the following too much:

Visual impressions gained during actual combat are more vivid than those gained beforehand by mature reflection. Nevertheless, they give us only the outward appearance of things, which, as we know, rarely corresponds to their essence. We therefore run the risk of sacrificing mature reflection for first impression.

The natural timidity of human's, which sees only one side to everything, makes this first impression incline toward fear and exaggerated caution.

Therefore, we must fortify ourselves against this impression and have blind faith in the results of our own earlier reflections, in order to strengthen ourselves against the weakening impressions of the moment.

These difficulties, therefore, demand confidence and firmness of conviction. That is why the study of military history is so important, for it makes us see things as they are and as they function. The principles which we can learn from theoretical instruction are only suited to facilitate this study and to call our attention to the most important elements in the history of war. Therefore, we must become acquainted with these principles in order to check them against the history of war, to see whether they are in agreement with it and to discover where they are corrected or even contradicted by the course of events.

In addition, only the study of military history is capable of giving those who have no experience of their own a clear impression of what I have just called the friction of the whole machine.

Of course, we must not be satisfied with its main conclusions and still less with the reasoning of historians, but we must penetrate as deeply as possible into the details. The detailed knowledge of a few individual engagements is more useful than the general knowledge of a great many campaigns. It is therefore more useful to read detailed accounts and diaries than regular works of history.

It proves that the influence of good principles, which never manifests itself as often as we expect, can suddenly reappear, even under the most unfortunate circumstances and when we have already given up hope of their influence. We must not give up hope until the last moment. A powerful emotion must stimulate the great ability of a military leader, whether it be ambition as in Caesar, hatred of the enemy as in Hannibal, or the pride in a glorious defeat, as in Frederick the Great. Open your heart to such emotion. Be audacious and cunning in your plans, firm and persevering in their execution, determined to find a glorious end and fate will crown your youthful brow with a shining glory, which is the ornament of princes and engrave your image in the hearts of your last descendants.

Napoleon has said that in war the moral element is to all others as three is to one. -

Moreover, as du Picq impressively demonstrates, while all other circumstances change with time, the human element remains the same, capable of just so much endurance, sacrifice, effort and no more. Thus, from Caesar to Foch, the essential factor in strategy is the human element, it remains the same in war as in strategy - and endures untouched.

John Boyed

"Machines don't fight wars, terrain doesn't fight wars. Human's fight wars. *You must get into the mind of human's. That is where the battles are won*". – J Boyed.

John Boyd, the great U.S. Air Force fighter pilot, believed to be the father of "dog fighting" as aviation engineer and tutor, he studied Sun Tzu and came to the conclusion that he, agrees with Sun Tzu - but Boyed was an analyst in heart and mind and seek to understand why?

Boyd, could also be describe as military philosopher, he was a scholar of what is known as epistemology: The How We Know What We Know type of science. Boyd described on several occasions his views on battle and the process of understanding it, he defined it as the process of creation and destruction. From Sun Tzu's work and Chinese beliefs he also equated creation with synthesis and destruction with the process of analysis. He coined the phrase; "This requires *mental agility* " and went on to describe it as a process of reaching across a spectrum of many perspectives. By looking at things from many vantage points – and then analysing each and everyone apart as it is prevalent in the equation by a process of analysis called the OODA loop, all the while intuitively looking for those parts of the disassembled perspectives which naturally interconnect with one another to form a higher order. This process has also been termed unpacking, a more general elaboration (synthesis) of what is taking place." To ascertain this agility of mind one needs to take the mind to the mental gym, for any Superior performance and mental agility is only cultivated through intensive rehearsal under simulated conditions that induce stress and that is a race against time, preferable done under pressure. By close matching the simulations to the most realistic level of reality, aircraft pilots are compelled to do a lot of simulator work during their careers to subconsciously imprint correct reaction to a stimulus of danger in simulators. Facing these scenarios repeatedly tightens the loops and allows for rapid almost automated execution and decision making potential. Socrates was right when he said, "We are what we repeatedly do. Excellence, then, is a habit." John Boyd went on and said. : "The race is not always to the swift or the battle to the strong, but that's the way the smart money bets." If the one side presented the other with a sudden, unexpected challenge or series of challenges to which the other side could not adjust effectively to counter such a threat in a timely manner. (What the losing side generally cannot do is move quickly in response to unexpected threats and opportunities due to its general un-preparedness). As a result, the side with the slower response was defeated and it was often defeated at a small cost to the victor. Moreover, the losing side was frequently materially stronger than the winner was. (The reason being that it does not have the corporate cultural characteristics required to do so, qualities John Boyd stressed such as decentralization, initiative and the tolerance for making mistakes that must accompany the growth of initiative, trust up and down the chain of command and reliance on self-discipline rather than imposed discipline.) I would also add that in many real-time competitions, the frame of mind is extremely important, as is moral. Winners have the right frame of mind, the mental vigilance like the Sheepdog and the flexibility of mind. In battle, this means physical, moral and intellectual courage. In business, it means the will to win, to grow to succeed another of John Boyd's most important contributions to military theory was his observation that war is waged at three levels, the physical, the mental and the moral. The physical level is the weakest and the moral level is the strongest, with the mental in between. Now the hard part comes. Remember, these three levels have to work in harmony. If we come across as the bully, pushing everyone else around, it isn't going to work, we're going to lose at the moral level and then we will lose at the mental and physical levels too.

Moving on to: Centres of Gravity in Joint and Service Doctrine

Clausewitz: *On War*, Theory & Centres of Gravity

Although our intellect always longs for clarity and certain, our nature often finds uncertainty fascinating. It prefers to daydream in the realms of chance and luck rather than accompany the intellect on its narrow and torturous path of philosophical enquiry and logical deduction only to arrive hardly knowing how in unfamiliar surroundings where all the usual landmarks seemed to have disappeared.

The concept of centre of gravity is perhaps the most critical element of operational and strategic warfare. By definition it means: "Stating that centres of gravity were not moral or physical forces themselves, but merely characteristics, capabilities, or locations." – by other definition and interpretation: The German "Schwerpunkt" and South African "Swaartepunt" – Direct translations favour a better description, it translates to the weakest links, points and vulnerabilities. No plan for a campaign or major operation can be executed quickly and decisively without identifying the enemy and friendly centres of gravity and properly applying combat power to degrade, destroy, neutralise, or protect them. This aspect is also a double edged cutting sword, let me explain; Napoleon described the centre of gravity as the weak point and went on to explain; the offensive should be aimed at the enemies weakest point. But where a point is obviously weak, this is usually because it is remote from any nerve or vital centre, or because it is deliberately left weak to draw the assailant into a trap... It is clearly suggested that what Napoleon meant was not point but joint...a joint however, is both vital and vulnerable...Attacking true vulnerability then by identifying a joint, is the key idea of centre of gravity, it's breaking a joint so that the arm leg neck or hand does not function any more, but an attack could be done in stages to totally immobilize the effort by attacking joint by joint or by moving on several joints simultaneously.

By exploiting several centres of gravity simultaneously, the enemy can be quickly thrown off balance.

The principle of Boyd's loop; he felt that the side which was able to get ahead of their enemy's thought process firstly by either acting or moving the faster, will be getting "inside" their OODA loop (Of Observation, Orientation, Decision, Act). Thus shortening the time line on their cycle opposed to the time line on the adversary's cycle would enjoy a distinct advantage. If one party is quicker at accomplishing the four parts of the loop relative to the goals on the battlefield, the other party is forced into a mode of ever increasing reaction time.

Causing imbalance and a loss of initiative, the one that leads is the one that dictates, thus with every continued cycle causing more and more confusion and desperation and breaking cohesion and the will to fight. The quicker thinking and acting aggressor is able to dictate the action by his own accord and can thus institute secondary loop at secondary objectives and centres of gravity, which will throw the adversary off-balance. As they attempt to counter one move, the aggressor comes with another and yet another, requiring increasingly defensive reaction. The result is a rapidly deteriorating position for the party whose OODA loop has been penetrated.

Clausewitz's concepts in the development of sound strategic campaign plans and firm operational focus support the ability of the concept to serve as a basis for effects based operations. "Theory is meant to educate the mind of the future commander, or more accurately, to guide him in his self-education, not to accompany him to the battlefield." theories are similar to his description of war in that they are a "true chameleon that slightly adapts its characteristics to the given case." Campaign design and sound operational planning, based on the concept of centre of gravity were and remain fundamentals of relevance and utility is the basis for the successful development and execution of any campaign or strategy. Armed with this as background, our operational focus and focal point for intelligence gathering and the underpinnings of the emerging concept and how to counter or ascertain them, will be the focus of effects based tactics.

Tactics and strategy;

What is "Effects Based Operations strategy" (EBO) and the 7 Pillars of Gravity

The concept of effects base strategy is a warring strategy that attacks the competitions centre points of gravity. In business, gravity refers to focal points/goals and objectives that unify strategic efforts towards achieving a specific goal. With EBO, we utilising several different strategies combined to reach our ultimate objective, we are focused on specifics, that create gravity – pulling all our efforts to the same point. One of the fundamental tenets of EBO is the ability to have simultaneous application of strategies, by different actors, utilising dissimilar tactics across each level of competition. Only focused on one overarching objective, uninhibited by; geography, ambiguity, artificial restrictions, competition and contradictions... Totally focused on how to create a huge effect with the least amount of effort from each actor. That in turn creates an impression of colossal unified action. With the main aim, of producing in the minds of people who sees, hears, or reads something about it, a strong alternative perception. Especially one that is deliberately intended or engineered to change a current perception or paradigm. Prepared with calculated execution and assessment that focuses on predicting and assessing what physical, and emotional actions combined will produce the desired behavioural effects to gain control over an adversary if we can succeed in influencing their perception – that will evoke actions that will lead to change. Physical actions - where the organisation is viewed as a solid structure, resting on pillars in the physical form. The pillars are its legs, that have to conform to the laws of gravity. That combined serves as the foundation of an organisation on which it rests, we can; shake, unbalance, break or topple and organisation if we can identify and understand their pillars and find their centre points of gravity to destroy it so to speak. With precision enabled parallel attacks against all systems virtually simultaneously. Consequently and simply put these are like the legs on a spider. By pinning down one leg, we arrest him, by breaking two or three we cripple him. By breaking five or more we incapacitate him, or throw him off balance, so let's just focus on an example of an acceptable area of competition to apply this strategy too. With advertising and marketing campaigns, our tactics must change and be more diversified; we must be viewing the competition as a system, selling their strong points. If we have to play catch-up then we are behind in the OODA loop, then we will find ourselves in head on contest if we play on their terms, by following their paradigm, they are in effect dictating the conditions. If and when you find yourself in this situation, then you do not have the initiative anymore. Nevertheless, by viewing the competition as a system, we get a much better idea of how they structured themselves for success, opposed to looking at it as a concept. By understanding any design, we get insight into its cardinal parts, which gives us a much better chance of forcing or inducing him to make our objectives his objectives and in doing, we have spent the minimum effort. We will gain the maximum chance of success, that is to say if succeed in taking away the initiative from them with our counter strategy. This works in two ways. The first focus is on isolating the leadership elements ability to command and control their system, by disrupting his systems, and then secondly to force the organisation into moral collapse, by making it seem vulnerable and ineffective. Whether we like it or not, strategy is a conflict of interest and minds. If we view EBO as the marriage of means with ends, then EBO becomes strategy making taken to the next level, more sophisticated in its approach. It becomes a tool, to fight off attacks on our systems and own strategy, a counter measure of sorts. The thinking behind it, is on shaping the behaviour of the adversary. EBO resonates with the ideas of prominent strategic thinkers in history like Sun Tzu and Carl von Clausewitz. These commanders realised and emphasised the importance of incorporating the psychological aspects of effect, into strategy, to the extent that physical action alone may not be enough to overcome an aggressor. We must by all means try to gain the psychological advantage, rather than having to achieve a physical objective only. Strategy as a norm, refers only to the definitive action-plan designed by an organisation. Its main aim is moving towards accomplishing long-term goals only. Strategy can no longer survive in this vacuum of residing only with the upper echelon of management. Where it only consists of sets of objectives, decision-making patterns, policies and procedures. Organisations need to strategise for optimal utilisation of resources, systems need to be complimented as and when needed, with immediate intervention - daily. For example, the traditional marketing strategy is the co-ordination and control of the four "P's" of marketing towards efficiently realising the marketing goals. The four Ps of marketing are **P**roduct, **P**rice, **P**romotion, and **P**lace. This is old school, the dynamics and volatility of marketing trends are no longer just physical concepts, and supported and driven by planning, we have seen some new and unique developments in marketing strategy and its development. By evaluating the natural marketing approach taught at business school, we find patterns emerging, where everything is done in phases or in step. We have to restructure and analyse inner and outer influence on the business environment, in order to understand what is attributes that are key selling points, and this develops the ability to forecast markets and predict future trends, and price. The fluctuation of pricing will become a standard phenomenon, where goods can become cheaper the one week, and then more expensive the next, depending on the markets. Therefore **P**ricing has been changed as a constant. If the stock market is showing a downwards movement, hold back production / buy and push **P**romotion, and down the price, for example, if it is showing an upwards trend, or seasonal events are in the cycle, like Christmas, then we push production and throw out specials, and up the price – we vary our marketing and advertising, as well as pricing scheme the same as seasons do. The bureaucratic school of conventional wisdom teaches us, to take conventional routes here; just place the add, fix the price and see what happens etc. Instead matrix strategy teaches us to be flexible in our approaches, we are taught to first look at the competition holistically, and then to position ourselves in the pecking order to see how "well we are positioned" in terms of targeting our target audience; with our campaign, our processes, our pricing and our ability to render quality service. You just have to find what the key initiating factor is that makes people buy, and run with it. These are the physical attributes. Today we have to mimic "success" – or the perception of things – in order to have greater market impact and value if we want to satisfy peoples "wants" as well, than just focusing on the product or service we are actually selling. We have to be able to distinguish what is actually selling the product. The effect that we have, the perception we create, the "want" we realise, the price, the quality, the service or the actual "need". We have to identify our product or service-enabling characteristics...are they satisfying peoples "wants" or "needs"? the point is this, all people have "needs", however once they are all satisfied, then they have "wants". You need a headache pill, but you want a beer. Two totally different emotional effects, that motivate us to get it. Therefore almost everything we sell, is either product or customer based and orientated. By incorporating the effect based strategy we are now not just only reviewing our objectives, we are also seeing where and how we can alter our competitors objectives and our own. Strategy is always opposed, in way or the other. Where we find it opposed by other, we have to give it the teeth it requires to chew through our oppositions counter strategy and survive. In order to attain this insight and focus to formulate a duel prong strategy; one that drives us, and one that protects us, one must eliminate the "fog of war" – first, (that which we cannot see, that which we do not know). Then the "friction" – (the resistance encountered at the centre point of gravity, our ideology – our culture and paradigm). Friction is caused by two opposing warring ideas at the point where it causes inner conflict when reflecting and contemplating these aspects. The aspects of morale, ethical and non-physical fair competition, and on means to support our own physical requirements of our systems, opposed to sharing it with that of "adversaries system", as a second dilemma. Because entities that become actors, be they, individuals, industrial or commercial organisations are heavily dependent on physical means, and information. More predictable and quantifiable information can be obtained by simply analysing the physical factors of any strategy. Physical means can be determined and analysed, to determine the risk and potential of every action contemplated. How?

With the -**The Seven Pillars of Gravity** -

"The Seven Pillars of Gravity" define the physical and abstract nature of our adversaries.

Strength and weakness, both physical and abstract, are mixtures of Yin and Yang. Where nothing remains stagnant, where strong becomes weaker, and weak becomes stronger in changing cycles. Where strength and weakness is brought about by influences. Then it stands to reason that we can influence things, to either make them stronger or weaker. By linking certain common attributes of business design to concepts, we can create models of any contemplated aspect of company design and relate it back to a physical form, to see where it is strong and weak. Then, by identifying and studying their objectives, we will be able to get a better idea of what is their strategy is all about, identifying their abstracts of reasoning, where are they hoping to go with it and what are they doing both right and wrong to get there. The picture becomes clear, then the abstracts of their strategy becomes concrete and factual to us. We deal better on factual basis as opposed to hypotheses and assumptions with finding solutions. We have now successfully identified the two crucial aspects of disseminating a design, and defined the physical and abstracts strengths and weakness of the adversary. Remember, every strategic aim consists of commonalities; the vision, mission and objectives. However, these attributes of strategy conceal the tactics used, it does not define the actual flow and direction for us, where one objective can become several objectives with smaller goals, that requires "things" in order to work. We can influence thought and the abstract of it, but we can create or destroy physical means. With strategy, something's are physical, clearly observable and tangible, and other things are of abstract nature – mainly referring to reasoning, culture, paradigms etc... Combined they form the organisation and its purpose. However, what they all require is a vehicle to bring them into effect, and that vehicle is systems. Systems need things and people to operate, so that makes them the perfect target, for it is the weakest, as it is the most reliant and vulnerable to change, influence and its dependencies. Where abstracts - their "objectives"- are seen as essential forces of strategy that cause "gravity" – weakness - because they need things to survive too, and they could exhaust resources and place burdens on systems. Objectives, with sub-ordinates, causes a polarity, that impacts on other parallel objectives, that impact on the total system at some point or stage. If unchecked it could cause failure, bottlenecks, or total systems collapse. Therefore, if we target certain main objectives and systems, we can cause the strategy and the organisation to fail. In order to achieve success in business one must achieve objectives and goals consistently and well. If we want to succeed whilst gaining momentum, we have to find ways to minimise risk and weakness, thus eliminate gravity, by closing the door on our competition, and as we do, we will gain some better competitive advantages. Our focus as organisation must shift to our ability to sustain systems, the ability to change objectives, and create situations that causes friction for the opposition, and not us, where the competitions system becomes stuck, or weak, because of the pressure we are exerting on them because of our strategy. By making them adhere to our tactics, then we can create and dictate the trend, either by destroying, or depriving them of their ability to stop us. This is also known as manoeuvring. In order to obtain this objective, we focus on physical means first, to understand what they are, and how are they structured to form the organisation. We can employ the *7 pillars of gravity model*, to serve as the focus point of efforts in planning our EBO. This gives us an ideal three-dimensional model of our radical strategy and that of the opposition, we are not designing strategy in a silo. By having analysed the physical attributes of the adversary, we take that data and deposit it into our model. Anything that can function on its own and is free and able to make decisions, as to where it will go and what it will do, has a determinable character, with attributes, like an organism, that leaves an influence and signature in its habitat. Depriving an organisation of its physical means, or distorting its gravity – making it weaker where it is weak already - won't always stop it, but a mix of both will, combined. Having defined the opponents systems attributes – then pillars emerge, it then gets broken down into the seven pillars.

The first Pillar is the core or leadership. - Here we build up a profile of who the leaders are, how they makes decisions, and how they get influenced. Their individual character traits, are they emotional, conservative, echo centric, or bureaucratic decision makers. If we ask the right questions we get the right answers. By finding opposing forces, like we saw in the yin yang model, we can draw many conclusions and assumptions. Chief executive officers leave trails and we can interview people to ascertain more information about them, providing us with a clear view of the brain behind the strategic direction, the guidance and control over the entire system. Breaking one finger, will render a hand useless. We don't want to take on the whole organisation just their weakest links. If we identify that their command and control element is it, then that is where we will focus on. "It and it alone is absolutely essential in the sense that there can be no substitute for command and control, and without the brain the body becomes useless, even though technically alive, it is no longer operating at the strategic level." The organising portion of the entities possesses will stall, the ability to decides the who, what, where, when and how, will become severed and useless. Direction and movement will depend greatly on the influence of the "head".

The Second Pillar is called organic essentials or physical means. - liken to food and oxygen for humans. Things that we cannot live without. Logistics; Service Providers, Manufactures, Transport grids, Warehousing, Transportation and Suppliers. The organisations life blood, where the heart and lungs pump blood and air as organic essentials without which, "the brain cannot perform its strategic function." Organic essentials are not of equal importance to the brain because, "a heart without a brain, is a very expensive, complex pump without meaning or ability to act or effect." We could start buying stock from the same supplier and be willing to pay more should he agree to only supply to us for the next year, exclusivity contracts, sole supplier mandates, this could include buying out the transportation contractor of our opposition and using them for other contracts that we have negotiated. Offering better services to his suppliers, buy buying bulk materials and selling the over flow to other suppliers. In short, everything that the businesses requires or are reliant on to function, as its support systems and life lines, is viewed here.

The third Pillar is the infrastructure or bones. - Blood vessels and muscles, they are important but we can adopt work-around capabilities to enable us to function without them. Infrastructure can move the organic essentials and support the brain but the body can exist without them. By spreading your vulnerability across a wide front by decentralising and flattening your organisational structure as a first step, you will in essence be out designing your competition. Here we focus on structural design and how to change the nature of the skeleton, of the beast. By streamlining structure, we will be speeding up and will produce faster turnaround times...The other aspect is a foot can compete with a foot and a hand with a hand, so do not try to break a market by introducing a structure that will not fit. Partnerships are not off the cards here as well, many big monopolies do this, they merely trade under different brand names but in essence all the working parts are the exact same thing, it is just the designs and interfaces that have changed. The customers are happy and high quality goods are under mass production, bring down prices so the same two seemingly competitors are flooding a market with high quality goods that their competitors just cannot match.

The fourth Pillar is population, cells. - The human capital and corporate culture they have -a human body can lose a substantial amount of cells (people) and continue to function effectively, we need to find out if this will hold true here as well. Is this organisation held together by, ethics and feelings of job security, loyalty and or financial gains for hard work, performance orientated.... If not what is the glue? What holds it together during hard and difficult times? Do a SWAT analysis, of the competitor.

The fifth pillar is the defensive mechanism. - That forms the protective ability of the organism to defend itself – its immune system. The interconnectivity of the human element with the systems and the set of subsystems, what type of interfaces and communication systems, protocols and policy within each pillar is seen to be fundamentally strong or weak, viewed as parts of the system, a microcosm of the larger entity. To relate this aspect of the human body model, how would a weak heart effect the system, how would an injury to the structure affect that organ, (if the chief designer were to resign) or the total loss of one part of the system, would it have a significant impact on the remaining parts.

The Sixth Pillar is understanding their strategy and design. – By taking these two ideas of interconnectivity and its effects, and interlocking them – how well are they aligned with their strategy – perfect, or asymmetrical. We create a model, which provides planners and strategist with the ability to examine the adversary as a system within a strategy, because it (the model) "tells us what detailed questions to ask and it suggests a priority for the questions that should follow". It is believed that the commander is at the heart of the strategy centre; the next pillar includes the organic essentials, or logistics. Lines of communications; the command and control structure, its interlocking networks that form the infrastructure or third pillar. Support staffs form the fourth pillar and the influences form the fifth pillar, is an applicable tool for campaign design and operational planning focus. Having identified all their centres of gravity – is it designed to be technically superior and expensive, or simple and multiple.

The Seventh Pillars of tactical and strategic advantage. Developing your own forms of attack and counter attack gives rise to the formation of "parallel attack." Parallel attack is the ability to strike at a vast array of "targets" across a strategic front. By having a decentralised structure, your system can function in silos, should the main system come under attack, the rest will still function uninhibited. Thus when "attacking" a centralised controlled structure, it is very easy to predict how it will respond with tactics and strategy, even when it is routed, so its history holds its future because of the pillars that support it. However, when decentralised, you have many autonomous "smaller heads" and " smaller pillars" that are strategically and tactically empowered to act compellingly different. How will you attack that? Hereby rendering them less susceptible to a single attack that will dislodge and defeat them. Thus attacking in parallel would cause significant damage and not enable the competition to rebuild his losses. Serial attacks are the opposite of parallel attack in which only a small number of targets are struck and in doing so, enable the enemy to quickly repair any damage. Instead of just focusing on only 1 or 2 targets, forces in parallel attack would disperse and simultaneously strike a wide array of targets, at the operational and strategic level. When targets are diversified, the perception and paradigm, the abstracts are better attacked, that the physical. In striking these simultaneous with parallel blows, the competition loses hope and balance, striving to achieve the effect of "reducing the effectiveness of the overall system." Just by changing perception. In this theory the centre of gravity is unpacked into the "Seven pillars of gravity", or the seven joints of balance, it also supports the linkage of this concept to executing effects based operations. This model views centres of gravity, as composed of both vulnerabilities and strengths, always changing, depending on how they are designed and approached. The Seventh Pillar is all about understanding and finding external influences to counter internal influences beforehand. The seventh pillar is an internal look at what we have, opposed to what they have, and how to best utilise it against the opposition if it comes to that, both in attacking him, or defending us from him, or a counter attack. How to hide our own vulnerabilities and exploit that of the competitions, what can we learn, apply, and share if need be, it is all about developing models of expertise, running simulations, and scenarios, to know the enemy is to know oneself it is said. This knowledge is formulated as doctrines to counter competitor's strategies and to be ready to attack them if they attack you. Battle is not the place where you want to face reality for the first time, and wish you had a few tanks as well. People who say, that no one will use tactics like this in business, it's too farfetched, and absolutely ludicrous, are naive.

"TAPS"

The corporate world is all about **TAPS: -Tactics, Accuracy, Power and Speed – "TAPS"**

Tactics; making the right moves at the right time; in the corporate environment, tactics are anything you would like to use in your favour, but remember this. Strategy and tactics are two interchangeable concepts, the one can give rise to the other, they are not exclusive, but inclusive of each other. Good tactics can give rise to good strategy, and a good strategy can produce new tactics. Change is part of organisational growth and survival in our modern global economy. If an organisation is going to grow and survive, it needs more than traditional strategic business plans; it requires good tactics as well... Company's can develop a strong competitive advantage through the strategic use of information technology – as a tactic.

Accuracy; Many start-up companies develop a business plan but rely heavily on their own experience and assumptions when it comes to business decision making rather than facts, than an existing company would use. While companies are on the growth path, mistakes become more costly. Especially where they hold on for dear life to existing systems, mostly a mixture of manual, and electronic processes. Because time progresses, we learn, and we realise that business decisions not based on facts, become costly, at this juncture - where business decisions become complex due to growth and expansion, a need arises for facts supplied fast, not guesses, then only do we need to incorporate technology. This belief, hampers the organisations growth. Technology has changed the way information is captured, stored, processed, analysed, distributed, communicated; and the organisational infrastructure which is used to reduce costs, increase profits, and gain a competitive advantage. Good intelligence, on the other hand is at the heart of avoiding blunders and conflict in organisations. When time and money are spent promoting decisions that are unlikely to succeed, managers can derail not only just a strategic plan, but their careers from backing initiatives from a declining dominant coalition beliefs in what we have is good enough, rather than an emerging one, that beliefs in technology. Yet, these blunders are avoidable, as technology has become cheap and easy to use. While we all agree on the need for timely and accurate intelligence, little effort is made on implementing it, and even less on how to acquire it, and utilise it effectively. Nonetheless, even as corporate systems generate data more rapidly and data volume increases, managers still often flounder in decision making and effective strategy implementation. This is largely because data by itself does not necessarily equal readily actionable information that is accurate. Accuracy only becomes a strength if it is precise, consistent, fast and easy to use.

Power; is a mixture of command and control, authority, influence, supremacy, means, and the mental and physical power to persevere and to overcome any stumbling block. Much of this does not come tailor made, it has to be exercised like a muscle, taught, bought, experienced and acquired. Above all, developing the minds power, and keeping it fit, by reading, joining courses and partaking in exercises and strategic games, has become essential. Continuous development and a thirst for knowledge. "Hos 4:6 My people are destroyed for lack of knowledge: because thou hast rejected knowledge". It's a learning curve to develop good "Tactical Power" that only comes with commitment to task. It is precisely the "excess of having too many realities" sold daily by ignorant and naive people, that precludes the possibility of the "singular unified perspective" necessary firstly, to lead the way to the successful implementation of strategic plans. Another dimension which measures the quality of a strategic response is its speed of implementation recognising this, to ensure a good speedy strategic response, with fast communication of information is imperative. In the digital era, power coincides with the emergence of *tactics*, *accuracy* and *speed*. Both on the physical and mental level. In an increasingly competitive marketplace with declining spending power, both internal as well as external, then good information is imperative to management decisions. The most important component of power is in the change equation, is knowing when to change, and what, and then making the decision to change, and implement the change in the shortest cycle. If resistance to change is wide spread, this will lead to the breakdown and irrelevancy of what was once a strong power, and weaken the whole organisation. The power to think critically and effect change, and keep changing effectively becomes a competitive advantage - a power. The ability to constantly keep moving and evolving the business paradigm is essential – a power. The most successful firms know how to keep moving, always staying alert and proactive with whatever they recognise as giving them power to change, and emerge successful.

Speed; only improves with time and experiences, experience that we benefit from, that taught us valuable lessons, only from prior experience can we deduce what the outcome will be when dealing with specific knowledge fields. Then we learn what to expect from having seen it in real time, and operate with fewer distractions and error afterwards. Expertise and experience are crucial elements that impact on speed, that renders better-developed reaction times to all anomalies dealing with time and speed. Taking one example; some cultures have accepted beliefs that prevail amongst most of their management teams, that impact on strategic decision. For instance using consensus, and having to get consent on all aspects, around getting approval. The process we use dictates the terms of reference for us, this also impacts on decisions and implementation, that follow, that starts a trend that impedes speed and delays outcomes, that could rob us of all success.

You have to get the mix right

When carefully looking at the attributes of strategic decision making, then the four core principles emerge, namely; tactics, accuracy, power and speed. Furthermore, the cultural traits we use – the format we use to think and position our perceptions will dictate the gravity of our thought, what the results will be, and how we will get them. It's a mix. Strategic thinking needs to have a format, to make it relevant. For example, decision making based on consensus takes time, it's mostly drawn out and exhausting. In the wake of this process, powerful surges of action never seems to emanate, as no one wants to take ownership after things were decided on - on censuses only, and not on facts and the merits of the case. Implementation does not coincide with speed either, as consensus evokes a wave of follow-on actions, that require even more consensus, diminishing speed. These seemingly insignificant acts, that occur daily as the norm in the decision making process, in fact robs us of steps forward, as we do not care to see that our culture is at the heart of our demise. Where we lose capacity, we lose interest. Where everything revolves around aspects of collective agreement, then it drains the total organisations power to perform, and therefore killing its power to gain speed. Time cycles, from decision to impact, is just not the top priority – where we need a collective to give the okay. All time-based competition, relates to standards and norms set by groups on how they will conduct themselves in thinking strategically, making decisions beforehand on how certain issues and actions for efforts used in the process will be dealt with. Most strategies are specifically designed around being time sensitive, providing for change control, to reduce one or more of the various types of lead times faced by the company. Change controls are implemented as an aspect of the decision making format and design, some principles are based on consensus, others on facts, others on figures etc. This is why we need tactics, they are implemented, using team building, organisational flattening, and flexible and automated manufacturing systems, and simultaneous engineering. The key challenge facing any company attempting to implement such initiatives, is to insure that there is a proper fit between how the company competes in the marketplace, with the specific timed process and strategies selected, and the specific implementation of tactics used. Tactics need to be multidimensional and smart, concentrating on principles, by having several different aims, qualities, or addressing divergent aspects – aimed at resolving identified specifics, in a timely and co-ordinated fashion.

The new age principles of business.

1. *Continued intelligence gathering in all directions*; from all sources available; electronic, practice, and academia - and responding to the capability gaps they expose.
2. *Designing unique strategy formulation criteria;* specific and unified ways and means, together with metrics attributes, to influence planning and decision-making for the future.
3. *Unification of force;* both active and passive tolerance for differences as a collective tool for preventing, when reasonable, or mitigating, when necessary, or bringing closure, when possible, to any form of conflict.
4. *Co-operation;* structured networking, to foster interoperability. Co-operation includes 'neutral buy-ins,' or 'non buy-ins,' if there is no cost associated with the objective.
5. *Arbitration;* to recognise the potential for matrix management and structures, and standards as a basis for conciliation. Particularly important issues are the memorandum of understanding; (co-operative agreements) and priority escalation criteria. (who will be taking the lead and when).
6. *Readiness;* getting ready and being ready to be tested, to acknowledge the causes and effects of factors on all operational fronts, as a means to ensure mental, materiel, and monetary readiness of processes and people to work together as a collective, to fight against waste.
7. *Main Objective;* which is prosperity, not at any cost, but directed towards a state of affairs in the future that is more peaceful, productive and harmonious than what is existing at present.
8. *Economy and union;* the over aching principle is the design and maintenance of interactive overlapping business plans for the utilisation of funds, manpower, and essential elements. That has to produce a master plan, which aligns all, where time will be required to facilitate a necessary or a chosen strategy, to ascertain the tactics and objectives for all.

9. *Education*; to equip every actor to be a better team player,' by promoting interdisciplinary knowledge and skills, and by fostering an awareness of other players who possess what you do not.
10. *Consequence criteria*; to study and contemplate the cause and effects of each decision taken, before going over to action, to conduct impact studies and assessment, as well as research where, and if required before taking major decisions.
11. *Growing competence*; the focus of each endeavour is on the growing of skills, by including, among other components: a willingness to take calculated risks, belief in ability and oneself, taking responsibility and using authority, performing within the means, keeping its legitimacy, and resorting to some element of luck, to allow for calculated error.

In Conclusion on War:

We are mostly only ourselves to blame if anything bad happens to us in business. With more prudence, wiser policies and a greater understanding of vision and the process of meticulous planning we could have avoided such danger, if only we became mindful of radical strategy. This idea is the philosophy of the grand strategists, and it is time tested. Whenever anything goes wrong, it is human nature to blame a person, or persons. Let other people continue on this trend and with stupidity. We will no longer be led by the nose, by only dreaming of the end result. No, trace it black, back to where it belongs, the blame normally resides squarely within; with poor internal politics, bad organisational culture and a lack of leadership.

According to Hirotaka Takeuchi and Ikujiro Nonaka: "... *Emphasis on speed and flexibility calls for a different approach for managing new product development. Under the old approach, a product development process moved like a relay race, with one group of functional specialists passing the baton to the next group. The project went sequentially from phase to phase: concept development, feasibility testing, product design, process development, pilot production and final production. ...*"

"*Under the [new] approach, the project development process emerges from the constant interaction of a hand-picked multidisciplinary team whose members work together from start to finish. Rather than moving in highly structured stages, the process is born out of the team members' interplay. ... The shift from a linear to an integrated approach encourages trial and error and challenges the status quo. It stimulates new kinds of learning and thinking within the organisation at different levels and functions.*"

Frederick M. Downey wrote:

Theory cannot equip the mind with formulas for solving problems, nor can it mark the narrow path on which the sole question is supposed to lie by planting a hedge of principles on either side. But it can give the mind insight into the great mass of phenomena and of their relationships, then leave it free to rise into the higher realms of action.

In countries subject to domestic strife, the centre of gravity is generally the capital. In small countries that rely on large ones, it is usually the army of their protector. Among alliances, it lies in the community of interest and in popular uprisings, it is the personalities of the leaders and public opinion. It is against these that our energies should be directed

Our doctrine does not consist of procedures to be applied in specific situations so much as it sets forth-general guidance that required judgment in application. Therefore, while authoritative, doctrine is not prescriptive.

Van Creveld writes:

The essential principles of strategy will continue to be determined by its mutual, interactive character; that is, the fact that war is a violent contest between two opponents, each governed by an independent will and to some extent free to do as he sees fit. The need to concentrate the greatest possible force and deliver a smashing blow at the decisive point will continue to clash with the need to outwit, mislead, deceive and surprise the enemy. Victory, as always, will go to the side that best understands how to balance these two contradictory requirements, not just in the abstract but also at a specific time, at a specific place and against a specific enemy.

Consider the words of Stephen Davis:

...the ability of its nodes to independently plan and execute operations requires that its centre of gravity analysis must be more of an art, requiring creativity both in the analysis and in the determination produced. The process must include the participation of a variety of analysts with an unconventional mind-set.

The "idea of fast transform of one's perspective suggests that, in order to win, we should operate at a faster tempo or rhythm than our adversaries." Echoing Sun Tzu, he further explains, "Such activity will make us appear ambiguous (unpredictable) [and] thereby generate confusion and disorder among our adversaries—"The aim of Boyd's manoeuvre warfare is to render the enemy powerless by denying him the time to mentally cope with the rapidity of flowing movements, or occurrences. "It is better to act quickly and err," von Clausewitz explains, "than to hesitate until the time of action is past."

General Ike Eisenhower:

" The thing about all power, it isn't the BIG decisions that way heavy, you can decide to invade Russia over dinner, take Waterloo on a whim. It's the detail the small stuff, it's easy to gamble a million lives. But what's hard, is to see how that can hurt one single person and if you can't keep that straight, you will lose your humanity – won't you? – General Ike Eisenhower Supreme allied commander D-day Normandy.

The birth of the "Power Management Matrix" - environment

Today, more and more organisations turn to the winds of change, just "hoping" and "trying" to find more multidisciplinary ways of doing work, getting feedback and motivating people. This is where it all seems to get stuck, with "hoping" and "trying", by having tried all the old methods to rejuvenate the organisation, without great successes. Mostly the organisation as a whole has become tired of acting out old clichés, travelling on the old and beaten path, going to bush retreats and the corporate get away. It has become a start – stop cycle. For one reason; they lack true unified common vision, vision that comes from radical strategy and the required insight to change people's perception, they do not have any true mental compass to navigate the waters of change with, as they have divergent visions and focus. For this very reason, no value added change ever takes place. Where and if we want to see real meaningful change, we have to intentionally create a certain amount of "chaos" in order to find balance and restore "real order" again.

The reality of the matter is one cannot just "hope" to become anything in life and not be willing to sacrifice and go through the required motions of – chaos – in order to reach the final stage, the realisation that change becomes essential and central for any rejuvenation to take place, this holds true in all spheres and dimensions of life, love, living and even for organisations.

The same with trying, trying is like flying, you can try all you like, but without wings, you will try flying all your life. By saying this, we understand that we are all bound by natural laws that require of us some form of action, wings and measures to follow, thus resulting in a desired consequence, because of it. We have to understand that the natural law of cause and effect is omnipresent. There will be no effect if there is no cause.

Consequently, we have to create a "cause": not just any cause, a justifiable one, that appeals to reasoning first, to get people to go over to action. By understanding these key aspects of social intelligence, and human behaviour we can get better critical insight into how restructuring of systems, cultural and politics of the organisation can be influenced, that will become a cause for people to change. This cause must be conceived out of necessity and want, otherwise it just won't work. No one person will go over to action if he or she does not understand the benefit to themselves first and if there is no urgency to do it. Because, everything starts from the first dimension, the self, the necessity to do this. Why do "I" have to do this, has to come from a need or want that has to be satisfied in order to achieve some personal goal. Either financial, political, emotional, or whatever motivates the individual. Nor will they do it if they are not confident that the result will not be worth their attempt, or effort required from them. We are now able to explain why and how social intelligence and human engagement works to develop insight on the importance of having unified focused and giving it personal attention; by focusing on personal goal setting, and challenges to sustain change behaviour, and performance management. It is very critical for people to feel intimately connected to issues that concern them, they need to internalise to adopt the beliefs, values, and attitudes of others, either consciously or unconsciously, in order to start stimulating excitement and creating insight about matters at hand. In order to understand strategy; vision, mission and goals, people need to connect with it on a personal level. This aspect explains why we connect with others deeply, or simply don't, why we change instantly or refuse to, it's because we have not made the connection, only when we share some form of commonality, and vision do we see a connection. If we do not see the reason, as being compelling enough, then we simple see no reason to connect. The cause, and grounds for justification to connect and act soon, or be acted upon, will only become a personal quest when we realise that the consequences are essential and vital to our own personal sustainability and growth as well as that of the scheme. To ignite action requires a total paradigm shift and then alignment with a understandable vision, that creates a reason to make the change. Without action, there will be no change or desired consequence ever. Moreover, change requires action, action, action and with every action there is a re-action, all actions creates friction that creates stress. This is the very reason why very few take to action, just to avoid the extra stress...of having to make a connection, and share a vision, it takes effort. Change comes at a price, we have the power, to make it very expensive, or cost effective. If we know the issues, we can deal with them.

Stress is easy to ignore and to deal with, either way; if we follow the paradigm of most managers – "it is something people need to sort out for themselves". Really!!! Is this still our belief, recent studies make it clear that stress has become too prominent of a problem sapping at scares resources in business to be ignored any longer – dealing with stress becomes a more cost effective measure, for it has a knock on effect. When we deal with stress at the company level, we create better unity, when not, we tend to see absenteeism, low work rates, and lots of negativity and friction, and it spread like cancer. While tensions and misunderstandings are normal and inevitable, if left unresolved they tend to result in hostility, then it brings on stress and ultimately a waste of resources. Many triggers, even compounded can lead to stress. Yes, stress is what they call it, managing people and business well, also includes changing their perception of stress and how to deal with it effectively. Large amounts of stressed-out people fill our environments, everywhere we go we hear how stressed people are. Stress is mostly self-generated due to our perceptual mind and triggers; that is to say, the way individuals perceive or think about a situation or event, from minute to huge, and how this will influence them emotionally, thereby determining how much stress a particular situation will generate and dislodge as emotion.

We also realise that we have become super **competitive** as a race; our offspring are all competitive, so much so that we are now even competing from within. We are tapping into our own personal resources much harder than ever before, this is not first-class living, and we know it by now, we see the evidence everywhere. Teenage suicide, depression and obesity are ballooning by the day. Are we not setting a president to be followed by the next generation, which would lead to more severe health and mental problems?

The older generation probably coped better with **pressure** and stress, mainly because they were not continually being asked and reminded about it, or even understood its effect, or have taken much note of it either – things were just so much simpler. Managing stress is all about taking charge: taking charge of your thoughts, health, your emotions, your schedule, your environment, finances, and the way you deal with problems. The ultimate goal is to live a balanced life, with time set aside for work, relationships, relaxation, and fun – plus the toughness of mind to hold up under pressure and meet challenges head on. Have we lost sight of the importance of teaching people life skills? We all know and understand that a certain amount of competitiveness is an essential part of our awareness, and being, as top predator we share a need like all living things to compete. This is a very basic need of all living things, forming the foundation of evolution itself, as per Dr Darwin's survival of the fittest theory. When things need to get done, why do we have to keep competing with ourselves and others to get a kick out of it, why not just to do it, can't we just enjoy the moment, and benefit from what we are doing without having to get rewarded, recognised or pressured to perform. This type of behavior can in turn lead to a drop in productivity if it becomes habitual, quite the opposite of what we had set out to achieve with a well thought out strategic plan. To much continuous focus on individual performance rather than solutions and principle, leads to a total slump in creativity and innovation. Could it be that we are breeding a generation of people who spend far too much time being over analytical, and introspective of their psychological state?

Our **conflicting nature**; we are in conflict with nature, earth, we have conflicting views, ideas, and perception. Conflict is generally the result of serious disagreement over needs or wants, or treatment, principles and freedoms, but mainly over the perception of these things, that creates differences, resulting in unwanted aggression, or depression, that we attribute to prolonged unresolved conflict.

Application of this principle to life's mechanism would mean that the more competitive creature has a better chance of survival. Even in sports, one of the best ways to teach children a spirit of fair play, healthy competition and the grace to take defeat in one's stride, is not the same as before.. Excessive competition sometimes makes it a stress-maker rather than stress-breaker. Competition, essentially a standard or scale of measurement, can be extremely beneficial, if only it is understood and applied properly. When a child seeks to take his first step, he naturally strives to improve each day, experimenting and trying new approaches. Such **experimentation and initiative** is random, we develop at different rates. As we grow older, our targets are the ones set by others and so try and achieve them, we become self-conscious when we don't, disconnected and therefore stressed – if we cannot keep up with the pack - we stand in conflict and feel disconnected. In this down turn economy, with so many parents worrying about money, it shouldn't surprise us that our kids are picking up on it. Almost every person has experienced it: that rush of dread in the pit of the stomach. The feeling that it's just not possible to do everything that needs to be done. Stress becomes negative only when the body cannot feel the rewards from the body's hard work, so too the mind. We need therefore to be mindful of how we utilise people, and how to make and break the pattern of stress, to work for us.

These aspects created the need for the "Power Management Matrix"

Why do we need to change our paradigm on management of people and strategy today? The "Power Management Matrix" strikes a delicate balance here, it gives people the required attention that will provoke them and shock them into action – because we have made the connection. This organisation has **Power**; a good mixture of command and control, authority, influence, supremacy, means, and the mental and physical power to persevere and to overcome any stumbling block. It has good **Management** that strives to creates simplicity by creating synergy in culture and thought processes, everyone is eager to go over to action, by creating and adopting one culture and one doctrine first. We start by changing the focus of our business design from the normative to the formative with **Matrix** design, seeking out more foreseeable victories and workable solutions to everyday problems.

Only when we acknowledge that pyramid systems no longer create efficiency consistently; then we move our thinking from current systems design and work distribution hierarchy that creates the traditional pyramid, towards designing a multidimensional work distribution matrix. Here there is a clear shift on where the emphasis is, we only utilise the systems approach, to enhance people's creativity and to create connectivity and structure, thus optimising cross-functional performance. These systems adapt to people's needs and not people to the system's needs.

We strive for less bureaucracy and more autonomy and call for more trust, streamlining of processes and systems, and to be more principle guided. Management is focused on capacity building and less coercion orientated. There is no one winner, or best of the best, things get done in a collective; it becomes we against them, not us, against each other. However, this is not the golden mean, or final solution to all problems created within enterprise. It also has its unique challenges that emanates from designing autonomous functional and creative work environments for people. People always try and beat the system. It is merely a new and refreshing integration, of new and old concepts that work. More focused on thinking and people orientated paradigms that aims to alleviate the causes of internal friction – we don't have to compete with our co-workers. It comes with new characteristics unique to applying such train of ideas; on the up side it offers higher resource efficiency, stronger integration, synergy and improvements in communication flow, both internal and external, with varying degrees of motivation and commitment. Nonetheless, on the down side, some disadvantages still include power struggles and conflict management. The challenge is to know what to expect next and to devise means to achieve balance, by anticipating the growth path, and navigating it through the treacherous waters of change.

Let's look at Traditional Matrix Management first, to get a better understanding of the matrix principle; it is a type of management system used by some larger organisations, which are mostly projects driven. Where they have many projects running concurrent, that are then organised within teams that work on a functional, rather than a typical project, basis. We will first explain matrix management in this context and then, cross over to the new paradigm on – "Interdependent Management" – or – "Power Matrix Management", derived from using individuals and organisations collective attributes, to give it power. As well as building in the required support systems, that actually works.

"The Matrix" as a concept

The disadvantage of conventional matrix management is the fact that employees can become confused due to conflicting loyalties, and systems, mainly because they feel that they only belong to one cell and not the total system. However, with Power Matrix Management this aspect is bridged and this is no longer the case; you have to work for all the cells, systems are universal and aligned, and you don't need to get to understand their thinking, knowledge, style and political culture – as it is equally the same. If we can function as a family, in natural terms with one culture and one style of politics; why not in corporate terms, we all do chores around the home and share the responsibilities of housekeeping. In order for the system to work, all parties must be willing to experience continued change and knowledge, they have to learn to adapt to different styles of management, thinking and culture, as well as knowledge. In order to get a grounded position eventually. They have to talk the talk and walk the walk, in order to progress, during this cycle of knowledge gaining, they get to know everyone and understand their paradigms whilst still young, as if their own. They also get to experience the influence of the global strategy and the organisation as one culture at every cell level.

With "Power Matrix Management", we use the same principle as with conventional matrix management, with the difference; we keep changing the experiences and influence people to be free agents and not to settle down and get into a groove, without having to change their focus. Our focus is on corporate culture and robust management development, a strategy in itself. Here we change the political corporate climate first, from competitiveness - one cell politics - to global villager's politics. We create synergy by introducing diversity; you cannot create synergy by creating divisions – with departmentalising, this creates cells in opposition – both physically they compete and mentally they build barriers. People only really get to understand one-and-other if they are joined by the hip and have to work side by side, out of necessity, if they have to rely on and trust each other. Granted, this will not work in all spheres of business, however the principle could be applied, to add value.

When moving from one position to the next, we do everything in a structured manner; call it a "career path" strategy. People only learn people skills when they are in each other's faces working out differences nose-to-nose and working as teams. We can only create abundance, from the formation of planned and structured corporation building strategies within an organisation and then move to the ideal position of interdependency if it is done in a structured manner. Companies will never arrive at abundance if everyone is holding onto their positions for dear life, because they see no future for themselves. Interdependency comes from a 360 degree vision of building competence, with traditional thinking we create leaders with blind spots, that entrench themselves in their positions and vigorously fight off contenders. Only from emerging from a full circle of growth and experience do we get true competence and global vision. With global knowledge and global experience growing, we create super conductors, people that channel energy, that are inclined towards action and that will jump at opportunity, a new breed of work force. This also diminishes stress, where we have the confidence of having global influence and support, by having have mastered all the facets of the business and change. Only then do we become productive individuals in our own right, with respect for others, when moving towards promotion. This can't work, oh really. Take the example of school training. We followed the same principle in school, first pre-school, then primary, then high, then collage, then university. Yet, we adopt a very different approach in business, why? This is the only way to create true, equal opportunity for all. Here we move in circles of trust, the trust is much higher, due to an ideology shared and experienced by all and the culture is in synergy.

I would like to illustrate this principle in simple terms; I have always been a keen pistol shooter, but it was my brother that inspired me with his skill and then taught me the finer art. I moved on and met with others even more proficient, that shared the same passion and vision, we exchanged knowledge. Eventually I arrived at a point of competence and then started teaching, as I taught my knowledge and even my skill grew and improved still. I then entered into competition and we formed a team, the competitive nature to achieve excellence inspired me to perform even better. This team won ten years in a row. In the end circumstances forced me to "migrate" from one level of competence to the next and I joined a rival team, with low skill, I taught them in turn the finer skills as were passed on to me, their competency and mine grew still, to the level where we now were real competition and we posed a serious threat, and the standard of the region elevated. This made me realise the importance of migration of skills and cross pollination. Where the vision and mission stays the same the culture will support migration and integration of core competency. It does not just develop others but also the individual possessing the skill, by having to refine it, repeatedly, in order to pass it on. Most skills are perishable, and needs to be performed repeatedly. The underlying principle here is, we were in the same culture, the gun culture; we shared the same passion, vision and mission.

The lesson: add the required attributes for success, before the fact and build it in as habitual. The unifying elements of culture are firstly that of symbolic culture. In other words, where previously, we focused on designing the structure as our primary focus of enterprise and strategy formation, then we filled the vacancies, and then only started to manage the people and their emerging culture with protocols afterwards. Only when the problems started surfacing and only then did we start managing them. With the design of business systems in this kind of fashion, in organisations, we have experienced many difficulties only afterwards, after the fact, by having followed this paradigm. We only define performance once the system is up and running and the culture have already been formed.

In pursuit of performance "The Power Management Matrix"

Somehow in the pursuit of this superficial thing "performance", we have also missed the real goal of structure, that of creating duality; efficiency and effectiveness. **Efficiency is seen as systems** orientated, going about doing things the right way. It involves eliminating waste and optimising processes. **Effectiveness is seen as strategy,** it is all about doing the right things, at the right time, or on time and in time...in a planned manner.

There is no point in acting efficiently if what you are doing will not have the desired effect - following the *"structure follows strategy"* paradigm. Today we recognise that this is only half the story. *"Strategy also follows from structure"* and how we construct it. Thus suggesting that understanding this duality and nature of strategic management as the least understood part of the management process. By implementing performance management and award schemes as the only performance boosting tool, we have effectively divided people into cells, cells that are not supportive of one and other, the one is purely focused on being *efficient* and the other on being *effective*. What we get as a result is quite the opposite. We have in effect created "champions" and "losers", we have left the question of how to create total performance unanswered. Remember the 80/20 Pareto Rule. Where 20 percent of people will do 80% of the important or profitable work. The problem is that you can't fire the other 80% percent because the rule would still apply. The key to effectiveness is that you're doing things that lead to results in the realm of your responsibilities only. Meanwhile the key to efficiency is getting your things done in a manner that consumes just the appropriate amount of energy and resources, involving others, and leaving more for others to share. What would the reality be if we could get everyone to perform at optimum, and not just some. In effect, we are only rewarding individualism, because in actual fact we are only getting 20% to perform to their optimum, the competitive people reap the rewards, over and over, jumping in and out of the equation, the rest become the tail that is just dragging behind. Defining performance itself thus stems from our focus point. When focused on efficiency or effectiveness only, things become unbalanced, we should be focused on both, to create balance, and as a result overall performance. People are either prone to be efficient or effective, seldom both. There is a belief that you can either get results fast or get it right, but you can rarely get them both at the same time, why not work towards a balance between the two.

The Radical Revolutionary Strategic Management Matrix For Predators

To create a 100% performance, requires a balance between efficiency and effectiveness. Where if effectiveness is concerned with quality, while efficiency with cost and speed. In principle they are opposed but you need both. We should not compare efficiency and effectiveness in term of importance. Their relationship is more of a necessity than a priority. Effectiveness is more of a goal orientated mind setting where efficiency is more of a process orientated mind set, that of measure in attaining the goals... It is also said that, you can be efficient with things but not people. With people you must be effective. Therefore, some people are efficient, other are effective - in orientation, by focusing on the development of leadership first and then the quality of the leadership required, we get and maintain the required performance from both schools, by shifting the focusing on developing managers that understand and embrace duality, then we start on a stronger footing. If performance can directly be derived from the ability of leadership that understands what true performance is, and how to get it, then it stands to reason that this becomes the key to performance focus. The systems thinking approach becomes but one thing and not the means, but rather the launching platform. Systems were created primarily to create obedience and uniformity – this equals efficiency, you cannot manage that which you cannot measure, thus efficiency requires a system to measure things by. Where managing people, we manage paradigms, then we get balance. As a result, we do not want to measure as much as what we want to perform and be effective, if we rethink our focal point on designing an effective performance management systems, then we arrive back at one thing; we require quality leadership. Leadership which can act with discernment and deliver, both attributes – efficiency and effectiveness. Where we define management and leadership attributes into aspects that will foster this type of culture we will be looking for: their ability to;

- *Demonstrate leadership as a earned responsibility rather than as a position of authority and power...this will create respect and trust.*
- *Demonstrate accountability and exercise responsibility for resource management, personal development, developing people and their life skills,*
- *Skilled in strategic thinking and process – as well as strategy formulation and implementation - understands the game plan.*
- *Builds unity and gets the best out of a diverse workforce - trough perception management, people skills and political culture alignment.*
- *Stimulates improved organisational performance – by building winning teams, and supporting systems. Connecting people with the focus, and vision.*
- *Fosters a climate of openness and fairness, that creates trust and ethical code.*
- *That continuously instils "Esprit de corps" - pride in performance, service, resourcefulness, innovation, team and quality.*

Some schools of thought on management still believe that people and their effectiveness are of lesser significance because of a systems only focus. Systems thinking in general have accomplished one thing; a breed of leaders that only know how to adapt to jumping hoops, by adapting to a mind-set (paradigm) of **only measuring things as a means of managing** and having a margin of measure of effectiveness and measuring leadership quality. Their primary focus is on how many hoops should be jumped in a certain time. Eventually people, and through time and practise, find the loopholes, by adapting "effectively" to the organisations rules and culture. Still in our pursuits of being more efficient and effective, this aspect alone does not create performance, it again creates obedience...and order. Something is missing here. Have we lost focus of what is truly important, should we not have turned our focus onto how many improvements were made in the line of service and products and what initiatives could or have been implemented successfully. Have we considered, that if we did not have as much red tape and hoops, to jump through, we would have more time to do other important stuff. Microsoft, have realised this very aspect and have changed their focus significantly to rid themselves of the burden of having too much bureaucracy.

What is truly lacking is the proper **"fluidity of the individuals expression of worth"**; our talent, skill and knowledge does not get used or developed to its full potential anymore. Systems thinking, and them thinking for us, have robbed us of our fluidity of worth, the freedom to implement and design change freely, as we experience difficulty, we rely on systems, no longer ones initiative. Initiative has been taken captive by to much policy and procedures – bureaucracy and systems, including technology focus... Managers need to be capacitated again in terms of this aspect, by teaching them *fluidity management*, and not by teaching them to implement more policy and procedure that restricts people like cattle in a crush. Strategy should be seen as a toolbox for creating initiative, and finding a way out. Whereas, policy and procedure, however necessary, has become arbitrary, because it keeps changing. Policy and procedures should be simplified, to only form a guideline and a matrix (template) within which a mandate can be exercised. Law should cover the rest. In an attempt to address specifics, policy and procedure should be created in a predetermined format, to give rise to interlocking systems to be followed. Let me explain; It goes without saying that one global policy that governs policy and procedure should be the first step in making policy and procedure work. This document will make sure that any policy or procedure interlocks with all aspects of the organisation, legislation and strategy. Without going into too much detail; policy and procedure must be streamlined and formed into one document endorsed by all departments and structures. Notwithstanding the fact that it must be practical and easily executable, in line with reality as it unfolds at the grass route level... to construct and repair all that is broken, the user must not become stuck and so too the organisation. Policy or keys should be universal, so that everyone can use them. Otherwise it just becomes dependency, call it mutualism, where everyone waits for the leaders – the gate keepers - to move on anything and everything, or say move – jump/act -, before they move or jump the hoop.

Most decisions leaders make and execute currently are based on assumptions, based on individuals prior experiences and knowledge, that is fading, and out dated. No factual tested data is incorporated, or at least very little, as a rule. Mainly because time does not permit, everything just becomes extremely urgent, and even hearsay will do, just get it done, or do whatever it takes, but get it done. The belief is that, things must be fast to be effective, if things do not happen fast enough or to our liking then we just force feed the system, even with coercion - do it now or else. Then we have the audacity to compare and complain if the results are substandard, if x can do it why cannot y do it as well? This thinking is based on the assumption that people that lead or manage know what needs to be done all the time, and how to do it, when and where, and that they will do it within the "frame work of policy" and deadlines. Regardless of their circumstances, work load, abilities, character, culture, or outside and inside influences and resources. This is the nature of systems and policy only thinking, no strategy is observable. They keep operating as a norm in a silo that does not consider any explanatory factors. When the focus is purely on **efficiency** then we still lack **effectiveness.** By having, and following a single minded focus as a norm, we tend to look in all the wrong places and make all the wrong moves, and decisions in order to rectify our insufficiency. The result is an organisation that becomes slow to act. All this is because of performance punishing. Those who use to set the trend, and work hard, have been overrun with to much urgency, policy and divergent tasks. Performance can be described as abstract; it is dependent on **fluidity**; fluidity of mind, thinking, ideas, trust and the ability to express all these attributes freely, even emotionally. All required to create true fluidity, or performance. For we all think differently, from different paradigms and frames of reference. We all need different things to energise us, but they only come with clear-cut freedoms. If policy dictates that thinking must seize, then it will.

The Radical Revolutionary Strategic Management Matrix For Predators

By virtue of implementing an abundance of rules, policy and legislation, we become the cause of systems failure. What we are in effect doing is, we are cordoning off the abilities of our human intellectual capacity. Our **"fluidity of expression of worth"** - with all the weight of rules and policy. The corporate crime scene starts here, with the arrest of all our human qualities – then we become the corpses - and the ability to express oneself - the crime. It just does not constitute quality thinking anymore where we are given an excess of does and don'ts, nor does it create performance as it is supposed to, just compliance. In general terms, we are creating a lot of conformity and no performance, it's merely an oversimplification of an idolised position.

Have we ever contemplated the possibility, that perhaps leaders and managers, which we keep in high regard, are themselves at times at a loss and seek new guidance? We find many more examples of this phenomenon, especially in middle management, of total disillusionment, in terms of what constitutes performance and what quality is. Should I use my initiative, **"fluidity of expression of worth"**; or just stick to the rules here? They just follow the example, the trend and start jumping hoops again as it is the prescribe culture, hoping to be recognised. Yet, it does not happen. Yet, they are expected to accept responsibility and even accountability, of great proportion, without a real say in any matter. The "boss knows best" and he or she will "decide", so rather await his or her decision first and until then, jump the hoops and stay under the radar. The perception is created that all they want is conformity to systems and policy, not performance, so give it to them.

Most enterprises find themselves in this scenario and then they wonder why, why performance is so poor, it is because trust is lacking and rightfully so. No one trust a leader or manager that has no skill, and in turn who does not trusts your instincts and ability or knowledge, in order to take and make the right decisions. If we just get measured, and we just keep conforming, when will we get time to think, plan, and do things. The question is who is to blame, the system, or the people in the system? Do they just assume too much about their policy and procedures, their systems and their people? We have to see, what adds value, and what pushes down on our people.

The next aspect that stuns growth and unity – is marginal vision. If managers assume that all is equal, by virtue of holding or having the same status, rank and file, then they are mistaken. For, talent and skill does not reside in a job title alone. The wise will know that talent and skill is not passed on genetically, it just does not spawn by promoting someone and giving them the title, it actually requires strategic development and time to mature, the law of the harvest to prevail. This in itself will not happen if we do not allow people to make judgment calls and to transfer ideas and skills.

To form any desired core competency required of a post, takes time and several repetitions, until you get it right. Performance is the art of mastering skills as taught by a practitioner: one at a time, by making decisions, by learning from them, acquiring from them the knowledge of what works and what does not work in a specific environment, and then only from having applied the acquired knowledge effectively, and having achieved results consistently, do they become practitioners in their own right worthy of any title. It never stems from just following a plethora of rules. The other phenomenon is that of following best practices blindly, they do not always fit by design; by saying this, we understand that best practices are only templates, and it goes without saying that we all understand that a template is specific and reliant on specific attributes to be present to fit and work. If any attribute does not exist in the new environment, or context, the template fails. Therefore, we should rather throw away this "key" as a concept and apply (strategy and principles) the "better practice" the **"fluidity of expression of worth"** instead. Better practices are based on principles that are tried and tested and not rules. They are flexible and interchangeable. Therefore, our "approach" to ascertain effectiveness and efficiency, starts with the focal point, that changes from systems to people. True fluidity of expression of worth; requires us to identify talent, develop skill and pass on knowledge, this translates into the freedom to implement and design change freely, by being able to use initiative and experiment with it.

This is the "Power" of the "Power Matrix Paradigm" or "Power Matrix Management" concept. We follow simple principles:

- Good strategy and bad execution. A common causes for poor results and moral. By just optimising cross-functional performance - people interacting with people. Then we see that teamwork translates into an organisation that understands that unity is strength, and as a result, we get more results, they become more focused, and stay focused, just by slowing down the emphasis on high performance and learning to stay focused, and being more strategic in how we use our time and resource, we can actually speed up our effectiveness and overall performance.
- Be customer orientated — get close to the customer, get to know him on a more personal level, rather be effective first and we will work on being efficient later.
- Developing entrepreneurship — give away control to get it, by giving people the authority to take initiative and affirming worth and potential. We create a global corporate culture of people taking responsibility.
- Productivity through people **"fluidity of expression of worth";** — affirm trust in your people, treat them with respect and they will reward you with trust and productivity. Catch them doing the right things at the right time, by doing this a culture of action will emerge.
- Active synergised culture development — the CEO should actively propagate synergised corporate culture development throughout the organisation, through promoting constant change, migration and growth.
- Stick to the things you know best — do what you know well, stick to the basics.
- KISS – keep it short simple – to much complexity encourages waste and confusion.

The design features of the "Power Management Matrix"

Next we look at the difference in designing work, between people and systems. Where systems follow rules and people follow principles – this becomes a design principle.

The first principle; that we all would like to follow, is doing a good job. We view everything we do as doing a good job; no matter what role we are performing. We all strive to be good at our roles as fathers, brothers, mothers and parents. Most of us are, because we are given our **"fluidity of expression of worth";** we pass this on to our children and the circle of growth becomes continuing. Then the family unit stays functional and intact. Therefore, this "job" is well divined to us, because we understand the paradigm of doing our best.

We all understand the principle of cause and effect, the vision, the mission and the added value if we act of our own accord. However, when it comes to defining the real job for employees in the workplace, we refer them to their job descriptions, as a "Paradigm" and reference point of what is considered to be good work. This is opening up a Pandora's box, (we have covered paradigm forming intensively in chapter one) and we will find many open ended interpretations because of this, this is not how we divine doing a good job, to people. Back to rules, people are not very good at following rules either, we cheekily have this natural urge to test the systems rules that we reside within, to see how far we can push them, or break them, this puts us in confrontation with management, just to see if we will get caught or reprimanded.

We all make different judgement calls daily, based on our own perception of rules and the scenario. This is what differentiates us and give us our unique personality, and power over people, we can choose, to obey and conform or not to. Where, as with principles on the other hand, they are universal truths, which relate back to us and our concepts of self-worth, ethics and morals, thus internalising things back to our mental and emotional authority, our consciousness, our pivot of existence, of what is right and what is wrong. We see ourselves as not only guided by rules and regulations, but by our consciousness as well. Principles forces us inward, where we seek and define for ourselves, our worth, values, and our virtues. It is for this very reason that we need to change our focus, from systems to principles, to moral authority by applying principles. By reiterating and defining what is a job well done, in terms of principles, we create synergy by doing so and oneness; one culture will emerge, as a work ethic orientated culture. Because we all function from a natural pivot of **"expression of worth".**

The problem leaders face here, is to get everyone aligned with any new way of thinking. We have been so accustomed and indoctrinated with systems thinking that it has become the custom and tradition of most, and therefore the most difficult mould to brake. When we rely too heavily on systems, policy, rules and procedure, in the absence of flexibility of structure, systems and the like, then we add very little value. Without having proper flexible structure and leadership in place, we won't see much initiative and experience unity. People are just not willing and able to take risks anymore, we just lean towards the other alternative – systems, the habit is indoctrinated beyond reasoning itself. This goes back, right back from the industrial age to the "Portland Cement" model, where the best practice for management and production style was developed, have we totally lost track of our current reality and its complexity? Have we forgotten the steps we took to get here; we were all first hunters, then we became farmers, and then we became industrialised. Different rules apply, nevertheless, why can't we cross yet another "Rubicon". The general thinking is that because everyone else is doing it, then so should we, but are they really getting it right, are we not finding ourselves in the "Information age" already and things need to change accordingly? Previously we had to "get all our ducks in a row", this becomes a self-consuming concept, of thinking and getting things done. It requires that all the "ducks", our workers, follow the rule, to get in line.

Not even in nature is this aspect ever perfected; you will always find one or more ducks falling from the line, not following the rule, "rules were made to be broken". People need room to make mistakes, do their own thing and experiment. This is an old paradigm of management thinking, that we need to fence people in, and if you do, you get people acting like sheep. With Power Matrix Management we do not want all our ducks in a row, we don't micro-manage, we want all our ducks to take off, experience freedom and flight, and arrive at their objectives, - again a natural phenomenon, a principle. That of growth, and evolution, of "migrating" ideas and not waiting the one for the other to get things done. This however requires true leadership and synergy of critical thinkers. Just like the ducks flying in formation, when migrating, we need to get people off. We want multiple thrusts, of energy, both mental and physical. With lateral thinking, the type of experimental process where young ducks learn to swim, and fly, whilst bonding and interact on a interpersonal level. The type of analytical (investigative) and formative thinking we see with our kids and animals, when used properly we can achieve so much more. Where people discover things, for themselves, they remember it, they share the experience and knowledge gained, they incorporate it and use it, and refine it. Opposed to the current reality of alternative thinkers that teaches "thinking outside the box". People often claim to be "thinking outside the box" to support views they hold that are mostly cliché, impractical, or different from the views of others, and in so doing conclude that they are right and others are wrong. If there is so much outside the box, why did we invent the box with ideas and thinking in the first place? Managers did, most of the time people are not given the chance to find out how to solve a problem – they are simply given the boxed solution, and told that the problem was their limited thinking, they should have used the system – and they should have looked outside the box. If everything great resides outside the box, and nothing inside the box, will learning to "think outside the box" help you become more creative? Contrary to popular belief, researched evidence suggests that thinking outside the box fails to produce the expected creative solution consistently. Moreover, and far from being a hindrance, past and current experience and training can actually be the only key to unlocking creative problem-solving minds. Creativity depends on mindset, and if we have experienced much we have great minds. Albert Einstein said that he wasn't smarter than anyone else, he was just more persistent than most.

The Goal

The ultimate goal of strategy is to discover the ***fundamental guiding principles*** that consistently determine the elements of cause and effect for us. That lead to better design, strategy, synergy (things working together) and performance. By highlighting the negative and positive outcomes, of using principles vs. rules, we create a bias for principled action. Principles strive towards finding a unified business theory that would unite the various forces of nature, and business, in a way that would explain - what seemed likely and ethical. Only by addressing uncertainties in a unified and structured manner will we arrive with consistent available probabilities. Companies that enjoy enduring success have core values and a core purpose that remain fixed through principles, while their business strategies are flexible enough, to accommodate altering practices in an ever changing world. This dynamic revolves around preserving the core while stimulating progress. Assessing our past so that we may predict and address the future challenges. With our addiction to control and to the extremes that we have become very competitive, it all has in effect paralysed us and prevented us from uniting people with ideas to address the urgency of any crisis at hand, in a "slow", calm and collected manner.

In order to achieve this aspect of principle guide strategy we have to develop our own basic set of principles required for our strategic development, that fits, and structure our alignment with doctrine – a set of never changing guidelines; which will form the outline, and ring fence the parameters of our final global or master strategy.

Now down to Designing a "Power Management Matrix:"

Matrix design is the intelligent choice, why? Mainly because it is structured and geared to deal with change effectively and fast. It sets a foundation for all concerned to work from in a structured and unified manner. It sets a standard of best practice to follow, where all things considered are tested against a yardstick. Plans are designed from information that is filtered, tested, and then validated to be correct, as well as factual, only then does it become our "business intelligence". Information not tested is just that, an assumption, information tested becomes intelligence. Where we use this as basis for our business assumptions, we refer to it as "business intelligence". Consequently, remember, "garbage in garbage out", if you do not take the conception stage seriously and give it structure – with the exodus strategy - and try and put in as much intelligence as possible, you will arrive with weak business assumptions and the chances are good it will all turn into garbage, bottlenecks and having to re-do it all over at some critical stage. Matrix design sets a standard for all initiatives to be followed - where initiative is described as the ability to act and make decisions without the constant help or advice of other people – acting on instinct. Only by having followed a set of principles that aligns these actions of getting ready to formulate strategy, can we count on initiative to truly work for us. The "exodus strategy", is the departing point where we guide our focus towards one common goal or objective with. The standard is the principles that need to be followed or that have to be conformed to when we ask of our people to us initiative, it does not dictate the process, only the requirements. Every matrix design is unique, unlike previous systems; the matrix is born from a self-realisation of the necessity for change, migration and what is required against the means available to achieve it, to effect change. There is no one wonderful system, or step by step method available that works perfectly. It's all about moving from the norm, to the form, by forming guiding principles aspiring to goals and objectives, that serves as building blocks and not plans for construction of a power management matrix. Let me explain in more detail.

The first phase of any strategy is the *idea phase*: however, with matrix management, before we get into brain storming, we first ring fence the specific idea, we unpack it to add value, to see if it is truly required, or necessary and viable to pursue. By doing this, we to stay focused, and within the means and requirements set to achieve the final objective. This is done by designing, a "exodus strategy", or formulating guiding principles beforehand. This way we do not think, or design outside the parameters that was set – and waste valuable time and resources, by just brainstorming and then going for it... No, here we stay and remain focused, and exert the least amount of energy, because we are focused as a collective, with the same direction finders on, we all are looking in one direction at a time. When designing core principles: "The smaller is to the larger as the larger is to the whole". During the idea stage – nothing is insignificant, no idea is bad. However if you put it on the table, be prepared to back it up and defend it. The first question is always, what do you want to achieve? Remember, we start with the end in mind, we have to clearly divine the final product and then reverse engineer or design it from that mental image, called the first creation. If you don't have a final destination, or concept, then take any road, strategy won't matter, will it? If you don't know where it is that you want to go, or what it is that you want to achieve, how do you want people and systems to get you there? Normally, managers and leaders want to fix things, but they themselves cannot give direction, because they themselves don't know, or understand why, and what is necessary, or how to get to the final destination, they can't see it to believe it, then they require vision and focus.

For instance; With Matrix Management, we create that vision, by having focus. The focus is supplied by the **"CAPS"** model to ring fence our idea, as one principle or standard, in the designing of strategy and vision. To recap; it starts with defining the **Concepts first** - people can better associate with concepts. We all have this ability, anything new is measured for fit against the library we have of concepts. Then by analysing it against our own, and templates that exist we find that it fits or not. Only by critically looking at best practice vs. better practices and concepts do we choose the best one, and then determine what do we still need to develop as attributes, to get a whole concept. This in turn creates more and better focus for leaders and followers alike, it highlights the specifics, the detail, problems and challenges, especially for those who are not all that strategically inclined. By conceptualising/ rationalising things into categories that we can understand or relate to, and it also rallies support. CAPS helps us to connect to strategy, and all its attributes, by breaking it down into rational form. Once the concept is understood, and designed, it flows. Then only do we look at the necessary **Attributes** required, to form the total desired concept. Attributes in turn to get broken down and scrutinised, in the same fashion. Until it becomes a dissected affair, clear and understandable. As we do this perceptions are created, questions and suggestions come to mind, both for and against. We have to address them here and now. We contemplate **Perceptions** that we will have to deal with, and look at ways towards managing them like politics; with "Reframing", and "Nero-linguistic programming", and form integration strategies to sell them, or market them. Then we divide the concept and attributes selected into **Structures** with their required **Systems**, and supports, either existing as they belong to a current structure, or design new systems with the necessary resources. When designing change we need one template to be followed by all, as a guideline for our plans to make them fit.

Two aspects have been addressed here; designing core principles that guide strategy creation , and creating a clear focus to see the vision. Why is this key to igniting good strategy and building synergy?

When creating the Matrix:

We must be able to account for a understandable mental image, a "concept" that becomes a symbol or "goal" that must be attainable.

Create the "Symbol"

The symbol becomes the key that opens the door to the awareness of contradiction.

A symbol is like a tree with branches extending in many directions, an excellent example of essential balance. The only constant is the final objective, to create fruit for instance. The appropriate CAPS model will assist to create a physical, emotional and mental concept, that can be defined by attributes.

Create the "Living mental model": The cognitive or mental model; relating to the process of acquiring knowledge and intelligence by the use of reasoning, intuition, or perception.

Create the "Look", what image does the company and its people want to put out, that also creates emotional context.

Create the "Quality" that can be verbalised, it creates imagery with characteristics, and it must be defined in terms of desired viewpoint – how do we want to be known, for the quality we offer.

Create the "Blue print": a design that can be followed, that is not sensitive to economic changes, flexible, and...simple enough to understand and execute.

The Matrix Mission:

•Must account for:

- A Strategy: In order for any business to adopt a diversification strategy, it must have a clear idea about what it expects to gain from the strategy and an honest assessment of the risks, before it can become a mission.
- Conventional strategic thinking suggests there are four possible strategies

Build or expanding strategy: here the company can either chooses to get investment to start expanding, or to increase market share and profitability, or polish up its image.

Investment strategy: here the company invests just enough of its profit's to rejuvenate to keep the market share.

Harvesting strategy: Great amounts of investment takes place, the company reinvents its self and its image, gearing up for future objectives, a long-term strategy aimed at building on all aspects of the organisation. Buying up bankrupt companies and turning them into profitable one's. The last order is to form strategic alliances, mergers or takeovers.

Separating strategy: By separating from sister companies, by phasing or selling out in fields in this market sector - in order to use the resources elsewhere such as investing in the more promising new markets. In short a strategic retreat out of a market.

The point is, to find the road to take, there are always many roads, many options, finding the right one is a question of experience and strategic insight and focus. We can only travel by one route and on this route, we will experience forces, which will either slow us down or speed us up.

Strategies are sensitive to forces. The correct incorporation of the external and internal environmental impacts or forces is essential, it needs to be considered beforehand, pertaining to:

- *Economic - factors*
- *Cultural – influences and impact*
- *Technology – scale and availability*
- *Demographics – distribution*
- *Government – laws and protection*

The correct interpretation of internal environmental impacts and forces, pertaining to climate:

- *The current political atmosphere, what do you feel, level of internal rivalry and corporate culture.*
- *The threat of new entrants and new ideology.*
- *The threat of insecurity and personal agendas.*
-

The next phase is the "*Conception Phase*"; only after we have collected all the aforementioned data with the CAPS principle can we start, if it is not properly executed - the beginning and implementation processes, our "exodus strategy" – then things will fall through the cracks at some point. However, the system is not perfect yet either, there is one element missing. Just like with construction, we now have a plan for a structure, however we need to level and prepare the mental and physical landscape first. This requires an ice breaking session, the likes of resolving personal issues between role-players first. We have to divine who will be the leading "agency", who will take the lead, and guide the process, get consensus. Then only attempt aligning group dynamics, and then only do we start formulating our exodus strategy. Having one corporate culture, this requires a total realignment in terms of paradigms and principles, for the entire organisation to follow. Every project needs to start from a clear slate. Therefore, we have to sort out politics first, or call a "seize fire', to anticipate the fact that we now have to work as a team. We have to have total synergy; or close to it, otherwise, this process will unfortunately fail. The secret catalyst is to start synergising small groups first, by applying the "domino effect", if we get 20% to buy in, then the rest will follow. We have to politicise and use symbolic means before any campaign starts to influence the collective. Matrix structures are not based on mutualism, where everyone is dependent on the person above him, as in pyramid structures. It's what is termed, **interdependency**: cross-functional performance - people interacting with people, it is an awareness of the reality of things and how they relate, that all life is connected, particularly with organisations and complimentary teams that are focused no longer focused on performance, rather concerned with positioning themselves in the knowledge and skill acquisition economy, in order to turn their employees' know-how into assets. By building on knowledge and skill acquisition we invest in competence, and we get better connectivity and networking. Where competence: refers to people we get; know-how, aptitude, abundance, maturity, wisdom and integrity. Where competence: refers to interdependence; we get elements relying on mutual assistance, support, cooperation, or interaction among constituent parts or members. The only way to achieve this is to migrate and create fluidity. In other words we have to explore, argue, share philosophy, test, analyse and experience as much as possible with people.

The *"filtering phase"*

Here we focus on qualifying and then quantifying the concepts we have come up with, and filter them with the following:

- The value and quality of the new concept or objective - what would the reality be if the situation did not exist?
- What would we like to experience and get out of this, both as individuals and as the organisation, and what are we prepared to put in, risk, and loose?
- What do we hope and set out to achieve?
- What do we learn from our surveys; the market survey, the risk assessment, and the performance gap analyses – it should show the projections, and enhancement we will get, and what will be required in order to get them.
- Are all the elements and attributes needed; identified, quantified and qualified, that are required for sustaining such initiatives for enhancement, the focus must be on continued growth, or staying power – or getting a greater competitive edge.
- Have we identified all the experience and competencies that will be required and the prospects that they will create, we need to unpack all aspects to see if they will add value, and to create understanding of the desired path. Remember, with systems we analysed all the required system attributes, with matrix we are operating from the other side of the stick, we are identifying the elements required to facilitate human capacity building and reward, but the principles of construction stays the same.
- When designing interlocking and alignment protocols, principles, for command and control, as well as the flow of information to build in cross-functional performance, it needs to be diagrammed, both up, down and sideways.
- Calculate the escalation and growth proportions, by forecasting at least five years beyond the inception date. We plan as if we are five years down this road, in terms of capital and operational budgets, as well as the incorporation of required resources and their escalating costs. The ripple effect and knock-on effect is also contemplated on all other systems as growth is projected, this will include training and re-training, as well as career path mapping.
- Then last but not the least, the profiling of work habitats, what type of personality and, experience/ qualifications will be required from the leadership positions, and work force to sustain , and grow, now, five years from now and even ten years from now, as well as the ergonomic design of personalised work stations and what will be required.
- The technological scale, and requirements, how will our current systems serve as future launching pads and foundation, with the focus on future integration, with other technological resources and systems contemplated?

We explain the role of "the paradigm alignment strategy", the self-concept and its influence on the individuals' perception, of how to handle stress and change their ability to cope with stressors. Here we teach: the concept of self-preservation:

- *Self-control, - esteem, - worth, - acceptance, - confidence and - actualisation.*
- *The importance of living with balance.*
- *The culture of interdependence and abundance.*

- *The handling of stress and interpersonal relationships.*

We are fully aware that if we up the performance we will up the stress proportionally as well. Under increasing stress, there is an evident decrease in productive thoughts and an increase in distracting behaviour - escapism. The greater the pressure to perform the greater the stress, the greater the distortion in perceptions of danger and poor judgment, the more critical and less tolerant people become - this often occurs. The greater the fear of failure, the more frustration and hostility it arouses and then everyone switches to survival mode - and its everyone for him, or herself. Consequently "crisis" management takes over, that spills over into a tendency to be aggressive or to escape. In a stressful situation (whether real or perceived stress), only immediate survival goals are considered which means that longer-range considerations must be sacrificed, and the system must be slowed down. We have to keep cohesion of effort, by continued rallying of people and their efforts. The aim is to - increase commitment, accountability, quality and motivation through a process of physically and mentally stimulating experiences, offered by the company. To create the team work ethic, in order to facilitate a relay mentality, what this means is when and where people are sapped, they can hand over to fresh team members. We encourage passing the ball, in order to score the goals as a team. People need variety - truth, but not to much.

Then the; *"Principle Alignment Phase".*

Just to re-cap on the steps;

- *The first phase of any strategy is the "Idea Phase': where we entertain an idea-informal*
- *The "Exodus Strategy"; where we unpack it to see if it will add value, if it will we come up with a concept. – more formal*
- *The next phase is the "Conception Phase"; aligning people and paradigms with the concept – very formal.*
- *The "filtering phase" here we focus on qualifying and then quantifying the concepts we have come up with - critical*
- *The "principle test phase"; here we test our concept further against our unification principles – absolute detail.*

The Ten Unification Principles of Matrix Management and Strategic Intent.

Principle One; Have a "Radical Vision"

First design the concept of your strategy with the aforementioned CAPS principle; the results will be referred to as the "Strategic Intent Statement".

"The Strategic Intent Statement" - is considered to be a high-intensity statement that tells people in the rest of the organisation exactly what your strategy's aims are and how do we see them accomplished, with them in mind. Set the stage for excitement and invention – with "Radical Vision". Vision requires action; action must bring about a sense of direction, discovery, and opportunity, excitement, progress and let's not forget diversity, that should always be communicated as worthwhile to all employees. The strategic intent statement, should not be vague, filled with clichés or catchy phrases. It has to be factual, and to the point. People want to know how do we intend doing this. Engage your employees, unions, and all role players concerned, you must communicate precisely what the objectives are, and who will be steering them. In order to explore a "strategic landscape of radical anomaly" effectively, where everything has to do with people and their power to perform, if the power to persist no matter the hardship is not kindled right at the start, then the project is doomed. Every company has a core competency, embedded in their corporate culture that makes them unique, to be seen as a collection of organisational strengths. These strengths give rise to power, either technological capabilities, and/or individual characteristics of leadership and innovation, and know-how that collectively deploys this strength to provide a core competency. Only with unique functionality that can be sustained and advanced, that will influence their ability to be more innovative and creative will they be consistent, and unified in their quest to achieve the strategic intent. The challenge is to build organisation with mission specific programs that taps into the companies unique DNA – the way they get things done best traditionally - in a way that not only builds excitement and participation, but more importantly – produces the fruits required from their labour. Strategic principles and intent should not focus so much on today's problems only, which are normally dealt with by company visions and missions, management, and bureaucracy as a rule, but rather be concentrated and focus on the fundamentals of strategic analysis and planning that is future focused. Planning a way out and forward, with strategy formulation, strategic choice, and strategy implementation to unearth tomorrow's opportunities, so that we do not repeat and arrive with the same situation, and problems and challenges we have today. Strategic intent needs to be successfully embedded, and communicated into every level of the organisation or it will fail, we must all share the responsibility and learn to plan our own initiatives to support the main thrusts. The perception of unity of effort must be radical, to be innovate and worth the effort. Stimulating passion for an organisation's long-term goals on all levels of the organisation requires high managerial skill, and reoccurring communication. This could lead to competition, competition is the way business gets done, and people need to learn to play the game by the rules. In the absence of rules, people tend to make up the rules as they go along, this becomes a

president. We need competitive people, but when they start competing to win for themselves, and at any cost, then they become a liability as well. Competition is good, when it is fair, and let's not forget, every entity is in competition for recourses, and it probably is not easier inducing enthusiasm for a strategic intent than it is for a strategy based on for instance the experience curve only. Where there is no trade-offs or balanced competitive practice, then internal competition among employees may for example lead to less unity, more bickering and strife - with respect to achieving set goals. If people - individuals start getting the credit – then schools out. Quite the opposite outcome as was intended, a challenge to increase efficiency by competitive and or other means should be a principle for engagement and competition, but it is tempting to argue that designing competition that is fair, is rather a question of principles, culture and implementation. People become predators when they compete, their fangs and claws come out. Strategic competitive predators, aim to collaborate to exist and befit together, using maximum core competency and minimum energy and effort to attain goals collectively. How we set our paradigm, to integrate strategy with people, and for them to compete as both individuals and a team, will be the final test of strategic brilliance. In the words of Bruce Henderson, who accurately pointed out that competition existed long before strategy: "If the animals were of different species, they could survive and persist together. If they were of the same species, they could not". In other words, if we all have the same competency level, and skill, we will not be adding value. Someone has to take the lead and some have to follow. Alternatively, we have to be of divergent backgrounds with dissimilar skills and competency to work together to solve a common problem - different species. More surprisingly, a predator may not be able to persist at all unless it does not have other predators, competitor also present. The presence of a competitor thus significantly increases the range of conditions for which a particular predator can persist to exist along with other predators – called facilitation. Facilitation - the process of making something easy or easier by doing it together - has been deemed as important as co-operative behavior, where the presence of the one, does not necessarily give rise – benefit - to the other, and missing as an essential part of strategic theory. Where all business is seen as predatorial, small to big predators preying on resources for its success and survival. This aspect also exist internal, where strategic, tactical and operations levels of management and personnel compete as predators in their own right, for internal resources, and therefore against each other as a result. The crux of the problem is resolved only where we have a common vision, shared by all, where we have commonality we have focus, where we have diverging opinion we get diversified vision, and this just leads to chaos. Therefore, in order to get clans of predators, to hunt together, you have to make space for all. Your strategic intent statement must be persuasive, simple, clear, and believable, or you won't sell it. It must also be realistic and challenging enough for the pioneers - big predators, and attainable enough for the doers, the small predators - or no one will buy it, and it must be repeated with relentless consistency, backed up by action and trust.

The designing of core principles for a business is no easy task: "The smaller is to the larger as the larger is to the whole" – during the idea stage – nothing is insignificant, no idea is bodged, where a good idea is simply squelched because of bad or negative energy, self-doubt and fear. Alternatively because the predator is small and insignificant, in the company of the bigger predators. Then the first question is always, which road we should take. Well, where do you want to go will the quantifying question? We need a common purpose, that everyone wants, or needs to pursue. Only after this aspect has been ironed out can we all jump in and share. What do you want to achieve, remember, we start with the end in mind, we have to clearly divine the final product and then reverse engineer or design it from that mental image, called the first creation. If you don't have a final destination, or concept, then take any road, it won't matter, will it? If you don't know where it is that you want to go, how do you want people and systems to get you there? Normally, managers and leaders want to fix things, but they themselves cannot give direction, because they themselves don't know the final destination, they can't see it to believe it.

When creating the Matrix vision:

• We must be able to account for:

– A comprehensible mental image, a symbol, or goal that must be attainable and that points in a direction.

• We do this by creating the "symbol" - Symbols are the keys that open the door to consciousness of paradox.

A symbol is like a tree with branches extending in many directions, an excellent example of integral balance. The only constant is the final objective, to create fruit for instance (an appropriate CAPS model will assist) to create a physical concept.

• Create the "Living cognitive model":

– Quality verbalised, creates imagery with characteristics, and they must be defined in terms of desired perspective – how do we want to be known, where and what is our quality we offer.

• Create the "Look", what image does the company and its people want to put out.

The Matrix Mission:

• Must account for:

A Strategy: In order for any business to adopt a diversification strategy, it must have a clear idea about what it expects to gain from the strategy and an honest assessment of the risks, before it can become the mission.

Conventional strategic thinking suggests there are four possible strategies;

Build or expanding strategy: here the company can either chooses to get investment to start expanding, or to increase market share and profitability, or polish up its image.

Investment strategy: here the company invests just enough of its profit's to rejuvenate to keep the market share.

Harvesting strategy: Great amounts of investment takes place, the company reinvents its self and its image, gearing up for future objectives, a long-term strategy amid at building on all aspects of the organisation. Buying up bankrupt companies and turning them into profitable one's. The last order is to form strategic alliances, mergers or takeovers.

Separating strategy: By separating from sister companies, by phasing or selling out in fields in this market sector - in order to use the resources elsewhere such as investing in the more promising new markets. In short a strategic retreat out of a market.

The point is, to find the road to take, there are always many roads, many options, finding the right one is a question of experience and strategic insight. We can only travel by one route and on this route, we will experience forces, which will either slow us down or speed us up.

The correct incorporation of the external and internal environmental impacts or forces need to be considered, pertaining to:

- *Economic - factors*
- *Cultural – influences and impact*
- *Technology – scale and availability*
- *Demographics – distribution*
- *Government – laws and protection*

The correct interpretation of internal environmental impacts and forces, pertaining to climate:

- *The current atmosphere, what do you feel, level of internal rivalry and corporate culture.*
- *The threat of new entrants and new ideology.*
- *The threat of insecurity and personal agendas.*

Principle Two: "Managing by set objectives."

Design a Matrix of opportunity and be innovative, seek innovative ideas, test them and work on them, develop systems and perceptions with attributes that can be sustained – until it can become strategically significant or an worthwhile objective to be pursued.

Every strategy must have specific objectives, broken down into goals, decisive and supportive to the operation and main objective. These objectives must be clearly understood, and formulated, designed qualified and quantified and or they will not be implemented accordingly. Taking and keeping the initiative implies action, mistakes, and learning from them, rather than reaction to situations, that causes bottlenecks and haphazard decision making. Staying at the forefront of innovation, means to be in the OODA loop, and taking the initiative constantly, and consistently, it implies dominating the situation, both internal as well as external, with decisive and swift actions, rather than allowing a situation to get out of hand, or a competitor to take the initiative.

Is leadership and management, managing by objectives (MBO)

- By the cascading of specific organisational goals and objectives.
- Do they have specific objectives for each section and individual?
- Do they allow participative decision making
- Do they enforce and give explicit periods for completion of work.
- Do they have a performance evaluation and good feedback system?

By structured co-ordination – in order to achieve maximum effectiveness, divergent tasks must be integrated, under a unit, logistics, strategic, operations, or tactical, in carrying out the overall strategy to achieve maximum effectiveness – things that belong together must stay together – fragmentation and waste must be eliminated.

Does management lead by objectives/ goals and apply "smart" principles to objectives.

- Specific
- Measurable
- Achievable
- Realistic and
- Time phased

  The beauty of Power Matrix Management is that it is totally flexible, scalable and a implement able design, that fits into existing structures and strategies; it offers a seamless transition to the new. By personalised design, it becomes a personalised choice. Here we plan both the indirect as well as the direct route to our goals, to circumvent the danger of losing our initiative. This gives us time to observe the plan as it unfolds in steps, with reaction and then to counter any negative feedback, before moving on to the next step. We work in a structured manner. We break up strategy, into smaller workable parts and we make our first moves count, to set the stage for the following moves – it's all pre-emptive. There are no rules only principles; so add whatever you are feeling comfortable with, it is a custom design. The golden line – our means - becomes increasingly evident as we progress and hit the course, we realise that something has changed, our focus – it has become one collective focus on one objective: on how to design better co-ordinated and structured work for people. Shared ideas lead to shared meaning. The more openly and honestly ideas are shared, the greater the level of trust will be, the more efforts will be aligned – and the more ideas will emerge.

Principle Three: "Resource management".

Always start qualifying and then quantifying things from the word go, until they become facts, tangible and reachable objectives. We cannot manage that, which we cannot measure.

Resources must not be wasted by allocating them where they will have less than a decisive impact. Responsibility and accountability, also dictates, that we have to inform; if we did not perform, if we have difficulty doing so, and if things just don't work. We have to be honest to be trust worthy. We have to unpack to add value wherever possible, and then prioritise the sequence of events out of the situation, and their priority during that phase. Identify your shortcomings and priorities and concentrate minimum essential resources to lower priorities, and mark specific actions for re-alignment with maximum effort and resources assigned. Resources must be positioned and moved in a co-ordinated fashion that supports the overall strategy to attain the objectives in succession, and in order of importance. Priorities change as situations change, and we have to be flexible and resourceful enough to meet them head on. For this level of manoeuvring to prevail, you must identify your priorities clearly, and the resources required, eliminate waste at every junction, qualify the requirements, specifics, and quantify them daily. Having specifics and details of your objectives and their requirements becomes paramount at the point of inception wherever action is required. By wasting minimum essential resources, we have more to spread, and the system moves faster, the focus of time and money must be on the primary objectives without neglecting the smaller details, problems, challenges and lower priorities – strategy is in the detail and facts. Unity of decision making, not necessarily consensus, is essential, someone must have the final say, in order to ensure maximum co-ordinated effort in accomplishing every assigned task, there should be only one individual responsible, and then someone that is overall both responsible and accountable.

Determine the most efficient use of your employees. This is where personal growth and experience comes into play. To know precisely who to assign to what, you need a system to determine the unique strengths and goals of your employees. Determine your innovators, organisers, communicators, leaders - find the employees with the strengths to match each objective.

Test your goals against the following to see if they have all the ingredients.
1. **Positioning** – location, arrangement, situation, view, role in team
2. **Flexibility** – opinion, method, style, perception, task, policy-procedure
3.**Economy of Resources** – waste, effective vs. efficient, situational appropriateness
4. **Exploitation** – management, utilization, exploitation, abuse, usage
5. **Organization** – affiliation, networking, club, social, brand, logo, vision, trademark
6. **Unity of Decision Making** – harmony, fluidity of worth, command and control, systems
7. **Co-ordination** – cause and effect, consequence, outcome, effectiveness, speed, quality
8. **Morale** – honesty, openness, fairness, competition, personal growth and well-being, reward
9. **Initiative** – parity in the concept, fair, strict criteria, endorsed, open, collective agreement
10. **Security** – privacy, data, professionalism, safety , protection equality, uniformity, culture
11. **Objective** – aim, purpose, goal, achievable, realistic, time phased, attainable, means available
12. **Simplicity** – accuracy, factual, timely, ease of use, straight forward,
13. **Concentration** – attention to detail, deadlines, structure, uniformity, directed effort
14. **Surprise** – initiative, tactics, strategy, ploy, awareness

Principle Four: "Improvise, Adapt, and Overcome".

The U.S. Marines have a motto to remind the troops how to perform under fire, even under the most dire conditions, *"improvise, adapt, and overcome"* We create multiple waves of strategy to achieve these objectives; of *improvise, adapt,* and *overcome* by filtering them; there will be strategy within strategy; that will give us pre-contemplated alternatives if and when needed - The exodus strategy can be explain as the:

- Strategy as the **plan** - a direction finder, guide, course of action - intentional rather than actual and specific, more ambiguous, it leaves space for interpretation, mistakes and initiative.
- Strategy as the **ploy** - a manoeuvre intended to outwit our competitors with, that require development at the moment of inception, contemplating situational appropriateness, but leaves space to retreat, and have more than one manoeuvre ready. It unifies the "game plan".
- Strategy as the **pattern** - a consistent pattern emerges with strategy, that of past behaviour we followed with great success, studied, to identify the paths of attack, the good habits, tactics, forming and reinventing it with new more imaginative ones, as we get going with the next. We have a history, to tell us what could, should and will happen, with some amount of certainty.
- Strategy as the **idolised future position** - the conceptual framework of determining our next course of action, primarily by guiding factors, such as, principles, vision and mission. It becomes a dogma, a ploy, and agenda.
- Strategy as the **perspective** – the guiding force, the structure to orientate us, by having interlocking strategy, we interlock at every level steering all efforts into one main aim, determined primarily by the master strategist, like the captain of the ship, that can be altered, several times, and still all the forces will arrive at the same destination.
- Strategy as the means to **gain the advantage**, or power – having the ability to place our competitors in a position of disadvantage through a flexible application of your resources. With the right person in the right place, your company will be able to maximize each and every opportunity.
- Strategy as the means to **alignment** – alignment of all aspects, by engaging your employees through invested and unified leadership, you can align your employees with the objectives and goals of the company. Unity of decision making – by ensures maximum co-ordinated effort exists, that in accomplishing every assigned task, goal and objective, then there should be only one individual held responsible.

Principle Five: "Create Power"

"Create Power" - *Purpose, Orientation, Worth, Energy and Rejuvenation* – daily, the **exodus strategy**.

For every challenge and objective, ensure people understand it, and their **P**urpose, **O**rientate your people daily, make sure they understand their contribution and intrinsic **W**orth to the company as being essential. Make people and their efforts count, **E**nergy goes where attention flows, keep them focused, and make sure you **R**ejuvenate perishable skills, and systems that have suffered, and that needs repair. Retain the best and rejuvenate the rest.

Principle Six: "Stay resilient to resist adverse effects and keep the initiative".

Resilience implies the ability to bounce back after hitting a stumbling block, or in the face of opposition and challenges, to gather the strength to continue. Resilience, is not a taught state of mind, you can't teach it in a classroom, you can talk about it though, it is a gift of experience, a result of incidents and accidents throughout life that leave a lasting impression. It teaches us life lessons, leaving us with scars, reminders of what it takes to survive or succeed against odds, and yes it has a lot to do with genetics, it cannot be passed on – like with good work ethics, you must want it, practice it to be good at it. Resilience requires both good administrative skills, and communication and teamwork of people and thing - skills, along with an awareness of wider strategic issues. Resilience is the first concept or principle that really shapes people and organisational growth and potential. We tend to rob people of developing this skill, by just providing the answers and solutions to them daily. We cannot just create enthusiasm and newness to keep people active most of the time, it seem to always just last in small bursts, with no apparent real need for it, people do their jobs either way, whether they are enthusiastic about it or not. Enthusiasm seems to be directionless and useless, it holds us captive, for a short while, and then burns out. It does very little for solving critical questions. The only constant factor that always emerges trumps in solving pressing issues, and critical questions, is resilience, that draws out persistence and imagination, it seems to arise out of a deep personal necessity to perform, and is far better directed at addressing specific issues, combined with imagination, it builds a lasting character with a goal focused nature.

True resilience seems to heighten and build on the back of an presence of harsh events lived and overcome, and an passionate internal desire to succeed against any and all odds. Therefore, as and when collapse appear, we seem to have this thing, that helps us all to face a challenge and get on with life and living. Therefore, we have to become more resilient, to resist collapse, and its adverse effects. The thing with resilience is this, it is not always present, only as and when growth becomes none existing, as a means to overcome hard and difficult times do we see people becoming resilient. Then resilience fades away again, at the point where no more growth is required and sustainability is achieved. This is a cycle of change, called the adaptive cycle, and then more active and adaptive management styles emerges because of these situations, people take more risks, and learn more lessons. Moreover, if we do not engineer events, and get our people to figure out things for themselves they will never learn these essential life lessons. We as managers must surrender control and allow for mistakes, if we want solid strategic managers to emerge with a resilient character, capable of solving complex problems, and taking hard decisions. In short, desired managerial skills only develop during conditions of crisis and uncertainty. Hence policies and procedures, rules, and guidelines to manage or develop a system have to recognise that there are deep unknowns in addition to the known processes and the uncertain ones that challenge us all on different levels. Be pro-active, but adaptive when managing people during uncertain times.

Structure and systems failure is also attributed to this principle. Where old structures and systems starts failing, due to radical shifts in power, or new management styles or ideas, politics or whatever the cause may be. We see a ripple effect occurring in layers. If the structure is not repaired, and the vacant positions not replaced very soon, with same, or similar calibre people, or systems, but with dissimilar components, then the whole system reverberates into eventual collapse. The collapse of ancient societies had this very characteristic in common - where the top religious and political controls collapse, thus triggering the gradual collapse of an established government. Along with it, its law, customs, and practice, then it impacts on culture, it becomes fragmented, a total loss of cohesion and control becomes apparent, low moral sets in, and it keeps unravelling until we just have the family unit that is left as the sole source of structure and survival. We need sustainability, to achieve balance in societies same as in corporate structure. Sustainability both conserves and creates energy, if structures and systems adheres to growth and responds well to challenges it becomes sustainable. However, it can also build dependencies, some of which become key building blocks to constructive change, or a slow demise. The aspect of resilience and its necessity to beat anarchy down, is a most significant, it can both form and destroy.

There is a dire need now, to get rid of the abundance of bureaucracy - off to much don't do this and don't do that - that block mental and physical improvement, to try to stabilise the structures. We need to experiment more, take more risk, and let our staff experiment, and to encourage experiments that link people, resources and processes in surprising new ways. Some, and perhaps many of those experiments will fail. However, some will succeed and set the stage for change.

The second key is to recognise that even if something is small and seemingly insignificant - as parts of organisation, structure or systems...it can become the cause for derailment. The removal of one individual or small group/s from a structure, can at times transform the bigger picture significantly, either good or bad. Alternatively friction will occur at this point, where resistors of improvement have been side-lined and are now causing bottlenecks throughout the system.

Principle seven; "What is to be learned" - Unpack to add value

Change that is important is not gradual but is sudden and also informative, it teaches us things about ourselves and our systems, policies and procedures if we stay aware. There is a common trait during sudden change observable in individuals, in ecosystems, in business, and in society. If change is not done in step, where every part migrates as a whole, the structure reverberates and collapses. Increasing inflexibility is experienced where change is slow at one point and very fast at the other, then slow periods of growth and increasing inefficiency becomes a norm. That brings about a period of total destruction of all old structures, and with it disappears recourses, skill and experience, followed by a fast period where uncertainty is great, in an attempt to recover or catch up, where novelty emerges, and where new foundations are formed, just to collapse, just for a new cycle to begin that will lead to the appearance of stability or total demise.

And these are the lessons that help in that process of dealing with turbulence:

1) We learn with grace and humour and patience to work with others from different disciplines and backgrounds.

2) That the difficulty to overcome challenges is held captive in the mind of the beholder. Uniform behaviour patterns emerge, where people see very little hope, they see failure everywhere. Then hope emerges again, their will to turn the corner is back, fuelled by smaller causes that are simpler...yet have a bigger effect.

3) Fix the smaller things first , before attempting to fix the grand strategy, this triggers initial ideas, that can be built on. One has to learn to develop senses that help us listen to intriguing voices that are hidden at grass roots level, that hold the key to getting the tail of the organisation through the door of change amongst the noise of the bigger animal. Engage your workforce with one-on-one's and hear from them what works. Help them achieve personal success, by helping and letting them implement things that they know will work. This will transform your company into a highly profitable and aligned organisation.

Principle Eight; "Do we have to replicate the driver?

A driver is something or someone that provides energy, resources or motivation for a process to work. Examples of driving force; internet, software, skilled labour, electricity, management, etc. At operations level, we are looking to have more drivers, this equals, production with scalability. At tactical level fewer and at management less. Production with scalability tries to replicate the process, without replicating the driver, the force behind it. This concept is not unique to matrix management. With people for instance. We realise that people get tired and require some timeout, that machines break down and no one can work, that motivational talks only help that long, that resources are depleting, and that long hauls of mental energy and drive is just not possible. However if you have good support and reserves, then this does not become an issue, but the strength of the organisation, it has something on the side, in reserve. Every strategy must have specific objectives decisive to the operational success, that addresses a replacement, or alternative for a driver, to see where it can make a process more consistent, and sustainable, without having to replicate the driver. These objectives must be clearly understood as mitigating, having the ability to soften, or overcome the impact of any accident, failure or disaster. We require initiative to be followed to plan a way out or around, should this driver "crash". Initiative here implies predetermined courses of action rather than reaction. It means totally dominating the situation, or being able to control it no matter what, rather than allowing circumstances to.

Principle Eight; *"Are people fighting side by side?"*.

The crux of any matrix organisational structure is twofold, the support services and operational people are fighting side by side, just like soldiers at war, although they belong to a different corps, suppliers (logistics) need to be closely knit with operations. We seek high functionality at the point where we are operational. Where resources are directly required, so the guy that is welding, needs to be able to pick up the phone, buy the rods he prefers best, from someone he knows and have a personal relationship with him, that has an account with the company. (Of course, the tender and procurement rules and policies will have to be followed but this will be done by the buyer who gets an email to say that x-amount was purchased etc.) The departmental buyer and the supplier also form a personal bond, by relating with the processing and payment component.

Your support services turnaround times and efficiency will become lightning fast, as the operational people have logistical people within their ranks, or have a certain degree of freedom in buying or acquiring what is critical and necessary to continue with the job at hand. No more bottle necks and dead locks. Due to procedure, that takes forever to get critical logistics to the point where it is required most.

The second prong; is *your middle managements*, needs to be enabled to the fullest extent and ability to exercises their talents and initiative, they have to be entrusted and empowered with budgets. Be held accountable and responsible for expenditure. If they just become yes sir no sir robots it will stifle the matrix. This normally happens where top management is too scared to trust middle management to deal with a certain amount of finances. This type of organisation breed's haphazard management, because finance arrives very late, this causes strife, backstabbing, mistrust and even corruption, the very thing they are trying to fight. By spreading the risk of corruption, we find it easier to wipe it out, so we intentionally spread it to middle management level. The Middle management is the meat in the sandwich and if it gets pushed like a hot dog, the sausage will pop out. Without well-capacitated middle management, the hot dog is just a bun. If you want to know if an organisation is healthy and if the top guy's know how to manage, just look at the middle management and see how much authority they have and you will know exactly what you are dealing with –fact.

Apart from this design criteria, the management matrix is pretty much a personal choice and more a frame of reference influenced by business design principles that work for a particular industry. In my opinion, the Matrix is an organisational structure; mission specifically engineered to deal with complexity and thus necessitates complex strategy, organisation and co-ordination to function effectively. It is not suited for types of business, rather the semi-governmental and large global enterprises. Nevertheless, it does lend itself greatly to decentralized companies gearing up towards becoming global enterprises, to start with the Matrix model as platform from the word go, will in this event make good strategic business sense.

Principle Nine; "The glue of matrix management"

The 3x3x3 principle:

The three most important fundamental guiding aspects of matrix structure is a definitive strategy that has the following ingredients firmly cemented:

- A crystal-clear, practically executable " VISION" statement.
- A modern day human resource management philosophy.
- A integrated value system and culture aligned with principle.

The assumption is that organisations need to develop flexible inter-personal relationships within the management component and with the work force. To exploit potential and to let individuals make judgments calls, these are all trade-offs towards a shared strategic objective.

This is a three-way junction: between three opposing forces;

1. *Functional manager* – you report to someone who use to do the job you are doing now that understands and can emphasise with you, guide you and assist.
2. *Project manager* - you report to someone who is merely coordinating efforts, checking deadlines, finances, budgets and who trusts you to be correct in your assumptions and facts, which reports to people who don't think like you – but need your expertise to get the job done.
3. *Matrix Management* – fuses both these components of management and leadership into the matrix, it harnesses all the strengths and weaknesses of both, plus the combined similarities and contradictions. In addition, this aspect is what baffles many a mind, the fusion of two opposing worlds and cultures of thinking, systems and management styles. The overalls and the white coats.

The Three Big Matrix Viruses

Traditional matrix systems makes use of multi-lateral reporting and coordinating structures, this practice kills enterprise. Because someone has power, he or she is top dog. One only needs to apply this principle to information systems in my opinion. We do not want any chain of command infringements; if everyone sticks to their chain of command then everyone stays in the loop and in line. However, we blame the structure and the organisation for a lack of discipline and commitment, because we as top management import viruses by jumping the chain of command. In addition, worst still, we can justify it and our actions, we are in total denial about our transgressions. We have to trust the second and third line unequivocally. However we have to be seen and heard to be effective as leaders as well, so good one on one relationships are encouraged, as well as taking control, of the whole section from time to time so that the grass roots get to feel and experience your presence and style.

Overloading the hard and willing workers and by being openly critical of other staff who do not "seem" to perform is a big no-no, thus causing infringements of discipline. Any ethical code of conduct, must be conformed to by the top management first, it all starts from the top down, it becomes contagious, just like lava flows from the top of a volcano. If the management and leader are not disciplined in their actions. They destroy synergy and discipline. Destroying everything it encounters, it destroys anything and everything that is not lava, so does all types of bad habits and agendas. If the "Boss" gets to do it why can't we, so what comes around goes around take note.

Do not split peoples' focus, have one team complete what they started and then move on to the next assignment, cloning work assignments causes suspicion, competition and duplication of work, it is never conducive, it causes stress and friction. Priorities get smashed and people lose their resilience and desire to perform. Do not ever second-guess your professionals over inexperienced peoples' comments and gossip. If you say you, stand by your management you should do so unilaterally and never generalize, nor merely assume. Any Matrix organisation becomes furiously competitive, junior people will try anything and everything to get ahead in the rat race, to win top dogs favour and some will even resort to maliciousness, rumours, planting seeds of distrust and even create perceptions to undermine their supervisors worth, this can only happen if they have the ear of top management. My General in the army told me once that "Sharks and Goldfish" have two things in common, one they know their place in the pecking order and two the smaller of the two fish have the good common sense to know not to leave the bowl for the deep blue see, because size does matter. So should we, we should not allow direct lines of reporting out of an existing command chain. It has more dilemmas than what it does advantage. Sever the person from the chain; no one can serve two masters simultaneously. Moreover, no General can lead an army if his divisional commanders are having tea with the King all the time.

Most managers want and demand magical results from the Matrix, the reality is that it takes more work and especially co-ordination to perfect and I think it appropriate to quote Mark Twain who once said that "name the greatest of all inventors – Accident". He was right; we want people to be making mistakes while they are still young and in charge of little, so the damage will be small and the learning curve big. Opposed to them only getting that freedom once into positions and the damage will be large and the learning curve of no significance, to little too late. Sometimes but not so much the greatest of inventions and breakthroughs comes from trial and error, setbacks and disappointments. In the same light, one can only get good at riding and jumping a horse, by actually doing it. However, it is only when have fallen from a horse that we realise the importance of balance and we learn to respect the horse, both are quite essential to riding and jumping, being reckless, only leads to insult and injury. Practice is the apprentice of knowledge and skill. Therefore, it stands to reason that like with everything in life we will have to go through all the phases of growth, with balance and respect. There is just no magical shortcut or quick fix formula to it – sorry.

Principle Ten; "Leaders have to actually lead and managers have to actually manage".

The other factor, leaders have to actually lead and managers have to actually manage in order for things to happen. This normally gets all mixed up, leaders still want to manage and managers now without a job because of this trend; tend to take on the leadership roles. The surest way to gauge this is by checking the emphasis of top management. How much effort and time and money goes into which direction, does the annual budget get spent at all levels, is there balance in the leadership style and management contingent, do they complement each other or do they stand in stark contrast to one and other, or are they also not evenly matched in terms of competence. Do they stand in stark contrast to one an others opinions? Leadership will determine where a company will fall and where it will stand strong. A true leader should be seen to be delivering, by delivering at four levels:

- **Employee satisfaction**, total focus shift from production to empowerment and equality, growth and investment in the labour force and commitment to task and strategy, with high moral and in general, a great investment in the human assets and capital, if the followers speak with respect of the leader and his abilities, then he is leading if not, he is managing.
- **The organisation should stand in high regard with its competition**, be viewed as proficient, professional and successful, a very competitive tough player.
- **Customers must associate the company with, quality;** product, efficient people and skilled, with great customer service ethics.
- **Things that delivers economic value. PEST**
- *Political,* correctness, in line with the politics of the country, such as BEE, black Economic Empowerment, equity and affirmative action, as well as labour laws. and their community, do they do any community based work, with NGO's
- *Economical,* is the company viable and run economical. Alternatively, are they wasting time and overspending. Is the strategy working, or just surviving?
- *Social,* safety and security issues, health and recreation issues, are they being address? Does the company fulfil their social responsibility commitments with pride, by ploughing back into the workforce, infrastructure, the community, or addressing safety and security, and other relevant social issues?
- *Technological,* how does the company make use of technology compared to its budget size, processes vs. that of the competition? Is enough provision made for evolution and compliance?

Smoke and Mirrors

There can be no meaningful dialog and connection between people and organisations; before "position" is established. Strategic thinking as a concept originated from this deeper understanding of the rules for engagement. The "things" that need to be present before we can go over to action, and follow natural dynamics - the forces that tend to produce activity and change in any situation or sphere of existence. All aspects that have greatly influenced how people fight in wars.

When we look at war again, it is an outside in approach. It is a process of getting leverage to get in and control things to our advantage. We all need to establish some form of leverage before we can engage people and establish position. Leverage is described as an advantage; an ability, skill or something, that gets people to like you, trust you or open up to you in the positive. In the negative; the aim is the opposite, it is to get people to agree to, surrender, or make way – because of the leverage you have over them. In this section we will introduce an outsider in view, on how to establish a steadfast "position" with people, by identifying the "superiority element" required in this "contest or competition" of willpower, to get position through leverage. Having, or acquiring an advantage puts us in an ideal position to pursue our goal – right or wrong. In most instances it is the absence of leverage that halts the possibility, where we have no path, position, finances or rapport, where we are not part of the team, organisation, or culture, then we need something else, a key, that which is required to get inside their "hearts" and "minds". When we are tasked with developing strategy as strategist, finding a way from the outside in, or a counter strategy for keeping "them" out and arresting advances against us, then we are confronted with a new set of rules and dilemmas – called the "Mask". Someone maybe brilliant at strategy on the inside, however, if you cannot see the forces that bend and shake the will of people, the natural dynamics, then you will fail if doing things from the outside in. The word "mask" explains this aspect, it is an assortment of strategic principles that people use daily, so that we can or cannot make the connection, and establish a position; the likes of camouflage, cover up, disguise, cloak and masquerade on the one side of the coin, and on the other, interrogation, probing, study, skill, ability, and behaviour.

Only by having the knowledge of how to open up a "front", do we get to lift the mask, and go beyond the purely obvious. It is a timely process, peeling away at layers of intrigue and perception. Understanding things as they occur naturally, in their environment, and how and why people act and react, only comes from the interest and study of these aspects. For this we need penetrating and interrogating skills. We have to seek out the vantage points for ourselves and use them as leverage. Aspects that create rapport – a link - with people are simple; the things that come to mind are; language, culture, ability, skill, designation, official authority and the list goes on. Every corporate environment is unique, and also share similarities, as any other. In one way or the other, there is something they want, need, or see as useful, finding that aspect is key to establishing a position, that will open up possibility. Where the essential strategic elements of strategy becomes hidden, and not accessible, we need to use different approaches to ascertain understanding of how their strategy becomes significant. If we cannot establish rapport and position with others, either because we are in competition, or indifferent then we need to be able to study their behaviour and movement. Each of these passions that people experience daily is reflected differently, and by so doing, we are perceived different and treated accordingly. Finding peoples passion is one sure fire way of getting them to talk, or getting an understanding of their power. Then, the game is on, then we have to start peeling away. We have all learned the art of social, economic and physical disguise, by trying on several masks until we find the ones that fit best the situation we are manipulating. We have all, to some extent adopted these characteristics and tactics of clocking our behaviour and intentions effectively, by masking them, and in our corporations as well, it surfaces in our everyday dealings. Whether we pretend to be happy, working, or giving it our best or not, either way we are pretending. However, the perception we create with our facial, and verbal – our masks - could imply quite the opposite of what we are really, and people could see us as being very happy and hard working or successful, but deep down inside we are just plain miserable.

The two most interesting things about masks is their purpose and usefulness. Masks have been used in war effectively both as part of the strategy and tactics. Strategy and tactics are of lesser usefulness if they are not masked, and unveiled at the decisive moment. Just like a poker player won't show his deck until the final moments, all the while manipulating people with his masks, so to with strategy. Masks main purpose is to act as disguise and to hide the facial expressions of the wearer as a tactic, for two good reasons. They say a face never lies, the eyes tell a thousand stories and in battle, you do not want the enemy to see your fear, your underlying doubts, and know your true identity. This is true for business as well. We don't go to the bank manager with a fear struck appearance when asking for an extension or loan, no we walk in there confident. This very aspect then becomes tactical, what we put up as a front, and use as a skill, what we would like others to perceive about us, our products and intent or the organisation. As strategist we have to find all the hidden, the real and factual.

The point is, we all have "masks" and so do organisations, "things are not always what they seem on the surface, or what people say or don't say they are". The same with organisations, they do not want everyone to see what is truly going on, or broken, although they desperately want to achieve their objectives, or fix what is broken. Then they tend to hire outsiders to come in and fix, plan, or give advice, very few get it right. Only those that do, are the ones that are aware of the existence of masks. This aspect transcends natural, sacred and economical boundaries, it even surfaces in our communication. It is all in our ability to disguise and allude to our true intentions and the truth. Being able to communicate effectively and listen cautiously is not a sure fire way to get things done, and create a position for yourself. The facts are; we can only take control when we are in control, and until then we are just fighting to keep our footing strong. This situation can only advance to a solid position when we start asking the right questions, and get inside their OODA loop. He who controls the question, controls the answer, controls the outcome and perceptions. Questions and their usefulness are more powerful in steering the course, and staying focused, to give you footing to advance to a steady position. Questions will give you clarity...the loaded question, the probing question, and then the ultimate question. These are classical probing tactics; having the ability to refer to something or somebody indirectly, without giving a precise name or explicit meaning, is called alluding, the balance between questioning and alluding becomes an exercise in delicate but focused negotiation and interrogation. Before we can constructively enter into any beneficial strategic thinking session, we have to break the barriers down that exist, without anyone knowing, this will put them on guard, the mental, emotional and physical barriers need to come down, by winning peoples trust, and earning their respect. We realise that this too is not always possible, as personalities clash, people don't trust you, especially when they have a different view or agenda, or there maybe other forces hard are at work here that no one is aware of. You must furthermore remember, that the new guy, or newness is not always a welcome flavour. Where anything newly introduced is immediately seen as strange in a tight-knit secretive, and competitive environment, it gets acted upon with suspicion, and gets probed, and only when we engage it, do we see it for what it is, and as it is. The tricky situations that strategist face daily, deals with the secrets of all things "foreign". In order to do so, we have to enter environments, peoples habitats, both physically and mentally, to try and understand the people; their cultures, strategy and systems, all the hidden elements.

Then we have to go with what we have, and act our instinct.

"Strategic thinking is the obvious precursor to any strategic development or planning session. It begins with exploration of the environment, an intuitive, visual, creative process that results in a synthesis of emerging themes, issues, patterns, connections and opportunities. It has two major components: insight about the present and foresight about the future."

T. Irene Sanders

Effective strategic decision-making mandates the true understanding, of things as they relate in their natural environment, from their context and content, their root and surrounding issues and influences, before any consideration can be made of the full potential range of options available.

Apart from the blatantly obvious, the vision and mission statement of the company and what people tell you. These things should give you only a good idea of what was, as it is history. Strategist concern themselves more with what is, because anything else is just an idolised position, and thinking, what's more important, we need to acquire additional information and test assumptions, and perceptions, to come up with a realistic strategic plan. In order to do this we have to fully explore the environment. Following is a list of the five main exploration criteria/ areas in the strategic thinking process that needs to be investigated, the "stuff", that hides behind the mask – the mental body.

First off – we need to do a political climate check, of the organisational and cultural aspects.
People like organisations want and need to be understood in terms of their culture and means, before we can even try to explore alternatives for them, we need to form a basis of common understanding with them. Both in terms of what they want from us and what they hope for us to achieve and return as a desired solution. We need to seek out their idolised position, by saying this, we recognise that it won't be a total concept, but as they explain it, they will normally define the parameters for themselves and us as we question their motives, and reason. What they have, as an initial departing solution is normally not what they really want, or need, and had in mind, or can afford - it is the ideal. All of us are to a certain extent eagerly

optimistic and overly confident in our ability to shape, and steer the future. Let me explain this; if you ask a child what they want to be doing one day, then they will or might be conservative in their thinking - a train driver sir - but ask them what they want to drive - a "Ferrari" - well then the sky becomes the limit. Clearly, these two will never merge, where the one prospect will never give rise to the other expectation.

Only when narrowing down their resolve – the ability to make up their minds for them as to what they need, and can realistically afford in black and white - do solutions become more realistic and so do expectations. We have now ring fenced the parameters in which things must take form. It is only here that we can actually say that we are ready to depart, and start determining the aim or objectives for the first time. The point I am raising here is wait before you start modelling strategy and creating expectations – people keep you to it, and the less they get of what they were hoping the less of a steady position you have. Wait for the close of the brief. Now we can colour it in, ask questions for clarity, are we talking total re-designing, or only new concept designs, are we talking fast tracking or stream lining? What is the nexus, the core of the relationship, between this strategy and other strategies they have in place? Why does this facet of the organisation require high-level intervention; and who endorsed it and why? I call it finding the "bull's-eye" - the core of the problem they want resolved; many strategist just go on the assumption that they know and have the answer, "what it is that the customer wants" – "but actually needs" – requires questions for clarification. Just because you have the "customers" brief in writing and listened to his wants, does not mean it will be the ultimate solution. Strategist are ultimate solution oriented. What you have is one view point. Remember the organisation is the customer not the individual giving the brief...i have seen many master plans dropped, and torn to pieces because it was designed on a single brief from one department head only – with one view point.

We only understand "wants" once we start the interrogation process ourselves and find them. Only by asking questions for clarity, until they shape the desired concept that everyone can associate with, do we have a master plan template. We do this from altering our own perspective, not from looking in, but from their perspective, looking out, seeing the solution as they see it fit, we become the architects of their imagination, acting inside their means. By introducing workable fragments, things they relate to and models they understand, of the envisaged final product built from their collective explanation and perspective, do we arrive with working concepts. Normally, we assume too much by just talking and listening, we need to listen to see, yes, talk to keep rapport, but we have to always rip at beliefs, at the model, and see if it is the right fit, before we just jump in and begin the tedious task of planning and designing. We need to see it all, and it must fit, from all available perspectives, to see the problem first-hand and ask ourselves, is this really the problem, and do we have the total solution? Or is this only the perceived problem, the tip of the iceberg, or an attribute of a bigger problem?

Is there not something deeper, sinister and underlying that they are not telling or missing here, or that they themselves have missed, or overlooked, or are not aware off, and last but least not talking about, their blind spot? Ask the right questions, to get the clarity you desire. Strategic synergy, refers to the ability of the strategist to look at everything in its smallest and most detailed form, and then weave it into one global concept. This is not possible, when working with assumptions only, it only comes from opening up the collective insight, like peeling away at an onion, layer by layer, until you find the centre stalk, the core of the problem. By seeing both the physical – the system and the structure - and the abstract – the people and their perception - as they exist in their natural environment working and existing, only then do we gain true strategic insight. What this implies is, people mask their problems, and deficiencies and sugar coat them, especially if the problem concerns them, pride is at stake here. Life is an endless battle, with conflict in many forms, and you cannot fight effectively unless you understand and can identify the root. We need to see the problem, in its many forms, with any group, and people there are agendas, alliances and hidden dark secrets. Disaster and Victory have the same origin, it happens in small steps, and then evolves to its final form. He who controls perception, controls peoples realty – and therefore the outcome. Terror and fear, keep people just as much captive as hope and denial, it is the ultimate way to paralyse peoples will, to either resist evil or to persist with conflict, it's all by "choice" and that choosing will result in either disaster or victory. The results will differ, however the recipe will stay the same. If we plan for victory, we are in essence also planning a disaster, it is a very fine line that exist, that they both travel on, it is just the end result that is uncertain, the rest is planned. People are originators, and catalyst for evil, and failure, once you have convinced yourself that they no longer have that power, then we move on and interrogate; policy, systems and procedure.

Revisit the organisational structure then, if you find no "evil", to see if your proposed strategy will compliment any of their existing strategy and structure and fix what's broken, to make sure they have the necessary resources and expertise, arbitrary resources might be available, but what would the results be, if they are used, or moved, what void would it create?

Think ripple effect, and cause and effect. People tend to fix problems by wanting to throw resources at it and then by so doing create even more problems. This necessity to think global, to make the structure work inline with new strategy emerging, only becomes evident once other systems, or sub-systems come under pressure or collapse, because of the new. Therefore, be mindful in assuming that resources and expertise are randomly available, for they very-seldom are not, even if managers think otherwise. Any change in direction, or strategy requires a total holistic approach, on all levels of organisation to see how it will integrate and impact on the old habitat. We need to ask the questions that count, when it counts, do we need to rewrite job description or re- define roles, policy and or procedures as well. By saying this, we could have a situation, where we move people around to jobs that they would rather do, from receptionist to debtors, for instance, thus creating new energy at the same time. Rather than saddling up a tired horse.

The next aspect is that of enhancing core-functions, this is the lifeline of the enterprise and must be protected, like a spine. In the final analysis, will the new strategy interlock at any stage with the core function, the vision and the mission? Let's go through our checklist before introducing a strategy we have to look at our:

Critical Observation of how they do things traditionally. Observation and orientation goes hand in glove, it is the preface of understanding, in order to see, we have to look wider, to gain a better understanding of the new battle plan, and what it will entail, we have to become aware of the battlefield and our vantage points. We create blind spots for ourselves and then blame bad feedback and input – that we allowed. When you are looking through diving goggles at a coral reef things are much clearer than what they would be without the vision aid. Strategic thinking takes on the same principle. We need to see with clarity, to think with clarity. People sell their personal flavour of clarity that they like best, because of personal interest and insight. How do we get un-obscured, byes clarity, by thinking what if? What would the reality be if the problem did not exist? Is the current reality the cause of the problem? If so, is it due to character or competence issues. The point is this; sometimes a plan or a strategy is just not what is necessary to change the reality. Sometimes it is just the peoples paradigm, which requires a strategy or makeover. Those character trait's of "willpower" that require tuning, their egos, their inability to see, understand, lead, manage and make sense of their reality. They are so close to the wall, their reality; that they do not see the door, the solution. Management style and support, is to be blamed for most of these crises, this creates blind spots, so it could be a small bottleneck, that would only require a systems change. This happens when we just cannot take criticism well; or we take it far too personal. The fact of the matter is this; this very aspect is quite essential the "fluidity of effective communication" in designing strategy, it needs to be unmasked.

Scrutinise and test Views. Views are simply different ways of thinking and expressing oneself, our core concepts and beliefs surface with our views. We become entangled in concrete, factual and abstract, emotional matter. In strategic thinking mode, we need to think three dimensional; analytical, global and critical to form a solid understanding of our task. Only then can we define our gaols and views clearly. Creativity spawns with insight and it is only with wisdom that it will translate into solutions. Solutions, spreads from finding creative views and synergistic methods and ways of seeing relationships where others only see complexity. What is significant is the turmoil it creates, that is required, the negative feedback, to give it the required certainty; only fools never differ, for non-see with clarity. The other aspect is job security, people have become survivors and they all seem to want to outwit, outplay and outsmart each other, to get recognition. People have become fearful of going it nose to nose, or differing with the general consensus, they feel that they might compromise their positions – or be ladled troublemakers. In fact they are, they rob themselves another's of the opportunity, to grow if they stop challenging convention. People in positions of authority should allow mavericks, and their thinking to be analysed and tested. To get clarity feedback. Some believe we have far to many "happy" employees in crappy jobs, getting run down, and beaten up, so that they just don't add their input anymore – why, what does it matter – because they are so unhappy in fact? We know that this seldom happens, oh really, the fact is it happens all over – people today work because they have to, most managers are badly informed, stupid, arrogant and self-centred – and won't give their people the time of day, but hay who cares, they get the figures. Critical thinking is paralleled thinking; it requires genuine feedback from all, be it unimportant or critical in nature it will serve no purpose, if it not spontaneous. Integrity and trust combined transforms to perfection, only if both parties can withstand the turmoil and friction it creates. This shows maturity, and great leadership. Only where openness in critical communication is encouraged, will trust prevail. Peoples interest should be focused at goal level and not at task, they have to find their own way of doing their task, within the means and training provided - themselves. Then team driven efforts, should be focused on creating visionary thinking and problem solving cells, and not just a targeted result. This creates the desired mental clarity we seek, for when everyone sees, what they are creating, they tend to all become more creative. This then becomes the second creation, the personified creation, my and our creation. People then take ownership and most importantly responsibility, for their creation. Creating effective and lasting strategy is an on-going process of thoughts aligned, with energy combined. Anything else is fragmentation, blurred vision and noise. Traditional crisis management strategy, where we have so many plans, but no one is allies, neither do they share in thinking, nor do they have the energy left, where no one can see the goal to believe in it enough, to even act on it.

What is their strategic driving forces? All strategy requires a driver and a force. The biggest driving force for human interfacing with strategy is trust, without trust nothing will stick. This is the universal "true glue" or "truth" of relationships formation. Be it with man and beast, or man and man, or man and machine, if we don't trust the relationship, it won't work. This is the force, that refers to our ability to adapt, improvise and overcome - behind relationships. If we can give every person a challenge each new day and make that challenge count, by rewarding trust, then they, your people will live full productive lives. Making the challenge of trust count, making it stick. We can only build trust by seeing potential in people, which they themselves do not even see. It is only when we inspire, one another that we realise that we have affirmed trust in that relationship. Trust and synergy are core values of any strategy, they become the drivers. However, competition emanates, we try to get better at it, and then become competitive, this is natural, but if managed badly then it becomes a bad and destructive habit. Do not set people up to chase the carrot, to get back into old habits. If you keep telling people that they are bright, have great potential and are bestowed with unlimited seeds of greatness, talents, then this is service unequalled by any motivation or incentive ever contemplated – however they have to trust you to believe it, and then see it in themselves their potential to realise it. It is only then that they will water their talents and develop them. That they realise that they can, can do things all by their own accord, that they have what it takes, affirm your commitment, affirm people, then they will start believing in worth and will follow you blindly (more on Nero Linguistic programming - NLP in a later chapter). If you treat them with dignity and respect they will bow to your wisdom, if you care for them as if they are your own children they will fallow and fall by your side, with you. Who we are to others is more important than who we appear to be to ourselves. How we treat a man is how he becomes, if we treat him as weak, then weak he will become. "We become that which we are told, if not by self, then by others". In short, we gauge the level of trust in the organisation and the way they get things done traditionally and habitually, their way. How effective it is, and can it be improved on, by changing perceptions.

How do they see their idealised position. If something like that really exists, it's merely a maxim for a good firm stepping stone, from the one to the next, to maintain essential balance and movement to the next "ideal" stepping stone, or "position". Life is fluent and so is time, just so is strategy, so to get to the ideal situation is a little presumptuous in my opinion. Your "ideal" position as outlined should include a next generation of ideal positions and even past that, to become a true ideal position. We also have life, change, and circumstance that prevail that inhibit us. We have to be realist, and plan past the point you are currently striving for, for when you arrive at the "ideal position", will it service, to assume that in the altering state we exist in, that the ideal position will now become a secure position, a final destination, once attained. This is not sound reasoning; it will deteriorate with time, to a less than advantageous position, whilst you are working towards it. If anything good, war has taught us that defence is a delayed defeat, a slow way of losing, whereas movement is a sure way of getting there. Therefore, the ideal position would be one that evolves constantly, as we move towards it, it is not something consistent. Movement, manoeuvrability, equates to survival and so do personal growth, it creates effortless movement, be it physical, intellectual or in whatever direction. The nature of matrix strategy, require a built in fluidity, duality, the human element and the strategy has to grow, to get to the idolised position, of continued evolution. The very conditions and principle needs to be prevailing in business to stay abreast and in the lead. Some will still argue, that it is inherently barbaric, that it is a relic of the past, and something to be forgotten for good – war, strategy and tactics. They might otherwise argue that it promotes conflict and deviousness. Well the truth is we have plenty of that in the world, the moral of the story is, it is human nature, and we will meet bigger and stronger opponents that has refined this art. The question is will we be vigilant and able to defend ourselves and our gains against them. Life and living only becomes significant and compromised in the face of imminent demise, business on the other hand and its lifespan, is determined by the ability to adjust rapidly, consistently and effectively to change. This principle should motivate and dictate your total thinking towards reengineering your strategy constantly. For strategy in itself requires global content. Therefore, daydreaming of the idolised position all day WILL NOT create the desired strategy to keep you at the spearheads end in the marketplace. All opportunities that may exist, currently or in the future, for you and your business will remain out of reach, if you do not actively talk and seek invention and new ideas. Fluidity of creative thoughts are born out of high speed trust communication networks, affirming the good in people, telling people that they can be more, if only they want to believe it. Rethink your strategies with people; in terms of dimension; firstly in terms of the core competencies and skills required in your business; secondly, instilling trust, and thirdly; affirming worth and fourthly teach strategy. This reminds me of a great poem;

DESIDERATA

Go placidly amid the noise and the haste, and remember what peace there may be in silence. As far as possible without surrender be on good terms with all persons. Speak your truth quietly and clearly; and listen to others, even to the dull and the ignorant, they too have their story. Avoid loud and aggressive persons, they are vexations to the spirit.

If you compare yourself with others, you may become vain or bitter; for always there will be greater and lesser persons than yourself. Enjoy your achievements as well as your plans. Keep interested in your own career, however humble; it is a real possession in the changing fortunes of time.

Exercise caution in your business affairs, for the world is full of trickery. But let not this blind you to what virtue there is; many persons strive for high ideals, and everywhere life is full of heroism. Be yourself. Especially do not feign affection. Neither be cynical about love; for in the face of all aridity and disenchantment it is as perennial as the grass. Take kindly the counsel of the years, gracefully surrendering the things of youth.

Nurture strength of spirit to shield you in sudden misfortune. But do not distress yourself with dark imaginings. Many fears are born of fatigue and loneliness. Beyond a wholesome discipline, be gentle with yourself. You are a child of the universe, no less than the trees and the stars; you have a right to be here. And whether or not it is clear to you, no doubt the universe is unfolding as it should.

Therefore, be at peace with God, whatever you conceive Him to be. And whatever your labours and aspirations in the noisy confusion of life, keep peace in your soul. With all its sham, drudgery and broken dreams; it is still a beautiful world. Be cheerful. Strive to be happy. ~Max Ehrmann, 1927~

Synergise the collective and remove the masquerades. Synergy is the working together of two or more people, organisations, or things, that deliver results greater than the sum of their individual efforts or capabilities would have. The great strategies and tactics that you will need to move and remove masks, are not only the consequence of study, and skill, it involves more than just strategic brilliance, it requires wisdom, and the will to overcome, fuelled by a passionate desire to persist against great odds. Forming and synergising pools of human intellect stimulates peoples individual passion, and the get-up-and-go mentality. Synergy will also translate in the formulation of new and fresh ideas, that one "Great business concept" will only come to mind by tapping into the collective source, through synergy of thought. "What you vividly imagine, ardently desire, you will evidently achieve", first as a person and then as a collective, only if we can live with synergy.

We need to formulate our collective ideas so that we can see them clearly from many and different perspectives; we have to unpack them in parts for others to see without a doubt, to be unmasked, in order to sell them in perfect clarity to all interested parties. The idea, is to add value. One cannot sell a half full or half empty type of business concept, or strategy to anyone anymore, it will not add value. People get despondent and are in general afraid to take the leap across the canyon of change, because of others who influence them to live in denial, by staying in the confines of known safety zones. What this world needs more of are more strategic athletes that run and find the new cheese daily. The world would have been a great deal smaller if we all believed that it was square. On the other hand, there is still reality and the laws of nature and how things are, affirm within yourself first and then take the much contemplated quantum leap: of affirming in others. Know that it will take time.

The Elements of Character

The elements of the human mask – character - only become relevant once we see the prevalence of it in its fragments. In each of the "strategic time spiral continuums" - explaining a link between two things, or a continuous series of processes required and forming, that blend into each other so step by step and become seamlessly and one concept or principle, that at some point it is almost impossible to say where it originated from, where the one takes over from the next, and to identify which one is key to the outcome of the strategic thinking process. We cannot shape blindly our plans and leave it all in the hands of faith and destiny, if the faith of human conviction did not lean towards follow into strategy itself. Therefore, true strategy is also a measured against the realisation of components mixed that will add the required and much sought after diversity and strength. We have to see, beyond the mask, to make sense of it. Practical examples are:

- **Prior experience** in strategic planning and thinking – this aspect will determine how effective time will be spent during planning and how close to the reality projections will be made,
- **The sophistication level** of the team in question, - the level of maturity and of technique, technical expertise, as well as the level of technology they will use, effectively of not.
- **Their consciousness** pertaining to available time-frames and resources, - their frames of reverence and effective utilisation of resources, how do they define and determine quality. How do they calculate the potential risk factors?
- **The point in the life cycle of the company**, only one in every ten companies make it past the ten year mark, do they take this into account and – how much credibility, experience, support and stigma is coupled, as well as status and financial backing, to this company or project.
- **How do they compensate** for the many other factors that will and can influence strategy that cannot be harnessed?

The importance of collaboration

In summary: We never know to whom, or where, or when, or how our strategic knowledge will become relevant, that's why I decided to do this chapter, to give you options, when you find yourself wanting to sell your strategy. For selling strategy is a strategy in itself, you have to satisfy their wants and add value to your service, your worth and that of the company.

Dominate with the wisdom of divergent strategies, strategy within strategy, this is the rule of the game of strategy, how do you dominate and become the victor with strategy, by having and understanding all the leverage it takes to get things in their intended orbit, and the next chapter deals with gaining this strategic advantage.

Rapidity is the essence of war;

It takes advantage of the enemy's un-readiness, make your way by unexpected routes and attack unguarded spots – Sun Tzu, - The Art of War.

The Rapid Dominance strategy; is a strategy within the grand strategy, it exploits the creative thinking and entrepreneurial nature of man to deal effectively with sudden change, by speedily reacting to it. With the onset of dynamically changing economic climates and business sectors, facing a down turn economy, several views and ideas on how to effectively deal with change and keep in step has emerged. This begs the question, is it not too little too late? Alternatively, is it not quite essential. In effect this turn, has opened up several completely new markets, brought down inflation, and has some good aspects as well. A sense of urgency has re-emerged, time and efficiency has merged, and has become of greater essence. Just by looking at new information resources; computer technology and cell phones are merging into new technology. The market has exploded with new, faster and integrated products. The course has been set and related technologies and systems will keep emerging to keep us on track with our faster changing reality.

It has opened up a new market, and industry catering for a void that opened, because of change, the world is advancing with systems and technology at a rapid pace. Superior portable infrastructure, software and computerised equipment is new in the news. Systems and network interlocking 24/7, anywhere at any time, has now almost become seamless, with the option of open connectivity, the ability to add on, or connect too more databases and resources as well as applications. The world has become one big interlocking global village. Nevertheless, the challenge of this day and age is still information management and processing it at the human interface level. Regardless of all the technological advancements made, this is and remains the bottleneck element. The slowest attribute is still the human components, which has to interrogate and disseminate the wealth of information daily. The point to make is this, the one with the most up to date information can make the best evaluation and steer the safer course with strategy. On the other hand, too much information and incorrect interpretation, could undo the whole concept. Therefore, new ways of dealing effectively and speedily with information has to be created. With appropriate integration we can benefit from technology and all its spin offs. When contemplating a strategy, any strategy, it requires fresh research and up to date information. Strategy itself only becomes relevant when it fits in with the current reality of things and how we get everyone to see it. Change has become the only constant and how we keep track of it will determine our future.

This lengthy introduction was done with intent; to point out how feeble a task it has become to stay abreast with all the new technology, information and research as they emerge. Nevertheless, the very nature of good strategy requires of us to be aware of any advances made in the respective fields. Strategy concentrates mainly on planning for research, technology, trends and timely information. We therefore have to re-look all our research and information almost daily, to stay current. All our assumptions are drawn from this pool of information, to become our business intelligence – which refers to skills, processes, technologies, applications and practices used to support decision making. Things are changing so fast, that we can no longer rely on yesterday's research and information today in certain instances. It becomes imperative and essential to prepare holistically. We only become conscious of reality once we "see" it; by having experienced it from different sources and paradigms. This creates "envision". Envision, is "encompassing vision", it encompasses as many attributes as possible, before we conceptualise our strategy. The passion of "vision" (seeing) only starts growing with enthusiasm when we find the relationships between our strategy and reality and how it is perceived, via our research and experiences. By implementing creative and critical thinking, we arrive with alternatives and solutions to complexity and thinking. Creative thinking stems from applying principles; we test our thinking by incorporating sound principles. We analyse this thinking by filtering it with critical thinking, a deeper understanding of how things fit, relate and interrelate, in relation to its parts, forming one whole in reality. This creates the required awareness of things and how they fit. We cut from the mental cloth of knowledge, experience and wisdom, the pieces required that will realise our goals, which will fit in with the constants of change, by refining it against our experience. Through independent intent and our will, we chart the course and set our sails with intent. However, success comes from realising that only through interdependence the process of seeking understanding first and then moving to be understood - will we find ways and means of realising collective objectives.

The Rapid Dominance strategy concept utilises one general approach to combine all aspects of initiative into one three dimensional model. Called "The Rapid Dominance Strategy". The purpose of which is to generate and evaluate as many ideas as possible for effecting "Rapid change" through the implementation of several strategies, and technologies that form one core strategy, as and when changes occur, we have to have flexible hovering strategies capable of turning and implementing the best of ideas rapidly into operational concepts. In order to counter the change effectively, without having to halt, or revise the main strategy, or propelling strategy. Hovering strategies are also referred to as "balancing strategies", like a hovercraft, glides on a cushion of air, over various terrains. The aircushion balances off the two opposing dominances of gravity and weight. The noticeable difference here is that there are several (free thinking) "waves of attack" of initiative, working towards one strategic goal, at the main strategic level; it is structured and organised, well-co-ordinated. The question is how do you co-ordinate strategy in motion?

The is the next step of co-ordinating strategy in motion:

The Hovering Strategy

"Hovering strategy" keeps the craft afloat, it is strategy untaught, it is a reflexive attribute, doing things on its own terms, at operational level, to counter any obstacle one encounters, it then becomes reflexive and instinctive. Its purpose is to use tactics, to overcome obstacles encountered at operational level, and requires inventiveness. This is in line with the "Art of War" principle, where we utilise conventional and unconventional means to reach our objectives. Therefore, "hovering strategy" could be termed unconventional strategies and the rest conventional strategy, only concentrating on the main objectives and keeping it on course.

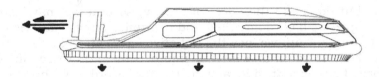

"Hovering strategy" -Explained in relation to a Hovercraft:

The significance of "Hovering strategy". Let's take this aspect to the next level and put it into practical terms, the air cushion under the hovercraft is the "hovering strategies", the frontline, more operational type of strategies, almost just plain tactics and utilised daily or short term. Emanating from a sound vision and mission as framework, by allowing innovation, initiative to flow uninhibited, at grass roots level, we have one force, lifting the system. The main strategy is the propelling force of the craft, that propels it, that which gives meaning to the core function. Although the two strategies are explained as being two parts, they must connect at some point to become one, although they work and exist in alternate states and in different direction. They also abide to different rules, and principles. Nevertheless, they rely on some of the same concepts and principles used in the grand strategy – like air (initiative). The big significance is this; the hovering strategy is confined, within a framework of the air cushion and can only go so far. Whereas the main strategy is not confined in any way by framework, only natural forces and factors will influence it. The other factor that differs is the co-ordination means, the command and control, like that of a rudder on the hovercraft – our intent - steering the strategy. Therefore if the main strategy is correctly steered by effective co-ordination, by utilising the rudder, the hovering strategy will have to follow. Mainly because it is confined within this framework of the craft and the terrain it encounters. The significant thing about the two strategies, the one requires the other; they are one thing, functioning along two very different paradigms – referring to an example that serves as a pattern or model for something, especially one that forms the basis of a methodology or theory. Strategist need to understand this concept. Without sufficient down force, the craft can't lift free of its gravity, thus it has no balance. As the down-force diminishes and the aircushion collapses, so does the crafts speed and balance due to the effects of gravity, until it eventually comes to a standstill, succumbing to the greater dominance of gravity. Gravity, relates to the circumstances generated in the organisation, where the management gives them forward motion directives, whilst they are operating from a downward paradigm. No matter how hard the main strategy tries to gain momentum and pick up speed again, or steer, it is and remains stationary, by virtue of its inability to break free of its gravity. We can deduct from this concept, that every strategy we design needs a platform, the craft and then the hovering strategy, the ability to do one thing and that is help the organisation break free of its own gravity. Gravity refers to (changing) circumstances and how to deal with it, as a real hovercraft would, transitioning, from cement, to water to sand, as it negotiates terrain each of these have "dominance", that it exerts on the craft. This aspect is blatantly obvious in organisations failing. Failing to realise that strategy requires two parts, one conventional the other unorthodox to work effectively. Dominance refers to our weakness and strength, the ability or inability to dominate certain circumstances that occur naturally, effectively, and consistently, if not they will dominate us and our strategy. This is how powerful, our hovering (balancing) strategy has to become; it has to not just influence, but dominate the effect of gravity, so that we may have to our advantage control and initiative. Once we have dominated and controlled circumstances we can use initiative to steer any course of events. Until we lose the initiative again and have to struggle to get it back. If initiative is lost, we have to adapt and fast, by improvising and overcoming our circumstances. This requires freedom of movement, and action, in other words, we have to give our staff the freedom to take and implement any actions required, as they see and deem fit, at grass roots level, to overcome dominance.

Let's just go back and revisit **"main strategy"**, the main strategy refers to the horizontal propulsion system of this craft. This system influences the "rapidity" – speed of the craft and the rudder the course, our speed will be determined by our ability to cycle through options, make relative choices and implement them. We have discussed the "OODA" loop, and here again it applies. Observation, is the clear awareness of circumstance, as and when they unfold, relative to our situation. Orientation, is the ability to find direction in relationships to the prevailing circumstances that puts one in a better position. Decision, is the ability to choose, the correct course of action under duress. Act, is the ability to go over from decisive thought, to rely on experience gained and to only go with our gut feelings at times, ones instincts, implying taking calculated risk. The faster we can complete the "OODA" loop the greater our "rapidity" becomes, this aspect works in both directions. The only difference is that forward it is charted, like a course on a map and downward, it relies on sharp wits and experience.

The significance of the rudder is that it steers our strategy towards its objective, the rudder is the co-ordination mechanism of strategy and resides in our ability to communicate rapidly and effectively. It combines the efforts and directs it in one direction. This is the niche of true leadership. It's the ability to co-ordinate all facets of enterprise, like a conductor and orchestra and choir, without adding weight. To produce the greatest of harmonious music, not noise.

" The whole secret of the Art of War, lies in the ability to become master of communication" –Napoleon.

Communication control, or command and control, both hold the same understood meaning; the art is in dimension; (according to Liddell Heart).

*The first dimension is the **Physical**: the ability to correctly identify physical means that could stop any attempt at rapidity or dominance, to ascertain the vision. This also refers to communication mediums and the dissemination and assimilation of information. In other word how we physically handle information.*

*The second dimension is the **Psyche**: the ability to stand firm in the face of duress and still be able to affect change effectively. The ability to make good decisions based on trust and not on suspicion. How we mentally handle communication and information.*

*The third dimension is the **Sensory** and broad communication: To make sure that communication channels stay open and uninterrupted, that information flows steady and correct. To ensure that perception do not cloud sound judgement. How we perceive information and prefer it, in terms of audio, visual, or both. Which medium gives us the best response?*

These aspects of dimension, will dictate how we act, or don't act with information. Personality, will be the covering criteria, we are only as good as what we are aware of our strengths and weakness, for we act on both equally well. Command and control is a skill and can only be perfected with practice.

On Goals: In order to reach the final objective we must reach goals, like milestones on a journey, but goals are not always queued in relation to the one logically following the other. This is linear thinking, non-linier thinking, would suggest achieving goals in a higher plain. By example, if the objective was to shop for food, then linear thought would dictate that we do it aisle by aisle until we have gathered the list of groceries we require. Non–linear thinking would approach this task   from a paradigm of effectiveness, our focus is fixed on the outcome and our flexibility on the process, whereby we will have several trolleys gathering the food simultaneously. Therefore, nothing stops us to achieve the unobstructed goals in the meantime, like playing a game of leapfrog; we can "leap" beyond certain goals for now and achieve others, whilst we wait for the obstruction to be moved to ascertain aforementioned goals. Goals should be seen as the smaller parts of strategy. Several goals reached will constitute an objective; an objective is a millstone, a measurable. Several objectives will constitute a main objective or a strategy. Several strategies will constitute our intent. Together all these strategies, form together like multiple waves, to form the core strategy or grand strategy. By virtue of following conventional and unconventional means; small and big waves of initiatives emerge. We are just utilising our time more effectively. By saying this, we imply that waves break differently; every wave is a wave, but it has its own character. If we allow our people to build their own wave making equipment, using their initiative and creativity; good hovering strategy will emerge, then we become an organisation intent on making improved waves. We create better wave effects, better strategy, as everyone gains the knowledge of strategy from practice. It is only when we find ourselves perusing strategy in this fashion, that we realise the importance of communication. Where we trade some space for time, in other words, where it could have taken days for one goal to be reached, we now put in more manpower and save time. This gives us space to rethink our next move and so on.

The concept of effective communication requires open source communication mediums – this implies connectivity – structured input and output of communication via all your mediums. Daily structured feedback and improved up to the minute communication can now be structured around one medium. The challenge is to get everyone to utilise the same medium successfully and to train them to use it effectively. We look at more streamlined systems, easy to use, with multi-faceted usage such as, cell phones, that have email, fax, internet and voice capabilities. The challenge is to get it to work without creating bottlenecks or total dependency. Bottlenecks should be breached, via contingency planning or routing. There will also have to be an important training and educational skills development component here, which will have to run in parallel with the implementation of any new and more technically enhanced systems - the challenge is to master our methods of communication. The full potential value of any system can only be harnessed if the people working on them are trained to utilise it effectively, just take a practical example here with the revision of Microsoft office. Every year or so new components and features are added, yet very few companies actually send their people to get retrained on the upgraded software, it just gets installed and that's that. Therefore, my point is this, if the Information and Technology component that has to deal with our communication is state of the art, but the operators do not harness a fraction of its capability, due to a universal culture of "failure to train people on communication systems", hereby the company is in fact wasting money on upgrading. The point in this, knowledge of technology has to grow in parallel, before it can become an effective tool. The Rapid Dominance Strategy relies on effectiveness; you cannot have multiple waves of strategy flowing out if you cannot manage it. It will result in chaos.

The Rapid dominance strategy is based on the military principles of "Blitzkrieg", it has the same effect as the crack of the whip, it is sudden, unexpected and fast and hits its intended target decisively. It is small yet has great energy. Summarised as a conflict put into motion, through careful planning, intelligence and research, that forms a deep understanding of the nature of opponents, their tactics and manoeuvres. Rapid dominance strategy, or attack, is introduced with lightning speed and accuracy, in waves, as soon as the one breaks the next one is ready to break, advertising, marketing, publications, product release, launches and then more outlet's opening up, etc. It is a well thought out plan, of fluidity. That creates a violent surprise, all efforts to stop it fails, as it changes shape and focus with every wave. This strategy is designed to achieve success and market share in minimum time, to cut costs and to produce turnover as fast as possible.

The problems experienced with most corporate strategies are that they become fragmented, the moment departments take ownership of strategy, it becomes fragmented, dislodged from the core, they rip the heart out and put their own in and massage it until it feels good. This is not what Rapid Dominance strategy is all about. Strategy requires control, the very opposite of human will.

In order to blend the two, it has to flow from one source. Strategy has phases; let's look at the phases of Rapid dominance strategy:

Phase one: Breaking open a front. – By identifying the opportunity.

It requires opportunity first, there has to be an opportunity that is created by merging circumstances that can be exploited.

> *"Rapidity is the essence of war; it take advantage of the enemy's unreadiness, make your way by unexpected routes and attack unguarded spots". – Sun Tsu, - The Art Of War.*

"The Encroaching – "make something happen" - strategy", has to be thoroughly researched, for it may only work once. You need to plan how you will manoeuvre, camouflage your intent, and then move in on the market. By surprise, and surrounding the competition, and then destroying his hold on the customer and ability to get them back. The first step would be to analyse and research effective ways and means of breaking into a market. The wave effect, start with the first wave, of opening up a front, by identifying a product, service or market that can be broken into. Being able to provide a better service with faster turnaround times and better quality, at a good price for instance.

Phase two; Find the weakness – their centre point of gravity.

We have to find the weakest "joints" in the market and exploit them, to our advantage. By saying "joints" and not "points" of weakness, we are implying that "points", are seemingly weak, but could prove to be insignificant when targeted, as opposed to "joints" that are always significant targets, for they are both vital and vulnerable. If joints are crushed, systems fail or collapse. This will require intensive, critical research and development of strategy, tactics and doctrine (the way we do things as an organisation).

Phase three; Command tactics – initiative and decentralised execution.

"Any favourable situation will never be exploited if commanders have to wait for orders, the highest commander and the youngest soldier must always be conscious of the fact that omission and inactivity are worse than resorting to the wrong expedient (methods)" – Molkte.

Fluidity of strategy flowing from initiative is the key to creating dominance, by virtue of the ability to act independently, but within the confined of the core framework and its guidelines, this aspect becomes indispensable in the scheme of fast, on the way to rapidity. This creates spontaneous waves of intent and rapidity once in place.

Phase four; the integration of effort.

Better described, as the *"Tsunami effect"*, where several waves of intuitive narrowly integrate at one point, where all seemingly fragmented efforts, spontaneously speeds up and create rapidity, all aimed at reaching one final objective with combined strength. This integration relates to teamwork, the interdependent effort, only through synchronisation by strategic means is this possible (planned and deliberated) means and by implication their timing, only with strategy can we achieve the powerful interlocking effect of unity of effort.

The final phase; Freedom of movement.

Once the integrated effort has passed, the fluidity flows back to its fragmented parts and every unit fights on its own terms. The main objective has now changed; this is the battle beyond the initial battle. The point where the aim is to break all cohesion and resistance left, which still exists in the theatre of operation, to take down any form of resistance, whilst chaos is still abounded and the initiative is on your side, leaving you with freedom of movement. Rapid Dominance strategy, also plans beyond the predictable, foreseeable and merely puts guidelines in place, to follow when the strategy goes beyond the initial planned expectation, or takes us beyond the initial objective. This type of strategy opens doors, as it unfolds, if we do not prepare, we may lose the opportunity that they present, by virtue of our disposition to wait until told to do so. By opening one front, we may open several others unexpectedly in the process; the plan of strategy has to compensate for such change and opportunity to be exploited to its full. For opportunity only comes seldom and if we do not take it someone else, will.

In conclusion; "throughout the ages decisive results in war have only been reached when the approaches have been indirect...more and more clearly has the fact emerged that a direct approach to one's mental object, or physical objective, along the line of natural expectation to the opponent, has ever tended to and usually produced negative results...to move along the line of natural expectation consolidates the opponents equilibrium and by stiffening it, augments his resisting power...in contrast, an examination of military history.....brings out the point that in almost all the decisive campaigns, the dislocation of the enemy's psychological and physical balance has been the vital prelude to a successful attempt at his overthrow..."(28:5 and 6)

In order, to improve our framework of understanding strategy we have to improve on the ways in which we aim. Culturally we have ring-fenced our strategy to only use the conventional and academically inclined ways to deal with reality. By only applying this wisdom of conventional strategy, we created for ourselves voids where seemingly good, spur of the moment tactics disappears through the cracks. By assembling strong mental machinery called the "Rapid dominance strategy", for us, and just by applying the principles we will fill voids and create effective and lasting strategy.

Following Nero Linguistic Programming as a principle and not a science

Nero linguistic programming is still relatively new as it is constantly evolving as science is; it was originally developed in the mid 1970's by John Grinder, assistant professor of linguistics at the university of California and Richard Bandler, a mathematician and programmer by occupation. Their work revolved around the concept of copying excellence or modelling it.

What is NLP exactly? In short, it is descriptive of the processes it refers to, **"Nero";** that refers to neurology, our nervous system – the mental pathways of our five senses, seeing, hearing, feeling, taste and smell, the pathways to our brain, the input channels. **"Linguistic";** refers to the spoken word, our language ability: the ways we build relationships and construct sentences to express whom we are, what we feel, see, hear, taste and understand. **"Programming";** having been taken from computer science understanding of loading "tested" data. The idea of "installing" or "installing" upgraded software and up to date "tested" data, data that is unequivocally positive and with refined quality. By installing this into the human computer, the brain, we are trying to enrich people's lives and perspectives, to undergo major paradigm shifts in thinking and relinquishing old scripts (programming) without fear. In addition, by doing so creating new more clearly understood models from which to navigate, operate and refer from and to which one can copy or simulate imminent success. There are many forms of empowerment, however this one is graphically better understood, therefore I will use it as a principle, to follow in the discussion on ways and means towards developing people, within organisations. This is not a quick fix, or a high, it's a system of levers. Archimedes said; "give me a lever long enough and a fulcrum on which to place it and I shall move the world". This concept is based on fact and science. The only proven way to gain knowledge is by intense exploration of the details and attributes of knowledge, or the association thereof and normally no short cut exists in this acquisition process. Only through prolonged cultivation of matter and by hard work and studying, do we ascertain knowledge, this is the pathway of ascertaining knowledge and only once applied successfully does it become our wisdom. Wisdom is seen as incorporated knowledge. Nevertheless, in this day and age of information and information technology highways, gaining explicit knowledge has become a matter of a few keystrokes and a few clicks of the mouse button on the Internet. With the advent of "Information on demand" we can research and tailor make our own unique "package of knowledge" and we can "feed it" into our system at will. By feeding we understand that people in general are indifferent to learning by means of reading alone, they are also differently inclined in ways of taking in knowledge and making it their own, some are visually inclined, others auditory inclined and some are both. It is said, that "nothing on earth is new", just focus on this saying; matter is never extinguished, nor destroyed, it only changes form. A carbon atom for instance, could have been part of an asteroid that had hit the earth billions of years ago, now part of the earth's atmosphere. It could move and be photosynthesised by a plant, that plant in turn could have been eaten by a cow, that could pass milk that you drink and then it passes through your system only to be exhaled back into the atmosphere. The point is this; every atom in our bodies was once part of matter that came from a star, which came from the big bang... the beginning of life. This code of levers are in all of us like carbon atoms, and little voices, they just need to be pulled; if anyone has ever paused and thought what is there to life, it must have happened during a major event, where the little voice inside started talking, like after a heart attack, or a car accident. These situations seem to pull at these levers in our sub-consciousness that make us change things in our life, that gets us to revisit aspects of our being, which are covered up by lifestyle changes we make as hard working individuals and we become more focused on what matters, and successful consciously. Only once we again experience life altering moments, the wake up calls comes and then do we seek answers to the basics again, to the fundamental questions of - there must be more to living, this can't be it, I have to find "it". Only to find you going back to that place they call "Inner Reality", where time waits for no man. Every human is born with this deep innate sense of finding, exploring and conquering knowledge in all its forms to some extent. It is only through our exploration and conquests that we elevate the inner being, the spirits needs above that of the ego, which gives us a sense of true accomplishment and a purpose to existence, with joy. NLP, strives to provoke the conscious mind, to become even more conscious, by becoming more inquisitive, to grow in levels of awareness, to experience altering states of existence, by pulling at your levers from time to time. In the pursuit of personal realisation and goals, we are faced with yet an another reality, that of business, that only plays by certain sets of rules that are not always aligned to who we are, and what we stand for, that makes us feel insignificant and unappreciated, betrayed. This aspect drives us back to be true to who we are once we suffer disappointment and setbacks, and we subconsciously seek ways to make it bearable... We practice new skills, renewed creativity, handling emotions, spiritual uplifting; we seek logical and spiritual deductions to all, in order to resolve issues, thereby growing mental agility and finding principles, the rejuvenation of ethics, norms and inner truth. This is all inconceivable without developing total predatory awareness, the predatory consciousness we seek to cultivate in man. If not, we just get depressed and give up our hopes and dreams.

Ivan Pavlov's work on conditioning and responses in the late 1904, is also incorporated in NLP and is referred to as "anchoring", to understand why, why we need to programme people, to survive change, disappointment and setbacks? This is an age-old concept for passing on survival training, by mimicking response to trained stimulus. Mental alertness comes from several experiences and training under stress or duress, that leads to automation of "perfect" response; this type of response only manifest during fight or flight behaviour and situations, true predator contact, therefore, if you get a trigger or stimulus that does not necessitate a fight or flight reaction regularly, then we stay unmoved and anchored in our comfort zone, of denial. The reason being, that only under duress, do we imprint automation of response that is effective. Consequently, we are bound by the circumstance that prevails in our lives, which form us and the way we will react...

The point is, we are all unique in the way we act and react. Everyone has his own unique set of scripts; patterns, habits, strategies, skills and programmes for doing anything and everything. This is because of our NLP. This very aspect can cause incompatibility and strife in relationships – obviously resulting in unwanted outcomes. We live inside out; we are that which we are or we at least what we think we are and project outbound. However, when we are analysed and brought to the realisation that our concept of self, is not all made out what we had perceived it to be, we come to other insights. For those that find themselves in jobs where everything is about what the company can get out of you, there will always be a sense that something is missing. This is simply because you cannot ignore your own inner needs and ideologies forever. At some point you will need to pay attention to your inner voice. Well, that's if you have one that's loud enough. This is the process of self-analysis. In addition, we then seek immediate resolve. How do I change this? Alternatively, we fight it off by going into denial and telling our self that it is not my fault, I did not do anything wrong, they deserve it and so on. Whichever way we choose to take, something is now missing; we all have a consciousness about right and wrong. A programme, a script to cope with our reality, as I perceived it. Then it has become corrupted; the very programme we require is missing, or none operative. This is always the norm; people cope with reality from their own perspective very well, only to come to a certain realisation that they are only holding on for dear life, only when we change our perspective to a total consciousness do we see altered states of reality that exist and that could coexist with our own. We all have bad scripts; programming is essential pieces of the thinking system, how we choose to change them, upgrade them, will ultimately alter our thinking and subsequently our reality. In addition, ultimately alter our destiny and sense of awareness or not. The point is this, I think one of the greatest lessons in life is the ability to truly learn from our past experiences, it was Einstein who said that doing the same things over and over again and expecting different results was the definition of insanity, then you begin to understand how important it is to reflect over your performance, expectations and aspirations to see where you could improve from your own experience. Now if you also consider this, against computer software that becomes out-dated, then so to do our programming. We have to keep our operating paradigms current, just as computers require it. Therefore, we have to keep reprogramming and upgrading. Naturally speaking, we must never stop exploring, learning, questioning, experiencing and conceptualising and let's not forget dreaming. These aspects of thinking clearer, comes from a childlike faith, believing without seeing. We become so self-consumed with control, and the life of capitalism, that we lose patience, everything must happen now and then resort to instant gratification.

NLP, can and will improve the emotional intelligence of people, it leads in understanding the self, by understanding our parts, in there relation to others, by shaping self-esteem (moral) first, by modelling people with concepts of professionalism, capability and confidence, we create focus and awareness, then arriving at the predatorial state – with wisdom. This might sound very insignificant, but let me remind you that we all modelled concepts until we reached a point where we understood them, in context and content and became models of concepts ourselves. Let's just take the concept of "love", we modelled love from childhood and as we grew so did the concept grow, until we grasped it in context and content. The point is, modelling is the foundation to grasping "content" (the substance, the knowledge, to be reasonably happy and satisfied with the way things are, a willingness to accept a situation or comply with a proposed course of action) and context (the awareness of the circumstances or events that forms the environment within which something exists or takes place), thus forming a concept, it gives us a framework of reference, from where we build further concepts, so we have to master basic concepts first in order to have a foundation to build future concepts with or on. NLP, is the scripting of concepts, the modelling of concept. We could use this to teach people coping skills with, all human skills that are required for heightened development, to enhance scripts and imprint new scripts... I see it as a total overall reprogramming of a mind, your staff, yourself, to live by one script, to form one culture, one language. We have some many "languages", because of diverse corporate culture within organisations that we cannot communicate effectively anymore. Everyone wants to make a statement, which represents his or her culture of thinking. Where on the other hand what we should be having is one culture, one corporate culture, that of abundance and interdependence only. It is a principled culture of entwined beliefs, accommodating all culture. Thus, generating a mechanism for building relationships, both inward and outward, NLP becomes the programming tool, to achieve this with, the more you hear it the more you will believe in its existence. People's minds are fertile but at the same time left barren, if we as employers do not start investing in planting new seeds, that of homogeneous corporate culture and sowing our seeds according to our true soil (desire to be real), or to that which we would like to leave as our legacy, the good. Then, carry on doing business based on pure capitalistic doctrine and forget the people, ethic and cultural impact and watch how the emancipation of man's virtues dissolves in to ego maniacs. Your organisation will eventually struggle, stumble and collapse. People are only as strong, as their leaders are wise and willing and the same can be said in reverse, it is all about what we stand for and believe in, and are willing to fight for. The ultimate aim of all strategy is to have an overall connecting effect, this works inward and outward. Inward, it moves you to revalidate your thinking, your character, your programming and worth; outward it expresses your logical and creative thinking ability, your insight, in forming concepts. Concepts, good or bad, make deep inroads into other peoples beliefs and systems and they have to go through the same process to arrive at the same concept, in order for the concept to be revalidated. Therefore, setting the bar this high will not be easy, if we are bad at conceptualisation, if we can't grasp concepts and form poor ones as leaders, our followers will be disillusioned. In order to achieve this height, for new concepts to take form we have to plough deep into the imagination and character, the inroads must appeal to both centres of the brain simultaneously, both the logical left side and the imaginative right side. For any concept to take shape we have to get both means and goals to go together, even if it seems impossible, leadership begins with a message, that begins with the visualising a goals, no matter how difficult or out of reach, it has to create hope, otherwise the concept is shallow, people can spot cheap and also shallow a mile off. The purpose of coaching is to remove internal barriers to success and to unlock everyone's potential, by addressing beliefs. Working to unblock the mind from self-limiting beliefs is challenging enough, changing perceptions and concentrating on the desired outcome, is reward enough in itself, it can have a dramatic and powerful impact on performance. Just like natural seed, the seed concepts are to be planted deep in the soil of desire; we first have to create an ardent desire, before we can even think of planting such a radical concept that will deliver the fruit's, or else, concepts like seeds, will be dried by the sun of circumstances, eaten by the birds of criticism, or washed away by the rains of conformity. To be or not to be is only by choices and decisive action, to become habit or be blown away by the winds of conformity to routine. Let us explore ways of making deep penetrating concepts embodied into global strategy. We can utilise NLP, to programme people, to be more and get more. Creating inroads, this is the intentional positive use of Nero linguistic programming. The creation of true inroads resides in the believe in the power of the soul, the imagination, in the seemingly impossible, by making it believable, with small calculated steps, actions and inputs, the opening up of minds and the desire for fruitful changes is calculated work, for the strategist this becomes the key to selling robust strategy; otherwise it will just remain shallow, just an idea, just another plan. Ideas only create power when they fuse context and content, again, two parts, coming together to form one whole in balance.

Leonardo Da Vinci explained the four keys to genius as;

1. *Studying the art of science,*
2. *studying the science of art,*
3. *learn to see and use all your senses,*
4. *study in the knowledge that everything connects.*

Einstein on the other hand, combined imaginative thinking with rational analysis to make his great discoveries.

Aristotle believed that it was impossible to think without evoking a mental picture.

Einstein enforced this when he remarked that my particular ability does not lie in mathematical calculation, but rather in visualising effects, possibilities and consequences.

We have to therefore "visualise" how our solutions will fit into the "context" of things, as they exist, by asking; what is the question that require a resolve here, in which the problem originated and then visualise how we will add value by adding new "content" to create the required balance and the visualise it. Yes, solutions, strategic solutions, are aimed at creating balance and by finding the dislodged parts that upset the natural balance of systems, by dissociated thinking and visualisation. What this implies is that as a norm, we tackle problems at face value only, we think we know the answers, we jump at conclusions, we assume and go with the first assumption, if we assume too much too often we will sink with our assumptions and become risk takers and even get branded as critics. If we take this statement and reverse it, we will be applying the philosophy of the anarchist, only creating imbalance. Anarchists think they know it all, they think they have all the answers, without studying the question that requires resolve, from different perspectives first. These two stand in stark opposing states, the critical thinker thinks from the soul and mind, and the critique from the ego and what's in it for me, by virtue of implementing the same means from different points of the same spectrum. We have to be aware of this as strategist; the very principles we use in strategy, both creative and practical thinking, can have the same and equal effect in reveres, if we just hand over our plans, when thinking about strategy, by implementing knowledge driven thinking, through the anarchist system, the idealist style of thinking. Strategy can create or destroy via the same means; it all dependent on our direction of thinking, namely our thinking paradigm. To illustrate this, for every man designing a projectile to be fired by a firearm, that will create more effect, there is the same amount of men designing bullet-proof vests, steel, glass and other defences. We sometimes unwittingly create strategy in dissimilar nature, not only directly opposing the other, thus nullifying the intent of both and leaving the question unsolved. The only way to beat this is with rapidity. Good nature, good will and good strategy are admirable, but it is only through awareness of dissimilar strategy that we design robust strategy, that is always faster and that stays one step ahead of the rest. NLP, utilise all the senses, to create a mental picture of the problem first and does not use logic and knowledge as a primary thinking key. Liddell Heart, is of the opinion that we should find our common ground first, (create on culture) and then find a common solution, that fits right in the middle of two opposing extremes of thinking, called the ideal concept. This will be the only real logical solution, nothing else will service. Not so, radical strategy is steps ahead of the mediocre thinking, in this regard; they will seize this opportunity and go beyond the fact and wedge that gap, wide open. Therefore, we have to think positive and negative, horizontal and both vertical and form a vision, get the whole picture, before arriving at any conclusion or concept. This process is called global thinking, where we also utilise all the senses and the left and right brain effectively, before arriving at the final conclusion. Moreover, the use of NLP, is the principle of programming people, to change their scripts, by using creative speech, sound, visualisation and relating it back to a common understanding of how things are understood by this sector of people, what they consider to be a good job, by using their cultural language, to explain these concepts. By utilising the visualisation of their old concepts and explaining it in new ways, by stimulating the left and right brain dominant thinkers, in new and both creative ways. We purposefully design the creation of conformity with the vision and matter, by utilising the abstract and the concrete issues of reality. **" By looking back on the steps by which fresh ideas gained acceptance, it can be seen that the process was eased when they could be presented not as something radically new, but as the revival in modern terms of a time-honoured principle or practice that had been long forgotten"** *–Liddell Heart.*

The Sum of the "Whole" is always bigger than the "Individual".

If this is true, then we are in fact **emphasising that "unity is strength", where the whole becomes greater than the sum of all its individual parts.**

Then this would furthermore imply that we should see better than average results within groups and teams, and from them. The unification aspect, that should constantly breeds better results, consistent with the individuals efforts and the groups success, to remain united and both productive as an entity, and still sensing personal growth and fulfilment should all be present, then it is a whole solution. Individuals belonging to such union subscribes willingly to the conditions set and benefits from it. This is the idea. Individuals should also be better-off and show improvements for it, thus benefiting from belonging and subscribing to harmony. Then why is this not the case in every instance? Why don't we all get to benefit from joining groups in this fashion? Why don't we all feel happy, chirpy and needed, as well as appreciated all the time when we join groups that become one entity, a whole?

Rules, law and contracts

Where and when we find people belonging to cells, groups, or institutions, or whatever they seek or use to unite them and unify their efforts with as a whole, then we find that there are unspoken rules; things that hide under the surface, that we all need to understand, before such unity will emerge into greatness, yet, people join daily, and others leave daily. Some make it in groups and others don't. Why? We all have a dire need to do things that gives us a sense of purpose and belonging first. We need to have a "social contract" with people, and or groups, just by signing several social contracts at different levels we feel a sense of achievement, with others, and a diverse range of opinions and emotions are stimulated because of this, that either motivates us to put in the required effort, or to withdraw. The term "social contract" implies the notion that people have, that if they want to belong to a certain order, or social unit or class they have to sacrifice their freedom and conform to specific rules of behavior, that dictate the actions desired. All in order to be invited, and made to feel welcome. Then it also "implies" things: – not always guaranteed – if you behave good and work hard – then rewards, benefits, and status comes as standard with this contract. Certain expectations are generated both ways, between the group and the individual. Either in writing, or in the open, or just below the surface and unspoken –where "it goes without saying". By association with groups, groups being two or more people, certain points of reference always emerge. Call it ground rules, club rule or social rules. These "rules" implies much more, it also suggests protection for the joiner by "law". We have to understand that here there is a distinction between the meaning of "law". We have two types of law, we have "universal law" and the "rule of law". The rule of law implies: "thou shall not" and universal law implies "principles"; time honoured, universally understood and tested aspects of human nature that refers to "wisdom, love, trust, forgiveness, kindness and acts of service". The belief is that law gives psychological, physical and emotional protection – it gives protection to a life in harmony with others, that law is kind, and also protected. Most of us believe that this is the way it is done, and we come to exist in peace and harmony, and that everyone prescribes to this. Even religion prescribes that we follow "law". The fact of the matter is, it's not the case. Law becomes meaningless if we can bribe and buy our way out. If some are above the law, manipulate the law, and get away with murder, then law becomes policy, for dealing with the weak and naive. Therefore a society that only follows the rule of law is doomed when they seek total unification, as "rules are made to be broken" and there will always be people to break them. Furthermore, people will have to die and get hurt in order for law to exist, if law cannot hurt you, punish you, or get you to refrain from certain behaviour, then you are above the law . If no one transgressed law it will have no purpose either. Therefore we all have potential to stun and shape each other's growth and potential at will, but is it lawful?. Thinking we are duty bound is simply respecting certain laws pertaining to us.

The need for self-discipline and moral good

Our potential for growth – in all dimensions - is the greatest reason for our existence, and therefore survival becomes an instinct that is primal and core to our being. It is the process of the unfolding of life and growth; we have to survive first in order to be able to grow. Consequently we seek safety in many aspects of the unfolding, by upholding traditional values, no matter how reasonable or unreasonable, as long as it is perceived to provide shelter – safety in numbers. Experiences and consequences, have taught us, history reminds us, knowledge teach us, and questions inform us, of this, ruins standing as reminders of what happens to us when we abuse power. It serves as reverence points for our direction finders both moral and ethical. When we become self-centred, we start suffering from a lack of self-discipline. Greed overtakes from selfishness, to the point of a blind ambition to ascertain only power or wealth. The laws of life, its principles, dictate that we will grow, either slow of fast, have it easier or hard, depending on the way we choose to live. If integrity and principles become the path we seek, then we will have it easy. If Intelligence is defined by how we make use of wisdom, history and view cause and effect. Then there can only be one power, the power to unite on the side to become one, and never exploitation, as it ultimately destroys cohesion and unity of effort and all the social contracts it is linked to.

The management perspective on groups

Managers for the most do not always understand group dynamics impact on strategy, and that continued growth in the group scheme is the essence of a "feeling" – we feel groups – we need to feel a sense of belonging and self-actualisation. The individual is in essence also a team of its own accord, that has parts, all have different needs that have to be satisfied at some point, and all needs change, as the one gets satisfied, the next becomes significant, it is a constant cycle of evolution, building or stripping away from the individual. Individuals therefore need to get something out of it, the group experience. It is not just the main stream belief that artificial massaging of egos, motivational talks and coercive rules that keep group activity going. If and when you see groups as being a "flat", as paper exercises with names and titles, then you have it wrong. Groups viewed as stagnant entities, does not exist, they are dynamic entities. We need to see groups and their true formation, from a different perspective. The flower box. Individuals in groups are elements of growth with potential, just like seeds growing in a flowerbox, being watered and growing every day. It is a give and take, a cause and effect action, a cycle. Seeds, become seedlings, that become sprouts, and then full plants, that grow, and compete for sunlight, water and nutrients, ultimately they compete for space, and eventually they will compete with one and other, it is a natural phenomenon. How to manage growth and the life cycles of groups is the business of strategy.

The individual parts

People often say that if both members of a team think the same then you only need one, could this be it? That if we only view groups as flat, then we will end up with too many likeminded people and that is why we have strife in groups, and groups collapsing. Why do we want to become one with a whole? Why do we need others? These are the questions that need focus. If i can make it on my own, then why do i have to conform to the pressures of the group and peer pressure and rules and law in order to get my needs satisfied? When the alleged reason of all religions read that the unity of efforts, is aimed at the united brotherhood, or to unite into one body as the ultimate goal. Nevertheless; this is no longer the case, where we all have different interpretations as to what this should imply, and how it should be applied in practice.

Somehow the "whole" idea, has becomes a "hole" through which all the good is sucked in. It is argued that we have to much diversity, politics, race, religion, and greed issues in this world, that makes it impossible to have great and exceptional teams. Furthermore then we also have the physical facts that complicate this process even more. Contrary to common belief, throwing people together and getting them to work, and deliver better results, is not just one thing. It is in fact two different processes that need to take place. Just by putting people together we are in fact not forming a "whole" either, it's just forming a team. It happens daily. We team up for the bus, train, and restaurants. Forming a whole is a long term process full of potholes, as we have to plan for the seed becoming seedlings, becoming bigger and then eventually fully grown. The life stages of the group that will form the whole needs better design and attention. For starters, people will only work together if they think that everyone is sharing an equal amount of work, responsibility, and are being treated and rewarded likewise. People in general are sensing fairness today on a higher plane of existence, as our society has become more individualised in its approach to social life. Young men and woman can now live and sustain themselves, without any help of their family or friends. They want their worth felt, recognised and rewarded. Somehow they feel that it is still going unnoticed, by adopting this principle of all are equal, and all is fair when all the parts form a whole. Forming is just the beginning. As time progresses, then things change, and people get promoted, get rewarded, and get lifted out, then things really start boiling. Especially with those left behind. They think that they are left with nothing more to prove, as empty shells of self-doubt and with pure remorse, with mental pain, in a state of total disillusionment. Once the whole starts to evolve, and people get promoted, get incentives and get given more attention, and accolades, then a rupture in the whole emerges. That creates suspicion, the total sense of worth seems to change, and so do they. It seems that for no lack of wanting and trying to achieve this oneness, this divine state of mutual co-existence, it just cannot bring anything good over an extended period of time, everything humane then seize to exist. Teams, team work and team dynamics take their toll on any group working side by side. The old saying of "familiarity breeds contempt" holds very true, especially in teams. This means that the more you know something or someone, the more you start to find faults and dislike things about it or them. However "familiarity also breeds content". We tend to concentrate more on global, than on the whole and its individual parts, including the individuals needs for reward, self-actualisation and recognition, as well as personal growth in this scheme. The culprit is following the sterile management style and orientation towards legalism, if they don't follow the rules, then we know what to do. People need rules. The principle of the "whole and all its parts" is still sound, it is the understanding and implementation thereof and the influence on human resources that are now in conflict, because of labour and other laws. Because of legalism, every sector is now protecting their rights and demanding them, pound for pound we have become self-righteous. There is no more room for trust and open communication, we don't share like we teach our kids to do at work anymore; it has become a me and them situation. This aspect has a great impact on all the good companies and workers can do and share, as a whole, and this is a reality that will not change soon, or ever, if we keep following and teaching one paradigm only, that of legalism.

We should re-look the way we seem to be forming teams and getting the parts to be more significant and unique. In a few words summarised by Aristotle in the *Metaphysics*: "The whole is more than the sum of its parts" it's the sum of individuals that form parts. We are faced with a different type of worker today. That no longer subscribes to "holism". We have moved from **"holism"** to **"individualism"** as a society. The term holism was introduced by the South African statesman Jan Smuts in his 1926 book, Holism and Evolution. Smuts defined holism as "The tendency in nature to form wholes that are greater than the sum of the parts through creative evolution." This held true in days where big families co-existed as units as a rule, where woman did not have careers, the philosophy was just brought across and implemented in the work place. Labour laws and rights was not on the cards back then, we operated along a totally different paradigm. Today we find more **individualism,** defined as the more moral stance and political philosophy, ideology, or social outlook that stresses "the moral worth of the individual". Individualists promote the exercise of one's own goals and desires as being first order and so to independence and interdependence has been redefined, to the extent that it promotes self-reliance while opposing most external interference upon one's choices, and social contracts, as to with whom to associate and co-operate with by choice, whether by society, state or another groups or institutions, that use to dictate the terms.

Excessive **Legalism and capitalism is also to blame:** It creates mist, grey areas, nothing is unbending and dedicated anymore. Everything and anything can be negotiated, bribed, corrupted , stolen or bought - he who has the money has the power over people. Meet the new "What is my rights generation?" Legalism and capitalism is also to blame for weak teams, as we are no longer a team to the end, it is purely a platform on which individuals compete for favour and position only – as taught by our schools system, that winners win big and looser lose all the time. Building strong teams in the presence of legalism and capitalism remains a challenge amongst the chaos and diversity of our time. This follows with, what is fair and to whom is it more fair? If we need groups, then we need to understand their mortar and bricks composition, in this era, and use the new. Groups need to feel a sense of uniformity and a need, a sense that i belong here and this is what i will get out of it. The whole idea behind teams are not equality that may come at the expense of the individual and impact on the overall effectiveness of the whole, but unification of effort, and co-operation. However today this translates to; if i as the individual become the light source of the light bulb – implying the group, that houses the whole - what if i get taken away, does the light bulb not become just a glass container? We are facing a situation here, where people can now demand to be recognised for their skills and achievements as individuals, even if they belong to a group. The workforce want their efforts noticed and rewarded remember, and on the other hand the company wants that extra that they bring, both as an individual and as a group, but don't want to pay a lot more for it. It has come down to old paradigms remerging; the rule of coercion, who is strongest, and who is the strongest in the contest of will - the union, or the company? Only by virtue of enforcing "discipline" without seeming "punishing" with rules will we manage this aspect, this is our aim as employers, what is yours as an individual?

If everything is important then nothing is important. If everything is priority then nothing is priority. In instances like this all cohesion between labour and enterprise has become lost. Strategy has become insignificant some say, as rules, and laws dictate how we get rewarded – and whether we qualify or not. We are slipping back into a time passed, where slaves did the bidding of their masters, and masters always have favourites. Companies can become slaves of their own devices and the power of employees through unions, rules, policies and practices as well. We all have become so aware of rights; both individual, constitutional and otherwise, that we have been over sensitised on rights and it is driving good will and strategy into extinction. Rights are outweighing worth, self-discipline and even common sense and good will. *The fact of the matter is this, you cannot get people's interest by violating their expectations.* One way to view this dilemma is by *revisiting principles that sustain and ignite growth.* Finding meaningful answers to truthful questions, and the; "there must be more to life than this" issues, is paramount. Just existing and protecting everyone and his or her rights, it's not living, it is existing. We have to change the paradigm. By means of studying behaviour that impacts on both mutual coexistence and rights, we might try to find the answer to this universal issue, for it has become just that an issue. Both economically and psychological it is taking its toll. These aspects and the nature of rights in modern society, and how they are individualised and perceived have influenced our behaviour, to think and act like legalist. Law is to be reinterpreted, it is not always clear cut, and it boils down to the philosophy of legalism, where there is very little room for compassion and real consensus when you have a minority versus a majority, with strong and weak competing. Where only rules protecting rights become significant in the scheme of groups and "whole", then anything else is of lesser importance. It is the conscious and unconscious beliefs of people and not rules that govern their life, and conduct ultimately, and it stays true for every individual. The notion that only rules can govern peoples actions effectively is unfounded. We have something called "fear" – the biggest motive for action, that propels people to do the unthinkable.

Fear

Fear plays a very important part in our daily life, and in human society as a whole. Fear comes in many shapes and forms and from many sources. It could be described as: an unpleasant feeling of perceived risk or danger, real or otherwise. It functions to make us alert and ready for action. Action that we have to encounter or initiate, whilst expecting or experiencing specific problems. Although unseen, fear is often the platform upon which common beliefs, hope and ambition are built, as it implies risk. Apart from ignorance, and a lack of knowledge and wisdom, seen as mental catalyst for fearing the unknown, we also have a natural fear of death, incapacitation, failure, victimisation and mockery, whereby beliefs are sustained, that give us "real" reasons to be careful. Those working for change must come to understand that if a society or organisation is to be transformed, their beliefs and resulting values that rule people's lives must be aligned with what they fear and fear most. Even if it seems realistic, and easy enough, people could fear doing it. Addressing fear, both in terms of personal, universal and or cultural beliefs, must remain a key and part of the change process. If we only follow systems design and laws, our inspiration to do more; by working harder, and living happier lives, begins to slip away until it withers away and dies. However, there is one type of fear we need to address more than others. The fear of going over to action: this is the fear that if we don't do anything about "it", we will remain living lives filled with problems and suffering. Where law governs everything, it creates new fear. Fear or paranoia is an exaggeration of what we perceive to be real, and forces our rational mind to keep thinking of ways out, and to stay in control of our situation and emotion, then principles cannot prevail. Fear is a powerful motivator, but it is mostly a negative one.

To motivate someone by eliminating doubts first, is always a better option. It is empowering people, and capacitating them to go over to action more often. Doubt destroys motivation to go over to action, and not even fear will persuade a person filled with doubt that they must act, when they are totally paralysed from within. Only if you can help a person get rid of their insecurities, by showing them "a way out", only then will you motivate them positively. We have become totally preoccupied with being evaluated by others, following their rules, and listening to their wisdom, and subscribing to their reason as fact. All the while fighting with our own "little voice" of reason, this then creates doubt. When we start listening to the inner voice, it becomes stronger, then it becomes in conflict with the outer reality. Then we feel intense anxiety at the thought of being in competition or even worst still in conflict with powerful or important people. Society, religion and any law, creates an expectation of evil. It is "evil" "to bite the hand that feeds you". If you are good, and you know it, then why do you conform to weakness, because they – the people that are important keep us in check, with fear, and self-doubt, and the possibility that evil exist, so that we don't take from them, position, and overtake them or disappear from them. For they create a perception, that they "protect" us from our fears, and ourselves, we know what is good for you – or so they want us to perceive it. If there was no evil, no death, no pain, no taxes, no depth...who would be able to control us. We may have chronic feelings of inadequacy when we are faced with situations of unfairness, and deceit, this is imprinted by the strong, not the week, influences in and on your life. Imprinters are the fathers, mothers, brothers, mentors teachers and friends, and if we get too close to our own "Success", we feel like a fraud or phoney, and we fear being found out. Because we can't have it all, it's not right, you have to think of all the losers and your friends. Then they ask us, why, why do we lack self-confidence, when we fear making our own success and happiness, it's because they all taught us, that money is the route of all evil and success is not everything. Although we may put on a show of bravado, a happy smile…in our hearts we know we were born to be great. So why do we not feel and experience it so very often, and even less in teams? Perhaps it is the absence of principles.

Principles had to make way for law…

Even higher order principles such as spiritualism, honesty and faith have to make way for current influences on our lives and society, that moulded our confidence in the past to take what is rightfully ours. As law is only a perception, it gets interpreted as we see it, and when we deem fit, there is law and then there is "THE LAW". The truth is, if a person feels that they merely exist, then it is because law merely exists, it does not grow in any spiritual dimension, just in perception. So if we perceive that we are not allowed to be great, or greater than the boss, then we won't ever go anywhere, because it is the law. Not that we will even if we remove the law, we have been conditioned to stand in line, and wait your turn, we are not allowed to grab and run with our portion of the cake, we just don't do that it is evil, bad, impolite and not right. Only they get to do it, we all have to make way for the boss, to step in and take and see what's left of the credit. They, the ones that make the law, and are above the law, that are on top are now interoperating law for us. Other aspects; the desecration of moral and ethical good, everything needs to be marginalised - to take or keep somebody or something away from the centre of attention, influence, or power to be fair. Stemming from other belief systems opposing our own growth and seen to be the only effective way to govern such elements of diversity is to implement the code of social conduct - law, governing all social habits, or so it is perceived. We cannot escape the eventualities of change, that life in general is the result of what we choose it, or allow it to be – it then becomes us, because it falls well outside our sphere of influence. I think it was Ghandi that said the purpose of life is pain – again a perception, not everyone's truth or reality. The "Status" of one's mental health and thinking is not a topic for open discussion in the work place either, as it is seen as our own weakness. We do not show or see weakness when we are ruled by legalism – it is just not allowed. We may talk about and raise disparity, and victimisation, and that will be entertained. Do we realise that this attitude has a two-prong effect; it has a direct impact on your behaviour as a person, you are compelled by law to be reserved, bias, and left to deal with your own problems and pain, so too your character and your culture, not excluding the wrongs and injustices of the organisation. Only when we come to the realisation that everything is interrelated somehow somewhere, then will we find truth again. We have to strive for normality, a point between two evils. The organisation is not inherently immune to the human pyramid of needs and its effect. Neither to the exploitation of law that it practices.

It is only when we stop looking outside ourselves for truth and for inner balance, that we realise the source is inside. Without deep routed fulfilment in oneself and the things that we do daily that create inner joy, nothing else will move the spirit. If our work environments satisfies only our "needs"; then why do we get all confused, why do we not get any sense of satisfaction on the job, that sense of purpose? It's because it does not satisfy our "wants" as well, "wants" are higher order principles that do not belong to the same plane as needs, it does not subscribe to rules, and the working environment does, we can only satisfy wants on one plane and needs on another. Only once we have satisfied lower order principles, needs, by doing our jobs the best we know how, can we satisfy wants, a higher order principle and be truly happy. Once we have satisfied higher, order principles, the principles of, unconditional service and spiritual fulfilment. If we get this wrong, then we seek fulfilment from the wrong source, or plane, as if a thirsty traveller would seeks water from a rock. There is no such thing as "job satisfaction" a job is what you get from it. These are inner and higher dimensional aspects of living and sources of living with joy. More on wants in a later chapter. We are talking about the question of parts forming a whole. It is all a question of orientation, a job is just a job, we hang onto our jobs as if it divines who we are. It's just a process, that gets us paid. "We ourselves feel that what we are doing is just a drop in the ocean. Although the ocean would be less because of that missing drop." Mother Teresa. Therefore we can aim to make our drop, or drops count, and even feel good about doing it, drop by drop. However, the truth of the matter is, we cannot focus too much on the individual, either, as this will build ego, and ego is a false sense of importance. This is also dehumanising our social nature, if and when individuals are raised above their scope, we create division, as perfection is impossible for all to reach, we need to rather create balance, by rewarding people more and some less, and not give them titles, but rather money or a prize, then we should be reaching it as a collective. We cannot pick and choose those who will be valued most, and who is valued less. For we all perform in that fashion, sometimes more, sometimes less. In this sense, it is better that "justice" of whatever quality be evenly distributed among a society, in the workplace. So, how do we get a "unified" experience?

Why not include animal behaviour herein to better illustrate this aspect, as well as to highlight the importance of the principle of seeking satisfaction in the right plane and living with interdependence on another plane.

Nature has many lessons to teach us about groups forming a whole. For some years now this has been my field of study, especially "predatorily" behaviour (in Dogs, Wolves and Wild Dogs) and how it relates to human behaviour. One common similarity and element is always present, a unique order and balance in the pack. Dogs have a pecking order; the "Alpha", the leader, is always in charge of leading the pack. The Alpha leader also has the responsibility to see to the hunt, breeding, enforcing territory and maintaining a steady pack culture. They never kill or cripple any member of the pack intentionally when settling disputes through fighting. Pack status, growth and size is widely respected and enforced daily as a matter of routine. The other significant member is the "Omega", almost the lowest rating in the pack, she is the care giver and play maker, in the pack, she will bring back food to the injured, groom, clean and look after the nursery and be widely respected. If and when clans split, they still belong to one clan and when they merge, it is a highly social event. Dogs spend a great deal of time on self-development, grooming their coats, chasing each other, play fighting, stealing "toys" and socialising. They are highly social animals, but defend their territory ferociously against intruders. They have remarkable stamina; they conserve energy running and spend more energy walking.

Therefore, they cover great distances without great effort. What is truly remarkable is their ability to hunt, here we see them working in waves, employing strategy and tactics and they will study a herd for days if necessary and only hunt small rodents and birds, until the situation is ripe for the big kill. The hunt starts by sending in the young to start the hunt, to see if their assumptions were correct if not, they stop. If correct, then they will disappear and out of nowhere, a second wave will emerge, this causes all cohesion in the herd to break, scattering them. They will isolate their target and run him down, by flanking him, from all sides until he stops, or is trapped. Then kill him with multiple attacks from the front, rear and at the abdomen, by rupturing surface arteries to reduce massive blood loss and collapse. Size is of no consequence, some of their targets in Africa, weigh more than the pack on the hunt combined. The other noticeable and remarkable thing is their "war cry", they chatter excitedly as they hunt and the chatter increases in pitch and length as the hunt concludes and then it stops.

Let's make initial deductions from this example, firstly:

- Pack order – everyone knows where he or she belongs, it's not fugue
- Leadership – the Alpha leader leads and guides, he know he is only as strong as the pack.
- Self – grooming and taking care of oneself, by looking inward for principles and truth
- Pack – social harmony and duty, with acts of service...
- Hunt – as a collective, in synergy and with strategy and tactics, on their terms.
- Chatter – The communication of individualised efforts to reach a common objective.

Strategists need to learn from initial and final deductions;

initial deductions create context,

understanding things as they occur by picturing them,

whereas final deductions focuses on content,

making sense of things through reasoning and deduction.

We first seek to understand and then to be understood.

By reading this story from a different perspective, try picturing the story and deriving strategic clues whilst reading it.

The Wild dogs in Africa, hunt in large numbers and take down game that can outrun, jump, sprint and smell better, even hear them before they can see them. This is only possible through their pack culture. "If the whole is greater than the sum of its parts" then we should see better results. Their survival purely depends on the pack; if the pack comes to demise so does their fulcrum for existence. However, it transcends this mere aspect, it relates to deeper than this, they look after the young, in turn. They let the small and weak feed on the killings of the hunt first.

They devour the whole carcass and regurgitate later, to feed their offspring. Before the hunt, they charge each other up with a war cry and then they go on the hunt.

By looking at the example and follow with analysis of what constitutes strategy, in parts, forming a whole. It's the leader who picks out the target (vision) and then initiating the hunt, to letting instinct take over (culture), which evolved over years of hunting (doctrine). Their clicking sounds and snarls form a network of coded messages. Giving them the ability to signal vocally (communicate) to each other as to which way to go, in short bursts (coded communication) or which tactic to apply by pointing with the tail (tactics). They function as one (synergy), yet every individual has some unique ability (attribute) and role in the hunt (system), a pattern always emerges. The leader seeks out the slowest or weakest prey and then isolates him;(mission) the pack moves in and kills him in an instant.(goal) Sometimes, he has been watching this target for weeks – just ignoring it, whilst hunting others,(planning) and then one day, without warning (element of surprise)he will guide and lead the attack on a really big animal, with great ease and success (strategic intent), just by studying him and how he reacts, doing a full (SWOT) analysis before they hunt the big trophy. Hunting is done primarily by sight (OODA). The older slower dogs, flank the prey and keep him moving.(stratagem) The younger ones chase him down and take turns doing so. Crystallising two concepts (MBO- management by objectives) (Waves of attack).

Achieving balance and natural order

There needs to be natural order, where leader leads, the managers manage and the workers work as one. I think you get the idea. It is the parts that fit, that make the "whole". There is no set recipe for success, every strategy is formed on its own terms, and so are teams and whole's. Nevertheless, the more you apply parts - ingredients, which work, the bigger the reference and the greater the whole becomes. Parts are two fold, not just the human components and their worth they bring, the physical, but also the abstracts of their reasoning, the principles of war. That forms the desired whole, then legalism plays its part within the greater whole. Business is not fair and so is life, sometimes we are on top and at other times we are at the bottom, we do have a choice however. We can choose how long we want to stay, where we want to go, and how we will let this affect us, and for how long.

They, the wild dogs of Africa can teach us many lessons for having to live inter-dependently. By living interdependently we become one with the whole, yet stay one with the self. The reason for this choice is that within a group we have better chances at attaining abundance of opportunities and shared responsibility and resources, to achieve our own personal goals with, for it is through people and their ideas, that we find a way out. We too, were designed to serve each other's needs, no matter on what plane. Different people and situations teach us, takes from us, and gives us, all at the same time. Negatives become positives, and positives becomes negative, it is a constant cycle of give and take. If companies pays us what we are worth, then we will soon be in business for ourselves. If managers gives us all the credit we are due then we will be managing them soon. Life in business is a battle of here today gone tomorrow, if you don't follow the set of rules.

Therefore, one can conclude by saying that the attributes that make "predators" successful as hunters and survivors, and team players are:

The Radical Revolutionary Strategic Management Matrix For Predators

Firstly they understand;

- Pecking order and their own preparation to get position.
- The Alpha leaders role and function, the leader that actually leads, prevents conflict.
- The importance of pack and culture, doctrines and value's – that creates interdependence.
- Their strategy, planning and tactics, that become references and not frameworks to life by.
- Their relationship building activities importance, that emanates from working together as a whole, benefiting from interaction.
- Their time spent on recreational activities, builds strong ties, that can open up opportunities.
- The way they empower their "young" by letting them feed first – applying the abundance principle, teaching us to importance of humility and abundance.

Why are they so successful? They are designed to hunt alone, but by choice and good judgement they rather hunt as a pack, structured to function as a collective, creating and sharing in the abundance they create due to their "inter – dependency" they live to realise the main goal of their existence, their purpose, the survival of the species.

This is all pack culture principles and characteristics. That of the "Predator" pack. This is the premise on which the word "Predator" was introduced into the Radical Revolutionary Strategic Management Matrix. To highlight the significances of symbolism, the symbol of the predator and what it stands for by implication. Strategist needs to align their thinking with this symbol.

The whole is purely a unification of desired and required parts:

Therefore, the most important thing on everyone's mind should be the creation of "predators" and "pack". In order for the dog pack to exist, they have to constantly hunt and kill, constantly meet objectives, or die because of the lack of meeting higher priority objectives. Let's not forget, they too, have laws to abide by, both natural and physical, yet they rise above the challenge. Nonetheless, how do we get people to align, without giving them symbols that they can freely relate to, we have to create envision, to instil the importance of unity. We are prone to make choices based on all "things" and not on our higher order necessity. People as a species have become brain washed to think, that it does not matter what the other person is doing, as long as it doesn't affect me – well it always does – look at global warming No one cares enough to make it stop, we are just to consumed with what's in it for us, and dam the rest. Self-sacrifice is a fast dying characteristic trait, we will go to War in the future over givens, clean water and air. Urgent things in our mind determine how we rank priorities and objectives. Without a symbol, or model to guide our collective thinking we think only linear, only about self. We choose and arrange our methodology based on our emotional state, means, and perception, based on what we feel like doing and not what requires doing, with little sacrifice. We mainly start our list with: The things we have to do, the things we want to do, the things we still can do and lastly the things we have always wanted to do but keep putting off. We do more every day but we seem to achieve less, by virtue of our inability to focus on the truly important issues. We seem to lose focus, speed and interest in all things important at some point. We work together, but by the end of the day - the "relationship" evaporates totally as we speed off home. We resume another culture and become family members the moment we open the front door, we take time to settle in, so we are shape shifting virtually every day as well, no wonder we are so tired. We are forced to act out of character, with other out of character people. Our very ability to adapt has scripted roles for us with different personalities, and different sets of truth in our diverse settings of life. Therefore, we have conflicting personality issues, pack and culture issues, how do we deal with all these conflicting issues. This is no new dilemma, the dilemma of crisis management and the rewards of the adrenalin rush and pressures of work, have become a norm, a custom. However, when we become stuck in one role, where the job gives the rush and becomes the rush, the body hit we like so much, that gives us a sense of purpose, then we have entered a danger zone. For legalism has given us power over people and a false sense of purpose and worth. Here we find two types of people, the ones that live for the job, the others that live from the job. This is our false misguided sense of purpose and worth and sense of living, we have to live in balance; nothing in our lives will change until this very aspect starts changing. The reality is, no one is indispensable; anyone can take over your "job" and title in a blink of an eye. This is the reality, so how can a dispensable person serve a purpose if it is only to work hard and long – is that your "purpose", your only part in the whole. No, we have to get balance back, in all spheres; work is as important, as family, as religion as self. This is the true whole and all its attributes. Only when we find the equilibrium in all our spheres do we find purpose again. Covey calls this our inner voice and it is only with inner voice that we can serve all spheres equally well.

The solution

There is synergy of mind, body and soul, only within constant renewal and only there does creativeness keep spawning. All things that are great, comes from within this framework of renewal, opportunity and enthusiasm. In summary; in this chapter, we have done three strategic things; we have sold an old concept in a new way. "The Sum of the Whole is always bigger than the Individual parts". People can now have one understanding of this concept. We have created a mental picture of the significance of such a concept – the flower box. In addition, we have rationalised it and reaffirmed its importance, its pitfalls and it use. "Interdependence" – a new paradigm for young people with independent ideas – that can unify parts to form one bigger whole. This is the first step of formulating Strategy, selling old concepts in new ways, so that they may change and become a new concept. The wisdom to see things for what they really are and not only for what they intend to imply or substitute. People require more wisdom...in this day and age.

Who is wise, and who is the wiser of the two?

Life in general is all about commitments and involvement. We have to decide daily how deep and how much we will get involved, and commit to doing so, or abstaining from doing these "things". Either personally, emotionally, financially, politically, and otherwise. This requires the aspect of wisdom, the ability to make these decisions wisely. **Wisdom** is described as all-encompassing reasoning. Starting with a deep understanding of people, their things: relationships, and events or situations that they find themselves in daily and how to best handle them. Wisdom is furthermore the distinction we draw as being essential to good living and survival. Defined as an empowering ability to choose or act wisely, and conduct yourself in accordance with principles, law, and religion, as well as social ethos and norms. The ability to produce the optimum in results, within short cycles of time, with the least amount of friction and energy. Thus also implying being both effective and efficient. The ability to apply intuition, perceptions and knowledge, and then filtering it with critical thinking, to become the knowing of what to do next; with the skill and knowledge of how to do it best, and still have the virtue, in accordance with a belief that knows right from wrong to do it or not.

Confucius stated that wisdom can be learned by three methods: Reflection (the noblest), imitation (the easiest) and experience (the bitterest). This is where strategy sorts the planners from the strategists, with their ability to understand things from a different perspective – that of wisdom. Wisdom sees everything in a duel state; dead and living, good and evil, right and wrong, cause and effect. The wise and rich see and understand this, that everything has two forces; a positive and a negative and an axis, or point that separates them and joins them. Knowledge is not wisdom, knowledge is better understood as the understanding of both fact and fiction. The ability to effectively manipulate and use knowledge, develops into wisdom. If we do not know how to use knowledge, harness it, we are lost to strategy, then we become mere planners. Where a Strategist; is a planner, an architect, a philosopher, a thinker, a leader, a manager, a councillor, a project manager, a scientist and an artist...a person with much knowledge and influence. He who becomes that which is necessary to achieve their objectives, are the "master minds", the grand strategist. For he gained knowledge of all things, and fused them into balance, thus ascertaining harmony, by crafting the ideal perception people want and like. He who controls perceptions, controls people's minds, and the course of things to come. We have taken the long route here in developing thinking capacity, by viewing things from many different perspectives, this is wise, and called wisdom. From this point forward we will get critical and break down all the knowledge and wisdom captured and start formulating things that we have learned, and deducted, with this book. From this point forward we will look at things as they exist in their opposing states and then become fused, by virtue of an axis. The grand strategist knows and understands the importance of the "Grand strategy", it can take on many forms just to succeed. It has many faces and many depths, it is calculated in its approaches. The grand strategy makes any tactic work better. The right strategy puts less pressure on people to executing tactics perfectly.

Opposing parts forming around an axis:

The importance of "Global thinking" is the centre point of the strategic canvas, global thinking is the ultimate quest of all master strategist and master strategies that revolves around the axis of wisdom. Global thinkers are the most effective, efficient and enjoyable people to work with; they have reached the highest level of total mental function. When you think globally, you are also focused critically, and then your mind works with both creativity and intent. Again, this comes from the deep understanding of opposing forces, parts – things - which fuse into a relation, to connect, like atoms to form a concept, towards creating meaning. This mental process is only possible by understanding the true nature of "opposing parts", and how they merge. Everything in the universe, even the universe itself, has opposing parts that revolves around an axis. This axis forms a polarity, or a split between two parts, both uniting and dividing them, asymmetrical and symmetrical all at once. It is fluid and yet it has structure. It has elements of Logic and Abstract, even the human brain is divided into two opposing parts, in terms of function, but in terms of design, they are identical. By following this principle – of two parts - forming the architecture of the Universe and its sub systems, it becomes supportive of the processes of thinking strategic. Everything is related in one way or the other. Where this happens we find duality; a situation or nature that has two states or parts that are complementary or opposed to each other at every level of the universe. As we break it down, from the Milky Way to the atom, we find the exact same principle and architecture re-occurring, following the principle of two parts and nature. Therefore, everything has two parts, both equal and similar, but different and unrelated.

Looking at the aspect is axis. Everything that contains two parts, has one axis, one common axis, around which its activity, spirals. Even our DNA. The moment we have two parts and one axis we have a system, with a unique function forming. Every system in turn is connected to other systems via its axis. Just take this analogy one step further. The same principle applies to the Earth; which is one part water and one part earth. The first part giving life the second sustaining it as it revolves around an axis.

Now we have a concept of creation, what is significant about this is that it works in opposing ways. From the one side it is creation; from the other it is destruction. By virtue of the axis around which the parts are arranged to form a spiral, the direction in which it turns will determine its effect.

Effect: is based on the direction in which the spiral is turned. If the spiral turns, clockwise in a horizontal plane, which in turn creates momentum in a vertical plane, causing it to move up. Then we can say that this is creation energy, or movement, thinking, accepting wisdom. However, if the horizontal plane turns anti-clockwise, then the vertical movement will be downwards. Then we can say that this is destruction energy, or stagnation, opinion and declining wisdom.

The significance of arrangements, the one preceding the other;

Thinking first, everything has to start with thinking, it starts from zero and returns to zero, no matter how far we go, forward or backward zero stays the centre. Why is this important, or significant? Well zero constitutes balanced thinking. If we start our thinking with zero, then we can determine to which side of the scale we want to move, destruction or creation. Be it positive or negative. People have been imprinted to think only positive, but they keep getting stuck on negative. This is because, the positive thinking has no axis and collapses the moment the stimulus disappear, same with negative. Our thought patterns should originate from the zero-zone, where there is an axis. If we want meaning and lasting thought, then it, itself concerns things that are positive and negative elements joining, before becoming neutral. So, in effect we have to think both positive and negative in equal proportions, to have a centre point, wisdom. This is how we decide to apply thought, that gives it meaning or not. By arranging it in positive and countering it with negative to see how much of what is left, this also vents all anger and aggression, scepticism and assumption, as we open up debate for both options. Here we make the first decision on which way we want our thoughts to turn, clockwise or anti-clockwise. This sets in motion our upward or downward spiral of thinking. Once again, if our zero-zone is not calibrated and true, if our thinking only spawns from -1 (minus one), negative or +1 (plus one) positive, just one dimension, we will create thinking without balance, without essence, just noise. The mind will chase thinking, around and around and it will arrive at the same point, one, one source and the source it originated from. However, if we start our thinking from the neutral, the zero-zone, we experience the freedom of going in any direction at any given time, without being bias or prejudice. Because of this, we are not reasoning from anyone specific paradigm all the time, either positive or negative, but from the source; at the source we have the freedom to choose, and trust our own thinking on thinking about one specific attribute, we may be in agreement with the plan, but not with the implementation. We can be both creatively and critically engaged in thinking, as well as spontaneously thinking and or be calculated all at the same time during any thinking spree, or think tank exercise without being judged or judgemental.

Consciousness originates from the premise that all knowledge is interchangeable, inter-related and renewable before it becomes relevant. We no longer fear NEGATIVE thinking, or thinkers, as we understand now, that it can interchange, any reasoning, either positive or negative. If we understand that reasoning is very essential, that we are purely regurgitating knowledge. That No new knowledge exists, it is only recaptured, reused, reinvented, restated. All knowledge goes through a process of metamorphosis; and this is it, now the group will start mutating these ideas towards its relevance and no longer see it as positive or negative but as how relevant it is or not. While all wisdom grows, in proportion to knowledge gained, tested and shared when dealt with in this fashion. We no longer prescribe to a perception that we don't want "negativity", no, we want it, and lots of it, because we want to turn it all to the positive and back. The realisation of the importance of working and thinking about things, is critical to draining noise. Building knowledge pools of critical thinkers, to manipulate knowledge and thinking effectively to our advantage through shrewdness and understanding, creates wisdom, and power.

Arranging the parts: Wisdom is the ability to see a relationship where others see none, only complexity. The ability to see relationships mentally like pictures and then applying wisdom and knowledge creates rationalisation; the ability to give meaning, to fit the abstract into the concrete, this creates context and content, the two parts of a whole. This is not nearly as important as how we arrange the contexts and content, to give it explicit meaning with intent. Meaning without intent becomes meaningless.

The golden arrangement of meaning;

- **Wisdom** first then follows knowledge = Creation
- **Knowledge** first then follows Wisdom = Destruction

Now think about it, apply the symbol of yin and yang here: The first, wisdom, the yin, the second knowledge, the yang, without this there is no centre, no pinnacle to unity and strategy. The fulcrum, around which the universe turns, is held in place by virtue of these two parts forming one, constituting balance and creating order, on the one side, on the other the complete opposite.

First things first. First put these two equations into perspective:

Wisdom /Abstract	Knowledge / Logic
Principles	Rules
Experience	Equation/ Formula
Tried and tested	Hypotheses
Faith	Fact
Understanding	Methodology
Empathy	Sympathy
Knowing	Understanding
Believing	Seeing
Evolving	Growing
Omnipresent	Neither here nor their
Patience	Time
Spiritualism	Humanism
Trail & Error	Right & Wrong
Embrace	Indifferent
Instinct	Education
Conservative	Liberal
Synergy	Compartmentalising
Harmony	Stress
Growth	Competition

Knowledge; Therefore, it is only through knowledge that we craft wisdom and thought wisdom that we realise the importance of knowledge and its usefulness. We cannot go without knowledge, knowledge becomes indispensable and our hot air, but wisdom is our balloon. We cannot interchange the two, there is a natural law that governs this, for if the hot air was outside the balloon and infinitely more than the balloon then the balloon would fall to the earth and meet its end. However, if the hot air is inside the confines of the material that makes up the balloon, the wisdom, then it grows, it will let the balloon rise higher and higher as the knowledge grows. Wisdom comes from applying knowledge with principles. This constitutes growth and creation. If we apply knowledge first and then wisdom we get the atomic bomb, we get death camps and war. For knowledge requires wisdom as wisdom requires knowledge, they are also inseparable; the one has no right to existence, or purpose, without the other. Knowledge stems from perusing these interests, wisdom stems from admiring them. They form the system of thinking and levers. Wisdom requires calmness, stillness and spirit. This is why we have the saying "listen with the heart and speak with the mind". For if, we listen with the mind and spoke with the heart. Things tend to get out of hand.

Why is this aspect of understand wisdom so significant then when dealing with strategy?

"Knowledge stems from perusing *interests*, wisdom stems from *admiring* them as they grow" If we look at the word interests, it implies; happiness, comfort, goodness security, welfare and health – the principles of self. If we look at admiring, it refers to – appreciative, positive, complimentary, favourable, sympathetic and deferential – implying respect – the principles of the universe and unity. Clearly we have to get balance between the two. Moreover, we can conclude that we require both knowledge and wisdom in equal parts. It becomes the compass when we need to find our direction, many people have great knowledge and the degrees and awards to back them up, but still they lack wisdom. We have evolved and are led to believe that knowledge is the ultimate quest and only quest to consciousness, now we know this cannot be true. If we don't understand this, we will forever blindly endeavour to find more and more knowledge, but the more we find the less we know. Therefore stock piling knowledge is useless. It is only when we apply wisdom that we create natural order and become wise. It is only, when we apply wisdom with knowledge that we arrive and know the place for the first time. I have had many encounters with knowledge centred personalities that want to reason everything out to the last atom – because it is fact. They would sacrifice wisdom at the cost of being proven right, being right is a question of perspective, it is not wisdom. If knowledge is power, then it becomes a personal quest and everything must be unequivocally predictable and tacit for knowledge alone to exist and become power. There is fault, if things are not of this nature. What they don't seem to understand is the universal law; you can read and study to gain knowledge, but you have to seek through it to gain wisdom. Also have the wisdom to know that nothing is always perfect and that one needs to compensate for it, by allowing it to flow, like puss from a wound to experience the power of healing. Because, without imperfection, perfection, would not have existed as it is.

Knowledge is but the messenger that learning has prevailed. One can gain much knowledge in one's lifetime, but never seek, nor experience the joy of wisdom. Many people are very happy and content to accept things as they appear at face value. Others sense that there is much – much more and move steadily through changes, in order to gain the experience it creates and the wisdom it leaves. Some just rush any experience and miss the opportunities created. Of course, there are those who fight to hang on to their beliefs and will not allow new experience to alter their mental state, while others actively seek greater understanding and risk, thereby they are open and receptive to receive wisdom. This is where the distinction comes in, between the type of cognitive action we engage in when dealing with the question of ascertaining both knowledge and wisdom. However, there is also a natural order, when we seek knowledge first, it puts us in the way of wisdom. Where wisdom is the experiment with knowledge that creates the truth one recognises in the external world, that corresponds with that, that already resides in the internal one, which is now awakened by virtue of this experimentation. Knowledge therefore is only useful and relevant in the context of changing conditions, and mind-set, when someone who needs to make a decision can synthesise the information into the current changing situation – and bring it into context, this is wisdom. With this added element of wisdom, the right decisions are made and the correct action taken more often than not. On the other hand, one cannot learn or teach wisdom - one must awaken it by acquiring relative knowledge and only pursuing that which is of intellectual value – this is wisdom divine. The more you seek knowledge in only one direction, the more it will pull you in many. Knowledge is bounded by title, and wisdom is unbounded and universal. Knowledge and wisdom then use two completely different processes to communicate with us, the one is the knowing and the other is the understanding. To know something is only that, knowledge. To understand something is to be able to act on that knowledge, being able to use it practically, and then comes the wisdom again, to know when to act on that understanding or not... Knowledge is only the doorway to wisdom; it is not the ultimate quest, it is only the beginning of the trail of fluidity and control.

Therefore, it makes perfect sense to choose wise in all things....

Now, that we have established why wisdom has to take preference over knowledge when we are thinking, and then knowledge over wisdom when we are absorbing things. We can move on to a more complex understanding of learned and applied knowledge. Wisdom combined with knowledge makes the *implicit* – the understood and implied become the *explicit* – the clear and factual, as if by mathematical equation. This is the job of the master strategist. Governments have for many ages been the self-proclaimed sentinels of human kinds contextualising; otherwise also referred to as the continuous process of embedding content into context; or how we should "see and believe" in things and distinguish them, this aspect has now become entrenched in enterprise as well – a total political view. That, which is considered, moral, ethical and acceptable today, was not so just ten years back. That which was once punished by death, only as recently as twenty years or so back, is now no longer a "serious" crime or a crime at all. We have created huge generation gaps in moral and ethical standards and principles through the manipulation of our educational system, segmenting generations. Today, we can send a man to the moon with all our advancements made in the theatres of science and knowledge. Yet, we still have to understand, what is understanding itself and how it guides and moves us. Mans need to understand "why" rather than "how" requires infinite calculations, which does not bring us to one common answer and knowledge, it is still the most complex of all aspects to contend with, yet it dictates every aspect of being, the who we are - human, our nature and character. This is purely the consequence of learned and applied knowledge. Knowledge encompasses many attributes, we get *explicit* knowledge and *implicit* and it consists mainly but not solely of data and information. Information becomes an inanimate object in language, only when we apply interpretation to it does it become interpreted and meaningful or not. Information is dependent on the current or prevailing situation at hand and the circumstances surrounding it, and influencing it. This aspect will determine whether the information is still relevant or not. The moment that information becomes useful it generates its own energy. Until its usefulness expires or evolves, energy can neither be created nor destroyed, so it stands to reason that information is neither created nor destroyed ever, it just comes into existence at a certain point in time and then fades back to where it came from. Information becomes knowledge that stays with us, once it becomes relevant to the specific situation and user, then it can be applied repeatedly to achieve the same desired results or outcome, that supports reality. This type of "Information" then becomes "common knowledge" if it holds its truth in the particular situation and will conform to our reality. Therefore, it can be said that knowledge is particular to its very situation. Furthermore, that knowledge grows and transforms as it gets challenged by new ideas and newer information in turn develops with advances made on the scientific frontiers and in the fields of research and development. Our prejudice/ biased towards information and especially new information and or the source thereof will validate or invalidate the information for us. Where we aim, will determine our focus in life and how we perceive reality. In many instance we are robbed from seeing the bigger picture by virtue of our own aim. For we aim too low or too high and we miss the target. The target being the truth, this is the reality of living, just as a rifle requires a scope; we require an aiming device that we can focus ourselves with, called wisdom. Dependent on our schooling and experiences we become more competent at aiming and focusing, or we give up and let others do the aiming, focusing and hunting for us, we become sheep and path minders. Without wisdom, there can be no personal power and emotional mastery, wisdom gives us this natural balance, a quiet space to analyse the choices at hand, to fill the gaps between stimulus and response. Without knowledge there will be no potential, without a transaction of wisdom the potential cannot be unlocked to its full potential, for every action we activate by exercising our choices, there will be an equal and opposite reaction. Our ability to predict and interpret the cause and effect theory will determine our mastery of universal code. Code being language, our common knowledge, that which links us with our fellow man and our ancestors. This code also brings with it a sense of a universal collective truth, which unifies all. This understanding of "right and wrong", which needs no explaining, when dealing with the aspects of the *implicit* and the *explicit*, is a fundamental code that is universal within the brotherhood of man. Wisdom is also referred to as mental intelligence; the knowing of the self and its weaknesses and strengths, its resources and its powers. There is a season for everything in life's cycle. Being able to motivate and generate positive frames, visions and contexts from within, throughout the circle of seasons, requires a resilience of mind that has the understanding that everything starts from within and with the self, guided by a higher being and purpose. This balance will only be accomplished through seeking out wisdom and not only knowledge, for wisdom has one path, it is said, that leads to one place, truth. Where knowledge has many that lead to many junctions in its pursuit, it unearths to the constraints of thought itself. Only with wisdom can these paths be navigated. Otherwise it will lead to the demise of reason and rationality, for knowledge only brings a man warmth once, liken firewood, so he will forever be in pursuit of wood only, to stay warm, however wisdom will guide a man to plant many forests, to build many fires, for it only requires one lesson in building fire, but many to sustain it. By developing and maintaining a healthy intense understanding for human emotional reactivity, its needs, it wants and its premise, we become a source of wisdom. This very aspect is where stress is either induced or reduced; everything revolves around choosing and choices available to choose from, this gives us the ability to act. Knowing; gives us the ability to navigate the choices. However wisdom; gives us the ability to see the relationships. When and only when, our influence starts at the core, as our worth grows, so will our influence and power. In the beehive where there is synergy and balance, the honey is sweet and the hive is armed and prosperous. Look at nature for an example of wisdom in action. The honeybee and the locust, the locust thrives on knowledge, the second it reaches maturity, it joins a school of seekers and they swarm, eating anything edible in their path and then dies having served no purpose, apart from leaving a path of destruction, here the bee has something to show for his labour, the hive, the family and off spring, interdependence, they all contributed and helped to raise the structure of their culture and organisation, by having served their purpose, that of service, crosspollination, so that many other may benefit and live from their worth. This is the nature of wisdom and knowledge in its singularity. These seemingly insignificant distinctions, can destroy our cohesion and strategy, the answer is programming quality leadership, with all elements required, both with wisdom and knowledge at all levels.

When Leaders get themselves trapped between a rock and a hard place

The key elements within any venture lies within the quality of your relationship, and relationships with others. The trap of leadership is in its paradigms; what do we consider to be good leadership characteristics. For instance if we believe that the essence of leadership is that you cultivate supportive followers, and then you will have succeeded at being a good leader. Merely having willing followers is not enough, because that places too much strain on you as they look to you constantly for guidance in every decision and situation. You need people that you can rely on to share the burden and act with initiative. The traps that are set in this path, of cultivating what you desire and require are many. I have taken the liberty to spell out some of the most common ones.

Leadership is about the ability to take control and to get people to follow willingly, by giving them the guidance they seek, it also involves a fair amount of planning, deliberation and good will and communication, a constant range of decision making and taking. Having neither ceiling nor floor; leadership is all about creating motion, by targeting emotion. The leadership position determines how much you get paid, linked to your task and responsibilities. The amount of action that will be required as well as the level of proficiency - will determine if you get paid. Therefore it is not the position that makes you a leader, it is what you do and how you go about doing it, that distinguishes one as a true leader, and not the title. Very few grasp this; this aspect distinguishes an excellent from an average "Leader". Things only get done by those who follow the recipe for success, the first step is to take "Action" and then to "See it, to, Believe it, to, Plan it and then to ultimately Do it".

The premise for defining true leadership is focused on **"action"** - a leader needs to take the first step and head in the right direction, through the door and leave it open for his people to be able to follow and make the journey, therefore, the leader becomes the path finder, he cuts down obstacles, navigates them and warns of danger, he paves his route to follow with directions and instructions, his followers become the path minders, they follow his instructions and directions to stay on the path.

The second aspect is leaders are also connected, they will stop on the path and let everyone pass, just to make sure they are still altogether, he must have the ability to take control and give control. Because of this, a relationship starts forming, trust develops and the confidence levels grow in the leaders instincts and abilities. The leader starts to develop a reputation, because of his well-executed actions and not because of his position, the leader becomes credible and his follower becomes loyal and dependable. The trust relationship develops and will grow and the end-results will better with every task, as he will develop leadership instincts within this collective. We need to make leaders understand that the leader is the catalyst for any action, the centre and focal point of his people and the likeness they strive for, each employees level of energy and commitment stems directly from the leaders influence, that which flows from the top will feed the bottom. This influence can range in the spectrum, from "The Officer and the Gentleman" profile to the "Overlord and the Skunk" profile. The leader must strive for emotional mastery – in order to become their icon. Followers tend to measure their own actions and contribution against leaders actions and contributions, the leader sets the bench mark for all measure as a standard for others to follow, his or her actions should in effect create passion that rubs off like pollen. Passion comes from enjoying any activity, and once started it fuels other passions again. Just like honey bees need to go out and find the flowers with the best pollen and bring it back to the hive, his hive (of passion) and then his passion gives others direction as he dances with joy and relays the navigation. This creates hope for others in the hive, the passion grows and action now follows and grows, with each return as the harvest grows. In addition, this creates a swarm of action all because of one bee; you cannot have passion if you do not have a sense of purpose and direction first, mutual understanding and insight, to act upon yourself first and find your passion, this is the first step towards becoming an active leader, that fuels others passion for action. True leaders, choose action over results and choose passion over status.

Leaders should strive to be balanced people, living balanced lives; in the sense that we look at how we do things as leaders with people. We measure others as we measure ourselves, the standards do not change; understand how others perceive you pertaining to this aspect, before you start measuring them out loud by your standards only. Find that which inspires you to get out of bed every morning and nurture it. Inspiration is what fuels a sense of purpose. "It's the start that stops most people", most people want to wake up fully rejuvenated and ready to go to work, this very seldom happens, every morning in our routine and boring lives, because there is just no challenge big enough to motivate them. Many people live and work in a routine environment, strict routine eventually creates boredom. This aspect gives rise to a false sense of safety. Yet, they all complain about the time constraints and how demanding life has become, they just don't have the "time" or energy for anything else anymore, outside the routine. The biggest problem with people today is that they think they can live a life without problems if they live this way, by removing themselves from neighbours, family, friends and colleagues because of their "busy" life style. If the task at hand has no personal gratification, then you are either; in the wrong job, in the wrong frame of mind, or on your way to a very hurtful place. To start with, all humans needs to do meaningful work, they are programmed this way, they all require a sense of accomplishment to reinforce their sense of self-worth and this is always attached to a sense of all worth. We will be listening, reading, following success stories and hoping all our life through that we will get the brake, the big accomplishments, success and the end product - MONEY. If we merely work to earn money, we will be doing just that for the rest of our lives, just work that is, to earn money. Note, every day is a unique opportunity to accomplish something good and also satisfying, in one-way or another.

We all live according to our income, so in effect the more you earn the more you spend. Leaders need to say we want to "live" and not just merely "exist", this aspect does not require great financial wealth. Financial wealth makes life easier, inspiration drives us to do more. If you are the manager handing out the work, that in itself is an art and art requires passion, we may not all appreciate this and would rather do what we would like to do, or have seen ourselves doing it, now change your attitude or change your job, if this no longer inspires you. You will find by changing your attitude towards your job for starters it will have a proportional profound reveres effect both socially, spiritually and emotionally, both on you and those that work with and around you. If the interaction was initiated in a positive and constructive manner, it will spark creativity that in turn goes out and comes back, it is a more positive and interactive way of coexistence, this attitude will relieve the stress and the work load on you. However the reveres are also true, if you are negative, then the work will be done like wise and create stress. Therefore, we need to consciously beware of how we act - our choices we make directly and indirectly filter straight back to the source.

People require clearer vision from leaders; the ability to **"see it" in order to truly believe it.** The understanding of the "third eye", that of wisdom, the Chinese call it "TAO", to understand the fundamentals of change, radical, revolutionary change and its consequences. These principles are applied daily, universally, but have we ever analysed them, the first one is that everything is created twice, first in your internal world, your imagination, your third eye or mind, in your "self". Then it transcends into the external world, your life. This transition is not automated; it requires a conscious choice of action. Whether to take it or withhold it. Everything man made that exists today was because of a process of thought and action; its mere existence is a testimonial to the power of thoughts put into action. Energy goes where attention flows. The process of "seeing" starts with a vision of the end-product in mind, "what you vividly imagine ardently desire you will evidently achieve". You have to "see" it to believe it. Create the porthole through which everyone must look at it, to see into the future, your future, their future. Support vision by giving it life and colour with interaction and action items, create hope and believe in it.

"Believe it" – This is the essential element of the process, no one will buy into anything if it cannot be seen as possible or if it is not reasonable or believable. Any achievement must add value, or become of value. We all want to lose weight, but do we believe we can? Yes we all know this to be possible and a reasonable thing to do, but do we believe we can? However, how will this change our routine, our life style, will it add "value", yes, but it will require action and all action requires some form of sacrifice in turn, on our part, so something needs to change and it is this change that requires a belief. What needs to change or be sacrificed and will it be worth the effort, to create the desired action now. We want many things to happen to us, however we put it off, for later, for some day. The catalyst is normally the "What is in it for me, or for us", if not instant gratification, then we can put it off. The same rule will apply throughout until someone changes the paradigm to what's in it for us. The win – win or no deal approach. Believing in oneself and in our abilities to effect change willingly must be one of the watershed topics of our time, very controversial and frightening to think that we can change our course willingly. Normally people want to and wait to be acted upon; rather than to act and be reacted to. To lose weight to some means undergoing a total lifestyle change and many are just not prepared to change the routine, for it will require sacrifice, they have become accustomed to the "believe", the habit of being fat. Habits reinforces lifestyle, work style and traits, if we aim to change we need to focus on *CHANGING OUR HABITS FIRST*. To believe we can, before we can change anything else...

"FEAR" being reinforced daily by others.

The "fear" of failure – we have been so conditioned to fear the shame of failure, that we would rather not attempt something than run the risk of embarrassment of " FAILURE" not realizing that by not attempting anything new, risky or dangerous, we are in fact guaranteed failure because there is no opportunity for success.

The "fear" of responsibility – If taking on a new venture by choice. Then there is the pressure to perform and should the venture fail, I will have no one else to blame. Realize this, you cannot avoid responsibility, you will either enjoy the rewards or suffer the consequences of your actions.

The "fear" of none-conformity – trading your passion for a pay cheque. Doing the acceptable thing, and never "rock the boat". Stay in your rut at least you know where that's taking you, even if it is only "nowhere".

The "fear" of "SNIOP" – (Susceptible to the Negative Influences of Other People). Isn't it amazing that those who are not doing anything spectacular with their lives will always find a way to stop you from doing something marvellous with yours? The sad part is we let them, the guilt and the unnatural fear of being cast out by the group of "friends" we hold so dear. We find ourselves to often and more often than not contemplating and second-guessing our abilities because of them and their own insecurities. The bottom line is this, we should not let ourselves be so consumed by what others might think, or say about us that we start doing what we think they would like us to do, say and be. This is especially true in younger immature relationships and with teenagers. However, we find ourselves still carrying those scripts with us into adult life, old habits die-hard, some don't. We have to reinforce new powerful self-enriched paradigms that emulates from enforcing positive habits of intellectual emotional maturity constantly, for any behaviour consistently reinforce become a habits over time. The only thing that stops you is the start, "it's the start that stops most people" from becoming successful.

"Plan it" – It is said that success is a process not a destination, with no short cuts or instant recipe and as such requires a plan or plan of action to give the processes direction to fuse the "see it" VISION "believe it" MISSION and "do it" GOALS and OBJECTIVES together in a systematic sequential logical way, that is time phased and outcome specific. With a due regard for processes, policies, procedures, logistics and resources etc.

"Do it" – the funny thing about ideas, they won't work unless you do something about them. Take **"action"**.

Things get done by people who are focused on "first things first", the ability to know how to prioritise and organise, they are result driven and orientated, people who are engaged in constant action. Do you measure your career milestones by promotions rather than achievements? Be proud of the promotions and recognitions but realise that they were received as a result of your actions that led to your greatest achievements. To go on getting recognition (especially from the self) you must keep on achieving results without losing balance to be a leader.

The Radical Revolutionary Strategic Management Matrix For Predators

Question all your actions, is this action to result in a real benefit to the organisation, or is this merely to enhance my status? Be result driven, let your achievements feed your ego. Don't be so busy playing at being an executive that you don't have "time" to execute and remember that you never compartmentalise your life on your way to the top. We need to stay the same person, no matter which role we are currently engaged in, if we are to retain our inner balance and our moralities at all cost. Then the oneness of person and personality needs to flow at home, work, socially, church, anywhere because we to live with balance. Furthermore, we need to live equally, in all spheres of life for balanced living to prevail. We need to spend equal periods of time and energy interacting with all our roles in life, that of father, parent, brother, son, teacher, member, executive... As well as dimensions; implying spiritual, social, economic, and family unit, in all of them we have a vital essential role and function to perform. Somehow our roles all "infringe" one upon the other in terms of scheduling and priority. How well we cope with this aspect will determine how we are able to live with balance and cope with life. In general, we build buffers and compartments in our mind between the different roles we have to fulfil. Each with their own unique diversity and complexity, gets a personality we take on, and a level of preference, the one challenging the other. However, this is not how we live; we don't go through a natural door in reality and cross over from one role to the next, just by walking through a house, seamless in terms of transition, back and forth. Then why do we see ourselves differently and wanting to act and behave differently when fulfilling our roles, from the one-minute to the next, this must be very stressful and wanting to be differently perceived in different situations takes tremendous amounts of energy. This causes friction within the self and evidently inner chaos. Because if one role suffers, they all suffer for they are all from one source.

That's why you need to be able to decide at every fork on the road, which role and function will take preference under the prevailing circumstances. For instance, you are at work, your wife is in a very important meeting and she is calling to ask you to fetch your son from school. You think about the role, as father and the dual responsibility you have as a parent towards your children. Then you think of the role that you are currently in and the responsibility towards your employer and the task and the role and function you have to perform here. Normally they are in conflict; this might even be an understatement... You have many choices the first is to accept the request or to reject it. Let's say you reject it, then you will be accountable to the wife and son later that evening and you will have to account for your decisions...If you accept, you can weigh your alternatives, seek help and pull a few favours in from a friend or family member, or do the job yourself. The point is our lives are seamless between our different roles and functions. We have the God given ability of "CHOICE" and the right to exercise this unique ability between our roles and functions, where roles come in conflict, ask yourself this, what would my reality be if the problem did not exist. Will my supervisor understand, can I take family responsibility leave, or put in normal leave – what are my options here? Every situation is different, but the fundamental premise is this, our centre of concern will determine how we make our decisions. If we are Family centred we will drop everything and fetch the son, if we are work centred we will not leave that space at any time and even at cost, pay someone to have the son collected. When striving for a balance centred lifestyle; we will see this as an opportunity to share some quality time with our son on the way home and we will work in lunch or get home later, but this is a good opportunity to build emotional trust accounts with the wife and son in the role as Father and Husband. This is not about image, but about seamless living and dealing effectively with circumstance. The qualification here is this, the job centred man will say the job needs to be done at all cost, I do not have time to fetch my son, the family centred man will say the family comes first the job second. The balanced man will say my job can wait, my son cannot. A very rational unemotional deduction of a problem viewed in context, this will be the reality if the problem did not exist. Time is of little consequence, for he is spending quality time with his son and he will go back to work content and spend quality time until he is satisfied with his work. Such is the relationship of balance, being able to make seamless changes, and transition between role and function.

Position is only perception, here on earth we look up at the moon, if you were on the moon you would look up at earth. It's all a question of emotional alignment, never trade passion for glory it will tarnish your legacy.

There are ten common traps "leaders" fall into:

There's a fine line between having a strong management style and being a bully. Life's stress and work pressure combined can sometimes lead even the best of managers into the pit of darkness, to behave in unacceptable ways, that never get noticed by top management, only by staff. Whilst their intention may not be deliberate, if it gets results then it starts forming a habit, if it goes uncontested. Managers who are only focused on positive results for their organisation and superiors will go to any length to get them. The impact of which has a profound effect on individuals that have to suffer their abuse. This can start eroding the fabric of confidence, shatter self-belief, and lead to poor work performance – which isn't good for them or the organisation. If you're aware of someone's bullying style, you may feel that the only option is to stand by and wish things were different. Well-wishing brings nothing other than more despair, it is only through action, that things change. However, in doing nothing and accepting what is or what has become unacceptable, then becomes condoned behaviour. People mimic success, even if it is flawed, if it gets results then it must be right. Managers breed second generation mangers, be aware, trends, behaviour and mannerism will prevail, it's a type of collective apathy' that resonates into all directions. Whilst it may feel impossible to challenge senior managers in an organisation, there are ways of doing this constructively.

Choosing "Status over Results"

It isn't the incompetent person who destroys an organisation, no; on the contrary, he or she never gets into a position to destroy it. It is those who have achieved something and want to rest on their laurels that clog things up.

Choosing "Popularity over accountability"

You may have grown up with your peers, you may even have started work together and now you are their manager. How do you keep their respect and friendship? When your responsibility is to perform and deliver, well in short the answer is simple; if you fail no one will like you any way. Treat your colleagues with respect, realise that they are professionals who value constructive feedback and who are also performance driven. Help them so that they may help you, people who accomplish things and do good work feel good about themselves – people who feel good about themselves and their accomplishments do good work. You are doing them a disservice by not holding them accountable. People need discipline and order.

Choosing "Certainty over action"

Nothing in life is certain we live in an ever-changing world. What was true yesterday may not be true today. Too often, we fail to act because we feel unsure of ourselves and the situations we find ourselves in, we use excuses to defend our predicament; "lack of information" "a lack of training" "a lack of resources" as an excuse to avoid us from having to take action. The fear of failure sets in and we lose hope and direction, we do introspection and we find more and more ways of going into denial and reasons for not going over to action. We can re take our strength by applying two rules, "first things first" and "don't sweat the big stuff" – this is not a simple rule, but very effective. First things first, deal with things that matter most in your life to us as a person.

The second truth is that basing our happiness purely on our ability to control everything in life is futile. The only thing that is sure is that we have control over our choices, we have to stop worrying about that which we have no control over, and in addition focus on what's right in front of us. Sometimes our noses are so close to the problem that we see no way out, if we just back up a little we might just get more perspective and even an answer or a way out. While detail is important, action and a resilient mind are more valuable. Don't get yourself bogged down in detail, the more detail the less certainty, all the while you wait for certainty, or perfection the window of opportunity could be lost forever. Ask not what the possible cost of making a decision is but what opportunities have been lost by not making one.

Nothing in life is purely black and white, simply solid, or pure – we have to apply our better judgment and wisdom in the absence of clear guidelines and in the absence of certainty, law and or legislation. The rule is where there is no policy or procedures, then we follow the presidents set, if there are none, then follow strategic principles that of; improvise, adapt and overcome.

The aforementioned paragraph is established business philosophy and literature all still valid and motivational in a general sense, when facing decisions of middle order importance, but when faced with contentious issues of a public interest and nature, then caution should not be thrown to the wind. The reality is one should also stay on the side of caution in today's litigations society, when and where the safety nets of procedures, are not hung – in place or lacking.

Personally, i would tread like a man in a minefield, in the event where the facts dictate that the consequences far outweighing the perceived progress should a bold decision be made to move forward, rather suspend your initiative, or escalate it to a higher tier for a decision, under these circumstances rather play it safe. Your best supporters today can become your worst critics tomorrow, your advisors can become your opposition overnight, it just takes one rooster to crow three times and then the blood flows, and the heads roll.

Being bold doesn't imply being blind and oblivious, stupid, every decision is a calculated risk no matter how big or small the stakes; decisions should be in the interest of the company when making bold moves. If your intentions are found to have been in line with the objectives of the organisation you could be pardoned should it go wrong, or there are ramifications and you are known to always act in the interest of the organisation, it all depends on the structure, type of organisation and leadership in place, but still it's risky. However, this dilemma of management and leadership calls for strong willed people who are not afraid of taking some risk, for if you risk nothing you could be risking everything. Invention only comes from having risked, tried and failed, until the solutions become apparent.

Choosing "Harmony over fear of conflict".

It is said that conflict is a sign of a healthy organisation, a good leader does not try to avoid or eliminate conflict he manages it. Therefore, it stands to reason if two people always agree, one of them is unnecessary. People who are passionate about what they do get excited very easily, to really get their creative juices flowing, you have to cultivate a culture of free willing expressions and ideas. This could create turbulence. Understand that turbulent meetings and gatherings are often a sign of real progress, an "aspire the corium". While tame meetings may mean that important issues are being ignored. Do you just receive lip service and empty promises; with many experienced people-nodding heads when you have meetings, is something amiss, most definitely, the will to fight and express is gone, everyone has this desire to express themselves openly. You cannot want participative management without handing down accountability. If you take the accountability away you strip any task of its "importance". Without accountability, the task and post is of routine nature and of little significance, anyone can do it why should I? Teach your people to avoid compromise, someone has to be accountable, responsible and in charge. Teach then not to take stuff personally, play the ball not the man.

Choosing "Invulnerability over trust, or building fortified castles"

Do you have a hard time admitting you are wrong, do you try to keep your weakness secret from your peers? No one likes to be wrong, or week, but creating the perception amongst your peers that they are not to criticise you or challenge your ideas, is disastrous for you and the organisation, it won't do much good towards nabbing that evasive promotion either. If you are confidant in yourself and your abilities then you will realise that the position you are in, is because of your unique ability and skill. The contributions you are making towards the organisation's overall results and not your "appearance" of being smart (clever) or more cunning, ultimately imbeds your net worth in terms of your contribution, this determines your worth and status. Beware of the boss that walks on water - syndrome. Do you ever have the fear of a subordinate being after your job? Here is the reality check; it is both your responsibility and duty to train someone to take your place, for if the organisation depends solely on you and your skills and expertise in your current position. Then you are truly in a very vulnerable position. How can you move up and on if there is no one qualified to take your post and run with it? This happens when we are not sharing or delegating...

The Radical Revolutionary Strategic Management Matrix For Predators

Delegation is not a "DIY" – or "if it has to be done I'd better do it" – type of practice and give the rest to someone else approach. By doing it all yourself, you are depriving your immediate subordinates of a learning opportunity. The job of a manager and leader is to get the job done not to do it, all this within the framework of time restraints, resources and benchmarks. Management is the art of getting things done through people and to utilise resource effectively. Imagine for one moment, a symphony conductor trying to play all the instruments by himself, impossible. Yet we expect to be in control by doing all the work ourselves.

Delegation and in this case, effective delegation is the art of giving clear to the point instruction sets, to a person who has the resources (both material as well as emotional) to cope with the task, along with the responsibility and accountability that is required by the task. Delegation does not stop here, it starts here, as from this point forward coaching and counselling may or may not be required depending on the task and the person performing it, progress monitoring and feedback become essential aspects of effective communication with delegation. Briefly, you need to micromanage delegation to staff in training, most people want to be checked and want to be helped along, especially when learning a new skill or task and praised as well and encouraged this greatly helps along the trust and growth potential of new talent. Veterans on the other hand only want, objectives and deadlines, and don't need a babysitter.

Do you as a manager allow your employees the benefit of taking risks, and making mistakes?

The usefulness of mistakes can only be measured, once mistakes have actually been made, and corrected. The question is always "what have you done with your mistakes?" Have you learned from them or not? Emotional mastery; is not being moved by emotions but by really making rational decisions about how you want to do this or correct that, by stepping back . Stepping back, and removing yourself from the equation, and emotion, gives you time to centre and balance yourself, and your thinking. This is a good thing and it develops streetwise managers that will carry you when the going gets really tuff. Just as change will remain a constant in our lives, making mistakes will remain inevitable. if we want to be good at change, and changing events and people, then it's not okay to accept people making mistakes. Especially if they are not planning on learning from them and finding ways to make things better as a result. The mistakes people make can tell you a lot about them, their strengths and their weakness. However, the way they go about fixing those mistakes or what they do with those mistakes will ultimately define who they are, or become. So instead of just accepting that it's okay to make mistakes, challenge yourself and others to take the responsibility to fix any mistakes made!

Practice has no substitute in life, no degree or qualification can pass down the experience and fertility of practical knowledge gained by doing things for oneself. For it has an emotional dimension that only gets captured during that moment of interaction, this is heightened by all the senses and become a primary fundamental survival resource. It becomes empowering, "i can solve problems". Especially in the event of stress and pressure, then we refer back to our automated practical experiences first. Good judgement comes from experiences and lessons learned from applying bad judgement in practice.

Are you trying to keep all the exciting jobs and projects to yourself?

A real leader creates a climate of growth for his employees by encouraging them to take on more responsibility. The growth of your business is dependent on your ability to develop capable people who can assume important responsibility. A good manager will delegate tasks in an area where they are weak, to people who have strength and potential to master their weakness.

Hogging the credit

The quickest way to de-motivate your people is to hog the credit, the key to an organisations success is to secure the drive potential, through commitment and enthusiasm of the few people who comprise of the organisations key decision makers and work horses and harness them, to form an internal work processing organ. Then harness the practically minded and have them perform the labour intensive tasks for instance, find the shoe that fit's.

Give people work they like and want to do, remove frustrations and distractions and empower them with resources and knowledge. Catch people doing things right for a change, you will be surprised at the reaction and even expressions you may receive and reward continuous growth and contribution. Remember this, the leader is only as strong as his weakest person and in reverse the team is only as good as their coach is wise, then again if the team does well the status of the coach enhances.

Fixing the blame rather than the problem

Fixing the blame is as old as mankind – Adam blamed Eve, Eve blamed the Snake and the snake did not have a leg to stand on. While it is essential that you always hold people accountable for their actions, it is important that you discover the cause of the problem.

All too often, who we think is a problem employee is often a bright employee with a real problem. The only value to finding out why something went all pear shaped is to learn from the experience of others so that you, yourself don't fall into the same trap. We lose out on great learning opportunities for growth and experience because we are so busy finding who is to blame, someone is always to blame and someone is always responsible. By taking this route we are actually treating a symptom and not the cause, we are wasting valuable time and not addressing the "real" problem. We lose opportunities daily, because we are so busy trying to find out who's responsible that you allow the problem to get worse, or lose an opportunity that you may have found because of a problem.

Attacking the person rather than the problem

It's not uncommon to get up close - in your face - and personal when things go wrong, this works when the relationship is very strong. When you feel a need to protect your image, you are more than likely angry with yourself and it becomes an egocentric attack on your person, then it is easier to direct one's anger and the negative attention at someone else, he's at fault, she did it. By having a mind-set of always wanting to be right at all costs, will inevitably create friction, both introspective because you are raising standards for yourself and other to such a high degree that it becomes very stressful. Outward this lifestyle creates enemies and suspicion. Sometimes, it is just a simple question of human nature prevailing and mostly this will hold truth, so it's the problem that needs to be fixed not the person. The person has developed this false sense of security within his or her insecurity to hide personal weakness and inabilities mostly fear of losing control. We have to change the perception and the attitude in order to change the person. When there is a problem the first reaction is to find the person – responsible - who "created" this problem. People are never the problem, it's their attitude, or perception that crashes or that is in conflict and contradiction with reality as we perceive it, as mangers this creates challenges and this can be fixed if we concentrate and focus our efforts on the rightful causes of problems, we will get to solutions much quicker. Criticise the performance never the performer. Someone had put this very nicely, we as people were programmed to run certain programmes during certain events and sometimes we run the wrong programme and this causes an invalid fault in the results it renders. The point is don't judge the person, don't hold a gripe, he has many good programmes and attributes that we can use, why denounce him for one or two bad ones that you have the power to change. We all have within us the power to change our outlook, our perceptions, attitudes and ourselves so why can we not change others for the better.

Furthermore rather use "I" communication rather than "you" communication when resolving disputes and defusing situations. As soon as you attack the person, you are at risk of destroying the relationship and you will find that people will try to either defend themselves or withdraw completely. It's not necessarily always the person who is bad; it is what the person did that is bad that needs review.

Punishment rather than discipline

Punishment is negative in that it aims to make a person feel bad or suffer for his actions while discipline focuses on correcting behaviour. We have to see it as an opportunity to correct behaviour by asserting authority; by changing the behaviour we build the person.

We all experience events and things physically (see, hear, touch, smell, touch) but we interpret the event in two ways;

- Intellectually – based on " knowledge", what you have learned
- Emotionally – how you feel, about yourself, your relationships, your beliefs.

Your emotional state will always determine your interpersonal interpretation of the experience unless you learn to control your emotions your emotions will control you. Always describe the problem in terms of behaviour and performance.

The importance of control and allowing fluidity of thinking

Control over thinking becomes futile if fluidity of free thinking seizes to exist, in favour of the purpose of having total control over thought. By applying overwhelming control and strict uncompromising guidelines of how to think, we are in effect inhibiting our ability to think and act in multidimensional ways and all functions of fluidity and reason subsequently succumb and seize to exist, the stronger the control the less the fluidity until it stops. Fluidity and control are both essential parts to strategy. Things need control and people need fluidity, to be effective, again, we need balance between the two elements.

That we must allow for margins of "imperfection" when working with people is true. We have become consumed, or rather obsessed with urgency and control, everything is time sensitive and systems were designed to take control and be time sensitive. Nevertheless, somewhere in our past someone took this concept and ladled it "time management" – which in itself is no natural concept; one cannot manage time - and turned the whole thing on its head for us. In the pursuit of glory, praise and our worth to be recognised, we moved away from structuring work, towards controlling it, yet another imperfect alignment, perfected by management. They want people to compete so that they can be right, others cannot be "right", how can they be, they are wasting time, by stealing glory, praise and being in control of their part of the system. Never, this can't be, people must leave these "higher order things" to the creator, the controller, the "Boss". To try to control time and consciousness is like trying to control time itself, it functions on its own terms and so do people. We cannot ask people to show awareness and create time. Because, both comes from the same source, fluidity, that is not theirs to control. However, strongly in denial we are about our insecurities, they manifest in the ways we manage people, either, with fluidity, or over bearing control.

More on this paradigm; they must live and do their personal private life's stuff outside company time, we expect then to hit pause – on their private lives and just live to work, they can carry on after office hours. Because knowledge can prove, we are wasting "time" with a formula we devised.

Once again, this is "common sense" and not "global thinking" talking; "common sense" reasoning turns everything into "fruit jam", they have the right to make a woman feel guilty about taking time off from work to take her kids to the doctor. (May I remind you; your mother took you to the doctor as well.) However, hey it's common sense; women spend more time talking and on the phone, or being away from their desks than men. Is this a problem? It should not be, but knowledge has taught us somewhere, somehow that this is a waste of time. It should not be. Always ask the "Control & Fluidity" question when confronted with these anomalies, "what would the reality be if the problem did not exist". Women are emotional creatures and if they have to ponder about loved one's health and other issues their fluidity is stopped, although they are at work physically, their minds are in another place, is this productive, they might be at the desk, as the boss instructed, but their worth is at home. People have emotional attachment and are where their minds carry them and so follows their worth.

The other aspect is work rates; women have faster work rates than men, but men can work for longer. Therefore, the one compensates for the other. It all relates back to reasoning dominance, how we perceive things should be from our perspective, when confronted with problems of time, management and work. Why not change the mind-set and send the woman home with her work, give her two, three days. I am almost willing to bet she will render better results, could we have split the scenario and duplicated it to test the results. I will take you back to knowledge centred thinking, it is destructive. Wisdom centred people have emotional connections and emotional bank accounts with their staff. Where knowledge centred people have full or empty physical bank accounts, they need more "money", they don't have enough " time" to give you the time of day, because "time is money" and to them everything relates right back to "common sense" in every argument they make, it's always back to common-sense. Well I am afraid that there is really nothing common about common sense for contrary to belief common sense is very *uncommon*, it requires wisdom, so it stands to reason that people, who reason with commons sense as a fail-safe, fail to understand the bigger picture. They are, in fact reasoning from denial, that they are in denial of the truth is always true. However, they perceive it differently, because their argument has too many anomalies and emotion in it, they reason from a premise of right and wrong. So, who is right? Both, in their own minds and cultures, they will be able to justify and even substantiate their thinking. However, which ones thinking will create and which one will destroy trust? Wisdom teaches us, that only after numerous trails and errors, that, only one ingredients is necessary to be effective at management. If they exist in the final equation then you are creating, or being creative:

Manage people with agility and enthusiasm

With mental agility and enthusiasm that is, we all have the ability to bring different styles and attributes to the table without having to reside to textbook answers. Practical experience will often win out over studied theory, therefore stay flexible, think agile and leave space for error and opinion.

Manage trust

Open up bank accounts with people and deposit into them trust. Because, during troubled times and times of conflict, trust is the only thing that will carry you through. That will keep the cohesion strong during troubled times, for if we lose all cohesion, everything is lost. Pay special attention to detail when planning, when executing and winding up, your strategy. This will identify risk, potential risk and blind spots; this should force you to plan for contingencies. Mitigation; is the process of having a strategy within an strategy, that only concerns itself with contingencies should things go wrong, there must be planning, should the tide change.

Dealing with risk

You have to embrace risk as if it is positive and even try to find ways and means to turn it into your favour; leaders separate themselves from the pack by taking steps to mitigate risks. By looking at the worst case risk scenarios, by weighing their options and taking the steps they deemed necessary and required, to mitigate risk, by viewing the aspect of risk objectively; one will see that the risk might not be so bad if managed properly. And if we at first don't success we will try and try again, until we do succeed, failed attempts, serve as lessons learned, not to be repeated again, it will never be the end of the line for us if we take this stance and should we succeed we have gained much. Wisdom, thus being wise, requires knowledge of the tried and tested variety, in order to grow from four dimensions of life. Gaining both wisdom and knowledge is not a spectator sport; you have to be into it to win it. Rumer Godden says, "Everyone is a house with four rooms: Physical, mental, emotional and spiritual. Unless we go into every room every day, even if only to keep it aired, we are not a complete person." By starting at home, with family, our church or religion, music, relaxation, our spiritual growth, our intellectual growth, acquiring all dimensions energy, this aspect, expedites the acquisition of balance and wisdom. This becomes your soil and seed towards creating global thinking, for your thoughts are tapped into four dimensions, the unity divided between wisdom and knowledge.

Pace yourself, find your balance

"Rome" was not built in a day, but don't be so laid back that people don't even seem to know you exist. Remember mostly you are in it for the long haul, for life.

Don't quit

Leaders need a never quit mentality, a die hard attitude; rather withdraw and regroup, if you at first did not succeed try and try again – someone said. Leaders are the one's that go the extra mile and their people just follow in that tradition. Not the other way around.

Agree to disagree

Most of the problems with maintaining momentum stems from focusing on the function of the business rather than the purpose of the business – and its core function. So keep the main things the main things; and the main things should always be the purpose of the business. However you need to encourage your juniors to work as a team, focused on the purpose of the business. Remind them that they do not work for you but with, and that they can trust you that their careers will never be jeopardised for disagreeing with management, constructively. All members of your organisation must be focused on consistency and accountability. Remember trust is not blind, people see through agendas and get hurt, trust needs boundaries, a vision, a mission a goal, trust takes time, allow for a learning curve, tolerate mistakes and lead by example, trust demands openness and honesty, learn to agree to disagree...trust no one or trust everyone, but don't trust them one by one.

You can never use, or exercise power effectively without having perfect balance.

Balance is a required element, that gives us power as strategist in order to guide, lead, and influence people and circumstances with. Power comes in and has many forms and sources.

Intellectual, physical, spiritual, financial, political, military, and anything that gives you leverage over an opponent, or in a specific situation, to gain the upper hand so to speak. Right through this book, the word "Balance" has been used. Balance is a universally understood term. In order to define this element and its usefulness, we have to look at it in all its facets, as there are many aspects that influence balance, and on differ levels. Balance in the true sense of the word and all it refers to, could be summed up in a few words. Balance is firstly a poise or *position* you have, that of self-confidence and a good composure. Secondly, *a sense of balance*; one can't balance if your senses can't determine where the horizon is, and what is up or down, or be able to feel forces of nature interacting on the body, like gravity. Like gravity and wet surfaces, they influence our physical balance when we slip. Balance is also connected to all spheres of existence. Balance influence our total balance in the emotional, intellectual, and even spiritual spheres. For example. Slipping on wet tiles, requires a sudden effective counter, running, screaming oh dear god, and then landing on your feet...after some wild pretzel impersonation and recovery moves – is a good way of visualising this. It, balance is all intertwined with everything, our senses, our surroundings, our food, air, water, everything plays a role. All are seen as being essential to the overall balance. Balance is the one thing and rule of nature that must prevail in all things connected, or we will come to harm and even demise. Balance is furthermore defined by looking at our *state of existence*. The emotional, mental and spiritual, as well as the physical being and aspects for things that influence our inner and outer is all because of balance, or a lack thereof.

Maintaining balance, is an attempt to overcome the environment and all its challenges, by searching for answers in all four spheres or poles of life daily. Daily we tap into the emotional, mental and spiritual, as well as the physical poles, to maintain a balanced centre and as result we live as functional and healthy individuals. Balance or a lack thereof, will ultimately influence how we go through life and deal with issues of individual balance. Balance furthermore transcends these poles of existence, it bleeds into and concerns our growth and development in all dimensions.

Physically balancing our lifestyles and well-being for instance relates to our ability to effectively conduct various physical activities; including recreational ones. Staying physically healthy and inculcating healthy habits, through physical exercise, eating habits, hygiene, and maintaining effective balance between work and rest is paramount to longevity and health. Emotional well-being talks to our emotional health. As Mother Teresa said, *"There is more hunger for love and appreciation in this world than for bread."* It is this aspect, the ability to clearly understand our emotions, connect with it, and others and their emotions. Then, the ability to cope with failure, learning resilience and so forth. Forcing ourselves to interact, it all becomes critical aspects for building meaningful relationships, at both work and home. Balance becomes more relevant today in our ability to deal with the ups and downs of life. Life and living has become a fast passed rollercoaster ride of ups and downs, sharp turns, feeling sick to the stomach, and then the highs, the screams, the rush. Spiritual well-being is connects our levels of self-awareness, charity, clarity, and sacrifice to have an understanding about the purpose of life, and our state of being and existence. It is about knowing who we are, our place in this universe, and our interconnectedness. Mental well-being relates to our intellect – our ability to think, our thoughts, understanding, values and beliefs. It facilitates our ability to create suitable mental maps to effectively navigate the world with balance.

It is said that for true strategy and strategist, to excel in the new era, they need to be groom to be well balanced. This level of activity and professionalism will only be reached where we reach a stage where persistent intellectual development of people is no longer just seen as required, but a norm for healthy and functional adult life. The way we think and gain an understanding of our world through the interaction and influence of genetic and learned factors will determine how we end up living balanced lives or not. A healthy sense of well-being is really important to all of us and starts with the way we think, this will determine our bias and balance in life. Research in this field includes information processing, language development, NLP and memory development to name but a few.

Jean Piaget the father of developmental psychology had this to say about our development and ascertaining balance; Piaget described two processes used by the individual in its attempt to adapt to change in his environment. Described as; Assimilation and Accommodation, both these processes are used throughout life as the person spirals through phases of growth and development in each sphere of existence. As we develop we accelerate development itself, with every cycle an ever increasingly pace of acceleration at adapting to the environment becomes apparent and more complex until adulthood is reached.

Assimilation, or absorbing things, is best described as the process of using or transforming the environment so that it can be placed in context, thus giving something meaning, and showing us where it fits, in our pre-existing frames of reference or scripts.

Accommodation is the process of changing reality, by influencing the thought processes in order to accept or incorporate something from the environment. Both processes are used simultaneously and alternately throughout life, the purpose of which is to achieve – balance – or equilibrium between the two poles of abstract and formal thoughts that influence our behaviour. This stability or balance is centrically part of the human DNA and make-up and presides in all three parts of the brain. Looking at the balance in human anatomy, every part has a counter part that is proportionally matched in every dimension and in perfect balance with each other. Piaget's theory is significant in that it describes how we master every level of emotional and intellectual growth, by challenging our environment constantly, both on the intellectual, spiritual, physical and emotional level, from infancy to adult hood, but some of us never achieve any form of emotional mastery because we become unbalanced along the way towards adulthood. Where we don't absorb or accommodate the right things, and can't find a fit for other emotional experiences and trauma. Only through successful adaptation to the environment, do we succeeded with on-going fruitful, and developmental relationship forming and building, this includes our peers, friends, family and parents influences as well as any role model on our mental modelling. We are thus the sum total of every assimilated encounter both emotionally, biologically, spiritually and even physically in nature, all our experience from infancy combined. Now that is a lot of data and influences both on the emotional and intellectual level that is required to form a functional balanced human being.

Therefore, it stands to reason that we are what we have been exposed too and have assimilated to a greater extent, this is where introspection comes in, have we been soul searching, have you ever paused for a second and just sat back and looked over the ocean and then up at the stars and asked yourself what am I doing here, what is the very reason for my existence and even deeper still what is my true purpose? If not to suffer, then what, and how and where do I fit? We have all no doubt at one or other stage of our lives, paused and asked ourselves deeply these questions.

Most of us focus so much on our existing state, that we lose track of our desired and ultimate state, we tend to anchor ourselves in the here and now. When in fact our minds are innately focused on accelerating our growth and potential and pulling us towards our final state, with good or bad, as we progress. If we are in a growth phases, and we are in a very bad place, unbalanced, then we will grow worse, the opposite is also true, good goes towards better and then great. Finding our direction to our desired state comes with learning balance, fulfilling a deep inner sense of purpose, it is not always easy. Nevertheless, we shut it out because the world prescribes to us best how we should think, choose, eat and live from day to day. Until one day, then that inner voice calls us to order, and we realise our balance is lost, and we shut down and break down emotionally and we are forced to become quieter and rethink our morality and values again, our integrated sense of well-being, honesty, integrity and love feels lost, our direction finder tells us we are in the wrong place and we are not serving our purpose, we are lost.

The only way to regain direction is to get the balance right again. "It's not that life is so short existing in it, it's that we take so long to realize that we have to start living it with balance" before we can accelerate to bliss. Picture yourself holding a compass when you are leaning over, it won't work well will it, it just goes around and around. This is true of many adults life's, they get stuck in compromising positions, no longer being able to stand upright, just leaning into "it". Like bracing ourselves against a harsh wind - focusing only on one aspect of life at a given time, this pulls us over - with all our might and at the same time trying to get the needle on the compass to stop, yet we seek direction, without ascertaining an upright balanced posture. Balance becomes impossible and even naturally it goes against the rules of nature itself. We have to stop existing in this state of imbalance and start living balanced lives. People who thrive on being busy, too busy to do anything but work merely exist; people who live have attained balance, emotional, physical, social and spiritually. This is a foundation for a solid happy (family) life, with deep emotional bank accounts and relationships built on deep routed trust. They have fulfilling spiritual, physical and social lives and always have time. We spend so much time worrying about, or hoping for, what might be and regretting what might have been, or reminiscing about what was, that we fail to experience what is, and what could be. What is, what is happening, what has transpired, what has changed. We fail to experience the magic of the "now" moments altogether, by trying meaninglessly to control every aspect of life, you cannot control those things that fall outside our area of influence, make peace with it and move on.

Life is too short to wait, worry and cry over spilt milk; you can have whatever you want as long as you are prepared to do whatever it takes and then to wait for however long it requires to come to realise itself. Things will never come to be without *taking action first*, that leads to restored balance. In addition, everything has a life cycle even success, so be patient in getting there and plan beyond that so that the journey neither does not end there. Now will never be again, what we lose now we lose forever and mind you that is by choice. The chance to say I love you my son, you look pretty my daughter and let's take a walk my wife, is now. Now is all that there is. Your life as you know it now is made up of constant flows of "now's" flowing eternally out of our today into your future, through your present and back into your past. The quality of your life depends on what you do with it, who you share it with, each moment, each now. You are the author of you present, the result of your past and the architect of your choices. By choice we change direction, and get balance back, in the gap between stimulus and response, how will you react is by choice and choice alone. The time it takes to make each decision is determined by your emotional mastery, are you in control of your emotions, yourself, your destiny and the quality of the decisions you make? How to get you there will be determined by your emotional power and self-mastery. This "power" comes from knowing and living with true balance, balance is power and power is self-mastery, they are one unity, the one fuelling the other. We all know that without power all things seize to exist or function, as power is the energy required to make all things alive.

What is this inner power?

Inner **POWER** is; *Purpose,* *Optimism,* *Wisdom,* *Enthusiasm,* and *Responsibility.*

Purpose; a life without direction or purpose is like a ship without a rudder, direction requires orientation. Orientation is only possible through balance, because achieving balance requires wisdom, inner wisdom that will give us our bearing in life, our true North, our purpose. That little voice inside you that tells you what is the right thing to do and what is not, that black and white thinking cap we turn down to a whisper. Alternatively, rather just listen to the world's voice, and see where that brings you.

Everyone has his or her own unique purpose to fulfil and this we know, by finding your "calf" you can carry it. If everyone can carry a work load that fits them, and by picking up that load, that "calf" every day we become more proficient at picking up "calf's". It is the start that stops most people from achieving excellence. Excellence is a combination of being both effective and efficient. As every day passes, we get use to our work load, the calf gets bigger and we get stronger and eventually we can pick up an ox, to every ones amazement and surprise, we can pick up any size of   cattle   eventually.
However, everything in life requires action first; find a "calf" that fit's you and pick it up, pass on the knowledge of calf carrying and soon everyone will be able to lift an ox. The point is you may not start a life fulfilling your purpose straight away, you may be required to suffer and toil and gain the necessary wisdom and intuition, that only comes with experience, serious hardship and compassion before you will find your purpose. Life is all about the encounters and experiences required for us to become great, that shape us and how we deal with them that form us. Like that rock spewed from a volcano, that falls into the river and rolls down to the sea over some time, to become a pebble, nicely polished and round. If not for the hardships and experience of the river that rock would have stayed a rock, such is life. We have to endure to come to perfection, to get

orientation, to start listening to the inner voice and form the required understanding of what constitutes balance in my life, before we will find our ultimate purpose. In the meantime, we will have to practice restraint and resolve in all our actions. - "Man's greatest legacy is to serve one and the other unconditionally; with love, with trust, truth and openness".

Optimism; your words, your dreams and your thoughts have the power to create conditions in your life and your future. Energy goes where attention flows. It is said that what you speak about you can bring about, what you emit you will attract. What you vividly imagine, ardently desire, you will evidently achieve. Never be afraid to dream, to believe and to speak about that which is your passion. However, watch your thoughts, for they become your words, those words become actions and actions become habits, habits influence your characters balance and your character determines your destiny. Tune your thoughts daily, into conversations to be more positive and to reflect your passion, packed with faith, hope, love and above all action. Optimism is a strange thing, it tends to rub off like excitement, it becomes contagious and grows like a forest fire, it just takes one spark to light the fires of optimism and action however keeps it burning. Remember, if it wasn't this, it would be something else, but there will always be something that requires our attention and action. Some nice and others not so nice, it's the sugar and spice of life, circumstances will always be part and parcel of who we are and what we do, or have done that brings it about or forces it upon us...deal with it.

Wisdom; we have covered wisdom extensively, but in short it is the knowing and realisation that no one can or will ever know everything, but it is the nature of principle centred living to endeavour to do whatever it takes to do the right thing and not just doing things right, that distinguishes us.

Enthusiasm; the ability to infuse energy into others and yourself – an inner drive we have, the get up in the morning and let's get to it, type of drive. It speaks and oozes of conviction, love, faith and desire - the commitment to self and task. Develop an unquenchable curiosity; learn as much as you can, about as much as you can, while you still can. It has been said that if you keep doing what you have always done, then you will keep on getting the same results. Well at the rate the world is changing and knowledge you will become an extinct item in no time, your services to your company will become redundant and so will you if you do not grow with the environment you are working in. Enthusiasm is a passion for life and living, it is a state of mind, the will to taste it all. The only way to really live is to constantly improve yourself in all four dimensions, emotionally, physically, socially and spiritually. Choose to learn from everything that happens around you, get to see a new learning experience in everything and turn it positive. Smile, your potential for resolving any issue will grow with each experience lived, and your resolves become unlimited, and you will become quite and still, and focused in the face of any challenge.

Responsibility; They say that no woman is ever just a little bit pregnant, or a venomous snake is just another reptile. You are, or you are not responsible, there is no grey area. Only people with balance has this power. We are not talking about managerial responsibility alone, and looking after stuff or taking care of your belongings. No, higher order principles, that of mastery, the total control over somebody or something. This is power. It comes at a price, you can't shift blame, you always stay liable, and never become a liability yourself. You keep your word, and people accountable, and live with accountability yourself, you understand that duty is service, and that dependability comes from trust, and thoroughness. We are talking about the higher order principles, taking responsibility for the moral and ethical values. Let me explain by telling you a story filled with principles. In life, everything we do or say reflects on our character and our emotional responsibility and mastery.

This short story is of a master builder that lost his balance when he needed it most.

This master builder was building houses all his life; he was loyal and trustworthy. The company was not doing so well anymore and decided that this would be their last contract. They instructed the man to build a few houses at the coast in a serene and tranquil place. The man was to retire on completion of his last house. The contract took longer than expected and the man got impatient and wanted to go on pension, he was bitter and angry at the same time because he never made it into a management position, and therefore only have a small pension to buy a small house once on retirement and to live from . The suppliers were slow to deliver the high quality materials that went into these up market seaside cottages. The customers wanted only the best money could buy. So he decided to get cheap materials and bricks for the last house, as there was only a few finishes that needed completion, and he did not think anyone would notice. He had only one thing in mind, to get this house finished. His back was killing him, from years of hard physical work. Upon completion, he handed over the keys and the inspectors signed off. His company gave him leave, and told him that they will let him know when he can come and fetch his final pay. He was invited to the grand opening as an honoured guest, and afterwards they would give him a farewell, of course, all at the same time, cheap he thought after 45 years of service. He protested with his wife, but she got him to go. The directors of the company were delighted at the building and craftsmanship so was the customers. After the ceremony they went up to the mansion, this last house had no owner yet and stood on the prime spot on the property and had cocktails stacked out on the sun deck. He was upset when he got his handshake and a gold watch. In true form he thought. The owners gave speeches and bid people fair well. The directors called the builder to the stage after all the keys had been handed out ceremoniously. He went up with a heavy heart, shook their hands, as they wished him luck and congratulated him on a job well done. He turned to walk from the stage and his wife – delighted - came on the stage and stopped him, she handed him a key and congratulated him on his life's work and his greatest accomplishment. He was astounded and asked her what are you talking about woman? She replied the last house, it's ours, the board of directors gave it to us...he started crying. So what is the moral of the story, do everything in life as if you are doing it for yourself, you never know it might just very well be and it normally is, if you think about it. We have a responsibility, a moral and ethical obligation to our self to do everything we do with honour and integrity, we owe this to our self. In reality, we seldom want to take responsibility, we distance ourselves with denial and contradiction, or we just stay clear of responsibility altogether. Is this wise? Do we still have power, and balance when we let others take all the responsibility, so we can stay blameless. Responsibility comes with conviction and wisdom, so one who doesn't know nor understand, has not been exposed to this truth. It is pretty hard to believe in truth, if you have none of your own making, nothing taught, nothing experienced. Some profess to know the truth, and be truthful, but their actions contradict their words, then they lack responsibility. We reap what we sow, only by sowing healthy habits in one self, and our lifestyle will we reap a healthy understanding of the importance of balance, and the use of power.

Balance;

Balance requires that we take on responsibility in all spheres of life and stay balance always, because we never know, when and where it will be required most; you cannot keep balance without personally taking responsibility for your actions or lack thereof, as well as behaviour and emotional reactivity to your environment.

The Radical Revolutionary Strategic Management Matrix For Predators

We serve many masters and have just as many roles in today's life, starting at home, most of us are fathers, husbands, brothers, friends and the list goes on. The point is each role dictates a certain amount of responsibility, and as we grow, we just keep piling on more responsibility that require action. With a required behaviour and emotional reaction coupled to it. If we go wider, we have social roles and responsibilities, physical roles and responsibilities and spiritual roles and responsibilities. Mentally we have to adapt to each role, this takes energy, not just physical, but mental as well, many forget we are spiritual beings and so it takes spiritual energy as well, socially it places a burden on us too, to act and behave responsible and in accordance with acceptable rules of behaviour. The point is, we draw from all four the poles of life's essence daily just to live with balance. However, in our busy lives we only tend to recharge the physical pole, we eat, sleep, drink vitamins and go to the gym now and then. We live life to the fullest and somewhere we find time to socialise, or some of us do – this is not living this is existing. We cannot run a car on one cylinder if it has four. Although we look at the revolution counter and we see it climbing in every gear every day to the max, in the red and we pat ourselves on the shoulder, you worked hard. We even hear the humming of the engine we feel and experience movement. In essence, we are living well - on borrowed time that is – just like the engine, the poles are there for a reason. We have to recharge our souls, spiritually, by hypnosis, quite time, spiritual work and proper relaxation and meditation. We have to spend social time in bonding and fostering new bonds, and strengthening old ones, all in the garden of social growth. Just like natural gardens, there can be no garden without a gardener. We have to feed our minds both emotionally, spiritually, chemically and with new information. Physically we need to eat better, sleep better and do exercises on a regular basis. These quadrants or poles are separate but not isolated from each other. The point; we have to realise the imperative importance of "I need to do this for myself, no one else will", and it needs to be done in a structured and organised fashion. Balance will not just happen overnight and by itself, it takes a deep sense of personal responsibility. One way of establishing instant order and cultivating instant balance is by lifting our sights, from where we are focused now, to where we should be focusing. To cultivate a rather critical sense of importance, the ability of knowing what matters most from what matters less. Being able to always take time to place first things first, and not to sweat the small stuff, is essential towards ascertaining and maintaining balance, the ability to say no and to be able to justify it and mean it. How does a workaholic do this? Without feeling guilt or remorse, easy you prioritise your roles and their importance to who you are and not what you are – John, Marry, no title. Remember a job is what you do, it does not define who you are. We move from existence with a title to livening with your mere name. So, if you had no title who and where would you be in this world, if that perfect job you have now, or relationship had to disappear, who would you be, where would you be. Ask this question to yourself and only listen to the inner voice of wisdom, your heart, turn off the worlds unrealistic expectations and judgmental attitudes, the over analysing, the false sense of perfection and security decree. Just be "You" and decide what would make "You" truly happy... This is not enough, we have to realise that we are only as powerful as what we are influential, meaning; if things fall outside our sphere of influence we cannot and should not try to control it, our efforts will be futile. Many things that we ardently seek to control seem to fall just outside our sphere of influence. The sooner we come to terms with it the sooner we will experience peace and healing, a sense of closure on all happenings falling outside that sphere. Alternatively, we could choose, to expand our influence, wealth, power until our sphere includes this aspect we wish to control. However, some things will never fall into anyone's control, no matter what. Once this becomes a rule for us, the sooner we will sense relief from great amounts of stress and pressure we would have otherwise have toiled with. Letting go of control issues must be one of the hardest things we can ever do, for that is where our security is founded, in our very ability to control every aspect of our lives. This is false; no person has this power or influence neither control everything. Once again, it is a perception, a very dangerous perception at that, but a perception nevertheless. Many people I know, sadly hold on to this belief, that someday they will control everything they want to control. Balance only requires a good character with self-control. What happens when we choose to ignore this, then the inevitable occurs, then we cannot seem to understand why we are finding ourselves in a hospital bed all of a sudden, looking up at the ceiling fighting to keep the breath in our lungs. When just five minutes ago, I was arguing the new plan or at least it feels like five minutes ago? Then all of a sudden the reality of our situation dawns on us as the doctors stick needles into you, our first things first are the reason for us being here, was it all worth it, will I live? Did my priorities in life serve me well, did I live with balance? Now it all seems so superficial, why, for whom did I actually do it? As for the first things first, now high on my list of priorities is air and living, something I took for granted while I was "existing". Only then, we realise that our endeavours to control everything in life was "absolutely" futile.

The Corporate balance culture, how does your organisation function - with or without balance? From which paradigm, the "systems" - efficient or the "human" effective – paradigm? Mostly operational focus is on systems and time, but where is the strategic focus then, on the near or far future, is it a benchmark or a question mark? In companies where the focus is purely on production, the wheels come off, because the more they produce, the bigger the demand on the other supporting systems; their suppliers of raw products, the warehouse and delivery systems, then things become unbalanced. You cannot merely focus on one aspect without contemplating the spin-off effect, the capacity to cope comes from being able to grow in all aspects not just one. It is a law, both for people and for organisations, the same principle applies – balance in all things and all spheres. Our strategic focus should be on relationships and results, structure, perception and strategy, every facet is interrelated, and affects balance. Balance has one common vision, mission and gaol everything else is of lesser importance. Our overall commitment should be to build capacity and increase productivity, both proportionately and systematically. This clear difference in focal point, on the business of line function is mainly disturbed by an upper management culture that never had to *work with people* as opposed to *working them hard*. Forcing the easier of the two choices right through, namely systems, procedures and time, because this way you don't have to treat anyone with respect, and feel responsible. Production is a measurable and you don't have to get your hands dirty as a top manager. You just scream and shout and everyone else does what they are told, with the "do it now and complain later" idiot mentality. This is why it is so imperative to work on one corporate identity, as well as culture and leadership roles. Many organisations lack of strategic direction, find themselves in a continuous cycles of crisis management, this is not the way to manage. This is haphazard conflict management at its best. Greatly due to the organisations in *imbalance*, you will find that all the control is centralised at the top and so is decision-making, everything is left to chance. This organisation is dying trying. Even organisations needs to conform to the law of balance, rather than following the control by any means management approach, discipline and command and control, is not the alpha and omega, it is but one pole. We should be capacitating and balancing our resources, getting to know and trust our people and do away with a lot of bureaucracy and irresponsible supervisors. This is the way to work, with people as your greatest assets and systems to support them, and doing justice to all the poles to get to balance and have power. This requires strategic alignment. The next chapter takes us through a strategic alignment model, that assist in getting the balance right again.

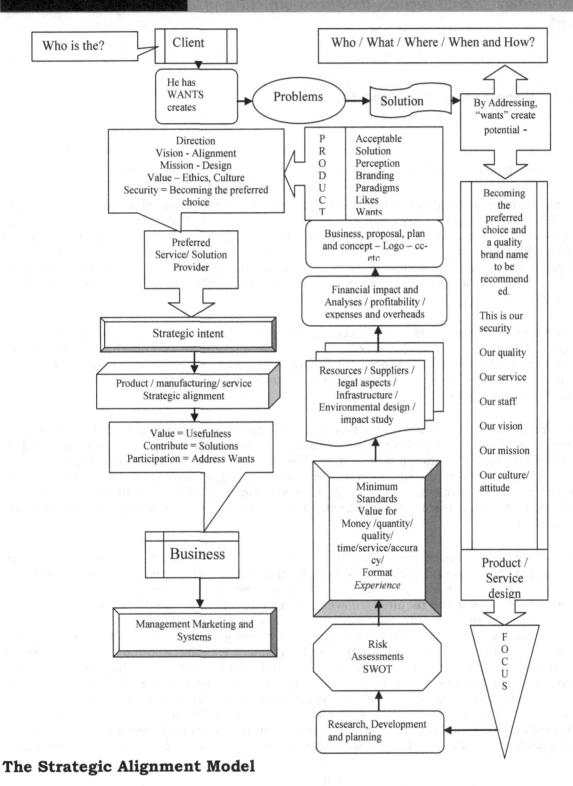

The Strategic Alignment Model

Modelling strategy is a good way of setting standards, with checks and balances in a model. It can take on many forms, as a flow chart of sorts that assist in the alignment of business practices and functions. Its usefulness resides within its simplicity, where it only depicts the basic structure of business formulation and alignment.

Strategic Alignment or Strategic fit

What do we hope to achieve with this model, either a strategic alignment or fit?

Strategic alignment or strategic fit is best described as the interrogation of strategies, ideas and concepts, to see if a specific strategy will give rise to a specific "need" or "want" as a requirement of that specific strategy. We understand that every strategy will have different aims, or benchmarks that will pull it either away or closer to the main thrust. This should be schematically depicted so that it can be traced, when we do alignment, we use schematics of the process like a map to orientate people with divergent backgrounds and levels of interest towards the process.

We all need and want "stuff", the way we get it is by applying strategy. Strategy is the plan/s we make to get it. In business terms it is several strategies small, minute and big that give rise to the master strategy. It also implies, a process of linking several strategies with the corporate vision, mission, goals, objectives, to see if these specific strategies do justice to a company's needs and wants - and other strategies.

It is not strategic intent; strategic intent has only one aim; that becomes a stepping stone, in a chain of strategic intentions, that keeps arriving with new results, until the final required result is reached. Strategic intent is therefore a result, that in turn becomes the predecessor to more results, before we can realise the main aim of our master strategy. Consequently, strategic intent, is the alignment of one strategy with several other strategies results - "intents" - in a chain of events, to deliver the final result contemplated, to see if they all work towards the final or main objectives realisation.

Whereas strategic alignments main aim is to test these assumptions we have first, as an intention, against the ideas and concepts we have in materialising these instances, to see if it (our ideas, plans, schemes) will work, to realise our main objective. By being able to answer the relevant questions, we get the required answers, as to how close we are with what we have, to prefect alignment, in other words how realistic is this assumption, concept, strategy we are entertaining in terms of both our ability and resources. Strategic alignment is a true reality check and validation exercise. It is also a calibration and alignment exercise, that confirms or validates that what we are doing is right, or that what we are about to set out to do will yield the desired results, and confirmation that where we are heading is in the right direction. Strategic alignment is the before, after and during process of strategy. Alignment is easy to state in terms of words or by definition, yet it is not so easy to accomplish in reality without any structure or model. Alignment deals with the flow and sequencing of events, in the lifecycle of the strategic process, by dealing only with the concept of things that implies; cost, workflow and distribution of resources and time, and not the detail of it. It looks at the plan holistically, both in terms of its effectiveness and efficiency, by focusing on the things we don't have in abundance, and how best to make them work to get what we want or need. All elements required to create a new product or service, without the detail, structured in a strategic manner to assist us in seeing the perceived end result. Strategy can be extremely wasteful if not totally aligned with the expectations that it creates, and has to deliver on. Strategic alignment is key to elevating organisational performance in a structured and schematic manner, by aligning that extra efforts with our goals perfectly we get less waste and margin for errors diminish proportionately to our continued re-alignment. Mainly it's because we become co-ordinated, systematic and chronological. It is essential if a company is to achieve its objectives fast, that we find the concept that is lacking, without having to re-evaluate the whole system of strategy, and all its process. The only way to make sure that it does, is to have a strategy, a plan, and then to evaluate the plan of action against it – this process is called strategic alignment. To see if we have everything we need, how much it will cost and how much time and effort it will require, before we reach our main objective. It takes the implicit – implied, and works it back to the explicit - the obvious and reality, by means of testing it to see if it fits.

Strategic alignment: or Fit, aims to do three things;

- To provide clarity on the nature and objectives of each strategy and its usefulness.
- To see if all the separate strategies, culture, and processes unite into the Grand Strategy.
- To deal with originality and find perfect alignment, by making sure process and people find and fit each other, to get what they set as an objective, to realise a need or want.

Strategy requires many things, however the main thing it has to have before anything else is focus, one focus to be exact – that leads to one common vision. If not, it's just pure chaos. If we do not share the same common vision we will find chaos in abundance. In life as in business, you are free to pursue any opportunity, and vision, need or want, however you cannot always afford to pursue everything all at the same time, or all opportunities you want. We all have other and current commitments, because you are already busy with one or more strategies, we never arrive empty, and we all have limited resources. Yet we want many things, for ourselves and our children, and others. In order to get these things we require resources. Nevertheless, no matter how big or how small, everyone is bound to the rules of strategic alignment, that states that we first give priority to the *things we have to do*, then the things *we need to do* , then the things *we want to do*, and then only to *the things we always wanted*, but never had the time or money (resources) for. If you don't have the means, or the ability then it can't become a "want", that you will satisfy soon. Strategic alignment creates a picture of this reality for us, that defines which things we can explore now, and in what order, and which ones to address later or have to avoid. Here we have to apply choice with reason, and decided which takes preference, then set our priorities, as things change, we need to be able to set priorities and queue, stop, or pause events in the strategic cycle of observation, orientation, decision and then action. All in order to contribute to our competitive advantage in keeping the initiative, and our momentum. Strategic alignment requires organisation, and vision, a model for this to happen effectively and daily, a simple straightforward well-structured model to cope with the prospects and fluidity and change of business, as well as our design and its alignment with strategic process and changing events.

Strategic advancement is truly the clear emphasis on the creation of growth, resources and potential, whilst striving for sustainability in all. However, it still needs something, that aligns all things in a certain direction, with complimenting strategies, thinking and initiatives that will or should give rise to new products, services and business models, and let us not forget the leaders ability to unify many visions into one vision backed up with entrepreneurial nature...

Strategic alignment deals with this aspect in five key questions. Can we answer the; Who?, What?, Where?, When? and How? If yes, we are aligned, if no, we are not. Although it is purely a strategic model in terms of identifying key performance areas, it is still the best fully integrated and strategically minded encompassing model to follow, especially when contemplating a new business, or analysing an existing business for performance deficiency, and strategic alignment. Is it really this simple? Yes, we cannot, and should not ever over complicate the obvious.

Business concept design and strategic alignment with the model

This section is a short overview of what strategic alignment would look like, and the steps followed to get the alignment right.

When we start from the understanding that a business originates in the market gap, where it fills a supply and demand function, or a need or a want. Traditionally the **business concept**, would be a focus on product or service first. Today, the reality of the matter is that you might have the best product and or service, but will lack the vehicle – the total business concept to do it with, to bring it to market. Thus implying that business formulation has become total concept today and not just a focus on product design, price, marketing, finances and service. (CAPS).

The first step is to find and identify the concepts you want to sell. Only by understanding and defining the customer that this concept would appeal to, do we find the fit in the target market, and then the targets become our focal point, not just the product. This again, requires strategic alignment, and only then will we be in position to formulise the intent of the scheme. The driving force behind having strategy to guide us in designing business concepts is the ability to plan in step, in order to have a structured approach towards satisfying a need or a want. Let me explain. In money matters there are two sides of the coin, that of satisfying the *needs* and *wants* of people, by either purchasing or producing the solution for *needs and wants*. *Needs* would imply or relate to things like, food, housing, spiritual things, social activity, and work. Defined as required, and necessary for survival. *Wants* on the other hand are goods or services that are not "necessary" for survival, but that we desire or wish for like luxury items, and status symbols. For example, one needs transport, but one may not need a plane to get to work. One needs food daily to survive, but does not have to have meat and beer at every meal.

With Matrix design, products and or services are designed from the potential client – needs or wants – perspective. We identify the GAP in the market and formulise a solution, based on either their "needs" or "wants" and financial abilities, all these aspects are aligned. Needs and wants originate from many different aspects, and only get realised once you have the potential to recognize them.

The first aspect is therefore identifying the "real client".

The Radical Revolutionary Strategic Management Matrix For Predators

There are three main levels in the potential **"Clients"** origin; that will motivate them to "need' and /or "want" things; we have to find the value we will add, the "want" we will fulfil, with our product or service first as a point of departure. No product or service will see the light and make it in the marketplace if there is no want or need for it. Then slotting products and or services into the right target market, all becomes essential towards making strategies work.

The client as a target. The first aspect is the scale or scope of our operation , how large or how exclusive do you want to be or go. Starting off small, or starting of big?

The scale of the scheme determines the core requirements; first in terms of target markets.

The highest spenders are **industry players**, professionals, company owners, and (international) corporations.

The middle level is – schooled labour, semi, and professional people, working for or owning micro, small, medium, large enterprise and projects .

The lowest level is the **individual** living on, or just above the minimum wage, or on the poverty line.

Then understanding the motivational force that drives most expenditure.

 Understanding why and how people in certain income groups spend money; and on what...comes first, with this exercise we define who the true client will be.

The first is their spending potential; this is directly linked to the "clients" sources of income, which gives them **their ability**. This could even extend to credit or loans. This aspect creates a demand, that seeks a supplier...

Define and narrow down the target customer, the true customer. Customers inclination to spend more on certain types of goods are dictated by either; an individual need, a unit need or a business sector need that makes them a client. This gives the "client" more spending and buying power, as the group becomes bigger. Therefore a client could be one person or a small business, or an international firm. Where needs becomes wants, that are then dictated by the following; we need many thing but want specific things, we tend to go after specifics first. Logic does not always prevail, when it comes to buying things, acquiring a service, or spending.

Spending is mostly motivated by;

- A need or want
- Self-gratification, luxury or status
- Desiring a personal experience
- Need to participate in sport and relaxation
- To gain the competitive edge.
- Or an essential element

Their life style, or industry demands as dictated by a need or want.

Evaluating the elements required of the strategic scheme against a business model

```
┌─┬──────────┬─┐
│ │  Client  │ │
└─┴──────────┴─┘
```

The first aspect in this model is the client; it stands to reason that this will be the fundamental focal points of the envisaged specific target group, of potential clients. In business you get what you "need", by giving the client what they "want", it's all about understanding the life cycle of "supply and demand" – which refers to the relationship between the availability of goods and/ or services and the need or desire for it among consumers; both individuals, groups, companies, industries and producers - driven by the force of "wants" and "needs".

In order for us to form a concept, of what is truly needed to fulfil a "want", and not just working on an assumption, we have to dissect the wants of our potential client. We need to; *identify quantify, qualify and then simplify* the target concept of the "wants" of the client.

Identify;

Where in the market will our service or product be required and by whom, or alternatively where is there a gap in the market for new goods, and or services, or where is there a need or want that cannot be sustained by current role-players...

Who is our client; an industry player, a group, or individuals, then we can identify its attributes. Is this client predominantly in a high, medium, middle or low-income sector that we want to target; where will we be targeting the market sector in terms of income potential. The reason for this approach is that the clients' acquisition patterns – their "wants" - change as we become increasingly wealthier and financially independent. Income to a large extent determines our spending behaviour and lifestyle preferences. This aspect holds the same truth for the industry players as well, being manufactures, suppliers, retailers and consumers, they are all potential clients, that dictate how they will acquire their wants and from whom, in terms of tender and procurement policy, contracts, terms, or cash.

As well as **what** they will buy at **what** price.

Quantify;

When will someone start spending. We start spending income in layers, as we progress and become increasingly wealthier so do our spending patterns and biases change, firstly;

- Low level income; addressing basic needs first, housing, food and travel etc.
- then according to our income we branch out socially -
- school fees, clothing, accounts and fuel budgets,
- Medium level income; then to fulfil our desires, we spend what is left
- on enhancing our living conditions, our need for socials status and nice things etc.

High level income; then we get to our "fit", we can now dictate the terms of trade, driven by our social status to make social statements of wealth and prosperity – here we make a plan to get what we need and desire to fit in with the industry standards or a specific social class.

This in turn is not the norm; customers are also influence by *personal bias* influenced by their individualised character, customs, beliefs and location. Nevertheless by aligning ourselves with the three major criteria for spending; **their ability, self-gratification and status**, we will be able to position the *where* our clients are, both in terms of how deep spending goes and on what do they prefer to spend money on. To identify the criteria they will most lightly follow as a norm, in their culture of spending. There is also risk involved, the higher the income level, the more credit, and higher purchase transactions people enter into. By looking at their preferred method of payment for instance; will it be by credit card, cash, terms, or on higher purchase etc. This is one common denominator regardless of class and income; however the interest and terms offered could become a draw card. That will tell us *how*, and how much they will spend. The top spenders stop spending first and start spending first again in down turn economies as they see growth. The key element to determine here is "what does the customer tell us about their wants" and preferences on purchasing, if we can align our whole business with all their "wants", not just the product or service, to that of the profiled targeted customer then we will be sure to attract that specific customer first. We do not need to do a lot of market research beyond that point, pertaining our clients spending behaviour. Furthermore, we don't have to be spending a lot of money if we can deliver what our customers "want" from start to finish, from the word go, if it is tailor-made to specification that is, now do we?

Qualify; Client behaviour in relation to the product or service on offer: Will this be a "Want" client or a "need" client; "wants" are totally personal or emotionally driven, a desire for a product or service, that needs fulfilling. "Needs" are life essentials, basics, the person still in primal buying mode due to his basic income, just wanting to fulfil his "primitive needs"– "a needy person" – for food, shelter etc. Needs deal with basics and essentials; we all require food, water, housing, clothing etc. – the basics, that stems from a basic requirement in order to survive and sustain ourselves. Never the less still a potential client. In comparison with first world living, this has become almost "irrelevant" to certain markets and goods as well as services. Even the poor buy brand names, - even if it is a poor replica - and designer jeans. A market has evolved for counterfeit goods, because of wants. However, "wants" in contrast belong to the upper echelons of middle to high-income society mainly, because they have the power to realise their wants – and

Who is the Client really?

they can afford to pay the high price tags to get it. Where we deal with the economics of scale, people with money create "problems that need solutions", and also a gap between these two extremes, due to their lifestyle and financial profile. When all our basic needs are satisfied and we have no need to fight off hunger pains, seek water and guard against predators, then we start to cross over the financial Rubicon into the "wants" arena. By wanting the better things in life, we create a culture of "wants" and a generation of "wantings" – kids that spend like their parents, they are predominantly very strong emotionally driven and satisfying spending habits inculcated by parents, peer pressure, media and icons. That translate spending patterns either social, personal, spiritual or physical and very specific to a person's character, lifestyle and taste. In other words, if you are conservative, you will buy items that segment, that will enforce your lifestyle and character; if you are liberal you will go with the trends, if you are physical you will go with health products and food, and if you are spiritual you will travel to experience spiritual things. Whichever way, they are mostly all short-lived personal victories that need to be relived, or sustained, so this is where markets are created, to serve diversified peoples' "wants" or alternatively "needs". We will focus on the higher order clients here – on serving "wants".

Simplify; Basically everything has turned to "wants" the moment we start earning, then the instant gratification culture becomes a ruling force in our lives for most. Mainly because of modern living standards. Early financial independence has liberated most people to a modern expectable living standard and let's face it, if we go without a slab of chocolate, or a beer for a while we will still "want" those things, they are in essence all responsible for chemical reactions that produce a sense of euphoria, causing joy, that livens up our spirit, that enforces their recurrence. Likewise, if we understand this aspect and we realise that everything is in fact a non-essential, in terms of sustaining life, once we have ascertained "wealth", then only a very small percentage of what we buy is driven by our very basic primal needs like "food" and "shelter" and the majority is just "wants". Then the client becomes a "problem" looking for a solution. Wants are also guided by our individualism. Dr. Kathleen Gurney, an American business psychologist and author of *"Your Money Personality"*, questioned 20 000 investors about their attitudes towards money, their finances and their investments preferences, before identifying 13 personality traits that she believes shapes our decisions about money: spending patterns have changed radically; one factor is that we have added a lot more low-income households to the equation of spending emotionally, because of immigration and family break-ups. Just to fill a void. This pushes some high-income households into the top of the income distribution who previously were closer to the middle. The second development is increased entrepreneurship, with layoffs and big companies closing, skilled and unskilled have taken their pension funds and have stated up their own businesses. Which takes some people out of the middle of the income distribution brackets and moves them either toward the bottom or the top...wants are now for everybody to pursue. If priced right, and it solves a problem, people will buy it.

Money personality traits, these are the key issues that decisions are made around:

- Involvement – the extent to which you personally want to be involved in, take responsibility and accountability for; IE. for managing your money, others, and things that you consider priority. Your level of involvement and commitment.
- Pride – the personal satisfaction you derive from the management of money.
- Emotionality – the degree of emotion you experience when dealing with money.
- Altruism – the degree to which you believe in generosity of others.
- Risk-taking – the level of comfort you experience when taking financial risk.
- Confidence – the degree of anxiety you experience when financial decisions are made.
- Power – the degree by which you desire for power, by influencing your behaviour
- Work ethic – your opinion on how your work ethic relates to your financial success.
- Contentment – the degree of personal happiness you get through your money.
- Self-determination – the degree to which you feel in command of your financial journey.
- Spending – your attitude towards spending and saving money
- Reflectivity – the way you reflect on past financial decisions and
- Trust – the level of honesty you think people have when handling money.

By understanding a person's personality and what drives him towards "wants", we are in effect then, tapping in to a culture, we can focus on the type of client we want to supply with "wants". If we do a profile, we will find that the result will give us nine spending personalities:

Types of client personalities;

Personality	Income	Education	Emotional drive	Risk favoured
Entrepreneurs	Very High	Moderate / highly	"Effort"	Low-risk
Cautioning	Average	Medium	"Least resistance"	Small
Predator	Average	Highly	"Influence"	Little
Optimists	Medium	Medium	" Impulsive"	Little/ medium
Perfectionist	Medium / low	Moderate	" Perfection"	Low-risk
Achievers	High	Highly	" Careful"	Low-risk
Gambler	Medium/low	Moderate	" Emotional"	Extreme
Manufacturer	Low	Low	" Prestige"	High
Banker	High / med	Medium	"Analyse"	Calculated

On managing perception and becoming the preferred choice.

Remember a perception about a product is stronger than the truth about it, because of the ever-changing marketing influences – so when designing solutions, design them around a strong perception you would like to create and back them up with truth and service.

Why?; work towards understanding how solutions are formed in the mind that truly address the problems of "wants" at the heart of it.

We have to study and understand the customers' specific "want", with years of research and study a pattern of influences have emerged where humans are faced with decision making, pertaining to finding a required solution.

He has WANTS

Solution finding have now become main stream. People are now following what works better today rather than what worked really well yesterday. It was observed for instance that where complex solution issues were contemplated, that they were broken down into their smallest understandable part for the client, to a level where it had meaning to the client, so that he could make sense of the subject. (e.g. a computer network – into computers, into parts – hard drive, microprocessor etc.)

This cascading dissection of data to its simplest understandable form is done in many fashions in the mind, almost instantaneously. What is significant about this is that the mind comes back with a wide diversity of possible solutions to work from; that motivates the client firstly, then tests his solutions against all his assimilated knowledge – from any source (e.g. TV, Internet, book, conversation word of mouth, labels etc.). This is where marketing and advertising steps in, it sets traps for this behaviour and catches this type of client. Moreover he confines clients to one or two options they understand and feel comfortable with, only then, does the client become aware of quality, price, status and value for money amongst other motivators. For an ideal solution to work, it will take three or more elements to become an ideal concept, before the client starts factoring it into his ideal solution, that he is contemplating. His drive to fulfil this "want" can overpower all logic depending on the customers maturity, experience in buying certain goods, products and service, and continuing spending habits and credit. With this in mind, we must make sure, that when we are selling concepts that are involved, we have to include a breakdown of the value they are receiving, for the take down, - the trick is to brake attributes down into bite size chunks, which shows, the value for money, the good quality, the performance, the components, their specifications, the detail and the benefits so that it makes sense etc. This relates to the marketing strategy.

Consequently, what we know now is that when we are faced with the designing of a total product or solution that solves the **problem**s" that people have, we have to know what the problem is clearly and not just concentrate on the traditional focal points of marketing a good product; the visual, texture, taste, smell and sound – that appeal to the senses only, we have thinking customers today with many options. However, do any of these options solve their problems?

Problems

Solution

We have to go well beyond the obvious of sensory input and move towards incorporating emotional and logical deductions that will appeal to the target as well. The emphasis and the attributes of selling ideal solutions have shifted; back to quality, after sales service, guarantees and warrantees, real value and service. The move is away from cheap and bulk, too fast and efficient sales and service, extending to online or electronic purchase, and after sales service, maintenance plans, insurance ext. We have entered a

Becoming the preferred choice and a quality brand name to be recommend-ed.

This is our security

Our quality

Our service

Our staff

Our vision

Our mission

Our culture/ attitude

new psychological arena here, where we break our product down into fundamental pieces that will find appeal with the client and rebuild it to have all the answers for the potential client to constitute a total solution, to a customer's problem, not just another product, but how to choose it, and get it effortlessly, in a working and reliable form. It should address the very important aspect of an emotionally driven desire, in making the final decision to "want" this, in contrast to the competitions variants, and of cost only. How well will this service or product address the "want" of a customer (on an emotional scale that requires three hundred and sixty degree solutions) will be determined by the close matching of the service towards rendering the desired product, fast and efficient. How will the product in turn match his "desired" solution, and against what criteria? In the absence of an ideal solution, a close matching one will normally do, to satisfy the "want" until next time, when someone else gets it to the client faster, fresher, and at the same price, any service or product must be viewed both critically and holistically during the design of an ideal product or service as well – to form the ideal concept; "the *ideal – real world solution is the ultimate one*". Before it becomes the preferred choice. On choice, research has shown that if you sell more than three choices in the same category, sales drop...limit options, and make it fast to carry out the door. How? We have to ask the right questions.

Who? / What? / Where? / When? and How?

Our product or service; needs to become the "Preferred Choice". Then, this is our aim and only then, have we established ourselves a new market with potential clients. By asking the right questions, of who, what, where , when, and how, we will find the right solutions...

What is our core business going to be? – "What are we going to do, sell, build and supply ext." In which sector are we going to slot in and with whom are we competing? This requires a full description of our service and product; its usefulness, value, quality and appeal and where it will fit into the market. How much taxes, and service fees will we pay, and how will laws impact on us etc. The focal points in designing a concept should be followed; with CAPS, to have a graphical representation, to work from. Then we should organise all our deductions and business assumption to make sense, into a format called a business plan. The basic business plan will cover amongst other things the following

Business plan Index

- Executive Summary
- Founders vision
- Company mission statement
- Company Strategic Positioning
- CAPS analysis
- Gap analysis
- Company Objectives
- Short
- Medium
- and long term objectives
- Company Summary
- Composition
- Location
- Expertise
- Products and Services
- Niche product range
- Sole import mandates and rights
- Target Market identification and Marketing Analysis
- our competitive advantage
- our market niche
- our dependencies
- our pricing objectives
- our ability to deliver
- Strategy and Implementation
- Strategic Alignment
- Financials

Many firms are no longer performing their core business function due to; expansion, integration, growth and restraints etc. They have deviated from the original business plan or concept. For whatever reason, the focus on core business should always stays relevant, for one simple reason. All the forgoing planning, design, structuring, recruiting and assembling of the original business revolved around one business assumption, the achieving of one specific outcome, the production or service, of the envisaged business. Thus, it makes good sense to realign any business as soon as it senses a deviation or shift from core business, if not, then balance will become an issue. Thus it is always a good idea to do realignment as often as possible, just like with a car wheel, the better the balance and alignment, the better the mileage...

Systems and resources; all things supporting the core business functions must follow suit, a business should never lose sight of its core function, as this is the pipeline of life into the business; this is what gives it identity and what created the perception. Never do anything in a business at the expense of core business; you will lose focus and direction. Alienating clients and service levels will exponentially fall below acceptable margins if the infrastructure and systems are not linked in tandem anymore to cope with new lines or services being co-opted. In short, make sure that the relevant resources are still there to compliment the structure to follow strategy. Design the business model with growth and expansion in mind. Without this, the firms infrastructure will break-up under any additional load if not properly capacitated; it's always just a question of time.

Who will be our clients then? – Start "Profiling". Some call it market research, or consumer research. The point is, you will have to know the; who, when, what, where and how about the clients you attract. This requires a customer profile, market profile, research, development and

> Business, proposal, plan and concept – Logo – cc- ltd. etc.

planning, a business proposal and ultimately a business plan. The question of demand and supply should features very prominently when addressing customer profile issues. Remember no business functions in a vacuum either, you have competitors, suppliers, new emergent products and services that will eventually render the old obsolete. Other factors; things like infrastructure decaying and outer influences that could impact indirectly and sometimes even directly on your clients, your service or product. Remember everyone wants a slice of the market. Risk assessments and mitigation steps, are crucial in this regard. Creating the full business concept requires critical thinking. If we are new to a market, then we will have to have an aggressive strategy, which has depth to survive the paradigm shift, with the entry and start-up phase in order to become a player, especially in big well-established markets. The "who", of who's, is not always as important as the "why", why will they become our clients, by understanding this, we create a concept for success that can be duplicated. Here we move from an uncontrollable aspect – the client – which is well outside our sphere of influence to an aspect well within our sphere of influence. We can definitely control our solutions and concept if we know and understand why people want it and buy it. This is within our domain of control and future driven enterprise. Do things that make sense, don't spend money on statistics and assumptions, which only become yet another hypothesis. Plan to plan and plan ahead - beyond the event horizon and thereby you will create a good business plan that addresses risk and builds in mitigation.

The need for a proper business plan:

- The need for a business plan is three fold;
- it creates a common understanding that serves as a road map for your agenda,
- it serves as a framework for setting goals and achieving small milestones and objectives within an action plan,
- it serves as a tool to get finance, funding, and input on assumptions made and could attract investors and partners.

Other considerations that will effect risk and could impact on our assumptions: **Where** will we be situated? Location-Location - Location – Strategically, in terms of feet or will we focus on infrastructure. On the internet it's very important to get search engine rankings right, do a SWOT analysis and risk assessment. This aspect will be greatly determined by the type of business, product, service and category of business contemplated; production, fabrication, supplier, warehousing, digital or transport for instance have different requirements, when it comes to situational appropriateness. Situational analysis is key to the environmental impact you will have in the market and in securing market share. Then we still have to keep in mind the systems that will have to support us; infrastructure, services suppliers, municipal services, levies, rates and taxes, climate and environmental impact, both ecologically, physically, emotionally and economically. Yes so many attributes to cover, but you get the idea of what is at stake.

Risk
Assessments
SWOT

Research,
development
and planning

When will our client stop being our client? Simple, from the first moment they used our service or our products and it does not satisfy their wants. If we did not leave a lasting impression they will no longer be our client. People sell products and services; products don't sell products or services. If our employees did not take a personal interest and responsibility, by instilling confidence in our customer, by offering a near perfect solution, they themselves must believe in the product. Remember the client is still in the open to options, when he comes through the door and depending on the first impression you make, you will either gain trust or raise suspicion, regardless of how good your service protocol or product is. It's always about the perception created. It could be about your people in your employment and the image they project to the customer, the time it took, or the quality - service, product, people, - that becomes an issue. On this aspect we will have to decide where will our service start and stop towards our clients? Firstly, keeping within the parameters of your mandate and service agreement. Secondly, be honest and deal with a win – win attitude in mind or no deal. Thirdly make it personal, make sure you understand what the customer "really" wants and not what you think he or she wants, or try and make the shoe fit, by bending an hammering at it. Finally, make sure they remember you as an honest, kind and a decent person or organisation. One, that is willing and able to satisfy their wants, even though he walked out the door empty handed, always leave the customer with a lasting impression; because referrals sell more products that advertising. Promptness, turns around more business, people expect as prompt a response to a Web query as they would to a telephone … Turnaround times, for products and service have become a huge factor in staying in business today. We have to devise this aspect as protocol, as business doctrine, to form part of our concept in our business design. By implementing and fostering a culture in the organisation of open, friendly and descent people, either through in-house training, or on the job training. See where you require skill, expertise and training, to up your game plan, the stakes are high. Start with the basics, discipline and responsibility, and that of taking ownership. Then identify the specific that customers want, and introduce them. Make everyone understand that they play a key role in the outcome, they own it. *"If it is not my job or task then whose is it?"* , solve this beforehand. This type of attitude kills speed, and eventually enterprise. Remember concept thinking is global thinking; we leave nothing to chance, we check all our blind spots before we leave the parking bay and enter the traffic, in the business lane. Have your people multi-skilled and trained ASAP. However, if all the tasks are the owners, then I (as the owner) have a responsibility towards seeing they are done, by developing systems and resource to support your solo career. By implementing a continuous improvement philosophy, regardless of the size of the business, the principles stay the same, we need to learn to develop good habits, that stimulate growth and accountability, we instil enthusiasm and commitment towards doing things right the first time out, every time, from the top down. Remember, that product or service knowledge is the next frontier to conquer, in the absence of scheme, the norm or precedent set will prevail and become the new set standard throughout. People adopt whatever goes around currently as the norm, ask yourself beforehand, is this, what you want for your business, is this the desired competence level. However if you give them the tools, resources and the training first, then nothing will stop them from forming a corporate culture, and performing at corporate level. Nothing motivates people more like being good at what they do and knowing what they do and getting better at it. Only by belonging to a group of likeminded people, who only settle for the best, do we become the best. What you put out there you will attract.

How will we become the preferred choice then? –

There is only one way, by creating a clear "focus" for all to follow, people want to know **what** to do, when to do it, **how** to do it, and **how much** of it needs to be done. The strategic plan plays this role. We all have to know what we have to offer in return for remuneration and recognition internally. Externally, how we are required to act, within the ambit of the scheme, this resolves both "personnel" and "client problems" by having readymade

> Direction
> Vision - Alignment
> Mission - Design
> Value – Ethics, Culture
> Security = Becoming the preferred choice

solutions available. Our Vision will be our alignment with our view towards finding solution to problems that creates "wants". Our Mission is to design, to follow and to refine our own solutions continuously, by utilising people's collective brainpower. Remember your employees are also your clients and if you don't align them with your business concept, character, and principles, they won't buy into your product or service either, then no one will. Our values can be measured in terms of ethics, culture and being service orientated – not just by the level of clients satisfaction, creating total overall quality (MQM) is the main aim. Our security resides in us becoming the preferred choice and building on that, by following statements mentioned here, to contribute towards finding better and faster ways of rendering service and products for a society big on instant gratification. How do we find better business solutions towards satisfying our clients "wants". Firstly, it's by informed choice, we will have to choose it, to become the preferred choice. Then we have to plan it, and align with it, until eventually everything is in place and we no longer have to re-do it, because it's done. As we get around to doing it, we will have to keep fine-tuning and re-aligning the solutions, to become the preferred solution in the market and even strive to up the stakes. By setting the unit standard for the industry, we take the initiative. Don't just follow the mainstream and their standards blindly, if it works for them, we can make it work better for us, it's all a perception, a mind-set. If they are fast, we can be faster, if you are thinking along these lines, then they are dictating, you have to be the one that is setting the trend, by improving "it", constantly, by focusing on "it" daily and not only by looking at "it" as a profit margin.

How, we will be keeping direction?

Only by following a unifying vision. As modern society is becoming more complex daily and is changing at an ever-increasing rate, so do their wants for direction and work. If we are not instep and marching to the beat of the same drum as a unit, we will find ourselves with plenty of product and no one buying it. Mainly because the vehicles we designed is not humming with harmony, it is clanking with turmoil. Internal influence can cripple any good origination, as do external. Focus internally first, as it is the one sure-fire way and place where you have the most impact and influence to control influences. Externally, we can only do our best, as the uncertainty about our economy and changing markets impact on strategy as well, our evaluation and alignments backed up with sound business assumptions, should be designed to create harmonised synchronisation between units, to change direction, with enough flexibility

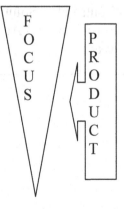

built in. This is the only way, to be flexible enough to weather any economic climate. Here we need to identify the aspects of our operations that are at risk. Risk that could be turned to advantage, and things that are solid should be identified. Therefore, we can safely say that strategy is no longer just the solution; it has rather become the framework for expanding solutions. Coupled to strategic alignment and re-alignment as a constant , until the course is clear and the weather good. People are the creators of solutions, or the architects of chaos. Finding the right answers to our daily dilemmas, stays with having focus, and a deep focus on people first, then this result will solve most of our daily problems encountered.

Can we hope to survive our competition and ourselves if we can't even work as a team?

This decade requires continued reengineering and reinventing, of everything and every paradigm ever held in business as sound. This gives us flexibility to effect change at a minutes notice, with confidence. Only with agile strategies like this, will we modernise our strategic frameworks and systems, too effectively utilise advancements in technology to its full potential. Only dynamic organisations, that perform radical changes with teams, focused on customers and employees as people, and not statistics, will turn the corner and then turn the profit. However, caution needs to be exercised when say this, we need to understand that old school and conventional holds strength like a buildings foundations, always have something conventional and old school that works. In addition, it is happening all over the globe, every second employee is complaining of "urgency addiction" and "chaos in the work place". It implies a "lack of true leadership" and un-sustained strategic alignment that gives no clear "direction". Too much change and newness for the sake of having it could also cost you dearly. As it impacts on structure. This is the first sign of procrastination having set in, where we have just added and not structured properly. Strategy follows structure where we make minor changes, where we make major changes, then structure follows strategy. Conservative pyramid styled cultures will not become like their name sakes, extinct reminders in the desert landscapes of business. They will always be around, although we are moving to a situation of smart MATRIX management structures that are, flatter, faster, inter-changing structures, with greater inter connectivity, fewer supervisors and bigger pay packages. Corporate culture liken peoples' attitude will determine their survival at the end of the day, in this new era and not the product or service, the secret is in its integration and design. I would like to predict that only corporations with a firm established corporate culture of interdependence in place and a flatter design would be staying on the frontiers of business and see the next millennium.

The second aspect; products and services:

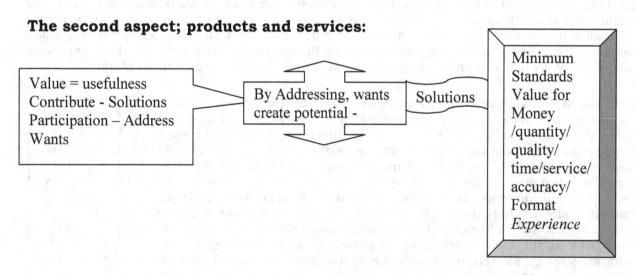

The focal points in design; business design; product design or service design, is no straightforward business in itself, but the basic principles are. Focusing on product or service design. Then the first aim is, that the service or product must have a purpose, or use. This is always true; it must contribute to the solution of a problem that exists, that can be solved to address a "want". Alternatively; it must be a brand new product or service altogether that creates a new market of "want". By virtue of the service or product coming into existence (e.g. Cellphone communication was non-existent until it came into existence, then it solved a problem of portable communication, and that of wireless communication, it supplied the ideal solution and it catered for every "client", that never existed, prior the invention. By addressing a "want", the cellphone industry opened up a portal of potential, for aligned new products and services, for new trade and industry. They planned beyond the event horizon, what was once just a rich man's toy is now a standard unmistakable tool, in everyday life.

> Product /
> Service design

The product or service design;

Regardless of whether it is a product or a service it needs to be designed, so that the same product or service can be reproduced consistently on demand – we require a "recipe".

This helps to get copyrights and patent rights etc. To protect the product for instance.

- To determine if minimum standards are met as well as to set benchmarks for quality and legal aspects.
- To establish run time estimates, of how long does it take to produce, what is the cost, its effectiveness, and will it deliver, the results contemplated.
- To determine accuracy or deficiency.
- To build and gauge experience that can be carried over.
- For buying or selling and even for facilitation and statistical purposes.

The third aspect is ergonomics: an ergonomic design is a design that strives for maximum comfort, efficiency, safety and ease of use, especially in the work place.

> Acceptable
> Perception
> Labelling
> Paradigms
> Likes
> Wants
> TQM

Ergonomics: The product or service must be appealing to the customer, either in terms of, value, quantity, time, service, accuracy, taste, appropriateness, format, experience etc. There must be one or several aspects that becomes another selling point. It must be an acceptable solution that comes close to the 100% fit mark and cost effective. The perception that the product or service creates must be one of "ideal fit or ultimate solution" It must leave a lasting cordial impression.

The labelling, branding or marketing must be perfect, we do not want to have to make excuses, or compromise in any way, we have to make sure that we can deliver to specification, and in a consistent and professional manner. When we have to deliver on what we promised. The paradigm and business assumption surrounding the product or service must be tested beforehand and proven, before it is launched into the open market. No one wants 43 000 000 cars pulled back to the dealership, no comebacks, no excuses and no bad products – this creates a stigma. The "like's" and "like-not's" must be carefully scrutinised after every launch, especially the media and critics opinions must be thoroughly investigated, they are opinion makers after all and influence customers. Public opinion is greatly influenced by the media and the perceptions they create. "Wants" must be analysed to see if it can become yet another opportunity, either to enhance, or launch yet another solution. MQM, Matrix Quality, Management, or otherwise known as TQM total quality management must become cardinal towards developing ideal solutions, we have to start with quality in order to finish with it. Nothing less will ever pass, there is just no short cut or cheaper way of attaining quality when we are addressing wants – you either produce quality or quantity anything else is a poor substitute or imitation. So choose the root you want to follow, quality or quantity, and then the strategy. This will also dictate price, when we look at the scale of economics. The old saying of "garbage in garbage out" comes to mind. The two different design platforms that exist here relates to – quality or luxury and exclusive goods and services vs. quantity, cheap commodity goods, they have very different criteria. In addition, one will have to follow these principles to be competitive. Choose which path to follow.

The fourth aspect

The basic steps in design stays the same no matter what you stand to design; start with the end in mind, break it down into concepts, and then attributes. Then we need to; *identify quantify, qualify and then simplify* the attributes, identifying what is the sum, if all the parts are combine, everything adds to cost and influence the final break even equation. Bells and whistles, marketing, transport and warehousing, will all have an impact on the final products life cycle and cost. In other words we can cost a product purely on the acquisition price, a purely circumstantial influence and therefore elevate the actual cost, of any concept product or service. Only when all the parts become one, at the point of sale, can we really say what the actual incurred cost of the total product or service is.

We can review this in step, ask the critical quantifying questions;

- **The Target market**; who will be the client and why? How much will it cost to reach him?
- **The required Technology**; what type of technology is available to support the product or service and what will be our profit margin? Will our focus be on quantity or quality or will it be exclusivity.

Production & manufacturing

- **Who has the wants assessment**; why will this product become or address a want and become the preferred product or service?
- **The Design specification**; SWOT, questions, what will be required to achieve this, will it be cost effective, will it be on the mark, will it ship well, will it (a-z)?
- **Then Concept development;** in terms of feasibility and marketability, CAPS
- **Selling the Ideal solution**; vs. selling the affordable & next best thing.
- **Concept vetting;** evaluating the many different options available.
- **Concept testing;** testing a few products first and getting Opinions.

2) **Designing & Engineering;** in terms of final product or service

Costing; every product has a price tag, that must fit the profiled market and our expenditure vs. income. No use selling anything if you cannot turn a profit. You must make it worth the while. The influence on this criteria, must be contemplated as well; evaluation of internal influences on quality, specification and adherence to compliance. Then looking externally at influences such as; suppliers, resources, raw materials, infrastructure, development, ergonomics, legislation and impact studies, the entire spectrum of attributes that influence, or could influence the concept. Or add to cost...hidden costs.

> Financial impact and analyses / profitability / expenses and overheads

> Resources / Suppliers / legal aspects / Infrastructure / Environmental design / impact study

Prototype or test phases; Could be a run up to the launch, with an opportunity for final design changes, specification changes and even material changes. This could cost a lot of money, have setbacks, and could not materialise. Decisions, to scrap or produce, must be taken daily, until the final, or finished product hits the floor. Always have a test run before wagering everything for nothing.

Marketing & sales strategy; going live and into the market, with advertising campaigns, adds, discounts, specials etc. Determine the mix, of your advertising strategy.

Continuous research & development; getting feedback, fine-tuning and alignment in line with market trends. How will we go about doing our research and development and gaining customer satisfaction?

The process of reviewing the "cradle to grave cycle"; Starts with assimilation and combination. We firstly need to assimilate the total time in labour and the cost of it, as well as the costs involved in procuring the components that forms the product or service. Thereafter we have to calculate the actual cost involved in moving it, storing it, selling it and the time and interest charged, calculated and added with the first process. Viewed as one continuum, taking the time and interest lost on terms, till we get the money in the bank. You have not sold anything, until the money is in the bank – this is the "cradle to grave" overview, an in-depth critical look at the life cycle of the product or service and its actual cost will determine actual profit or not. The least obvious normally chips away at profit harder than the most obvious it seems. This aspect of micro financial management, becomes a numbers game, when the numbers grow, in every dimension, so do the costs and it chips away at profit, if not gauged continually, any change in inflation, taxation, or the environment can ruin the scheme. Growth and expansion could become the one thing you are striving for, and also the very thing that kills your profit. That is if no protection is built in for hidden cost escalation and economic indicators that form part and parcel of the total product or service design and a sound financial management plan.

The fifth aspect is;

Management of the systems and marketing; No business can exist if it is not built or designed around some system that creates the structure for business, the bridge between product and client. The system can be very simple or immensely complex, depending on the nature and extent of the business, its needs and requirements. The system is the proverbial "Habitat" in which the business exists. With that much said, every habitat has one thing in common, in the sense that if one aspect is taken out or one relationship is severed, it will affect the whole system. Such is the nature of systems in business as well.

Management Marketing
and
Systems

Let's look at these relationships that could influence the business internally;

- managements – skill, style and character
- theft – theft or damages incurred
- climate sensitive business – global warming
- natural disasters - insurance
- personal relationships –partnerships, group dynamics and culture
- culture – existing, forming, or breaking up
- systems – in tandem with work or not effective
- attributes – all present or some missing or dysfunctional
- attitudes – of work force and management
- unions – call a strike
- perception – internal and external

Will determine the corporate culture and environment.

However what is truly significant is the effect, it has on effectiveness itself.

The management's focus and leader attitude, will guide people, people are very aware of impeding factors on performance and strategy and how to compensate for it. The driving principle behind this is to allow energy at random and not to control it. When it comes to motivating people, the job lies squarely on managements shoulders, select them well. Typically the mind set of managers will dictate how the system revolves, either on its own steam, or with great effort. The level of initiative allowed will dictate the speed at which the structure will function. The way we structure, will also influence the way we communicate and the speed, as well as effectiveness of it. Information systems are either direct contact or sequential. Furthermore, it will also influence the degree of professionalism and mutual respect; where systems are aligned to create empowerment, to liberate peoples' energy and creativity towards pre-agreed-upon purposes within the guidelines of shared values, we find growing professionalism and creativity. There's less bureaucracy, fewer rules and regulations, more close knit involvement, tackling bureaucracy at the root, doing away with restrictive measures. Management should be improvising and adjusting not plaguing and disrupting people.

Becoming a formidable **"Service Provider"**: The magic of any transaction had no sooner disappeared, as the moment; the "want" was fulfilled. The secret is after sales service, customer loyalty program , incentives, and discounts on bulk, or pay later options. Every interaction between us and our customers are transactions and we have to make a good on, and deposit in the trust department. If we cannot utilise this interaction to our advantage, we are doing the customer and ourselves a great disservice.

Therefore the emphasis is always on service and transaction, the before, during and after aspects of connectivity and building report, the follow up call, to see if all is well with the service or product, did we address the "want", how can we improve? Our level of service rendering determines our very survival, we have to have three levels; the before, the during and the after. What this entails is the grouping of services that compliment and relate to each other.

For instance **"Administrative functions under one leg"**, along with information Technology departments, Finances, Projects, Research & Development, Procurement, Tenders and Corporate & Legal for instance will be sorting under the co-ordination of one person, dually qualified at the head.

The second leg will be a more **"Operationally and marketing inclined leg"**, with Sales, Production, Creditors & Debtors department, Production and Transport and Warehousing under the same leg.

The last leg will be the **"Human resource, Training & Development leg"**, Logistics, Strategic and Infrastructure, Contractors, Repair & Maintenance departments.

This is the structural difference; the term managing across borders comes to mind, when we look at the human infrastructure role and function. The emphasis has shifted, we have transitioned to the collective responsibility and accountability to perform a task to specification, the one for all and all for one culture. This is only possible when and where we have a collaborating mind-set, guided by principles regularly enforced.

Developing corporate competence plays a decisive role, with matrix management.

The strength of any company is determined by its quality of human resources, this inner core strength is only acquired primarily through experiencing growth by learning, observing and forming good working habits and skills, thus translating to the required paradigm of interpersonal growth, the acquisition of personal 360-degree balance. By extending or maximising effort, we have to know our true strengths and weaknesses and not just the self "perceived" view. This is our growth potential inhibiting factor, losing cohesion and balance between role and function, between reality and perception, by creating blind spots, by giving more to one and by taking from the others without the promise of giving back more than what was taken, people in general don't mind giving, but they want to know that somewhere somehow they will receive some sort of dividends or enjoy security because of their giving, this aspect is entrenched, everyone is developed all along. The integration of individual thinking and activities into the corporate agenda called interdependency.

Three aspects that effect balance in any organisation are:

- The unchecked development or degeneration of essential skills.
- The degree to which individual's capacity is effectively utilised or inhibited by the organisations management, systems and or bureaucracy.
- The quality of work and training, that gives personal satisfaction, right throughout the organisation.

This could be projected on a personal level and corporate level. However, it can also influence the company as a whole. For instance, a successful strategic initiative yields great dividends and may unexpectedly develop capabilities, which could be applied to different fields that are starving. Where a group for instance was working as a team and they have developed a certain proficiency in a certain field. Management comes and moves the members to a new division after the project is finished to use that new knowledge to spearhead another direction or initiative...this is the nature of matrix management, it is intended to breed expertise that can be redistributed across the organisation. They say that good business sense is required in order to run a business. Business sense is really common-sense if you think about it. If you do what works, and you get dividends, then you are in business. When you think about trade, trade begins from the fundamentals of book keeping, retailing, pricing, and delivery of goods. Good business sense also dictates that you need working capital in order run your business smoothly. What business sense tells you is that consumers want more promotional information to guide them in their purchases. Is this not just plain common-sense? We should have the mental maturity to understand that we are serving peoples' "wants" and this requires information and adaptation. If we adapt successfully and supply on demand we have closed a deal, and conducted trade or business. Thus we are service providers of a higher order. Satisfying needs brings less emotional well-being than satisfying wants. Where needs are basics to be serviced, wants are all emotionally motivated in origin. We must not lose sight of this by developing the perception of being just another service provider, and not a *"sole" provider* of a product or service, we have to do our customers a higher service by selling him ourselves as a only source of information and fulfilment first, then our product, and our service comes second to this. In order to become a formidable *sole service provider* that satisfies wants, we have to control our inner and outer human influences. We can do this by creating external influences to counter internal influences and visa-versa. Alternatively, we can choose to control them ourselves –referring to our urges for personal self-gratification, we have to switch it off whilst we are in "sole provider mode" and transition, to such a nature of giving. Business sense teaches vision, mission, ethics, corporate care, charity, courage, humility and defining your business properly. If we cannot we will fail our product and our service, our moral, ethical and spiritual being must act as one, with restraint and professionalism. Business sense is acquired more through real life experiences, insightful observation, and learning the hard way. If anything, people are stripping away the catalyst of emotions to buy, once they have become habit, then it becomes trend and routine, and I think that pattern will continue. We have to have our inner influences harnessed, to generate positive results for us, and it is only by cognisant practice and finely tuned observation that we get the business mix right that works for us. That fits us, at every interaction, be it with our colleagues and clients, that we form these predator characteristics. Personal experiences and observation, equates to wisdom, and business sense. They are all factors lubricating your business activities for success.

How important is trust in strategic terms anyway?

We all think we know what "Trust" is from our own experience, but we don't know much about how to improve it, and where it weighs heavy. Why? I believe it is because we have been taught to look at "Trust" as if it were a single entity." Trust or even just the perception of it, becomes a key element in every aspect that deals with our communication, co-habitation and interaction with others. Thus, any strategy we wish to deploy, or develop will need ingredients of trust.

However we need to understand that trust is not just one thing, a word, a statement of honesty and integrity, far from it. It is the precursor to everything strategic, what needs to be in place, before we move, think or apply our minds to trust, there is the need to establishing a premise, some sort of credibility first. This type of credibility is at the centre of people's ability or inability to influence others, into trusting them, and therefore make themselves approachable and communicable to others. We need to be in a position to trust the intentions of people to do the right thing, make the right decision, and make choices that, while maybe not exactly what we would have decide on, will work either way. We have not given trust much attention have we? If the element of trust is taken for granted then we are already losing focus of key elements, then so will follow integrity, loyalty and honour. The old saying of birds of a feather flock together has merit here. Our true character is often revealed by how fearful or greedy we are .Trust builds just as much as distrust destroys. Only by being organized and focused on instilling and protecting trust as a principle can we help by not becoming the problem or even worse creating it by destroying trust, or by abusing trust. The concept of trust has been an object of much study by researchers of, psychology, sociology, economics, management and marketing, the one common denominator is fear and uncertainty, the prelude to trust or distrust. The word trust comes from the German word "trost" which means comfort. Note however that many languages (e.g. Dutch or German) do not distinguish between the words trust and confidence. Trust is having the confidence or faith in another person to do what they say they will do, or to be comfortable with them, this takes willingness. A willingness to take risks maybe one of the few characteristics common to all trust situations. To take risk daily means believing in the honesty, integrity, and the reliability of that other person. This equates to trusting. For a society to function properly, there needs to be trust, trust is of much importance precisely because its presence or absence can have a strong bearing on what we choose to do and in many cases what we can do as people and a collective. Trust runs in every vain, a core component of any relationship and a crucial factor *in the lives of people*: It makes our social life *predictable*, it creates a *sense of community for us*, and it *makes it easier for people to work together*. Often we imply more than one thing when we use the word trust. We use it to describe what we think of what people say. We also use it to describe behaviours. We use it to describe whether or not we feel comfortable sharing certain information with someone else. And we use the same word to indicate whether or not we feel other people have our best interests at heart, vs. furthering their own interests.

There are observable and distinguishable elements that give rise to trust;

1. **Competence.** Refers to the presence or perception of the presence of ability that gives us a level of trust in people because of their ability. In many instances we place our trust blindly in people and even things by virtue of a set of standards or code we have of competence. A Doctor, Pilot or Dentist is for instance viewed as competent by virtue of their title to perform a certain task. Competence in general refers to how well you "appear" to be at your given job or task or in a specific situation, where you can be seen as competent by projecting confidence and seemingly having knowledge of the subject.

2. **Worthiness.** A trustworthy person is someone in whom you can place your trust and rest assured that the trust will not be betrayed. *Worthy;* having worth, merit or value being honourable or admirable and deserving, or having sufficient worth. Worth and worship both come from Old English "weorth", worth value. Worship is composed of this word "weorth", worth, + ship (a suffix meaning condition, office, etc. as in friendship and sportsmanship), hence worship was originally the condition or office of being worthy, thus worthiness, a person with dignity.

3. **Alliances.** Mainly for mutual benefit. An alliance is a primary form of structured co-operative collaboration between two entities for whatever reason. Stemming from sharing information, combining resources, capabilities, and core competences all in order to pursue mutual interests. Alliance also implies shared means "co-operation between two or more people, groups, firms that produces better results that can be gained from a single action. Alliances are risky but they are a fundamental necessity of both short- and long-term strategy that requires skill to forge and trust to keep it going.

4. **Respect.** Comes in many forms; self-respect, mutual respect, respect for authority, society, law and order. In order for trust to be established, one needs to respect the boundaries of law, both natural and spiritual, as well as written. These boundaries create a solid foundation upon which further respect can be built. Respect should be independent of bias, of whether or not you like the person, as a person, an authority figure, a servant, master or slave. Perhaps half or more of the people in situations you deal with on a daily basis you wouldn't care to know on a personal level. Nonetheless, that does not mean that our personal feelings about people should cloud the amount of courtesy and respect that we show them. Understanding and acknowledging other people culture and traditions, this builds respect and in turn creates trust.

5. **Appearance.** Trust is integral to the idea of influence or persuasion. You can either be influenced or persuaded to trust things, people or animals based on the

appurtenance - an accompanying part or feature of something - it generates, either physically or emotionally. Influence or be influenced. There are always two choices: either you can persuade others to help you or you can be persuaded to help them. You have to look or act the part if you are going to establish immediate trust with a person or client. Aristotle believed that three characteristics need to exist to be trusted, either as a speaker, or authoritarian. People look at the intelligence of the speaker - correctness of opinions, or statements - the character of the speaker - his reliability a competence factor, and honesty - a measure of intentions, and the goodwill of the speaker (favourable intentions towards the listener). I don't think this has changed much even today. Your appearance creates the environment for trust to occur. If you are engaged in business then you must look, act and be professional. If you are looking for trust in a relationship, then you will have to dress to match their lifestyle. Birds of a feather flock together...

6.   **Positivity.** Does not mean having a blind faith, it means being assertive and influential. People have a tendency to believe negative things far easier than those powerful positive statements of "think outside the box" crap. Avoid being more than positive; just being neutral, yourself, at first, when meeting people. The purpose of this is using negatives constructively, to make yourself appear trustworthy. Once people believe you can be trusted, persuading them becomes far easier. With this technique you can openly admit the weaknesses or disadvantages associated with your proposal. This is an excellent persuasion technique because it disarms the listener, by suggesting to them that you are an honest person and someone who can be trusted. Once you can be trusted, they can then be persuaded. By then affirming others, this builds trust and motivation to react and inter act with you. Being able to create win-win situations in business and in personal life depends many a time solely on one's ability to influence others without undue aggression and with both parties' interests in mind. Most people are not aware that every human interaction involves a complex process of persuasion and influence, and being unaware, they are usually the ones being persuaded to help others rather than the ones who are doing the persuading. Every hour of every day, at every level in every organization, influential people succeed and non-influential people usually don't.

7.   **Responsibility.** Is often used synonymously with such concepts as accountability. Trust is built on the basis that you take responsibility for your actions and deeds in life. Knowing what to do and when to do it, as well as what not to do. By denying responsibility for the mistake or projecting the blame away from our self we are seen as childlike, irresponsible, and essentially telling people that you haven't learned from the mistake, and cannot take responsibility for your actions, and that you won't help to repair the damage and that it will probably happen again in the future.

8.   **Listening.** People have a desire to talk about themselves, and to be heard. Some ideas they want to bounce off people, so an easy way to build trust is to have a receptive demeanour. Let the people talk to you about their life and the stuff that is important to them. This will have a reciprocal factor of drawing you into their lives and building trust.

9.   **Empathy.** Empathy and sympathy are two ways of gaining trust. Where empathy is a standoff approach, just words, our ability to see the world through others eyes by "walking around in their shoes." But from our perspective. Empathy reduces the level of tension between both of you and facilitates trust building through mutual understanding. Where sympathy is actually going through the emotions, and experience grief first hand.

10.   **Honesty.** We need people in our lives with whom we can be blatantly as open as possible. To have real conversation with people may seem like such a simple, obvious suggestion, but it involves courage and risk, we can never be blatantly honest with people we meet. We can be respectfully honest. You want to be truthful in both your personal and your professional life. Honesty facilitates trust building by letting your counterpart know

that what you are telling them is truthful and genuine. A trusted relationship is one where the person will risk making the other person upset by telling him something that they may not want to hear if they know it will help them out in the long run. Human nature dictates that honesty and openness is the best policy, however, it has many risks. Once a word spoken, it never becomes silent if it caused thunder to be unleash, like a spell it will be remembered. Try to conceal a flawed word, or action, and the world will imagine the worst.

11.   **Patience.** People don't enjoy being rushed through things, or having things dumped on them. Patience equals wellbeing, organisation and skill, as well as professionalism...a calm demeanour builds trust and confidence. Giving a client ample amount of time to think things through rather than pressuring them to sign the contract is an example of using patience to build trust.

12.   **Common interests.** For it is mutual trust, even more than mutual interest that holds human associations together. Our friends seldom profit from us but they make us feel safe and significant because we share certain things in confidence. Having shared interests provides you with a forum upon which you have a basis to talk and exchange ideas. The more interests you share the better. Common interests are the best way to meet people because it's something that both of you know and it's something that both of you enjoy.

13.   **Enthusiasm.** This is the amount of effort, energy and persistence you use towards making things work. People want and need to be around other people who are motivated to forming healthy relations. If you meet someone for the first time and they give you the "shrug-off" or are looking around the room while you are talking to them, then that does not convey much enthusiasm to continue talking to them. However, if you meet a person and they take a keen interest in what you have to say by actively listening and maintaining good eye-contact, then you feel like they are enthusiastic about you and your life.

14.   **Loyalty.** A trusted relationship is one where you can count on the other person being faithful to their word. When people honour each other, there is a trust established that leads to synergy, interdependence, and deep respect. Both parties make decisions and choices based on what is right, what is best, what is valued most highly by both parties. A person who is loyal always holds their end of a promise expecting the other to do the same. They have a high level of integrity to do the things that they say they will do consistently.

15.   **Values and beliefs.** Trust is associated with sharing of values and beliefs. Beliefs are the assumptions we make about ourselves, about others in the world and about how we expect things to be. Where values are about how we have learnt to think things ought to be or people ought to behave, especially in terms of qualities such as honesty, integrity and openness. Sharing any commonality of values and beliefs finds people and builds trust.

16.   **Culture.** Culture can divide and unite; it has the ability to cut both ways, as it entrenches religion and language. To achieve high levels of personal trust in a culturally diversified environment, that forms one working culture, individuals must find and develop shared values and beliefs in the work space, in line with their own culture. This involves a strong individual identification with norms and ethics that transcend universal boundaries, and precipitate into the organization and its member's culture. Address the animosity between management and employees. Foster good communication between all stakeholders and aim for one unified work culture.

17.   **Good communication.** In order for trust to flourish in any given relationship, there has to be a good line of open communication between parties. Good communication involves making sure that your ideas are accurately "faxed" over to your counterpart and that miscommunication is avoided. This involves exchanging information between each other and over-communicating rather than under-communicating. It means telling the

person how you feel and transmitting your interests, values, and goals so the other person can understand you better. Good communication involves the ability to openly discuss conflicts and issues that are inevitable on the road towards relationships. The other part of good communication is being able to read and speak good body language. You want to be sure you are sending nonverbal language that is consistent with your spoken words.

18.   **Security.** Is defined as the state of readiness for interaction with someone or something. In psychology, trust equals a belief that a person whom you trust to do what you expect from them, will act accordingly, we all trust policemen, as they are supposedly protectors. According to Maslow's Hierarchy of Needs, people have a need to feel safe and secure in their environment. As we meet people, spend time with them, and establish a relationship we naturally estimate how much we can trust them. We approach each person beginning with our natural inclination toward trust or distrust. In addition as we learn more about each person, primarily from first-hand experience, we have reason to trust or mistrust them.

19.   **Similarity.** Why do we trust people we perceive to be similar to ourselves? Surprisingly, the answers are simple. Trust between people is based on the perception that efforts between the parties will be reciprocated easier if we are like minded or from the same culture.

20.   **Self-sacrifice.** Self-sacrifice is one of the most important components of a trusted relationship.

21.   **Persuasion** is how we are influenced to trust based on our environment and life experiences. The persuasion to trust a person can be brought about by our peers, our needs, family relations, and the availability of opportunities which support our way of life. Persuasion motivates us to accept and trust people, ideas, principles, faiths, and respect authority.

22.   The **perception of competence** is made up of your perception of an ability that others with whom you work, or socialise with can perform competently at whatever is needed in the current situation. Where a friend of a friend would take charge of a boat...we perceive him to be competent, as he is a relation of a relative that I trust.

Trust is therefore relative to the situation, the people, as well as our level of awareness and mind-set. Trust is not the same "thing" for everyone; it differs from person to person, and from situation to situation.

The meaning of trust transcends common belief

Trust is a *feeling* of comfort and security, how comfortable do we feel and how secure is the measure of trust we derive as an answer.

The *two dimensions* of trust are identified as *goodwill* and *competence*.

The Radical Revolutionary Strategic Management Matrix For Predators

Trust is the *necessary precursor* for:

- feeling able to rely upon a person, or team.
- The ability to co-operating with and experiencing teamwork with a group,
- taking thoughtful risks, and
- experiencing believable communication.

Trust depends on two independent components; *intent and ability*.

Unless you intend to fulfil your agreements and keep your word, there is no trust. Nevertheless, intent is not enough, you have to deliver on your promises, and that requires the ability to do what you promise.

Trust is also a form of social manipulation that aims to change the perception or behaviour of others through underhanded, deceptive, and/or even abusive tactics. Social influence is not necessarily negative. For example, doctors try to persuade patients to change unhealthy habits. Identified the following basic ways that manipulators control their victims with false trust:

Perceived Positive reinforcement - includes praise, superficial charm,

superficial sympathy (crocodile tears), excessive apologizing; money, approval, gifts; attention, public recognition.

Negative reinforcement - includes nagging, yelling, the silent treatment, intimidation, threats, swearing, emotional blackmail, the guilt trap, sulking, crying, and playing the victim

Intermittent or partial reinforcement - Partial or intermittent negative reinforcement can create an effective climate of fear and doubt, for example in terrorist attacks. Partial or intermittent positive reinforcement can encourage the victim to persist - for example in most forms of gambling, the gambler is likely to win now and again but still lose money overall.

Punishment – in any form

Abuse; encouraging or couching people to start abusing stimulants, to gain their trust, taking negatives and turning it to positive control and advantage.

Trust can be abused, bought, controlled, manipulated, broken and built, all in just one sentence. It is a very fragile, yet very powerful, a drug of social manipulation.

Addressing Influences Through Specific Strategic Management Interventions

The last aspect left on the road towards solving the problems created by strategy on the way to solving others, is the consequence of influence. For every action, there is an opposite reaction. Human nature, and personal character traits combined with outside influences forms baggage, every person you meet, and work with comes with his or her own baggage, some have more some have less.

It is just part and parcel of our composition; we come willing and able, prepared to do our best and equipped to do our worst. Politics will have a profound influence on the effect of the total corporate culture and work ethic and effects collaboration in general. Call it "political will". Therefore, it makes sense, that we still have a choice in the matter, but it is not whether to join in or stay out of it, politics that is. Rather we only have two choices in this regard, the first is to use it and become an active "politician" or have it abused by other political "pigs". Let us take a very critical look at the importance and significance of having healthy co-ordinated company politics versus uncoordinated political rivalry, the very likes of the classical backstabbing, opportunism and bickering.

"Political correctness" *is in fact nothing more than blind conformity to an idiotic belief, a term widely used, that actually describe the rape of people's freedom of association and liberties, their inability to make decisions for themselves.*

Portals of influence on strategy

The influence of observation; Mans greatest and higher order activity is that of contemplation and rationalisation. Company politics is a direct result of this higher order influences, practiced by our key employees and their effect on the company, let's analyse them:

The social dragnet influence; The basic appetite of man evokes a multitude of "wants", in that once they have freed themselves from the burden of basic needs and have escalated to fulfilling wants, they move to the ultimate level of existence, that of emotional and political fulfilment. This is all due to an innate programmed pursuit to seek out and find more means of improvement and gratification; either in social class, in power, status, or even spiritually. Once we are free from realising our needs and wants, we start to function from a different set of paradigms. These paradigms stems directly but not exclusively from; intellectual superiority, wealth, status, race, gender, positions or whatever gives you an ability to exercise influence over people and create wealth. Man's driving desire is staying in pursuit of the ultimate pleasure and all things pleasurable, his last greatest conquest. This is where all willpower is tested, where man gets to choose his pleasures, and then to abstain or indulge. When we find ourselves consumed with winning even if it means to win at any cost, then having abilities and power becomes dangerous. Too much power corrupts, we all have faced similar decisions when confronted with prospects of pleasure or exercising your power, and have had to weigh it against our own belief system and live with the consequences thereof today. In Pursuit of power and pleasure there is always the possibility of getting hooked on it, pleasure especially is abound in many forms, by crossing legal boundaries, or just ethical, or even religious, we get hooked, thus infringing on the moral fabric of society. Those who fall prey before its beauty and give into its magnetic powers have very little consciences left, as pleasure in itself drains consciousness and enslaves those that worship it to live with denial. The word addicted, also means slave of desires, and living with denial, this becomes habitual in nature and a viscous cycle is then created if not broken. Wickedness spawns as a result of perusing pure selfish greed, lust or desire; one has to resort to cowardice and succumb to the belief that this is the right thing to do by "me", in order to live with oneself, we have to change the truth, to suit and sooth our burning soul.

The abuse of trust, in the workplace normally coincides with these social activity going unchecked in the work place, where the win-lose mentality is observed, and power is misused. Alternatively, abuse of power is more prevalent where personal satisfaction becomes an issue, this could be linked to personal addiction to pleasures, that could ultimately devastate the business where and if key players are involved, in some extracurricular activity, that could directly impact on the success of any business. This aspect will become prevalent faster towards the top echelon of management who has the means and influence and in some instances even middle management level, than at employee level. Aristotle warned us - man needs to be compelled, in order to have a social affectionate relationship, governed by rule and law. Where all man are not born equal, therefore there will always be class.

The anti- social influence; Reason is the means used to influence, and once the means becomes effective it becomes power, to achieve desired results with. Then we require more reasoning, thus we become stronger at reasoning, and the influence we exert grows. Power, cannot be obtained without having conflict, we must all therefore struggle and by struggling, we get into situations of conflict that creates winners and losers. The only means to survive conflict is to protect, by either fleeing or attacking. Therefore, without any self-control, we will find ourselves constantly at "War" with each other – mentally as well as physically- *("man's nature makes him totally unsuited for social life" -Thomas Hobbes)*. In conclusion, we need to have established good self-control as a mental mechanisms, that stems from a principled balanced centre of living in a world of abundance, the paradigm that there is plenty out there for everybody and put this win-win paradigm in place, as orientation mechanism, to deal with anti-social behaviour effectively.

The influence on social equilibrium. Two key aspects that have a major and both significant bearing on our social equilibrium are integrity and fairness. Where corruption and injustice against people occur, social equilibrium is impaired as a result. Which combined threaten to weaken society, and social systems, even government as a whole. So often, the problem is created by ideology and not with the people within the system. Politics corrupt people faster than people can people. They just find themselves learning from the pros and are influenced to look the other way, or submit themselves to corruption. All man desires is to gain the approval and avoid the disapproval of other man, even if they have to do wrong to get it. Which in itself gives rise to all sorts of wants, gaining approval and avoiding shame is what renders man socially interactive and complex. Personal passion will override any other passion of sorts, always with consequences; causing, anger, envy, frustration and even hate if it is perceived to be in contrast with what is ethical. Deep frustration emanates from this; frustration is the cumulative result of total indifference that creates polarity, between the two extreme forms of living. Resulting in the classic eventuality of total indifference "they do not understand us/me" to be empathetic is to build bridges; to be indifferent is to burn them. People do not want you to always agree with them, just listen and try to understand, that is all they ask. Please just put yourself in my situation for a minute here and then I will listen to what you have to say. Man is all about self and self-interest; if we do not create a utopia of abundance and rule it with principles then we will have failed man and his quest for fulfilling his personal interest.

Therefore, the only effective way in dealing with social conflict would be to apply rules of "engagement", by applying sanctions on certain types of anti-social behaviour. This would only be possible in a genuinely compassionate and spontaneous environment where trust prevails.

"From each according to his ability, to each according to his needs" *– Karl Marx.*

The influence of our Social and Political environment; the working environment should become the system that forms our social habits, it is said that 72% of our emotional state is influenced by the senses and how we perceive things through them. Thus what we feel, see, taste, hear and smell, all culminate in how we feel. How we feel is how we act, and how we act is how we live, and are known. The why do we then only concentrate on the cognitive aspects of reasoning, wisdom, and knowledge only when designing strategy and politics.

Consequently, we are very perceptive; this makes sense that we should have things to focus on daily that influence us in a good manner. We should focus our environmental design in engineering corporate environments and politics, to satisfy all the senses as we spend most of our wakened life's at work, through the incorporation of scientific and medical data, that would enhance working environments, both physically, ecstatically, emotionally and even environmentally, to appeal to all the senses and physique. Our relationship with our environment will influence our ability to feel, thus our mood to.

The influence of group dynamics; group dynamics has all the attributes of disaster woven into it, just as life and living has all to do with socialism, habitation and mutualism. Although we have greatly explored man as a single entity in this book, we must not lose sight of the significance of how group dynamics and peer pressure still has its influences on the adult individual. For when any individual wants to align and join a group he will be seen as "raw material" or "foreign" and will be moulded by such a group until he or she either fits or get rejected. This will cause some new distinguishable characteristics typical in nature of that of the group and its peers. Humans become that which works in order to sustain. In order, ascertain their wants they will adapt to any situation. We are all highly adaptable creatures, we will indulge in activity that we perceive to be worthwhile perusing it in order to belong or feel significant and thus adapt accordingly and so will our paradigms. When we sense that we no longer belong, or have out grown the group we will become the hunter again and move on, a very natural progression, where and when our sense of worth and focus change on life and what really matters living, we become analytical of ourselves and introspective, we re-orientate. This is also our origin of work related stress, depression and anxiety, both having to please ourselves and others, all in order to belong, all at the same time, this shape shifting calls for great measures of personal sacrifice and energy. This requires detachment from the true self, our very real nature, if prolonged it gets aggressive and we become depressed or even destructive. This is not self-sacrifice; this is character suicide, the spiritual decay of having to live a double life, with the clichés of modern standards dictating living standards and norms.

Greed is aroused without knowing where to find your moral foothold, reality seems valueless by comparison with the dreams we once had, we then acquire a strong thirst for unfamiliar pleasures, nameless sensations, all of which lose their savour once known – Emile Derkheim.

Where the influence of rationalisation steps in; The universal truth of rationalisation is that no one is truly rational. We all sometimes find ourselves living and acting totally out of character, for various reasons. Conflict tends to do with rationalisation whatever it wants, and we do things even if and when they do not make perfect sense. Every human would like to believe that he or she is acting rational; however to what extent is this perceived rationality going to be influenced. This aspect becomes crucial, it become circumstantial, as alluded too, our cognitive ability to stay truly focused and content and even on course, with our principles, is governed by how best we deal with our circumstances.

Rationalisation is best described as a systematic organisation of facts; the act of organizing something according to a system or a rationale, that was brought about by a certain influence.

The influence of doing right; Ask anyone if they are doing the right thing and the answer will be an unconditional Yes!! Yes, really, and by whose standards, we can't say. Even little kids are in this mode of justifying their actions right or wrong, we can all defend what we are doing daily. A defence of the real truth or denial, either way it influences reality, it is all about the difference between people and their natural focus and need for justification. We don't want to be caught out, or be in the wrong, ever. This creates one of two options, between two opposing choices; *"doing the right thing, vs. doing the thing right"*.

Herein we find some secrets and truths, and the real truth at failed attempts at enterprise transpire. It is reasonably clear now and very apparent that the way in which you approach anything in life, will ultimately be the main factor that will determine the facts. Paradigms and conceptual reasoning guide us in the choices we make, and this is why we read books. Critical thinking on the other hand will determine our focal point in the spectrum of thought, and this is why we reason. How we determine our focus on what is right, by "doing the right thing" or "doing the thing right", will ultimately determine the outcome, by virtue of this choice.

The first aspect is paradigm alignment – a way of thinking about thinking. The classic White and Black hat situation, the question is not so much, will it work, but rather how do you work on influences to arrive at a situation of **social equilibrium**? Now here is the one word that sums up diversity when trying to reach equilibrium. "Agendas". Office and company politics are all about personal agendas that become group agendas that become political agendas, that in turn create perceptions, which start influencing people and unions paradigms. That if not managed could create chaos. Be it to come to grips with newly found power, the proverbial "power trip syndrome", or the prospect of a financial gain. Whatever the focal motivation or points are, they create momentum towards a specific goal, people are by nature very competitive and if the goal is to compete then we revolt. Revolution in itself comes from pure frustration and disillusionment with the system and its politics and ways of doing things, and finding an influence or power to fight back unites and polarises people. Then you find that people put on hats.

The White Hats – *"doing the thing right people"* mostly *"politically' motivated*. The "white hats", the guy's that like playing it safe, that like to criticise, these people are mainly concerned with you and what you are doing. Somehow, it is never about them and how they can assist and how they create the problems you will have to face; by failing to plan, or manage effectively – they are too busy "doing the right thing". They question, with what are your results – they are results driven, statistics is there measure. If you come with any alternative, guaranteed they will be referring you back to "policy" and "procedure". Some of them will even quote it verbatim, why, because they either have the degree, the authority, the position and even the political mandate. People with agendas, mainly concerned with furthering an agenda to dictate the paradigm on what is perceived to be rational and logical ways and means of doing things, shaped from this paradigm. People and their thinking influence how things get done...

The Black Hats – *"doing the right thing people"* mostly focused on *"practicality"*. Where on the other hand, the "black hats" the practically minded operational guys who have the expertise as their first qualifying degree and some even degrees and diplomas. This group will mostly be concerned with the margins of error and the risk involved, armed with lessons learned from prior experience, measured not so much by how they did it then, but rather what had been learned and what could be applied through doing it now, or the "old fashioned way". The black hats tend to align with others like-minded, sharing their knowledge gained from experiences, with current situations and thinking. By applying a tried and tested type of methodology, in effect, the white hats work from the conception to the objective and the black hats work from the objective to the conception. "Academically minded" vs. "Practically minded" paradigms differ widely, especially when it comes to paradigms of implementation, causing them to clash as a result hereof.

The influence of E; reaching objectives via two influences, either being *effective* or *efficient* when performing tasks, these two words describe the two ways practiced towards ascertaining a successful outcome, in whatever matter. White hats tend to want to be *effective* all the time. Whereas black hats, tend to want to be *efficient* most of the time. Being "Efficient" is better described as doing what you do and doing it very well, on the other hand, being "Effective" requires that you are doing what needs to be done, to help you reach your final goal or vision, in a predefined manner.

This can be divided in to group and personal levels of work ethic. Personal effectiveness is closely related to ones level of education and understanding, the key to effectiveness is that you're doing things that lead to results in the realm of your responsibilities. Meanwhile, the key to efficiency is getting your things done in a manner that consumes just the appropriate amount of energy and resources, another way to look at these differences is to equate leadership with effectiveness and management with efficiency, when your intention shifts to being more effective as a leader or manager, you demand thinking of alternative nature and origin and you can achieve more of your worthwhile goals in much less time, by applying this paradigm of fusing the two core beliefs into one. By choosing the things which will make you more effective beforehand, instead of doing more and more to achieve efficiency, without taking stock of what is really required, to up performance and create expertise.

Experience and expertise are the accumulation and integration of effective and efficient, if you master both, then you become experienced, an expert.

- Efficiency; is the relationship between the amount of work done(increasing efforts) and the energy expended during the work
- Effectiveness; comes from taking the time to stop, plan and evaluate,(strategic stance) rather than running faster and faster
- Efficiency; doing things right
- Effectiveness; doing the right things
- Effectively; a level of ingenuity is required in getting things done
- Effectiveness; Doing things "right" by repeating them

The influence of corporate cultural development: Company politics is the result of personal insecurities, and disputes or unfairness– where we are wholly and solely to blame for not being able to manage this diversity. We should always be aware of "outside influences" and their impact on our "inner influences". From the Art of War – Sun Tzu. This uniqueness works visa-versa, so it stands to reason that if you want to change "inner influences" you have to introduce "outer influences" and on the other hand, if you would want to change outer influences you have to create inner influences to affect the desired change or create balance". Give people a reason to form groups and they will...

- **Forming –** groups begins to form; members are measuring themselves against other that step forward as leaders and trying to determine where they fit into this group or not.
- **Storming –** internal discontent as members explores each other's "hidden agendas" and counter them by any means.
- **Norming –** growing interdependence of group; interaction begins to normalize, as they find more and more common ground.
- **Performing –** group has established structures and relationships and is working together to achieve the task(s) at hand.

Counteracting conflict caused by interpersonal influences: Whenever we are working with people, and pushing them to start performing, including groups, then we can expect tension at some point, some competition even, and then if prolonged conflict. When conflict emerges, then the thrill of the "hunt" has died down, and reality now sets in, it has actually now become work, and hunting takes effort, and self-discipline, and we start measuring, and checking who is not bringing their pound of bacon. This is human nature, when we are set to compete and perform its fun, until we have to do it repeatedly, where it becomes routine, and expected. Then we internalise, what is in it for me, what will motivate me to carry on.

We always tend to internalise, because we are all selfish, and Selfishness and self-serving-interest gets tested, to see what's in it for me, or what will I have to sacrifice to get the deal, mirrored against our level of commitment towards the "TRIBE", and concern for others. Then the moral and ethical tests gets applied, of what's right and fair in this instance, we filter things that concern us. Then only do we establish risk, to see how people might get hurt, or undermined in the process, this process creates influences on the inside that others feel and experience as emotions on the outside. Emotions translate into energy and then concepts, ideas, notions and thoughts. The level and intensity of rivalry – stems from our eagerness to win, and winning is based on a selfish fulfilment and sense of gratification, governed by our morality, which will determine to what extents are we prepared to go just to win. Our level of concern for others, and our sense of self-serving acts as the two most important catalysts for conflict between people. Human beings are inherently violent and competitive, and this trait surfaces where we feel threatened, and afraid, as well as humiliated, uncertain and undermined. What is clearly observable in on our bonds with people is how we emotionally get charge up or rundown with our own emotions as they get influenced by others energy, it is all dependent on the level of conflict or ecstasy we experience when in contact with people, a force we all share, called emotional energy. Energy gets moved by influences and reactions, they become apparent and exist by being empathetic – feeling with emotion - or just sympathetic – just acknowledging emotion - or having no remorse – showing no compassion at all, just staying rational. Our state of emotional energy gets filled up or run down by others, our environment, addictions, emotional wellbeing, health climate etc... whether we like it or not. However, the most profound impact is between people. People make people feel good, or bad, with their energy. These levels of emotional interaction with others directly influence our behaviour, and this in turn can lead to conflict. The point is "We feel each other", emotionally daily. Conflict between people is a fact of life, and it's not necessarily a bad thing either. In fact, study has proven a relationship with frequent conflict may be healthier than one with no observable conflict. The belief that doing nothing, by abstaining from violence, and being neutral, and none confrontational is always good is apparently not. No, this stance does nothing to resolve future conflict, it only avoids it, and in fact only serves to increase the tendency to become violent as well, and escalate the intensity of violence in the future. We tell people how to treat us, by the way we dress, present ourselves, speak, and by the image we portray, it is the same with organisations, and with strategy. If there is no code, then each individual will apply his own, by either following sound proper principles, which will formulate the strategic directives and influence the managements style.

War is a self-serving behaviour, a battle of wills, which uses violence in an attempt to force or alter beliefs and culture, on either side to unite around one idea. As a strategic effort of war, we aim to align an indifferent entity with a new reality. By not applying principles we find a "struggle of wills", then people start to polarise others and then we have "war". Warring ideas, and practices, complicates the process of strategic thinking, planning and management, it creates conflict between emotional truths and raises interpersonal conflict between personalities; that spills over into race and gender issues and conflict. This then creates unbearable amounts of tension for the bystanders. People in general have no interest in creating conflict with others. Most of us know enough about human behaviour to distinguish between healthy and unsuited aggressive relationships. It is always in our best interest to maintain relations which are smooth, flexible, and mutually beneficial.

The observers; none confrontational types, what is the influence on their behaviour and the bulk. The person who only does "things right", will never find him or herself in trouble or in the path of aggression, or aggressors, they will never learn anything useful either, because they just keep repeating what they do well, and are told, over and over again. Run and hide, even unknowingly at times, they will not distance themselves from their paradigm of following the set routine and procedure on the path of least resistance. Even if it means that it is at the expense of not doing much more, they will in effect do nothing significant about solving any underlying problem either. In fear of being targeted. The price tag coupled to a paradigm of "doing the right thing" only, could become very costly. Mostly in terms of time wasted to conform to bureaucracy, or a false blind sense of achievement, as well as conformity to norms, perceived to be the correct. They never contemplate looking at getting better results, in order to deliver the same results by other means rather than the norm. We may be very busy when we keep applying the norm, we may even seem very efficient, but we will only be truly effective when we begin with the end in mind...and not leave everything to chance, policy or routine. This requires critical thinking, strategy and reverse engineering, of the highest order. Don't let stale influences keep people prisoners of route, habit and policy.

Therefore, this is not always a viable option of continuing with the norm only, it could have a knock-on effect at some junction, where the normal way of doing things crystallises everything, and then nothing is done. Normality, can stonewall many a good implementable solution that are otherwise lost in translation, due to enforcing bureaucracy constantly that coincides with repetitive and outdate norms. We need a little chaos now and then, a little spice, and fear, and joy. If not the "marriage" becomes routine and mundane, and we take things for granted, and leave things for later. This aspect could become your proverbial "Achilles' heel", due to the inflexibility of administrators, leaders and managers to adopt some bits of change, in step with change itself, as and when things change. Procrastination is not our enemy, our enemy is holding onto routine, and bureaucracy for dear life, and this is the best form of procrastination, it is the enemy of mind-set, and freethinking, and it will start weighing heavy on every aspect connected to it. If and when, this aspect becomes an entrenched ideology, where we just do things according to the norm in an organisation; or where everything is cast in stone type of mentality, policy only, then for sure the norm will prevail. We cannot solve problems the same way we are creating them, and use it as a defence mechanism against inefficacy, and idiocy. An unequivocal immovable paradigm develops and affects everything and nothing all in the same instance. Every aspect of the organisation, with people in key positions that manage, will only be able to manage what they understand, and nothing else, with bureaucracy only. It destroys the balance between two extremes, between effective and efficient – if no change occurs ever, then we become trapped by virtue of our focus and paradigm. People who just "do the right thing" always, will inadvertently do more harm to the process of growth and development of any scheme in the end. Just in terms of slowing it all down like a dead weight, with too much "required policy", that will create loads of paperwork, signatures, bottlenecks, budgets and approvals. All for what end, it never delivers. Today we live fast, those who cannot do fast must make way. They, who only see the "wall of policy" and procedure as the norm, become themselves immovable and impenetrable, this they cannot grow, or move faster. The conclusion is that little to no progress will be made in an environment subjected to total bureaucratic dominance. In addition, many results are left to chance, if only they, the "white hats", could step back from their wall of policy and procedure, they will see, like the "black hats", that all walls have one or two things in common, they all have doors and some even windows and cracks. These doors and windows could be unlocked, or opened with the keys of initiative. Do not just let one influence prevail and dominate. If we only let one influence prevail, then it will start to dominate how we do things, make sure to have all the good influences sustained and entertained. Diversity is strength, it is a mind-set; we just have to change people's focus from keys to codes. So that anyone having the code, can proceed with their tasks in life, unhindered, and the tedious task of locking and unlocking with keys become an out-dated phenomenon.

The influence of polarity; Understanding the influence of mental maturity on personality.

Certain character/ personality traits become vital towards performing specific key functions, forming effective groups, and creating leadership traits, they all combined become attributes of success. However only certain types of personality's work well together, others do not. Sorting people by their different personalities has gone on for thousands of years, and understanding their polarity and influence has changed history. This practice has left us with the systems that can assist us greatly, it can help you find a system that will shed light on your own personality and the personalities of those around you, and how to best engage them and provoke them to deliver on excellence.

We need to tread careful not to oversimplify the study of human changing character aspects and that of the mental condition, for it is much too complex and way too complicated to be summed-up under one label. Strategy is the process of contemplating everything that can and will influence performance, and the speed of change. Therefore defining personalities for specifics needs and fit, is not unforeseeable. Here today and certainly more in the future we might find ourselves hiring personality traits first and then qualifications, and not just volume. We could have fewer better suited people doing the same job as opposed to many under-qualified and unsuited. Psychology has found striking patters that consistently deliver success, and patterns often have to do with contrast and similarity when dealing with behaviour. By studying this similarity and patterns certain visible traits have surfaced, and we can now to a certain degree of safety state and predict how these personalities will react and act under certain conditions. Call it the selection of true mental maturity, over convention. It's all about getting people with good mental ability and health.

Merriam-Webster defines mental health as "A state of emotional and psychological well-being in which an individual is able to use his or her cognitive and emotional capabilities, function in society, and meet the ordinary demands of everyday life. True mental maturity on the other hand is an intellectual state where an individual is functioning mentally at his highest capacity, and a functioning rational adult. This union requires at least three of our four major supporting character attributes to be present and fully developed to maturity for us to function at this higher level.

In terms of defining mental ability and health, educators stated that this should only include elements that could be developed: Such as a sense of;

- moral responsibility and sound ethical and moral behaviour;
- capacity for enforcing and excepting discipline;
- a moral and ethical sense of values, goals, and processes of a free society;
- standards and norms of personal character expression and ideas.

What this implies is, without the basics in place you cannot build anything useful, like teams, or leaders. If the people we take on or consider for employment are not aligned with the four basic cornerstones of good behaviour then we are getting in rotten apples. We all have one or more dominant trait that we primarily exercise to maturity; this is not enough to be truly effective or mature. We could be seen to be adults because of our age, but still behave like juveniles. Mental maturity is mostly only observed after 30 years of age, here as strong sense of responsibility materialise and we start to realise, and identify that our juvenile charter traits needs to be expanded and developed to reach full maturity. Yes, mental intellectual maturity truly depends greatly on how we have developed our governing behaviour traits. Our less developed dominant attributes throw us off balance, at times when we need them most, because they are not developed to full maturity, and this has a profound influence on our thinking, behaviour and results, not to mention our public opinion. We have four dominant personalities, of which one takes preference and the others follow on, here they are:

The Practical personality: A personality that likes to keep the bigger picture in mind; the creator. Temperamental personality, that is fairly extroverted. The practically minded, analytical, creative an architect, they can keep their finger on the pulse and keep tracking many projects and operations all at once, they resort to being creative when confronted with a problem or situation and can spot creativity and talent and harness it. However, some alone time is crucial for those of this temperament, they are sensitive under the surface, compassionate and thoughtful. Generally struggle with following tasks all the way through. They see potential; either as threat and both as opportunity, white and black in their distinctions with no or little grey areas. Enjoy social gatherings and making new friends. Only once they have reached maturity do they, live with balance and strive to keep it in all things; this personality can inspire people with their leadership abilities and talents. If not inspired themselves and appreciated, they become withdrawn.

The Visionary personality: A personality that thinks in pictures; the dreamer. Tend to be self-content and kind. They can be very accepting and affectionate. They may be very receptive and shy and often prefer stability to uncertainty and change. They are very consistent, relaxed, rational, curious, and observant, making them good administrators and diplomats They are emotionally driven, their empathy and understanding of people is profound because they can see – mentally - what it is like to be in another's shoes, they all have a tendency to be relaxed, they are broad and open minded, open to new challenges and well organised, once they reach maturity they live with balanced, this personality relies on systems and support and can see the relationships that can be the most efficient and effective means to progress. If not they become self-analysing and self-destructive in their behaviour.

The Authoritarian personality: A personality that enjoys being in charge; the leader. A person who is a doer, and not afraid of hardship. They have a lot of ambition, energy, and passion, and it rubs off, and they try to instil it in others. They see others as week, and cowardice. They don't trust others, and keep secrets. They can dominate people. Many great charismatic military and political figures are authoritarians. They like to be leaders and in charge of everything. They get inspiration through ideas and thoughts rule their minds, they are great listeners, they like and demand structure and order, they must have an audience and must have the facts to move forward. Although they have a tendency to be too aggressive and assertive to a point where they drive every one away, once they reach maturity, they reach balanced; this person never gives up and has an inner sense of concern and fairness. If not they become pessimistic and criticizing.

The Spiritual personality: A personality driven by emotions and feelings, the spiritualist. A person who is a thoughtful thinker. Often very considerate, can be highly creative in activities such as poetry and art - and can become occupied with the tragedy and cruelty in the world. Often a perfectionist and self-disciplined. They are often self-reliant and independent the point of withdrawn. They are very sensitive to people around them and their surroundings and have a profound ability to reach out to others. Although they have a tendency to involve themselves in other people's business and problems excessively and deeply, they have strong views and are guided spiritually, for guidance and relief, once they have achieved maturity and balanced, then this person can be a powerhouse of inspiration to others. If not they go into solitude and become very defensive.

The influence of desire. Human beings are naturally born selfish, just like animals, and therefore we at times behave as such, or irrational. If most, if not all our behaviour is flung into the psychology pot and roasted to see our behaviour, if it can be described and digested, then we will go hungry for sure. We can explain a lot and predict very little about human behaviour. Remember psychology is not a "science" based on a fact, but a belief based on the appearance of something scientific, just like religion. Consequently psychology is the best answer to the problem of diagnosing human behaviour. Most of what propels us can be traced to one source, desire. Desire transcends reason. Most of our desires are either self-motivated or circumstance orientated and we crave fulfilment. Either instant or delayed gratification will do, but mostly instant. This pressure to satisfy a want is called desire. Desires pressures us to give rise to subconscious needs, literally controlling and overriding reason at times, and influencing our every move, to the extent that some desires become habits and automated, and burnt into our Nero pathways. Like smoking. The highest desire is to be spiritually enlightened or looking for something that emulates joy and ecstasy. Desire equals **"Will"**, and the one with the most **will-power** is almost always the one that full fills the most desires. Both willpower and desire are two poles of the same thing, they cannot exist the one without the other. The word **will** in the dictionary is defined as; *the action of willing or deciding to do something; the exercising of the mind with conscious intention towards initiating a chosen action.* You always act upon the strongest emotion and that is desire— subject to the absence of pain, hunger, and need for shelter – warmth, shade, and the basics of human needs. **Power** is a measure of an entity's ability to control the environment around itself, including the behaviour of other entities and elements. Combined, it becomes Willpower, the strength to act, or forbear from acting, in the pursuit of a goal. Includes two powers, that of;

- Self-discipline, training and control of oneself and one's conduct, usually for personal improvement.
- Self-control, the ability of a person to exert his/her will over the inhibitions of their body or self.
- Willpower also implies something basic; the will to live, the will to succeed against all odds, the will to prevail against great suffering...survival.

Basic human needs always act as a restraining influence; so that we may not go outside our means, and just keep perusing desires all day, and stop to fulfilling higher order needs through reason. Reason dictates that we must have food in our bodies, be healthy, be warm or cool, depending on the weather. Only when the basics are grounded, do we move up, to sex and family, safety and security, and then total desire. Desires are somehow suppressed when we have no means to fulfil them, then our most basic of human needs take preference and get all our energy, and then only sex becomes second and higher order as it is free. By desire, and desiring to be someone better, some place nicer, or with someone loving, or wanting something, we start the process of creation, and we create expectations, that create hope. **Desire and hope** are the two strongest motivators to achieve any goal with. However, it is also a double-edged sword. Spiritual leaders teach that "free us from desire". Why, and then they go on and say that, "desire is the root cause of all suffering" and even evil. I thought that desire is a very positive and powerful emotion and the first step to any achievement and self-up-lift-ment. However what this implies is, it is rather the temptation/s that pursuing of desire brings, that we should caution against, it is the *binding* effect of desire with forbidden fruits, and unscrupulous ways, that the caution is against. That we must free ourselves from temptation to do no evil in pursuit of unspeakable desires, and not desire per se, as it is a human emotion. Unbound desire gives rise to aggression where it is not realised, the need for power and dominance is also a last resort to get what we want and take it no matter the implications. Arrogance and ignorance is dangerous, bounded with desire it becomes lethal. Desire is not the culprit; desire is a gift and a force. The problem comes in with how we work with it, and to what extent do we abuse it. Desire, also can evoke a paired interaction among individuals, where they pair up, or team up and force people to compete for attention, favour, grace or whatever, here we determine hierarchy and test dominance. The freedom of choice and the binding of desire to action give rise to competition and conflict, on the one hand, and on the other to self-fulfilment and success. The predator and hunter within must learn to resist people that wish to dominate us with selfish desires. We will and should all ultimately become immune to their evil venom, to the disapproval of our fellows, when we desire more approval, recognition and better for ourselves. We should pursue desires, test everything and keep the good, and leave those behind that do not support and want the same things for us. You should be able to say that if the only weapon an opponent has against you is his disapproval, then he is very poorly armed man and no match for you. We all would like to think that we are not bound by desire, that it cannot tempt us to be selfish or devious, cunning and or manipulative, and lure us. That we have total power over it, and not it over us. If we think this we are mistaken it does. Desire in itself is consider to be a liberty, a freedom to do exactly what one chooses, when it is not distorted by patterns of ignorance, and greed, then it is a very powerful influence on us, and others, a force of growth and evolution, a true power of up-lift-ment and achievement. Whether it becomes a source of bondage or liberation for us depends upon our relationship with it, and how we bound it and with what: what level of self-knowledge – wisdom - we have of using it and not it us. The Freedom to choose and the intelligence to measure your actions against principles, and then to do, or refrain from pursuing your desires, for what you desire is important, but not always rational, reasonable or attainable. Remember that life itself is one big conflict, a battle of wills, and willpower, the conflict between the strong and the weak and the smart and the stupid. Do not make the mistake of idolizing someone to the point where you are becoming them, and not working on becoming you. Your own life and achievements are all that matters, when one looks back, and not that of others. Let others inspire you, and then you them, but remain focused on harnessing all your power and creating your own realities and legacy.

The final strategic influence and challenge - our collective cognisance.

Cognisance describes a knowledge or awareness of something. In this instance it is a sense of self-awareness and realization. Total awareness is a state of mind that explores in all four wind directions simultaneously, that makes us vigilant, curious, contemplating and cautious all in the same instance. Then we become socially aware as well, not just mission orientated, systematic and calculated, no we mix, and feel the energies at work, we feel what others are thinking and saying about us, and how this influences us to withdraw or excel. Creating a clear and certain mental anxiety, that all our thoughts are somehow connected, and people can influence our thoughts and perceptions. Only with true critical thinking; the thinking about your thinking, and self-evaluation, do we fosters correct perceptions, and actions, which lead to the correct emotions and further actions to match any given situation, because we are aware of what and how people think and perceive certain actions and words.

Perceptions, emotions, and actions are a balanced trinity for creation, essential for awareness and strong strategy.

We have covered perception, and actions, we will now soak on the importance of evoking the right emotions in people, to get the balance of creation right. Why is it important to calibrate people's emotions during strategy? No aspect of our mental life is more important to the quality and meaning of our existence than emotions. What we feel and how we feel matters more than anything else in this world. Our reality consists not only of the present state of things, but our perceived past as well. Only when our awareness of all things human and significant to the cognitive balance has been formed, will the strategic trinity make visible that which we desire, and experience as emotional burst of excitement, and manifest in one way or the other, that which we vividly imagined. Only by gaining awareness of all things significant strategically and utilizing knowledge and incorporating wisdom well, do we end up having balanced perceptions, emotions, and actions that form the strategic trinity of creation.

For example, we often mistakenly assume that others act upon influences that are identical to our own, and in the very same fashion as we would. Given the same circumstance, it seems likely that everyone else would behave the same, but we don't. Then we get hurt, frustrated or confused. In reality, there is more to triggers for behaviour than just environmental circumstance. There is emotional influences that run deep, that move us, or harm us; combined they either lead to passion and excitement, or agitation and turmoil, that create perception and results of its own nature, requiring some form of action. We all differ vastly in our individual experiences, and patterns of thinking, just as much as we do in physical appearance. Whatever programs we have assimilated into our neural pathways, and our genetic tendencies, and all what we have learned, our total sum of being manifest in our emotions. Feelings does not define our current emotional and physical state, and the orientation and degree of sophistication we have achieved, neither, nor our spiritual and mental development. However, all this will altogether have bearing on our thinking and behaviour, in one way or the other. All too often it is our emotional buttons that get pushed, that awaken dark or light, which will determine the path that determines what circumstances we are born into and encounter throughout life most. This aspect complicates the psychology of our business as strategist, and the "nature vs. nurture" dichotomy concerning human behaviour and how to influence it from a strategic perspective.

The Nature vs. Nurture debate covers to what extent do we get our skills, attitudes, and so on directly through our genes from our parents vs. acquiring them from our experience. Some scientists think that people behave as they do because of their genetic predispositions or even "animal instincts." This is known as the "nature" theory of human behaviour. Other scientists believe that people think and behave in certain ways because they were taught to do so. This is known as the "nurture" theory of human behaviour. Either way, and until they have figured it out, we need tool to fix people, service them, and keep them fine-tuned.

Nevertheless, confusion sets in when we fail to reconcile people's behaviour with our own, or are at a loss to explain it, then we get frustrated with them, "they are stupid". Humans have an inherent tendency to deduce other people's intentions only from their actions. Then a paradox arises, because reality now conflicts with our own assumptions of correct actions, and our attempts to solve this paradox without growing further awareness, creates much confusion. The trinity of creation is not in balance, if it does not have equal amounts of good perceptions, emotions, and actions for the trinity to exist. This aspect only puts our minds through the perpetual grindstone, where we race to find the answers. Now we need to check whose perception is out of sync with reality, and a process of new awareness starts. In such cases, our perceptions are skewed and even devastated if we were not made aware of distinctive differences on human behaviour during intense situations of strategy and planning, as well as execution. We have to be aware of all things in heaven and on earth to be at a higher level of consciousness as the strategist.

Divergent Thinking is the growing of awareness so that we may understand that creation is impossible without balance first; and to have one reference point to work with, this binds us, around a sense and purpose to form unity. Unity between our perceptions, emotions, and actions, as a group is necessary before we can create with intent, this is referred to as unity with intent, where we have the same perception, emotions and perform the same actions. This is however a desired state, and for most a steep learning curve, and to some extent for us all; we all have experiments and experiences with human nature, good and bad. One thing we have learned, without one common vision we only have chaos, a vision shared is a vision realised. Many a life lessons we have learned and some may have to re-learn them, that not everyone is kind, predictable, gifted, sane, honest, and most importantly - like us. So we can't influence them all...

We can only allow, prevent and influence things that have less freewill or will-power than us, and that we are more cognisant of. In other words you have to be wiser, smarter, and more informed in order to be in a position to influence people in general. Furthermore, we can only exercise our freewill over people if they allow it, over objects that we have means over, and over beings and animals that have less freewill than us. Then, only with proper awareness to direct your will in the right direction, will you be able to do so with others, of the same strength as yourself and stronger. If you cannot control your will, then you will be commanded and lose your willpower. Then nothing will happen that is greatly significant. Where we do not perceive fairness, we seize to contribute. Fairness or justice is the **perception** that any relative deprivation of our rights are relatively under control, and we are all sharing and sharing alike.

Exercising our freewill is not a matter of struggle versus no struggle at all, what you have to do and the way you have to do it is incredibly simple, it's by choice. Whether you are willing to do it, or not, that is the distinction, for everything we experience, we do so because we were willing, of our own free will. The difference between hard and soft applications of our will, comes with the amount of power we give it to succeed, willpower is like pedalling a bicycle in thick sand, and making progress, it's like attempting to get indifferent people going in a direction, and then one gets it right, with much effort. It's a totally different approach from the norm, from people doing the same thing because they are willing, doing same on a flat road for instance, with likeminded people, opposed to doing it in sand. Willpower is the adrenaline when you have nothing else left to make it in time with, you best effort.

Since childhood we have only assembled some likeminded people around us, because they will – think, and share the same beliefs as us. We associate better with people that do not struggle much to convey a message or their will, sharing the same language and culture is a rule. Someone we can relate too and communicate effectively and effortlessly with. This is natural, but when we work we do not have this luxury and we have to work with diverged personalities. The chameleon effect, a psychological phenomenon, this effect is similar to the nurture theory, in saying that people imitate the behaviours of others around them that yield required attributes or results; that are successful, and smart, or powerful etc. The environments in which we live with the people around us affect how we behave - resistance to change is futile, as it is all around, and this change is also a change in energy, and cognisance.

The fact of the matter is too little influence, too little progress, and progress becomes slow. Too much influence and progress becomes impossible. The bike in the sand analogy, best describes how an environment can impede the best of intentions and even machinery for us to form and work with. We can use, influence or resist it, only when we are aware of its nature and effect. The greater the competition, the higher the initiative and creativity spawned, to overcome the ingenuity of the other. The purpose of true reality creation is to remove unnecessary friction in the internal environment as well as influences and perceptions, so that creation can take place in harmony and collaborative to focus on the external environment as the only enemy, and have no enemy within to deal with - so that the resistance is just right internally for good collaboration and initiative. You can't manage others if you can't or won't influence them daily, and they must be influenced properly, and not be bullied into submission. Remember the standard practiced is the standard that will prevail, therefore don't use tactics and measures that you don't want deployed and used against you. Influencing others is a fundamental managerial activity, and an art. Being effective at influencing others usually doesn't mean using your leverage only, to push them around ... but sometimes it does. It's more a game of catch and release. The best managers actually use a range of influence tactics, and balance them off with rewards...influence is neither an enemy nor a friend, it is a very sharp sword that cuts both ways, if not carefully and skilfully used, it is never a good substitute for common decency or straight forward negotiations...or reason.

The Strategic Time Spiral Continuum

Whether you think you can do a thing or not, in either case you are right.

The Strategic Time Spiral Continuum starts off with this notion, by looking at our thinking premise and culture first, and how any paradigm shift could influence our overall thinking at the core.

If indeed we were ever in doubt about the power of our thoughts, this ability to think, that informs us whether we are capable or not of doing things as perceived. Then this is proof enough. The mind functions mostly with perception – insight - and distinction – the ability to recognise difference. These two elements give us the ability to distinguish true from false, certain from probable, consistent from inconsistent, only from using our own opinions. That is to say, it is always *our thinking* above all else, and not our inner-self, our "nature" and "nurture" linked with the clutter of many ideas in our minds and the heat of our emotions, that will always influence our behaviour ultimately. No, it's thinking, it is all about thinking, thinking becomes the compass, it even transcends into our worth, status, judgment, character, culture, health, religion, and the list goes on, literally everything we are, do and say. Because of this, our mindset will also filter into our strategy, and so too other people's ideas – mindsets - and cultures that we come in contact with. Influences keep seeping into our mental fibre, like water seeping into the earth...likewise thinking penetrates everything we connect with on the cognitive level.

The way we should be thinking

Strategy therefore both exist or fails because of our own way of thinking. From the very start, any strategy needs to influence thoughts, in the direction of thinking critical, that is to say we need both conceptual and analytical thinking, in order to create something worthwhile with strategy.

Critical thinking becomes the sum of many parts, it also requires background skills such as imagination and creativity, logic and reasoning, **conceptual and analytical thinking**, these skills gives us reflection and feedback. Critical thinking's main aim is to find new and innovative ways of solving problems. **Critical thinking** is also accepting nothing at face value, but rather examining the truth and validity of arguments and evaluating the relative importance of ideas. It then leans on two attributes, *conceptual and analytical thinking to make it both effective and efficient. Where* **Conceptual thinking** is the kind of thinking that allows a person to "see" something that others may have missed. Like pattern recognition, mismatches, links, solving enigmas. It tends to be more creative, artistic, and instead of just working on any detailed analysis, it looks at other means, as an alternative, we rather look at the bigger picture. It also emphasizes looking at random un-related ideas, and then shifting of our point of view by looking at how problems were created, rather than just how to solve them. Then there is also ***Analytical thinking***, the kind of thinking that instead of focusing more on the bigger picture, looks at the opposite, it focuses on a smaller scale by making detailed analyses, studies, testing and examining specific issue and using this detailed analyses to create new knowledge and insight. If we ourselves are not aligned in this mindset, to design and create with opposing insight, duality, then likewise we can't replicate the patterns of conceptual and both analytical thinking that will be required in strategy.

Furthermore, strategy needs to serve a purpose. It needs to get us excited and involved, even emotionally attached. Its primary purpose needs to be served, it needs to solve a problem we have. Therefore we all need to think we can do this thing called strategy first, before we will arrive at this stage *of having fun with it, and doing it* right. For this to happen, we need to be readied. People need to be ready to be tested. They need to be conversant and confidant enough with strategy, and in their own self before we can get them to perform at their ultimate level, and deliver with their ingenuity. This sounds simple enough, it's not. The mind seriously needs to be prepared for change, any radical strategy, it's not a turnkey process. Thus it is all about cultivating specific mindsets first, that can deal with turmoil; that will influence right thinking, and cultivate self-control, to guide our emotions that can lead us astray as well. It is only when we know ourselves and our abilities well, that we become aware that our emotions are not reactive impulses to be suppressed, but signals — coming from within our soul, a deeper consciousness — warning us of the hidden implications of our actions. Only with a readied balanced self do we become aware of the multiplicity of thought we require to make sense of extreme forms of creation. We have to brake with conventional thinking patterns first, before we enter radical strategy, to break free of the taught *dualistic* thinking we have been indoctrinated with.

The way most of us are programmed to think today

When we think **dualistically** we are doomed to fail - Dualistic thinking is the way most people think and act today, it is the "us vs. them", we are superior they are not, syndrome. It even transcends the obvious, it becomes a victim mentality. It's their fault they made me this way. It's his or her fault. Never, do we take stock, and own up. When the facts speak for themselves, we were not all created equal. We are who we are because of what we are, by choice. **Self-esteem** withers at the point where your confidence in your future reality seizes to give you steadfastness, in the belief that you have everything you need to reach that future. If not, then you believe that its others that will make you happy, and a better person. This is not the case. It is only you, that can make you happy. Stop looking for others to blame for your incapacity. Laziness, forces incapacity, and in turn it forces you to seek out alliances to feel safe, then you are doomed. Then you are no longer thinking, just following. These unholy alliance form from weakness and incapacity to think, and most importantly **act** with esteem – if you don't believe you have and can add value. Again, it's our thinking only and not others that will determine our future. When we rob ourselves of our worth due to our thinking, then we will repeatedly succeed in **diminishing** ourselves in the presence of others, when we believe, or perceive that we are inferior. Because of this, like-seeks-like, we then have weak seeking out weak to form bonds with. When you **feel that others are more superior** - and constantly judging your thoughts, your culture and ideas, then you are lost to dualist behaviour, then you would rather align emotionally than intelligently yourself with your future. These type of alliance has the potential to breed conflict, with serious complications. It then tends to bring out the worst in people, to some, a false sense of belonging, superiority, and internal comfort to know that they are part of the "inner circle" of something great. Just how great they haven't been able to figure out yet, but they are assured it's great. They then feel reassured that their thoughts and sense of worth are commonly shared "values", therefore correct ones, and feel vindicated that they are right and others then, must be wrong. It's a blind conformity to an absurd reality of perceived power, power that does not exist to better itself, only to enslave. This way of thinking only diminishes self-esteem, with the result that we find inflated egos, or a warped sense of reality emitting, thus making them feel like they belong to something different, that gives then power, and worth. When in fact all that we require to prosper in peace is that each individual should only do their own personal level best, without being judged. The dualistic behaviour traits we employ daily are determined not only by the nature of anything we are observing and learning from, but also by social systems of class and politics and social structures we align ourselves with, even culture. Things that others have taught us that we have adopted, on the back of the likes of politics, religion, faith, schooling, tribal beliefs etc, it just keeps re-enforcing false hope and beliefs. Many people today are doomed by their victim mentality. They take no responsibility for their own self image, and who they have become, it's always someone else, that made them this way. When we should in fact only be dealing with the universe in critical though, this would be considered sound reasoning. We have to follow concepts.

Start thinking with concepts. Here we only deal with images and concepts that our mind has power over. The ability to conceptualize patterns into form, that will relate back to a known concept, by converting the thought experience into an idea, then, once we have the idea, at that time only do we start with actual strategic execution – called a continuum. That is to say conceptual ideas breed strategy that solve problems we have. We can use this to better ourselves, and to better our strategy. However, when we conform to any dualistic behaviour on the side of working as a collective, it corrupts this thinking, then we only see us and them again, and abstracts, we become locked in the conscious mind that peruses short lived pleasure only, with self-indulged and selfish behaviour as prime focus. The selfish animalistic desires that arise which are capable of ruling humanity. These desires spring from the self-will of the intellect of humanity whom worships the world as a symbol of their material success. Here the human intellect cannot develop, as it becomes lacking in spiritual orientation, we were born spiritual beings, and it cuts itself off from all that is divine. This blocks any previous notion of growth, as we become the victim, with a victim mentality that directs us likewise. Back to nothing. People in this frame of mind cannot build, construct, develop, act, or do anything creative or worthwhile, only survive from day to day, they become a cult unto themselves, and strategy will never serve them. Strategy like thinking is a gift from the divine.

This is the ultimate knowledge required towards having and developing good strategy, hence forth we will be looking at all the elements and attributes of radical and revolutionary strategy and speak of how a continuum starts.

The definition of a continuum is; something that translates into specific strategic behaviour that directly impacts on our performance, and that of others, where performance in turn is shaped by our own perception of what the realization of this thinking should look like, and how we are going to cultivate it...

Solving some of the problems thinking and strategy creates

If we focus on this aspect of building or designing comprehensive strategies; then our strategies should be able to shape and change people as well as their thinking. This is what this chapter is all about, if we shape their behaviour first and foremost and manage their perceptions prior their interaction with any strategy, then we are off to a great start. Understanding the importance of thought at all the three levels of managerial action and their unique thinking processes, and how it gets impacted on, is critical, as thought and instructions cascade, it brings about unique strategy- within strategy, thereby changing face at every level. From the operations and then follows tactical, it keeps changing as a continuum forming from the main focus to where it reaches implementation. It is the creators of strategy that sets the context for all to follow, from the strategic level, to operations, which in turn set the context for the rest, and it will depend greatly upon, how they pass down their own day-to-day tactics and guideline, and reach the coal face with strategic communication and shaping behaviour thus resulting in correct actions or inactivity.

Ultimately, refining the quality of our thinking is up to us as individuals. Most of us are not that optimistic to think that's going to catch on, the majority of people are inherently passive, so we have to do it for them. With behaviour shaping and perception management as tools, we start by focusing on how we communicate, and then only on what we communicate - to become relevant. When we purposefully and attentively steer our **strategic conversation**, then we influence people by giving them focus. We supply the mental hooks and thought material they have to work with. We make it our business to get them to perform their required functions especially well, by feeding them mentally that which they need. Mainly it is because they understand what is expected and required implicitly – clearly now – and have nothing more to focus on or think about. We have to create a legion of doers to assist the few thinkers. Let's face it, not everyone is endowed and gifted, with critical thinking, then better they just do something. Only by keeping our strategic conversation critically focused, can we accomplish this goal. The fact is that what we think about morally, has no relationship with what is real, consequently, as long as the paradigm we function with delivers results, and harms no one, then it does not seem to bother the overwhelming majority of people. Most of our bad ideas that lead top strategies today, especially bad political ideas and its implementation with "so called strategy" fails dismally and no one cares. This is morally wrong. However, no one cares enough anymore, the results of global warming etc... is proof of this on a global scale. It is not all about *Reality*, or *Morality*, it's about getting the job done, it's all about the perception of it. If we don't turn out to wound others with our actions, and if they injure no one at all, then it's all okay. This is just human nature, we are all selfish, and if I have to look the other way, so that I can have my turn next, then it's all good. This implies that bad thinkers don't get weeded out of the thinking population pool, and then multiply faster than you can say scum... We will always have their influences prevailing and have to cater and be aware of these pests. This is one of the biggest problems strategy creates, it creates and empowers bad thinking as well, if we are not careful. Then even grand strategy becomes susceptible to these influences, what do we allow and what must be blocked? It all needs to start with us deliberately shaping the overall perception – our corporate culture, and then only designing the focus of what we want to create, by staying focused on influencing *reproductive behaviour first,* prior to designing any strategy, way before bad influence start seeping in. We have to split the real critical thinkers from the doers, and teach the doers reproductive thinking only.

Reproductive behaviour is behaviour that is focused on minimum waste, and maximising output, being highly effective and efficient, and it also informs and explains what is considered to be success and a job well done, and what is waste. We have to entrench this aspect to become culture, and habit before we can depart with a strategic continuum... Reproductive behaviour is a set *pattern* for achieving success that we eventually use daily, moulded from our own prior learning and experience. Something we can duplicate that explains to others with ease, like principles, that deliver required results consistently and accurately...how to perform this act and get rewarded. Naturally it comes from **reproductive thinking,** this is thinking that becomes "automated" – a good habit or trait that has formed – and used consistently for solving problems with. *Human behaviour is highly adaptive and situational*; that is to say, it operates at different levels of reason, at different times, and in different situations, to ensure that individuals will survive or adapt quickly to change in order to survive or succeed. It does not lean towards the rational of theory or science – as we would like to believe. No, most of our actions are deemed to be instinctive, it's more of a gut (emotional) feeling that informs our decision making mostly. We instinctively know if things will or won't work, in known environments – that is to say familiar places. In these instances where we use our previous experiences and what is already known, more often than science and theory, in order to solve a known problem with, or to inform us on the best course of action – we refer to us following our gut. This is very common thinking. For example, when a person is given several known problems to solve, on a daily basis, they deliberately examine the relationship among its parts to see if there is a pattern they recognise, and once they see the pattern they just act. By looking at problems as patterns relating to concepts, we start seeing where things fit in, and we get to process them faster. That is fits in with the totality, until we reaches the "aha!" moment, by only using what is already known, and matching it with things (patterns) we understand – then we create internal order.

"Unknown" problems on the other hand – are things we have never encountered before, they take longer to solve, with the *"known unknown"* elements present, which refers to circumstances or outcomes that are known to a certain degree to be plausible or possible, but it is unknown whether or not they will be realized exactly as contemplated with certainty. Where we face substantial limitations and unknown risk, we will never really cure the emotional anxiety of the unknown. Rather, we can learn to understand the creative process and work with the process and break free of the hold the anxiety of the unknown holds over us. The hardest truth we will ever have to face is learning to stay focused and be happy with what is, as it is, in the realization that everything is perfect just the way it is, even the anxiety we feel when our world seems to crumble, or when faced with the complexity of the unknown in the now situation. It's part of a pattern, a cycle, busy shaping that often involves the application of critical thinking to see the connections made, and patterns formed. We deal with these instance by thinking both **conceptual and analytical,** and looking to see where the patterns we recognise will emerge.

Solve problems with Pattern Recognition

Only when we use different levels of consciousness to solve different types of problems with, do we find patterns that reoccur randomly amongst all problems we get to solve. The conscious brain identifies with the past and future in finding solutions faster if it is focused narrower. The non-conscious brain only recognizes the "NOW". Our memory spans for the two components differ dramatically, as the conscious brain is limited to about twenty seconds, while the non-conscious brain remembers everything it experiences forever. Some of it at a conscious and others at a subconscious level. Nonetheless, we know things without "knowing" how. We need to start trusting our instincts, our gut again. Because if we focus people we get meaning emerging, and this pollinates others thinking too, to follow the pattern to experience the meaning for themselves – people require focus. We were never created victims of our own thinking and desire, it is only when we lose focus of what is truly important that it corrupts us. We only become victims due to our early experiences, in following patterns that become addictive and harmful, and the resulting misconceptions that were reinforced by others that then crystallised into habits for ourselves. We carry about ourselves and about life the thoughts, dreams, nightmares and scares of our past and the realities they created. Do not trust your negative patterns of though and the emotions that attend them. You can change any thinking and thereby thought that control behaviour, but you must first take full responsibility for every thought, emotion, and behaviour you created a habit from, before attempting to alter them.

Solving the problems we created for ourselves, that set beliefs and views bring, is a human flaw we all have, and a burden we share. There is a tendency to derail the views of others, because I want to be right, or its not time to change yet – this comes with perception - the things that gives meaning to our own experiences and events. This is called a bias. Perceptions that are in contradiction to others perception is called a bias. Explaining our cognitive biases as an attribute of a mental process, that individuals go through when they have to make a computationally complex judgment, we do get the answer, but refuse to reconcile with it. Instead of making the difficult judgment, we unconsciously substitute an easily calculate virtual reality in its place - a heuristic (Heuristics are escaping strategies used, somewhat rational though loosely related to a truth, to form an argument against the judgement, that is not necessarily true, but seems so on the surface of it). In other words we can lie, and fool ourselves and others in to believing in pain, suffering and wrong things, because we are in denial.

These counterproductive mental strategies are simple rules that everyone uses everyday when processing information, they generally work well for us; however, they occasionally cause serious systematic errors, aka, cognitive biases that stop us from going over to necessary action, because we don't want to, or don't believe it will benefit us. Whenever or not we are taking action by responding to our correct thoughts, or not, either way it's inevitable starts evoking action, internally it evokes emotion, and for every action, there is a coinciding memory, which serves as an interpretation for us of our perception of this specific event. It is very important not to "think:" in the middle of emotional spells, but simply to allow the flow of that emotion to exit. Emotion distorts thinking if we allow it to take lead, and then it evokes bias, as we feed it rationality. This is the dual system of thought that creates the meaning we seek in all we do, the rational path and the emotional path needs to work in balance. The experience, interpretation, memory, and desire test needs to balance inward, before we will get outward the required results. We need to get our "aha" moments from balance. Rewards outwards, informs us if we connected inwards or not. Only if we are happy with our thought, will we be happy with others thinking. All of this seemingly automated behaviour is very closely connected in the time spiral field, of social behaviour and beliefs, and can be accessed intentionally to create change. The good news is we can change ourselves, and people, and their bias, on a personal and cultural level. We need to create change in people's habitual behaviour patterns in order for all to align, connect and focus on the ultimate goal. Perception management is a goal alignment and focus creation tool. Without aligning everyone's focus perfectly before we start, we will be losing cohesion and effort, and chaos will ensue. This is part of behaviour shaping, people shape their behaviour in line with others in order to get results, rewards and pleasure, and then it becomes a habit, that starts forming a culture. Once the behaviour is successful, then they will want more. Behaviour shaping sounds like a very complicated concept, but it's actually very simple, shaping consists of breaking the behaviour you want down into tiny little increments, or steps, thus forming a pattern, and then training/ explaining them to others, one step at a time.

Behaviour patterns like anything strategic deals with thoughts that become focused. Once we decide to act on the vague concept of a thought, it becomes a reality. Repeatedly entertaining the same thought produces the habitual traits we need, called behaviour, and behaviour starts resonating a pattern to be duplicated. Thinking the same thoughts and attracting positive results enforce a belief, thereby generating the pattern, that will render the same results, if copied. Some thoughts are so empowering that the patterns are just assimilated. People see, they like and adopt the behaviour. This process of following patterns subsequently produces a tangible outcome, it creates a habitat for success breeding habits. We become more like the likeness of the people we keep close company with cognitively, than the people we have as family. Habits enforce our physical experience of reality too, that with time becomes part of our total character.

Understanding behaviour is equated with being able to predict with a certain amount of conviction, for a given subject, what the behaviour will be at a given time. We aim for this, in order to create certainty and predictability in all things strategic. The more we understand human behaviour, the more power we will have in influencing and changing it. Behaviour psychology is advancing almost daily, governments, media, armies, corporations and the like are using it to keep their population in control, and to steer and influence public opinion. Do you honestly think we have become immune to mind control, pacifists maybe yes, now they use it even on our children too.

This is strategy performed at its pinnacle, as mental warfare and mind control. We need to get a taste for it, and a feel. In order to defend and both attack if need be.

Here we look at strategy from an entirely different and more mental prospective. Removed from the norm of the step by step theoretical formulation of strategy taught daily. All good but by now we know there is more to it. We want to move strategist towards higher order strategy in this book, with forms or pattern recognition. The "Gut instinct" is basically a form of patterns and recognition, we have all done it and will keeping do it. The more you practice self-reliance, the more patterns you will intuitively start recognizing, that lead to success. Highly intuitive and successful business people will tell you there are patterns to success. However it's not all set in stone either, what will work for one won't work for all, it's mostly *situationally appropriate.*

The need to be intuitive

You need to be cognisant and intuitive all the time, tapping into the collective until you experience that "aha" moment. Where our reason, imagination or interest are not engaged as one, focused, then we have difficulty connecting, then we are no longer intuitive, open to possibility, and experiencing and learning things. This is the only time where you will start seeing the pattern, where reason, imagination and interest are all engaged as one mental kaleidoscope, then you are intuitive, then you are receiving the gift of the gab. People often let themselves be talked out of very good ideas just because they are not intuitive enough, or lack the strength of self actualisation. We are not all created equal, no, generally you're either better with either people or things. Not both. We get practical and theoretical, musical, artistic and the lot, all patterns or models emerging from within us, from our DNA code, that make us better at some things and poor at doing other. However, becoming intuitive, and then tapping into the greater consciousness, is by choice...

The Power of Cognisance

Now we can look at strategy as a mental form, requiring a pattern for success. From a cognitive point of view of course (cognitive -relating to the process of acquiring knowledge by the use of reasoning, intuition, or perception) to create a new reality with. Becoming cognisant is having cognisance; an awareness of your own individuality an intuitive awareness; "he has a feel for animals" or "it's easy when you get the feel of it". The you also get a general conscious awareness; "a sense of security"; "a sense of happiness"; "a sense of danger"; "a sense of self" a clear and certain mental fear of the unknown. It's a person that is aware of himself, his surroundings and the things unseen, that influence us daily. The influence of an individual's needs and desires both have a strong impact on the direction of their behaviour, and if very strong it will influence others around them. This is the strong at mind, the cognisant people, the ones that are creative and in tune... now we also have those that are not so.

Especially if they have personal needs that are yet unsatisfied, then no amount of behaviour shaping, or pattern enforcement will get them to shape their behaviour according to a required pattern. If we want to be able to show people the way with strategy, as it really transpires, and becomes significant, then we need to capacitate them to solve personal problems first, and solve their own needs. You first need to have personal focus, before we can create strategic focus. The thinking behind the idea of shaping behaviour is described by observational learning, the learning of a new skill or set of behaviours by observing another person perform these skills/behaviours, and getting a result or reward that they too would like. For example, you have to work to get money; or steal, or bribe etc....seeing how this works, observing the pattern, makes the learning curve shorter. Seeing is believing. Now you can satisfy a need via one chosen way. However, is this the right way? This is why we want patterns to make sure people solve problems the right way – legal – in this instance.

We need forms or ideas to give us insight

Strategy starts with these things called ideas, us solving problems of want or need, or just things we are entertaining and want to realise. Ideas are also the product of our thinking, and not just academic and scientific reasoning joined that forms a concept or idea only. No! far removed from it, academics and scientists are just tools we use to find patterns with, where ideas jump in and out of consciousness daily as a fact of life. Now in order for any of these great idea to take shape, we have to think about them, then become conscious to capture them, and pin them to a point in space, and start thinking about them critically first. Thinking critically implies that we have to wipe away all other thought and distractions, and channel all our mental energy into realising one idea and solving the problems it creates, one at a time. Here our ideas get subjected to a pattern of thought that is systematic, and specific; dealing with one or all aspects of reasoning critical. Be it either academic, rational, scientific, emotional and or creative thought patterns that we apply etc, before it will necessitate form that will give it structure. This "pattern of thought" we subject our ideas to will determine the direction of thinking to follow on. The way we start with thinking - with ideas - will determine if they will be successful or not. *It's the start that stops most great ideas from seeing the light,* and not always the process we refer to as strategy. Critical thinking deals with recognising cognitive patterns for the design of things, it makes up the components that we need, for strategy to ultimately make sense and deliver. By thinking both *conceptual and analytical,* and looking to see where the patterns are that we need to recognise. To give our ideas form.

Plato was the one who gave us more of this insight, by promoting the theory of forms or ideas to explain how thoughts strive to become reality. This theory goes further and entertains forms or ideas that come from perfect models; timeless wisdom, and things emanating from patterns in nature and the universe, and also things we know to exist as a race without having studied them. Nothing is new, it's just rediscovered, reused or reinvented etc. Plato argued supplementary that ideas are ultimately real things existing, blue prints of something that already exist, like patterns re-emerging in other time spirals in time, called continuums, where they become a new reality. Where one idea sparks several other ideas, forming a totally new concept at a different point in time, where it then becomes reality, this then becomes the design or form of that idea, and starts a continuum.

Designing the strategic continuum with intent

The entrenched norm is to start planning, or brainstorming first, when we talk about formulating strategy. You will find the white board at the front with the words, VISSION, MISSION and GOALS written on it. Well it's time to break this mould. We need to create narrow focus first, on the idea we want to realise and nothing ells first. It needs to be our intent, our focus, our mission our vision. That of - *Designing with intent*; if all designs have one thing in common, it's that they all have specifications and patterns. We have to invent ways out of the now and into the future. Invention requires new attributes. Invention means to come up with a unique idea, thought or fabrication; a new object, device or process that no one has seen or used before. Something that we all can relate to, and we are going to use it in order to understand and transfer strategy better. All aspects of design influence our environment, both socially and physically, and especially in the way we use things and consequently also our own behaviour. However, if we can design our strategy's to influence behaviour first, then we will in effect also change paradigms, and habits, and have pre-empted things that cause bias, and error. This we have now established.

Critical thinking clarifies goals, examines assumptions, discerns hidden values, evaluates evidence, accomplishes actions, and assesses conclusions.

We now understand that we need to change and influence behaviour at the point where it needs to create one focus, and vision. Here at the start of the formation of any idea, to become a strategic continuum. Reason being, we have all seen how using only planning as a departing concept to form this strategic aspect with has derailed us in the past. Planning sessions as the main forerunner to any strategy has run amok with us, as everyone comes with his or her own great (dualistic) idea, that points us in many different directions, and it becomes time consuming to work through all the politics. This process has wasted and killed brilliant ideas. We need to design with intent and focus, this reflects an new approach towards incorporating behaviour shaping – by following the duality in design principle. This also proves that through design we can shape not only strategy but behaviour as well. Thereby designing a strategic pattern for interaction. Pattern recognition becomes a new tool. Where we become aware that all things have a pattern, a life cycle, from cradle to grave. Four seasons, become a year, tyres wearing off, then you get a blow out, it all has patterns, both observable and predictable.

Patterns also relate to form, clearly observable in Architecture, error proofing designs, by testing them, putting warning labels on products, instructions, and supplying instruction manuals. Daily people adopt patterns, that with time become habits to work with, they must make many decisions as to how they will solve some problems. Each problem becomes a pattern design. It is given a name, (driving, eating, dressing etc.) and segmented in to criteria – (home, work, social etc). Patterns can also be copied, and passed on, a pattern is also a reverence model, or template that can be successfully duplicated with the same predictable outcome when applied. Opposed to our traditional definition of planning; planning is typically any procedure used to achieve an objective with, great, this explains a lot.

When in fact what I should say is. Only once all the objectives are set, clear and specific in every way, only then can we use the planning tool, to take us from our objective to action, to the final goal. This is where the tool "planning" then becomes useful.

How do you explain strategy like this to people? When strategy as a process and tool to deal with complexity, is in itself diverse and complex. Especially where people are at different levels of competence and skill. Then how do you make it relevant to all, because it concerns everyone of us?

When things become specific, they become known, then only do they become clear, after that they become observable and therefore more real – this is the life cycle of creating understanding with all who reason.

The thing about behaviour shaping is this, it takes time. Where *Certainty* creates passionate belief, and trust, *Hope* only weathers away like a flag in the wind. We don't want to invest time only to get to the end of our journey and find fragments of our reality. With the designing of strategy we aim to create more certainty, especially if strategy can be "seen" by all concerned. Because of this, we use the word design and not plan intentionally. So that we may better explain how differently we attack the commencement of any strategy. To design something, implies that we require exact detail, specifications, and facts. To plan something implies that we are not sure of the outcome, we are taking a chance, and it's okay to work with assumptions only or mostly. How many times have you heard them say we have a NEW PLAN. Implying, that everything you have worked on before is now nullified. Where with design, we just change what doesn't work and carry on, we don't change direction, and total work environments. To design something is to make a detailed drawing or graphical representation of something - that shows how it is to function or be made - first to scale and then full size. Then emphasizing specifics of each aspect; like features, use, appearance, convenience, cost, and efficient functioning.

Strategy creation – with this mindset, begs for more perfection from people, they can truly see the long term effects, and a detailed holistic approach, from start to finish. We need to explain to people the terminology, the paradigms, before we explain the process, this gives them reference points in their own strategic discussion.

Being more Strategic

Being - Strategic implies; being calculated, and of sound reasoning, having actions performed with intention, based on specific calculation, directed at achieving a goal. Having alternative plans of action, backed up by tactics to get the initiative. If you want to be strategic you require strategy. Strategy should be seen as; always evolving, and it becomes a *seamless process, called a continuum.*

Now the Continuum

A continuum is a continuity of one idea, as it evolves and grows, it starts taking form, losing its imperfections, forming from a composition of elements evolving into a concept, in order to realise a specific idea. The strategic continuum has one goal, aimed at specifically realising just that first idea. Continuums should be seen as strands forming a rope. Several continuums combined could have as its sole purpose to only realise one grand idea. This is why strategy needs to be designed at its start, from the start. Here, at the start, we require specifics for this type of alignment of continuums to come to exist in harmony. If not, its "like a river in flood" – we have endless ideas – and assumptions - flowing in all directions, all un co-ordinated, and even unrelated, in the minds of people. Where no part or portion becomes distinguishable at certain times anymore. Then we find that the left doesn't know what the right is doing, then strategy becomes overwhelming and complex. Subsequently with more time it just becomes too much to handle, plain chaos and everyone shies away from it. Just like a river in flood, we get out of its way. This is just brainstorming it. Then when we get all these ideas on paper like bricks of all shapes and sizes it just does not work well when we start building... that was then, this is now.

Today we do things differently. We have learned from the past. Having a clear vision for any strategy implies having specifics, and references to work from. In order to create clarity about what is expected we need to work with specifics, just like baking a cake becomes a delicate science experiment. If we deviate, or miss one ingredient it could turn out a flop. Where strategy starts running away from us, it's because we started off *planning it* and not *designing it*. When you design; you tend to make notes and identify the ingredients, and the amounts and specifications of each, right down to the last detail. We do this with something as simple as baking a cake, why not in business, why do we think taking short cuts will deliver better results. When the same patterns emerge for creating something from elements. We need to get back to basics; to strategic parts and design elements. With elements in mind, the how to be strategic becomes more import, than why. Because we now understand why we need to make sense of strategic design and incorporate all elements that create clarity. When we seek clarity through the design of strategy, we create an amount of certainty for all. Only if we break complexity down into parts, can we slow it down, and start understand it. Here time as an attribute of strategy slows down as well, the river of ideas then spreads out and flows slow and shallow, and then becomes observable, clear, we can identify nuts from bolts, and bricks from stone, clearly and calmly. Start slow...

The troops need to be trained and readied for war. This is not a rush job in the military, neither should it be in enterprise. Armies use soldiers, well conversed in doctrine, and battle talk, fighting fit, trained in tactics and strategy. They use strategy to reach their objectives. We have now adopted from them strategy, but we need the whole concept. We need soldiers trained and ready to use our strategy. Sometimes we expect just too much from strategy. We expect strategy to get the troops trained, armed and into the air, see and land – at ready. This is not the job of strategy. Strategy has one general job, and that is to get results with people. Not to train them, and develop them as a rule, except if it is fittingly designed as a training strategy.

Therefore, and before we kick start any strategy. We need to do it with some trained people, with "commanders", thinkers that can lead the doers. That we involve in the design of the main or core continuum. The main or core continuum is the foundation of all that is to follow, and needs to be designed well. This will be the "design specification", or framework in which everything must happen. This main continuum requires *six forming strategic elements* to be present to support the core idea. The more elaborate the idea the more detailed the scheme, thus it could require lots of continuums, to realise it. Here we need to design and decide on the amount of "sibling" continuums we want and will use – that will also be influenced by behaviour changing paradigms we have adopted. Every creation starts with just that one idea, especially when given attention. It then gets energy and evolves with time. Any idea needs more ideas to evolve, and these ideas then form a way of thinking, called a paradigm. It takes one and not several paradigms to support several continuums, and not the other way around, to make the initial idea grow. As the idea evolves, it speeds up taking less time and more effort, and then our awareness takes over, this then starts a *strategic continuum*.

A Strategic Continuum

A Strategic Continuum; is a continuity of one idea along a designed path. It's the initial idea, that gives birth to more and bigger ideas, that link up, to form a composition of elements evolving the concept, until that idea is realised. Consequently, a strategic continuum is a culmination of several continuums assisting the core continuum to become a reality. It also has duality, in that it too in turn also start evolving and manifesting in a focused manner; either the theory or conceptualisation of each idea forming, aiming towards giving form to the original idea, by introducing it to a process of forming, that will give rise to a concept. Where at some stage it must then start to produce results, as contemplated, or the process – and its continuum disintegrates. At the end of a continuum's life, it delivers one of two results; either a concept, or a theory. A concept comes from combining attributes, that form elements. A theory comes from several ideas combined, that become a pattern for success.

Following Patterns for Success

Any success story has a run up, or a build up, it doesn't just happen by accident - rather by incidents building up over time and then coming to conclusion, that created a window of opportunity. History repeating itself is proof of this, were we see incidents reacquiring action, and then later on transpiring into accidents, if we could not see the pattern, pre-empting the fact. If history has any value as a guide, it indicates that we should pay attention to the information being provided to us, by studying patterns, or being aware of their existence. *We are not successful because of what we do daily, or at any given minute, but because we don't want to repeat the same mistakes over and over again.* Same with incidents that lead up to causing accidents. Incidents can cause both, good and bad things to happen. As we build ourselves or our organisation, we see patterns emerging, and at some point, we experience an incident, where we get paid out in dividends, for the effort and time we committed, or we pay up. Only with incidents and accidents do we become successful, the more incidents we create the more and the faster we move. The more accidents we experience the faster we come to demise, if we cannot learn to avoid accidents and create, or learn from incidents then we will have no future. The difference between an accident and an incident is the end state. While the end state in an incident is always recoverable, it is not so in an accident. Especially where we have followed patterns for success, where incidents then happened that created meaning. Meaning in the form of, rendering results that are positive by having followed a pattern, and then devising a strategy, we can then avoid accidents. Accidents happen more often where we are unable to identify the patterns that lead up to them. We become successful because we were made aware of the importance of following some patterns, and avoiding others. When we are successful, it's because we have experienced growth and rejuvenation. This inspires us to utilise and explore more with finding patterns for success. They say success breeds success because it becomes a spiritual pattern. Here in this instance we have a sense of worth and purpose developing, created by these incidents as rewards. Alternatively, we are stressed, or distressed in the absence thereof. In the absences of tools to promote ourselves and our talents with, we become lacking in patterns. This create stress. Psychological distress stems from three patterns emerging: a) from conflict in any form, conflicts of wishes, fears, and fantasies; b) from an absence of perceived meaning and patterns for success, life, work, family loses its meaning; and c) from frustration, the need to progress as an individuals or in a group, is overcome by feelings of restraint by circumstances. **Success** is otherwise governed by self-image and attitude, talent, resilience and ultimately by the choices we have made and skills we mastered, called a pattern for success. Take note, we may all have the ingredients, and never be as successful as what we had hoped. As we all follow an internal pattern as well. Some call it destiny, that derails our outer environments inputs to create incidents and accidents for us. Then the stages of mans development also has bearing on our levels of success, where after forty for instance we lose our will to fight, bleed, and get physical. We relinquish the will to reason repetitively with subordinates, we would rather say how it should be done once and that's that, and rather resort to calm, and meditation to compose and enforce our will. Following these patterns, just guarantees one, that we have the best chances of becoming successful, it is also situational and both incidental. You have to be in the right place at the right time so to speak. Like winning the lottery requires of one to have a dated lottery ticket. Now, this is why having one single pattern for success that works for all, is impossible. Mainly it's because of internal and both external forces that impose specific patterns of experiences required on us, which consistently produces precise outcomes, that influence and control our environment. For example, when I go somewhere, I need to make a picture of where I'm going and how to get there in my mind. This requires calm and focus, and I gather information. When I have enough information, I then move into action, and trust my unconscious mind. That's my strategy for driving somewhere for instance, when I do it successfully, I was aware of all the incidents in my environment. When I don't do it successfully, it's usually because I haven't gathered enough information, my pattern for success –with navigation and driving – has not yet been formed. So, I don't have a clear picture of how to navigate, or drive, and then I may even take the wrong turn or get lost, or be involved in an accident or incident. Do you use a strategy when you go somewhere? Of course you do, although you may not have been aware of it until this moment that it is your patterns for success that aids and guides you. It informs these ad-hoc strategies we use daily. Strategy is in our thinking, and then the detail, that renders the design...that delivers the outcome. If we take one wrong turn, even if the design was perfect, we will not reach our goal. This is incidental patterns that impact on our behaviour, what we do after that will inform us if we got it right or not.

Strategy as a designed affair

Strategy requires a design first, then some planning; where planning aims to steer, and inform the gathering and dissemination of data to capacitate an idea to start a continuum with, to give it form – consistent with the design specification. We cannot follow continuums if we did not design or planned for them. If they disintegrate, it's because we have left out one or the other. Never the less, as they grown, they too become susceptible to influence, then we have to fix what is broken. Strategic design is like tracking ideas in space, that lead to required actions, or should, that lead to process that must render specific results. Planning also assists in the transference of these ideas and resources, from one to other continuums. Starting up other continuums for action, could be a result of planning, once the resource becomes available, or when the previous result renders a product required to proceed with the next stage and continuum. Design gives us a recipe, that combines all this planning, to duplicate and follow with success. Strategy that combines all these designs – with more planning, resources, and give it action. Strategic continuums create the type of clarity we need to orientate people with, when we work with continuum, we work with specifics, distinguishable parts of our strategy segmented from the rest, yet part and parcel of it. Now we have the ability to delegate, outsource, and re-design a continuum at will. Because we can quantify and qualify what we are working with. We can better gauge and influence; our performance, cost, time, and progress. As well as gauge influences caused by duality, both internal, as well as external forces, either attempting to assist or destroy our continuums.

Duality – the influence that both assist and plague strategy

We have been informed that **forces** and **influence** both work with duality in on our design, planning and strategy. They are dually involved in who, what, where, when and how we do things. Every day you see the failures of those who could not *influence - influences, and force* others, and the successes of those who could make their ideas and agendas stick. Forces and influence, are used mostly by a small minority affect the behavior or beliefs of the bigger majority, believing that it was their doing. How is this possible? What factors influence and inform, our tactical, interpersonal, political, social, financial, operational, and strategic decision making to name but a few… next we have influences partner in crime, force.

In science, *force*, usually means either a push or a pull. So what is pulling or pulling your strategy? What is the driver? One of the basic features in physics is the occurrence of forces that keep matter together. Is this the driver? There are for example, the forces that keep the cells together to build up the human body, and there is the gravitational force that keeps us on the ground and the moon in orbit around the earth - what is keeping the strategy together? In physics, a **force** is "any influence that causes a free body to undergo an acceleration or alternatively to decelerate". Otherwise it is the driver; the thing that accelerates us? Force can also be described by intuitive concepts such as a push or pull that can cause an object with mass to change its velocity (which includes to begin moving from a state of rest), i.e., to accelerate, or which can cause a flexible object to deform. Implying that, we have both internal and external forces and influence, that is working in on every continuum. They either create or destroy, add or protract, depending on their duality. This "Duality" implies having two things; acting as one when combined.

There is a mental aspect to this as well, the thinking behind the union – the joining of elements, that also works with duality. Duality is in every aspect of strategy, this is the lesson here. It informs, and influences what have been chosen and combined to form a continuum. Here duality deals with one part certainty and one part complexity, that directly influences the tapestry of creation of strategic continuums. Consequently, and the point is this, we have two levels at the start of creation; one mental, or cognitive, our thinking mind, and the other the physical. Thus forming yet another duality, between inner space and outer space, two aspects influencing and determining the creation path. Therefore we can say that strategy, when seen as a continuum; has a main path, a spine, the main idea that is cognitive, and then the physical creation of that idea. Where everything relates back to our thinking, and either attaches or detaches the physical side. We require the elements of strategy to guide us, because of our thinking. Without strategic elements in place we will be driving creation towards its finality or demise – because of our correct or incorrect thinking.

Creation always moves, as it starts as a cognitive process, that flows and gathers attributes to give it form. *To create is* to think of something as caused by a particular culmination of circumstances, or attributes at one point, and it then gets life and evolves, into a situation or concept. When we combine concepts with physical elements, and deliver on the idea, we have created successfully. Creation is never stagnant, or fixed at one point, it moves and grows, and evolves, and forms the foundation of what is to come. Therefore it is always good to think and then re-think any idea, before we let it loose to grow. Ideas deal with both certainty and complexity – hand in glove, as we engage with it and disengage. It is cause and effect, action and reaction, duality always. As the creation moves on, it creates consequential derivative attributes, new things, that will impact on its balance, its duality, that are either more complex or more certain. We have to learn, and take this to hart, that in life as in strategy - everything affects everything else that follows, as a result of the first union, and the duality.

The first matrix union

The rest of this chapter will describe everything emanating at the first union. *The first union*, is where the joining of an idea to invention, starts a succession of interlocking events, actions, and results, that forms a matrix of unions, that are supposed to render a contemplated result. That in turn will influence the succeeding results. From here on forward, we will be looking at all these elements that interlocks to support the first union. This is the first step of creation that deals with how things need to follow in succession to deliver a result contemplated. Here, we have to expect both the unexpected as well as the desired results and prepare accordingly. Short cycles from first union to where we deliver are best, the longer the cycles the more error can occur, and the longer it will take to fix. However, we must not lose sight that there are still outside forces that will once again influence any creation, both seen and unseen. Forces keep prevailing throughout the whole process of creation – from cradle to grave – certainty and complexity take turns in influencing and confusing our decision making. With creation we bring at times something into existence that normally did not exist before. If this is the case, then we find new, and sometimes unseen characteristics as a result, or new attributes emerging as a result, that we could not have anticipated, or did not expect. Then, *we find uniqueness emanating as a result of our creation.*

Uniqueness emanating as a result of our creation.

This then either gives us certainty to carry on, or raises doubt. At these junctures, we will always find a condition or temperament, called a characteristic that we can identify. That is typically unique to a specific alignment of attributes, that we can work with. Seek the familiar and work from there to the unknown. All things are of its own unique nature before it became complex – rock was sand before it became a mountain, water was rain drops, before it became an ocean, steam was warm before it became a cold cloud. In combination we get new characteristics, with some uniqueness that points us back to the origin. Some things are better understood at its origin than in its final state. Unions that have two states or parts that are either complementary or opposed to each other, create elements of uniqueness, and similarity. For instance fried eggs and bacon equals breakfast. Both states affects the uniqueness emanating, if they were eggs and toast, it would not be breakfast, or bacon and cheese it would not be breakfast, all as a result of the union. The point is this, we want to create more certainty. In some instances when we join things, then we can be certain of the results, in others not. In the one part we can control certain aspects with certainty, in the other part it takes on its own temperament and character. Therefore we have as a result, both certainty and uncertainty living side by side during the creation process of strategy. These aspects create conditions that require both specific, scientific and general action and foresight. Where in some instances, we again have to control, and in other just influence and then anticipate certain eventualities and plan mitigating steps to overcome them. Furthermore, every creation has new and unique issues we will never be able to anticipate, or control. Things that we won't know until they are there. We can either behave instinctive – or strategic in these instances or both, all in order to come to understand things better, and deal with them likewise – especially when we get to meet them for the first time. Thus we should always expect the unexpected so to say, when creating. That we will have to deal with constants, change, and variables is a certainty, and clarity can also be found in understanding without seeing.

This is why. Strategy creation should become much more than just a paper exercise – called planning a strategy. We need to prepare people both mentally to see creatively and speak constructively. Not just academically. Judging from the aforementioned. There is just too much happening and resulting from certain choices and decisions that we make, daily, that could have far reaching consequences, and affects on the total strategic habitat, and to still want to just do things willy-nilly. These affects could only become noticeable years later, and then prove to be catastrophic. There are many things we need to; argue, gauge and test, before we just start implementing them. It has to become a focused, holistic, continuous affair – a strategic continuum.

Strategic Focus is gained by applying the OODA loop, with Observation, Orientation, Decision and Action...or on a tactical level; we Improvise, Adapt and Overcome. These are the things we need to prepare our "troops" with. If there is no time, or direction, at least they still have options. Starting with recognising that duality in all things exist, and because of this things can go "wrong" and pear shaped if we are not careful. Being able to see if building blocks belong together or not, is a question of having dual focus. Just like sperm and egg cells, water and fire, left and right feet, are either similar or dissimilar parts of each other, we need to see all duality both relevant at times, and then irrelevant at other, only then are we off to a good strategic start. Therefore, creating with duality in mind creates more balance and certainty, learn and appreciate the higher order understanding of creating and working with *elements of strategy*, and its building blocks.

Starting with the forming elements of strategy

Six forming elements need to be present before designing strategy. They have been identified as being fundamental to the overall success of any strategy. If applied and present during the design phases of strategy, you will have far greater success with strategy formulation. Here are the strategic elements required of good strategy. People need to be trained in these elements before they are allowed to create strategy or participate in the design thereof.

Perception management and alignment; is a companion to business philosophy, and planning of good strategy. If we depart from the assumption that everything we deal with strategically is based on someone's perception, then perception is of either "things" or "facts". Furthermore, a strategy should point into a direction, or give direction, this direction is based on some form of bias and alignment, of strongly held perceptions. Then alignment is of either "belief", or "orientation". These two aspects have become focal in strategic circles, where strategies are now concentrating on both things that people believe in or perceive to be real and "facts", that they get from being orientated towards a belief or science, and aligning this with strategic objectives. If our perceptions is open and eager, our managers well trained and experienced, and our alignments are spot on, then we have armies ready to serve. Perception management, is a term that originated in the U. S. military. "The definition relates to actions consistent to conveying and/or denying selected information and indicators to foreign audiences. Specifically aimed at influencing, emotions, motives, independent reasoning, as well as intelligence, systems, and leaders at all levels. Furthermore, *the aim is to influence people's beliefs, and opinions, that ultimately result in a desired altered behaviour. Consequently, altered behaviour brings about actions favourable to the originator's own objectives.* In utilising various ways, perception can be manipulated – managed - to combine bits of "truths" about things and "facts", so that eventually it becomes a new reality and a fact."

In the words of the political philosopher Samuel P. Huntington, we use our paradigms to:

1. order and generalize about reality

2. understand causal relationships among phenomena;

3. anticipate, and if we are lucky, predict future developments;

4. distinguish what is important from what is unimportant; and

5. show us what paths we should take to achieve our goals.

The 360 degree perspective *refers to us being able to understand the implications and limitations of design, planning, resources, thinking and strategic actions.* We need to attack everything strategic with an open mind, free from undue influence and bias. Strategic thinkers have to have the cunning abilities of mental modelling - creativity, and insight; the ability to see creation in the mind, and find the necessary relationships required to manifest them. We need mental architects that can design all this, in steps, and be able to design systems for them that will deliver on value creation, consistency and continuity, until we reach the completed end state. In order to be able to design systems with value creation, and quality in mind, we need to be open, to connect to attributes and essentials of strategy, as well as new resources at any given time.

The third competency is ***creating focused understanding and intent;*** *which means looking at better ways of getting more leverage, and getting the whole organisation to the event-horizon, as well as keeping initiative to carry on.*

Only by focusing our efforts faster and narrower with focused intent, do we create continuums. Continuums must and will give us the ability to focus our attention and efforts as a collective on specifics first, to resist diversion, and waste of resources and efforts, and duplication, through well structured work. It is with co-ordinated design and engagement that we structure and create meaningful work, that that precipitates into meaningful results, by means of focused intent, and to concentrate all our efforts as a whole for as long as it takes to achieve the main objectives.

Thinking in time spirals *means being able to bring past, present and future assumptions, as well as relevant aspects into the strategic equation.* Time spirals connect us only through awareness. Only through awareness do we create better decision-making models, make better strategy, resulting in stronger continuums and as a result speed-up implementation and minimise the error margin. We need more from strategy today, "Strategy" is no longer just a buzz word. It is a designed way of thinking, unleashing pools and pockets of potential, backed up with a wealth of ideas. Channelling ideas to become a focused energy – starts a continuum. Strategy in the past was only driven by future focused intent, it must now be changed to create action, continuity and sustainability. If we hope to deliver on the promise of the visions of tomorrow – we need all three these attributes. We have to change our mindsets, our paradigms, to see every strategic action, as an opportunity that creates possibilities. We have to use them to see where we can close some gaps between today's problems and tomorrow's reality, for ourselves and our organisations. Strategic interactions, show us time spirals, these connections between, past, present and future, and it also serves as a learning experience that creates an awareness of old problems, addressed in new ways. Time spirals also relates to history repeating itself, so to climate patterns and incidents and accidents in nature – volcanic eruptions, tsunami, earthquakes etc. By being aware of time, its impact in the past, our history, we may predict with some certainty the present and future, and how to utilise effort at best, as yet another valuable resource.

Critical thinking, the fifth strategic competency is *being skills development driven, by ensuring that both academical, tactical and practical skills are taught and transferred.* By developing intellectual capital, with both imaginative and critical thinking. Critical thinkers need to be identified, even trained, and then utilised at the core of the endeavour, to run with the core continuums...they need not spread their influence to every aspect, if the core is solid. The continuums that will follow, will flow with the same solidity of thinking, by taking from the president and examples set to follow.

The final strategic competency is developing of ***intelligence***; By specifically *identifying personal attributes that enable people to succeed in life, and by developing them.* Developing knowledge, and passing down skills, and behaviour patterns that breeds success. This is also referred to as developing and protecting intellectual capital. This also includes life skills, developing self-awareness, empathy, self-confidence, pride, and self-control. Next level intervention, where we develop instincts, which means being entrepreneurial, and focused on network creation, we create human capital and emotional intelligence, by developing minds. Through and with our business and self actualisation programs, thus enriching people's knowledge. Knowledge has to become a power. They say that anything really worthwhile having, starts with having the courage to go out and find it. Courage is never seen in the absence of fear, this is self-sacrifice, not courage. Courage is driven by fear, then believing in others, and yourself more than in this fear. This creates the flow of strategic energy, and starts a strong continuum of spiralling and stratagem.

Spiralling and Stratagem

Stratagem is also referred to as tactics. Tactics are used at the coalface. Stratagems aim is to create better decision-making models and speedup implementation at the coalface. Stratagem is tricks we use to do things faster, smarter, more efficient and effective – also called tactics. Tactics do not stand alone, they are linked to a strategic move, or moves. Spiral dynamics is a process of giving tactics resources at specific time intervals when needed. It is the outer-environment connecting with the inner, giving thought body, purpose, and meaning – by linking it with resources and time.

Where a strategy starts to deliver, it's because the tacticians are getting the resource, when they need it and how they need it. Strategy then gets meaning, all because of the tactics used, the recipe, that becomes a tool for success. Then it is referred to as a spiralling strategy. Everything works like a machine. Inferring to its growth that is on time and in time. This is where time becomes relative to success, this is where strategy takes over from planning, by combining all the tactics, and continuums, and then scheduling it to fit against a time-line. To achieve strategic momentum - spiral growth - we utilise whatever is available or required at a specific stage of development, and give it a certain amount of time to perform. Just like with babies, some stratagem/ tactics with babies are only useful at a certain stage of development. Just like breast milk, precedes formula, then follow soft solids, and then chewing, that becomes a pattern making up the transition from milk to solids in baby food. The same principle applies. Same with stratagems/ tactics, it needs to be situationally suitable, appropriate and time sensitive in order to achieve specific desired results we wish to acquire, in a specific time frame. This is where the stratagem part becomes strategy. Where numerous tactics made several continuums produce the desired result – not just any result – and in the required time, and time frame. As an example, a baby only needs milk for so long, then soft foods, and then it can take on solids – all consistent with his age and development. This is a changing of continuums, with the core continuum being "food", the one naturally progressing in time, until it hands over to the next continuum.

Stratagem is also defined as; being a trick for surprising or deceiving an opponent as well as any trap, scam, or method devised or used to attain a goal or to gain an advantage over your opponents. Getting the initiative. It could also be described as **"Tactics"**. Which also involves utilizing leverage for gaining a person's or people's confidence and trust, through extortion, fear, politics, faith, or by whatever means. In short, stratagem or tactics are used to help our strategies along, or parts of it. Stratagems are the things we feed ideas to make them grow into assisting, our sibling continuums – it becomes a method of doing something to assist the main continuum, that works every time.

Strategic Spirals are simply – a way of describing a process of things happening in time, stemming from events and human influences, that started affecting growth and new beginnings for many. At the core, we always find some sort of initiator, a catalyst, ideas, planning and a tactical approach. Nothing ever start from nothing, all things start from something. This concept started by us looking at the usefulness of Spiral Dynamics to explain certain attributes of strategic design to people.

Spiral Dynamics is a theory of human development introduced in the 1996 book *Spiral Dynamics* by Don Beck and Chris Cowan. *Spiral Dynamics (Snippet from Wikipedia)* argues that human nature is not fixed: humans are able, when forced by life conditions, to adapt to their environment by constructing new, more complex, conceptual models based on a systems of core values or collective intelligences, applicable to both individuals and entire cultures. This is what Radical Strategy is all about and this book. It's this type of fusion that allows for planning that allows the forces of this world, to release mental energy, that allow us to handle and solve the new problems in specific timeframes, as if we knew they would exist, in which specific actions take place in that specific timeframe and we counter tragedy with new knowledge and skill never seen before. Only by travelling back in time, and witnessing time travelling through spirals of time and seeing things change, do we get a better understanding of what it implies as we go forward in time. From the ice age to industrial age, was a shift from one timeframe to the next and from one paradigm to the next. This implies one full circle, that made up a time frame, and a leap in evolution. That connects two aspects with time. Like a relay race of one idea giving rise to the next as part of a growing continuum. Where spirals are on the outside, disconnected in some way from the thinking process, just supporting ideas, actions, and results with tactics or stratagem in time, to help the continuum along. Any idea when given attention, creates energy, that creates more ideas, this forms a continuum of the original idea. It is only when we couple it to time that it becomes relevant. Now, on the outside of the continuum, we have spirals spinning, that uses other forms of energy. Continuums use brain power, spirals use physical sweat and energy, methods, to help this continuum along, that takes time. The time spiral starts as a pin-prick, then spirals out and goes faster and wider. With every completion of a cycle a time period is closed and the next opened. We go from intro to epilogue with every completed cycle. Some have short time spans in the beginning and they get longer as the scheme gets bigger and more elaborate. How we make decisions and control our emotions, how our genes shape our desires and how our personal futures are being shaped by a reward system that adapts in response to satisfying experiences...will determine where and who we will be in time - tomorrow. Remember, everything affects everything else once it becomes connected. We too develop and grow in parallel with our strategies, just by hitching a free ride on the outside. This world needs more leaders, and even better, some heroes to help us save ourselves. Again, we need true leaders, and action heroes, people that do stuff, not just talk about them. What is a hero? I argue that a hero is someone who possesses and displays certain heroic attributes such as integrity, compassion, and moral courage, heightened by an understanding of the power of situational forces, with an enhanced social awareness, and an abiding commitment to social reform through action.

This type of social action and reform must bring about more champions, hero's. Patterns for breeding better people and managers must be forged. People who come from nowhere, and just make things happen as if by miracle. Heroism is a social concept, and, like any social concept—it can be explained, taught, and modelled through education and practice. I believe that heroism is common, a universal attribute of human nature and not exclusive to a few special individuals and comic books. No, we have heroes in every family, town, culture and office. Heroism is just a choice away, a way of portraying the relevance of what we need to pursue that is worthwhile, with our time, in relation to it affecting our growth, by choice. "Historically, the various fields and branches of what we know now as Psychology have attempted to adapt to new developments, and explain them. We have to "MOTIVATE" people – was a drive at one time. These studies no longer are relevant and totally outdated. We now know motivation does very little for growth or understanding. However, too often our social and academic textbooks still reflect the outdated products, assumptions and world views that once fitted perfectly in the absence of true knowledge, the age in which they were created and popularized, now inadequate to their task. Therefore we need some heroes, people that will come and solve problems for us. People that can think, act, and that can explain these attributes and concepts of success - the strategic spiral dynamics - and strategic thinking, someone to feed our ideas and make them grow.

"Stratagem" and "strategy" are what we feed our ideas - so that they may become continuums that deliver working concepts. "Stratagem" and "strategy" come from the same Greek word but

are spelled differently. The reason for this difference is that "stratagem" was taken from the Doric dialect of Greek, spoken in the south, while "strategy" was taken from the Athenian or northern dialect. The two words have very similar meanings but a strategy is usually a more complex plan, comprising of several stratagems – actions, methods, tactics for accomplishing individual steps. That create *"a meaningful coincidence"* - Grand Strategy.

Getting people to think strategic and critical is painful, it's not routine, it's out of the ordinary.

Much of man's thought processes are basically mechanical or automated. Most of our actions are due to automatic responses to stimuli. We don't have to think much, and we prefer not to, as the brain uses the most energy and oxygen when thinking critically, thinking is hard work for the body, and painful, exhausting. Our survival depends on us getting people to start thinking again. We have to design our way out, as we did, designing our way of life into routine. We have designed a place where we can be lazy. This is why we designed everything in our lives, so that it becomes routine, then we only have to use the minimum of brain power to make it through a day. All caps screw of in the same direction. All cars are driven in the same fashion, with the same control layout etc. Getting people to think strategic is painful, it's not routine, it's out of the ordinary, described as *"a meaningful coincidence"*.

Jung noticed that if two events were *not causally related, but connected by meaning, it had purpose,* therefore, this established that a human mind was needed to see a connection – and it must be cognisant (awake and thinking) and not automated to do just that. When you notice the same coincidence happening often, then it takes on meaning when it creates significance, at that point it becomes a synchronicity. We have all heard people say, it was just a "stroke of luck", "stroke of genius", "coincidence" or "by accident", it has to do with fate. These instances are only noticed when we are aware, and prepared that they might exist. We only find things that are hidden, if we are aware and interested in them. Like Easter eggs. In strategy, synchronicity is an occurrence that creates understanding of new, and the unknown, that exist outside our sphere of thought, that influence us, call to us, and try and inform us of what to do. The more you are aware of the world, and the things in it, and how they work, and fit, and influence each other, and us, the more success you will have in life, and with strategy. This teaches us to trust our intuition, and first responses. Instinct plays a great, if not vital role in survival as well as strategy. If asked to write down your sharpest instincts, i am sure you will frown. However, if you are thrown into a lion pit, I am sure we will see what instincts are all about. Use it, develop it, and it will serve you well. Instinct or intuition is also influenced by perception, so observe how people influence your perception, as it can and will influence your intuition. Many tacticians said in hindsight that they went on pure instinct... there must be something to it.

Therefore, strategy exists because of various meaningful combinations of connections, continuums (ideas), that gives it purpose. Stratagems assist in forming these meaningful connections, and combining it into one thing, that gives it purpose, and as a result becomes a strategy. Strategy does not just exist because of theory, and practice. Rather lessons learned from necessity and coincidence.

Not only does strategy truly become relevant for all, because we know or think we know how it works on the surface, and as a result say it does and will matter to others. No, that's definitely not how, I have heard this many a time, if we keep it – strategy that is - simple and superficial, everyone will understand it. This approach failed miserable. Just look at attitudes towards strategy in general, no one wants or cares much for it anymore, they just don't see the need for it. Maybe this way they will get to know more about it, but understand it? Strategy is for analytical people, creators, thinkers, its deep, involved, encompassing, and only the CEO knows what is best. Yeh right. Today no strategy can make it if it does not become superior through a thorough understanding of the process, and critical thinking, only when we see all things critical, and understand how they are attained, combined, and aligned in the exact sequence, in a time spiral continuum, then do we create superior strategy – or the ultimate strategy - Grand Strategy.

The one thing that is clear as day, is this; we need to better design and align our strategies with our and others reality, and their culture for it to matter. In order to do this, we need to see in entirety, the totality in psychology of all the aspects that need to be present to connect strategy with the human element. Only by giving strategies *meaning,* so that we can see its purpose clearly, through all our senses, perceptions, ideas, attitudes and feelings, and feel how they influence us, and our own strategies and reality, will we design better strategies for all. Strategy needs to become a team sport. The human aspect can only be defined as the ultimate strategic catalyst, the key driver, which corresponds to the expectations and tendencies of the group, and their collective knowledge of human behaviour when combined with strategy. By focusing on finding all the meaningful dualities; *nothing just causally related, but specifically connected by meaning, to give it a purpose.* Then will we realise for once and for all, that Newton was right, when he said everything in this universe is somehow connected. Only in an environment consistent with that in which these expectations and tendencies were formed, can we with certainty say how it will transpire and render a result by watching it unfold first hand.

We cannot design outside the cultural framework, and knowledge and reference of known environments for the people we are designing for. This, includes smaller aspects such as appropriate behaviour in, and treatment by other people as part of that environment. Knowing - What is in, and what is out? We cannot design strategy for the unknowns of cultures, it needs to flow from a strategic continuum, something existing – an idea - to something greater, with form. Strategy does not flow from nothing and become something.

This "idea" or "notion of something" is referred to as a - *first union*, where thinking meets the harshness of reality, where thought becomes focused on the joining of a idea, with reality by giving it detailed attention. This should starts a succession of more factual and detailed comparison, matching in with critical thinking, and mental events, rendering results, that will influence the succeeding results, and perceptions, and if matched with reality, will start a continuum. The aspect of Continuum, can be explained in relation to man. The continuum – or idea of a man – the *individual* seen as a concept. The individual being self sufficient and an entity, yet he also forms part of the next continuum - family – yet another idea - of what several entities joined would look like – called *family*. Where we have several solo identities merging to form one new continuum, a family. Which in turn is part of – yet another idea - of what several families joined would look like – a *clan*. Then *clan's*, become *communities*, and *species'* continua, just as the continuum of the human species forms part of that of all *life*. So too, do just one idea. Any idea has the potential, in the right place and time, to give rise to more complex and bigger ideas, eventually forming more complex and bigger continuum, influencing the path of strategy and making it more complex. It always just starts with that one big idea, and developing it for a culture. One idea becomes many, that becomes a concept, that renders a result, from following one idea – or continuum. What is your strategic paradigm? Implies - What are you focused on specifically that guides and informs you strategically? Which continuum are you focused on – implies – what part of our strategy are you most concerned with? Strategy needs new reference points, to make space for all the enhancements. We need new knowledge and people attributes incorporated into the equation of strategic discussion. Less cliché, more practical and scientific... we can see and hear who read what book, by listening to the clichés dropped in meetings – we will be doing "Business Unusual" from today – aha... come on, we need leadership not a show-off. Most of these buffoons don't even know what it implies when they drop it into conversation, these "pearls", they just like the cliché.

Strategy that is in pursuit of knowledge, aimed at developing intelligence and concerned with people should be our aim

In order to create this aim, the ultimate warpath, the framework strategy, a strategy in pursuit of knowledge and concerned with people. Then we need a totally fresh perspective on how we view and explain strategy to people. We need radically different strategic perspectives and paradigms, training and literature to inform us what to look for and what to work with and on. As if we were reinventing strategy from scratch. Making it the starting point of any business training. If knowledge be their power, then so be information and communication, that becomes our business intelligence combined, then it becomes a knowledge base. Where knowledge becomes both a product of our collective interaction and is also used as a tool daily. Then it implies that we are now working intelligently. Schooling people in custom made strategy, and utilizing technology that deals with information at much greater degrees of efficiency than ever before to get them to be intelligent, is a hard stretch of the imagination, if not reality. Feeling that someone else is more intelligent than we are is almost intolerable. Then comes the denial, he is only strong at.. or because of. We take things personal, when we are rated on our brain power - or the idiot scale. Never insult or allude to a person's intelligence in a group setup...

Knowledge based strategies, the tools to do strategy with intelligence

Stop, there are two things we need to grasp here first, when we are talking about intelligence, we are referring to a continuum. In life as in business there are certain things that require brains and other brawn. This is one place you need to decide which one will serve you best, brain or brawn? Then next, we can add value to any endeavour and organisation by protecting, developing and servicing what we have as core- intelligence. Core-intelligence revolves around a certain skill, and knowhow, to perform tasks, and or other functions with. Where we become better, faster, and more economical with the help of either brain or brawn or both types of intelligence. Now the question here should be, do we have enough "intelligent" people left out there to pull it off, to figure it out for us. To understand that we need to protect that which makes us strong, as if it is not always a given. Because we cannot mimic core-intelligence. In the realm of **Multiple Intelligence -** with Howard Gardner's Theory of Multiple Intelligence, it defines eight kinds of human intelligence for us:

1. Mathematical-logical (problem solving, fix or repair, program)
2. Spatial (dance, sports, driving a bus)
3. Bodily-kinesthetic (acting, mime, sports)
4. Musical-rhythmic (composing, playing music, clapping)
5. Verbal-linguistic (reading, using words, public speaking, storytelling)
6. Interpersonal (social skills, reading other people, working in a group)
7. Interpersonal (introspection, self-assessment, goal making, vision, planning)
8. Naturalist (able to distinguish among, classify, and use environmental features)

Where Mathematical-logical and Verbal intelligence then represent *core intelligence.*

This covers human intelligence. Then we also get I-Phones, electronic, and software tools, gadgets, and machinery that are intelligent. Furthermore we also have rational or emotional and spiritual intelligence too. Not to mention, practical skills that also related to core intelligence. People with above average ability in any of the eight areas of intelligence, have **special intelligence**. This world rewards people who develop skills associated with their special intelligence, provided that they have the minimum core intelligence skills required of their profession. Therefore, it truly takes a lot of things to get intelligent people to build and develop more intelligence for us, along with their strategy. Intelligence becomes integral and indispensible to strategy, a continuum, because most of it is entrenched in people's minds first, it needs to be extracted, and used carefully. Intelligence is so complex in nature, and expensive to re-create, duplicate, and takes much time to develop. Therefore we need to develop a specific structure to work with intelligence as if it is a scarce and rare commodity called intellectual capital. Intellectual capital becomes a company asset, losing just one intelligent person could have a ripple effect that could destroy some endeavours. We need to take stock of who we need, want, have, and who are vital to our livelihood. What is true intelligence then? Some say its people savvy or personal intellect - the ability solve problems etc. Then we get what's out there, information, information in addition becomes intelligence when we have verified it to be either factual, scientific and or true. Here we need to start looking critically at reality, before we embark on developing critical mass, with intelligence driven strategy creation. Before we even start incorporating into our doctrine knowledgebase strategies, systems and tools, we have to test to see if it will have a greater effect and deliver on its promise. Knowledge and intelligence are two components of strategic design. We have to test and see if our industry and people are knowledge orientated, or skill orientated. What is our basic function, and which tools serves us best, and is knowledge one of them. There is no reason to go after knowledge if we are working in a coal mine for instance. However, intelligence is core to any endeavour big or small. Don't get it mixed up, knowledge based strategies are not the same as intelligence. Neither get into anything just for the sake of having it, it is very expensive, and perishable, also very maintenance intensive. If Knowledge is a big yes, then this concept should become the first step in the introduction of any new strategy. We all need foundation, employing knowledge base strategies as a broad spectrum prerequisite to strategic design serves this purpose. If we work intelligently, we are working faster and both smarter, with less waste, with the least amount of effort. Explaining this, the deeper nature of strategic thinking, and design, the fits of continuum, with the individual, and the firm, the total strategic process, builds greater vision and focus with people. They see thing in a 360 degree fashion, and as they exist. In order to do this, we need to make things simple first. We need to adopt a departing strategy. A knowledge-based strategy, to guide the design of all the firms' other strategy, this is to ready the firm in totality first, and all employees for strategy, everyone gets his basic battle training. We should consequently start with the primary aspects of developing our intangible resource: our people first, the intellectual capital. By looking at their levels of competence and development – their intelligence.

Looking at peoples work environments – and designing intelligence

The environments we work in dictate the level of our effectiveness. Our operational habitats, our working spaces, benches, desks and aesthetics, will impact on how people traditionally do things here, because it is of consequence, and Industrial Psychology teaches us these things. Sharp people with sharper minds need the sharpest tools to do their work with. People, daily wish to avoid anything in the negative, with negative consequences; even places, other people and situations that make them uncomfortable, aggressive, or just feel bad. This includes, smell, taste, association, temperature and humidity, all of this impacts on how well we perform. People all over, desire things in the positive, results, effects, and places, we even look for them daily, that first positive to build the rest on. Behavioural shaping, and learning assumes that *people's environment* (their surroundings) cause *people* to *behave* in certain ways. Our environment could be conducive or corrosive and stressful, even depressing. The more prestigious and technologically advanced an environment is, the more prone people are to become professionals dominating such environment, becoming experts at every attribute and feature of its design. Again, this is not true for every culture, group or person. Some prefer the outdoors, being on the ocean, in a hole, or in a jungle. The point is, like needs like to grow. It's no use having trained rocket scientists, and then they only have surfboards, sand and sun to work with. Just like scientist will be most comfortable in labs, and sales people on the street, so too do we need to design our work spaces with these specifics in mind. Start by re-designing work areas to assist people, to capacitate them, and to create an atmosphere of professionalism. This is on the physical level, on the mental level, we need flexibility, creativity and connectivity – in line with their function and requirements. We need everyone to think, see, feel and believe one thing when they walk in; "Things are happening here, and I am part of it, because everything just works great, looks great and feels great, it even smells great". Otherwise we have failed at re-designing work spaces. What's more is, we want real interactions, emphasizing "live" interaction between people. Cell phone shops are doing this, with stand-up coffee bars encouraging impromptu meetings, and dialogue. The aim is; one, to improve on our total networking capability first, people need to communicate, to create and renew connections. Then, the transference of knowledge across various levels and parts of the organization via any means takes place. We learn to communicate at all levels; formal, informal and structured. Again, all within reasonable limits. Humans are social creatures, creatures of habit, they need to see others work, think, and listen to how they communicate in order to define and understand their own work, and work ethic. We measure our selves by what others do in the same situation, say about themselves, and handle themselves at the same level or with the same means. This then gives us justification, a reference point, before they will be happy with themselves and the amount of work they do. They need this familiarity in others actions, and habits, to gauge their own worth to have any sense of value. We value what other say, especially about us. Now, all this is all good, however the hard truth of the matter is this, if the transference of knowledge can't be connected to measurable or visible improvements in performance -- including improvements on the bottom line -- then the knowledge revolution will be short-lived, and so to the ultra modern office space, and deservedly so. If we don't get greater returns on our investments in people and their environments, then it's just no use. This is the final measure. You can bring a horse to water, but you can't make it drink. If your people are not clever enough to use all the advancements and changes to better themselves and their work, then sink the ship. Get new people, start over. This knowledge can be adopted in our strategy. Communication and sharing of ideas, problems, knowledge needs to be soaked into the human fibre, to become entrenched. Where People are seen as true assets in business; where we can get them to work intelligently trough design, training, communication, intelligence and strategy, then the company may profit, from these results of structured and planned human interaction, and depend ultimately on only people for their continued existence. At this stage, groups or individuals are tasked to plan and then execute interventions to facilitate and promote awareness of strategic communication and to find the value of networking and promote specifics. Starting from soft interventions to hard and complex, we live the way we work, at work. We cultivate this and start the implementation of the knowledge. Then where our tactical inputs are required, we are ready, for designing and planning phases tailoring interventions in order to address particular barriers identified in the prior continuum, and the particular targets we need to address with new continuums. The organization that wants to build competitive advantages has to create internal leverage with its capabilities.

People are seen to be constantly extending themselves into their own world by both tangible means, such as arts and craft, interior design, starting gardens and taking up hobbies, then why can we not harness this creativity in the work place? All intangible aspects, that all corporate associations need, incentivize for, buy, yet we have in abundance. It's not just an idea, it's also a fact, and these attributes we seek only gets dislodged in an open environment, starting with open communication, and consistent conversation, that we at times turn strategic when we need their creativity to spawn, building and relationships. It deals with the golden triangle of influences, the internal, external and interpersonal influences. We are not interested in the fuzzy pursuit of knowledge, no , it must yield results that can be duplicated, or it just won't make the grade. This gives rise to intervention strategies, that assist with things that impede knowledge transverse, and that hamper strategy Executing a knowledge-based strategy is not about managing all knowledge; it's about nurturing the people with the required knowledge, and getting them to mentor, tutor and oversee specifics, and fragile aspects of our strategy. Knowledge-based strategies begin with a strategy itself, it is a start up, get the troops ready for war strategy, not the warehousing and collection of knowledge. Because knowledge has to become central to strategy formulation, design and implementation, we need tacit more than historic. Tacit refers to things people know, that are only used at certain junctures that help us cross the river of circumstance and arrive dry, because of previous experience and knowledge gained. This type of knowledge that is not general, or used daily. Knowledge that only becomes relevant and apparent at an instance that taps the brilliance of a lifetime of experience. Without this foundation, of knowledge and management in place, we cannot manage, let alone plan, and strategise. Management has become a key strategic task, and we have very few people qualified to manage, due to the lack of training, experience and knowledge transference. Where the challenges facing managers for achieving success in today's complex and dynamic environments, has become pure complexity, requiring reason. Reason without knowledge experience and training translates into disaster. A major challenge facing strategic management is engineering and managing the individual and group level knowledge that facilitates better strategies and invokes commitment. A knowledge management strategy should be presented.

Strategic talk, focus and alignments

Fists remove any conflict, either perceived or real. We have to be realistic here as well, we will always find...*resistance* to any form of change In no way must this just be seen as conflict, people stonewalling us. No, in these instances, its mostly uncertainty, and detachment from the known environment that spawns fear and resentment of the now unknown, that with time escalates, and builds up and causes frustration and eventually anger erupts overtime if not defused. Focusing on conflict removal first, and then open communication is an indispensable force in keeping any system stable. Making our conversation strategic also helps, as it becomes a battle language that means the exact same thing and it implies. Using strategic "lingo", could assist greatly in cleaning up communication problems, and execution orders. The world is made up of two kinds of people – the few who learn and grow, and the many who don't because they just don't see the need now, nor ever – yet – they will tell you, they want to. They just don't see the necessity yet, so it will allude them, it is our duty to inform them, and make it stick. We only grow as individuals by actualizing our own human potential. However, if we don't see our own potential in others and help them grow, how can we see any possibility for growth in the future, or potential in others. Nevertheless, as people with our own normal share of problems, we too grow by resolving those problems, by growing in self-awareness, group awareness, and cultural awareness. All in different ways possible to evolve knowledge and wisdom. If we don't, then we lead average lives, then we will find that others may start exploiting our strongest talents, and make a great deal of profit from us, and we won't understand why. Life is not just a question of fit, just to fit in with the group, or make it in any culture. No, it's about becoming your own person, and being happy with what you have become. When living unbalanced, we become unsure and weaken ourselves, by neglecting or avoiding our weakest, or least-rewarded attributes. As a result, our constitution may become over-developed in one area say knowledge – with all the assistant stress and exhaustion to our systems – while our other capabilities say health, may waste away through under-use.

The face of strategy has changed totally, in line with this orientation from people to develop themselves, how we see our role and function, and work, as well as interact with each other's strategy has changed to. It's no longer just a top management or business line function, or plan only, no, it's a customised game plan, that concerns and connects all, even horizontally, people are consulted. It comes with the rules, and directions up front. Strategies today are in-depth and complete – master Strategies. It unites people with processes and systems with resources, and it will keep changing, and so too has the tools, and influences. It has attained unique flavours, and characteristics' from those that practice it, over many business sectors, regions and continents. Strategy has become entrenched in ideology and perception, showing internally consistent characteristics of culture that distinguishes it from other cultures strategy. The more we grow closer with communication, the further apart we grow with our culture...

More people think strategic today, and there are even more of them coming, therefore more strategies will originate in different forms and dimensions. From different sectors, perspectives and cultures, we will see people and companies competing for space, resources, and time, more and more each day, all in different ways. Thus things are happening faster, and faster. Mainly because people are better enabled and educated to solve problems for themselves today than what they were, say ten years back. Mainly it's because we have vast arrays of diverging resources and affordable technology available to us, and even readymade strategy. We have quick fixes, takeaways, DIY, affordable consultants, fast forms of communication, and things good to go, that did not exist just a year back. Thus, keeping in step with changes in: business philosophy, and technology is very pertinent, as it all becomes essential but no longer crucial to successful strategy. *The point here to make is this; many now capitalise on this "instant" aspect, and are selling instant, as "strategic solutions", when in fact most, if not all of these solutions are not long-term, therefore not strategic at all, but perishable, so you will need more.* You have been conned into thinking your dilemma is solved. They are in fact just essentials, things, nice to have, a quick fix and not sustainable. When in fact what we need more of now is long-term, practical, sustainable, affordable and crucial solutions from our strategies. If we look at global indicators we will see that the pool of resources and energy is decreasing, and shrinking rapidly, especially with the rate of pollution we are generating, we have now become the most wasteful generation ever.

Because of this, it is said that the next World War will be fought over "clean water", and we are leaving our children to fight that one, now there is a scary notion.

IF superior strategy exists, it is because of *focus*... Then it stands to reason, that what we focus on more, we will get more of, then why aren't we all seeing the bigger picture? Mainly, it's because we are consumed with ourselves only, our perceptions, and self gratification, we are a very selfish generation, almost to an oblivious extent. Consumed with self, the new era of self-awareness; that focuses only on image, fame and fortune. Focus starts with thinking, and perception, if we focus on health for instance, how do we prioritise it and against what? Instant solutions come to mind - drink a pill - and fix a problem, in this case health. Just like vitamins are essential to good living, but not crucial. When in fact, what we rather need more of is clean air and water – a long term *focus*, more realistic to our health, as water and air influence our food sources, habitat, and our bodies directly, daily. Then why are we not focused on what really matters?

Very crucial for superior strategy, is one's long term focus. We have to distinguish and focus ardently on the vitals of **strategic elements**, the things that directly impact on the end result, things that will truly matter in the long term. In the medium and short term we are busy with *stratagem*, in the long term with strategy. However, we can all deliberate on this aspect and best methods and practices towards formulating and focusing these good strategies all we want, and we will fail, when the crux of the matter is simply this. Studies have found that; Strategy never fails during the formulation phases, only at implementation. Maybe it's because this is the one, and only time we see the total results of the process, the error of our ways and focus, and then only do we see our flawed assumptions, and want to start fixing. Then its normally too late.

Now that we have identified the one common aspect of most failed attempts at strategy how are we going to fix it? What if we could fix the blame and problems before hand? By concentrating on our focus points first. No matter how we go about building things, normally the cracks only appear once the building is finished, or fails, or years later. No matter how well we are qualified to lead, direct and manage, if we are not focused on the cardinal – key - aspects we are lost. We should be more critical of our perceptions and assumptions when dealing with our continuum – still embryonic ideas - and developing it. We need to take more time at the stratagem level, to test, evaluate and contemplate critically if this option on the table is the best, and will it work the way it is contemplated or supposed to, etc. Only by focusing critically on our phases of development, planning and influences, and things that really should be tested, and double-checked, beforehand will we arrive better off. Studies have shown that where strategies are put through thorough second and third round testing, the implementation is normally flawless. By implication, if we look back at the continuum – all the ideas that formed and originated from the original idea, and the stratagem - supporting actions that supported the main idea. Then we should be able to clearly see the process from cradle to grave, and be able to make a cardinal judgment call, and yes, or no, with certainty. It is only by better evaluating our perceptions and paradigms with critical thinking beforehand, that informed decisions are made, that guide our thinking on further and future strategy formulation and execution. When all our inputs become validated, then we will see less cracks. The other aspect that covers focus, is alignment and timing.

Alignment and timing.

The "past" "present" and "future" is the only place where time exists. We hear this repeated often. But how can that be? Time is not what we think it is. We perceive time to run in a straight line, only forward, and we can see where it came from, in the past. However, what if, time is composed of multilayered and multidimensional spirals, spiralling outward like a cone, of synchronistical arrangements, in chronological order showing historical events that happened. That becomes linked with timelines that intersect, where at each intersect, we have events, incidents or either accidents happening. This is then called a strategic time spiral continuum. Where time consists of two variables in the strategic continuum, the one is speed, when varying the time allotted, it either speeds up a process or slows it down, more time equals slow, and as it runs out we have less time to do more things in, so it speeds up - fast. Then time also becomes a resource, the amount of time utilised or with specific time frames, referring to specific dates and time allocated to reach objectives in, refers to measure, an amount of time. As well as cost and actual time available or used, then time equals money. Time is also relative and impacts on us with things like; seasonal time; that consist of less day time hours, more night. As well as seasons, where certain things sell at higher rates during December for instance, as what they would during March for instance...

Time also impacts on location, day here night time there situations. Winter and summer, the Northern and Southern hemisphere differing in seasons and climate over time frames, even time zones from East to West, it all impacts at some intersect. Time also serves as a tool to synchronize work with, it becomes an event pacing tool, to get others there on time. Trains, planes, ships all function on time, these aspects of it... schedules become a measure, of how much time spent, and how much production we got from it. At the point where things become time intensive, or labour intensive and reliant...with goods to market, production turnaround time, time spent in research, unlocking innovation, and testing. Where on the one hand we can accelerate time, by throwing more resources into production, and on the other hand we can't, where crops take a set specific amount of time to grow and mature. Therefore in some instances we can manipulate time, in others, we are at its mercy, just having to wait. Time can also be used to queue events in relay, so that it take an exact measure of time to complete a specific cycle. Time is also used to differentiate work, and create order. It's used to schedule certain work in certain time slots, whilst it is also used to create order. To create time slots, interim, medium term and long term, is but one example of this. Now we have slots, and order, the one has to precede the other. Time also has set rules; there are 60 seconds, in a minute and so on. We can't shorten it or prolong a minute. It is set, and universal.

Systematic and procedural alignment of process needs to be managed. Superior holistic strategic thinking; requires from us to evaluate all we do, in step, in time, by utilising proven approaches that aligns in the exact sequence, in time, all the essentials and critical elements in a time spiral, that creates momentum and a continuum. This implies that, we need to start the process with the pre-identification of needs and short comings, and it should be done beforehand, with required essentials to be intermeshed with management processes and business culture as well as philosophy, to gain a superior end product. In short, how we focus on each step we take, and evaluate who, what, where, when, and how, will determine whether we are going the long way or all the way. We have to be holistic and thorough, take more time planning and deliberating, testing and doing research, and thereby spend the minimum of time developing and producing results – "so fast". In order to become "so-fast" we have to be so-slow – in planning, then production becomes –"fast", and we become "so-fast" in the end. Before we move on anything strategic we need to think it through, from cradle to grave, it needs to pass through some standardised best practice as filters, testing, and analysing results, before we move to the next level, this way less failure will be observed at implementation. Alternatively, if strategy as a process is not consistent with measuring things and testing ideas against the prevailing and changing environment, with all its influences, and the people in it, against its objectives, and ours, then we are not focused enough on critical elements, rather just on essential outcomes. In life, anything that matters enough to us, we will give effort, if it doesn't, we will just do the minimum required to get by, and not care much what the outcome/ consequences will be.

Therefore, strategy today requires greater insight and awareness beforehand, of what is at stake, and what this strategy will do for us, the organisation, its people, or whoever, so that it will matter enough to all the stakeholders. This is referred to as strategic focus, people need to take ownership, to make a strategy important enough, to stick to its reality, as everything we know and have about strategy today, has and will change. Just like dry bubblegum won't stick to wood, strategy too, needs to be chewed, and also requires some saliva. Same with strategy, it always looks good, and is well presented and packaged, however it requires outside influences, and elements, a lot of instinct, and maybe a small percentage of luck to make it work.

We now have some unique tools we can use, to identify some of these influences, and elements, such as sociological insight, referring to the study of the origin, development, and structure of human societies. It also deals with the behaviour of individual people and groups in society, their approaches and perspectives on living, - focused on the forming of healthy perceptions - and how our own senses of what "the real world" is becoming and should look like, to assist us in modelling people friendly strategy, when we have to look at our strategic focus.

This becomes the strategic time spiral continuum – an ongoing focus on what creates excellence at the micro level and superior strategy at the macro level. Thinking in time spirals means being able to bring past, present and future assumptions, and all relevant aspects into the strategic equation, to create better decision-making models and speed-up implementation. By having one constant as a driver of your culture, and its people, influencing their thinking – a stratagem, a essential component. Balancing off against the other fluctuating element of time and influences.

In this continuum, we plan things in time spirals, or we couple a time value to a strategic and operational task. How much time will we need, and how much of this time, is spent as effort, administrative, logistic. Coupled to the cost. We focus on it twofold, getting two things for the price of one;

- *Strategic Focus* on planning - then breaks these aspects down into a sequence of events, time, cost, and resources required, that can be duplicated. The example of a small business, starting with;
- *Customer/ problem statement knowledge* - emphasizes paying close attention to customers desires and providing them with total solutions, or solving needs and wants, through strategic intervention.
- *Then concentrating on Product or solution design*– sub-focus on investment, and providing the best technology and quality available in products, alternatively solving or fixing a problem.
- *Then designing Operational and Strategic Excellence* – sub-focus both on efficient and effective outcome and costs controls, to provide the lowest costs alternatives to operation, product, or solution creation.
- *Tactical Focus.* If you look at the *time* a shop owner for instance spends on his business, you will find it can be broken down into three categories. These are:

- *Administrative and Operations* – the time you spend keeping the routine day to day business running
- *Crisis* – the time you spend solving unanticipated problems
- *Breakthrough* – the deliberate actions and planning – strategic planning and tactics - and time you spend on creative efforts to improve performance in the long run.

What happens here is, that if you are not focused on both tactical and operational, that the first two categories of the one or the other will grow in importance, and consume all your time and effort – energy goes where attention flows – until it occupies all your time and they push out your breakthrough time. Maintaining a *Strategic Focus, amounts to a* combined initiative, between strategy and tactics. With the developing of *Strategic Goals* to execute new or better directives, and finding workable solution daily to the challenge of invention and creation, influenced by change in short time spirals, affects the total process of growth – and remains the challenge of maintaining balanced focus. Picking one of these as your lead focus represents a smart thing to do. This is very important, it does not mean that you don't try to do well in the other two. It means that you don't try to do all three equally well. Having one tactical and operational focus point is a good start. Trying to be all things for all customers puts you on a path to failure because customers will not behave in a way that profits your business. Business is just too hyper-competitive for you to succeed doing all three better than anyone else.

Pick your *Strategic and Tactical Focus,* and then lead and run with it. Where we understand that strategic here refers to the "what and why" and tactical refers to the "how." Then We will get things done, if we get people to understand both, and focus on designing and doing things in step, and designing from both the tactical and strategic perspective, we will arrive with better rounded strategy, then we can copy the process and duplicate it.

You begin this process by selecting your *Strategic Focus* and limiting your goal to critical elements only.

When we incorporate this thinking into the succeeding steps of our *Grand Strategy*, we get sustainable growth throughout, both on strategic as well as operational level.

What gives us a greater degree of certainty, planning and spontaneity, or strategy and people knowledge?

In business of any nature today as in society, we need things to get into their intended orbits and start their own continuum, a life path, or intended journey. We need more certainty from strategy making; we need things to work as we expect them to – first time out. With superior strategy in place, things need to gain and keep momentum, and not drop out of orbit, or come to a grinding halt, just because the drivers are not there. If this is still the case then we need to stop and ask. What's missing or what's blocking my focus?

Failing to plan, is planning to fail they say. With good reason. The difference between planning and strategy is this. Planning is always subject to the known, we plan around things we know, and assumptions we have. Strategy is a course we draw, into the unknown, by taking small known steps with planning. The shorter the range the more accurate the outcome generally is, and then we call it planning. Planning makes way for strategy. Where strategy is seen as dealing with medium and long range issues, as well as dealing with a greater degree of uncertainty, resulting from a limited knowledge of tendencies, condition, and influences at long range. This creates complex issues, and dilemmas. Now, with any complexity, comes challenges that could threaten us, some aspect of fear could forces us into action, other enables us to begin to get people to think about the problem. We all react totally differently when confronted by fear. Our views of the world could change instantly, as a result of fear, and in different ways. As the reality of people changes so too do people's views, beliefs and perceptions – all of which relies on a perceived degree of certainty, about what was, what is, and what will be, for it is mans very existence that requires aspects of certainty and some untarnished belief, in order for him to flourish. When this certainty is threatened then we see spontaneity take over, spontaneity only comes from being able to do and learn things for oneself, developed in an environment that allows for mistakes, and gives guidance. Successful learning processes always require a degree of error, risk, fear and planning, and then spontaneity develops. How, and when it will be successful, no one can know, the future cannot be predicted with any degree of certainty, if we have not studied our past... only the wise leader knows just how unsure any strategy really is, how fragile, however he believes that it will carry through, if it was given a great effort....during the first union.

No theory, book or system will alter how you see yourself and the world, if we do not stop and contemplate its necessity or usefulness critically. If we don't, then something normally needs to break first, before we reach for the tools to repair it, or to challenge us, before we act, such is our nature. They say "prevention is better than cure", and "vigilance saves the day... However we also have something called "informed" choice, if we get information we do have a choice whether we want to act on it or not, then we can be pre-emptive, and do introspection, or not. Things that concern us are becoming more philosophical, and almost spiritual, we tend to talk more, give advice more and do less, especially for others, this brings me to *Strategic Spiral Dynamics, and closer to the time spiral.*

What *is Strategic Spiral Dynamics?*

Well, firstly Spiral Dynamics on its own, is a powerful model and predictive theory of human development and Cultural Revolution. It has emerged as a powerful instrument for understanding the complexity of human behaviour and understanding. Maslow got the leg up way back, and we followed him blindly around, for some time, and parked his brother Spiral Dynamics. Well, now he's the new thing, spiral dynamics has been successfully employed around the globe for conceiving and implementing real-world integral solutions to social conflicts and for catalyzing individual evolutionary transformation, and it is now leaping into strategy. All great things are only born from necessity, strategy has identified that there is a necessity to link culture with strategy, and so to time. The need for a new robust and more comprehensive model for strategy has emerged because people often mistakenly utilize the process of strategy, or the word strategy, to solely imply a financial review and confuse strategic planning with budgeting, and benchmarking, as well as normal day to day planning.

Most great plans aren't strategic. They are just very nice, well thought out deliberated and structured plans, plans never the less, or high-level ideas on paper.

The Radical Revolutionary Strategic Management Matrix For Predators

There is No strategy behind the Idea on paper or a plan. Strategy has a generation of business processes, business philosophy and management integration, a value chain, and drivers that enables value reference modelling of all business processes and provides product quality, operations excellence, and customer satisfaction – as well as initiative. Plans in general cannot do the same. Strategic planning is rather a process by which an organization defines its strategy to successfully achieve its fundamental purpose. Most people are challenged with developing a strategy, I see it, time and time again, the tendency to approach strategy making as a purely systematic, just follow this recipe like approach, where it is rather an analytical and very emotional process in my mind. It also needs to be stated, that there is no one single approach for strategic planning that will work for all organizations. The process must be tailored to the specific circumstances in order to suit the culture of the company. As a result; there should be more focus on ensuring the right cultural content, than just getting the right amount of commitment. People get to, and become committed as they have to do the labour, and start seeing results. We need both, elements of internal culture and commitment. If we have a situation where we start off just massing commitment we will eliminating the strategic planning process, and we will only serve to increase the number of *attention deficit disorder* (ADD) people that already exist, the mindless, and clueless managers that just conform to lip service, they do very little but tend to have a lot to say. This is endemic in Africa society.

They just focus on day-to-day business, and as a result they become short sighted, exhibiting the short-term behaviour that has severely weakened so much of western business philosophy, and replaced it with hap-hazard management, and it will continue if we are not guarded and aware, then we will become short sighted too. Unfortunately, a lot of effort will still be expended but little strategy will be made, that will stick, and count, if it is not a focused endeavour. The acid test of whether strategy is still needed or not, is whether it informs and constrains decision making by compelling leaders to align their functional goals and day-to-day decision making to the goals of the enterprise, and stretch them over longer periods, to become medium and long term. The only way to accomplish this is through strategic; communication, education and collaboration. The process of aligning people's hearts and minds is a difficult one that requires ongoing group discussion, and wrangling. No one can "do" strategy for someone else, it's a leader's job and one that is also done collectively, never individually, transcending knowledge and knowhow, and breaking into culture. Creates pressure, and tension, that not everyone has the stomach for. Normally those who are strategically gifted have a tendency to only emphasize the quality of the idea, and the process emanating over the quality of the commitment and action required. Never approach strategy making as a purely analytical exercise, or trade off, we need to get beyond the obvious, because not everything is as it seems on paper... If you want strategy to stick, to matter, thus gaining essential commitment in the quest to "get it right" or "get it done right". Then it is all part of addressing "sticky issues" too with strategy... Furthermore, the reality and truth of the matter is, strategy is never done, there's always more, and the better the strategy the sooner we need a new one, and more of it.

The pressures of dealing with a interlinked society and its cultural influence, and culture, across many global divides. This aspect has profoundly affected how we structure and deal with cultural diversity, as well as strategy. On the one hand we want to be treated in business the exact same as our counter parts across the globe, but on a cultural level we still want to keep our identity. Is this sound reasoning, can we have both? I say no. In so far as cultures are concerned, any culture emits signals, that tell themselves important stories, amongst themselves, and perceptions start forming, and they then become biblical truth, of either privilege or deprivation. It transcends the individual it becomes "we" verbalised as a certain sector of society now, and how we are included or excluded. This is our dualistic nature, but do we ever correct the "belief", as the reality becomes more and more apparent and different from what we perceived? For we have today too many conditions affecting the mental health of society's members, because we made one big mistake, we labelled them, you are; black, white, male, and female, and brought these labels into the strategic equation too. Politics corrupts even the saints, following these respective confining definitions blindly, leads even strategy off course. Now we move in tribes because of this, tribes makes us stronger, and so to our beliefs, and the old ghost stories can let a new consciousness emerge, that really no longer exist. The point here is this, if we begin to recognize that **how** we think about important matters, from which paradigm, is so much more important than **what** we think as a person, a group or a nation in general, because of perception! Thinking and paradigms affect every aspect of our scope and core, that bleeds into and informs our strategies. What you put in you will get out, be aware!

On the other hand, strategy to some extent and in certain sectors has become somewhat of a fuzzy discipline itself, corporate strategy has growing schools of diverging thought on how, when, where, and why – one thing is for certain, the strategic landscape is complex, and becoming more so , changing in uncertain and new ways, daily. The speed of change is in step with our speed of progress, should we miss a gear will we be out of sync? It's how we add value, and define for ourselves the borders of our scope and imagination that ultimately defines our strategic brilliance. If we do not go faster and explore further our capabilities, then within our environments and personal limitations, we will become fuzzy, then strategy becomes a home brew. Strategic limitation is only forged by imitation, or cloning, it has become endemic...we are all talking about the same thing, but yet we have different words, and labels for it. Too much labelling has occurred, the balanced score card, value chain, drivers, systems...what is it again we were focusing on, it becomes a plethora of buzz words – of which everyone has his or her own trickled down version of what this animal should look like and do, if we don't actively set rules, and reference points to keep our strategic conversation specific, on topic and simple, we will disappear in the fog of war. The simpler, the better a strategic idea the shorter its life span.

All things are plausible in strategy and thinking, however not always possible, especially where we deal with issues of productivity vs. resources against time and finances available. Strategic alignment with intent, always impact on time cycles, you need time to measure and calibrate, and adjust, and eventually see the new results against the old, and evaluate the variances and then start it all over, or not. It takes time to grow a tree, and then to prune it, and pick the fruit, and so on. All signs of growth and not decay are time sensitive. Without making a meal out if it, specifics takes careful judgement, and time to develop. We tend to overstate the obvious, as indicators of growth and performance, and sometimes they are not indicative of what is really wrong, right or changing, and we tend to spend more time and energy doing something than what is necessary. We need to find and identify more realistic indicators that inform us of specifics, specifics we require, not just generics. State-of-the-art indicators are required, which will force us to find new and innovative ways to manage people, systems and resources with. Based on who they have become due to our strategic intervention and not only on what they have delivered. Indicators still need to change the things that will inform us, as to what we have to measure, and how to measure success and how to measure it in terms of our industry, and our strategy. Incorporating catalysts and influences that are part of the information they surrender, which will help us change, as time changes, and so too be able to measure the environment we operate in. We have to keep being vigilant, and find more ways of informing our decisions.

The time spiral continuum has everything to do with new ideas, and models that inform us of our "intent" and alignments required with all elements of strategy, notwithstanding the aspect of time allocation and utilisation. Where spiral dynamic assists us in plotting, the chain of events, and the time and resource we require at a certain point on a scale, to link objectives with required action at specific intervals, and see the growth path. The difficulty with this is, identifying the exact action steps to get from the strategy to is operational implementation, and the day-to-day tactics implemented, and resources needed to make it a reality, in step with time frames, and relaying it schematically in a spiral diagram. Spiral dynamics as a science offers profound systemic insight into individuals, organisations and cultures merging – and why they do what they do well to be effective, consistently. *Spiral Dynamics* also argues that human nature is not fixed: humans are able, when forced by life conditions, to adapt to their environment by constructing new, more complex, and conceptual models of the world that allow them to handle the new problems in more effective ways. When we are dealing with time, and strategic competencies – and models that gives us new insights and options, then we become aware of opportunity and innovation. Then the law of time becomes relevant where things need to come together to work, where we require structure and connectivity. The Law of Time is a universal law and principle. It states that time is the universal factor of synchronization. Synchronization implies designing and affecting harmony and organisation through following principles of design. When employing one's strategy it is important to recognize the correct timing to do so. Learning the elements of each move makes them seem segmented, but in reality they are fluid connections in motion. This is also the critical element of timing. Timing of *techniques* comes from repetition. Timing of *attacks* comes from lots of sparring. Timing of *defence* comes from failing and being submitted to blows. We have to practice, test and re-align until we have near perfect alignment.

The more time we devote on any project the bigger it grows in dimension, and the more time consuming it becomes, the more variables we have to deal with, and the larger the command and control gets. The reward is that eventually in time, it manifests, in one way or the other, and it comes to conclusion. However, when we look at this from a strategic point of view we don't want to just let things go and grow in their own direction, we want to control aspects of the process, to cut cost, time, resources etc... We want efficiency and effectiveness. Now we deal with strategic concepts, and in this instance time as a principle. Let me drive the point. Notice how daily people are talking about time as if we have it in reserve, like a resource, and we can manage it with pinpoint certainty. "I will see you at five", and then he only arrives at 05h30 – with "sorry traffic". The fact is, we cannot store time, control time to an absolute certainty and predict its path and therefore it is not a resource. Therefore, I still find it strange that we are taught time management – absurd. Time management implies that we get a box of time and now have to cut it up so that we can allocate it to a day as we get to the office, here is your time, manage it please. Implying, we are all working at the same speed, and can perform tasks in the same time and equally well, and fast, and efficient, no matter how many distractions we have to deal with, not to matter, telephone calls, emails, and nature calling, even hunger pains, and smoke breaks, oh and traffic, no we are all blissfully equal when it comes to excuses, as to why we are running late, and are not on time.

When in fact we should be taught prioritization of tasks, in terms of the strategic matrix; into administrative, logistical, and operational criteria.

The time spiral also deals with repetitive and none repetitive tasks, and actions. Daily prioritization and tracking of tasks, and task action maintenance which deals with task, of a reparative nature, like stats and their deadlines as a key measure of progress. As a norm repetitive tasks require drivers, and lots of action maintenance – resources and logistics - to make sure they are generated and produced in and on time. We need specific outcomes and champions for every aspect of our strategy, in terms of it's strategic importance, its tactical relevance and its timing for action and revue. When working with predictions and time, we predict which tasks are more important and critical and arrange them in order of importance, then we queue them, and then we go over to action maintenance.

Taking our strategy over to action

Action plans, and action items are important elements of strategy execution, because this is where the strategy meets the tar. It implies the following. Action maintenance is charged with the active engagement and co-ordination with tasks so that they come to an expected conclusion, with some learning loops, this is the goal. So that we do not do things repeatedly and keep getting the same results, we must learn and carry this learning right through. Action maintenance is independent authorities that crack the whip on the strategy. Now, by assigning responsibility and accountability as well as deadlines - we will keep doing it until we get it right, how is up to the drivers. We all realise that any task and predictions rely heavily on knowledge of any present conditions, but present conditions are largely invisible until we get to the event, and start performing it, only then do we get to know mostly how long it will take for real, and what will actually be needed.

Intent is the ultimate infusion of all intentions, imagery and actions, focused on realising one objective. Vision without intent is just n few words without power. It lacks essence.

Time, the last matrix element

Dealing with the dimension of time, time has everything to do with our intent, it is the velocity indicator, which dictates our effectiveness when using intent, to pass through the curtains of night and day, to see what tomorrow will bring, with time. The "past" "present" and "future" is the result of time, and the only time that exists. We hear this repeated often. If Time is seen as being composed of multilayered and multidimensional spirals of synchronistical energy that intersect, and at each intersect, we have, events, incidents or accidents happening. Then Time consist of two variables in strategy, the one is speed, and by varying the time allotted, it either *speeds up* a process or *slows it down*. The more time we have, the slower we go, and as it runs out we have less time, this then implies, that we only have a specific measure of time, to do more things in. Consequently, so it speeds up – we go faster to make it in time. The amount of time utilised or with specific time frames, will be referring to specific dates and time allocated to reach objectives in, this becomes and refers to a measure then. In business everything cost money, and if you can measure it you can charge it. Actual time available or used, equals money, either spent or made.

Then time is also relative and impacts on us with things like; seasonal time; that consist of less day time hours, more night. As well as seasons, where certain things sell at higher rates during December for instance, as they would during March for instance...

I would argue that most strategic problems with time usages and measures of it, are in fact communication problems. They are also policy and execution problems. That relate back to communication...

What is Strategic Conversation;

Strategic conversation reiterates the importance of accurate and timely information transfer as an operational enabler, it enables the delivering of business concepts, definitions and doctrine. With respect to a rapidly evolving information environment. It relates back to effective communication, the ability to process information, and to create understanding. By wilfully engaging with others on the key strategic attributes and principles of strategic design, in order to advance the strategic interests and objectives of the organisation. Strategic conversation then becomes relevant to the entire organisation as an institution tool, especially at the service level, where we start dealing directly with our clients, or products, on the tactical and operational levels. This is where we need to impact, we must feel, see and experience the strategy growing and coming alive. This must then translate in to more strategic conversation. This includes all operational actions, even supporting our public diplomacy/ relations and opinion. Strategic conversation is the process of integrating issues of audience and stakeholder perception, behaviour shaping, and paradigm alignment, into planning and operations at every level. Strategic conversation should aligns us with others, stakeholders, plans and objectives, the inner and outer environment, and connects us with support, and resources, those initiatives of a higher order concern. Constant feedback, analysis and assessment are necessary to ensure that efforts support desired outcomes.

Policy and execution problems

When our strategic messages lack credibility it's because we haven't invested enough in building trust and relationships, and we haven't always delivered on promises....We hurt ourselves more when our words don't align with our actions. The essence of good communication: is having the right intent up front and letting our actions speak for themselves. We need to apply principles. We shouldn't care if people don't like us; that isn't the goal. The goal is credibility, and we only earn that over time... now how to the act into action.

The nine principles of strategic communication; that drives action, people and organisations, that becomes the act, that brings about action. In order for this to happen we need certain traits;

1. Driven leadership – where leaders lead with structured strategic communication, and guide with principles and best practices.
2. Credible people – respect and truth in all aspects of work
3. Designed dialog – structured multifaceted exchanges of ideas and concepts, resulting in focused aligned strategic communication.
4. Unity of effort – at every levels; from administrative, operational and strategic, all coordinated and structured into one continuum.
5. Rapidity and responsiveness – act with lightening speed and decisive action, becomes spontaneous, and intuitive.

6. Seek understanding in everything; deep comprehension and study of the inner and outer environment – with cognisance.
7. Pervasive and resilient – no matter what, we will succeed or finish what we started, with our die hard attitudes, anything is possible.
8. Results driven – narrowly focused on intent and delivery.
9. Consistency and continuity – focused on doing and designing things that will prevail; that will persist and sustain itself. Through constant evaluation, and re-design, with constant planning, analysis , execution and review, that creates meaningful coincidences...

There can or will be no action, without the acts of true leadership and cunning. One of the challenges is the need to foster a better understanding of the relationship between "listening" and "communicating", between superiors and officers, between management and employees. "Strategic listening" is imperative if we are to understand strategic communication as an overarching philosophy intended to guide the way to action. The ideas contained in this functional concept and other related guidance of people to perform tasks well must be critically examined, fleshed out and adopted within our educational institutions, training venues, and be high on our career path lists. The innovation and adaption of cunning, being pursued in the strategic time spiral continuum, and cognitive strategic arena, influence our operational expediency. Only by having exceptionally cunning managers capacitated and trained in this understanding of leading "men", can it be transformed into art, in the field of operation. Only then, and when, will it translate into institutionalized strategic actions across the organisation, that becomes a culture of true, and cunning leaders. If middle management fails to adopt, adapt and improvise, they will never be able to overcome diversity, and chaos, thus never overcome indecisiveness. In order to achieve this we need to;

1. Carefully select the members of your design team. Here we use two criteria for selection - first make sure you include those who can, and will, contribute positively to the content of your resultant design. Secondly, make sure you also include those who are positioned to drive the successful implementation of the strategies within the design, the plans. Implying that we need true leaders - both formal (per the organization chart), our appointed leaders and both informal (natural) leaders, people well liked and respected to play the political card. Open with predesigned instruction sets (make your intent clear and ring fence the project with guidelines and parameters to work in) on perception management and alignment outlines that need to be adopted, that need to form part of this continuum.

2. Remember that strategic design is more than an event; it's a matrix of thought, a process of thinking, and design, that delivers comprehensive strategies, that starts with the first union. Only once you've developed the concepts, then only starts the design, then the planning, and ultimately follows the action plans...if done right you will have a "Grand Strategy" emerging. Now we start the real work.

3. Ready your managers with reproductive thinking, and pattern recognition skills, ahead of time. Make sure they all study and understand the definition, and the importance, of terms - like, "intent", "critical thinking", "continuum" and "envision". Make sure they all understand the critical role they play in both strategy design, intent, development, implementation, and execution. The full cradle to grave concept. Strategy needs to be monitored closely. A workshop (with an applicable case study) on the "strategic continuum" that will be followed, should be held to have the design evaluated, and having an overview of the total process works best.

4. Involve employees (doers) beyond those on your planning team at this stage. Ask

them for help, and give input, get the buy in. Be intuitive. Have them participate in pre-planning surveys, testing, and dry-runs, to "bubble up" issues for discussion at your up-coming strategy sessions. Be sure to offer them feedback on the outcome of those sessions. Remember, asking for their input implies a promise to feed back. If you forget that feedback, they'll feel cheated.

5.   Gather applicable information prior to your "open to the house" strategy sessions, where all aspects are explained, and left open to scrutiny and comment. Very painful, but a necessary evil. Here we ask critic, and strategic thoughts to be exchanged. Here we clarify goals, examine assumptions, discern hidden value, we unpack to add value, evaluate evidence, see what our actions would accomplish, and measure if it will be enough, and then we close the session and assesses our conclusions. Then, prior to your next strategy sessions, gather and share this information amongst the members of your planning team.

6.   Hold your next finalisation and sign-off sessions away from your office. Avoid the interruptions and distractions which so often arise when planning team members' meet at offices. It's too easy to step down the hall to check a message, and return much, much later. Don't fall victim. Meet "off campus."

7.   Allow enough time for your final action plan design sessions. Strategic thinking involves thoughtful discussion, testing and evaluation at this late stage. This simply takes more time, and find the patterns for success. Those who rush, end up with an inferior design.

8.   Encourage open strategic communication, and avoid dualistic behaviour to grow. If you're the boss, you'll play the most difficult role in the process. For you'll walk the fine line between being an active participant and coming across as "too strong." As the boss, you're in a position of leadership. Others will simply hear your voice as a bit more loud than any of the others. Tone it down a bit and encourage others to participate.

9.   Communicate your strategy, again, and again. Once you've developed your strategic plan, let your employees know of your strategy. Focus on strategic talk, and focus people on the goals and objectives with alignment. After all, it is they who will help with its implementation. And don't just tell them once. Tell them again, and again.

10. Keep your plan alive with spontaneity. Pick your strategic and tactical focus. Maintaining a strong strategic focus and alignment, amounts to a combined initiative, between strategy and tactics. Have your employees develop specific action steps (tactics) to implement your strategy. Monitor progress of those action steps at daily, weekly and with quarterly review meetings. Remember, it's one thing to develop a strategy, and quite another to implement it. This is real work! You'll need to manage it as such.

11. Link your strategic plan to your budgeting process. As part of your action plan development (see #10, above), estimate the resources required to accomplish all of the action steps - thus implement the strategy. Those resources should include: people, money, facilities and equipment. These estimates feed nicely into the budgeting process. So your budgeting cycle should (ideally) follow your strategy development and your action plan development. Implementation is where you'll spend the bulk of your time and resources. Make sure you take implementation seriously. Integrate your plan into the day-to-day operation of your business.

The four basic principles on which all strategy resides can be summarised in one word, *Power*.

The use and abuse of power has become entrenched, even endemic, especially at all levels of government, and it is seeping faster into corporate entities, than ever before.

Moreover, it is individuals that cause the cancer, not the culture. Daily we read in the media how certain individuals have abused their power, have become corrupt, stole, or left a company ruined, because they were not fit for the positions they held office over, or abused its power. Abuse of power extends individuals, now even organisations are bullying and forming monopolies, controlling whole markets, this even extends to countries, enslaving their people. The point to make here is this, power exists, and people use it daily. How we play, or don't play, the power game is what makes us strong or weak at the game of politics. Political beliefs, views, principles and opinions, fashion power. *Politics consists of social relations involving the use of authority, influence and power. Furthermore it refers to the regulation of peoples affairs within a segment of society, or industry or religion, or government, and the methods and tactics used in these instances to formulate and apply an agenda as policy, law or religion.* As it too, is part of strategy. How we view the relationship and influence of power, between us and our peers and their principles, will also predict our strategic success. How we view power, use it, and manage with it, will ultimately determine our long-term survival or early extinction. As you may, or may not have surmised, this chapter is all about power, and politics, and those who are more powerful than us.

The principles of strategic power refer to four set elements: *The Warpath, The Grand Strategy, Influence and Overall Leadership* that will determine how, where and when power will be used. You need to be cognisant and intuitive all the time, tapping into the collective until you experience that "aha" moment. Where our reason, imagination or interest are not engaged as one, focused, then we have difficulty connecting, then we are no longer intuitive, open to possibility, and experiencing and learning things. However, if we are strong, then strategy will remain standing, on the other hand, if one leg is weak it will eventually collapse as the weight of strategy unfolds and becomes heavier on this foundation, of our personal and corporate perception. What do these principles hold as their secret, for one they are all unique in every situation, they shift in balance, and take turns at controlling our thinking and strategy, let's look at them.

The Warpath

The combination of two words; "War and path". "War" implies a behavior pattern of organized violent conflict, and it can also be seen as the last resort, where **war** *is an* **extension of politics**, *but by other means.* **"Path"** *then, is seen as the way: a course of conduct; "the path of virtue"; " a way especially* **designed for a particular use,** *"genius usually follows a revolutionary path"... the "warrior's path" or the way of the warrior, who uses his power, where fighting then becomes a way of life. It also refers to power-play between two entities, (even internal rivalry). Furthermore, it also explains the "mood" of someone, or something, (the company is on the warpath), even a corporate culture,(these are war mongers, always on the warpath)...descriptive of power on a course to reach an objective violently if need be as a last resort...*

The "warpath" is the way we do things traditionally as people first and then as an organisation, it's a culture that we adopt to make our "way" of doing things the norm, to reach objectives with. Warpath, is a hostile mood in which a person goes to work against one another, with everything they have, to enforce their will. How it influences the overall strategic direction, is determined by how we influence our corporate culture, and how we refer to things, as they exist. The manner in which we do things; manipulate, scheme, drum up support, go nose-to-nose with others, and plot, to get our way, is referred to as our "Warpath". If the leader is strong and achieves much, then his warring path and his ideas will trickle into our corporate culture, this aspect will be governed only by mimicking this thinking, mythology, and corporate language, as well incorporating political views, biases and personal aspirations. The systems and levers of the "Warpath" is described as a way of life in the organisation, a course of action and intent, leading to violent clashes of will, and persistence. It's also the path of genius and revolutionaries.

Grand Strategy

In short, its comprehensive. It's the overarching strategy that combines all effort into a design, that aids, and directs all strategic action. Key factors of this strategy may include market, product, and/or organizational development through acquisition, diversification, joint ventures, or strategic alliances. Grand strategy at its essence refers to a collection of plans and policies that comprise of some deliberate effort to harness political, operational, tactical, and economic tools together. Functioning as a designed affair to advance the intent, objectives and interest of the continuum. Grand strategy is the art of reconciling ends and means that creates purposeful action. It informs and translates effort, and action into what leaders think and want. Such actions are only constrained by the factors of leadership. These things explicitly expected from managers and leaders; like specific skills and proficiencies required, coupled to the office or title. For instance; financial proficiency, managerial, administrative, strategic and organizational proficiency, coupled to the limitations of the environment, its budget constraints and the limitations inherent in the tools of the trade, and furthermore influenced by the macro environment and its resources. Its informed, and informs, seen in the context of the global economy. Grand strategy is all about using everything at your disposal, and translating it into tactics and strategy...to achieve the objective of the scheme.

Influence

Also known as, "*The Psychology of Persuasion*", where one person takes advantage of a position of power over another person. The decision to comply with someone's request is frequently based upon either persuasion, or coercion. Any profitable tactic to gain probable compliance.

The opportunity to exploit persuasion tactic is due to three characteristics of the *Rule of Reciprocity*:

The rule is extremely powerful, often overwhelming in the influence of other factors – apart from persuasion, or coercion - that normally determine compliance with a request.

The rule applies even to uninvited first favours, which reduces our ability to decide whom we wish to owe and putting the choice in the hands of others.

The rule can spur unequal exchanges. That is, to be rid of the uncomfortable feeling of indebtedness, an individual will often agree to a request for a substantially larger favour, than the one he or she first received.

The cascading of power and influence

In any enterprise today, we have people who use and abuse power. It has become truly essential that we develop an instinctive capability to want to influence people, and understand the best ways to do it with. However, this becomes a double-sided sword, and all power comes at a cost. This cost will influence our strategy – both good and bad. The use of power and influence needs to be checked and balanced. We need to draw up budgets to firstly see if we can afford it. As Wayne Dyer once said, we come from being NOWHERE to NOW HERE – only by the forces of influence, but at what cost? We all were born with a sense of power and purpose. We all have that "something" that we know makes us; faster, better, stronger, wiser, likable, sexy, adorable, wise, cunning, sharper, and so too the list goes on. The point is, we use it, that gift to get our way. To get what we want when we want it most.

Now, importantly, we have to look at the influence cards played by leadership, and the use of power, and coercion...

The Radical Revolutionary Strategic Management Matrix For Predators

- *Alliance building* – "out of sight settlements/ agreements"
- *Coalition building* – "canvassing for support"
- *Cronyism* – "supporting the leaders personal interest"
- *Deal making* – "you scratch my back and I will scratch yours"
- *Divide and rule* –"dirty tricks"
- *Empire building* – The misuse of organisational
  - infrastructure, position and people, to advance oneself.
- *Power mongers* - manipulate the system and its people. In
- their pursuit for control, power and domination, will do
- whatever it takes to eliminate competition.
- *Half-truths* – one sided interpretation to boost the presenter
- *The Hidden agendas* –People in pursuit of alternative higher
  - personal goals, by utilizing and exploiting the current system
  - as a vehicle / stepping stone, for a future position in another
  - sector with greater prospects...
- *Bedfellows* – sexual innuendo or sleeping with the boss for
  - favours, mostly a better position. Alternatively, to form a
  - pressure group, to halt initiatives, side-track the system or
  - destroy someone's credibility.
- *Spin-doctor* – people who create an alternative truth to fit
  - their reality, by mixing facts with perceptions – in order to
  - cover up their mistakes and flaws – an art form developed at
  - government level.
- *Sponsorship* – is support by a powerful director for a junior –
- mutually beneficial.
- *Window dressing* – fending off scrutiny, by masquerading and
  - doing things that please the director, seemingly aligning with
  - the powers, without doing anything productive or
  - constructive.
- *The rule of reciprocity* - This rule requires that one person try
  - to repay what another person has provided. You owe me, or
  - I owe you. You love me, I will love you. The rule for
  - reciprocation allows one individual to give something to
  - another with the confidence that it is not lost. This could be
  - seen as a gesture to gain trust or to expect it in future.

The sense of future obligation according to the *Rule of Reciprocity* makes it possible for various kinds of continuing relationships, transactions and exchanges that are beneficial to society. Consequently, virtually all members of society are trained from childhood to abide by this rule or suffer serious social disapproval.

Compliance with someone's request is frequently based upon the *Rule of Reciprocity*. It could also be used as a tactic to gain probable compliance, to give something to someone before asking for a favour in return.

It's all "Power-play", the methods for using certain influences as a power tools, to get leverage, initiative, support, or control. It provides for shortcuts, for getting things fast, and then real fast. The question is this, at which point do we need to start determining when to behave ethically and professionally and then at other times, ruthless and calculated like true revolutionaries. How do we get the balance right? How do we wage "civilised" war on our business path, and face our opponents in the business arena? It's all about appearance. Everything just needs to appear, civilised, decent, democratic and legally responsible, oh, and fair. Cleverly disguising their manipulations of people through the use of influence, by playing the ethics and moral cards when in trouble, makes people back off. This then becomes their power over others. Their ability to influence and control every situation, by manipulation , coercion and compliance. Strategy is not for the faint-hearted, those that live in denial, that think that no man wishes them harm, that life is fair. It's all about shifting perspective, and altering paradigms, through influence. There are a few rules to power play. In short;

- Don't bite the hand that feeds you – don't make an enemy of the one that you serve under.
- He who walks alone walks further faster – there is very little usefulness for friends in a work environment, acquaintances, and networks yes – by all means, don't get confused.
- T-bone your internal opponents – crush their will to fight you – never let them know what you are busy with, until such time that it is time to reveal – this way they won't see it coming, and won't have time to prepare.
- Don't elevate your status beyond your means, by over stretching yourself you will reveal your vulnerability.
- Disappear from time to time, and then emerge an erupting volcano, never just be a somebody, be that someone that they need, and come to for advice or something. Make your presence felt.
- Protect your reputation and honour at all costs – and fight tooth and nail if someone attacks it, or attempts to tarnish it...
- Partner with lions, not lambs – surround yourself with a few strong people.
- Get people to believe in a paradigm by repeatedly, enforcing it, until they preach it as if a belief themselves.
- Caution, always pick your words wisely. Especially, when you are trying to impress people with words, the social shortcut, the more you say, and not make a point, the more common you appear. Making a point, is key to controlling conversation, otherwise we become very vulnerable to the manipulations of others. He who seeks to exploit such influence for self gain, now has means. Therefore, keep the initiative, erupt and retract, erupt and retract, just like the volcano. It lets people stand in awe, when you speak, and wait in anticipation, when you say nothing.

Overall Leadership

Refers to leadership as both an art, and a privilege, and the business of everyone in a position of power... this includes both natural and appointed leaders.

Serving "Number One"

In the negative; Is no fun when he is in fact a zero. This is the thorn in most organisations side today. leadership flows from the top, mark my words, from the top. If there is a void, then it's because there no real leader. It's not the people, the strategy, the systems, or the resources, its just the absence of power. Then you get yet another reality, that of political appointments. Political appointments have the tendency to be just puppets, using their positions, the trend is that they only look out for themselves, their family and friends first, only in it for the money, and to further their own agendas, and political future, and then you have people getting appointed that have no business in these positions today as a matter of politics. Then the emphasis of what management implies and signifies shifts to a warped reality. It's like having a red Mini with a Ferrari badge on, it's just not the same thing. It's all window dressing. They tend to use power to prove that they are right and able no matter what the results of their actions, at any cost. On being right at any cost... it is nothing less than self-preservation, and comes at a high cost, you pay for it in efficiency, effectiveness, and consistency - all-round. In an ethical organisation, they give emphasis to being content; over being right all the time, getting along, sorting out differences and moving on becomes the norm – a team effort.

Ethical and un-prejudiced conduct, is the suit to wear today and no longer just playing in favour of mainstream party politics. Leaders have to make trade-offs between these two extremes. In order to become good leaders, we have to be able to point fingers at one another and rub shoulders with staff – and differ – from time to time. We have to take a firm stance at some point as well, otherwise everything just becomes ordinary chit-chat, and you cannot just let everything slide into chaos. Order requires two elements; discipline and mutual respect. Self discipline and mutual respect needs to prevail before structure will emerge to hold things in place, such as leadership – a natural order of things as they exist.

Ethics should become the leadership's edge – this won't happen in an environment where talk is cheap, from "command and control" practitioners – in disguise. Codes of good conduct are necessary, however not to the extent where it becomes a 50 page document; that spells out every single aspect of conduct, it needs to be to some extent, almost standard rules. In most cases, the "lack of discipline" is actually a "lack of inspiration" and management skills. People who cannot manage, and lead, rely on rules, policy and procedures. Blind conformity to rules, codes of ethics, and so forth and so on, creates stagnation, everyone is just too afraid to act. Then rules seem to be applied differently, as we deem fit. "Ethical people" – shout foul, at every opportunity, as a means to wedge themselves into control and distract attention away from their own wrongdoing. Ethical behaviour is not behaviour guided by rules, but by principles. Behaviour that only satisfies self-interest is unethical.

By only serving "number one" and his interests, by dancing to his tune all day and night – you inevitable steer away from a human attribute – that favours fairness. It creates an atmosphere where everyone wants their worth to be noticed and realised – you just cannot move forward, or ever have closure in a self-consuming environment. Then the plot is lost, and you no longer serve a leader, you serve an ideology, an organisation, an objective. Where leaders think they are gods, it creates a culture where someone always has to win and someone has to lose, thus no one really gets close to the cheese they just get to smell, and even see it. But taste it, never

How do people become susceptible to this blind conformity?

People prefer to say yes to individuals they know and like – this is human nature, for the very simple reason, they then will also be liked. This simple rule helps us to understand how *Liking* can create un-sober influences in the work environment. Especially where people avoid conflict at all cost and polarise around existing only with harmonious influence. Here, they seem to forget that without friction / conflict, very few good things we have today would have ever existed, otherwise and or because of it. On the other hand, too much conflict and unhealthy relationships defeat this principle as well, no matter how you play it, it needs to balance out. Between friction and harmony, one day the one the next day the other. Compliance practitioners are – mangers that force their will – by playing on people's perception of what is right, in order to cover up their own weakness and insecurities. The will force compliance all day, every day, by emphasizing certain factors of ethics and/or attributes that they can control. Thereby they increase their overall attractiveness and subsequent effectiveness, without moving a finger. Compliance practitioners may regularly use several factors to get what they want, by manipulating the truth to suit themselves to increase their power... they control sheep – people living in denial of the truth.

Dr. Robert B. Cialdini, Professor of Psychology at Arizona State University, has spent over fifteen years in the scientific investigation of these processes whereby people are persuaded to reach their decisions. Here are some of his findings;

Physical attractiveness is one feature of a person that often may help to create some influence. Although it has long been suspected that physical beauty provides an advantage in social interaction, research indicates that this advantage may be greater than once supposed. Physical attractiveness seems to engender a "halo" effect that extends to favourable impressions of other traits such as talent, kindness and intelligence. As a result, attractive people are more persuasive both in terms of getting what they request and in changing others' attitudes.

Similarity is a second factor that influences both *Liking* and compliance. That is, we like people who are like us and are more willing to say yes to their requests, often without much critical consideration.

Praise, is yet another factor that produces *Liking*, though this can sometimes backfire when they are crudely transparent. However, generally compliments most often enhance liking and can be used as a means to gain compliance.

Increased familiarity, through repeated contact with a person or thing is yet another factor that normally facilitates *Liking*. Nevertheless, this holds true north principles when that contact takes place under positive rather than negative circumstances. One positive circumstance that may works well is mutual and successful cooperation.

A final factor linked to *Liking* is often association. By associating with products or positive things, those who seek influence frequently share in a halo effect by association. Other individuals as well appear to recognise the positive effect of simply associating themselves with favourable events and distancing themselves from unfavourable ones.

In further research studies conducted regarding *obedience to;* there is also strong evidence of the strong pressure within our society for compliance when requested by an *authority figures.* The strength of this tendency to obey legitimate authorities is derived from the practices designed to instil in society the perception that such obedience constitutes correct conduct. Additionally, it is also includes genuine authorities because such individuals usually possess high levels of knowledge, wisdom and power. For these reasons, deference to authorities can occur in a mindless fashion as a kind of decision-making shortcut. When reacting to authority in an automatic fashion there is a tendency to often do so in response to the mere symbols of authority rather than to its substance.

Our attention to symbols and towards *actual evidence of authority* and status, where we are not all that alert to the trust-enhancing tactic used, in which a communicator may first provide some mildly negative information about himself or herself. Then, this can be seen as a strategy to create the perception of honesty, by making subsequent information seem more credible to those listening.

An emerging *sense of independence*, which brings to importance of such issues as autonomy, freedom, and self control, where individual rights and freedoms are in question. People are especially sensitive to these restrictions.

There are many ways, we have addressed but a few, to give you an idea of the wealth of tactics available. Ways that leaders create control mechanisms; to create their own little "The People's Army" principle – living for an utopia or principle that can never materialize. This first army relies on crisis management, they emerge as victors to the crises that they create, with experience to resolve problems. Otherwise, everything is routine – this style of management will lead its army straight into battle - to one of two eventuality's; either emerging with great spoils or into bitter chaos and defeat.

The point is this; it is of no use to create sound strategy, for an organisation that is still on the march, or on their warpath, with no strategy and internal focus. That just goes forward regardless, blind and unperturbed in several directions at any given time.

The second army is one who picks their battles well, and test many routes before marching, weighing options and threats, they use their collective strength to define their aims and desired outcome – the revolutionists. They will only go on the warpath if it will lead to success, they have become, balanced, and organized as well as disciplined in their ways.

The leadership style

Serving number one

In the positive; The leadership style and corporate politics, has everything to do with power, and how we see our envision; the leader and his leadership is cardinal to the direction strategy requires, without direction it is just a plan. Direction encompasses more than just the way, it requires will, call it political will, to show us the path. This political will is summonsed by the board of directors.

We find the following corporate board styles:

- Rigid and tight control style – the rubber stamp board.
- This board functions around the ambit of strict policy and code, the rules – military and police.
- Interpersonal ethics style- the country-club board
- This board is more concerned with being gentlemen and ethical behaviour and conduct is the prerequisite.
- Task orientated style– the representative board
- More project styled and event management orientated, concerned with economy and efficiency in delivering a product on time.
- Professional association style – the professional board
- Most prevalent of all boards, especially in corporate enterprises, concerned with managing the totality of the enterprise.

Summary on how to beat the game

Many people in organisations must rely on the influence, negotiation and persuasion skills from their leaders and peers, rather than just their authority, to get things done – and most of them do not even have a title, yet, but they get things done. Your title becomes your authority, how you build upon it, becomes your own strength and influence. Start the change, with a new influence, by changing the paradigm of managers and management. Managers and management – these two terms are mutual and at the same time exclusive: it also implies that no matter what your title is, you cannot use it anymore as an excuse not to get dirty and down in the trenches with the rest – so to speak. One of your biggest challenges as a leader is getting people to do what they need to do in order to reach the organisation's goals and objectives.

Unfortunately, many leaders go about it in ways that are guaranteed to produce dismal results. By talking about rewards that are too far into the future and unrealistic, and if this carrot and stick trickery fail, they start playing the part of the authoritarian again, does any of this sound familiar?

Conflict and fighting are generally unpleasant and unnecessary. The fact of the matter is, that it is essential; you cannot have a decisive win, victory, or success, without having had a good fight.

Mostly with your own, if you did not fight for it, how can it become yours, how can you claim the victory, without having had challenges.

Challenges

The reasons for this are plain and simple – human nature can endure many challenges and even unfairness, it is stronger than the force of the people who play the control game well, the coercionists. However, in this day and age everyone is just watching out for their own jobs, because work is scares, so they crop up and crop up, until it becomes just too much. The game has to stop, we want out. At some stage we retaliate – as is our nature - and it can manifest itself in many forms – at this stage it is mostly too little too late, we have become the prey – the sheep.

Anything is possible however, from passive resistance to full out confrontational behaviour, sabotage and or self-destruction. No one wants to be compelled to do things that are forced upon him or her that go directly against their constitution.

The result of these games in the work place and on the corporation is a watered down version of what was contemplated and the more things are done in this fashion, the more the trickle slows down, competent people resign in droves, or the dictators resign. Many good men have been drowned in the misery of others, by only having attempted to reach out and extending them friendship, a helping hand, and then they too went down. The same with too much innovation, and change. We drown in our own confusion, when turmoil erupts, and people revolt. If and where change is necessary, make it feel like spring-fresh, exciting and peaceful. Leave friends for weekends. This should at least include a greater sensitivity to people's feelings at work, and you can detach whenever you feel like it. Beware, arrogant ambition flows into the sacrifice of holy cows; the common good, is replaced with, obnoxiousness, vindictiveness, spite, and selfishness.

Beware; Natural law dictates that; every action, has an equal and opposite reaction.

Focus on the principles of a correct management style; by saying this, we imply that you are no longer allowed to force your own will on anyone, especially if you want to expand your influence. If you cannot make a sound argument, judgment, or decision as a manager, then you cannot manage people. You need to work on your people skills. If the collective consistently resist, then you have to revisit your plan of action, your presentation skills and work on your sphere of influence. You first have to build rapport, via structured communication. Before you can gain influence – this in itself is a strategy.

Structured communication, via informal – and formal roles, some examples are:

- **Be more social around business – in the sense of decision-making that flows from a directive in your strategy**: The business contributes to social advances, encouraging networking among executives. This has been sighted as the most important factor in business today – social and strategic communication in the organisation. It builds trust and one-on-one interactions at different levels. It also diminishes the Game of power struggles. People like to be heard and once that bridge is crossed they like to listen.
- **Less risk tolerant and more purposeful.** This lone-range style of management creates stability, within departments and the organisation; We now have core business as our first priority and long-range goals as our aim – this creates stability.
- **Less control oriented systems, procedures and protocol, more relaxed management.** The delegation skills of executives tend to allow others to support them at their own accord, whilst the executive pursues their strategic interests – and look after the infrastructure, resources and development arena, as a primary focal point. Executives today feel and tend to want to manage all aspects of the business, because they don't see the value of exercising restraint. If all Executives just stick to calibrating strategy – the intentional revisiting of structure resources and strategy. The resources, infrastructure and development challenges will surface, in a global picture. Remember, implementing a plethora of checks and balances, is called – micromanagement. It shows little trust and weak self-esteem.
- We teach people how they can treat us by the way we treat others. If you want to know the values of another person, watch how they treat people who serve them.
- Within the context of the global economy we need all our managers – to become "inspiring and influential". With a style that complements both the person and as a result encourages overall stability, with a fixed emphasis on moving forward and growing as a person, a company and a collective.

Our listening should develop

Understanding, that listening to conversation takes up two thirds of the total reasoning process. Then, replying effectively is the result of having listened with intent, or intuitively. If not, then we have failed at communication. Politics, power and communication run hand in glove. A leader therefore should be listening more, so that he can communicate narrow; clearer more to the point - thus better. It is only when we get to know communication, that we really get to understand people. Some lessons learned in the past, have become gems in the future, pearls of wisdom some call it. Supporting people is much more effective than just advising them. The truth of this matter is that people in general learn more from mistakes than just applying these experiences willingly. Communication is just not effective if we don't apply reason, as managers we have to listen attentively before we act. Subsequently, we will be in a far better position to teach, guide, give advice and support employees, fellow workers and management alike. Just like with children, you can repeatedly warn and advise them about potential danger, without effect, but should they get hurt, be sure they will have learned a great deal more from their experience than what they would have done listening to advice otherwise. We also need to gauge all our interaction, by being intuitive, and decide how to convey and when to convey lessons learned, or get people to just listen to some wisdom. Until such time that you have proven yourself, you will just have to let go under certain circumstances and just cushion the learning experiences with people, until they realise that you are truly wise and have learned that it's good to trust your instincts and follow your advice. Being a leader is all about being a Father figure; both strict and disciplined, as well as wise and trusting. By endeavouring always to contribute towards relationships with fellow employees, we build trust – not friendship. The best performing children, are the one's that get equal measures of love, trust, and discipline. This imparts empathy, guidance, respect, support and understanding as well as freedom to make their own decisions. Leaders should keep this in mind, that people need to love what they are doing, feel trusted, and know that they will be disciplined if they don't perform or behave badly – just like pigs.

Identifying pigs without principles before it is too late

If you are a "Pig" you will conform to some "principles" as long as it suits you, you chop and change the interpretation, you apply it here and not there, these principles are always influenced by the politics practised in the company and endorsed by the few in power, the chosen clan of pigs. This is the proverbial "wolf in sheep skin group" a corrosive "political party" or personality in business. They deal from the win loose paradigm. They believe they are the victims, and everyone is out to get them. They believe that there is only so much pie to go around and only the fittest will survive and get to share it. They serve a greater darker master, that of self-interest and will do whatever it takes to get a bigger share of the pie, normally the Lion's share and eventually the whole pie. Mostly, you will find them seeking self-gratification along the lines of public recognition, a prestigious position and favouritism, they produce nothing much and they never bring in the numbers, or amount to much. We all know personalities like this, we might even be one, and have never realised it before. Nevertheless, at a cost, they leave a trail of broken spirits and disgruntled employers behind them as their legacy, if we empower them and give them titles, and authority...The methods these devious pigs are using, is entrenched in exploiting diversity in all forms. Let me explain. We said that within diversity lie strength, but also treachery. Any person who has not discovered the true meaning and benefits of principle and spiritual centred living for him or herself and made it his life ambition, and guiding belief system, will sell his soul to the "devil", or the pig without knowing it. The pig, in classical literature is also referred to as an opportunist. The opportunism usually refers to a person or group betraying the fundamental principles of abundance for the purpose of self-gratification. The principle of abundance deals essentially with an environment where competition becomes futile, there is enough to go around for everyone. We have grown beyond our own needs, we have realised that we are serving a greater purpose, and it is best served as a collective. One can only find harmony if the collective has one purpose, and pursues it willingly. We have matured to the point where we realise and accept that there is enough for everybody to share, no matter which way you look at it or argue it. The theory of abundance is necessary for any long-term successful coexistence, plan or business. Often this aspect is overlooked by pure ignorance and human nature gone unchecked, the lack of capacity towards understanding the significance of spiritually orientated and principle centred living. In its absence we find political greed. Greed creates a perception that the short-term interests of the individual will be best served if he becomes an opportunism, and joins others who pursue same. Pure short sightedness on the part of the opportunist, chasing every perceived prospect of some immediate gain, this will be just another driving force, derailing any good intentions still left. Nevertheless, opportunism generally does not hurt the short-term interest of an organisation or group much anyhow. It is mostly medium and especially long term that it balloons, and then explodes into toxic waste. Inadvertently derailing any prospect of any future long-term strategic intent and potential. Through destroying essential relationships and formations of trust, especially the report structures are sabotaged by means of constructively overriding them or by-passing them. Owing to unholy relationships being formed, between the likes of key and senior management and their very junior employees. Giving them direct contact, thus by passing formal command and control, right through to the upper echelon of management. It is through this type of relationship formed, that trust is broken at all interceding levels between tiers of management. This action has yet another effect, the formation of cells within these tiers, the followers and the non-followers. Better described as company political party formation, each becoming openly critical of the others favoured affiliations, views and perceptions. Now, as time goes on and the situation is allowed to evolve, it tends to form more pockets of resistance. It undermines the very fabric essential in formulating strategic plans for various reforms. Because of people's strong desire to be recognised, they start to compete, in ingenious ways, the one undermining the other, at first it is harmless, like lion cubs playing. Then, with time, they, like the lion cubs become serious, up to a point where it becomes personal and ferocious. Then it becomes a battle of brainpower and favour. People who practice "opportunism" have little empathy and sympathy for others, they have very poor people skills and normally suffer from poor self-image. They feel it their duty to always judge others from their own perspective, even openly; they belittle others by virtue of sharp wittedness and sarcasm, even jokingly, just to serve a personal agenda. They are the typical one track minded people, hell-bent on elimination. Their way is the only way, and this is makes them dangerous, power and arrogance combined spells sure disaster and chaos. The term "opportunism" is also used to indicate the practice of "selling out" to the new corporate culture and its views or its principles for either personal gain or the prospect of some form of a promotion. Self elevation, and making sure everyone knows how important they have become – is a daily ritual, of egocentric babble.

A to Z constitution of principle centred living:

Simple, yet practical truths, and ways of enforcing and instilling good behaviour.

A. *Don't spoil people too much*, to the point where you're in fact robbing them of their worthiness. Their potential to appreciate what they have achieved in life through hard work. The things that they have achieved themselves gives them pride and joy. For anything worth having has a price tag, every person knows fully well, that we value those things most, that we had to sacrifice time, love, and energy for. We are also brought up to know what we are entitled to and what not. Only "things" that one had to work hard for, by having sacrificed are truly worth having, remember this always. It is within all human's nature to "want" things they don't really need. Human's will always be testing each other's good nature to see how many of these "things" that you have and that they "want", you will sacrifice on their behalf because of your relationship with them. Learn to say No when you feel that you are being exploited and mean it. You will never be doing anyone a favour, by just giving away your hard earned things that they "want" without putting in any sacrifice themselves. Realise that anything given without work will become meaningless to them anyway, once they have filled themselves with it, they will hate you. The truth is that there are no short cuts in life. Food and clothes as well as medicine, can be given. Houses, cars and electricity should be earned. Life in itself is about making transactions and learning from it, followed by patience and perseverance, we need to teach the poor this aspect, so that they may come to power in principled living. They need to understand the required effort of each need and want, its price tag, and without currency, we will never be able to afford it. Effort becomes currency, without effort there will never be a win-win situation, only win-lose or lose-win, and lose-lose. This in itself is not conducive to growth and development of any people, or nation in any way. We only promote poverty, and dependency, by throwing things at the poor and needy that makes us feel better, without teaching them the gift of principles. You will be doing yourself and them a great disservice by indulging in the practice of free hand-outs. This practice could also be interpreted as discrimination. Because we take away their pride, and reduce them to nothing - just beggars and thieves. This is a universal principle, of nothing for nothing. "They say that No good deed goes unpunished", this is where this saying comes from...

B. *Never use force in any fashion or form as a means to get things done.* It only teaches your subordinates that muscle is a means to get leverage over people. This then becomes a means, and eventually all that counts, and it is fast, takes little effort and patience. People who grow up within an environment with much coercion and persuasion via violent means, tend to become reckless, and they too learn how to use it, and will shift their focus towards ascertaining such perceived power, and more of it, as a means to get their things done. People in general tend to respond more willingly to being led and taught by someone that they consider being knowledgeable, and respect, than what they do to people using forms of coercion power.

C. On the other side of this coin, all *humans instinctively crave for stability and safety in any environment* that they find themselves in. Safety in terms of their jobs being secure and security in terms of being cared for and looked after. This aspect is only to be found where true order prevails and as a means of keeping order one needs to be firm. There needs to be rules and discipline, and it needs to be applied fairly at all times. We all inherently prefer firmness, it builds confidence, (not referring to arrogance or autocratic means) but rather an open honest straight to the point type of interrelationship based on truth, so that everyone knows where he or she stand.

D. *Allow for mistakes to be made and don't see them as problems either, but as opportunities for personal growth and leadership.* Understand that the road to competence is long and dangerous. If you have never been lost until you have found your way again, then you will never know the value of knowing how to find direction, and you will never find your way without getting lost. Therefore, don't make people feel that by making mistakes they are in actual fact committing sins. They, as you have, need to find their own way and what better way of building competence than emerging from incompetence victoriously. However, if we do not see the relevance of this aspect, we will be creating blind followers with no confidence in themselves, or their leaders, they will all feel that they are no good and start walking around with canes.

E. The next trait is *consistence* in terms of your perception, judgment and resulting actions. It is very hard to conform to this aspect of consistency, we are all-human and change things. If and where things change to fast, people get lost as well, or they feel out of place, and uncomfortable. Change, is forever influencing our conceptualised moral and ethical stance on matters arising. Nevertheless, be as consistent as possible by any measure, and where you have to move from one premise to the next, explain yourself accordingly. Perceived inconsistency confuses people terribly, they become very disillusioned because of this and they then resort to start looking for the cause. This is a sure-fire way to create division in the ranks and elicit a lot of emotional criticism.

F. Very important, *don't ever commit to making a promise based on any other promises made to you.* Or on information passed on to you, that you have no means of verifying or controlling. Promises should only be made on things that are well within your sphere of control. Don't make this fatal managerial mistake ever. A promise is a contract to deliver. If you don't, then it reflects badly on you, no matter what the excuses may be, or who or what is responsible, people lose faith and trust if they don't get what they were promised.

Your word is your honour. In fact so much so that where promises are broken more than not, it totally degrade your trustworthiness and creates suspicion if you cannot deliver on promises made. You might even come across as being incompetent and run the risk of being branded a liar, or as being devious.

G. *Never treat other people unlike the way you would like to be treated yourself, or expect to be treated in the first instance.* Respect cost nothing. So too does good manners. The old saying of, do not do unto other as you would have done unto yourself. Don't make people feel small and insignificant in your presence, if you are, then you are in fact making fire under your house, - lots of enemies with the people you live or work with. No one is your enemy until we make him or her our enemy. This type of behaviour will usually also spawn "Big Shot" behaviour, where everyone will become an expert unto themselves, to protect themselves from possible or even perceived future belittlement.

H. *Don't do things for people that they can do for themselves,* you will become the pack mule and ultimately everyone will eventually feel comfortable with dumping their responsibilities in your lap, or should that read on your back? This will create inner unwanted conflict.

I. *Do away with an "open door policy' when it comes to bitching and moaning,* it is one of the key ingredients to starting up office gossiping and creating division and suspicion. In line with this, never allow bad habits to attract attention, and then it takes months to sort out. The hot stove approach must be followed where bad, or incorrect behaviour is reported, rectify any bad habit immediately. Gossiping and email abuse especially, and any other form of instigation. Rather implement a formal grievance procedure policy where every "accused" is rightfully afforded the opportunity to defend him or herself, by first having reduced every accusation to paper before it is entertained.

J. *Endeavour, never to correct people in front of colleges,* they might take it personally; they will take much more notice of your concerns in private. However – there are certain instance where it is called for...

K. *In the heat of conflict, try to determine what the question is that requires a resolution.* By trying to reason with anyone in the heat of battle is futile, for some reason people in general create a mental block. Their hearing tends to be less than what it should be and so to their co-operation and response. It's all right to take any remedial action required to solve the question, but let's not talk about it until later.

L. We generally tackle *"wrong behaviour"* by asking the person concerned to explain his or her behaviour, like with our children. With adults, this approach backfires; it stands to reason that if he or she knew it was wrong they would not have resorted to such behaviour in the first place, or would they? If adults start behaving like children then it is because we treat them as such. Rather move your focus from trying to understand the motive or frustration behind the irrational behaviour towards trying to understand the frustration that caused such behaviour. In this way, you will effectively find the answer and solve the behaviour problem amicably as well.

M. Universally all people are endowed with the seeds of righteousness, moreover don't always resort to preaching as a means of trying to correct behaviour, you will be surprised to learn that *everyone knows the difference between right and wrong.* Rather apply discipline, by pointing out clearly the consequences of crossing the line and the inevitable results that will follow if the behaviour does not change.

N. They say that *honesty is a virtue, but don't over tax honesty too much,* strangely enough it has the opposite effect, people are easily frightened into telling lies. They do this in an effort to try to protect or defend their image. Image is an emotional matter and so is lying, so it's okay to lie if it will keep the image intact.

O. *People tend to become deaf towards others that nag, so stop nagging and begging.* Realise that you have a responsibility to fulfil, firstly towards your employer and then yourself, to be fair but also firm is very expectable and even required, this requires some form of nose to nose interaction at times, you will be amazed to see how junior supervisors are able to do this.

P. The only way to protect your organisation from disastrous consequences is to *get your staff to learn from experience before they become leaders*. This in itself is a required life cycle in the scheme of becoming an effective leader. The more you tighten the noose the more you suffocate the enterprising spirit of man; therefore you will have to do the complete opposite and let go. In the initial stages this will require a lot of 360° thinking and explaining, by letting go you will have to be very specific about what you want and by explaining the consequences, responsibility and accountability as well as the desired objectives clearly, before you attempt to let go. The more you do, the better the habit starts forming, until it becomes a ritual or trait.

Q. *The breakfast of champions is good continuous feedback.* Without feedback, we have no measure of our progress or success. Once again you cannot manage that, which you cannot measure. The measure of quality positive feedback will and should become your benchmark of achievement and the openness of the relationship, all other systems and measures to gauge performance by should become subordinate to this.

R. *Never forget the fundamental concept of actions specifically aimed at achieving greater understanding*, to stimulate our reasoning, and converse our enthusiasm into encouragement and better responses. This in itself requires a lot more listening and less over-analysing. Moving away from biasness and a lot of talking, a total seamless ability to exercise self-control.

S. Learning is conceptualised through experimentation and analysing of things as they exist naturally and the reasoning for their existence, therefore questioning the reasoning of anything's existence to ascertain logic and insight should be encouraged as it is a very natural process of thinking. We *ask questions to ascertain truth.*

T. The question of *spending quality time.* Quality time spent weighs far heavier in the corporate environment, especially on maintaining and forming of crucial individual relationships, by spending too little quality we create distance. The principle of out of sight out of mind, out of touch, creates a sense of out of reach. We should spend time with individuals within our organisation and outside and we should make those interactions count. Quality time is always measured in the fact; in how we spend our time that counts and not the amount of time we spend in doing so that really amounts to something worthy of mentioning.

U. *Do not concentrate on rewarding small achievements*, people may learn to enjoy poor or average performance because of it, be wary your focal point for benchmarking performance and rewarding it accordingly. Our ability to motivate and grow will be determined by our ability to recognise and appreciate the true ability to perform consistently and effectively. We should not award burst of achievement rather shift our focus on extraordinary continued performance and reward that.

V. *People who ask honest questions should be endured*, if you don't they might resort to seek their required answers elsewhere.

W. *As a leader and or manager do not ever think that it is beneath your dignity to apologise*, any honest apology makes for an immediate substantial deposit of trust into that persons personal bank account. Furthermore, acknowledge that you do not know everything and that every interaction, is still considered to be a learning experience by yourself daily. Be more human, be open to criticism and respond with optimism. Leaders need to be seen to be human to be effective, even icons make mistakes. That way you will not be judged on a pedestal and be criticised in an unforgiving manner. This releases undue pressure.

X. *Don't let people's fears arouse their anxiety, or yours* and then they will become more anxious and bewildered, show courage and wisdom in such instances. This will instil trust and camaraderie.

Y. *Treat you colleagues the way you treat your family and friends*, with kindness, compassion, truth, trust and empathy and they will become your closest allies.

Z. *Remember we all learn more from role models and stewardships than what we do from critics and books.*

When you get an idea you have 2 choices.

1. Think on it then Act on it. Or

2. Think on it then Sit on it.

This world is changing fast, and so should we. We can no longer just rely only on one school of thought, when in fact we require a matrix of knowledge, and possibilities to inform us of all our available options, giving us 360 degree vision.

To some degree it's just not happening, we are still stuck with basics. The most basic of methods are used in traditional strategic management (even today still) to describe a working model, just by plainly observing the winners and looking at what makes them win. Then creating a model from that. Thus taking for granted that that becomes a winning recipe for all who copy and paste it. It's totally absurd. Then some start adopting and merely adapting the model to fit again somewhere ells. This was strategy then, from a business school perspective. Then we also have Sociology, a Psychology perspective. They too used only the most basic of method in economic sociology, also just by observing large numbers of firms and looking for any pattern, that could aid them in explaining social differences in behaviour, thus psychology, that lead to success. Two different prospective that have never really met. We have to some extent succeeded in mixing it all up, both the practical, and workable knowledge, that have served us well, and by incorporating of these two extremes together to design a concept. The Strategic Management Matrix for predators with. It's result was a matrix of ideas, continuums, and tools. I truly hope it will serve you well.

Teaching people the basics, with acronyms, gives us shared reference points. Firstly, let us review in brief the cornerstones of this process; we explored everything about the precepts that drive us, and our strategy. Even the way we think and form perceptions that creates our paradigms (all in chapter one). Then how we see our reality (in chapter two), then we moved over to things effecting our character and our thinking (in chapter three), then - who we are, will determine how act and what we say or do. The rest of the chapters built us up, to revisit our frames of reference. We covered attributes of success that stem directly from our paradigms, formed from as early as childhood, our knowledge, our wisdom.

Create more Shared Reference Points with Acronyms;

CAPS: Defining the - who, what, where, when and how as a concept.

- C- Concepts
- A - Attributes
- P – Perceptions
- S – Systems

TAPS: The way to deal with the complexity of strategy.

- T – Tactics
- A – Accuracy
- P – Power
- S – Speed

PEST: Dealing with influence from outside that impact on strategy.

- P – Political influence
- E – Economical influence
- S – Social influence
- T – Technological influence

SMART: Integrating optimization tactics in your plan

- S – Specific
- M – Measurable
- A - Achievable
- R – Realistic and
- T – Time phased

Then we moved on and grew the concept of "radicalism" and the importance of the "Can do" attitude, developing the predatory drive and instincts, to give rise to mental vigilance, vigilance of mind, body and soul – creating an internal focus for us, on things, and how they relate inward – by having external focus. These attributes, then combined and incorporate with the use of wisdom and knowledge, forms our strategic sense, and means. Thus giving us concepts to work with, call it our seventh sense, our strategic sense, the ability to see and predict with a certain amount of certainty – logically – and with the same amount of imagery - creativity - the outcome of any strategy.

Having a good in-depth understanding of human nature helps us to formulate our thinking and make it strategy, the duality between our left and right dominated thinking mind combined, gives us insight into human emotional reactivity. Where we acknowledge inner conflict with the self, and find the outer influence causing it and visa-versa. We moved on to see the difference between radicalism and denial and its influence on action. People in denial; criticise, complain, compare, fight and put themselves and their interests forward in the place of strategy, thus causing it to fail. Where strategic "predators" are people who only seek to live with integrity, they communicate strong intent. They are people – pack orientated – in their approaches, great visionary people, pioneers with a deep caring, they make conscious decisions based on facts and the understanding of human needs, desires, and follow through on them with intent. They motivate others by doing so and become experts in seeing the bigger picture, by pioneering the way, true leaders that give power to the people they serve, to use their own wits to solve problems and create opportunities; they are courageous people, models of human mental liberation. This is all in line with the methodology of strategy taught here, it is all principle guided. As humans technology and businesses evolve, we can no longer be focused on designing one system at a time either, we have to fragment systems, smaller is faster and more to the point. Flatter is the way to structure port-to-port communication and hierarchy. Systems, like hovering strategy, that sustain and release pressure from building up in the main system, due to bottlenecks. Bottlenecks cause frustration and rogue information from filtering back as a result of lockups, things stand over and it creates more pressure on others in the systems that are reliant on the first mentioned and visa-versa.

Pick your battles

Pick your battles wisely; fight one at a time and treat your enemy reasonable, as you do your friend, or they might take from you your victory, by making your opposition harden themselves and hate you and turning your friends against you, thus turning victory into despair. All great generals, have lost their nerve and then emerged the stronger for winning it back, when you do, let others run the show, then recompose yourself, emotion is all powerful and all human, like riding a wild horse, the more you lose your balance, the more you will learn to keep it.

Any army requires Structure and organisation

Napoleon was a good example of this, obsessed with structure and organisation, he intentionally had built in flexibility into every tier of his structure, the lesson is simple, a rigid bureaucratic structure is centralised and locks the organisation into linear thinking and strategy. Where opposed to this, a segmented structure, (the matrix) gives you options. He believed that strategy started with structure and it must suit the prevailing circumstances. By deliberately facing our fear of change and of losing balance and control, we condition ourselves to its presence, by doing exactly that, we force change on ourselves and then our anxiety grows less, our balance stays on course and so do we stay in control. Life and leadership is a race, only in the relay, do we go faster and further, learn to delegate and relinquish control, give compliments and credit where it is due and punish the ones that do not play by the rules – balance is control and not control itself.

Sometimes the directions we seek in life are written on the outside of the box, whilst we seek for it only on the inside.

In situations where we are tested, stay calm, force on yourself a mental determination to overcome any obstacle. By removing yourself from the equation, the intensification of one's confidence and ability only notches up our strength, once we realise that everything has its natural time and place and something's we just cannot change and only time will change it for us, we just have to except this and carry on; with the things we can change. This serves as a counter balance, when our balance has shifted. Every engagement be it physical or mental or both, has to do with the instances where resistance crumbles and balance gets shifted. Change is the best master of balance; the more we change the better we balance, change every aspect of thought and find new meaning, new footing and new balance, do the same with control. This becomes one of the aspects of war, namely fluidity, manoeuvrability, momentum; this exploits situations of chaos, where we create uncertainty, thus winning back the initiative, just by changing the inner focus and our composure, to reflect as strength, outward. That which has mobility, fluidity, has life and endless possibilities. Keep your balance to keep the control.

Adapt core strategy

Miyamto Musashi, author of the Five Rings, teaches us that in each interaction, we must adapt our core strategy to that of our opponent and the prevailing circumstances, keep changes active, habits crystallises thinking. We only require one shift, that of perspective, then we change the paradigm and our balance shifts, be like thunder when emotional and like a lake of ice when calm, this is how to shift inner balance. Strike with decisive and deliberate force, do not play the spectrum of being angered steadily and then wanting to strike, we have to explode into action, it is mentally disorganising and unbalancing if we have a build-up. Fight or get ready to fight, a barking dog loses his esteem, but a biting dog never his respect. Explode into action with relentless determination to succeed, or wither in the storm, this is shifting your outer balance, only you will know when it will be best to do either or neither.

Plan as if you are planning for War

War then you say has everything to do with corporate strategy it seems, yes; even in the boardrooms, we find it. The likes of character assassination, deceit from a good colleague, becoming the escape goat, deaf by strangulation of initiative, sabotage of ingenuity so that agendas may prevail, undermining of authority and worth and the last one and my all-time favourite, masquerading true intentions and playing to the audience and the leader, telling them exactly what they want to hear. Just to get the mule to do all the work. How does one overcome this, well several generals realised that no one can be trusted with plans alone, everyone has an agenda, so he who walks alone walks faster, sees more, hears more and stays vigilant and is less likely to be distracted and lose direction. The very purpose of our life is to seek happiness through training the mind. - Dalai Lama. These are pearls of wisdom, in strategy wisdom always wins over knowledge, the feeling of having nothing to lose is created by wisdom, wisdom stays forever steadfast, whereas knowledge forever changes form and therefore becomes a destructive force when not harnessed by wisdom. Where, opposed stands wisdom as fluid and resilient. This is the very reason why this book is aimed at thinkers and thinking strategic. When something has been improved due to critical thought having been applied, it ripens into clearer ideas, which create order and instil calm, accordingly, for one to be content with what he has as knowledge only, indicates a lack of effort on his part. While the wise realise that only with continued improvement of thinking will clarity remain and knowledge become obsolete. This is the very aim of strategy, not to create friction or war, but mental balance in all spheres of life and everyday living. However, without war and friction there will be no peace, just winners and losers, as we are all creatures of desire and it is desire that requires knowledge to exist. This is where we all start our suffering, because we want and want more, this is fine; nevertheless, this creates opportunities that create friction and competition, with the result that we have to have winners and losers. People change their perception, only if they see the necessity, therefore make it essential that they have to run in the race. Remember this; there is no such thing as winning; there are only people that fail less often. "Success favours the bold, trying is like dying, a slow process that leads to demise". Thinking only, brings more risk of failure and we become content with failing, by setting our sights lower and lower still. It is only through action that thinking stays relevant and clear. Remember this, even winners fall on bad times, these instance should be used, to cultivate new strengths, new tactics and to review old doctrine. Constant metamorphosis and changes make us stronger. Willpower is only rejuvenated if everyone believes that the goal is attainable.

Once this foundation is laid, move on and become the – Classic_ "One-Minute Manager": written by Kenneth Blanchard, Ph.D. & Spencer Jhonson, M.D.

Strike the balance between, being the tough autocrat and the nice democrat. Remember this; results are only achieved through people. Stop making all the decisions, let people start thinking for themselves. Make it clear what the task is; the responsibilities that go along with it and then hold them accountable. Get people to set goals, their own, one minute goals – write down what needs to be done and then do it - and keep them to it, this is their performance contract. Keep this informal performance contract standard; show them the benchmark for good performance. The benchmark is to solve your own problems effectively, either by doing it yourself or getting people to help you do it. The difference between a problem and complaining is this. A problem only exists if there is a difference between what is actually happening and what you desire to be happening. If you have not found the difference yet, then you are only complaining. With one-minute managers -you hardly get any help; you have to figure it out on your own. Why, that way it is your success and yours to claim, you have evolved as a problem solver - rightfully, when the praises come. Proper feedback is the gauge, if you give feedback on you progress and resolve – your work rate and efficiency is gauged, that will lead to recognition - referred to as one minute praises. Catching people out, doing the right things, is the undying philosophy – it makes them feel good about themselves and want to do more meaningful work... that keeps them in suspense – wanting to be caught out doing something else right again. It stimulates true and not just enacted positivism. Then, we get the one minute reprimand, the moment a mistake is made, the facts are analysed and then a conclusion is reached – brake even – where it was a legitimate mistake, or a - reprimand, where it was a careless mistake.

Coming up with a Grand Strategy; is the final aim of strategic management

Grand strategy is all about using everything at your disposal, and translating it into tactics and strategy...to achieve the objective of the scheme. In short, its comprehensive, relying on emergence and systems for its survival...

It's the overarching strategy that combines all effort into a design, that aids, and directs all strategic action. Key factors of this strategy may include;

1. market,
2. product,
3. and/or organizational development through acquisition, diversification,
4. joint ventures,
5. or strategic alliances.

By definition; Grand strategy at its essence refers to a collection of plans and policies that comprise of deliberate effort to harness political, operational, tactical, and economic tools, and combining them together. Functioning as a designed affair to advance the *intent, objectives and interest* of the continuum. Grand strategy is the art of reconciling ends and means that creates purposeful action. It informs and translates effort, and action into what leaders think and want. Such actions are only constrained by the factors of leadership. These things explicitly expected from managers and leaders; like specific skills and proficiencies required, coupled to the office or title. For instance; financial proficiency, managerial, administrative, strategic and organizational proficiency, coupled to the limitations of the environment, its budget constraints and the limitations inherent in the tools of the trade, and furthermore influenced by the macro environment and its resources. Its informed, and informs, seen in the context of the global economy.

Dealing with the jargon of strategy.

"Strategy" - is how we turn what we have into what we need to get that which we want. It is the conceptual link we make between the targeting, timing, and tactics with which we mobilize and deploy resources and the outcomes we hope to achieve." - Marshall Ganz

"Objective and Tactics"

Best analogy I ever heard:

The objective is to win the war.
The strategy is to take the hill.
The tactics are "skinny guys behind the trees, fat guys behind the rock".

"Strategic planning" - starts with *strategy formulation itself; however, the first aspect of strategy is* how to create strategy. Strategy formulation is the process of determining appropriate courses of action beforehand through analysis first, before we go about designing in a formal and structured manner, the act of creating strategy is an extremely complex process demanding sophisticated cognitive and social skills called "emergent strategy". The challenge is to have people thinking critically, finding the best solutions together and validating them before planning the final course of action, "a mixture of precocious accuracy and curious errors", "there is a co-operation of things of unlike kinds" - Aristotle.

"Strategy formulation" - serious radical strategic innovation calls for both a holistic and micro analysis approach referred to as Strategy *formulation. Strategy formulation is the prelude to any strategy, every strategy has a purpose, and here we define that very purpose, in terms of the;*

- *Vision,*
- *the Mission,*
- *the Objectives,*
- *the Goals and the*
- *Emergence.*

Then using Strategy vs. Tactics

There is always much confusion about the terms **strategy** and **tactics**. In addition, much of what is called strategy today is often really just **logistics**, so how does it all work? How we understand and refer to strategic terms, and relate to them will ultimately impact on our overall efficiency. For instance;

What do these words mean? In exploring these terms we'll also have to consider a new term: **Grand strategy**. In many situations there is a lot of overlap between the meanings of these four terms, but that doesn't mean that you can use them willy-nilly and not be laughed at.

Grand strategy is political. It sets the long term and short term goals both in and out of war. It decides who to attack when and what the goals of a war are to be.

Operational strategy or just strategy is the planning and the execution that leads to the fulfilment of the goals set in grand strategy. If the goal of a war is to capture an island with three cities on it then the strategy decides which order to take the cities in and what sort of force will be required.

Tactics is the deployment of troops to execute the strategy. Tactics often includes small set pieces of troop movements and deployments that are known to be effective.

Logistics is all about making sure that the troops are where they're meant to be before the fighting starts and that they have all the support (normally supplies, but can include other things) that are required.

People seem to confuse these two issues with strategy. Tactics divine how we are going to get it i.e. by force. Strategy only comes into play, where we want to start off on our quest, to give us a collective measuring point, against the desired objective. Then tactics takes over, until such time again when and where the organisation hits a preverbal bump. It could also constitute a junction on the path that they had set themselves to achieve their envision, that now reveals itself, with two or more opportunities as a result and we choose the one that we think is the better option.

Effective strategy formulation gives us unique insight into the rationalisation behind having strategy, by looking at its birth right, and the very reason for existence, validity and viability. Innovative thinking is excellent, but it always has a price tag. Strategy formulation has become the prelude to all innovation, both as an essential and required process to fuse all business decisions with innovation.

We only revise Strategy - Where the reality has changed;

- Either financially – we don't have the means anymore.
- Physical – the market has changed drastically, or our position in the market has changed, our ability / capacity is no longer sufficient, etc.
- Alternatively, strategically – this option and direction is no longer viable, we have to change our direction to survive.
- This is the point where strategy will be required to solve, a problem, or address an issue that will require vision, hindsight and foresight, as well as organisation and expertise.

Otherwise, it is all just managerial tactics. (Tactics that are revised as many times as what is necessary.)

True emergence of radical strategy

New things emerge every day, and it's all because of someone's strategy. Hence the term "*emergence*", generally used in strategic conversation to define an "emerging strategic assumption that is radical". This can equate to markets, products, raw material, and technologies etc... the elements and attributes of emergence has both attributes of the old and the new. These aspects also translate into views, assumptions and perceptions generating. Where view points on strategy formulation become radical, implying that we find ourselves at a juncture, with two perspectives here, that of "weak emergence" and "strong emergence". The term "Emergence" itself is described as how we categorize things systematically, and try to make sense of them by analysing them by themselves as individual parts or sub systems of the bigger systems; as well as objectives and frameworks that strategy has, having an effect on strategy. Weak emergence is essentially a term borrowed from reductionism philosophy; in which "local causes create local effects". The cause and effect theory applies here, where as in strategic terms it refers to new properties of alternative thinking of strategic nature, that is merely part of an old strategic language, or old model that is "required" now, by approaching strategy formulation from the humanistic point, and not purely from a systematic point of view. From the bottom up and not top down as is the belief. In order to describe the fit of any new system in relation to the old and their behaviour or impact with a focus on change and renewal. Emergence is thus better defined as an absolute renewed look at bringing innovation to life, in line and consistent with current technology and trends both on the local front and globally, to reach higher order objectives with, and not purely entertaining (new) strategic dialog at top management level. It requires independent dialogue, listening to "different voices, styles, and ideas" that come from the people who deal with the real pressures and forces of integrating change daily, expressing and exposing the forces in real meaningful terms, creating a polarity of business logic and operational logic, working in their different ways towards problem solving, to reach the same objectives.

Modernisation of Strategy

Modernisation as a business term has become a buzz, especially since the late eighties until now. Much emphasis have been placed on modernization. Strategy itself has been dominated by educated paradigms; business formulation, case studies, and management methods to guide strategy along this path of modernization, with new ways of formulation. With the effect that the West has been increasingly looking at science and so too the East, attempting to close the cultural gap, by combining several theories, to arrive with new theory and answers. One such theory has made waves, the reductionism theory of science – that deals with the analysis of something into simpler parts or organised systems, especially with a view to explaining or understanding things so that common people can understand issues that are more complex. Systems thinking originated because of this. On this view, in order to explain any event in the world we reduce it down to its fundamentals, as well as incorporating natural laws, and forces that influence change, to create a global understanding of business and its functions. In recent years, reductionism has been dramatically challenged by a radically new paradigm called emergence. According to this new theory, natural history reveals the continuous emergence of fresh phenomena, new structures, and new organisms with new unique powers, Darwin's theory , however they all still conform to natural rules and laws. Our collective consciousness is consequently required to solve these dynamics - forces that tend to re/produce activity and change in any situation or sphere of existence of new emergence.

Concept forming

Furthermore to this, emergent dynamics also plays with images, vision, symbols, history and social organisation, it transcends the pure conceptual form, but is never free of expectations to react true to its nature, and design. According to this view, when we think about emergence we are in fact in our mind's eye moving between two different vantage points, both from the understood to the unambiguous, back and forth, from the tangible to the theory. We see the trees, and the forest, at the same time, and make a distinction between the two. We see the way the trees and the forest are inter-related forming a system, with noticeable sub-systems. To see in both these views we have to be able to see their details, but also ignore some insignificant facts. The ability to determine the cut off line when dissecting is the ability to think holistic, and global. To quest to find that which connects strategy to the opportunities as they unfold is the criteria. However, leadership today seems imprisoned in not only academically taught social and corporate behaviourism, but also with their thinking belief on strategy.

Brian Quinn's famous quote: *"A good deal of corporate planning ... is like a ritual rain dance. It has no effect on the weather that follows, but those who engage in it think it does. ... Moreover, much of the advice related to corporate planning is directed at improving the dancing, not the weather."*

In an effort to work with everyone's ideas, and assumptions, we will have to start decreasing the amount of (emergent) fragmented assumptions (data), into workable form. There are two distinguishable options used today.

Common understanding

Working towards common understanding, only through the analysis of simpler parts and organised graphically depicted systems, explaining or understanding will come about, so we have to MAP it. By reducing multiple aspects to its own class – sorting things that belong together; into facts, assumptions, properties, attributes, concepts and systems, and its subsystems, to form one understanding of each ones usefulness will we see patterns and logic emerge.

Repair and maintenance of strategy

Designing and building robust systems requires designing and building of proper infrastructure, in support of growth and development, which takes more consideration as well. Strategy is not a "hot-air-balloon" that drifts over the business landscape and drops in on its objective, on the contrary, it is a massive heavy machine, like a tank, that moves, future focused, requiring constant re-supply and maintaining of its own internal structure and systems that support it. Future thinking and doing will accomplish far more with this approach, in far less time, with only a fraction of the effort of than what you have been giving it in the past. Performance is only accelerated once quality time has been invested in perfecting two types of strategy, "the Master plan", or "grand strategy" and "hovering strategy" or "maintenance strategy". The game of life is won behind the scenes, internally, by looking after our pennies we look after our pounds; time well spent on preparation and good maintenance is a good rule of any strong military force. Implementing and utilising strong modern theories of self-organisation, preserves previous efforts, and gains. Take note, today, business and governmental organisations face something of a "perfect storm" of problems, because they did not look after their infrastructure and resources, they did not, renew, protect, and maintain their gains, this now has profound implications for current and future leaders the world over. If your strategy does not set you apart from the competition, chances are it will fail, therefore make sure your employees understand how important it is to look after what we have, to maintain it, and renew it, before it is too late, furthermore, to work towards effecting interdependence, this can help put some teeth into your unity. The implementation of "Hovering strategy", could counter the influence of continued consequential repair and renewal or replacing of assets, at all levels of an organisation. Maintenance strategy is required, someone to take care of the "tanks" maintenance while we make "war" type of scenario. By adopting hovering strategies, we are providing for a maintainer of the total system, that forms the support structure for the system.

Defining objectives

When defining new objectives in relation to the changing global context, as being both effective and essential elements, by studying previous systems and strategy and the forces that they contended with, and the way they do or could reoccur, will be time well spent. Why old objectives still exist in the first place, might be explained better, only by fully understanding their past significance and usefulness, which has large scale implications for most new strategies future.

Strong emergence implies that if systems can have qualities not directly traceable to the old systems components, but rather to how those components interacted(was structured) to give it existence; and one is willing to accept the new system on the same design, then it is not so difficult to account for how the new system will react in reality. Nevertheless, a better assumption, than taking on something (totally) foreign. Therefore, there are no guarantees in life; it becomes an educated, deductive, and informed opinion. Where new qualities cannot be simplified or simplified further to the systems level and its resident parts to see what made it work well, when we just know it works and therefore should work again if constructed in the same manner; we do not always have to know exactly why, and then this design becomes a relevant choice. Where the

~ 535 ~

whole is greater than the sum of all its parts, and it works, then the parts significance becomes unimportant. The strategists then is left to determine the size and complexity of systems being designed, by choosing its blue print, structure and the relevant interactions we want to consider as part or parts thereof, thereby defining the systems boundaries and elements as well as attributes reminiscent of the old working concept designed as one thing. It combines two seemingly paradoxical mindsets: one is the objective – the aim based on facts rather than thoughts or opinions on parts and their significance, and the other, the subjective reasoning based on someone else's opinions rather than on pure facts as the evidence. This is the emergent property of strategy, it is both weak and strong in that some deductions are based on facts and others on personal assumptions and prior experience; this aspect itself may be either very predictable or unpredictable and unprecedented to some, it could also be flawed in its deductions, and influence the whole systems evolution. Either way, emergence presenting itself as being strong or weak; in fact or perception, is still emergence either way. Therefore, a code of practice that enables companies to understand their innovation processes as cardinal to the success and outcome of strategy, resides in the ingredients that go into *strategy formulation*, it becomes the catalyst to all system and functions for future use. Therefore, it is good and both required, encouraging creativity at a strategic embryonic level, requires caution, caution needs to be exercised to determine the risk and implication, during the process of innovative strategy formulation. Every action has an equal and opposite reaction, consequently, we need to have quality and reality checks in place. We have to continuously test our facts and our assumptions and our theory, as strategy just keeps becoming more and more complex as it unfolds, strategy formulation needs to concerns itself with behaviour, analysis, facts, hypothesis and assumptions first, and then only with its properties that relate to the factual.

The systematic process

The systematic process of strategic planning combines spontaneity at the level of emergent of ideas that are not yet tested, we assume much first, and then we apply the rule of caution, with the focus on creativity and chance. Spontaneity and chance are aspects of causes of effects, as they adapt and manifest to become the new. Nothing commands systems to conform to a certain structure of rules; instead, the interaction of each of its parts within its immediate surroundings causes the complex chain of processes leading to some form of order within chaos. Within the sphere of moral actions, it must involve free choice, without free choices, we will not find any interaction or initiative otherwise, and only humans are capable of deliberation when they are faced with the subject of choice. Traditionally we remove this aspect of choice from the equation of strategy formulation because we act on the side of caution. This knowledge, of all the cardinal forces influencing strategy in its making is centre to good strategy formulation. Emergence as a process of formulation of strategy without any formal structure is referred to as the complexity of strategy, as new ideas emerge they should be tested, and analysed first before we move to the next idea, and so forth and so on, quality, MQM, become a value chain activity. Strategic formulation and ideas that come about in this fashion, as formulating principles, whereby the right person or idea seems to hit on the right path - *emerge* - the emergence of strategy – at exactly the right moment when faced with a dilemma, this is its key to formulating good strategy. Only where strategist stay in the OODA loop, do they remain cognizant of the circumstantial influences as well as the progress of their strategy, then do we come up with revolutionary and radical resolve to potential pitfalls and problems by having our finger on the pulse. Just when a problem occurs or a necessity for change the solutions must arrive as fresh and appropriate, the emergence of strategy in tandem with its momentum. Potential new and diverse solutions also emerge as substance for renewing and reviewing of the structure and creating uniformity. Remember *strategy formulation* is an on-going and never ending process; it is a combination of both matter (it has to matter to materialize) and form (the manner in which it is presented or shaped) whatever constitutes change must have the *potential* for growth, and the flexibility to change form. This requires attributes of both the old and the new converging, strategy formulation, and strategy are two processes occurring in parallel, describing how a "thing" that is contemplated now is capable of doing better and better "things" for us vs. what we initially contemplated. This creates the attribute of self-organisation, and reorganisation, which should be expected of humans thinking, that where we create situations of common interest, we find the middle way through dialogue, towards the means to achieve common goals with. Strong cognitive relations forms in this fashion where there is open dialogue, because we start trusting and drawing from each other's strengths, co-operation and teamwork is the spin off, then a new wider middle way emerges between several opposing ideas; that now has made room for more people, cultures and parties. This culmination is essential before we can truly plan the strategy of the strategy, referred to as the setting up for *strategy formulation*, defined by the strategic management matrix.

Only then can the strategic journey start in all earnest. Now it is the right time to progress and start thinking concepts and attributes; *identify, quantify and qualify* your assumptions with analysis, incorporate knowledge and theory, find the target, and the envision, then only move on to the actual planning. This is the foundation work before we can jump in and plan, in order to proceed to draw up grand strategic plans. This grand strategic plan is the culmination of all the knowledge of afore mentioned chapters.

The strategic plan

The question now is what is a "Strategic plan" again? Exactly how do we draft it, where do you start, what is its intended purpose, what and whom do you need to do this right and in what format should it be done?

It is said that a strategic plan is both a means as well as a tool; it can be used to attract investment and capital when coupled to a business plan. However, for most, it is better described as a graphical representation of the effective utilisation of resources, fused with streamlined systems, in order to create a structure to ascertain certain goals and objectives with.

Structure includes forms of measure (a measurable); in other words a gauge that aligns multiple initiatives on one time line to complete highlighted aspects of a planned nature in relation to subsystems;

- The unrelated processes that influence the scheme as it starts unfolding – viewed as being part of a chain of events the will have an influence on the planed process – the global overview.
- The planed processes, it aim is to set in motion the scheme, to predict and determine all subsequent events that should follow, in order to arrive at a favourable foreseeable outcome as planned, and in what way this will be done – the strategic scope

- The positioning of activities and resources in a certain manner of strategic logic to create optimum output, and production as a measure of progress and success - the project or life cycle of events.
- The supporting planed initiatives - the additional steps in a process that once implemented, in a predetermined and pre-emptive manner, aims to mitigate risk, and waste – the risk scope
- The structure of command and control; who will be in charge of what, and take responsibility and control certain events as they unfold, and who will be accountable, all in order to realise a shared objective whatever it may be in a structure fashion – the structuring of coordination and feedback

"The strategic plan" then has as its main purpose the role of relating ideas into concepts, for people to understand and start aligning with it and to become pro-active – firstly in understanding, then selling the concept, secondly in explaining what will be required in detail, and how it will be accomplished in sequence of events, within the means available. The aim is to take the initiative and pass it on to the lowest level of organisation, to set in motion a chain of events where everyone knows what is expected and what is at stake, and to initiate the formalisation of systems that will effectively and both efficiently drive processes towards realising the predetermined objectives.

The strategic plan in its physical form is an organised, well-structured and comprehendible document; the format of which is of no consequence – whatever suits the role-players, it describes the scope of the schemes requirements, and this in itself will dictate how professional and elaborate the requirements will become, and its format.

This format

Could also include a:

- Business plan
- Financial plan
- Operational plan
- Action plan
- Project plan
- Marketing plan

The important aspect here is to remember that strategic plans form the focal departure point for strategic conversation making, as the journey unfolds to its realisation. Strategic plans focus us on what is at stake and what is up for grabs, it also ring-fences the boundaries for us, both in terms of cost, size, time, resources and whatever is required, called the business matrix – the boundaries of the scheme. It becomes the axis around which the scheme revolves and evolves, and how the objectives are to be understood, interpreted and implemented in step, and how the goals will be ascertained to realise the vision.

Good strategic planning is always clear;

- It is clearly spelled out in terms of specifics and deliverables, as headlines - visions
- In terms of the (who, when, where, what, and how much), as instruction sets.
- Coupled to a time line and scale – the scale of time refers to how resources will be required and utilised vs. the time and money available to achieve a specific goal in, the deliverables
- As well as what will be allocated to each objective, the resources within in a certain time frame, and constraints, the objectives and goals.

It should also define the measurable; how or what the criteria for success will be and how it could be measured, these aspect will determine and influence the global success ratios, or the Master plan otherwise referred to as the "Grand Strategy".

The success ratio of any strategic plan is determined by the weight of the objectives and goals; that are pre-set. they are quality check points or milestones, where we stop and check our alignment and the quality of progress as we carry on, more precision requires more checkpoints, speed requires routing, the term you cannot manage that which you cannot measure – becomes very relevant in the light of the aforementioned. The focal points for measurable outcome within every measurable time line, of each process, being from cradle to grave, or tracing its life cycles become a management prerogative. Goals and objectives are termed outcomes, milestones are the stages were we orientate and adjust smaller aspects that affect the bigger picture, and it shows how far we have progressed in the life cycle of each monitored aspect of the plan, in relation to achieving one specific goal or several at that point in time. Call it a systems check. The unit standard with which progress gauged will differ from plan to plan, and from industry to industry, normally the size and scope of the plan will dictate what will be effective. Therefore, it will be in context with what stands measured in terms of objectives and goals. The drilled down version of an objective referred to as the goal/s. Where goals are understood to be the subservient to objectives, and do not have the same implicit meaning in strategy, in other words; not all goals are in support of the same objective, however all objectives are in support of the main objective, and many objectives are in support of one final key objective. Many or few goals may be required towards achieving only one specific objective, where on a higher plain you could also build in secondary objectives to strengthen the aim of reaching the final objective. Good strategy will have complimenting and supportive objectives, in favour of the set objective, on your way to the main key objective. Consequently, before going for the main objective and securing it, we might want to secure several smaller objectives, this will imply taking the long route. Where we have a contingency plan, a plan B in support of the global plan, should the initial objective fail or only met partially – by having more secondary objectives built in to run in parallel or in support of the main objective, then only do we secure a better foothold. Furthermore, the relationship between goals and objectives best explained as graphical representations of (business) assumptions becoming real. Something taken as a starting point from a logical deduction (a business plan) that has no proof rather than given as a premise of the collective understanding of the scheme; of what things could be like if successfully executed through our strategic means and capacity. We utilise the strategic plan to serve as concept to contemplate this, however the strategic plan is the blue print (or the building plan) of this vision, where we create the vision in reality, we fulfil the vision of the business plan and its aim.

The strategic plan therefore can also be called the battle plan, that describes the tactics on operational level, that deals with the aspects of ambiguity and deals in specifics and measure; strategic plans solves the problem of complexity, by utilising structure – a vehicle created to handle all the complexity of the task at hand. We start thinking critically only when we can see how relationships will form once the plan and the resource merges with time and budgets. By having carefully analysed potential problems against possible solutions beforehand, we have in essence eliminated many blind spots. We create order and confidence in this fashion, by showing how it's done in concept form; with what, and by having calculated how much it will cost. We have minimised waste and geared up for efficiency; we have arrange resources to achieve the aim, by having planning for all eventuality. This gives us options, flexibility, and the initiative all the while the scheme unfolds.

Understanding the definitions and terminology used;

What is a strategic plan?

If something is "Strategic"; then it is premeditated, calculated, well thought-through, studied, examined, measured, and then designed; in other words, not done spontaneous. The word "plan" refers to; a diagram, an arrangement, a scheme, and idea, or proposal, a map or a document that explains this. In many organisations, this method is viewed as a process for determining where an organisation is going to position itself over the next year or more -typically 3 to 5 years, what they need and how much it will cost, as well as who will be required. In order to determine where it is going, the organisation needs to know exactly where it stands, then determines where it wants and how to cross the gap to get to where they want to be. The resulting document called the "strategic plan". Strategic planning itself cannot foretell exactly how the market will evolve and what issues will surface in the coming days in order to plan your organisational strategy, that is where we enter the matrix, and learn how to better control these influence on our design and planning.

Never engage with the same winning strategy for too long or the opposition will adapt to your tactics, wave-breaking strategy is the answer; focusing the strategic design on several smaller initiatives and tactics all aimed at ascertaining the same objective; but with differently organised goals, is the solution. Keep your strategy and intent covered for as long as possible; until the final blow is struck. The idea of utilising multi-dimensional wave-breaking strategy arises from understanding that the opponent as a "system" or "organism," that needs to be dissected (CAPS assessment), that evolves and adapts to our advances, becoming simultaneously more complicated and less complicated depending on how we reach our objectives, and how fast. We cannot solve problems that originate because of our course of action, tactics, and strategy, by using the same kind of thinking and strategy repeatedly, that we used when we created them. Your strategy must shape form strong to stronger, but take on the character of water, to seem formless, just like water's formation adapts to the ground when flowing, it avoids the high and assembles around the low first, thus going after weak and avoiding the strong, until it is surrounded, and ready to rise to that point. Strategy is many things: *planning, pattern analysis, positioning, ploy* and *perspective,* by collectively defining and understanding these aspects, it gives rise to collaboration and cooperation in an instant, it is about the preparations, people involved, and actions taken before the first step in linking the means or resources at our disposal with the ends or results we hold in view. Tactics, of course, is the second step. Strategy is concerned with deploying resources where tactics is concerned with employing them to the best of their ability. Without some goal, some end in mind, there can be no use for strategy and tactics; it will consist of aimless flailing where action taken just for the sake of having action. Strategy, then, is *relative and both circumstantial*, which is to say that it exists only in relation to some goal, end, or objective. If someone asks you, "What is your strategy?" be sure to reply, "In relation to what?" Tactics are doomed to failure when they applied without a sophisticated knowledge of the adversary or objective pursued, of how an objective be met, and therefore how it is likely to respond or adapt to the tactics being used against him. We cannot prevail without breaking the cycle, by utilising the same winning strategy for too long or the opposition will adapt to your tactics, we have to change shape, replenish, and re-train. One of the most difficult tasks of strategic management, which confronts any manager, is the ability to keep strategy alive, to change his plan in an instant, to alter this thinking in relation to the current reality, and to stay in step with changing circumstances. We need to be continually improving our resources, training, infrastructure and individual strengths as well as corporate strengths to stay at the forefront of covering and overcoming our weaknesses. If not they will become the areas target by our opponents in turn, or in retaliation to countering our winning strategy. Furthermore, no strategy exists in a vacuum, it collides with forces that both oppose and assist it, the moment it rolls out. These forces come in the form of emotions, perceptions, paradigms, ego, hope, fear, and greed described as internal forces; the collective knowledge and experience that gave birth to our strategy and the understanding of human nature. The understanding of each market's phase of growth and risk involved within the targeted segment within that market, the patterns that are viable, the market's volatility as well as its intrinsic characteristics; ratios of supply and demand. It all conglomerates to become the collective external forces that try to balance out with our strategy; to make space or way for it, or to block it. All business strategy has one thing in common, its own intrinsic weight that will influence the market, which can tip the scale, either for or against us.

What is strategy?

A strategy is a long-term plan of action designed to achieve a particular goal, strategy relies on objectives, goals, and tactics. The word derived from the Greek word *"stratēgos"*, which in turn was derived from two words: *"stratos" meaning* – army- and – *"ago"* – the ancient Greek for leading an army.

What are tactics?

A tactic is a conceptual action – a method - used to implement a specific strategy to achieve a specific objective, to advance toward a specific goal. A tactic is implemented as one or more tasks. These concepts can be defined in a hierarchy:

- The Business plan
- The Grand Strategy
- The Strategic plan
- Objectives

- Goals
- Tactics
- Tasks

As it flows from the top, it develops unique characteristic and attributes at each level.

What is a business plan?

A business plan; is the embryonic state of a vision, or idea, which is based on assumptions. Described as a formal statement of a set of business assumptions, the reasons why they are believed attainable, and the plan for reaching them divined as goals. It may also contain background information about the organisation or team attempting to reach those goals. The goals are defined in terms of;

- The competitive advantage
- The market niche
- The dependencies and assumptions
- The pricing objectives
- The ability to delivery

Then we design a grand strategy to make it all work

What is a Grand Strategy?

Grand strategy; refers to a complexity of power, residing in strategic elements, both prevalent and indispensable for achieving very large-scale objectives. For an enterprise, the Grand Strategy includes calculations and research by experts on the business assumptions made in relation to what will actually be required to achieve various and diverse objective simultaneously. It is very critical of the actual economics of scale and resources, the level of expertise and experience, as well as their availability – are they realistic expectations or not. It also includes an overview of impacting factors that have to be present in every strategy, as well as the format presented in, referring to the subject fields, and *subject matter experts* that are required to be present in formulating each strategy; i.e. as legal requirements, financial backing, marketing, viability study, SWOT analyses etc. The grand strategy normally includes studies; such as market research based upon business assumptions; especially in relation to labour related issues and requirements, contractual limitations, culture, and economic stability in the sector ventured into. Grand strategy focuses primarily on the repercussion of company policy and procedure, law, climate and economical indictors to asses risk and both potential. The focus of grand strategy is both global and ultimately unifying; with the main-focus on long-term sustainable development, with the emphasis on sustainability, where several projects and strategies will be forth coming, the grand strategy or master strategy will be the backbone and corners stone as reference framework for all other strategies emerging. Some have extended the concept of grand strategy to both include and describe multiple-tiers of strategies, at various levels of organisation in existence, in relation to the global context, formalised along one guideline or principle that needs or requires alignment with the initial agenda of the company and its core business. How will this add value to our business? Is the question grand strategy asks, as a departing aim and philosophy for new strategy. Grand strategy becomes the constitution of the company, guided with formal rules and principles endorsed by the entire organisation. In other words, multidimensional strategies governed by one strategy, the grand strategy.

The six components that make up a Grand Strategy;

1. It's clearly defined **objectives**; divided into main objective, and secondary objectives. Some even include the subservient goals of a particular strategy aimed at specific future expansion and growth avenues, operations are redefined based on facts, trends and research rather than thoughts or opinions.
2. **Situational assessment/ analyses**; the current conditions that characterises judgment about something based on an understanding of the situation then vs. now, a method of evaluating performance and attainment by reprioritizing objectives and goals.
3. **Operations and tactics**; the act of making something carry out its function, or controlling or managing the way it works, the supervising, monitoring, and coordinating of activities as they unfold.
4. **General dynamics**; identifying the forces - the condition/s of being effective, valid, or applicable that tend to produce activity and change in any situation or sphere of existence, that impacts on the relationships and power between people in a group.
5. **Resources**; anything drawn on or utilised by a company for making profit; personnel, capital, machinery, or stock.
6. **Review**; to examine something critically, to make sure that it is adequate, accurate, or correct in its assumption and application.

Ascertaining of several diversified **objectives** is the focal point of all grand strategy, in pursuance of one key objective. The ultimate objective of this hierarchy, in strategic terms, is to determine the correct content of all components of operational strategy; its goals and their attributes. At each subservient level, we also find those things strongly related to ultimate ends; including values, visions, worldview, and ideology that tend to connect the dots with the vision of the grand strategy. The charter or constitution of an organisation is its grand strategy - a formal written statement of the aims, principles, and procedures that need to be followed (a dogma) in all matters of strategy.

Assessment refers to the in-depth analysis and interpretation of facts, in relation to the perceived situation, the reality of the strategic terrain, as it was, as it is, and as it will be in the near and foreseeable future, shaped by critical insight and judgments as to what is realistic and possible under the circumstances. Through purposeful threat analysis and constructing of contingencies for strategy as part of any strategic assessments, we require mitigating steps and provisions incorporated. It also has to do with "knowing the enemies of strategy" and being able to prepare effectively for any shifts and changes in the strategic landscape, to counter blind spots and anomalies experienced at operational levels, in order to proceed with achieving goals whilst balancing the forces that work in on it, as and when it unfold.

Tactics refer to the techniques employed at operational level to achieve goals with in relation to the objectives. Here the question is whether we are doing things right, or doing the right things. It is about the how it should be done, and not the way it should be done, the systems to be used; the financial systems, the acts, regulations and procedures, vested in departments and people, the way the organisation does things, and prescribes to us how to go about accomplishing our goals. Tactics tend to focused on details of action and engagement – the rules of engagement. Operations, in turn, are the co-ordinated activities that groups and organisations engage in to further their strategic plan. Generally, operations involve the simultaneous employment of many tactical capacities and advantages.

Dynamics is the understanding of the order inside chaos, it works from within to outside, if it is rotten inside it will manifest on the outside, both with people and organisations this holds true. The interplay between several strategic actors energy against several others energy within the same section of their environment, influence it either positive or negative. We cannot act in contradiction but aim for harmony and synergy in planning events. Dynamics is the sum of our focus, we cannot control other people no matter how hard we try and instead we have to change their focus to change their effect. The grand strategy must prepare for effective coordination of effect, of several strategies; each strategy in turn must prepare for the ensuing chaos and battle for supremacy, within the options and opinions that become available to the players vs. what is available to their opponents. There must always be something in reserve, a provision made for absorbing losses, or regeneration, and reengineering to soak up the spill-over effect. The stress and uncertainty that tends to knock strategy of its tracks, positively and creativity must be the focus, focus perpetuates into working environments becoming working habits, positively recreating the work culture. Critical analysis allows the strategist to correctly locate, correlate, and plot these necessary interim requirements to fuel the process (milestones and secondary objectives) or intermediate objectives (strong points) on the road to the ultimate objective. Resistance creates feelings of what we do not want; the more we focus on this the more create of it, where instead we should focus more on what we want. The fear of the unknown drives us to question ourselves, the process, our creativity, and ability. Vision, mission and goals, will only deliver if we believe it, then we can achieve it. Just like a car, driving on a road at night with its headlights on, it can only see the immediate, and consequently the driver can only react to what it sees. Likewise, the critical evaluation informs us about crucial decisions that we should take in advance, highlighting priorities, and dictating the sequences of actions required in averting and overcoming any problem or obstacle. It is an ongoing process, the utilisation of the OODA loop gives us options; as to what we should be concentrating more efforts on stays current, what should we do first becomes apparent and what next and last becomes a mere choice. There is a dynamic relationship between the components of strategy and the processes of strategy that help it along – between the main objectives, secondary objectives, goals and their attributes in relation to its dynamics - the forces that tend to produce activity and change in any situation or sphere of existence. Consider the results we achieve with strategy as being the domino effect worthy and representative of our efforts and wants. The outcome of any strategy is a true reflection of the energy and contemplation we had put into it, nothing more nothing less.

Resources are about institutions, suppliers, material, organisations, money, and people. Resources must be amassed and managed to reduces waste and optimize potential. Closely related is the concept of infrastructure; however, resources and infrastructure are not related. Access to lots of resources does not automatically translate into strong infrastructure - the large-scale public systems, services, and facilities of a country or region that are necessary for economic activity, including power and water supplies, public transport, telecommunications, roads. Rather, strong infrastructure depends on how effectively people, money, and other resources are organized, and integrated, to exploit it to its fullest potential seen as one system.

Finally, **review** is the critical component of continuing on the path of great strategy, systematically assessed strategy is an ongoing pursuit. Assessments provide the structured and required feedback, as guidance to all levels of strategy and management, on how to improve on strategic plans and achieve strategic envisions.

The key attributes of strategic planning; Strategic planning aims to minimise waste, of resources, time and energy; and expedites execution.

The ultimate purpose of strategic planning; is to join the organisation in with its resources, to maximize proficiency at all levels, to increase chances of success, and save on energy, to create decisive action. The spin-off is less stress and better structured work and instructions, with proper coordination that spill over into a high-spirited workforce, the mental, emotional, physical, and spiritual energy is focused, energy goes where attention flows, a holistic required processes to reach full speed.

Great achievement only happens when we have both great vision and passion combined

In conclusion I leave you with this:

"They say that Lt.'s and Capt.'s study tactics, Majors and Col's study strategy and Generals study logistics! For sure, you can have the best agency or army in the world, but it will grind to a halt without structure. Every facet of management belongs to its own corps."

Several tables were created to explain certain business concepts and views used in this book.

Time allocation.	Time spent –have to does	Philosophy –time spent on still can does	Intellectualising – time spent on – want to do
Vision	Give control – who takes it willingly	Potential growth	Personal growth
Mission	Shared responsibility – who picks up the slack.	Willingly take responsibility	Building competence
Planning	True to vision, did we move towards it	Robust dialogue	Big ideas win
Implementation	True to benchmark, did we ascertain it or not	Best idea	Crossing the Rubicon, risking, breaking out
Execution	True to form – the way we do things	Champions	Margin of success
Evaluate	Return on investment	New Results	Evaluate Personal performance, the self

The plans	Strategic plan	Business plan	Operational plan
Level	Organisational	Departmental	Business unit
Responsibility	Organisation	Department	Business unit
Alignment	Top down	Should link both	Bottom up

Developing the required culture:	Culture – requires leadership	Nature of business – and tasks	Perception management –require detail
Developing	Follow through- plan, do, evaluate	Stewardships assist where possible.	Setting clear goals and objectives
Explaining	Vision and mission, daily –realignment.	360 degree vision, abundance	Principles and perception management.
Active involvement	Affirm your people; their worth, see commitment.	Know yourself	Get to know your people

Required frame for Steps to conceive the ops plan with

Systems involvement	Scope for improvement	Process to benchmark	Agreements
Personal level	What I can do	What I will do	How I will do it
Group	What we can do	What we will do	How we will do it
Business unit	What we can do with budget	What we will do within constraints	How we see ourselves doing it
Department	What we can do to assist	What we will do to assist	Our commitments

Developing the trust regime, required within corporate culture:

Desired ability	Philosophy	Deposit	The Gift	The Art
Ability to earn trust	Over time –act consequently	Time	Empathy	Mastering Principles
Ability to give advice	Must be consequential and logical	Balance between radical and subsistent	Wisdom	Applicable Knowledge
Ability to build relationships	Listening –first seek to understand – before seeking to be understood	Service – and commitment to service - discipline	Self-sacrifice – putting others needs first.	Love of service - reliability
Ability to build culture	Mixing the ideals of all	Creating Understanding	Negotiator - navigator	Creating Vision

The Kaizen concept

Kaizen – continuous improvement	Method	Self - actualisation	Work environment	Productivity
Change – in steps	Small changes –steps – towards the big change.	Personal commitment to change	From the group for the group	Individualised concern, towards improvement
Realistic	Personalised design – focusing on the parts	From the people, for the people, by the people	Fast tracking processes	Saving in time and cost

The Radical Revolutionary Strategic Management Matrix For Predators

New habit	Document the process	Implement the processes	Describe the significance	Cross pollination
Constraints	Framework of freedom	Uninhibited	Gratification	Increases
Principles	Stop doing stuff that does not make sense	Change or enhance the process	Reduce waste and unnecessary work	Incremental improvements
Motivation for kaizen	Reward – merit's -	Inventors of progress	Team kaizen	Innovativeness

Generate energy:

	Vision	Mission	Task
Elements	Know it by heart	Support	Clearly defined
Love of task	Confident in oneself	Confident in skills	Start and finish
Passion	Expanding Influence	"Can Do" attitude	Achievement
Commitment	Receiving Credit	Thank you	Trust in competence

Infused energy

	Understanding	Contemplating	Dissecting
Curiosity	Things	Relationships	Prospects
Test knowledge	Teaching it	Applying it	Failures
Focus	Different perspective	Different schools of knowledge	Building 360° vision
Willingness to change	The significance of required change	Personal growth and advancement	The coping mechanisms
Acquiring balance	The relationship	Ways to achieve it	The benefit's
Physical development	Benefit's	Means	The growth
Consciousness	Systems	Relationships	Attributes

Adding value, the company that holds the most value, to the nett value holds the most power. Tactics shapes perception.

Evaluation Matrix.	Adding value vs. adding quality	Price vs. quality	Quality vs. quantity	Quantity. Vs. per unit (production) cost
Role-players	Co-operation	Competition	Balance	Efficiency
Design	Packaging	Turnaround times	Cost at point of production	Transportation node -method
Branding	Selling Benefit's	Reward customer loyalty	Branding bulk assignments = advertising	The higher the quantity the lower the cost
Packaging	Insurance	Deduction damaged goods	Swap around	Replacements, warranty
Distribution	Generic Pre - order assignments	On time delivery –small assignments	Bulk delivery or timely deliver	Rail, Road, Air, boat, or post
Marketing	Slogan	Provision to match any offer	Discounts per volume - booking	Rebates – for early payment

Advertising vs. Networking

Mix it up, to get the better concept	Advertising campaign:	Target audience – generalised product concept	Budget and research determine size and effectiveness	Inform them of the new – advantages, price, quality or attribute
Networking your agenda:	Tactics differ			
Define a specific objective –target - customized		Wide vs. spot on – waste margin		
Established Contacts determine hit's			Big layout vs. little cost	
Warm them up to new ideas, prospects				Effort vs. time spent

How can I deliver to the customer the right quality and quantity, when he wants it, and where he wants it?

The difference between principles and values:

Principles	Objective – Global view	Unchanging	Universal frame of reference	Based on Truth
Values	Subjective – Bias –one sided	Varying to condition	Personal frame of reference	Based on Perception

Examples: the difference between principles and values.

Principles	Honesty	Self-sacrifice	Integrity	Fairness
Values	Relationships	Money centred	Fame	Pleasure

The two side of knowledge tacit and explicit

Explicit knowledge	Precise	Clear	To the point	Understandable
Tacit knowledge	Implied	Derived	Own assumption	Understood

The Radical Revolutionary Strategic Management Matrix For Predators

This is the Kaikaku – the Chinese for "transformation of the mind", working with others to achieve radical change.

Kaikaku – leaner is faster – a war against waste	Competition cannot pick it up improvement	Break up work into manageable pieces	Collective responsibility for quality	Flatter organisational structures
Daily improvements in communication and quality	Removal of all none valuable waste, time waiters, ineffective equipment	Removal of waste work, filing, sorting, reports, transport	Removal of none essential paperwork, inventory, registers, clock cards, overtime	Removal of none essential communication -meetings
Even workloads – shared responsibilities	Self-development and improvement of moral	Creates understanding of parts and systems	Creates understand of the whole	Creates better managers and supervisors
Find the root cause of the problem	Look for the solution that solves the problem for real	Develop abilities, skills and the brain	Shared vision and mission, all focused on collective quality	Solutions is everyone's prerogative
Keep asking why until you understand why, then explain it to someone else	Reproduce the problem see how others solve it	People are recognised for leadership by colleges and superiors	People can mutually educate themselves by learning from others	Productivity is the result of operations and systems combined
Multi - skill – and cross skill development	Constant improvement – learn from others mistakes – by watching them solve it	Report defects and bottlenecks and how it was solved	Solve the problem quickly – get help if necessary	Managers must give subordinate the time and opportunity to solve problems

~ 551 ~

The Characteristics of "Principles": at the centre of living with balance.

They thirst for knowledge, as diverse as possible...	Always seeking new knowledge, read, learn, listen and observe – the knowledge forming required wisdom.
Live to serve others.	They live to do better, by doing more for others.
Positively charged personality.	They are forever optimists, rationalists and hopeful.
They affirm the good in people.	They validate the good and work on the bad
To live a balanced life's	They seek balance in all four spheres of life.
They live life as an adventure	Change and risk is their spice to conform to, adapt to
Thinkers, creators	They build, they design and seek synergy in life
They exercise self-restraint	They lead and live by example, they stand in high regard and truth and trust is their pillars of strength.

The four stages of moral

Poor -Moral	Leaders do everything	No discipline – co-dependant
Low -Moral	Leaders do productive things	No accountability – no trust
Moderate -Moral	Leaders do difficult things	No common vision- us and them
High -Moral	Leaders do maintenance	Shared responsibilities – everyone is accountable
Abundance -Moral	Leaders become stewards	Synergy

Team building matrix:

The Poisons of teamwork	Ego	Naiveté	Insecurity	Temperament
Personal agendas	Wrong person	Lack capacity	Introvert	Catalyst - for conflict
Frustration	Stupidity	Lack direction	Anger	Autocratic
Miss alignment	Self-gratification	Lack vision statement	Maliciousness, sink the process	Revolt
Disillusioned	Wrong place, wrong group, wrong topic	Sapping energy -waste	Politics, take sides, split group	No significance – no results
Glue of teamwork	Ego	Naiveté	Insecurity	Temperament
Clear vision – the bigger picture, know why this is important.	Unifying purpose – forces ego shut down – focus on service.	Team builds capacity, from collective knowledge and experience	Introvert – extrovert, everyone must give, in turn, structured team	Catalyst - for finality, closure, result
Calm	Creativity	True direction	Neutral	Natural
Sense of Purpose	Complete task	Get vision	Team work	Oneness
Sense of worth and necessity	Right place, right group and right topic.	Create Energy forming, norming, storming	Perception – shared views, bonding	Significance - results

The Radical Revolutionary Strategic Management Matrix For Predators

Measuring company value, profit and progress – with a baseline analysis checklist.

The "Global Thinking Matrix."

Why? MQM	Measurable: Kaizen - TQM	Information management	Relationships formed	Just-in-time/ results
Identified **Critical success factors: CSF**.	Have we made any improvements in quality? Are we listening to "voices"	Has the vision been adopted, with first things first?	Has self-discipline and work ethic improved because of first things first?	Has the vision been accomplished? Is it reflecting in the global culture?
Profit margin – financial figures –in relation to production cycles.	"Burn rate" Where do we spend what and how much and why? Where do we make /spend money and why?	How did we identify, quantify and qualify this? Are we adhering to the "Law of the Harvest?"	Who worked on this initiative, how did they convey this info and to whom, how long did it take to fix.	Was any processes held back, due to this discovery, if so "why". Why was it not fixed? How will we solve this?
Amount of **"Waste"** eliminated and perceptions managed.	Have we become leaner? How much leaner could we still become? Test assumptions, research and development.	Are we moving towards a paperless environment? Is the info available to all? If not, why not?	Are we effective in creating one culture, that of "abundance". Interview disgruntled customers. Report	Have we changed the perceptions and what is the new perception created as a result.
New step-in-step – Developments "Incubation strategy" we help them – they help us.	Are we following through –if not why not? Do we satisfy wants?	Do people understand their tools, their trade, their mission and their worth and feedback?	Did our network, produce any new allies, did we tell them how to communicate with us.	What changes are we contemplating? Where, when, what, why, how?
Objectives reached in line with vision. Remember:	What steps are presented /suggested towards alignment – are we	Are the systems coping with the changes envisaged?	Who needs to lead the process here? And why? Have we given credit where it was	Have we hit the bulls-eye, what are our deviations and contributing factors?

"Unexpected great service" the customers take it personal.	implementing	What can be outsourced - hired?	due?	
Consistency in "zero fault" production	ID –Bottle-necks and the route cause.	Have we re-aligned our strategies	Have we found the defective relationship in the system?	Are we producing flawless results?
"Why" factor	Ask "why" until you understand it.	Ask "why" until you get it	Ask "why" until you are part of it	Ask "why" until you are just-in-time with it
The Whole Performance and efficiency: of Strategy, Tactics, Systems, Structures, Logistics, Marketing, Branding, Suppliers and Resources.	How well did our suppliers, departments perform. Did they deliver just in time, is their quality still acceptable and has it more range? Look at better ways of integration and implementation.	Turnaround times, did it improve and if so why? If not Why? Fast beats slow. Did the customer get "Instant gratification"	Have we deposited into personal bank accounts or are we overdrawn? (How and why not?) If so, how?	Who is still not happy, not performing, not up to par – How can this be changed? Are we forming good habits? Do we deliver on strategic intent?

The Probe Matrix:

	Who	What	Where	When	How	How much	What if	CAPS	Deliverable/ Benchmark
Quantification									
Qualify									
Identify									
Main focus, vision									
Methodology									
Profiling									
Time frames									
Delegation/outsourcing									

The Radical Revolutionary Strategic Management Matrix For Predators

Strategy, concepts									
Symmetry and synergy									
Infrastructure									
Logistics									
Pro-service providers									
Procurement									
MQM, principles									
Tenders, providers									
Draft, hard copy, Final									
Implementation									
Calibration									

Acknowledgements

To the people that helped me and inspired me, a great thanks, and a special thanks: to Johan Campbell, for his inspiration and guidance. To LTC (RET) Dave Grossman for his great contribution, LTC (RET) Roland de Vries for teaching me strategy.

Moreover to all the other co-authors and contributors, who helped me edit, do spell checks- it has been a pleasure working with you all, because I learned more from you than you think and stand humble before you and thank you from the bottom of my heart for the opportunity. From a "Boertjie"

Last but not least. To my wife, my children. To my family and friends for real perspective on the things in life that matter, that last, family.

my Creator.

Copyright

This Books Reference Table of Strategic Terminology

References and sources;

Principles of Strategic Management **Implementing Strategy: Core Competencies, Reengineering and Structure.**
Professor G Gomes: http://www.csuchico.edu/mgmt/strategy/

ON SHEEP, WOLVES and SHEEPDOGS By LTC (RET) Dave Grossman, RANGER, Ph.D., author of **"On Combat,"** an extract from this book, http://www.killology.com/military_bground.htm &   www.killology.com with special thanks.

The seven habits of highly effective people: Restoring the character ethic. New York: Simon & Schuster. Covey, S. (1989).

Conflict Research Copyright ©1998 Conflict Research Consortium -- Contact: crc@colorado.edu

Got A Second? American Handgunner, May, 2001 by **Ken** J. **Good**

Principles of Strategic Management Copyright 1995 Richard D. Irwin, Inc. and Professor G Gomes:
http://www.csuchico.edu/mgmt/strategy/

General Psychology – W. J. Jordaan, J.J. Jordaan J.M.Niewoudt –McGraw-Hill Book Comp. Copyright 1975

Reframing in Business -Copyright © 2002-3 Veryard Projects Ltd http://www.veryard.com/demcha/reframe.htm

REFRAMING - Robert L. Sandidge & Anne C. Ward Chapter 11 from Quality Performance in Human Services Copyright 1999 - Brookes Publishing.

Dr Leandro Herrero : **Behaviour** the blueprint for change –Unknown

The 4 P's - Mind Tools material is published by Mind Tools Ltd of Signal House, Station Road, Burgess Hill, West Sussex, RH15 8DY, United Kingdom ©**Mind Tools, 1995-2004. http://www.mindtools.com/pages/article/newCT_05.htm** The idea of the Reframing Matrix was devised by Michael Morgan in his book ' Creating Workforce Innovation

Creating Workforce Innovation: Turning Individual Creativity into Organisational Innovation by Michael Morgan

Recipe for Revolution: http://killeenroos.com/3/revolutionrecipe.html - **Killeen Harker Heights Connections**

Dr Leandro Herrero : Management :Behaviour: the blueprint for change http://www.thechalfontproject.com/

Levers of Organization Design -Book: Robert Simons

A Theory of human motivation, psycol. Rev. 50 (790-796) - 1943 Abraham Maslow

Sun Tzu On The Art Of War -Translated from the Chinese with introduction and Critical Notes .BY LIONEL GILES, M.A. Assistant in the Department of Oriental Printed Books and MSS. in the British Museum
First Published in 1910 http://www.kimsoft.com/polwar1.htm. This publication is based on an Etext version provided by the Project Gutenberg. Dr. Giles's commentaries are included for the benefit of those who are not familiar with the Ancient Chinese History (500 BC).

"OODA Loop" Col John Boyd, USAF (Ret), coined the term and developed the concept of the "OODA Loop" (Observation, Orientation, Decision, Action)

A Chinese Parable - Gwee Li Sui Singapore: Landmark, 1998 - http://www.postcolonialweb.org/singapore/literature/poetry/gwee/parable.html -

A Chinese Parable -Who Wants to Buy a Book of Poems? (1998) - Gwee Li Sui

A Special Report From David Lazear - Understanding of Intelligence, with special thanks **http://www.davidlazear.com/Special_Report.html and** *www.DavidLazear.com.* MiQ™ - A Different Kind of Smart

What is strategy ?– John R Boyed

The Nine Aspects of Life~ William Arthur Ward

Mao Tse-Tung. Selected military writings. Foreign language press, Peking, 1968

Mapping: K9 Unit Management, Reinier Geel, Trafford publishing 2004

The Rapid dominance strategy: Mobiele Oorlog Voering, Roland de Vries, f.j.n. Harman uitgewers -1987

 The Rapid Dominance strategy -Reinier Geel on Mobility and manoeuvring - EMPD forum. Strategic workshop 2000 - Blaauwpan

Critical Thinking For The Military Professional -Col W. Michael Guillot:///http://www.airpower.maxwell.af.mil/airchronicles/cc/guillot.html.Document created: 17 June 04 *Air & Space Power Chronicles.*

Dogmatism/Legalism (from *Sources of Chinese Tradition, Vol. 1,* trans. and ed. Wm. Theodore de Bary. Columbia University Press (USA: 1960).

Strategy formation patterns, performance and the significance of context:http://www.findarticles.com/p/articles/mi_m4256/is_n2_v23/ai_19498954/pg_2 – from -**Journal of Management**, March-April, 1997 by Dennis P. Slevin, Jeffrey G. Covin

Control - First things first - Stephen R Covey - Published by Simon & Schuster Publication date: March 1, 1994 -

"The institution, its resources and the environment" (Rowley, Lujan, & Dolence, 1997, p. 15)

Master Of Military Studies From Air Force Fighter Pilot to Marine Corps WAR FIGHTING Colonel John Boyd, His Theories on War and their Unexpected Legacy - Major Jeffrey L. Cowan, U.S. Air Force Academic Year 1999-2000

Manoeuvre versus Attrition: A Historical- Antal, Maj. John F. USA. " Perspective," Military Review 72, no. 10 (October 1992): 21-33.

Defining Air and Space Power- Baner, Maj. Carl. USAF.. Unpublished research paper. Maxwell AFB, AL: Air Command and Staff College, March 1999.

"Avoiding Information Overload." Bateman, Capt. Robert L., III. Military Review 78, no. 4 (July - August 1998): 52-58.

"Beware of Simplistic Solutions," Drew, Lt. Col. Dennis M. USAF. Air University Review 36, no.2 (January-February 1985): 102-104.

"**Informal Doctrine and the Doctrinal Process: A Response,**" -Drew, Lt. Col. Dennis M. USAF. Air University Review 35, no. 6 (September-October 1984): 96-97.

Competing Visions of Aerospace Power: A Language for the 21ˢᵗ Century. Unpublished research paper .Faber, Lt. Col. Peter R. USAF.. DTIC ADA-325593. Newport, RI: Naval War College, February 1997.

Type Orders in Joint Air Operations: The Empowerment of Air Leadership Fischer, Maj. Michael E. USAF. Mission-. Thesis. Maxwell AFB, AL: School of Advanced Airpower Studies, May 1995.

Manoeuvre Warfare and Marine Corps Aviation. Individual Study Project Haley, Lt. Col. Stephen D. USMC.. DTIC ADA-222249. Carlisle Barracks, PA: U.S. Army War College, April 1990.

Air Force Fighter Acquisition since 1945," Hallion, Dr. Richard P. "A Troubling Past: Air Power Journal 4, no. 4 (Winter 1990): 4-23.

"**Synchronization and the Corps,**" Johnson, Capt. Mark D. USMC. Marine Corps Gazette 78, no. 11 (November 1994): 28-29.

Knobel, Maj. Philip E. USMC. "Revise FMFM 1, Warfighting," Marine Corps Gazette 77, no. 10 (October 1993): 31-33.

Kohler, LCDR. Matthew J. USN. Maneuver by the U.S. Navy in 20ᵗʰ Century Blue-Water Operations: Selected Historical Examples. Thesis. DTIC ADA-312821. Fort Leavenworth, KS: U.S. Army command and General Staff College, June 1995.

Krieger, Col. Clifford R. "USAF Doctrine: An Enduring Challenge," Air University Review 35, no. 6 (September-October 1984): 16-25.

Lauer, Maj. Stephen G. USMC. Maneuver Warfare Theory and the Operational Level of War: Misguiding the Marine Corps? Monograph. DTIC ADA-240346. Fort Leavenworth, KS: School of Advanced Military Studies, May 1991.

Lemelin, Capt. David J. USA. "Misunderstanding Synchronization: An Army Perspective," Marine Corps Gazette 78, no. 11 (November 1994): 26-28.

Lind, William S., Colonel Keith Nightengale USA, Captain John F. Schmitt USMC, Colonel Joseph W. Sutton USA and Lieutenant Colonel Gary I. Wilson USMCR. "The Changing Face of War: Into the Fourth Generation." Marine Corps Gazette 73 no. 10 (October 1989): 22-26.

Lind, William S. "Defining Maneuver Warfare for the Marine Corps," Marine Corps Gazette 64, no. 3 (March 1980): 55-58.

Lind, William S. "Reading, Writing and Policy Review," Air University Review 36, no.1 (November-December 1984): 66-70.

Lind, William S. "Some Doctrinal Questions of the United States Army," Military Review 77, no. 1 (January - February 1997): 134-143.

Matthews, Col. Lloyd J. USAF. "The Speech Rights of Air Professionals," Air Power Journal 12, no. 3 (Fall 1998): 19-30.

McKenzie, Maj. Kenneth F., Jr. USMC. "On the Verge of a New Era: The Marine Corps and Maneuver Warfare," Marine Corps Gazette 77, no. 7 (July 1993): 62-67.

Meilinger, Col. Phillip S. USAF. "Ten Propositions Regarding Airpower," Air Power Journal 10, no. 1 (Spring 1996): 52-72.

Nelson, Maj. Denny R. USAF. "Seeking A Forum for the Mitchell's," Air University Review 35, no. 5 (July-August 1984): 85-86.

Pennington, Reina "A Commentary: Prophets, Heretics and Peculiar Evils," Air Power Journal 10, no. 2 (Summer 1996): 65-68.

Peppers, Jerome G. "On Commentary and the Air Force Officer Corps," Air University Review 36, no. 5 (July-August 1985): 111-112.

Schmitt, Maj. John F. USMCR. "Command and (Out of) Control: The Military Implications of Complexity Theory," Marine Corps Gazette 82, no. 9 (September 1998): 55-58.

Schmitt, Maj. John F. USMCR. "If Not Synchronization, What?" Marine Corps Gazette 81, no. 1 (January 1997): 54-60.

Schmitt, Maj. John F. USMCR. "Out of Sync With Maneuver Warfare," Marine Corps Gazette 78, no. 8 (August 1994): 16-22.

Shobbrook, Maj. Timothy J. USMCR. "Synchronization and Maneuver Warfare: There's a Place for Both," Marine Corps Gazette 81, no. 1 (January 1997): 61.

Simpson, Maj. James M. USAF. The Battle of Arbela an alternative approach. Student Research Report. DTIC ADB-039445. Maxwell AFB, AL: Air Command and Staff College, May 1979.

Spinney, Franklin C. "Genghis John," Proceedings 123, no. 7 (July 1997): 42-47.

Szafranski, Col. Richard USAF. "Twelve Principles Emerging from 10 Propositions," Air Power Journal 10, no. 1 (Spring 1996): 73-80.

Trout, Maj. Robert S. USMC. "Dysfunctional Doctrine: The Marine Corps and FMFM 1, Warfighting," Marine Corps Gazette 77, no. 10 (October 1993): 33-35.

Vincent, 1st Lt. Gary A. USAF. "A New Approach to Command and Control: The Cybernetic Design," Air Power Journal 7, no. 2 (Summer 1993): 24-38.

Vincent, 1st Lt. Gary A. USAF. "In the Loop: Superiority in Command and Control," Air Power Journal 6, no. 2 (Summer 1992): 15-25.

Walters, Maj. Eric M. USMC. "Synchronization: The U.S. Inheritance of Soviet Military Doctrine?" Marine Corps Gazette 78, no. 8 (August 1994): 23-26.

Watts, Lt. Col. Barry D. and Maj. James O. Hale USAF. "Doctrine: Mere Words, or a Key to Warfighting Competence?" Air University Review 35, no. 6 (September-October 1984): 4-15.

Watts, Barry D. Clausewitzian Friction and Future War, McNair Paper 52, Washington, D.C.: National Defence University, 1996.

Wilson, Lt. Col. Gary I. USMCR. "New Doctrine or Slipping Into the Past?" Marine Corps Gazette 77, no. 10 (October 1993): 44-45.

Wyly, Col. Michael D. USMC (Ret). "Doctrinal Change: The Move to Maneuver Theory," Marine Corps Gazette 77, no. 10 (October 1993): 44.

Wyly, Col. Michael D. USMC (Ret). "Re-establishing What?!" Marine Corps Gazette 78, no. 8 (August 1994): 27-29.

Spinney, Franklin C. "Aviation From The Sea"

Boyd, Col John R. "Pattern for Successful Operations"

Four Star Investor: George Smith Patton, Jr. (1885-1945)

Trading as Mental Warfare Brett N. Steenbarger, Ph.D is at www.greatspeculations.com

Manoeuvre warfare - William S. Lind is Director of the Center for Cultural Conservatism at the Free Congress Foundation

On War. ed. and trans. Michael Howard & Peter Paret. Clausewitz, Carl von. Princeton, NJ: Princeton University Press, 1976

The Essential Boyd. Belisarius. 1 Jun 2004 Hammond, Grant T.

Genghis John. Defense and the National Interest. 9 Oct 1998. 17 May 2004

The Art of War. Trans Richards, Chet. Interview. Spinney, FranklinTzu, Sun.. Samuel B. Griffith. London: Oxford University Press, 1963

The OODA Loop. Belisarius. 3 May 2004. Boyd, John

Patterns of Conflict. Defense and the National Interest. Dec 1986

Strategic Warfare: The Enemy as a System Colonel Warden January 1995

Pointing the Way; the translation of *Faith in Mind* used is that of Master Sheng-Yen. Jos Slabbert's website / Recreated: (Narrative impression & 7 Pillars of Gravity)

Strategic Futures – Ronald a Gunn – assimilation only (reflect on his work)

Jim Clemmer – WWW. Clemmer.net – firing on all cylinders – (assimilation only (reflect on his work))

Peter Drucker – the Practice of Management 1954 –MBO Management by objectives, assimilation only (reflect on his work)

Pest analysis – Steeple, assimilation only (reflect on his work)

Steven R Covey, First things first, copyright 1994 / Simon & Schuster UK ltd.

The I Ching, book of changes, fate and fortune / 1996, children's leisure productions ltm. David Dale house, new Lanark Scotland 1998.

Taylor Andrew Wilson, mind Accelerator, a Volition thought house publication, ISBN ;0-973-19710-2

Johan V Campbell – "The leadership trap" – "Campbell's Model" with permission, rewritten

Johan V Campbell – " Thoughts to live by" written and published by Johan V Campbell - ISBN 0-620-32205-5 j.v.c@mweb.co.za - www.motivate.co.za

Dr. Kathleen Gurney – "Your Money Personality; what it is and how you can profit". Extract only.

Peter Savage –"Who cares Wins" Mercury 1995.

John Gray – "How to get what you want" Vermilion 2002.

Steven R Covey, the 8th habit, Simon & Schuster UK ltd. 2004.

The "One-Minute Manger": written by Kenneth Blanchard, Ph.D. & Spencer Jhonson, M.D.

The 33 Strategies of War – By Robert Greene – ISBN –10 1 86197 993 2.

Rule of Reciprocity - Dr. Robert B. Cialdini, Professor of Psychology at Arizona State University, *Taken from Influence. Science and Practice*, Robert B. Cialdini, Scott, Foresman and Company, 1985; Summary notes.

Ethics –The Leadership Edge; How to sharpen strategy with values and trust. By Laurance Kuper, Published by Zebra Press, 2006. ISBN; 1 77007 103 2.

The Secret – Ronda Byrne - http://electexiles.wordpress.com/2007/12/08/the-true-secret/>

Goleman, D. (1995). Emotional intelligence. New York: Bantam Books

Jürgen Trittin Ecological materialism - http://www.eurozine.com/articles/2008-10-09-ozolas-en.html

Liedtka, J. M. (1998), "Linking Strategic Thinking with Strategic Planning", Strategy and Leadership, 26(4), 30-35.

http://www.journal.forces.gc.ca/vo7/no3/harries-eng.asp Canadian national defence journal

The Nine Principles of Business War; by Author: Greg Langston http://www.leader-values.com/Content/detail.asp?ContentDetailID=871

Http://en.wikipedia.org

Strategic Focus http://www.hpstrategy.com/html/grand_strategy_steps.html

Marine Corps Functional Concept for STRATEGIC COMMUNICATION (SC). Extracts...

The Radical Revolutionary Strategic Management Matrix For Predators

A Final word:

The Three wishes (in memory of Schunelle)

Life is not a place it is a journey it is said, the journey is one of self-discovery, learning and keeping the faith in the self to do the right thing and to do right by others. The fundamental principle is to live a life of principles. Principles are values and beliefs. They come from following role models. They speak of a good upbringing with a solid value system that enables us to choose it is the difference between right and wrong. The difference between doing the right thing and doing things right – that is the spiritual principle.

Only three wishes:

My first wish would be to become wise in the ways of life, so that I may find my purpose; one cannot lead a life without purpose. In order to find that purpose we must struggle with ourselves daily in the choices we have to make and by making the right choices we find meaning. Living is not about breathing; it's about personal experiences that form us. Life is a gift, to be used to pursue our need to find truth and once we have found truth and meaning, we will find our purpose.

My second wish is to be righteous and incorruptible, to live a life of openness, kindness and to serve my fellow man. One can only serve your fellow man if you do it without thinking, without a reason. Thinking is the one thing that separates us from animals, but yet animals care more, they serve; they nurture one and the other. Why can we not just be honest in all our dealings?

My last wish is for resilience of character – resilience is the ability to bounce back after a serious incident, to be able to cope with whatever life throws at us. To be flexible, to be the least, to be strong, but always to be yourself.

In summery I would say; I have many adventures to live, many ordeals to face, so I will take life one day at a time. A good support system will carry me trough, so if I want to do this thing called life right, I will have to do the right things. – Reinier Geel

Another fine Management book by Critical Minds

Other titles by this author

The Radical Revolutionary Strategic Management Matrix For Predators
K9 Unit Management

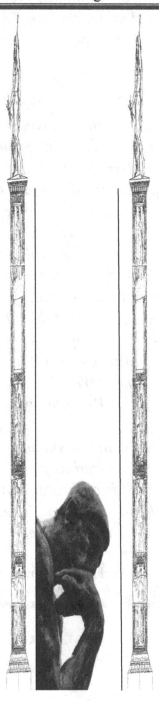

*This book is Revolutionary
in many ways, it is also
Extraordinary in every way
imaginable. Nothing like it has
ever been written.*

*A
true Strategic Miscellany of
divergent knowledge and
wisdom, combined, into one
Matrix. With all the fields
of knowledge necessary to create
the concept of strategic trinity.
Written
with remarkable true
insight about what cripples and
what excels strategy. With
strategic insight, bleeding into
military principles, some history,
and philosophy on War, with the
Art of War, Sociology,
Psychology.*

*Mixed with a good dose of street
smarts, as well as practical tools,
all fields of Strategic Wisdom
and knowledge combined in one
book. Have never seen it done?*
It's here...
The Radical Revolutionary Strategic
Management Matrix For Predators